RATIFICATION

———— ★ ————

The People Debate the Constitution,
1787–1788

PAULINE MAIER

SIMON & SCHUSTER
NEW YORK   LONDON   TORONTO   SYDNEY

Simon & Schuster
1230 Avenue of the Americas
New York, NY 10020

Copyright © 2010 by Pauline Maier

First Simon & Schuster hardcover edition October 2010

SIMON & SCHUSTER and colophon are registered trademarks of Simon & Schuster, Inc.

For information about special discounts for bulk purchases, please contact Simon & Schuster
Special Sales at 1-866-506-1949 or business@simonandschuster.com.

The Simon & Schuster Speakers Bureau can bring authors to your live event.
For more information or to book an event contact the Simon & Schuster Speakers Bureau
at 1-866-248-3049 or visit our website at www.simonspeakers.com.

Designed by Level C
All maps by U-W Madison Cartography Laboratory.
Illustration credits are on page 590.

Manufactured in the United States of America

10   9   8   7   6   5   4   3   2   1

Library of Congress Cataloging-in-Publication Data

Maier, Pauline, 1938-
    Ratification : the people debate the Constitution, 1787–1788 / Pauline Maier.
        p. cm.
    Includes bibliographical references and index.
    1. Constitutional history—United States. I. Title.
    KF4541.M278 2010
    342.7302'9—dc22   2010027709

ISBN 978-0-684-86854-7
ISBN 978-1-4516-0636-2 (ebook)

To the memory of my mother,

Charlotte Rose Winterer Rubbelke
(February 23, 1917–November 8, 2009),

and my fellow historian, mentor, and dear friend,
Thomas N. Brown
(April 27, 1920–October 23, 2009)

The United States, 1787–1788

CONTENTS

★

INTRODUCTION

———— ★ ————

Playing Games

T his book tells the story of one of the greatest and most probing public debates in American history, one that occurred at the end of the American Revolution and involved far more than the handful of familiar "founding fathers." It is the story of how "We the People" decided whether or not to ordain and establish the Constitution of the United States.

The drama formally began on September 17, 1787, when the Constitutional Convention (or, as contemporaries called it, the federal Convention) adjourned and released to the public the Constitution it had written in secrecy. At that point the Constitution was nothing more than a proposal. In fact, it was a proposal from a body of men who had acted without authority since the delegates had been appointed to propose changes to the Articles of Confederation, not to design a new government. The federal Convention specified how the Constitution should be ratified: not, they said, by the Confederation Congress with the unanimous consent of the thirteen state legislatures, which was required for approving amendments to the Articles of Confederation, but by special ratifying conventions elected by "We the People" in each of the states. And approval need not be unanimous: Once nine states ratified the Constitution, it would go into effect among those ratifying states.

Debate over the Constitution raged in newspapers, taverns, coffeehouses, and over dinner tables as well as in the Confederation Congress, state legislatures, and state ratifying conventions. People who never left their home towns and were little known except to their neighbors studied the document, knew it well, and on some memorable occasions made their views known. What the people and the convention delegates they chose decided had everything to do with making the United States into what George Washington called a "respectable nation."

————

The most surprising thing about this book, perhaps, is that it wasn't written long ago. There are shelves of books on the federal Convention, far more than have attempted to tell the story of ratification. (In this book the convention happens between the Prologue and Chapter 1, when the delegates are leaving Philadelphia with printed copies of the Constitution in their bags.) I suspect most Americans think George Washington was inaugurated a week or two after the Convention, if they think about it at all. They assume ratification was automatic, which it was not.

I don't mean to imply that historians have neglected the subject. Many books on the Convention include a chapter or two that give a quick summary of the ratification process. There are also a handful of books that might qualify as general histories of ratification. One, which discusses both the federal Convention and ratification, was written in German and is only now being published in translation. Two others tell the story almost incidentally while exploring the role of the "Antifederalists" or the background of the Bill of Rights and, perhaps for that reason, did not tell it altogether successfully.[1] The authors of those two books struggled with problems of organization with which I sympathize. It's no easy thing to tell the story of an event that happened in thirteen different places, sometimes simultaneously.

Other historians have backed away from telling the full story, I suspect, because the documentary record is massive and widely dispersed in both central and local archives throughout the thirteen original states and other parts of the republic. Faced with a subject that might demand more than a single working life to study comprehensively, historians have done what they are trained to do: They examined "workable" parts of the subject—ratification in a single state, for example, one group of contenders, or the arguments made during the ratification struggle. (*The Federalist* alone has inspired something of a small industry.) Alternatively, the distinguished historians Forrest McDonald and Jackson Turner Main studied ratification as a whole to answer specific, limited questions: Was Charles Beard's economic interpretation of the Constitution right? Who were the "Antifederalists"?[2]

Breaking a complex topic into pieces and delegating the parts to different authors is another way of tackling outsized subjects. There are two fine books with chapters by different authors on ratification in each of the original thirteen states.[3] I have used those books (and the other studies of ratification) with great benefit, but, because they look at the states separately, a lot of the story falls into the cracks between chapters. They miss the ways contenders learned from what came before, to say nothing of the tension when—as in February 1788, after the New Hampshire convention adjourned without voting—it looked as if the Constitution's prospects could easily unravel; or in June 1788 when, after eight of the required nine states had ratified, three state conventions met simultaneously.

They miss, too, the popular excitement, which reminded me at times of Americans' obsession with the final games of the World Series, but with greater intensity because everyone understood that the results would last far longer than a season. The analogy is, I think, appropriate, since politics was in a real sense the first national game, and the debates about the Constitution marked the beginning of American national politics. Indeed, the ratification contest was the first national election, although it was more like a series of primaries than a presidential election since the votes were cast not on a single day but successively, in one state after another. Over and over observers tried to calculate how what happened in one state would affect what came later, which itself served to bind the nation together more tightly. One Massachusetts observer commented in November 1787 that newspapers, which were filled with news and commentary on the Constitution, were "read more than the bible at this time,"[4] which was saying something in New England. And as discussions spread from the press and taverns to homes, the arguments even involved—in a world where politics was supposedly confined to white men—women. The "whole story," in short, is something more than the sum of its parts.

The state ratifying conventions and the debates that surrounded the election of delegates to those conventions are at the center of the book. It describes only the beginning of the newspaper and pamphlet debates—"the war of printed words"—and not in great detail except where they had an obvious impact on the debates in state conventions or upon the electorates that chose delegates to those conventions. That means readers who want a careful analysis of *The Federalist*, for example, will have to go elsewhere. Except for the state of New York, it was less influential in 1787 and 1788 than in later times, when it was too often read as if it were a dispassionate, objective analysis of the Constitution, not a partisan statement written in the midst of a desperate fight in a critical state.

At one time I worried about telling the stories of a series of conventions all of which discussed the same document. Then I remembered that Americans and other human beings spend a lot of time watching the same game played night after night, week after week. No one game is exactly the same as the others. Similarly, the conventions in each state played out differently. To add to the interest, they all began (unlike, say, baseball or football games) with the delegates, or players, negotiating the rules by which they would play. It wasn't always clear, moreover, for which team some players fought, or if they were on a team at all, and every convention brought an entirely new set of players. How a convention developed depended on the character of the state, its history and traditions, the relative strength of the contenders, the strategies they took (which were reflected in the rules they adopted), and occasionally some outside event. What happened in earlier conventions also changed the "game" in certain particulars for those that followed. That's why no two conventions were identical. Each had (and has) its own fascination.

Each also had its own cast of colorful characters. Some of the "usual suspects" had roles to play, including George Washington, James Madison, Alexander Hamilton, Patrick Henry, even Thomas Jefferson, who was at the time in Paris, where he would witness the beginnings of the French Revolution. Others such as James Wilson, William Findley, Rufus King, Edmund Randolph, George Mason, Edmund Pendleton, Melancton Smith, and James Iredell are less familiar today, to our loss. But the real delights of this broad-based story, I think, are the local figures whom almost nobody has ever heard of before. Some are nameless, like the townsmen in rural Richmond, Massachusetts, who attended no fewer than four informational meetings before deciding that the Constitution in the form proposed was no darned good. Others are faceless: Few portraits survive of the backbenchers in the conventions, who often came out in the days immediately before the vote and expressed their convictions with a wonderful, honest eloquence. Or the portraits, as with more famous founders, are often of them as old men, which obscures how young many delegates were—in their thirties, an age when they often had to juggle responsibilities to their young families with the public responsibilities they had assumed. Participation in their state ratifying convention was for most their one brief part in history, what the New Yorker Gilbert Livingston called the greatest transaction of his life. The way they played their roles helps us understand why Nathan Dane, another relatively unknown person who appears in these pages, referred to Americans as an intelligent people. We owe them our attention, and they reward us richly for hearing them out.

————

What made it possible for me—in my sixties—to take on this sprawling subject is a landmark editorial project, *The Documentary History of the Ratification of the Constitution* (or DHRC), which has been published since 1976 by the Wisconsin Historical Society. There are to date twenty-one thick volumes in print, most of which pull together documents on ratification in individual states. The editors scoured newspapers, major archives, and even local libraries, where they sometimes found material that I suspect no historian has ever used before. The size of the documentary record varies dramatically for different states. Pennsylvania received one volume; the records for Delaware, New Jersey, Georgia, and Connecticut together take up another. Virginia, however, required three volumes, Massachusetts four, and New York five.

In the end, the DHRC lays the foundation for something of a revolution in our understanding of the ratification of the Constitution. Unlike the modern editions of the papers of Washington, Jefferson, Hamilton, and Madison (which I have also used with great profit), the DHRC documents the grass-roots story of the people and the Constitution. To be sure, its volumes include hundreds of letters by the men with familiar names, but they also reproduce a collection of records that tells how the towns of Massachusetts and, to a lesser extent, Connecticut responded to the Constitution. The DHRC includes a letter that tells of a friendly fight over the Constitution at a home in Biddeford, Maine; accounts of joyful celebrations of ratification in several states, and also of the "fracas" in Albany on July 4, 1788, after some fifty "Antifederalists" celebrated Independence Day by burning the Constitution, which was for them a perfectly patriotic act. These volumes, in short, reach down to the people and the places they lived.

The project still has five of the original thirteen states to cover: New Hampshire, South Carolina, Maryland, North Carolina, and the renegade Rhode Island. But it has completed work on eight states, including the four major state conventions that marked critical stages in the ratification process—Pennsylvania, Massachusetts, Virginia, and New York. I should say the editors completed work on those states, which get the lion's share of attention here, in the nick of time for me: The final New York volume came out just as I was finishing the book. For the five states not yet in the DHRC, I had to depend on old-fashioned research and far less comprehensive documentary records. I was also more dependent than usual on the work of others. Fortunately, some of that work is magnificent.

The recording of the convention debates is, I think, a part of the story of ratification as well as one way we learn that story. In brief, "shorthand men" often recorded the debates for publication in contemporary newspapers, whose daily reports were later pulled together and published as books. In some states, Federalists hired individuals to record the debates for subsequent publication as books without the intervening newspaper stage. The printed "debates" were never exact. They gave summaries of speeches rather than complete texts and often favored the Constitution's supporters over its critics. The debates of the Pennsylvania convention are the most extreme example: They included only the speeches of two leading Federalists, as if nobody else were there. Occasionally the shorthand men simply missed parts of the debates. In transcribing their handwritten notes, they might well also have imposed a coherence on the debates that was lost to listeners or that depended on a use of voice and gesture and so would have been lost if spoken words were simply translated into print. By coordinating the published debates (where they exist, which they don't for all states) and official journals with newspaper stories, letters, and the private notes delegates sometimes took during the conventions, the DHRC helps get around those problems. It makes it possible to tell some stories—the final part of the New York convention, for example—that were almost impossible to tell before.

The DHRC also helps historians avoid the pitfall of repeating the Federalists' version of the story and their descriptions of their opponents uncritically. Let me be clear on this: I have no doubt that we need to understand the Federalists' understanding of the Constitution. In many ways they provided the intellectual foundations of American government. For that and several other reasons, good and bad, we tend to believe everything they said. From a certain perspective, they won, and winners generally tell the stories. The Federalists were intelligent and articulate, the kind of people with whom historians tend to identify and so to trust. After two hundred years of stable constitutional government (with one notable and very bloody exception), it's hard to find fault with those who supported ratification of the Constitution as written. What they said seems wise and persuasive, which is to say true.

But the Federalists also controlled the documents on which historians depend. They owned most of the newspapers. They sometimes paid those who took notes on the convention debates or subsidized the publication of their transcripts. In some places, above all Connecticut, Federalists forcibly blocked the circulation of literature critical of the Constitution. In Pennsylvania, as one little-known letter in the DHRC proves, they even tried to suppress evidence that anyone had anything negative to say about the Constitution, and so to suggest that everyone was simply shouting "huzzah."[5] They were not trying to distort history. They were struggling to win a very tough fight on behalf of what they understood as the nation's welfare in a world where the rules of the political game were different from those of today.

And sometimes what they said was questionable at best—that those who opposed ratifying the Constitution as written simply continued an older opposition to central government, for example; or that they were mostly state officeholders worried for their jobs; or that they opposed the Constitution for some other personal reason, not from a commitment to the public good. That's getting ahead of the story, but it helps explain why I decided to use the word "Antifederalist" for critics of the Constitution only where it appears in quotations, almost all by Federalists, or where the designated persons willingly accepted the name, as in the upper Hudson Valley of New York. The words we use, especially names, shape the stories we tell, and "Antifederalist" was a Federalist term. To use the Federalists' language—to tell the story in their terms—tends to give them the game, or at least to tip the story further in their direction.

I make no case against other historians—including the editors of the DHRC, to whom I am greatly indebted—who refer to all people who opposed ratification of the Constitution without amendments as "Antifederalists." They are following an old historical convention and will no doubt insist that they need some word for the people they call "Antifederalists," which I understand. Moreover, there is some evidence that, once the ratification fight was over, "Antifederalist"—like "Quaker" or "Puritan," both of which began as terms of opprobrium—lost some of its old implications. My sense, however, is that the Pennsylvanian William Findley spoke for many others in 1796 when he said that the people who raised objections to the Constitution during the ratification struggle were "called Anti-federalists, as a name of reproach," and then added, "I do, and always did, treat the appellation with contempt."[6] For that reason I preferred to type out "critics of the Constitution" and its synonyms over and over.

I have, however, used "Federalist" for the supporters of the Constitution because they accepted the name, which they also invented. Even their opponents sometimes spoke of the "so-called federalists" or the "feds." I nonetheless use the term with some hesitation because it tends to suggest that there was something called a Federalist party in 1787 and 1788, which there was not, at least in anything like the form that emerged later, and that the fight over the Constitution was a two-sided contest between them and the opponents they called "Antifederalists," which, again, it was not. But there's time enough to get into that.

This book follows logically from my earlier work on the Revolution. (I would say it culminates that work, except I'm not ready to down-tool yet.) I began writing about the local resistance organizations that evolved into a movement for American independence in *From Resistance to Revolution* (1972), and in *The Old Revolutionaries* (1980) I wrote brief portraits of the men who led that resistance. Then, in *American Scripture: Making the Declaration of Independence* (1997), I described the state and local "declarations" of independence that preceded and made possible the familiar Declaration of Independence that the Continental Congress adopted on July 4, 1776. That long-term exploration of the local and popular foundations of politics in the Revolutionary era seems, in retrospect, to have led inevitably toward a book on the people and the Constitution. It feels almost providential that the DHRC finished publishing its volumes on the most critical states just in time to let me to write that book.

In the course of studying ratification, I also came to realize that few adult Americans have read the Constitution, at least since they were in high school, if then. I'll confess a personal dream that the book will make them better acquainted with the document (understanding, of course, that some provisions have since been changed). I propose a voluntary quiz after finishing the book. Readers might measure their understanding of the Constitution against that of the freemen of eighteenth-century Belchertown, Massachusetts, who described their reasons for considering the Constitution a threat to their rights and privileges as follows: "1st. there is no bill of Right[s]. For other Reasons See artical 1 Section 2-3-4 and 8[,] artical 2d Section 1 & 2[,] artical 3d Section 1 and [Article] 6. With many other obvious Reasons."[7] What was so obviously dangerous about Article I, Sections 2, 3, 4, and 8? Article II, Sections 1 and 2? Article III, Section 1? Article VI, and (though this might be too easy) about not having a bill of rights? (Checking the Constitution is fine; there's a copy of it at the end of the book.) For extra credit, what might the freemen of Belchertown have been referring to as "many other obvious Reasons"?

Finally, although the acknowledgments will come later, I need to thank the late Barbara Tuchman, whom I heard speak long ago, while I was still a graduate student. One idea she proposed has remained with me over the years. A writer can build suspense in telling a story, she said, even if the reader knows how the story turned out, so long as the writer never mentions the outcome until it happens at the proper place in the story. This book is, among other things, an effort to test that theory.

For the experiment to succeed, however, requires readers who are willing to play a game. They need to forget for the moment much of what they know about the American past and return in imagination to another time when there was no Constitution, when the federal Convention had not even met, and watch events occur, step by step, unaware of how they would turn out.

It's almost Christmas in 1786. An early winter ice storm had kept a retired general in northern Virginia from collecting his mail from the nearby town of Alexandria. Now, at long last, he is ripping open a letter from Richmond. . . .

Pauline Maier
Cambridge, Massachusetts
January 25, 2010

. . . whatever veneration might be entertained for the body of men who formed our constitution, the sense of that body could never be regarded as the oracular guide in . . . expounding the constitution. As the instrument came from them, it was nothing more than the draught of a plan, nothing but a dead letter, until life and validity were breathed into it, by the voice of the people, speaking through the several state conventions. If we were to look therefore, for the meaning of the instrument, beyond the face of the instrument, we must look for it not in the general convention, which proposed, but in the state conventions, which accepted and ratified the constitution.

—James Madison in Congress, April 6, 1796

J. C. A. Stagg et al., eds. *The Papers of James Madison*, XVI. Charlottesville, 1989, 295–96.

PROLOGUE

———— ★ ————

The View from Mount Vernon

A few days before Christmas in 1786 George Washington received a gift he didn't want. It was a letter from Virginia's governor, Edmund Randolph, trying to pry him out of retirement.

The envelope included a copy of an act passed on December 4 by the Virginia general assembly appointing delegates to a convention in Philadelphia "for the purpose of revising the federal constitution" and the names of seven delegates the legislature had chosen. Washington's name stood at the top of the list. Randolph explained that the assembly was alarmed by the "storms" that threatened to bring the American nation to a quick end, as its enemies had predicted. "To you I need not press our present dangers," Randolph said. As commander of the army Washington had witnessed the inefficiency of the Continental Congress and could see the steadily "increasing langour of our associated republics." Now only those "who began, carried on & consummated the revolution" could "rescue America from the impending ruin." Randolph urged Washington to accept the legislature's unanimous choice of him as a Virginia delegate to the Philadelphia convention.[1]

His appointment was not a complete surprise to Washington. He had tried to head it off in November, after James Madison, a leader of the assembly and former member of the Confederation Congress, warned him that the legislature was going to choose delegates to the convention and that Washington's name would probably be first on the list. It was "out of his power" to accept such an appointment, Washington replied. A few weeks earlier—on October 31, 1786—he had notified state chapters of the Society of the Cincinnati that he would not stand for reelection as the society's president and would not attend its second triennial meeting, which was scheduled to convene in Philadelphia on the first Monday in May—a week before the federal Convention would assemble in the same city. Washington gave the Cincinnati several compelling reasons for his decision: His private affairs had become seriously "deranged" by his long absence during the war, and they now needed his "entire & unremitting attention"; he was deeply and "unavoidably engaged" in a project to open navigation of the great rivers flowing through Virginia; and, after so many years of arduous service, he yearned for "retirement & relaxation from public cares." Moreover, his health was not good: He had recently suffered a violent attack of "fever & ague, succeeded by rheumatick pains" such as he had never before experienced. How then could he pick up and go to the federal Convention without offending "a very respectable & deserving part of the Community—the late officers of the American Army," who made up the Society of the Cincinnati?[2]

In fact, Washington had another, more pressing reason for backing away from his association with the Cincinnati, which he explained in confidence to Madison. When he had first agreed to head the new society in 1783, he thought of it as a fraternal organization whose main purpose was to take care of officers' widows and other dependents. Then, to his surprise, a pamphlet by South Carolina's Aedanus Burke provoked an uproar against the Cincinnati and, above all, its plan to pass membership on to the eldest sons of Revolutionary War officers. Critics such as Burke said that practice would lead to the creation of an hereditary aristocracy, which was totally at odds with the republican system established by the Revolution.[3]

Washington accepted reelection as president at the Society's first general meeting in 1784 after it proposed several changes in its rules, including the elimination of hereditary membership. But some state chapters refused to ratify the reforms, so by the fall of 1786, as the Society's second general meeting approached, Washington found himself, as he told Madison, in a "delicate" position. He didn't want to seem disloyal to his fellow officers, who included some of his dearest friends and confidants, nor did he want to support an institution "incompatible (some say) with republican principles." Under the circumstances, he simply could not attend the federal Convention in Philadelphia while the Society of the Cincinnati was also meeting there. That was his excuse, deeply felt and, to Madison at least, clearly explained.[4]

Washington was more circumspect with Randolph. He was grateful for the honor conferred on him by the general assembly, he wrote the governor, and in general stood ready to obey the calls of his country. However, there were at the moment "circumstances" that "will render my acceptance of this fresh mark of confidence incompatible with other measures which I had previously adopted" and from which he had "little prospect of disengaging myself." The legislature should replace him with someone "on whom greater reliance can be had," since the likelihood of his nonattendance was too great.[5]

Randolph refused to take no for an answer. Neither he nor the members of Virginia's council of state, to whom he showed Washington's letter, saw any need for Washington to withdraw immediately. It would be as easy for Randolph to appoint another delegate in Washington's place "sometime hence" as now. Perhaps the obstacles to Washington's attendance would somehow disappear, or the national crisis would become so severe that it outweighed all other considerations. "I hope therefore," Randolph wrote, "that you will excuse me for holding up your letter for the present." James Madison also urged Washington to leave the door open for a later acceptance in case "the gathering clouds should become so dark and menacing as to supercede every consideration, but that of our national existence or safety." Randolph and Madison played Washington like expert fishermen, and Washington, who no doubt understood full well what was going on, decided not to fight.[6]

As a result, when newspapers throughout the country announced Virginia's election of a delegation to the proposed federal Convention, Washington's name remained at the top of the list. No American commanded admiration and trust like Washington, which was precisely why Randolph and Madison were loath to let him resign. His appointment was "a mark of the earnestness of Virginia" and an invitation to other states to send their best men as delegates to the proposed convention. Indeed, by appointing a notably strong set of delegates—which included Washington, Randolph, Madison, the distinguished jurists George Wythe and John Blair, and also George Mason, who had drafted Virginia's state constitution and its influential declaration of rights—the Virginia legislature meant to convey a sign of its zeal "and its opinion of the magnitude of the occasion."[7]

The proposed convention needed all the support it could get. In late 1786, its chances of actually meeting, much less accomplishing anything, were remote at best. It looked like another in a long line of failed proposals to strengthen the Confederation. This time the call for a convention had come from a handful of state delegates who met from September 11 to 14, 1786, in Annapolis, Maryland, to discuss giving Congress the power to regulate the trade and commerce of the United States. Only five of the nine state delegations showed up on time, though more were on the way. Rather than wait (as usual) for the laggards, the delegations already present called on all the states to send representatives to another meeting in Philadelphia on the second Monday of May, 1787, "to devise such further provisions as shall appear to them necessary to render the Constitution of the Federal Government adequate to the exigencies of the Union." Then the meeting adjourned. The delegates had received no authority to call a convention from the state legislatures that appointed them. Moreover, Article XIII of the Articles of Confederation said that any alterations in the Articles had to be "agreed to in a Congress of the United States, and be afterwards confirmed by the Legislatures of every State."[8] Did that mean Congress had to initiate or at least endorse any meeting called to propose changes to the Articles? If so, would the states elect delegates to a convention that was, in the language of the day, "irregular"—that is, called in a way that seemed to bypass the established procedures of the Confederation? *Should* they?

Virginia said they should. On November 23, 1786, the state's general assembly adopted a beautifully crafted act that endorsed the call for a convention and authorized the election of delegates. The act, which Governor Randolph forwarded to the other states as well as to Washington, said the crisis had arrived when "the good people of America" had to decide whether they were to reap the fruits of independence and a union "cemented with so much of their common blood" or give way to "unmanly jealousies and prejudices, or to partial and transitory interests," and "renounce the auspicious blessings prepared for them by the Revolution." The assembly argued that the proposed convention would be a better place to discuss reforms of the federal system than the Confederation Congress, where those debates "might be too much interrupted by the ordinary business before them," and where various highly capable individuals could not participate because they were disqualified by law or "restrained by peculiar circumstances." It called for the appointment of seven "Commissioners," by "joint ballot of both Houses of Assembly," and authorized the governor to fill any vacancies if those elected declined to serve. On December 4, the legislature chose its delegates (or commissioners). Virginia, the largest and most populous state in the union, won considerable honor for its early support for the convention—although New Jersey had, in fact, chosen its delegates a week earlier.[9]

Washington's name added to the impact of Virginia's action. Suddenly the convention began to look like an event worth taking seriously. The Pennsylvania assembly specifically cited the Virginia precedent on December 30, when it became the third state to elect delegates to the convention. By mid-February, North Carolina, New Hampshire, Delaware, and Georgia had joined the list. That made seven of the thirteen states, which was not enough to assure that the convention would meet, especially since some of them made their appointments contingent on Congress's giving the convention its approval. That so many states were willing to participate was nonetheless remarkable considering how unlikely it seemed at first that anything would come of the proposal.[10]

TO GO OR NOT TO GO

Letting his name remain on the list of Virginia delegates was one thing; going to Philadelphia was another. Washington had questions to ask, and only a few good ways of getting answers while he remained at Mount Vernon. He scanned newspapers for information, and he picked up more news from a stream of visitors so steady that at times his home seemed like a tavern (though one where the proprietor always picked up the tab). Above all, however, Washington relied on his correspondents, many of whom were old officers of the Continental Army. Over the next four months a surge of letters between them and Washington laid out the problems that made the nation's situation critical, discussed what constitutional changes were needed to remedy those problems, and evaluated the likelihood that the Philadelphia convention would do what had to be done.

Soon after receiving Randolph's letter, Washington asked General Henry Knox what the "prevailing sentiments" on the convention were and how well attended it was likely to be. Knox's friendship with Washington went back to 1775, when Washington took command of the Continental Army camped in Cambridge, Massachusetts, across the Charles River from Boston. It was Knox, a portly onetime Boston bookseller, who had led the expedition that dragged cannon from Fort Ticonderoga on Lake Champlain to Dorchester Heights, where that artillery helped convince the British to evacuate Boston on March 17, 1776. He was with Washington through the rest of the war, during the devastating campaign in New York and Washington's critical victories at Trenton and Princeton, through the miserable winters at Morristown and Valley Forge, and on to the trenches at Yorktown in 1781. Knox was a leading organizer of the Society of the Cincinnati in 1783. Two years later he became the country's secretary of war. Situated as he was in New York and in close contact with members of Congress, he soon became a major source of information on national affairs for a network of correspondents.[11]

Washington also wrote to Connecticut's Colonel David Humphreys, who had been an aide-de-camp during the final years of the revolutionary war and became a particularly trusted and beloved member of the commander's military family. Like Knox, Humphreys had served with Washington from the battles of Long Island and Harlem—which Humphreys described in his *Essay on the Life of the Honorable Major-General Israel Putnam* (1788)— through to Yorktown. Washington gave Humphreys the honor of delivering to Congress the flags of the defeated British and German troops, along with his official report on the British capitulation of October 1781. Humphreys was with Washington when he surrendered his commission to Congress on December 23, 1783, then accompanied him back to Mount Vernon, where Humphreys joined the joyful celebrations of the commander's homecoming on Christmas Eve. A member of the Cincinnati, a poet, and a diplomat, Humphreys corresponded regularly with Washington between 1784 and 1786, when he served as secretary to the American commission negotiating commercial treaties in Europe. After he returned to America in 1786, Humphreys stayed at Mount Vernon for six weeks, working on a projected biography of Washington, before returning to Connecticut, where his home town promptly elected him to the state legislature.[12]

Washington considered Humphreys a reliable source of information on the attitudes of the Cincinnati, "the temper of the people, and the state of Politics at large," particularly in the northeastern part of the country. He told Humphreys about his exchange of letters with Madison and Randolph, then asked the question that troubled him. If the issue of his attending the convention "should be further prest (which I hope it will not, as I have no inclination to go)," Washington asked, "what had I best do?"[13]

"No inclination" was an understatement. During his eight years away from home while commanding the Continental Army, thoughts of Mount Vernon had been Washington's greatest solace. He tried to write his plantation manager (and distant cousin), Lund Washington, on a regular basis and to direct from afar major renovations of his house, taking respite from war with thoughts of plaster, paint, and newly planted groves of trees. He complained when letters from Virginia failed to arrive since that denied him "the consolation of hearing from home, on domestic matters," and he dreamed of the day when he could join those who, in the words of the prophet Micah, had beaten their "swords into plowshares" and he too could sit at peace "under his vine and under his fig tree" with no one to make him afraid.[14] Once, in 1781, as the army marched toward Yorktown, Washington rode his horse a heroic sixty miles in a single day to get home for a brief visit. It had been over six years since he had seen Mount Vernon. Except for one additional short, sad visit to bury his stepson, Jackie Custis, he would not return for another two years.[15] Then, with his military service over, he fully intended to stay put.

Washington made his intentions emphatically clear in a long circular letter he sent to the states in June 1783, as his command neared its end. Washington called on Americans to commit themselves to "an indissoluble Union of the States under one Federal Head," which was essential, to realize the promises of the Revolution. He stressed the importance of "a sacred regard to Public Justice," which demanded paying the nation's debts, including those to the officers of the Continental Army. Washington also urged the states to abandon "local prejudices and policies" where necessary for "the interest of the community." He could not be accused of any "sinister" purpose in expressing these convictions, he said, because he was determined to take no part in "public business" after the war and to pass the rest of his life "in a state of undisturbed repose." He bid "a last farewell to the cares of office, and all the employments of public life."[16]

Six months later, when he submitted his resignation to Congress at the Maryland State House, Washington repeated his renunciation of future public office. "Happy in the confirmation of our Independence and Sovereignty, and pleased with the opportunity afforded the United States of becoming a respectable Nation," he said, "I resign with satisfaction the Appointment I accepted with diffidence." He was not, Washington emphasized, retiring simply from the army but "from the Service of my Country," indeed from "all the employments of public life."[17]

His military service made Washington a hero; his retirement made him a legend. To observers everywhere he seemed an exception to the rules that normally governed human beings. A Caesar or a Cromwell might exchange military for dictatorial political power, but not Washington. He became the American Cincinnatus, a man who left the plow to save his country, then took it up again when the danger had passed.[18] In late 1786, however, Washington's renunciation of public office complicated his reflections on whether or not to attend the federal Convention. If he accepted a place on the Virginia delegation, would he be going back on his word? Would he destroy the foundation of that very prestige that made his name on the list of Virginia delegates so influential?

Above all, Washington wanted to stay home. By 1786 he had fully realized his youthful ambitions for glory; his reputation was so monumental that it seemed he could harm but not enhance it. He was finally free to do what pleased him most. When he first returned to Mount Vernon, he had to remind himself every morning that he was no longer "a public Man, or had anything to do with public transactions." By February 1784 he could write Knox that he was "beginning to experience that ease, and freedom from public cares" that "takes some time to realize." He had come to feel like "a wearied Traveller" who, "after treading many a painful step, with a heavy burden on his Shoulders, is eased of the latter," having reached his destination. With obvious delight he wrote his beloved Marquis de Lafayette—another member of his close military family—that he had "not only retired from all public employments, but I am retireing within myself," and "tread the paths of private life with heartfelt satisfaction—Envious of none, I am determined to be pleased with all." That was his new order of march: He was determined to "move gently down the stream of life, until I sleep with my Fathers."[19]

There was much at Mount Vernon to solace the soul. Washington's home looked across the wide Potomac toward Maryland, surrounded by lawns, gardens, and flowering trees. The rest of his estate also had a certain natural beauty. An early twentieth-century visitor who tramped through lands that Washington had visited on horseback, day after day, could still find there, as meadow larks sang and the scent of honeysuckle filled the air, reason enough "to understand how there came to be a poet called Wordsworth." (He was, however, also struck by the extremely poor quality of the soil.)[20]

Managing the plantation was a complex job not altogether unlike administering the Continental Army. By buying or leasing adjacent lands, Washington had built an enormous estate that by 1786 ran some ten miles along the Potomac and inland as much as four miles. Less than half of its

8,000 acres was cultivated, and he divided the arable land among five in-
dependently administered farms, each with its own work force, animals,
tools, barns, sheds, and cabins. Washington generally visited all five every
day, riding a circuit of some twenty miles, and kept careful records for each.
He also owned a ferry across the Potomac, a fishery, a gristmill that served
his neighbors as well as his plantation, and a variety of "manufactories" that
produced commodities for his plantation such as linen and woolen cloth that
he would otherwise have had to purchase.[21]

But the plantation and his financial affairs had fallen into disarray. Washington's new secretary, Tobias Lear, discovered that Washington had lost
some £10,000 sterling—a fortune at the time—during the war. Moreover,
expenses at Mount Vernon persistently outran the plantation's earnings.
There was little Washington could do either to pay his creditors—cash was
hard to come by at the time—or collect from his debtors, many of whom
were relatives. He could, however, try to make his plantation profitable.[22]

Addressing that problem engaged his natural talents, which were less
literary than technical and managerial (which is perhaps why we have more
trouble "knowing" him than others of his generation who were more at ease
with the written word). Washington had little formal schooling; he never
attended college, and his interests tended toward the practical. As a young
man he had been a surveyor, which required mathematical skills; technical
devices always fascinated him (or, as one observer put it, he had a leaning
toward "mechanics"). Now Washington developed an avid interest in the sci-
entific approach to agriculture, hoping it might reveal ways of teasing more
bountiful crops from his weak and exhausted soil.[23]

He corresponded with the English agricultural reformer Arthur Young,
who sent Washington volumes of the *Annals of Agriculture,* to which Young
was a major contributor. Eventually Washington owned thirty-two volumes
of the publication, which he carefully studied, copying passages of particular
interest, as he frequently did throughout his life. Young offered, as a "brother
farmer," to supply Washington with "men, cattle, tools, seeds, or any thing else
that may add to y[ou]r rural amusement." Across the Atlantic and the impediments of time that distance brought, the two men discussed plows, farmyard
design, soil, seeds, and crop rotation. "Agriculture," Washington volunteered,
"has ever been amongst the most favourite amusements of my life." He celebrated the establishment of an Agriculture Society in Philadelphia, and he
wished that other states would found more such societies so their members
could correspond with each other and inform the public of "all useful discoveries founded on practice, with a due attention [to] climate, Soil, and Seasons."[24]

Meanwhile, Washington carried out his own experiments, attempting to
increase soil fertility with manure or with soil dredged from the bottom of
the Potomac, and he began a complex system of crop rotation that involved

planting in succession corn with potatoes and carrots, buckwheat, wheat, peas, barley, oats, and red clover. His letters on farm practice have a warmth and enthusiasm unusual except in those he wrote to old friends from the Continental Army's officer corps. Those who knew him best—Humphreys, who described Washington's love of farming in the biography he wrote, John Jay, or the Marquis de Lafayette—recognized his passion for agriculture and so knew how to please him. In February 1788, for example, Jay sent Washington some English rhubarb seed that he had reason to think was "of the best kind. . . . If the seed prove good," Jay continued, "you will soon be able to determine whether it will flourish in your climate, & in what Soil & Situation best." In return, Washington offered to mate one of Jay's mares with his Spanish Jack, a noble jackass that he'd received as a gift of the Spanish king. When Lafayette sent Washington another jackass and two jennies from the Isle of Malta, Washington described them as "the most valuable thing you could have sent me." Although "not quite equal to the best Spanish Jennies," he told Jay, the animals would help him "establish a valuable breed of these animals in this Country."[25]

After the war, as Washington told the Cincinnati, he also took up another of his old projects, one that first attracted his attention in the early 1770s: to develop the Potomac River into a major route to the west. Thomas Jefferson, a fellow Virginian, shared his enthusiasm. "All the world is becoming commercial," he wrote Washington in March 1784. It no longer made sense to speculate "whether commerce contributes to the happiness of mankind" since "our citizens have had too full a taste of the comforts furnished by the arts & manufactures to be debarred the use of them." Virginians must "endeavor to share as large a portion as we can of this modern source of wealth & power." Jefferson wanted the Virginia assembly to invest tax revenues into opening "the upper waters of the Ohio & Patowmac"—connecting the Potomac with rivers or streams that flowed into the Ohio and finding ways around the waterfalls that obstructed navigation—but critics always said that public money was carelessly managed and so "spent to little purpose." If Washington superintended the project, however, fears of poor management would disappear. Would that, Jefferson asked, "break in too much on the sweets of [your] retirement and repose"?[26]

Washington agreed entirely on the "practicability of an easy, & short communication between the waters of the Ohio & Potomack." That route had advantages "over *all* others." He described his prewar efforts to extend navigation of the Potomac through a privately owned, incorporated company, which still seemed more promising to Washington than the prospect of getting tax money for river development. Was he willing to take the lead? Perhaps, he wrote Jefferson in March 1784, "if that undertaking could be made to comport with those ideas, & that line of conduct with which I mean to glide gently down the stream of life" and "did not interfere with any other plan I might have in contemplation."[27]

In September 1784, Washington began a trip—part pleasure, part business—that he had long dreamed of, a journey of some 600 miles up the Potomac and through the Appalachians to the Ohio Valley, where he owned vast stretches of land. The route was much the same as that he took as a twenty-two-year-old Virginia militia officer thirty years earlier, at the start of his military career, and again in 1755, when he joined General Edward Braddock on an expedition up through Virginia and Maryland and across the Appalachians to a site near the Monongahela River where Braddock and some 465 of his men met their inglorious end at the hands of a few well-positioned Indian and French soldiers. If Washington hoped to find a way to alleviate his financial distress in that ghost-ridden west, he was disappointed: A mill he hoped to sell was in such disrepair it found no buyers, and his lands were filled with squatters who refused to acknowledge his title.[28]

That was vexing, but Washington had become absorbed with another quest: to find the best way to link the upper reaches of the Potomac with the Ohio River, which formed at the junction of the Allegheny and Monongahela rivers and flowed down to the Mississippi, that great highway of the interior. Everywhere he went he asked questions, made observations, and speculated on how best to tie the river systems together. He also met James Rumsey and first saw Rumsey's invention: an odd-looking boat, somewhat like a catamaran, with poles on its sides that drew power from a front-mounted waterwheel to push the contraption upstream, against the current. Washington was delighted with the device, which he thought would help solve the problem of navigating the Potomac. By then he was hooked. He assumed leadership of the project to develop the river—not from necessity, as he suggested to the Cincinnati, but with passion. Washington became president of the new Potomac Company, which, thanks to his efforts, received charters and financial support from both Virginia and Maryland. The mass of the company's capital would, however, have to come from private subscribers.[29]

If the Potomac Company succeeded in tying the west to the Atlantic via the Potomac River, the value of Washington's lands in the west would increase. So would that of his Mount Vernon estate if the town of Alexandria, only nine miles away, became a major trading metropolis. But he wrote Knox that he hoped for the project's success "more on account of its political importance . . . than the commercial advantages which would result from it, altho' the latter is an immense object." If the settlers filling the west, generally immigrants with no historical bonds to the United States, could not easily trade with the Atlantic coast, they might attach themselves to the Spanish to their west or the British to their north. Washington feared they would "become a distinct people from us," with "different views" and "different interests, & instead of adding strength to the Union, may in case of a rupture with either of those powers, be a formidable & dangerous neighbour."[30]

THE STATE OF THE NATION

The Potomac link with the west would be, in short, a bond of nationhood for a nation in desperate need of bonds. The very possibility that western settlers might switch their allegiance to Britain or Spain testified that the "continental belt" remained "too loosely buckled," as Thomas Paine had put it in *Common Sense*. In fact, the "continental belt" had never been adequately tightened, as Washington and his fellow officers knew from painful wartime experience, and the union became even weaker after the peace, when the need for national government seemed less pressing. The basic problem was, as one of Washington's correspondents put it with admirable succinctness, "no money."[31] Under the Articles of Confederation, Congress had no power to levy taxes. The struggle with Britain began when colonists denied Parliament the right to tax them on the principle of "no taxation without representation." With independence, it seemed safest to keep the right to tax in the state legislatures, where the people were directly represented. The Continental Congress could legally print money, and it did so to finance the opening years of the war, but its currency depreciated to the point of uselessness. Congress could also borrow money, which it did. And in the 1780s it began to make arrangements for surveying and selling government lands in the west, but it would take time before those sales produced a substantial revenue stream.

In the meantime, Congress depended on annual payments—requisitions—from the states to make interest and principal payments on the war debt and to cover current expenses. But none of the states paid all of their requisitions, and Georgia paid nothing. A few states began to pay interest on the portion of the national debt that was owed to their citizens. The part of the national debt that was owed to foreign nations, however, remained the sole responsibility of Congress. In 1781 and again in 1783, Congress asked the states to let Congress collect duties on imports (an "impost") so it could at least pay its debts. But amendments to the Articles of Confederation required unanimous ratification by the state legislatures, and Rhode Island refused to ratify the first impost amendment. State consideration of the revised 1783 impost dragged on into early 1786, when the states that had not acted were urged to ratify the proposal quickly and avoid the "fatal effects" of Congress's defaulting on its contractual obligations.

Virginia congressman Henry Lee (an ex-army officer known as "Light Horse Harry") wasn't optimistic. The members of the New York legislature, he told Washington in February 1786, were "violent enemys to the impost," and he feared that "even the impending . . . dangers to the existence of the Union will not move them." In fact, New York ratified the 1783 impost amendment but insisted that the duties levied by Congress be paid in New York's paper money and collected by state officials. Congress refused to accept those conditions. "Part of the principal of our foreign loans is due next year," Lee noted, but Congress had "no certain means . . . to pay even the interest." Massachusetts delegate Rufus King reported that employees of the Confederation "begin to clamour" because they had long gone unpaid, and the handful of troops beyond the Ohio River was starting to mutiny and desert. The country's situation, another member of Congress commented, was "indeed wretched—Our Funds exhausted, our Credit lost, our Confidence in the federal Government destroyed."[32]

In 1783 Washington had called on the country to pay the debts Congress had incurred during the Revolutionary War as a matter of justice and honesty. To default on the foreign debt would also undermine the country's capacity to borrow abroad in the event of another military crisis. "We have it in our power to be one of the most respectable Nations upon Earth," he wrote in October 1785, when the problems of national finance were already abundantly clear. Nobody could deny that "our resources are ample, & encreasing," but by denying Congress a share of that wealth "we give the vital stab to public credit, and must sink into contempt in the eyes of Europe."[33]

There were good reasons for his fears. One incident after another demonstrated that Congress's sorry financial state left the United States at the mercy of other nations. When Britain excluded American ships and American exports from the West Indies and also blocked American imports into Britain, Congress could do nothing. The British imposed those restrictions, Washington said, on an assumption that the states could not unite against them; he predicted—incorrectly—that Britain's shortsighted policies would provoke the states into giving Congress power to regulate trade.[34] Congress could not retaliate after Spain closed the Mississippi to American shippers in 1784. After meeting with the Spanish negotiator Don Diego de Gardoqui, Secretary for Foreign Affairs John Jay found he could get commercial privileges from Spain only if the United States gave up navigation of the Mississippi for twenty-five years. When he asked Congress for permission to negotiate a treaty on those terms, he succeeded mainly in causing a profound split between Northern commercial states, which were willing to vote "yes" to enhance their trade over the Atlantic, and Southern states, which saw their future and that of their western lands tied to the Mississippi. When the Barbary States of North Africa began seizing American ships in the Mediterranean, the United States could neither pay them off, as Britain and other European countries did, nor respond with force. It had no navy.

Moreover, its army had shrunk to some 625 unpaid, poorly equipped men, mostly in western Pennsylvania—too few to prevent squatters from moving onto Indian lands, which threatened to provoke open war at several points along the western frontier. The United States was becoming "the sport of transatlantic politicians of all denominations."[35]

Congress could not enforce the powers it clearly had under the Articles of Confederation. The Articles granted "the united states in congress assembled . . . sole and exclusive right and power" over "peace and war, the sending and receiving of ambassadors, negotiating treaties and alliances," and "regulating the Indian trade." Nonetheless, New York negotiated a separate treaty with the Iroquois, with devastating implications for national policy.[36] Congress could not even assure compliance with the peace treaty it had negotiated and ratified. In late 1785, the British formally refused to evacuate their posts in the northwest, arguing that they were not obliged to honor the peace treaty while the Americans violated it. In particular, they charged that the treaty's fourth article, which said creditors would confront no legal impediments to recovering the full value in pounds sterling of all bona fide debts previously contracted, had been violated by the states. An investigation by John Jay confirmed the charge and discovered that both New York and South Carolina had also violated the treaty's sixth article, which prohibited further prosecutions of Loyalists for wartime activities and future confiscations of Loyalist property. Jay concluded that there was almost nothing Congress could do to end those practices or to compensate the victims for their losses. "Our affairs," he wrote Washington in June 1786, "seem to lead to some crisis—some Revolution—something I cannot foresee, or conjecture." He was more "uneasy and apprehensive" than during the war, when "we had a fixed Object," and when he believed the Americans would "ultimately succeed" because "Justice was with us. The Case is now altered—we are going and doing wrong."[37]

Meanwhile the Confederation Congress remained in a state of paralysis. Under the Articles of Confederation, Congress could not engage in war, enter into treaties or alliances, coin money and regulate its value, determine the expenses necessary for the country's welfare, appropriate money, or essentially do anything of significance without the consent of nine state delegations. Even lesser matters—except for adjourning from day to day—required the consent of seven states. A state needed at least two delegates (and could have as many as seven) for its vote to count. If its delegates were equally divided, its vote was so recorded but did not count. However, for long periods of time too few delegations were present for Congress even to attempt anything of significance. In April 1786, Rufus King complained that there had been nine state delegations present on the floor of Congress on only three days since the previous October, which meant that his staying there through the winter was a "mere farce. . . . Foreigners know our situation, and the friends of free Governments through the world must regret it."[38]

When, finally, nine states (but no more) were present, Congress needed their unanimous consent to exercise its major powers. That was all but impossible because of sectional jealousies and conflicting interests. "Every State," Henry Knox complained, "considers its representative in Congress not so much the Legislator of the whole Union, as its own immediate Agent or Ambassador" to represent its particular views. How then could the United States become a republic that could "rival the Roman name"?[39]

Washington knew all these problems, as Governor Randolph acknowledged. In 1785 Washington described the Confederation as "little more than an empty sound, and Congress a nugatory body." It seemed extraordinary that Americans would confederate for national purposes but then refuse to give officials who were "Creatures of our own making—appointed for a limited and short duration—who are amenable for every action—recallable at any moment—and subject to all the evils they may be instrumental in producing, sufficient powers to order & direct the affairs of that Nation." He saw no threat of tyranny in expanding the powers of the federal government since the members of Congress were "so much the creatures of the people" that they could have no views or interests apart from those of their constituents. He did, however, see reason to fear "the worst consequences from a half starved, limping Government, that appears to be always moving upon crutches, & tottering at every step."[40]

By 1786 Washington's dream of a "respectable nation"—that is, a nation that could be "considered on a respectable footing by the powers of Europe"—seemed increasingly remote.[41] The very future of the republic—a government without hereditary rulers, in which all power came from the people—seemed in doubt. Washington shared John Jay's fears that "the better kind of people" would be "led by the Insecurity of Property, the Loss of Confidence in their Rulers, & Want [Lack] of public Faith & Rectitude, to consider the Charms of Liberty as imaginary and delusive" and adopt "almost any change" that promised "Quiet and Security." American affairs were "drawing rapidly to a crisis." Requisitions were "a perfect nihility," he wrote Jay in August 1786, and "if you tell the Legislatures they have violated the treaty of peace and invaded the prerogatives of the confederacy they will laugh in your face. What then is to be done?" Things could not go on as they had; "I am told that even respectable characters speak of a monarchical form of government without horror. . . . What a triumph for the advocates of despotism to find that we are incapable of governing ourselves, and that systems founded on . . . equal liberty are merely ideal & fallacious!" Experience showed "that men will not adopt & carry into execution, measures the best calculated for their own good without the intervention of a coercive power. I do not conceive we can exist long as a nation, without having lodged somewhere a power which will pervade the whole Union in as energetic a manner, as the authority of the different state governments extends over the several States."[42]

Popular unrest in the fall and winter of 1786–1787 brought these fears to a peak. Discontent was "not confined to one state or to one part of a state" in the northeast, Henry Lee told Washington in September 1786, but pervaded "the whole." Soon David Humphreys reported that although General John Sullivan, then the president of New Hampshire, had put down an insurrection there "without effusion of blood," in Massachusetts, where the event remembered as Shays's Rebellion was under way, "everything" was "in a state of confusion."[43] Was America following the pattern of previous republics, which ended after a plague of anarchy led law-abiding people to invest power in some strong leader who could restore order? "For God's sake," Washington implored Humphreys, "tell me, what is the cause of all these commotions?" Were they provoked by licentiousness, British influence, or "real grievances" that could be redressed? "I am really mortified beyond expression that in the moment of Acknowledged Independence we should, by our conduct, verify the predictions of our transatlantic foe, & render ourselves ridiculous & contemptible in the eyes of all Europe."[44]

Washington's correspondents—above all Humphreys, Knox, and General Benjamin Lincoln, all old army officers—sent Washington detailed reports that were heavily slanted against the insurgents in Massachusetts. Rufus King came to a different but correct conclusion: He wrote John Adams, the first American minister to Great Britain, that heavy, direct taxes on polls and real property, levied by the state in the midst of a commercial depression, along with pressure from private creditors, had driven farmers in several Massachusetts counties to obstruct tax collections and close courts until the legislature could grant them relief. "You will see this business greatly magnified and tories may rejoice," he told Adams, "but all will be well."[45]

King might have added that the situation in Massachusetts was an extreme case of a widespread problem. In the 1780s, to pay their war debts and requisitions to Congress, the states had increased taxes to a level several times what they had been before 1776. Moreover, except for New York and Pennsylvania, which received substantial revenue from taxes on imports, the states depended primarily on regressive taxes on persons and property, which caused widespread discontent. Some states averted rural insurrections by issuing paper money or providing other forms of tax or debt relief. But Knox, who, as secretary at war, went to Massachusetts to investigate, insisted that high taxes were only the "ostensible cause of the commotions." The insurgents, he said, were not simply poor but also "desperate & unprincipled men" who paid little or no taxes; they resented their inferiority to the wealthy and sought to take advantage of the government's weakness to redress the imbalance. They planned to "annihilate all debts public and private" and pass laws that would redistribute wealth by making unfunded paper money legal tender "in all cases whatsoever."[46]

Lincoln, who led Massachusetts troops against the insurgent followers of Daniel Shays, later echoed Knox's claims, while Congressman Henry Lee managed to exaggerate them. The insurgents wanted not only to abolish debts and redistribute property, Lee claimed, but to reunite with Britain. The "malcontents" supposedly had close ties with Vermont (then seeking independence from New York), which "it is believed [sic] is in negotiation with the Governor of Canada." Lee also reported that a *majority* of people in Massachusetts opposed their government—not, as Knox claimed, a fifth of the people in some counties—and "the same temper prevails more or less" in all the New England states. "In one word, my dear Gen[era]l," he wrote to Washington, "we are all in dire apprehension that a beginning of anarchy with all its calamitys has approached, & have no means to stop the dreadful work."[47]

A sense of helplessness made a bad situation almost unbearable. Congress could only call for troops to help Massachusetts by pretending they would be used against Indians: The Articles of Confederation did not give it a clear and indisputable power to suppress domestic insurrections. The states seemed equally powerless. Massachusetts, whose constitution Washington considered one of the most "energetic in the Union," had now seen "its laws arrested and trampled under foot." Its government, Humphreys reported, lay "prostrated in the dust. And it is much to be feared that there is not energy enough in that State, to reestablish the civil Powers." The state treasurer couldn't even borrow money to supply a volunteer army. Lincoln himself had to raise funds for the expedition he led against the insurgents, which he did by urging a group of wealthy Bostonians to lend "part of their property if they wished to secure the remainder." Meanwhile, Knox reported that the strength of the uprising was growing, "& it is expected that they will soon take possession of the Continental Magazine at Springfield," where there were "ten to fifteen thousand stand of Arms in excellent order."[48]

Lincoln's army actually suppressed the uprising with relative ease, and the Massachusetts government reclaimed its old effectiveness after the spring 1787 elections. A surge in voting participation (three times more people voted than the year before), provoked by severe and partisan reprisals against the "rebels" enacted under Governor James Bowdoin, gave Bowdoin's opponent, John Hancock, 75 percent of the popular vote. Sixty more towns also sent representatives to the legislature, which grew from 198 members in 1786 to 266 in 1787; and then, after it became a more genuinely representative body, the legislature adopted a conciliatory position in place of the Bowdoin administration's hard-line policies. Soon order returned, even in embattled sections of the state. The problem was hardly as serious or as intractable as Knox had claimed.[49]

Washington, however, believed the frenzied reports he received. In a letter dated December 26, 1786—the same in which he asked for advice on the convention—he thanked Knox for his clear "advices" and asked him to send more accounts of the events in Massachusetts because he could depend on them, unlike the "vague & contradictory" accounts in newspapers. Not even Lee's charge that the insurgents sympathized with Britain seemed untenable: The British were certainly fomenting discontent among Indians on the frontier, and Washington was sure they would also take "every opportunity to foment the spirit of turbulence within the bowels of the United States" in order to "distract" our governments and encourage divisions. The "commotions" gave "a melancholy proof of what our trans atlantic foe have predicted; and of another thing . . . still more to be regretted . . . that mankind left to themselves are unfit for their own government." The whole episode seemed to Washington "like the vision of a dream. My mind does not know how to realize it, as a thing in actual existence, so strange—so wonderful does it appear to me!"[50] Governor Randolph thought the uprisings in Massachusetts might even persuade Washington to go to Philadelphia. At least he should not resign from the delegation, Randolph urged in January 1787, "until time shall disclose the result of the commotions now prevailing."[51]

A crippled national government; state authority trampled into the dust; a people incapable of self-government; a revolutionary cause on the brink of failure: The situation amounted to a crisis of unprecedented importance in the young republic. For those caught up in that frame of mind, the entire future of the United States was at stake. Washington was not, he acknowledged, an "unconcerned spectator" of these developments.[52] He had already compromised his retirement from public affairs by becoming involved with the Potomac Company, which he saw as a way to promote union. Now something more had to be done. But what? And was the proposed convention a feasible way of doing what was needed?

WHAT IS TO BE DONE?

Americans had been designing and redesigning their governments since 1776, when the states enacted the world's first written constitutions. In devising new governments for the states, the Americans built on deep colonial precedents and could act with a confidence born of experience. By contrast, the national government was new; it seemed at times to threaten state power; and its most obvious precedent—the supervising authority of Britain—did not encourage trust. The colonists had, after all, spent over a decade questioning, resisting, and finally throwing off the authority of the British government. At every step, the effort to establish a formal plan of government for the union met resistance and delay. The Continental Congress had worked on the Articles of Confederation for over a year before sending the document to the states for ratification; it took another three and a half years before the Articles finally went into effect in March 1781—seven months before the Revolutionary War finally ended at Yorktown.

Now, in late 1786 and early 1787, some of Washington's correspondents mused on what changes in national government would resolve the country's problems and shared their ideas with him. To a man they proposed giving the national government a more complex structure, like those in most of the states, with separate legislative, executive, and judiciary departments. They also proposed a more centralized national government, one to which the states would be clearly subordinate.

It was a big mistake for the Articles of Confederation to put all of the federal government's powers in Congress, John Jay wrote Washington on January 7, 1787. Congress was too large, too open, too subject to private ambitions, and too oblivious of character, honor, and dignity to govern effectively. He proposed a new government that divided power among a legislature, an executive, and a judiciary. The legislature should be bicameral, with a popularly elected lower house and an upper house whose members held office for life. Executive authority could be entrusted to a "Governor General" whose powers and term of office were clearly defined and limited. With the advice of a special council whose members were drawn from the judiciary—much like the council of revision in Jay's home state of New York—the governor general should be able to veto acts of the legislature. How much power such a government should have was, Jay thought, worthy of "much Thought," but he was inclined to think "the more the better." The states should be left with only those powers necessary for regulating their internal affairs, and the national government should appoint and have power to remove from office "all their principal Officers civil and military."[53]

Henry Knox sent his ideas to Washington a week after Jay. He too proposed separating and balancing power among three branches of a new central or "general" government. Again like Jay, he advocated a bicameral legislature, with a lower house whose members held office for terms of one, two, or three years; and an upper house whose members had terms of five, six, or seven years. Knox would place the executive power in a governor general chosen for a seven-year term by both houses of the legislature, but "impeachable by the lower house and triable by the Senate." The governor general would appoint judges who held office on good behavior, but who could be impeached and tried just like the executive. Knox also expressed a strong preference for a single national government rather than an association of governments. Certainly all national laws should be obeyed by the "local governments"—Knox didn't even use the word "states"—and "if necessary" such laws should be enforced by "a body of armed men" kept for that purpose. Knox's "rude sketch" of a more workable government was dramatically different from the Confederation, but anything less, Knox thought, would "hazard the existence of republicanism" and risk either having European nations divide up the United States or "a despotism arising from highhanded commotions."[54]

Was the proposed convention a good way to get such radical but necessary changes? Even the advocates of reform disagreed on that. Some—including Rufus King, who was as impatient as anyone with the imbecilities of the Confederation—thought that proposals for changing the central government should come from the legally constituted Congress and be submitted to the state legislatures for ratification, following the procedure described in the Articles of Confederation. Knox, however, considered that route to change absolutely hopeless: Congress's recommendations were too ineffectual, the state legislatures too recalcitrant. Getting the unanimous consent of the states for essential changes to the Articles of Confederation would be impossible. John Jay proposed instead that Congress declare in plain, strong terms that the Confederation government was inadequate to achieve its purposes and recommend that the people of the states "without Delay" elect delegates to state conventions, whose sole purpose would be to choose deputies to a general convention. That general convention could then enact constitutional changes, without any further process of approval, based upon "the only Source of just authority—the People." What Jay proposed was not, however, what the Annapolis meeting proposed. And as more and more states chose delegates to the Philadelphia convention, it drew support from men who, like Rufus King, still questioned its legality but by February 1787 had come to think it was more prudent for the partisans of change to back the convention than to oppose it. However, King, like Jay, doubted "that much Good" would come from the convention.[55]

Washington's correspondents agreed, in any case, that mere amendments to the Articles of Confederation would not do the job. If the Philadelphia convention recommended only measures to prop up the Confederation, Knox wrote, it would be a step backward, "assisting us to creep on in our present miserable condition, without a hope of a generous constitution" capable of shielding the country from "the effects of faction, and despotism." The convention's recommendations might even exacerbate the country's problems, producing, as Jay feared, "endless Discussions, and perhaps Jealousies and Party Heats." Knox—but not Humphreys—saw a remote chance that, if the convention were well attended by a "respectable set of men," it would propose a more energetic government and the country would accept it. Certainly the convention was, as the Virginia legislature had argued, a more likely place to produce such a proposal than Congress, whose peculiar voting requirements could sometimes keep measures with clear majority support from passing. Even an imperfect proposal from the Philadelphia convention would get men thinking about the subject, and so might serve, Knox suggested, as a "stage in the business" of establishing a "good Constitution."[56]

DECISION TIME

So long as opinion on the convention was divided and its outcome remained uncertain, Knox and Humphreys both thought Washington should stay home. By attending, Humphreys said, Washington would offend the Cincinnati and violate the retirement from public affairs he had announced in resigning his military commission. At some point he might need to do that, Humphreys said, but "the Crisis is . . . not yet come." Washington's "personal influence & character" were "the last stake . . . America has to play." Rather than risk his reputation needlessly, Washington should wait "for the united call of a Continent entire." Knox said the same thing.[57]

Their advice coincided with Washington's inclinations. In February 1787, he wrote Knox confidentially that he did not plan "at this time" to attend the convention—which suggested he might still change his mind. Above all, he wanted "to do for the best, and to act with propriety." He favored the "shortest course" toward getting the federal government the powers it needed for fear that, like a house on fire, the building might burn to ashes while people argued over the best way to put out the flames. He did not think Congress was the most "efficacious" route to constitutional change "for reasons too numerous to enumerate." Washington also said that he found Knox's proposed plan of government more "energetic" and "in every point of view" preferable to the defective government in place, but he thought no such system could be established until major turmoil shook and perhaps destroyed the "political machine." The states with their "darling sovereignties," as well as governors, legislators, and "a long train of etcetera" whose importance would be weakened or destroyed, would oppose such a "revolution." Then Washington pulled back. Perhaps, he said, he spoke from ignorance since he rarely left his farm or spoke with people other than those who visited him, and so he had little acquaintance with "the Sentiments of the great world."[58] Clearly, however, Knox and Jay had started Washington thinking in concrete terms about what might be done. And wasn't the convention already scheduled for May the "shortest course" toward change?

Meanwhile, circumstances began to shift. Between November 1786 and February 1787, while the crisis in Massachusetts was at its height, Congress was incapable of doing much of anything since fewer than seven states were represented. When, finally, nine state delegations were present, Congress still needed the agreement of all to exercise its most important fiscal and military powers. James Madison, who had returned to Congress in 1787, reported that it made "very slow progress," even on issues that required the assent of only seven states. To Humphreys, Congress seemed to be "in a state of mortal stupefaction or lethargy."[59] On February 15, New York finally and definitively refused to ratify the 1783 impost amendment without disabling conditions. A week later, on February 21, Congress adopted a resolution, introduced by Rufus King, that endorsed a convention of state delegates at Philadelphia on the second Monday of May "for the sole and express purpose of revising the Articles of Confederation" in ways that, when approved by Congress and the states, would "render the federal constitution adequate to the exigencies of government and the preservation of the Union." That quieted anxieties over the legality of the convention proposed at Annapolis. Within a few weeks, Massachusetts, New York, and South Carolina had joined the list of states that had elected convention delegations. Madison sent Washington the names of the delegates, which included those of many powerful, respectable men, and predicted that even Connecticut and Rhode Island, where opposition to strengthening Congress was strong, would eventually join the other states in Philadelphia.[60]

Washington's fears of offending the Society of the Cincinnati also began to give way. To be sure, some state chapters still refused to enact the reforms proposed by the Society's triennial meeting in 1784.[61] But correspondents assured Washington that men who were once "mortally opposed to the Cincinnati" had come to see it as a force for "our political preservation." Who, after all, had opposed Shays's Rebellion more ardently than Benjamin Lincoln, the president of the Society of the Cincinnati in Massachusetts, and other ex-officers of the Continental Army? "The clamor and prejudice which existed against" the Cincinnati "are no more," Knox assured Washington. Those who were most against the organization now say "that the society is the only bar to lawless ambition and dreadful anarchy to which the imbecility of government, renders us so liable."[62] There was also reason to think that Washington's fellow officers would cheer his decision to attend the convention: William Moultrie, president of the Cincinnati in South Carolina, congratulated Washington on his "call" to join the Virginia delegation and his decision "to forego all other considerations," quit "the desireable Sweets of retirement, and accept the appointment" from a "regard for the general Interests of America."[63]

Of course, Washington had made no such decision, although many people, he said, had "indirectly, and delicately pressed" him to attend the convention. Then, in early March, a new consideration, potentially more embarrassing than all the others, occurred to him. Might his failure to attend be considered a "dereliction to Republicanism," a refusal to respond to the needs of his country for some unspecified but dishonorable motive, and so injure his reputation? Again he asked Humphreys and Knox for advice: Did the public expect him to attend the convention? He needed their response fast, as Randolph was likely to ask him to decide at any time.[64]

Three days later, with the convention only two months away, Governor Randolph again urged Washington to join the Virginia delegation. Every day seemed to bring some new crisis, Randolph said. The Confederation remained "the last anchor of our hope," but Randolph had come to doubt that the Confederation Congress would survive the year. The letter took thirteen days to arrive, which puzzled Washington, who said he always had his mail collected in Alexandria once or more often twice a week. He took four days to answer the letter because he was "indisposed"—that is, he was physically unable even to acknowledge receipt. He would go, Washington replied, if his health permitted and also if nobody had already been appointed in his place, which would be "highly pleasing" to him because, aside from his old reservations, he had suffered so severe an attack of rheumatism in his shoulder that at times he couldn't raise his hand to his head or turn over in bed. If the governor still considered him a Virginia delegate, he needed to know so he could make arrangements to get to Philadelphia early and mend his fences with the Cincinnati.[65]

Was that a "yes"? Not entirely, but a few days later a letter from Knox pushed Washington toward a firmer consent. If Washington attended the convention, Knox said, he would no doubt be made its president. If the convention proposed only amendments to the confederation, his reputation would suffer. But if it proposed "an energetic and judicious system" with Washington's endorsement, that would be "highly honorable," enhance his fame in "the present and future ages," and entitle Washington "to the glorious republican epithet—The Father of Your Country." The persons chosen as delegates, Knox said, were generally men of "wisdom and vigor," which made him so optimistic about the outcome that his opinion had shifted "greatly in favor of your attendance." Since many states had decided to send delegates because Washington was on the Virginia delegation, his absence would be "chagrining." His presence would give the convention "a national complexion" and "more than any other circumstance" encourage acceptance of its proposals. As for the Society of the Cincinnati, if Washington went to Philadelphia a week early and attended the society's meeting, that would "rivet" the members' affections and remove all embarrassment over his attending the convention.[66]

Humphreys gave the opposite advice. He thought the convention would do nothing of importance. Rhode Island had refused to send delegates, and Connecticut seemed likely to follow its example or that of New York, two out of whose three convention delegates were "antifoederal. What chance is there, then," he asked, "that entire unanimity will prevail?" Few people had "sanguine" expectations, he said, and none of the people he consulted thought Washington should attend.[67]

The reasons for and against his attending the convention seemed to Washington "near an equilibrium." If not all the states attended, or if they sent delegates so "fettered" by instructions that the convention would be unable to act effectively, "I should not like to be a sharer in this business." Only if the delegates could "probe the defects of the Constitution to the bottom, and point out radical cures" would it be "an honorable employment." He wrote Madison that "a thorough reform of the present system is indispensable . . . and with hand and heart I hope the business will be essayed in a full Convention." The central government needed a "means of coercion" to force obedience to its ordinances; without that, "every thing else fails." His wish was "that the Convention may adopt no temporizing expedient, but probe the defects of the Constitution to the bottom, and provide radical cures, whether they are agreed to or not." That would "stamp wisdom and dignity on the proceedings, and be looked to as a luminary, which sooner or later will shed its influence."[68] In short, like Knox, he saw a strong proposal from the convention as a step forward, a stage in the creation of a respectable government, even if that proposal never went into effect.

Finally, on April 9, Washington unambiguously accepted his position on the Virginia delegation, protesting all the while that his assent went against his better judgment and repeating once again his reservations. He yielded, he told Randolph, "to what appeared to be the earnest wishes of my friends." He still feared that the convention would not be well attended and that its members would be so "fettered" that they could not rise to "the great ends of their calling," which would put him in a more "disagreeable Situation" than any other member of the convention.[69]

Soon he received abundant support for his decision. Benjamin Franklin wrote that he looked forward to seeing Washington at the convention, "being persuaded that your Presence will be of the greatest Importance to the Success of the Measure." David Humphreys reported that the Pennsylvania delegate Gouverneur Morris "&some others" had asked him "to use whatever influence I might have to induce" Washington to attend. Knox predicted that there would be "general attendance" at the convention and that the delegates would have "ample powers to point out radical cures for the present political evils." Washington's presence was considered "highly important" to the success of the convention's proposals, which had a good chance of being accepted because the mass of the people were already feeling "the inconveniences of the present government" and wanted change. Washington's failure to attend might indeed provoke—as he feared—malicious charges that he preferred to impose change by force. "On the other hand the unbounded confidence the people have of Your tried patriotism, and

wisdom, would exceedingly facilitate the adoption of any important alterations that might be proposed by a convention of which you were a member"
and, Knox added, "president."[70]

Nobody shared Washington's conviction that "temporising" proposals
would bring dishonor on the convention more than James Madison, who had
warned Washington about his election as a Virginia convention delegate.
"Radical attempts, although unsuccessful," Madison said, "will at least justify the authors of them." In April, two months after Jay and Knox had sent
Washington their ideas on how to redesign American government, Madison
described his own more fully developed proposal of what "radical" transformations the convention might adopt.

Like Knox and Jay, he wanted a "well organized" and "balanced" government with executive, legislative, and judicial departments. Madison
remained undecided how the executive should be structured or what powers
it should have, except that it should control the militia. There should be
national courts, at least for hearing appeals in cases where the litigants were
foreigners or inhabitants of different states and for exercising admiralty jurisdiction. At minimum, state judges should swear to uphold the national as
well as their state constitutions.[71]

Again like Jay and Knox, Madison thought the legislature should be bicameral, with the members of one house chosen by the people or perhaps by
the state legislatures for a term of years he did not define. The other branch
should have fewer members who served for longer terms that were staggered, so experienced delegates would always predominate. Madison did
not say who would choose the members of the upper house, but he insisted
that representation in both houses should be in proportion to population,
and not, as in the Confederation Congress, the same for every state, large
or small. Getting agreement on proportional representation, he thought (in
what proved to be a massive misjudgment), would "not be attended with
much difficulty." Northern states would approve because they had the larger
population, Southern states because they expected major population growth
in the future, and "the lesser States must . . . yield to the predominant will."
Proportional representation, moreover, would help reconcile the larger states
to giving more power to the central government. Its powers should be substantial, including "complete authority in all cases which require uniformity,
such as the regulation of trade, including the right of taxing both exports &
imports," and setting the terms of naturalization.

Madison did not propose consolidating the states into "one simple republic," which seemed to him as unwise as it was politically unattainable. He
was ready to retain local governments wherever they could be "subordinately
useful." The national government, however, should have a veto or "negative
in all cases, whatsoever on the legislative acts of the States, as heretofore exer-

cised by the Kingly prerogative." That seemed to him "absolutely necessary," and "the least possible encroachment on the State jurisdictions." Without that "defensive power"—which could, perhaps, be exercised by the upper house of the legislature—every power given to the national government would be "evaded & defeated" by the states. He also suggested that the national government, empowered with the ability to veto state laws, might serve as a "disinterested & dispassionate umpire in disputes between different passions & interests in the State," and so as a check on majoritarian abuses of minority interests.

The new government, Madison thought, might include a "council of revision" consisting of "the great ministerial officers" to review laws before they went into effect. The plan of government should include an article "guaranteeing tranquility of the states against both internal and external dangers," and the "right of coercion should be expressly declared." Above all, to give the new government "validity and energy," it would have to be ratified by the people, not the state legislatures. That was important because "inroads on the *existing Constitutions* of the States will be unavoidable." In other words, popular ratification would take the power of decision away from those agencies of state government that would suffer the greatest losses of power under the proposed new national government.

Madison had already given Governor Randolph his plan of government; and he sent it to Washington as a fellow member of the Virginia delegation. There was now no going back, not even when his rheumatism forced Washington to carry one arm in a sling. Then, within days of his departure for Philadelphia, he received an urgent message that both his mother and his sister in Fredericksburg were deathly ill. He rushed there, found them better than expected, and returned to Mount Vernon on April 30, with plenty of time to leave early, as planned, so he could mend his fences with the Cincinnati before the federal Convention met.

But instead he went back to visiting the parts of his plantation, supervising the planting. On May 3 and 4 he took along his nephew George Augustine Washington, who would manage Mount Vernon in his absence, and explained to him "the Nature, and the ord[e]r of the business" at each place as he wanted it carried out. He also committed to his diary a detailed scheme for raising Irish potatoes in straw that had been described to him by a gentleman in Fredericksburg: Put the seed potatoes on ordinary ground; cover them with six inches of straw, and add more when the vines poked through, until, finally, a good crop could be harvested with relative ease. Washington also calculated the probable yield per acre.[72]

The man was dawdling. Perhaps he dreaded the divisions and perplexities Humphreys said he would inevitably encounter at the convention. And perhaps he sensed that leaving his retirement once would lead to other such occasions, robbing him of the private life he treasured. Or was he held back by those fears for the success of the convention and the impact its failure would have on him personally that he had described to Governor Randolph in early April?

In those final days at Mount Vernon—or perhaps earlier, in late April— he drew up precise and careful summaries of the plans of government he had received from Jay, Knox, and Madison.[73] Not one proposed a "temporizing expedient." Each called for the creation of a new central government divided into executive, legislative, and judicial branches, clearly superior to the states, with substantial power and the capacity to enforce its rightful authority. Whether the convention would propose so ambitious a program and whether such a plan could be ratified remained to be seen. These plans were at least a beginning, a step toward the creation of a true nation, one that could defend its borders, pay its bills, enforce its laws, and hold its head high in the community of nations. That was all he dared to hope for.

On May 8, Washington finally set out for Philadelphia.

ONE

———— ★ ————

The Morning After

By the morning of September 18, the day after the convention adjourned, David C. Claypoole and John Dunlap, publishers of the *Pennsylvania Packet*, had printed five hundred official six-page broadsides that included the Constitution, the Convention's letter to the president of Congress, and its additional resolutions on ratification procedure. All three documents were signed by the Convention's president, George Washington. The Convention's secretary, William Jackson, tucked some copies into his baggage before he left for New York, where, two days later, he delivered the Constitution and the accompanying documents to Congress. Departing delegates scooped up copies to give governors and legislators in their home states, plus a few extras for friends and family members. Washington himself took a small pile of the Dunlap and Claypoole broadsides. Before leaving Philadelphia he sent copies to Jefferson and Lafayette and later mailed others as a courtesy to Patrick Henry, Benjamin Harrison, and Thomas Nelson, all former governors of Virginia.[1]

It had been a long four months since Washington happily met a delegation of old friends from the Society of the Cincinnati at Chester, Pennsylvania, on Sunday, May 13, and proceeded with them to Philadelphia. On his arrival, he noted in his diary, a set of artillery officers "saluted as I passed" and "the Bells were chimed." There was—no surprise—a crowd outside the Philadelphia boardinghouse where he had planned to stay during the convention. Instead he decided to accept the insistent invitation of a friend, the financier and ardent nationalist Robert Morris, to stay at his home. At first Washington had turned down Morris's invitation for fear that "the tardiness of some States" and discord among the delegates would drag the convention on for a longer time than he wanted to trouble a private family. Even so, he had no idea how long he would be in Philadelphia—through most of the growing season and into harvest time.[2]

The Convention was supposed to assemble the next day, but it took a week before a quorum of seven delegations arrived. Washington had anticipated the delegates' "tardiness." Still, it put him in a bad mood. "These delays," he complained, "greatly impede public measures, and serve to sour the temper of punctual members who do not like to idle away their time."[3] The Virginia delegation used the time to prepare a plan of government to lay before the Convention, so Washington found a good use for his neat summary of the Jay, Knox, and Madison proposals.

Once it settled down to work on May 25, the Convention unanimously elected Washington its president, as Henry Knox and David Humphreys had predicted, and adopted rules of proceeding, including one that forbade delegates to print, publish, or in any way communicate anything said during the debates to the outside world "without leave." That allowed the delegates to speak freely and change their positions when persuaded by others; it also let the Convention do its work without having to contend with outside criticism. As the Convention's president, Washington was responsible for enforcing the secrecy rule, and he personally honored it with scrupulous care. As a result, his correspondence reveals little about the Convention other than chronicling the arrival of new state delegations, which was public information. He wrote Knox on May 31 that ten delegations were present and that another from Maryland would arrive soon. Once New Hampshire's tardy delegation arrived, only Rhode Island would remain unrepresented. A few days later he told George Augustine Washington that eleven states were present (the New Hampshire delegates would not arrive until late June), but he could send no other information except that the debates were more harmonious than he had expected.[4]

As the weeks turned into months, Washington's thoughts turned regularly to Mount Vernon, as they had during the war. He pored over the reports that he insisted his nephew send him every week, and he wrote careful replies. There wasn't "the smallest prospect of my returning before harvest," he reported in early June, "and God knows how long it may be after it." In Pennsylvania, "fine rains" were constantly watering the land; was it the same in drought-parched northern Virginia? He sent detailed instructions for running the farm—what to plant where and how to prepare the ground; which crops to note and compare with others—and on making improvements to the house. His questions were endless. "How does your Pompkin Vines look?" he asked in early July. "And what figure does the pease—Potatoes— Carrots & Parsnips make? Does your Turnips come up well, and do they escape the [Hessian] Fly? How does the Clover, and the other grass seeds which were sown this spring look?" And did the rye, "which was so very thin when I left home, come to any thing—and how has the Spelts & flax turned out?" How much "orchard grass Seed are you likely to save—and what are your prospects of Timothy seed?"[5] Finally, on September 9, he wrote his nephew what he thought would be the last letter he would send him from

Philadelphia because the Convention would probably finish its business within the week. "God grant I may not be disappointed in this expectation," he added, "as I am quite homesick."[6]

It took another eight days before Washington could record in his diary for Monday, September 17, 1787, that "the Constitution received the Unanimous assent of 11 states and Colo. Hamilton's from New York (the only delegate from thence in Convention)" and was signed by every member present except Virginia's Governor Edmund Randolph, Washington's neighbor and old friend George Mason, and Elbridge Gerry of Massachusetts. The delegates then "adjourned to the City Tavern," had a dinner, and "took a cordial leave of each other." He could only marvel at the momentous work the convention had done, meeting often for seven hours a day for five or six days a week since May except for a brief ten-day respite in late July and early August while a Committee of Detail prepared a draft constitution. (During that break, Washington went trout fishing with the Pennsylvania delegate Gouverneur Morris. He also took the opportunity to visit the site of the army's old winter quarters at Valley Forge, where he found everything in ruins. On his return, he struck up a conversation with some farmers on the cultivation of buckwheat and its use in fattening livestock. "About 3 pecks of seed," he recorded, "is the usuall allowance for an Acre.")[7]

Homesick or not, he had to finish some "private business" before leaving Philadelphia on Tuesday, September 18. Before setting out he added brief letters to the copies of the Constitution he sent to Thomas Jefferson, who had gone to Paris as American minister to France, and the Marquis de Lafayette. He could not fulfill his promise to describe the proceedings of the Convention, Washington told Lafayette; the enclosure would have to "speak for itself." It was the product of four months' work and "is now a Child of fortune, to be fostered by some and buffited by others." He would not guess how the country would receive it, or "say anything for or against it—if it be good I suppose it will work its way good—if bad it will recoil on the Framers."[8] Perhaps he needed to say no more. He had, after all, signed the Constitution, and to all the world that looked like an endorsement.

THE CONSTITUTION

That document would certainly surprise those who expected the Convention to recommend amendments to the Articles of Confederation: The Convention instead proposed an entirely new government. A letter to the president of Congress that Washington signed "By unanimous Order of the Convention" explained why. It said the delegates considered it unwise to place all the powers necessary for an effective general government in one body, the Confederation Congress, as the Articles of Confederation had done. As a result, to empower the new government required that it be entirely redesigned.[9]

Moreover, ratification of the Constitution would not require—as both the Annapolis meeting and the Congress had assumed—the consent of Congress and the unanimous consent of the state legislatures. "We the people of the United States," it began, ". . . do ordain and establish this Constitution." A resolution of the Convention, separate from both the Constitution and its letter to the president of Congress, explained how the people would give their consent. The Constitution, it recommended, should "be laid before the United States in Congress assembled," and then "be submitted to a Convention of Delegates, chosen in each State by the People thereof, under the Recommendation of its Legislature, for their Assent and Ratification." When a state convention ratified the Constitution, it should send "Notice thereof to the United States in Congress Assembled." Another resolution described how the Confederation Congress should put the new government into effect once nine states—which Article VII of the Constitution said was sufficient to ratify the document—had given their assent. In that way the new government would be firmly founded, as John Jay (and also James Madison) had argued, on "the only Source of just authority—*the People*," although by a method different from the one Jay had proposed to Washington the previous winter.[10]

The power of the new central government would be divided—as Jay, Knox, and Madison had proposed—among three branches, the legislative (Article I), the executive (Article II), and the judiciary (Article III). The legislature would be bicameral, as, again, Jay, Knox, and Madison had proposed, but in other ways it fell short of their wishes. Each state would have two "Senators" in the upper house, and a delegation in the "House of Representatives" or lower house proportioned to the number of free persons in their population and three fifths of "all other Persons." (The "other Persons" were slaves, a word the convention assiduously avoided.) Senators had to be at least thirty years old and citizens of the United States for nine years; they would be chosen by the state legislatures. Representatives, who would be elected by the people, had to be at least twenty-five years old and citizens for seven years. All members of Congress had to be inhabitants of the states they represented (Article I, Sections 1, 2, and 3).

The number of representatives in the House, according to Article I, Section 2, "shall not exceed one for every thirty Thousand," although every state would have at least one representative. That section of the Constitution also specified the number of representatives each state would have in the first Congress after the Constitution was ratified, before a census could be taken. Virginia, for example, would have ten representatives, Massachusetts eight, New Hampshire three, and Rhode Island one; together the states would be able to send sixty-five members to the first House of Representatives. That made it smaller than several state legislatures.

Representatives would hold office for two years and senators for six, a long period by contemporary state standards, although their terms were staggered so a third of the Senate came up for election every two years. The Constitution put no limit on the number of terms representatives and senators could serve, unlike both the Articles of Confederation and many state constitutions, which imposed term limits to avoid, as the 1776 Pennsylvania constitution put it, an "inconvenient aristocracy" of entrenched officials with no immediate knowledge of the people's needs and feelings.

A census or "enumeration" of the population would be taken within three years of the Congress's first meeting and every ten years thereafter. It would be used to adjust the allocation of seats in the House of Representatives and also direct taxes, which were to be apportioned among the states in proportion to their populations, using the same formula as for representation. The Constitution did not define "direct taxes." However, Article I, Section 9, referred to "Capitation" or poll taxes, which were levied on all adult men, as a direct tax. Most people also considered taxes on real property such as land a direct tax. Direct taxes were levied on individual property holders and could not be avoided, unlike "indirect" taxes such as duties on imports, whose cost was usually added to the price of articles that people could choose not to buy. When assessed per acre rather than by value, land taxes also put a heavy burden on farmers whose land was not particularly valuable. Direct taxes were for those reasons especially feared: They could drive people to ruin.

The Constitution gave Congress substantial new powers. One of its new powers was tucked away in Article I, Section 4: "The Times, Places and Manner of holding Elections for Senators and Representatives" would be set by the various state legislatures, "but the Congress may at any time by Law make or alter such Regulations, except as to the Places of chusing Senators." The reason for the exception was clear: Since the state legislatures would choose senators, for Congress to set the place where senators were chosen would be to let it say where the state legislatures could meet, which was too great an infringement on the states. But why could Congress interfere with state electoral arrangements at all? That provision of the Constitution would come up again and again in the ratifying debates.

More important, Article I, Section 8, which listed the main powers of Congress, said it could "lay and collect Taxes, Duties, Imposts and Excises" to "provide for the common Defense and general Welfare of the United States." Congress could also regulate commerce with foreign nations and among the states, establish post offices and post roads, enact uniform laws on naturalization and bankruptcy, and coin money and regulate its value. It could grant inventors and authors the exclusive right to their inventions and writings "for limited Times" in order to promote science and the arts. It could create courts inferior to the Supreme Court and pass laws to punish crimes on the high seas "and Offenses against the Law of Nations." Congress alone could declare war, and it could "raise and support Armies," although no appropriation of money for that purpose could be for more than two years. It could also "provide and maintain a Navy."

Congress would have the "coercive power" Washington and others had found so conspicuously lacking in the Confederation. It could "provide for calling forth the Militia to execute the Laws of the Union, suppress Insurrections and repel Invasions." It could also "provide for organizing, arming, and disciplining, the Militia," which was primarily a state force, and make rules for governing the militia when it was in service to the United States, although the states could appoint officers and provide for training the militia under rules of discipline prescribed by Congress. It also had exclusive legislative power "in all Cases whatsoever" over a new district of no more than ten miles square that would become the seat of government for the United States. Finally, Congress could make all laws that were "necessary and proper" for executing the powers vested by the Constitution in the government of the United States or any of its departments and officers.

The new Constitution did not, like many state constitutions, begin with a bill of rights, but Article I, Section 9, put some limits on the exercise of congressional power. Congress could not suspend habeas corpus except in cases of rebellion or invasion when the public safety required it; and it could not pass bills of attainder or ex post facto laws. If those provisions protected individual rights, another limited Congress's capacity to extend freedom: It could not prohibit "the Migration or Importation of such Persons as any of the States now existing shall think proper to admit"—in plain language, it could not end the importation of slaves from abroad—until the year 1808. Nor could it grant titles of nobility or tax articles exported from any state.

Limits on state power in Article I, Section 10, reflected the delegates' determination to prevent the state legislatures from violating property rights. The states could no longer "coin money; emit Bills of Credit; make any Thing but gold and silver Coin a Tender in Payment of Debts;" or pass any laws "impairing the Obligation of Contracts." Nor could the states lay duties on imports or exports except where necessary "for executing it's inspection laws," and the money collected had to be turned over to the United States Treasury. The states were explicitly denied the power to keep troops or ships of war in time of peace, enter compacts with another state or with a foreign power, or engage in war without Congress's consent unless actually invaded or in imminent danger.

The Constitution entrusted the executive power to a president who would hold office for four years and, like the members of Congress, could be re-elected indefinitely. The president had to be at least thirty-five years of age, a natural-born citizen of the United States or a citizen of the United States when the Constitution was adopted, and a resident for at least fourteen years. The president's pay could not be increased or lowered during his term of office, nor could he receive any other compensation from the United States or the separate states. The Constitution also provided for a vice president, who would become president when the president died, resigned, was unable to perform his duties, or was removed from office. The vice president would preside over the Senate, but could vote only to break ties.

The provision for electing the president and vice president was the most complex in the entire document. The president would be chosen by electors in each state equal to the number of senators and representatives it had in Congress. Those electors, who were chosen in whatever way their state legislature decided but could not be members of Congress or hold another federal "Office of Trust or Profit," would meet within their states and vote for two persons, one of whom had to be from another state, then make a signed and certified list of the votes cast and send it, sealed, to the president of the Senate. He would open the returns and count the votes before a joint meeting of Congress. The candidate with the highest number of electoral votes, provided the number represented a majority of the electors, became president; the candidate with the next greatest number of votes became vice president. If nobody won the votes of a majority of the electors, or if more than one candidate managed to do that and each had an equal number of votes, the House of Representatives would choose the president from the top two candidates (if both had majority votes of the same size) or among the top five (if nobody had a majority vote). In making that decision, each state had only one vote, and the winner had to have the votes of "a Majority of all the States"—not only of the states whose representatives were present and voting. If no candidate clearly won the vice presidency, the decision was instead thrown to the Senate.

The president—now the head of the government, not, as before, the presiding officer of Congress—would have considerable power. He was "Commander in Chief of the Army and Navy of the United States, and of the Militia of the several States" when it was called into the service of the United States by Congress. Acts of Congress required his consent to become law, but if he made no decision for ten days (unless Congress adjourned in that period), the act would go into effect anyway. If the president refused his consent, his veto could be overridden by a two-thirds vote in both houses of Congress. The president was not required, like some state governors, to make appointments or veto laws only with the consent of special councils. He did, however, need the consent of the Senate to make treaties or appoint ambassadors, judges of the Supreme Court, and several other major officers of the United States. The Constitution referred to "executive Departments" but said nothing about them except that the President could require opinions in writing from their principal officers.

Article III, Section 1, placed the judicial power of the United States "in one supreme Court, and in such inferior courts as the Congress may from time to time ordain and establish." Judges held their positions during good behavior, although they could, like the president, vice president, "and all civil Officers of the United States," be impeached (indicted) by the House of Representatives for "treason, bribery, or other high crimes and misdemeanors," tried by the Senate, and, if convicted by two-thirds of the senators present, removed from office. To help keep the judges free from manipulation, they had to be paid "at stated Times," and their compensation could not be lowered while they remained on the bench.

The federal judicial power extended, according to Article III, Section 2, "to all Cases, in Law and Equity, arising under this Constitution, the Laws of the United States," and treaties negotiated under its authority. It would also try cases affecting ambassadors or involving admiralty jurisdiction and controversies to which the United States was a party, between "a State and Citizens of another State," between citizens of different states, between citizens of the same state who claimed lands under grants from different states, or between a state or its citizens "and foreign States, Citizens, or subjects." The trials for all crimes except impeachment would be decided by jury and held in the state where the crime was committed. There was no similar provision for trial by jury in civil cases. The third and final section of Article III defined treason in a way that was meant to prevent it from being used, as in times past, against political enemies. Treason against the United States would consist "only in levying War against them, or in adhering to their Enemies, giving them Aid and Comfort." Conviction required "the Testimony of two Witnesses to the same overt Act" or a confession "in open Court."

The rest of the Constitution addressed other miscellaneous issues, which, however, were often of great consequence. For example, Article IV repeated a provision in the Articles of Confederation that said the citizens of each state were entitled to all the "Privileges and Immunities of Citizens in the several States." It also provided for the extradition of criminals from one state to another, for the return of persons "held to Service or Labour in one State . . . escaping into another" (i.e., runaway slaves), and for the admission of new states to the union. And it decreed that "the United States shall guarantee every State in this Union a Republican Form of Government" and protect each of them against invasion and also domestic violence (including slave insurrections) on the application of the legislature, or the executive if the legislature was not in session.

No longer would amendments require Congress's approval and the unanimous consent of the state legislatures. Article V said amendments could be proposed by either a two-thirds vote of both houses of Congress or a convention called on the application of two-thirds of the state legislatures.

Amendments would go into effect when ratified by three-quarters of the state legislatures or by special conventions in three-quarters of the states, and Congress could specify the method used. No amendment, however, could end the foreign slave trade before 1808, and no amendment could ever deprive a state of equal representation in the Senate without its consent.

Article VI stated that all debts entered into by the United States before the adoption of the Constitution would remain valid thereafter. All officers, legislative, executive, and judicial, of both the United States and the several states, would be bound by oath or affirmation to support the Constitution, "but no religious Test shall ever be required as a Qualification to any Office or public Trust under the United States." Moreover, Article VI, paragraph 2, said the Constitution itself, the laws of the United States enacted under the Constitution, and treaties made under the authority of the United States "shall be the supreme Law of the Land," and the judges in every state were bound by it, anything to the contrary in the constitution or laws of their states notwithstanding. Finally, Article VII said ratification by nine state conventions would be sufficient to establish the Constitution among "the States so ratifying the Same."

The document received "the Unanimous Consent of the States present the Seventeenth Day of September in the Year of our Lord one thousand seven hundred and Eighty seven and of the Independence of the United States of America the Twelfth." Thirty-nine delegates from twelve states signed "in witness whereof," including, as Washington noted in his diary, only one delegate for New York, Alexander Hamilton. Thirteen delegates had left the Convention before its end, some for pressing personal reasons, and some— including Hamilton's two colleagues, Robert Yates and John Lansing, Jr., and Maryland's Luther Martin—because they heartily disagreed with what the Convention was doing. Three others, as Washington also noted, stayed until the end but refused to sign. In short, sixteen of the fifty-five members who at one time attended the Convention did not put their names to the document. That suggested it would meet some opposition when announced to the world.

A MIXED BAG

In fact, many of the men who signed the Constitution and who would become its most powerful supporters in the months to come left the Convention with mixed feelings. By all evidence, they had won a stunning victory. The Constitution was no "temporizing" solution to the country's problems. In many ways it resembled the plans of government proposed by Washington's correspondents, including Knox, whose ideas Washington had considered revolutionary the previous February. But the match between what they wanted and what they got was not exact. The advocates of national power had to yield on some points to win on others—or to keep the Convention from failing altogether. As the delegates said in their letter to the president of Congress, the Constitution was the fruit of "mutual deference and concession." They did not pretend it was perfect. The delegates claimed only that the Constitution was perhaps "liable to as few exceptions as could reasonably have been expected," and they hoped it would prove able to "promote the lasting welfare" of the United States "and secure her freedom and happiness."[11]

James Madison was more pessimistic than that. Having witnessed the failures of the Confederation while a congressmen from Virginia, he became one of the strongest promoters of the federal Convention. In preparation for its sessions, Madison, a graduate of the College of New Jersey (later Princeton), undertook a systematic examination, through a trunk of books sent from Paris by Thomas Jefferson, his friend and onetime colleague in the Virginia legislature, of ancient and modern confederacies, and he also summarized the major problems of American government during the 1780s. Although Madison was short, shy, and relatively young (he was thirty-six in 1787), his intellect and learning had won him respect among his more senior colleagues, including Washington. He helped write the plan of government that the Virginia delegation prepared while it waited for the Convention to meet, and he would later be called "the father of the Constitution," a title he had the grace to decline since it was, as he said, the work of "many heads & many hands."[12]

More important, he was not altogether happy with what those "many heads" decided. On September 6 he sent Jefferson a description and assessment of the Constitution, putting critical phrases (in italics below) in code. If the Constitution was adopted, he predicted that it would "neither effectually *answer* its *national object* nor prevent the local *mischiefs* which every where *excite disgusts* ag[ain]st the *state governments*." He had strenuously opposed the equal representation of states in the Senate, and he would have liked to change several other parts of the document. What bothered him most, however, was the Convention's refusal to give Congress a veto on state laws. That power, he insisted, was essential to keep the states from continuing to infringe national authority and to violate individual rights.[13]

Alexander Hamilton shared Madison's pessimism about the Constitution, but for different reasons. Born out of wedlock on the island of Nevis in the West Indies in 1755 or 1757, Hamilton had come to be educated on the North American mainland in the early 1770s thanks to a fund collected from his neighbors who recognized the boy's extraordinary talent. He attended King's College (later Columbia), became an army officer, serving for a time as aide-de-camp to Washington, and married into New York's wealthy Schuyler family. A lawyer by profession, Hamilton was as assertive as Madison was reserved. On the last day of the Convention, he declared that "no man's ideas were more remote from the plan than his own." His fellow delegates understood, since Hamilton had described his preferred form of government earlier in their deliberations. It was much like those Knox and Jay had proposed to Washington, with a central government that appointed the states' chief executives as well as officers of the state militias, which Hamilton thought should be "under the sole and exclusive direction of the United States." He would give the federally appointed state executives an absolute veto on the laws of their states to make sure no law went into effect that was contrary to the laws or Constitution of the United States. Morever, to make the federal government more like that of Britain, which Hamilton considered "the best in the world," judges, senators, and the executive or "governor" would hold office for life or "good behavior." He would sign the Constitution despite his misgivings, Hamilton said, because the alternatives were "anarchy and Convulsion on the one side," and, on the other, a remote chance that the Constitution would do some good.[14]

Gouverneur Morris, Washington's fishing partner and one of the most influential nationalists in the federal convention, said he also had objections but would support the Constitution "with all its faults" as "the best that was to be attained." And Benjamin Franklin, at eighty the oldest delegate and the only one, thanks to his achievements in science and diplomacy, who came anywhere near Washington in stature, confessed that there were "several parts of this constitution which I do not at present approve." He thought, however, that he might change his mind in the future, as he so often had over his long life, due to "better information, or fuller consideration." Franklin consented to the Constitution "with all its faults, if they are such," because the country needed a general government and he doubted that another convention could produce a better one. He called on each of the other members of the Convention who held reservations to "doubt a little of his own infallibility" and sign the Constitution "to make manifest our unanimity."[15]

Henry Knox was not a delegate, but he seems to have received reliable information on the convention's proceedings despite the secrecy rule. He too found the Constitution "short of my wishes and of my judgement." He described it, as did Morris and Franklin, as "the best which can be obtained under present circumstances." Knox considered the states "an insuperable evil in a national point of view," but he could not see how "in this stage of the business they could be annihilated." Like others, he supported the Constitution because no better alternative was possible and said that "all those who have wished for a national republic of higher and more durable powers" should strenuously support its ratification.[16]

Washington, too, had his reservations. He had voted in the course of the Convention for a list of losing propositions—to require, for example, the consent of only seven states to ratify the Constitution. He had also favored requiring a three-quarters vote of Congress to override a presidential veto.[17]

His main concern, however, was probably with the Constitution's provisions on representation. His only recorded intervention in the Convention's debates came on the final day, when he supported a motion to change the statement that "the number of Representatives shall not exceed one for every forty thousand" to "one for every thirty thousand." He had always considered "the smallness of the proportion of Representatives" among the "exceptionable" parts of the plan, Washington said, and he hoped the change would be adopted, which it was.[18]

It is not entirely clear that the change resolved his doubts. Once before he had expressed discontent with the Convention's work—on July 10, in a private letter to Hamilton, who had returned to New York. "I *almost* dispair of seeing a favourable issue to the proceedings of the Convention," he said, "and do therefore repent having had any agency in the business." At the time the Convention was debating what came to be known as the "Great Compromise," by which states would be represented equally in the upper house of the legislature but representation in the lower would be proportional to population. During the Convention's debates, Madison expressed fear that without a system of "just representation"—which for him demanded proportional representation in both houses—the new government would be denied one power after another and so would end up "as impotent and shortlived" as the Confederation. Moreover, Madison said, the sixty-five members proposed for the first federal House were too few: They "would not possess enough of the confidence of the people" and could not "bring with them all the local information which would be frequently wanted." On the day Washington wrote Hamilton, Madison had tried unsuccessfully to double the size of the first House. The Convention's refusal to go along with Madison probably explains Washington's distress. Like Madison, he thought the power of the new government would depend on the fairness of its representative system, and he roundly criticized those "narrow minded politicians"—no doubt small-state delegates who insisted on an equal representation of the states—who opposed "a strong & energetic government" on the pretext that the people would not accept it.[19]

In any case, Washington, like so many others who put their names to the document, saw the Constitution as a mixed bag. "I wish the Constitution . . . had been made more perfect," he wrote Benjamin Harrison soon after the convention adjourned, "but I sincerely believe it is the best that could be obtained at this time." Since it opened "a constitutional door . . . for amendment hereafter," and so a way to remedy its imperfections in the future, he supported its adoption "under the present circumstances of the Union," which seemed to him "suspended by a thread." If the Convention had failed to come to an agreement—or, by implication, if the Constitution were not ratified—"anarchy would soon have ensued."[20] No longer did he think of the

Convention as a first step toward the development of a strong national government sometime in the future. Now he wanted the Constitution ratified. But there were limits to what he would do for that cause. He had, after all, attended the Convention and signed the documents it issued, committing his name and reputation to the Constitution. Wasn't that enough?

At long last, on the afternoon of September 18, Washington set out for home along with his fellow Virginia delegate John Blair. He was in such a rush that he refused to wait when heavy rains prevented him from crossing a ford at Head of Elk (now Elkton), Maryland, and tried sending his carriage, loaded with baggage, over an old abandoned bridge. He and Blair took the precaution of getting out first, which was wise because the bridge gave way. One of his horses, still in harness, dropped some fifteen feet, and the other came close to following, which would have destroyed Washington's carriage. Fortunately, workers from a nearby mill managed with "great exertion" to save the horses and prevent further damage. On September 22, Washington finally arrived at Mount Vernon, "about Sunset after an absence of four Months and 14 days," and resumed his life as a private man.[21]

The newspapers continued to arrive, however, along with a steady stream of speeches, pamphlets, and reports on the ratification process. Washington's correspondents shared with him not just the news they received, good and bad, but their hopes and their fears. Mount Vernon became a fine vantage point for watching the drama unfold in one state after another. And occasionally Washington would do something to help get the Constitution ratified—so long as it did not make him leave home again.

THE DISSENTERS

George Mason was not a dissident by nature. He was a builder, not a naysayer, the man who drafted Virginia's first state constitution and the powerfully influential declaration of rights Virginia enacted in early June of 1776, whose affirmation that "all men are born equally free and independent" found its way, with some variations, into several other state bills of rights as well as the Declaration of Independence. Left to his own devices, the sixty-two-year-old planter—seven years the senior of his neighbor George Washington—would have happily stayed at his elegant home, Gunston Hall, near the Potomac in northern Virginia, a few miles from Mount Vernon. But when provoked, as he was by what he called "the precipitate, & intemperate, not to say indecent Manner" in which the convention acted during its last week, he became a fearsome fighter. He left Philadelphia, Madison reported, "in an exceeding ill humour indeed" and went home "with a fixed disposition to prevent the adoption of the plan if possible."[22]

Mason's political involvement before 1787 is best described as irregular. He served briefly in Virginia's house of burgesses in 1758–60, then skipped several sessions and did not seek reelection. He supported resistance to British taxation and drafted the powerful Fairfax County Resolves of 1774, which called for the collection of provisions to relieve Boston, a boycott of the East India Company, and the appointment of a Continental Congress "to concert a general and uniform Plan for the Defence and Preservation of our common Rights." He also participated in Virginia's Revolutionary conventions—extralegal legislatures—in 1775 and again in 1776, where his work on Virginia's constitution and declaration of rights earned him a fame that he, unlike other members of his generation, did not crave. He once described himself as a man who seldom meddled in public affairs, "content with the Blessings of a private Station" without regard for "the Smiles & Frowns of the Great."[23]

Public service was an obligation of class for wealthy eighteenth-century Virginians, but time and again Mason fought off the call of his country, particularly when public service would take him away from home. He refused election to the Continental Congress in 1775 and again in 1777, and he served much of his term on the state's committee of safety—an appointment he tried to avoid without success—in absentia. (He claimed, however, that he corresponded regularly with the committee, considering it every man's duty to "contribute his Mite to the public Service.") Mason sat in the house of delegates during 1777–81 but refused to return three years later. He would regard any attempt to elect him, he wrote the sheriff of Fairfax County, "in no other light than an oppressive & unjust invasion of my personal Liberty." If elected, he would "certainly refuse to act, be the Consequences what they will."[24]

Mason had strong reasons for refusing public offices. His first wife, who died in 1773, bore him twelve children, of whom nine lived to adulthood, and he thought that his large family and the demands of managing his plantation had first claim on his time. Beginning in his thirties, moreover, Mason suffered from chronic illnesses that made attendance at meetings difficult. Intermittent attacks of gout, which affected his hands, feet, and stomach, with aftereffects that lasted for weeks, often kept him at home or, as in 1779, left him weak and exhausted. Fatigue no doubt caused or reinforced Mason's equally chronic impatience with inflated oratory, political maneuvering, and colleagues who acted with less intelligence and incisiveness than he did.[25]

The best-known portrait of Mason, painted in the 1750s when he was in his twenties, shows a chubby man with a cherubic face. Except for the set mouth and intense eyes, it probably gives a false impression of his appearance (some observers said he was tall and muscular) and certainly of his personality. Mason was known not for his geniality but for his intelligence and also his knowledge, despite the fact that, unlike many influential men of his time, he never attended college. The oldest son of a wealthy planter who drowned when George was only nine, he was taught by private tutors and then read extensively in the library of his uncle, John Mercer. There he absorbed the natural rights philosophy of English Whigs such as John Locke and became so learned in the law that people often assumed he had been trained as a lawyer. Mason never seemed to suffer the discomfort that Washington, who also lacked a formal education, sometimes felt in the company of educated men. Mason more than held his own in that crowd. When appointed to the committee charged with drafting a state constitution along with James Madison, Edmund Randolph, Richard Bland, and Thomas Ludwell Lee, Mason commented that the committee was, "according to custom, over-charged with useless Members."[26]

Washington, by contrast, commanded Mason's highest regard. The two men had much in common: They both owned and managed large plantations in northern Virginia (Mason had over five thousand acres), and both put a high value on their private lives. They also shared a thirst for lands in the west and a commitment to developing the Potomac River. Washington and Mason worked together as Truro Parish vestrymen, as arbiters in local disputes, and in defending American rights against Britain during the 1760s and 1770s. Washington asked for Mason's counsel on both private and public affairs, and Mason sent Washington dozens of fruit tree grafts—which should have sealed their friendship. Washington, however, never seems to have returned Mason's affection in equal measure. They clashed on some issues in local politics, and Washington perhaps suspected Mason of impropriety, or at least of an ardor that strained the limits of propriety, in defending his personal financial interests. Or was he simply upset by Mason's refusal and that of other "Men of abilities" to leave their vines and fig trees when the country desperately needed their services?[27]

And yet in 1787, when the country needed him again, Mason responded. He accepted his appointment as a Virginia delegate to the Philadelphia Convention, although it took him farther from home than he had ever gone before. He arrived on May 17, a few days after Washington, along with his son, John, and a couple of slaves. Like several other delegates, Mason moved into the Indian Queen Tavern on Chestnut and Fourth streets, near the Pennsylvania State House, where the convention would meet. He had never been to a major American city before, and he soon complained about the "etiquette and nonsense so fashionable" in Philadelphia. But he showed up at the Convention day after day, served on major committees, and became one of the most active participants in its debates. His health seemed unusually good: William Pierce, a delegate from Georgia who wrote some short, perceptive descriptions of Convention members, said Mason had "a fine strong constitution." To his delight, Mason discovered that his fellow delegates included "many Gentlemen of the most respectable Abilities; and, so far as I can yet discover, of the purest Intentions." Their company seemed to energize him: No longer did he have to endure the mediocrity that added to his misery in the Virginia assembly. "America has certainly, on this occasion, drawn forth her first Characters," he wrote his son and namesake in early June. Mason was finally in his element, among his intellectual peers.[28]

The apparent transformation of his politics was no less amazing. Mason had been no friend of efforts to give the Confederation Congress power to regulate trade or to collect an impost on imports. He said that giving an independent source of revenue to a central government that possessed military power would pose a danger to American liberty. In short, Mason had what another Virginian, James Monroe, called "Antifederal Prejudices." By the beginning of the Convention, however, Mason recognized the magnitude of the crisis facing the United States and the importance of establishing "a wise & just Government" that would affect "the Happiness or Misery of Millions yet unborn." The challenge was so great, he wrote, that it "absorbs, & in a Manner suspends the operation of human Understanding." The eyes of the people were turned toward the Convention, "& their Expectations raised to a very anxious Degree. May God grant we may be able to gratify them."[29]

At first Mason acted hand in hand with delegates who wanted to create a substantially stronger central government. He apparently supported the plan of government the Virginia delegation proposed in the opening days of the Convention, a plan that closely resembled Madison's pre-Convention ideas and included a congressional veto on state laws. He was ready to tear up the Confederation and start over. When a New York delegate said the Convention had authority only to propose amendments to the Articles of Confederation, Mason answered him: There were, he said, crises when "all the ordinary cautions yielded to public necessity." The Convention would submit its proposals to the people for ratification, and the sovereign people had power to do whatever they chose to do, including accept or reject whatever the Convention proposed. Moreover, once the powers of the central government were no longer placed in one body, the Confederation Congress, but were divided among various branches of government, Mason was willing to strengthen the central government. He understood that the United States needed what Mason was ready to call a "national government," one whose power came from the people and that could enforce its powers on individuals.[30]

Mason wanted to preserve the states, and not just as administrative units of the nation, but he was willing to free the national government from state influence on one point after another. He favored letting the people—not the state legislatures—elect members of the lower house of Congress, and he thought congressmen should be paid by the national government, not the states. He served on the committee that proposed the Great Compromise on representation, which kept the Convention from dissolving, and then probably used his influence at a caucus of large-state delegates to reconcile his colleagues to the loss of proportional representation in the Senate. In short, Mason contributed more than his share to the design of a national government with "extensive powers," although, like any son of the Revolution, he wanted safeguards against the abuse of those powers. William Pierce described him as a man "of remarkable strong powers" with a "clear and copious understanding," who was "able and convincing in debate, steady and firm in his principles, and undoubtedly one of the best politicians in America."[31]

Mason continued to support a strong and active government in August, after the Committee of Detail presented a draft Constitution based on resolutions the Convention had approved. He disagreed with delegates who thought Congress might not have to meet every year. Such men underestimated how important Congress would be, he said, because "the extent of the Country will supply business"; in addition, Congress would have not just legislative but *"inquisitorial* powers" that could "not safely be long kept in . . . suspension." Mason was responsible for giving Congress the power to "declare"—not "make"—war, which he saw as a way of "facilitating peace," and supplied the phrase about giving the country's enemies "aid and comfort" in the constitutional definition of treason.

Mason wanted to require a two-thirds vote of Congress for all laws regulating trade to protect the interests of the exporting South against a Northern congressional majority. But he defended that provision from a nationalist, not a sectional, perspective. For the new government to be "lasting," he said, it had to be so constructed that it could command "the confidence & affections of the people," which required protecting minorities against abuses by the majority. He thought that requiring a supermajority on trade laws, which were sensitive given sectional economic differences, would help accomplish that. Mason also passionately condemned not only the slave trade but slavery itself as an institution that retarded industry, discredited labor, and fostered tyrannical habits in owners. Slavery was a moral evil, and "providence punishes national sins," he predicted, "by national calamities." He lost on the issue of the slave trade because, he charged, delegates from South Carolina and Georgia agreed to let trade laws pass by simple majorities in return for a provision precluding the abolition of the slave trade until 1808.[32]

Then suddenly, on August 31, Mason told the Convention he would "sooner chop off his right hand than put it to the Constitution as it now stands." He wanted certain points decided before he voted on ratification procedures—or he might want to bring the "whole subject" before another convention. The same day he scribbled a list of "objections" to the Constitution for the Maryland delegates, hoping to enlist their support in fixing what was broken. Once that was done, he said, "the system would be unexceptionable."[33] Mason thought the "aristocratic" Senate had too much power, but he could not get the Convention to give some of its advisory functions to a council of state in the executive branch (although Franklin, Madison, and

James Wilson seemed sympathetic). Nor could he keep the vice president from becoming ex officio president of the Senate. He considered that provision "an encroachment on the rights of the Senate," which should be free to choose its own presiding officer. He did, however, see to it that the House, not the Senate, would choose the president in the event that no candidate won a clear majority of electoral votes. And he contributed the phrase "high crimes and misdemeanors" to the clause on impeachment of the president.[34] For an impatient man, Mason invested enormous attention in details. He knew they were important. They would determine whether the government would be a blessing or a scourge to future generations.

Edmund Randolph also developed reservations about the Convention's proposal. Several of Randolph's objections coincided with Mason's: He too thought the Senate was too powerful, Congress's power too broad, and also that the federal judiciary would pose a threat to state courts. Randolph suggested letting state ratifying conventions propose amendments to the Constitution, which could be put into effect or rejected by a second general convention. Franklin seconded the motion, but Mason managed to have it set aside until the Convention could see the polished form of the Constitution being prepared by the Committee of Style.[35] The Committee of Style did not, however, solve the problems Randolph raised, nor those Mason listed on the back of its report.

Nor did the Convention. Between September 12 and 17, the delegates went over the revised version of the Constitution one last time, considering a mass of changes, accepting some but turning down most. Twice they rejected efforts to increase representation in the first House of Representatives.[36] When North Carolina's Hugh Williamson noted that the Constitution included no provision for jury trials in civil cases, another delegate observed that jury trials were not proper in all civil cases. Maritime cases, for example, were generally decided by judges specially trained in admiralty law. Mason saw the problem: A general principle would be enough, he said, and he thought that if a bill of rights that supported the right to a jury trial along with other civil rights were added to the Constitution, "it would give great quiet to the people." A draft could be prepared in a few hours using state bills of rights as models. Elbridge Gerry of Massachusetts moved to create a committee for that purpose; Mason seconded the motion. Connecticut's Roger Sherman said the existing state declarations of rights were sufficient protection; Mason answered that the laws of the United States would be paramount to the state bills of rights. He might have added—as the delegates well knew—that not all states had bills of rights. Still, not one state supported Gerry's motion.[37] Later the delegates rejected motions to protect freedom of the press, to include a phrase protecting the people's liberty against standing armies in time of peace, and, again, to guarantee jury trials in civil cases.

Those additions were unnecessary, they said. They could endure no more delays; they wanted to go home.

Randolph, who had done so much to bring the Convention together, found himself in a painful position. He worried about the "indefinite and dangerous power" the Constitution gave Congress, but he did not want to differ from the majority after so long and arduous a labor. To save him from that embarrassment, he formally moved that state conventions be allowed to propose amendments to the Constitution, and that a second general convention convene to accept or reject those amendments before the Constitution went into effect. Again, Mason seconded the motion. The Constitution, he said, had been written in secret, "without the knowledge or idea of the people." After a broad public debate, a second convention would "know more of the sense of the people, and be able to provide a system more consonant to it. It was improper to say to the people, take this or nothing." He had sufficient reservations about the Constitution as it then stood that he could neither sign it nor support its ratification in Virginia. But "with the expedient of another Convention as proposed, he could sign."[38]

Charles Pinckney of South Carolina called the idea of a second convention a prescription for disaster. He too disliked parts of the Constitution, but only "confusion and contrariety" could result from letting the states recommend amendments to the Constitution. They would all propose different things, and the delegates to the general convention would be too shackled by instructions from their home states to agree on anything. That "general confusion," he feared, would finally be concluded "by the Sword." Elbridge Gerry, however, endorsed the project—then "supported" the motion with a speech that effectively snuffed out whatever hope it had. He too had objections to the Constitution, which he proceeded to list. As Gerry criticized the allocation of three-fifths representation for slaves, the length of senators' terms, and Congress's power to tax, to regulate commerce, and to raise an army, delegates no doubt saw the real possibility that all their hard-won compromises would dissolve into nothing.

Or were they more concerned with Gerry's charge that Massachusetts would not have enough representatives in the first federal Congress? If the states fought over their particular interests in that way, what chance was there that the Constitution would be improved by the process that Randolph, Mason, and Gerry supported? Gerry, in short, seemed to prove Pinckney's point. Not one state delegation voted in favor of Randolph's motion. The Convention then approved the Constitution with the handful of changes it had made.[39] But even Franklin's eloquent speech, calling on his fellow delegates to doubt their infallibility and support the Constitution, could not persuade Randolph, Mason, and Gerry to put their names to the document.

MASON'S OBJECTIONS

Soon the list of objections Mason wrote on the back of the Committee of Style report became something of a platform for critics of the Constitution. The document, he said, did not include a bill of rights, or a "declaration of any kind" for preserving liberty of the press, trial by jury in civil cases, or against "the danger of standing armies in time of peace." Mason (like Washington and Madison) objected to the small size of the first House of Representatives, which gave the people "the Shadow only of Representation" (although he later noted that the problem was reduced by the convention's decision on its final day to change the provision, so there could be one representative for every thirty thousand rather one than for every forty thousand people).

Senators had too much power, he said, given that they were to be chosen by the state legislatures and therefore were "not the representatives of the people or amenable to them." The Senate could alter money bills and propose appropriations of money, including the salaries of officers it appointed; it had power over the appointment of ambassadors and other public offices, the enactment of treaties, and impeachments. Its close connection with the president, the senators' long terms of office, and the fact that the Senate would be "almost continually sitting" would destroy the government's balance and allow it to usurp "the rights and liberties of the people." Since treaties would be the supreme law of the land, Mason thought the House of Representatives should have to consent to them, not just the Senate.

He continued to think that letting Congress pass "navigation acts"—laws regulating trade—by simple majorities put the five Southern states, which grew products such as tobacco and rice for export, at the mercy of the eight other states. He feared that Congress would pass laws that allowed merchants of the Northern states to demand exorbitant freight costs and to monopolize the purchase of commodities, paying prices that served their interest "to the great injury of the landed interest" and the "impoverishment of the people." Requiring a two-thirds vote would instead produce "moderation, promote the general interest," and remove an "insuperable objection" to ratification of the Constitution in its current form.

Mason also feared that Congress would abuse the "necessary and proper" clause, using it to create monopolies, to define new crimes and "inflict unusual and severe punishments," and in general to extend its authority so far as to threaten the powers retained by the states and rights retained by the people. On the other hand, he opposed Congress's constitutional incapacity to interfere with the slave trade for twenty years. Further importations of slaves, he said, "render the United States weaker, more vulnerable, and less capable of defence."

He objected to the fact that states could no longer levy export duties on their own produce (as Virginia had long done on tobacco) or pass ex post facto laws, which he claimed legislatures always had and always would pass "when necessity and public safety require them," so the provision would be honored in the breach, inviting other infractions of the Constitution.

Because the president had no "Constitutional Council," Mason said, he would turn to "minions and favorites," become a tool of the Senate, or receive advice from a council composed of executive department heads, who would readily agree to oppressive measures to avoid inquiry into their own misconduct in office. Mason proposed a council composed of two men from the Northern states, two from the mid-Atlantic states, and two from the South, all appointed by the House of Representatives, with each state having one vote, for six-year terms of office with two of the six councillors coming up for reelection every two years. When necessary, the council's president could act as vice president. Then the "unnecessary" office of vice president could be eliminated from the Constitution: Because the vice president had nothing else to do while the president survived, the Constitution made him president of the Senate, which violated the separation of powers and gave his home state "an unnecessary and unjust preeminence." Mason also objected to giving the president power to grant pardons for treason, which would allow him to shield from punishment persons he had instigated to commit crimes and prevent discovery of his own wrongdoing.[40]

Mason's fears were a lot like Randolph's. Mason thought the government under the Constitution would begin as "a moderate aristocracy" and then, over time, become a monarchy or "a corrupt, tyrannical aristocracy." Randolph predicted that the convention's plan of government would "end in Tyranny."[41] Mason and Randolph were not like the New York delegates Robert Yates and John Lansing, Jr., or Maryland's Luther Martin, all of whom left the Convention early because they had no taste for anything except amendments to the Confederation. Randolph's continental vision was well known, not least to Washington. No one, Washington wrote Randolph in November 1786, after the latter's election as governor of Virginia, was more aware of the crisis in American affairs and the urgent need to take steps to avoid ruin than Randolph, and so nobody was better qualified to hold the "reins of Government." Without Randolph's skillful negotiations, Washington's name might never have appeared as a member of the Virginia delegation to the federal Convention, encouraging the participation of other states. Randolph had also presented to the convention the Virginia delegates' plan for a powerful new government.[42]

Mason's support for a strong central government was of a more recent vintage, but his record at the convention showed that his conversion was total. He believed in a national government whose authority came from the people and could be enforced on individuals. He was willing to invest substantial power in the central government—far more than the Confederation held—

so long as the government included structural checks on the misuse of that power. Mason also insisted on provisions to protect minority interests and the people's rights.

Although the Convention's Constitution failed to satisfy him, he did not question the need for fundamental change. He wanted to perfect the Convention's proposal, not abandon it. That was why he and Randolph stayed to the end of the Convention. In October, when Mason sent Washington a revised list of his objections, he said they were "not numerous" and could easily have been removed by "a little Moderation & Temper, in the latter End of the Convention."[43] Later that month, Mason expressed hope that the state conventions would all meet at about the same time. If, after consulting each other, they agreed on "a few necessary amendments" while "determining to join heartily in the System so amended, they might, without Danger of public Convulsion or Confusion, procure a general Adoption of the new Government."[44] There he would be disappointed: Thanks to differences in state politics and legislative schedules, the ratifying conventions would be spread over a long period of time, from November of 1787 through the following summer. As Mason anticipated, that complicated the task of amending the Constitution by common consent of the states.

It would, in truth, have required a significant recasting of the Constitution to meet some of Mason's and Randolph's objections: their unhappiness with an imperfect separation of powers, for example, and what they considered the overly intimate relationship of the Senate and the executive. But neither Mason nor Randolph asked that everything they wanted be accepted. The sovereign people, or their representatives in the state ratifying conventions, would decide what changes should be made, and then another national convention would sort through the various state proposals, enacting some, perhaps with modifications, and rejecting others. Mason and Randolph insisted, however, that the people and their chosen representatives should be able to adjust the Constitution to their wishes *before* it went into effect. What right did the convention have to tell the sovereign people to "take this or nothing"?

Although Washington acknowledged that the "imperfect" Constitution might need to be amended, he argued that amendments could be enacted *after* it was ratified, using the process described in Article V. Randolph thought it was better to repair the Constitution earlier, when he assumed that amendments could be adopted by a simple majority of states, not the three-quarters required to amend the Constitution after it was ratified. Once ratified, moreover, any constitution should be changed as little as possible in the interest of stability. More important, if the people were allowed only to accept the Constitution as written or to reject it, Randolph feared they would reject it.[45] If its rejection brought, as Washington predicted, the onset of anarchy or the "general confusion" that Pinckney thought could only be ended by "the sword," the consequence of forcing the people to "take this or nothing" could be disastrous.

Although Randolph did not sign the Constitution, he kept his options for the future open. He was only thirty-four, a generation younger than Mason, and still had political ambitions he did not want to hazard. He had not decided what position he would take on ratification in Virginia, he told the Convention, but he did not want to deprive himself of the freedom to oppose it if "that course should be prescribed by his final judgment." Mason, however, had no ambition for public office and he was not a man to hedge his bets. Without the prospect of a second convention, he declared, he would neither sign the document nor support it in Virginia. Like Washington, he was anxious to go home. Not, however, before winning some allies. He was, after all, "one of the best politicians in America."[46]

TWO

───── ★ ─────

"Take This or Nothing"

lbridge Gerry was a strange ally for George Mason. A New Englander, slender and of average height, with a broad forehead and a long, sharp nose, he was nineteen years younger than Mason, and a college man to boot (Harvard 1762). Gerry had no hesitation about taking on public office: He represented Massachusetts in Congress between 1776, when he signed the Declaration of Independence, and 1780, and then again between 1783 and 1785. But Gerry, unlike Mason, had no family to leave behind. He remained a bachelor until January 1786, when, at age forty-one, he married Ann Thompson, the daughter of a New York merchant, who was sometimes called "the most beautiful woman in the United States."[1]

Gerry came from the town of Marblehead, on the coast north of Boston, where his father had made a fortune shipping dried codfish to the West Indies and southern Europe. After Harvard, Gerry joined his brothers in the family business. That made him one of those Northern merchants whose interests Mason saw as distinct from and potentially at odds with those of the South. But Mason was not a narrow Southern partisan; he wanted constitutional provisions that would prevent regional cleavages, a goal Gerry shared. And by 1787 Gerry was no longer a fish merchant.

When his new wife, accustomed to New York's sparkling social life, found provincial Marblehead intolerable, the Gerrys moved to Cambridge. They took up residence in Elmwood, a mansion off Brattle Street that was once the home of Loyalist Andrew Oliver (and today of Harvard's president) and assumed a style of life very different from that of Gerry's frugal childhood. He had built the inheritance he received on his father's death in 1774 into a fortune during the Revolutionary War, in part by securing supplies for the American army through contacts in Spain, and then he gradually left behind his involvement in overseas trade to take up other profitable activities, such as speculating in public securities and, later, land. Upon his marriage, Gerry began to refuse public appointments, citing, like Mason, "private concerns." Yet, thanks in part to Shays's Rebellion, which made him fear for the future of the republic, Gerry agreed to attend the Constitutional Convention as a Massachusetts delegate. At the Convention he was, according to William Pierce, a "hesitating and laborious speaker"—he struggled with a stammer—who nonetheless spoke extensively but was only "sometimes clear in his arguments." Gerry's love for his country was, however, beyond dispute.[2]

Like Mason, Gerry had worked to resolve the conflicts among Convention delegates. He chaired the committee that proposed the Great Compromise on representation. But he could be hopelessly inept politically—as when he spoke in favor of Randolph's motion for a second convention in a way that doomed the proposal. On that occasion he rattled off a long list of problems with the Constitution, but Gerry's main reservations were much like those of Mason and Randolph. All three worried about the lack of explicit protections for basic rights, the close ties between the Senate and the executive branch of government, and the way the "necessary and proper" clause could expand congressional power.[3] Before leaving Philadelphia, Gerry copied Mason's list of objections to the Constitution, and during a long stay in New York—where, thanks to his marriage, he had family ties—he showed it to others who also had reservations about the document.[4] Later Gerry would carry his concerns back to Massachusetts.

Meanwhile, on the day after the Convention adjourned, Mason wrote Richard Henry Lee, an old ally in Virginia politics who was representing his home state at the Confederation Congress in New York, and probably enclosed another copy of his objections to the Constitution. A fourth-generation Virginian and a member of one of the state's first families, Lee was tall and thin and as a young man had red hair, although the best-known portrait of him, by Charles Willson Peale, shows a white-haired man in profile, with a high forehead and aquiline nose. Like Gerry, Lee had been an active participant in the independence movement. On the order of his home state, Lee had presented the motion that "these united colonies are and of right ought to be free and independent states," which the Continental Congress adopted on July 2, 1776. He had served as president of Congress in 1784–1785, and so understood the problems of the Confederation, but Lee's experience during the struggle with Britain had made him an outspoken defender of liberty, particularly against threats posed by a powerful central government. Mason also showed the list of his objections to Robert Whitehill, a member of the Pennsylvania legislature, who made a copy for himself; it survives, in Whitehill's handwriting, among his collected papers.[5]

Before the end of September, both Congress and the Pennsylvania legislature held important debates on the Constitution in which Lee and Whitehill played prominent roles. Contenders differed less on the Constitution itself, which almost everyone found better than the Confederation but imperfect for one reason or another, than on just what Congress and the people were left to decide. Did they have to accept or reject the Constitution as written by the Convention? Or could they try to fix its imperfections before putting it into effect? Mason, Randolph, and Gerry had argued in the federal Convention for letting the state ratifying conventions propose amendments. Their fellow delegates voted them down, but that didn't settle the issue, which quickly moved to the center of the country's debate over the Constitution.

CONGRESS

Congress was meeting in New York when the Philadelphia Convention adjourned. Attendance had been meager through much of the previous year, and it was particularly lean in the summer and early fall of 1787, in part because no fewer than ten members—almost a third of the thirty-three representatives who attended Congress in late September—also represented their states in the federal Convention. Richard Henry Lee had refused to serve as a Virginia delegate in Philadelphia because he thought the appointment conflicted with his responsibilities as a member of Congress. Few of his congressional colleagues shared those scruples. Most of them remained in Philadelphia until the federal Convention adjourned, although one of the congressmen/delegates—Georgia's William Pierce, the man who wrote brief descriptions of his fellow delegates—left to fight a duel in New York, then began attending Congress on the first of July.[6]

Now the other Convention delegates made their way to New York. Four had already taken their seats on September 20, when Congress first received the Constitution and the letter and resolutions that accompanied it. More delegates arrived by September 26, when Congress began discussing what it should do with the Constitution. By then eleven states were legally present, each having at least two delegates in their seats. Only one Maryland delegate was present, so Maryland's vote could not be counted under the rules of the Confederation. Rhode Island had no representative at all. On September 15 that state's general assembly sent the president of Congress a letter explaining that the state had sent no delegates to the federal Convention because of its "Love of true Constitutional liberty" and "fear . . . of making innovations on the Rights and Liberties of the Citizens at large." In Rhode Island, it explained, the people at large chose delegates to Congress, so the assembly could hardly appoint delegates to a Convention that "might be the means of dissolving the Congress of the Union." The letter did not explain why, if Rhode Island held such esteem for the union, the state had no representatives in Congress.[7]

Those who advocated ratification of the Constitution as written wanted Congress not only to transmit the Constitution to the states, but to endorse it without "any examination of it by paragraphs in the usual mode of doing business." They also wanted Congress to act quickly: According to Nathan Dane, a delegate from Massachusetts, its supporters were "extremely impatient to get it thro Congress, even the first day that it was taken up."[8] That they did not get.

Criticisms of the Constitution surfaced quickly among delegates who were not yet its opponents. Already on September 23, the Virginia delegate Edward Carrington urged James Madison not to dawdle on the way from Philadelphia to New York because the same "schism" that divided Virginia's delegation during the final weeks of the Convention had reappeared in Congress. Carrington and Henry Lee—Washington's old correspondent, and a cousin of Richard Henry Lee—favored the Constitution (though Carrington, like so many others who argued for ratification, said he did not agree with "every article"), but Richard Henry Lee and William Grayson were on the other side. That meant Madison had the swing vote on the five-man Virginia delegation.[9]

It was hard to think there was no connection between the two "schisms," and, in fact, soon after the Convention adjourned both Randolph and Mason had written Richard Henry Lee explaining why they had refused to sign the Constitution. Lee, however, had a mind of his own, and Congress faced one major issue beyond those that were of concern to Randolph and Mason.[10] On February 21, 1787, the Congress had endorsed a Convention for the "sole and express purpose of revising the Articles of Confederation" and reporting any proposed changes "to Congress and the several [state] legislatures," whose approval would be needed to put those revisions into effect. Instead the Convention had proposed an entirely new form of government, and its resolution on ratification said the Constitution should "be laid before the United States in Congress assembled" and "afterwards be submitted to a Convention of Delegates, chosen in each State by the People thereof, under the Recommendation of its Legislature, for their Assent and Ratification." What was the Congress supposed to do with the Constitution laid before it? The resolution did not say. It did not require Congress's approval. Nor did it preclude Congress from trying to fix a few obvious imperfections before forwarding the Constitution to the states.[11] In any case, what authority did the Convention have to tell Congress what it could and could not do?

On the first day of debate, Nathan Dane moved a long, convoluted resolution. Since the Convention had not recommended alterations to the Articles of Confederation consistent with the instructions it had received from both Congress and the several state legislatures, the resolution said Congress had no authority to express an opinion on its proposal. However, out of respect to its constituents and "the importance of the subject," Congress would send copies of the Constitution and the other documents from the federal Convention to state executives for submission to their legislatures. When a

South Carolina delegate said the resolution seemed hostile to the Constitution, Dane admitted that he thought the "consolidation" of power under
the Constitution would not work except with the support of an army. The
Constitution would "oppress the honest and industrious" and advantage only
the privileged few. Still, he was "open to conviction, and, if convinced, will
support it." He was also willing to change his motion so that it seemed more
"neutral."[12]

The next day, September 27, Richard Henry Lee proposed a substitute
motion. It said Congress had no right to recommend a plan that subverted
the present government of thirteen states in order to establish "a new confederacy of nine states," but he nonetheless thought it "respectful" of the Convention, in which twelve states had participated, to transmit the proposed
Constitution to state executives so they could lay it before their legislatures.
New Jersey's Abraham Clark offered yet another proposal: Congress should
transmit the Constitution and the other documents from the Convention to
the states with no comment whatsoever.[13]

Which resolution was better? Virginia's William Grayson, who admitted
he was against the Constitution, preferred Lee's because he thought Clark's
suggested approval. Lee agreed: "Congress don't send out anything but such
as they approve," he said. If so, Clark responded, didn't Lee's resolution—
which would also transmit the document to the states—imply that Congress
approved the Constitution? Dane apparently saw no such implication in
Clark's resolution, which he preferred because he "wished to steer in the
channel of neutrality." James Madison, however, objected to both proposals.
Any resolution that did not explicitly endorse the Constitution, he said, implied disapproval. "The question is, whether on the whole it is best to adopt
it, and [we] ought to say so."[14]

But could Congress endorse the Constitution without debating it clause
by clause, and perhaps suggesting ways to improve it? Connecticut's William Samuel Johnson claimed that the federal Convention was, in effect,
a committee of Congress whose report Congress "must approve or disapprove." It did not, however, have to approve every part of the document.
Congress needed only to say that it was "upon the whole" better than the
current government. South Carolina's Pierce Butler, who, like Johnson, had
been a Convention delegate, agreed that "the question ought to be on the
whole" of the proposal. "The state of the country [is] contemptible abroad"
and there would be anarchy "at home" unless the Constitution was adopted.
Lee remained unconvinced. There were both good and bad things in the
Constitution, and he thought "civil liberty will be in eminent danger" if it
were adopted as written by the federal Convention. At least the state conventions should have the right to propose amendments. But an overwhelming
majority of Congress, ten states to one, agreed to postpone Lee's resolution

and moved Clark's—to forward the Constitution to the states without comment—to the top of its agenda.[15]

Then Virginia's Edward Carrington proposed another substitute resolution: Congress should say that it had considered the Constitution and "do agree thereto." It should also recommend that the states call conventions "as speedily as may be" so the Constitution could be "adopted, ratified, and confirmed." That was too much even for Henry Lee, a supporter of the Constitution, who thought Congress would subject itself to disgrace if it adopted a resolution expressing approval of the Constitution without carefully examining it and proposing amendments wherever the delegates thought they were necessary. He wanted Carrington's motion postponed so Congress could debate the Constitution paragraph by paragraph. But Madison, Rufus King of Massachusetts, and William Samuel Johnson, all of whom had been members of the federal Convention, insisted that Congress could not propose amendments to the Constitution.[16] They did not, however, have their act together or their arguments synchronized.

The relationship of Congress and the federal Convention, Madison suggested, was like that of a bicameral legislature, with the Convention serving as a second house (not, as Johnson had argued earlier, a committee of Congress). Neither house could unilaterally amend an act that required the approval of both. Since the Convention (unlike any legislative house known to man) had adjourned for good, Congress could only approve the Constitution as it stood. Madison also thought it unlikely that Congress would agree on what alterations should be made. On that issue, he said, critics of the Constitution differed significantly with one another. If, however, Congress proposed amendments, there would be "two plans" of government in play, that from the federal Convention and another, somewhat different, from Congress. Some states would accept one and some the other, causing confusion. In fact, Madison argued, if Congress proposed an amended version of the Constitution, the proposal would fall subject to all the "trammels of the Confederation." That is, ratification of the congressional version of the Constitution would require, like amendments to the Articles of Confederation, the unanimous consent of all thirteen state legislatures, not just the approval of nine state conventions.[17]

King took another tack. The idea of the federal Convention originated not in Congress but in the states, he argued, and the Convention had submitted its proposal to Congress only "to satisfy forms." Congress therefore "cannot constitutionally make alterations" in the Constitution. Johnson agreed and, like King, seemed to suggest that any amendments would have to come from the people or the state ratifying conventions they elected. These arguments were inconsistent, but they led to the same conclusion: The Constitution "must be approved or disapproved in the whole" by Congress.[18]

Richard Henry Lee considered that position not just wrong but counterproductive. To say that Congress could make no alterations in a report
submitted for its consideration was the "strangest doctrine he ever heard."
If Rufus King—and, by implication, Johnson and Madison—wanted the
Constitution sent to the states unchanged, "let it go with all its imperfections on its head, and the amendments by themselves," separately. "To insist
that it should go out as it is without amendments" was "like presenting a
hungry man 50 dishes and insisting he should eat all or none." Amendments
would make ratification *more* likely, "as capital objections will probably be removed." The idea that the Constitution had to be agreed to "or nothing else"
supposed that "all wisdom centers in the Convention" and that nobody outside the Convention had anything to contribute but a quiet nod of approval.[19]

But what "capital objections" did Lee have in mind? Before anyone in Congress mentioned specific objections to the Constitution, those who wanted it
approved as written sensed that they needed to explain and justify the omission of any explicit protection for several basic rights. The states appropriately
enacted bills of rights, they argued, because the people needed to reserve certain rights from state legislatures, which had "unlimited powers." By contrast,
under the Constitution "powers are enumerated and only extend to certain
cases," so "a bill of rights [is] unnecessary." Richard Henry Lee disagreed.
Finally Nathaniel Gorham suggested, quite sensibly, that Lee propose the
amendments he wanted. Then Congress could consider whether or not they
were expedient without wasting time guessing what the man had in mind.[20]

Lee had a reputation for giving succinct, eloquent speeches, in the course
of which he made gestures with a hand covered in silk to disguise the loss
of several fingers during a hunting accident twenty years earlier. "Universal
experience," he began, proved the necessity of "the most express declarations
and reservations . . . to protect the just rights and liberty of Mankind from
the Silent, powerful, and ever active conspiracy of those who govern." The
new Constitution should therefore "be bottomed upon a declaration, or Bill
of Rights, clearly and precisely stating the principles upon which the Social
Compact is founded." In specific, it should protect the rights of Conscience,
freedom of the press, and the right to trial by jury in both criminal and civil
cases. It should say that "standing Armies in times of peace are dangerous
to liberty" and ought not to be allowed without a two-thirds vote in both
houses of Congress. The bill of rights should also state that elections for
members of Congress should be "free and frequent," that the right administration of justice required the "freedom and independency" of judges, that
people had a right to assemble peacefully to petition their legislatures, that
citizens "shall not be exposed to unreasonable searches" and seizures of their
papers and possessions, and "that excessive Bail, excessive Fines, or cruel and
unusual punishments should not be demanded or inflicted."[21]

Lee also proposed changes to the institutional structure of the new federal government. He wanted a council of state or privy council of eleven members chosen by the president to advise and assist him in exercising executive power. Its assent would be necessary for civil and military appointments. Taking those responsibilities from the Senate and relocating them in an executive council would remedy the Constitution's "dangerous blending of the Legislative and Executive powers." Lee also proposed to eliminate the office of vice president and allow the Senate to choose its own presiding officer. In that way he would avoid the creation of a "Great Officer of State" who was sometimes part of the legislative branch (when presiding over the Senate) and at other times part of the executive. The office of vice president, he said, also added unnecessarily to "the Aristocratic influence" in the new government and would give his home state "unjust and needless preeminence."

Lee wanted the Constitution to provide for trials by jury in civil cases over property; to cut back the jurisdiction of federal courts in actions over property between citizens of different states and between Americans and foreigners; to enlarge the House of Representatives, and to increase the percentage of votes necessary to pass new laws or amend old ones. Finally, he proposed changing the Constitution's provision on representation in the Senate so it stood "on the same ground that it is placed in the House of Delegates thereby securing equality of representation in the Legislature so essentially necessary for good government."[22]

Did Lee know that the federal Convention had nearly dissolved over the issue of representation? Those congressmen who had served in the Convention were, in any case, painfully aware that the Great Compromise, which gave states equal representation in the Senate while keeping representation in the House proportional to population, had bridged a division among delegates so deep and emotional that it had threatened to destroy the Convention altogether. What Lee proposed—representation proportional to population in both houses of Congress—was what Madison and other advocates of a substantially stronger nation also wanted, but they had been forced to yield to representatives of the smaller states in order to get any agreement at all.

Even William Grayson, who had not been at the federal Convention and had powerful reservations regarding the Constitution, sensed that Lee had gone too far. It seemed, he said, "precipitate to urge a decision in two days on a subject [which] took 4 months" to prepare. And if, as other congressmen argued, "we have no right to amend, then we ought to give a silent passage, for if we cannot alter, why should we deliberate"? In any event, he saw no need for a "hasty decision. In 2 or 3 years," he said, "we should get a good government," one that would, he suggested, address the country's basic problem—"a disinclination to pay money"—more effectively than the proposed Constitution.[23]

The next day—Friday, September 28—Congress approved a rewritten version of Clark's earlier resolution. It acknowledged receipt of the Convention's report, then "Resolved unanimously" to transmit the Constitution and the accompanying documents to the state legislatures for submission "to a convention of delegates chosen in each state by the people thereof in conformity to the resolves of the Convention made and provided in that case." The word "unanimously," Richard Henry Lee explained to George Mason, referred only to the decision to transmit the Constitution and related documents to the states, but it was inserted "hoping to have it mistaken for an unanimous approbation" of the Constitution itself. He was correct: Even Washington thought that the "apparent unanimity" of Congress would mislead people into thinking it had endorsed the Constitution. "Not every one has opportunities to peep behind the curtain," he wrote Madison; "and as the multitude often judge from externals, the appearance of unanimity in that body, on this occas[io]n, will be of great importance."[24]

The Constitution's supporters did all they could to assure that the public did not peep behind the curtain. Congress's debates remained secret, like those of the federal Convention, and its official records did not even include the amendments Lee proposed. After New Jersey's Abraham Clark said they would "do injury by coming on the Journal," lines were drawn through Lee's motion on the rough manuscript journal so it would not appear on the official record. The *Journals of Congress* were not printed until late November—and then gave no information on the debates of September 26–28 beyond a list of the states officially present, although they included Congress's unanimous decision to forward the Constitution and accompanying documents to the states.[25] Nor did the press fill out the story: The New York newspapers, the usual source for news on Congress, failed to report that it had engaged in a two-day debate on the Constitution. A few scattered references to the divisions in Congress appeared, mainly in the Pennsylvania press, during October, but the general public remained unaware of how limited Congress's unanimity had been for a full two months. Then on December 6, the *Virginia Gazette* in Petersburg published Lee's proposed amendments with a long letter he had written to Governor Edmund Randolph on October 16 explaining his reservations on the Constitution. The letter and amendments were then widely reprinted.[26]

The debates in Congress nonetheless served to harden divisions over the Constitution. Nathan Dane, who had previously supported strengthening the central government and who, in the opening days of the congressional debates, had expressed a willingness to be talked out of his doubts about the Constitution, later announced that if there could be no amendments he "will stand excused to vote in the negative." Other delegates also had doubts about parts of the Constitution although they acknowledged that it provided a remedy for the Confederation's problems. Their suspicions grew as the Constitution's supporters insisted that they approve the document as a whole. "Your prediction of what would happen in Congress was exactly verified," Lee wrote Mason on the first of October. "It was with us, as with you [in the Convention], this or nothing; and this urged with a most extreme intemperance."[27]

One big question remained unanswered: "Is it the idea of [the] Convention," Richard Henry Lee had asked on September 27, "that not only Congress but the states must agree in the whole, or else to reject it?"[28] Rufus King and William Samuel Johnson suggested, though in language that remained somewhat ambiguous, that the states—or "the people," who met in state ratifying conventions—were the proper source of amendments. Would that position triumph, or would the states and the people, like Congress, be denied the right to propose amendments? In other words, were the Constitution's supporters going to insist, as Mason sensed even before the Philadelphia Convention adjourned, that the sovereign people "take this or nothing"?

THE BIG RUSH

The supporters of the Constitution in Pennsylvania, like those in Congress, were in a hurry. Immediately after the Convention adjourned on the afternoon of September 17, the state's congressional delegation requested an audience before the Pennsylvania general assembly, the state's unicameral legislature, which met upstairs in the Pennsylvania State House while the federal Convention occupied its usual quarters. At eleven o'clock the next morning the delegates formally presented the Constitution to the assembly, which had moved back to its first-floor chamber. According to the *Pennsylvania Gazette*, the Constitution was "read publicly in the presence of a large crowd of citizens, who stood in the gallery of the assembly room, and who testified the highest pleasure in seeing that great work at last perfected, which promises, when adopted, to give security, stability, and dignity to the government of the United States."[29]

Benjamin Franklin, who was president of Pennsylvania as well as a Convention delegate, suggested on behalf of the delegation that the assembly offer a ten-mile-square part of the state as a "residence" for the new government.[30] Perhaps by acting fast and becoming the first state to ratify the Constitution, Pennsylvania would receive the honor Virginia got for being the first state to endorse the federal Convention. That, in turn, might increase Pennsylvania's chance of becoming the site of the nation's new capital.

The assembly had the advantage of being in session and, as a result of its location, officially receiving the Constitution from its Convention delegates before any other state. It also had a majority of members inclined to favor a national government like the one proposed by the Convention. But the assembly was scheduled to adjourn on Saturday, September 29, and would not meet again until after the annual election of members on October 9. Could it call a ratifying convention before Congress had officially submitted the Constitution to the states?

In the meantime, the Constitution's supporters orchestrated a series of petitions asking—as one from Germantown put it—that the Constitution "may be adopted, as speedily as possible, by the State of Pennsylvania, in the manner recommended by the resolution of the late Honorable Convention." On Tuesday, September 25, the assembly ordered two thousand copies of the Constitution printed in English and another thousand in German for distribution throughout the state.[31]

Finally, on Friday, September 28, George Clymer, a Philadelphia merchant and Convention delegate, moved a set of resolutions calling for a state ratifying convention that would meet at the State House in Philadelphia on the last day of November. Even the first of Clymer's resolutions, recommending the election of delegates to a ratifying convention by qualified voters in the same manner by which assembly representatives were chosen, awoke opposition. Why such haste? Because, replied Daniel Clymer (a cousin of George), it was "the general wish of the people that we should go forward in the measure"; and there were only a handful of people against it, including four or five "leading party men" in Philadelphia who he thought would be "ashamed to show their faces among the good people, whose future prosperity they wish to blast in the bud." Robert Whitehill, the representative from inland Cumberland County who had copied Mason's objections to the Constitution, replied that all the petitions the assembly had received were from the Philadelphia area and represented "but a small part of the whole state." By Whitehill's estimate, not one Pennsylvanian out of twenty knew anything about the Constitution. Pennsylvania was, after all, divided by a broad band of mountains that made the spread of news westward slow and irregular.[32]

William Findley of Westmoreland County, in the far west of Pennsylvania—an area Washington had visited and explored time and again—also questioned the ratifiers' "precipitancy." The Constitution was no doubt "wisely calculated for the purposes intended" and "very deserving the commendation it received," Findley said, but "nothing is perfect," and the assembly should take time "to make it as agreeable as possible." Whitehill added that the proposed resolutions had taken him by surprise. He never dreamed the assembly would act before Congress had forwarded the Constitution for the state's consideration. What if Congress proposed alterations or amendments to the Constitution? Until Congress acted, who could know "what sort of a plan" it would send out for debate? The impropriety of acting before Congress had completed its deliberations, he said, was obvious.[33]

Findley added that for Pennsylvania to act before hearing from Congress would violate the Thirteenth Article of Confederation, which required Congress's assent to changes in the terms of union. Americans were not considering the Constitution from a "state of nature," unconnected, he insisted, but on "federal ground," under the Confederation. Only "absolute necessity" could justify acting before Congress went through its "usual forms" and recommended the Constitution, which it would surely do since it had for years been "begging" for the powers it granted. Then why not delay action until the next session of the assembly, when the results of Congress's deliberations would be known and people throughout the state would have had an opportunity to study the Constitution and instruct their representatives how to proceed? Delay would not necessarily lose Pennsylvania the "honor of taking the lead," Whitehill said, since other states were unlikely to act more quickly.[34]

Neither Findley nor Whitehill expressed opposition to the Constitution. Findley even said he was "in favor of federal measures" and that "the people generally are disposed to have a [national] government of more energy," while Whitehill "had nothing against the principles of the proposed plan." But the unseemly haste of its promoters aroused their suspicions. "I don't know any reason there can be for driving [the Constitution] down our throats, without an hour's preparation," Whitehill said, unless it was "a plan not fit for discussion." The supporters of Clymer's resolution, Findley suggested, might "have some object in view which is not understood."[35]

Findley's arguments for acting with respect for Congress's authority had the curious effect of pushing some of the Constitution's supporters—the supposed champions of the nation—to argue that the Confederation had collapsed so totally that its decisions were no longer binding. That left Findley and his cohort to defend the continuing existence of a federal union.[36] Nothing, however, provoked the partisans of quick ratification more than Whitehill's suggestion that Congress might propose amendments to the Constitution. The Convention submitted the Constitution to Congress, according to Daniel Clymer, not "for alteration or amendment," but because it was the "proper channel" for sending it to the several states. Not even state conventions could adopt some parts of the Constitution and reject others: "They must adopt *in toto* or refuse altogether for it must be a plan . . . formed by the United States, which can be agreeable to all, and not one formed upon the narrow policy and convenience of one particular state."[37]

The Constitution, Clymer added, was "framed by the collective wisdom of a continent, centered in a venerable band of patriots, worthies, heroes, legislators and philosophers—the admiration of the world." (Later Pittsburgh's Hugh Henry Brackenridge went a step further, predicting the Constitution would be "the wonder of the universe.") Writing the Constitution had required "mutual concessions—mutual sacrifices" of local interests on behalf of the general welfare. Now, Clymer suggested, further changes were impossible, whether by Congress or the states. Why would the United States "submit to the amendments and alterations to be made by a few inhabitants of Pennsylvania?" Hesitation was "criminal." Pennsylvania should embrace the Constitution and "the glorious opportunity of being foremost in its adoption."[38]

Others on Clymer's side noted that Virginia had not waited for Congress's approval before endorsing the federal Convention and electing delegates to it. Now Pennsylvania had the chance for similar glory if it led the country in ratifying the Constitution and encouraged the other states to follow its example. To wait for Congress was to squander the advantages that allowed Pennsylvania to become the first state to act. "I don't see, for my part, what Congress have to do with it," Brackenridge volunteered. He was willing to wait a few days for news from New York, but now, with the assembly session on the point of adjourning, it was "improper" to delay any more. Waiting to hear from Congress, George Clymer said, would be "to attend to forms and lose the substance." If the assembly called a convention right away, it could meet in November and ratify the Constitution by December. If, however, the issue was left for the next session "it will inevitably be procrastinated until December, 1788," and nobody would let the country's existence remain in jeopardy that long or "run the risk of a final ruin." In any case, there was no doubt that Congress favored the Constitution. Indeed, Clymer claimed, a gentleman who had come to Philadelphia from New York told him that "the members of Congress were unanimous in approving it," although it would take more time for them to send official notice of that decision.[39]

Some assemblymen argued that it made no difference what Congress did. The Articles of Confederation had no authority in this case, since the Constitution was not an amendment to the Articles. The government set up under the Articles had proven "totally inadequate" and "incapable of affording security either within or without," so the Constitutional Convention proposed "a different organization" to be established under "the AUTHORITY OF THE PEOPLE." The Constitution, moreover, had to be ratified by nine state ratifying conventions, not the unanimous consent of the state legislatures, as amendments to the Articles required. By implication, Congress's consent was unnecessary; the people could act without it. In answer to Findley's plea for the continued authority of the Confederation while the nation contemplated adopting a new form of union, Brackenridge said Americans were "on the wild and extended field of nature, unrestrained by any compact." Under the circumstances, "the former Articles of Confederation . . . are inactive and have no efficacy," and the Pennsylvania legislature was free to act "independent of Congress or Confederation."[40]

Such arguments did not persuade Findley and Whitehill or those assemblymen who sided with them, but that did not stop the assembly from adopting the first of Clymer's resolutions, providing for the election of a ratifying convention in general terms, by a vote of 43–19. The division reflected the usual partisan split in Pennsylvania politics, with the Republicans, who wanted to replace the state's radical 1776 constitution, voting in the affirmative, except that nine of their Constitutionalist opponents (who defended the state constitution) joined them. Whitehill, Findley and most other Constitutionalists were in the minority. The assembly then adjourned until four in the afternoon.[41]

At that point the conflict turned from words to action. Only forty-four members (including the speaker) returned in the afternoon. Another nineteen stayed away, leaving the assembly two members short of the two-thirds quorum (of the entire body of sixty-eight elected delegates) mandated by the state constitution. That technique—postponing a vote by not showing up—had been used in the past by both sides in Pennsylvania politics. Nonetheless, the Republican majority was quick to condemn the absentees for shirking "the duty they owed their country." The assembly sent its sergeant at arms to collect the missing delegates. He found all but two at Major Alexander Boyd's boardinghouse, where many members of the state's Constitutionalist party stayed when in Philadelphia, but they refused to return to the State House.[42] The assembly could only adjourn until the next day, then try again to persuade the missing members to come back.

Early the next morning—Saturday, September 29—an express rider from New York brought an unofficial copy of the resolution Congress had adopted the day before, unanimously agreeing to transmit the Constitution to the states for submission to ratifying conventions (but not, as George Clymer had claimed, unanimously approving the Constitution). Nonetheless, the assembly's sergeant at arms—now accompanied by its assistant clerk—could not get the absentee legislators to return to the State House. He found a few assembly members on the street but soon lost sight of Findley, who "mended his pace" when he saw the clerk behind him, turned a corner, and then disappeared. Those dissenting legislators the sergeant and clerk managed to reach simply would not comply when told the speaker and house members had sent for them. The news from New York, which the assembly's officials carefully conveyed to the absentee assemblymen, made no difference at all. The resolution from Congress "had not come officially," one delegate said, "and therefore he would not attend" the assembly. The sergeant and clerk tracked down other absentees at their lodgings but had no more success there. A woman thought to be Robert Whitehill's maid told the clerk that Whitehill was home; she went upstairs to fetch him, stayed there a suspiciously long time, and finally returned to say that Whitehill was not at home after all.[43]

Then, the assembly records say, two members who had been lingering at Boyd's boardinghouse, James M'Calmont and Jacob Miley, suddenly appeared in the room where the legislature met. They had been forcibly seized and dragged to the State House by the sergeant at arms and three men who supported a quick ratification of the Constitution, including William Jackson, who had been the federal Convention's secretary.[44] M'Calmont and Miley brought the number of assemblymen who answered a roll call to forty-six—exactly the number needed for a quorum.

M'Calmont protested that he had been "forcibly brought into the assembly room, contrary to his wishes," and "begged he might be *dismissed* from the House." That led to a debate of a sort worthy of a university faculty meeting. M'Calmont's presence was essential for the house to do business. But could it hold him against his will? M'Calmont asked for the rules on absenteeism to be read, then offered to pay the five shillings fine for members whose absence robbed the assembly of a quorum. That provoked "a loud laugh in the gallery." The rule applied only to members who did not appear and answer the roll call, both of which he had done. One member said M'Calmont couldn't be "detained as in prison." Another seemed to think locking the doors to prevent his leaving would be just fine. When M'Calmont tried to flee, spectators in the gallery "called out *stop him*," and a crowd at the door forced him to return to his place. Then the house formally voted against giving him a leave of absence and, its quorum safe, went on to finish its business.[45]

M'Calmont tried to make the best of the situation. He moved to have the convention meet farther west in Carlisle or Lancaster and to put off the election of delegates to the convention by one, two, or even three weeks, but he failed time and again. The assembly decided that elections for convention delegates would be held throughout the state on the first Tuesday in November. The convention itself would convene two weeks later at the State House in Philadelphia. Finally, after issuing warrants for members' pay (with M'Calmont collecting the sums due for the absent members) and thanking the speaker, the Pennsylvania assembly adjourned.[46]

THE COST OF VICTORY

The Constitution's supporters had won the battle in the Pennsylvania assembly, but there was a price to be paid for their high-handed victory. On Saturday, September 29, the same day the Assembly adjourned, sixteen of the seceding members signed an address to their constituents that would be republished throughout the states, awakening suspicions not only of the Constitution's supporters but of the Constitution itself. The address explained that the seceding delegates had opposed efforts to call a convention before the Assembly had even received official instructions from the Confederation Congress. It also noted, correctly, that the majority's haste was at odds with Pennsylvania's state constitution, which prevented the assembly from approving even "trifling" measures without time-consuming delays. But the majority proved determined, and only by absenting themselves from the assembly—and so robbing the house of its quorum—could the minority prevent it from attempting to "surprise" the people into electing delegates who would approve or disapprove a Constitution that would "entail happiness or misery forever" before the greater part of the state had seen, much less examined, that new plan of government. Only the "outrageous proceeding" against assemblymen M'Calmont and Miley, who were violently seized from their lodgings by a number of Philadelphians, "their clothes torn, and after much abuse and insult . . . forcibly dragged through the streets to the State House" and detained there "by force, and in the presence of the majority," kept the minority's plan from being successful. The dissenters nonetheless took credit for having the elections held later than originally proposed.[47]

Then the address turned to the Constitution itself. The federal Convention, it said, violated the instructions to its members, which empowered them only to propose amendments to the existing Confederation, not to devise an entirely new form of government. If the people, after "mature deliberation," decided the proposed Constitution would promote their political happiness and preserve their privileges, they would no doubt choose delegates who would ratify it. But would they be able to support the expense of so elaborate a new central government as well as that of their home state? Was a national government that had three branches, none of whose members were chosen annually, and with senators elected for astounding six-year terms, be more likely to enhance or to reduce the people's burdens? If, after ratification of the Constitution, their state government was annihilated ("which will probably be the case") or reduced to a mere corporation subordinate to the nation, would the central government be able to serve their needs? Did the country really need a national judiciary, and was the proposed "continental court" a threat to the continued existence of state judiciaries? Would a central government empowered to collect "internal taxes" with the help of "a few faithful soldiers" serve the people's best interests? Were the people prepared to accept a Constitution that gave no protection to freedom of the press, abolished trial by jury in civil cases, and included no provision against "standing armies in time of peace"?[48]

For a group whose spokesmen had at first expressed no profound opposition to the Constitution and accepted the need for some alternative to the broken-down Confederation, the dissident Pennsylvania assemblymen raised an impressive number of arguments against the Constitution. They questioned the structure of Congress (though not yet the small size of the first House of Representatives), the cost of the new government, and its right to raise "internal taxes" and maintain an army; they expressed fear for the future of the state governments in general and the state courts in particular, and they strongly suggested the need for a more explicit protection of basic rights. Public debate of the Constitution, which the "seceding assemblymen" helped open, would turn in good part on just those issues.

The haste of those who supported ratification and their intolerance of opposition had again converted men who had hoped to "perfect" the Constitution into its opponents. But maybe they knew the enemy. Pennsylvania's Republicans and Constitutionalists had squared off against each other since 1776, and the state constitution that the Constitutionalists defended was radically different from the proposed new federal Constitution. It had an annually elected unicameral assembly and a weak executive in the form of a popularly elected supreme executive council whose presiding officer— currently Benjamin Franklin—was the president of Pennsylvania. Certainly the state constitution put little stock in separation of powers: Its main check on power came from the ballot box. Pennsylvania's constitution was closer to a direct democracy than that of any other state. It also included an elaborate Declaration of Rights. If constitutional perfection as Constitutionalists like Whitehill and Findley understood it was embodied in the Pennsylvania constitution, their Republican opponents had reason to fear any amendments to the proposed federal Constitution that they would propose.

The issue of amendments, however, extended well beyond Pennsylvania. Although the Continental Congress deleted all mention of Richard Henry Lee's proposed amendments from its official journal, it could do nothing to prevent their private circulation. In late September and early October, Lee sent copies to Elbridge Gerry and George Mason, as well as to William Shippen, Jr., his brother-in-law in Philadelphia, and also Boston's Samuel Adams, a "dear friend" with whom he had "long toiled . . . in the Vineyard of liberty." A few weeks later he sent them to Edmund Randolph, mentioning (as he had to Shippen) that Randolph might "make such use" of his letter "as you shall think . . . for the public good." Lee no doubt argued for amendments to the Constitution when he met privately with a set of delegates to the Pennsylvania ratifying convention in early November, as well as with other contacts in Chester, Pennsylvania, and Wilmington, Delaware.[49] Unless "some such alterations and provisions" as he had proposed were incorporated in the Constitution "for the security of those essential rights of mankind without which liberty cannot exist," Lee told Gerry, "we shall soon find that the new plan of government" would prove more "inconvenient" than anything under the Confederation. To "avoid Scylla we shall have fallen upon Charybdis": That is, the nation would have gone from one extreme—a government too weak—to one dangerous in the extent of its powers.[50]

Lee still thought that "the new Constitution (properly amended)" included "many good regulations." He was also convinced that the changes he proposed would "by no means interfere with the general nature of the plan, or limit the power of doing good." Above all, he wanted to "restrain from oppression the wicked and Tyrannic" by explicitly protecting those basic rights whose loss would not serve "any good social purpose." The American people, Lee wrote Samuel Adams, had not fought the British only to be "brought under despotic rule under the notion of 'Strong government,' or in the form of *elective despotism*: Chains still being Chains, whether made of gold or of iron." The "corrupting nature of power" made it essential for public safety that "power not requisite should not be given" to government and "that necessary powers should be carefully guarded." Amendments should be incorporated into the Constitution before it went into effect since threats such as "the Oligarchic tendency" from the close connection under the Constitution of "President, V[ice] President, & Senate" were "not within the compass of legislative redress." Why couldn't state ratifying conventions propose amendments that a "new general Convention" would weave into the Constitution's fabric, making it "fit for freemen to wear"?[51]

All of this seemed so sensible that Lee stood amazed at the effort to hurry the Constitution through "before it has stood the test of Reflection & due examination." The "violence . . . practiced by the Agitators of this new System in Philadelphia to drive on its immediate adoption" suggested that government was "a business of passion, instead of cool, sober, and intense consideration." The amendments he proposed would not prevent "the exercise of a very competent federal power" but were "such as the best Theories on Government and the best practice upon those theories have found necessary."[52]

If Lee discussed his proposals with Washington during a visit to Mount Vernon on November 11 and 12, he no doubt received a cold reception. Washington certainly did not take kindly to the constitutional objections that George Mason sent him on October 7, with no sense, it seems, of how much hostility they would provoke. Washington wrote Madison (who was attending Congress in New York) that Mason had carefully distributed his objections among the seceding members of the Pennsylvania assembly, who repeated them in their published "address." Washington thought Mason was also behind Lee's arguments. Mason, in short, had caused the opposition to the Constitution in both Congress and the Pennsylvania assembly, and for no good reason: Madison insisted that there was little if anything worthy of serious consideration in Mason's objections, which he dismissed, one by one.[53]

Even to discuss changing the Constitution would be, from the perspective of its supporters, to open Pandora's box. Where would it stop? Lists of proposed amendments would be as different as the people proposing them and the interests of the states and regions from which they came. To "perfect" the Constitution, its major supporters claimed, would undo the compromises that brokered different visions and different interests, compromises that could never be renegotiated in a second convention where delegates would be bound by more restrictive instructions than those the state legislatures had given delegates to the federal Convention of 1787. That was Charles Pinckney's argument in Philadelphia when Randolph and Mason first proposed a second convention. For those who thought the Constitution good enough and the best they could get under current circumstances, Pinckney's argument remained persuasive. It would, moreover, take time to hold a genuine, wide-ranging national debate on the Constitution, collate proposed amendments, and convene another convention to sift through the pile of proposals. And what the United States lacked, the champions of ratification said over and over, was time.

The country, they believed, had this one last chance at becoming what Washington called "a respectable nation." The cost of failure would be high: Foreign countries might pick off parts of the United States while Americans stood helplessly watching, with Spain taking Kentucky and Britain claiming Vermont. The conflict at home between poor debtors like the followers of Daniel Shays in Massachusetts and the men of wealth who helped put them down would escalate as the country dissolved into anarchy. Going back to government under the old Confederation was unthinkable. It had collapsed under the weight of its flaws. The strategy of the Constitution's supporters was to go for broke, to get the process of ratification off to a quick start in Pennsylvania and then to keep the ball rolling. How hard could it be, anyway, to get nine states to ratify?

———

In New York during the final weeks of September, Alexander Hamilton tried to calculate the odds of ratification. In a set of "Conjectures about the new Constitution" that he composed but never published, he listed considerations that favored ratification: the "universal popularity of General Washington" and the prestige of others who framed the document; the good will of the persons engaged in commerce, creditors, and men of property, who wanted a government capable of protecting them against domestic violence and "the depredations which the democratic spirit is apt to make on property," and who wished "for the respectability of the nation"; a widespread understanding among the people that the Confederation was inadequate to preserve the union or to protect their safety and promote prosperity. On the other hand, several forces worked against the Constitution, including the opposition of a few dissenting members of the Convention, of debtors, of state office holders and others who would either lose influence and power or might hope to gain it by fighting the adoption of the new government. Hamilton also noted the strong popular opposition to taxes and to institutions that "may seem calculated to place the power of the community in few hands and to raise a few individuals to stations of great preeminence," and he anticipated opposition from foreign powers that "will not wish to see an energetic government established throughout the states."

If the Constitution failed, the consequences, he thought, would be catastrophic: civil war, the dismemberment of the union, the establishment of monarchies in its various parts, maybe reunion with Britain in reaction to the chaos. If the Constitution was ratified and a strong government established with Washington as president, the federal government might "triumph altogether over the state governments and reduce them to an entire subordination, dividing the large states into smaller districts"; if not, struggles between the general government and the states would probably lead to a dissolution of the union. "But," he concluded, "it is almost arrogance in so complicated a subject, depending so entirely on the incalculable fluctuations of the human passions, to attempt even a conjecture about the event." It would be eight or nine months "before any certain judgment can be formed respecting the adoption of the Plan."54

In the meantime, those who favored ratification would find it increasingly difficult simply to write off critics of the Constitution as a handful of disreputable persons opposed to the public good, as Daniel Clymer had done in the Pennsylvania Assembly. Once criticisms of the Constitution mounted, its supporters had to defend sections of the Constitution about which, in truth, they themselves often had reservations, and they had to make sense of the system of government it proposed in ways that went beyond anything said or even understood in the federal Convention. The result was one of the greatest outpourings of political writings in American history. In sheer volume the mass of published essays and speeches is bewildering. But arguments soon took on patterns, with later contenders repeating and developing what earlier ones had said.

That debate in print first took shape during October 1787, just before the first state ratifying conventions met. And it began in no small part thanks to the address of the Pennsylvania Assembly's minority and one cantankerous Philadelphia printer.

THREE

★

A War of Printed Words

The National Debate Begins

By Wednesday, September 19, two days after the Convention adjourned, six Philadelphia newspapers had printed the Constitution. Within three weeks at least fifty-five newspapers had published the document, and another twenty joined the list by late October. Many printers, following the example of Philadelphia's John Dunlap and David Claypoole, published the Constitution both in their newspapers and separately, often along with the letter to Congress and the resolutions on ratification that the Convention issued, as a pamphlet or a broadside. Before the end of 1787 there were as many as two hundred separate printings for the benefit of "We the People," who would decide, directly or indirectly, the Constitution's fate.[1]

The press was the mass medium of the eighteenth century, the only way to bring both news and commentary to a broad public audience. The popularity of newspapers soared in Revolutionary America: By the late 1780s, the United States had about ninety-five newspapers, over twice the number at the time of independence. Moreover, the newspapers of 1776 were weeklies, but those of 1787 were often published two or three times a week. There were even a few that appeared daily to satisfy the hungry reading public.[2]

What the newspapers would print for the benefit of the sovereign people during the ratification process was itself the subject of debate. Printing the Constitution was fine; publishing commentaries that found fault with it was something else again. Essays on behalf of ratification had no trouble getting printed: Already during the summer of 1787, while the federal Convention labored away in secrecy, newspapers carried articles advocating the adoption of whatever strong national government would be proposed.[3] Once the Convention adjourned, more essays appeared describing the Constitution and singing its praises. A debate, however, requires two sides. To get criticisms of the Constitution into circulation took a few more weeks and a sturdy dose of stubborn courage.

Once they got going, the newspaper debates were more than a mere prelude to the more decisive debates in the state ratifying conventions, which were about to begin. They influenced electors who chose delegates to the conventions and provided those delegates with an array of arguments that they could adopt, perhaps modify, and repeat.

"FREEDOM OF THE PRESS"

For those who saw the Constitution as the country's only alternative to ruin, any opposition to its quick ratification was akin to treason. The response to the first published criticism of the Constitution, in Philadelphia's *Freeman's Journal* on September 26, nine days after the Convention adjourned, was characteristic of much that would follow.

The essay's anonymous author questioned "with diffidence" only a few parts of the Constitution and admitted that most of his objections were "of an inferior magnitude only." He questioned the provision that said the number of representatives "shall not exceed one for every 30,000" (unlike later writers, however, he objected because he thought that ratio would make the House too large and unwieldy in the future), and he disagreed with giving Congress the right to make or alter state provisions on the times, places, and manner of electing representatives and senators, "except as to the places of chusing Senators." He did not like having a new Congress meet in December; he thought poll taxes should have been outlawed, and he suggested the Constitution should be more specific in describing the size and function of juries in criminal cases. However, the essay acknowledged that "our situation is critical," described the Constitution in general as a "well-wrought piece of stuff" that promised to insure the happiness and respectability of the United States, and concluded that "on the whole" the Constitution deserved "the approbation of all the states."[4]

As criticisms go the essay was pretty mild, but it provoked a vicious denunciation in the *Independent Gazetteer*. What "in the name of wonder" inspired such a "daring" attack, the response asked, "at this awful crisis, when the fate of America depends on the unanimity of all classes of citizens" in support of the Constitution, which was a "masterpiece in politics." If the name of the *"Antifederalist"* critic of the Constitution became known, he might well suffer "the just resentment of an incensed people, who perhaps may honor him with a coat of TAR and FEATHERS."[5]

Threats like that encouraged writers to continue the standard practice of publishing essays under pseudonyms. In Boston, however, Benjamin Russell, publisher of the *Massachusetts Centinel*, announced in early October that he would print no essays that raised objections to the Constitution unless their authors left their names "to be made public if desired." That would clearly discourage critics of the Constitution from speaking out. The local tradesmen and artisans (known as "mechanics") who strongly supported ratification "had been worked up to such a degree of rage," one Massachusetts official noted, "that it was unsafe to be known to oppose [the Constitution] in Boston." Some writers defended Russell's policy as a way of making sure foreign enemies of the United States were not secretly fomenting fear and discord among the people. Since no similar distrust fell on those who supported the country's "happiness and prosperity" by advocating ratification of the Constitution, they could apparently go on writing without divulging their identities. Other commentators, however, charged Russell with violating freedom of the press since his policy would curtail the range of arguments available to the public. And in Philadelphia, a writer who took the pen name "Fair Play" answered the threats leveled against those who criticized the Constitution by insisting "that the LIBERTY OF THE PRESS—the great bulwark of all the liberties of the people—ought never to be restrained" (although, he added, "the Honorable Convention did not think fit to make the least declaration in its favor").[6]

The freedom such writers defended went back to an earlier time, when colonial printers had to appeal to a broad range of readers to stay in business; they took a neutral stand and justified necessity by defining a "free press" as one that was "open to all parties." That way of operating came under pressure as the market for newspapers grew and the Revolution raised doubts about the wisdom of giving "all parties," including Loyalists, ready access to the reading public.[7] State partisan divisions during the 1780s also made it difficult, and sometimes unprofitable, for printers to remain impartial. On the other hand, the establishment of a republic, in which all power came from the people, gave the argument for a press open to all parties a new ideological foundation: To exercise their responsibilities intelligently, the citizens of a republic had to be fully informed of different views on public issues.

That concept of a free press was, in any case, different from the standard Anglo-American understanding of "freedom of the press," which referred to the freedom of printers to publish whatever they wanted without "prior restraint" by the government. Printers remained liable to prosecution for "licentious" uses of that freedom, and liberal defenders of freedom of the press insisted that truth should be a defense. The emphasis, however, was on the freedom of the press to monitor and criticize persons in power and the policies they adopted.[8]

In 1787 no government prevented the publication of essays critical of the Constitution. The problem lay instead with the array of city dwellers, from wealthy merchants to rowdy sailors, dockworkers, and also many tradesmen and mechanics, who almost to a man favored the Constitution. The establishment of a new national government with power to promote and defend American commerce promised a new prosperity for men whose livelihoods depended on trade, which had been hard hit during the postwar depression, and they were not inclined to quibble over proprieties. Because the great majority of American newspapers were published in eastern port cities and towns, their trade-oriented subscribers and advertisers had an influence on the press disproportionate to their small part in the country's population, which remained over 90 percent rural.

In the end, proponents of the Constitution found an effective alternative to threats of tar and feathers and other forms of physical punishment: They could influence editorial policy by canceling or threatening to cancel their subscriptions to "offending" newspapers. Advocates for freedom of the press could insist that the American people needed access to the full range of opinions on the Constitution. But were individual subscribers—or groups of like-minded subscribers—obliged to pay for newspapers that published essays they considered profoundly subversive of their own and the country's best interests?

The first public criticisms of the Constitution appeared, appropriately, in Philadelphia's *Freeman's Journal*, which proclaimed that it was "OPEN TO ALL PARTIES, BUT INFLUENCED BY NONE." In the spring and early summer of 1787 its publisher, Francis Bailey, had printed items favorable to increasing the powers of the Confederation. By late summer it had become critical of the federal Convention. The *Freeman's Journal* was, in fact, closely aligned with Pennsylvania's Constitutionalist party, which supported the state's "radical" constitution of 1776 and whose members provided the rank and file of the federal Constitution's critics in that state, and probably the bulk of Bailey's subscribers.[9]

That a rival Philadelphia paper, the *Independent Gazetteer*, also became a major source of essays criticizing the Constitution is more surprising. Its owner, Eleazer Oswald, generally spoke for the state's Republican party, whose members wanted the Constitution ratified quickly and without changes. Oswald—an old enemy of Bailey, whom he once challenged to a duel—also operated the London Coffee House, an important meeting place for merchants and their political allies. In August, before the federal Convention adjourned, the *Independent Gazetteer* had published essays advocating the "speedy establishment of a vigorous continental government," which reflected the opinions of its clientele. Similarly, in September, the paper included the piece by "TAR and FEATHERS" that attacked an early criticism of the Constitution.[10] But Oswald was tough and hot tempered, sometimes to a fault. When his old supporters tried to prevent him from publishing criticisms of the Constitution, he refused to give in. Oswald had firm convictions on the role of the press in a free country, and he was not about to let anyone, even his best customers, tell him what he could and could not print.

An Englishman who migrated to America at age fifteen in 1770, Oswald learned the printing trade as an apprentice to John Holt, whose paper, *The New-York Journal*, had been allied with New York's radical Sons of Liberty in the years before independence. Later Oswald fought in the Continental Army under Colonel John Lamb, a prominent New York Son of Liberty who would later be at the center of his state's opposition to ratification of the Constitution without amendments. Before the Revolutionary War was over, Oswald had gone into business for himself and almost as quickly found himself at the center of a controversy over freedom of the press. In 1782, after his *Independent Gazetteer* accused the Pennsylvania supreme court of bias, the court ordered his arrest for publishing a "seditious, scandalous, and infamous LIBEL." A rash of newspaper essayists rushed to his defense; one took the precocious position that, rather than restrict the flow of information to the public, even false newspaper attacks on the conduct of public officials should go unpunished. The prosecution failed when the grand jury refused to indict Oswald.[11]

Five years later, those who tried to keep criticisms of the Constitution out of the press met their match in Eleazer Oswald. According to one observer, he was the only Philadelphia printer who dared to print the address of the Pennsylvania Assembly's dissenting members. When supporters of the Constitution threatened to cancel their subscriptions if he continued to publish such pieces, Oswald did not cave in. They were "very welcome" to do that, he replied, so long as they settled their accounts first because "whatever might be his *own sentiments*, his *Press was Free*, and he would *support its Freedom*." His old allies knew him too well to think Oswald would give in to threats, the observer added, or they would have proposed some other form of punishment.[12]

Men like Oswald were rare. Only twelve of over ninety American newspapers and magazines published substantial numbers of essays critical of the Constitution during the ratification controversy.[13] Many noteworthy essays that criticized the Constitution first appeared in an even smaller handful of newspapers, including Oswald's *Independent Gazetteer*, Bailey's *Freeman's Journal*, and also the *New-York Journal*, John Holt's old paper, which was now published by Thomas Greenleaf. Oswald, who had married John Holt's daughter, helped his widowed mother-in-law sell the *New-York Journal* to Greenleaf in January 1787, and Greenleaf sometimes sounded a lot like Oswald. If printers were "easily terrified into a *rejection* of free and decent discussions upon public topics," he wrote in early October 1787, the "inevitable consequence" would be "*servile fetters* for the FREE PRESSES of this country." Greenleaf promised to give "every performance, that may be written with decency, free access to his Journal." For their persistence, Oswald and Greenleaf suffered verbal attacks, canceled subscriptions, and threats of mob violence.[14] Their insistence on maintaining what they understood as a "free press," that is, one that presented the people with criticisms as well as hallelujahs for the Constitution, helped start a widespread public debate on the Constitution, which they then kept going.

HITTING THE PRESS

Public debate of the Constitution began for all practical purposes on October 2, when Oswald printed a broadside edition of the address of the Pennsylvania Assembly's dissenting minority, then published it again the next day.[15] Before then newspapers had carried only a few pieces critical of the Constitution. The *New-York Journal* had published the first of seven essays by "Cato," who suggested that the people could propose amendments to the Constitution. "Cato" inspired an outraged response by "Caesar," who again insisted the country had to accept or reject the Constitution "IN TOTO" and the people should "just take it as it is; and be thankful."[16] The impact of the Pennsylvania minority's address was, however, out of all proportion to anything that preceded it.

By early November, the address had been printed twelve times in Pennsylvania (including as a broadside in German) and sixteen times in another seven states. By contrast, the first essay by "Cato" was printed or reprinted only six times in three states (twice in New York, three times in Pennsylvania, and once in Massachusetts). The story of how dissenting members were dragged to the State House, which the address described, accounts for much of that interest. Answers to the address were quick in coming, but they could not kill the public's interest in what the *New York Morning Post* described as "an Event perhaps unparalleled in any Age or Country," the "political and outrageous FRACAS" in Philadelphia "in consequence of a virtuous minority of the Legislature refusing to vote against their Conscience." The "intemperate & violent Measures" of the Pennsylvania assembly suggested, as George Mason charged, that the Constitution's advocates dreaded "a thorough Knowledge & public Discussion of the Subject" and wanted to get it ratified before it was submitted to "the Test of impartial examination."[17] Before long the Constitution's supporters understood that the Pennsylvania majority's actions were a political mistake, one serious enough to throw the Constitution's fate into doubt.[18]

Two days after the seceding assemblymen's address appeared in the *Independent Gazetteer*, Oswald printed the first and most widely circulated of eighteen essays by "Centinel," who went beyond all predecessors in his outspoken attacks on the Constitution and its supporters, including George Washington and Benjamin Franklin. Many contemporaries thought the author was Pennsylvania supreme court justice George Bryan. In fact, "Centinel" was Judge Bryan's twenty-eight-year-old son, Samuel, who, like his father, was an ardent supporter of Pennsylvania's state constitution.[19]

"Centinel" found the proposed government too complex, too powerful, and too removed from popular control. The Constitution lacked provisions safeguarding liberty of the press and other rights that "most free constitutions" protected; indeed, he said, it had "none of the essential requisites of a free government." These flaws were not innocent mistakes: The framers fully expected the new national government to melt the states "down into one empire," which was incompatible with "democratical principles" and freedom. The Constitution was for "Centinel" nothing less than the "most daring attempt to establish a despotic aristocracy among freemen, that the world has ever witnessed." The "wealthy and ambitious" conspirators behind the plot had tried to lull the people's suspicions by recruiting two "illustrious personages" to their cause, taking advantage of the "unsuspecting goodness and zeal" of one (obviously Washington) and "the weakness and indecision attendant on old age" of the other (Franklin).[20]

What was to be done? "Centinel" did not deny that the country needed a federal government, or even the need for a central government more powerful than the Confederation. But he rejected the proposal in hand. He proposed calling another "general Convention" whose members would be informed by the current debates over the Constitution, which was only a "first essay" (or attempt) on the "difficult subject" of designing an appropriate government for the United States. Moreover, the second convention that "Centinel" had in mind would not amend the Constitution, like the one Mason and Randolph had proposed. It would start over.[21]

And there was no hurry. The Constitution's supporters claimed—as "Centinel" observed—that the nation's situation was "so *critically* dreadful, that, however reprehensible and exceptionable the proposed plan of government may be, there is no alternative, between the adoption of it and absolute ruin." But "Centinel" said there was no crisis. Europe was in too much turmoil to threaten the United States, and the danger of internal dissension was insufficient to justify adopting a form of government that threatened "*despotism*." Exaggerated fears were as out of place as the "frenzy of enthusiasm" for the Constitution that had seized Philadelphians. The occasion called for "free and unbiased discussion," so "Centinel" invited all who were capable of understanding the "abstruse" science of government to help the people "make a proper judgment" on the Constitution.[22]

The first "Centinel" essay was printed or reprinted nineteen times from Massachusetts to Virginia. That fell short of the thirty total printings scored by the address of the Pennsylvania minority, but it compared well with several of the more popular essays written in support of the Constitution.[23] The fight was on.

JAMES WILSON AT THE PENNSYLVANIA STATE HOUSE
No longer could the Constitution's supporters simply claim that "the people" wanted the Constitution ratified quickly, as they had during debates in the Pennsylvania Assembly. The address of the dissenting Pennsylvania assemblymen and the more developed, hard-hitting, radical arguments of the first "Centinel" essay demanded an authoritative answer. James Wilson, a Pennsylvania delegate to the federal Convention and one of the most active participants in its debate, took on that task. On the evening of Saturday, October 6, he rose before "a very great concourse of people" at the Pennsylvania State House and gave a speech that would become a basic text for defenders of the Constitution as well as a major target for its critics.[24]

Wilson was born in Scotland in 1742, the eldest son of a devout Presbyterian farming family of modest means. His parents wanted him to become a minister of the Church of Scotland, and after spending four years at the University of St. Andrews studying a broad range of subjects including Latin, Greek, philosophy, science, mathematics, and history, he began at the university's theological school. After a year, however, his father's death forced him to leave the university. He served for a time as a private tutor for a gentleman's family and began looking for better ways to realize his ambitions, which he found, like many Scots of his time, in America. Wilson arrived at New York in 1765 and soon moved to Pennsylvania, where he became a Latin instructor at the College of Philadelphia. He began studying law in the office of John Dickinson, a distinguished lawyer and one of the most popular writers on behalf of American rights and resistance to Britain in the decade before independence. Wilson was admitted to the bar in 1767 and became a successful lawyer in the town of Reading, then in Carlisle, and eventually in Philadelphia, where he moved with ease in the society of wealthy merchants. In 1774, he published a pamphlet that questioned Parliament's authority over the Americans and quickly achieved political prominence. Between 1775 and 1777 he represented Pennsylvania in the Continental Congress, where he signed the Declaration of Independence, and was again returned to Congress in the 1780s. In Pennsylvania politics, Wilson was an ardent critic of the state's 1776 constitution.[25]

The man had enemies who took exception to his politics, his "aristocratic" friends and manners, as well as his readiness to represent Loyalist clients, and who were further put off by Wilson's prodigious arrogance. "His lofty carriage indicates the lofty mind that animates him, a mind able to conceive and perform great things," one of his detractors wrote, "but which unfortunately can see nothing great out of the pale of power and worldly grandeur. . . . Men of sublime minds, he conceives, were born a different race from the rest of the sons of men." A defender agreed that Wilson had a "lofty carriage," but for good reason: "A man who wears spectacles must keep his head erect . . . to prevent them from falling off his nose."[26]

There's no doubt that Wilson thought very well of himself, and to some extent justly. His fellow Convention delegate William Pierce said he ranked "foremost in legal and political knowledge." Government was his particular interest, and Wilson knew in detail "all the political institutions of the World" and could trace "the causes and effects of every revolution from the earliest stages of the Grecian commonwealth down to the present time." Pierce added that, although "no man is more clear, copious, and comprehensive," Wilson was "no great Orator." He drew attention not by "the charm of his eloquence, but by the force of his reasoning." Wilson spoke a full 168 times during the federal Convention, more than any other delegate except his colleague (and partner in arrogance) Gouverneur Morris,[27] and some of his speeches—condemning the small states' insistence on equal representation, for example—are among the Convention's most memorable. On October 6 he became the first member of the Convention to defend the Constitution publicly.

Alexander J. Dallas, the editor of the *Pennsylvania Herald*, described Wilson's speech as "long and eloquent." Its length is hard to measure since the *Herald* printed only what it described as the speech's "outlines"—or, more exactly, a condensed version of the oration. Its eloquence was probably more apparent to the people who heard Wilson deliver it than to those who can read only the truncated version that Dallas published. Wilson liked to keep lists of opponents' arguments, then answer them one by one, a technique he would use again in the Pennsylvania ratifying convention. That broke his speech into fragments and robbed it of rhetorical sweep (until, perhaps, its end), but it facilitated the effort of Federalists elsewhere to take from Wilson's oration answers to what were already becoming, less than three weeks after the Convention adjourned, stock objections to the Constitution.[28]

Wilson had to explain why the Constitution did not, like several state constitutions, include a bill of rights. The reason, he said in one of his most influential arguments, lay in a critical difference between the constitutions of the states and the proposed federal Constitution. Through the state constitutions, the people gave their state governments "every right and authority which they did not in explicit terms reserve." The federal Constitution, however, carefully defined and limited the powers of Congress, so that body's authority came "not from tacit implication, but from the positive grant" of specific powers in the Constitution. Under the state constitutions, "every thing which is not reserved is given," but under the federal Constitution "every thing which is not given, is reserved." It therefore made good sense to add bills or declarations of rights to state constitutions, where they imposed constraints on what would otherwise be unlimited state powers. But it would be "superfluous" to say Congress could not do something—interfere with freedom of the press, for example—that the Constitution gave it no power to do.[29]

The argument was not entirely new. The Constitution's supporters had made the same point without Wilson's mind-twisting language during the Confederation Congress's debates a week earlier, but the press had not reported those debates. Wilson, however, went a step beyond his congressional predecessors. It would be downright dangerous to add reservations of rights to the federal Constitution, he said, because statements protecting rights could be "construed to imply that some degree of power was given, since we undertook to define its extent." In other words, some clever person—no doubt a crafty lawyer, like Wilson himself—could argue that Congress must have a power that was not explicitly given to it, for example to control the press, because it would make no sense for the Constitution to limit a power that Congress did not have. In that case, a federal Bill of Rights might actually be construed to give Congress powers that threatened basic rights.[30]

Because the Constitution mentioned jury trials only for criminal prosecutions, critics charged that it "abolished" trial by jury in civil cases. Not so, replied Wilson; members of the Convention simply found the problem "too difficult" since not all civil cases required juries (admiralty courts and equity courts, for example, did not) and state practices were far from uniform. The Philadelphia Convention therefore left the issue to be settled by congressional regulations.[31] Worries about a "standing army" were also unfounded. All governments, including the Confederation, had to "maintain the appearance of strength" even in times of tranquillity, and the exercise of military power was safe "under the controul and with the restrictions which the new constitution provides" (but which Wilson apparently did not specify). Concern over Congress's taxing power was equally misplaced since most federal revenues "must, and always will be raised by impost"—that is, by duties on imports. Congress would levy direct taxes only in times of emergency. Pennsylvanians, moreover, had much to gain from the establishment of a "competent and energetic federal system." The state had assumed responsibility for funding that part of the federal war debt owed to Pennsylvanians, and it would be freed of that "extraordinary burden" once the federal government could pay its own debts. Taxes, Wilson suggested, would actually go down in Pennsylvania once the Constitution went into effect.[32]

Critics charged that the Senate would become home to a "baneful aristocracy." Not so, Wilson replied, because its power was limited: The Senate could do nothing of a legislative character without the consent of the House of Representatives, and nothing of an executive nature without the president's concurrence. But was the equal representation of states in the Senate fair? In the federal Convention Wilson had opposed that provision; now he chose to celebrate it as an example of "mutual concession and accommodation." That did not really address the objection. He said nothing about a senator's six-year term of office, which was unusually long for the time, or the lack of term limits, which "Centinel" said would allow senators to be reelected indefinitely.[33]

Wilson did, however, answer charges that the Constitution would reduce the power of the states and then destroy them altogether. The new government could not function without the states, he argued. State legislatures would choose senators and decide how presidential electors were chosen, and the franchise requirements for electing members of the House of Representatives were defined by each state's rules for electing members of the largest house of the state legislature.[34] If there were no states, a good part of the Constitution could not be implemented.

For Wilson, in short, no objection to the Constitution had merit. He nonetheless found it unsurprising that some writers criticized the document since "it is the nature of man to pursue his own interest, in preference to the public good." Those who had or wanted state positions collecting revenue or dispensing justice were behind the opposition to the Constitution, he suggested, because they thought those responsibilities might be transferred to the federal government. A man who feared for his job raised objections to the Constitution "not, in truth, because it is injurious to the liberties of his country, but because it affects his schemes of wealth and consequence."[35] The charge that opponents were defending their private interests rather than the public good was standard in eighteenth-century politics. Still, Wilson's comment, repeated in one form or another by many supporters of the Constitution, was hardly calculated to win over men who genuinely believed that the Constitution threatened the rights and welfare of the American people.

There were, in fact, parts of the Constitution that Wilson did not like. But after four months of debate at the federal Convention, he concluded, like Washington and other nationalists, that nothing better was politically possible. Any serious problems could be fixed later through the process of amendment described in Article V of the Constitution. And so, "in every point of view, with a candid and disinterested mind," Wilson asserted that the Constitution was "the best form of government which has ever been offered to the world."[36]

———

The *Pennsylvania Herald* reported that the crowd frequently interrupted Wilson "with loud and unanimous testimonies of approbation" and again cheered repeatedly when he finished his speech, demonstrating "the general sense of its excellence" and persuasiveness.[37] But Wilson was preaching to the converted: Philadelphia was a Federalist enclave. He had answered the assertions of the seceding assemblymen and "Centinel" only in part. Wilson's speech nonetheless became a landmark in the ratification debates. An account of it first appeared in an "extra" edition of the *Pennsylvania Herald* on October 9, and then it was reprinted in every state except perhaps Delaware, which probably received copies enough from nearby Philadelphia. Federalists throughout the country welcomed Wilson's speech—and then silently absorbed his arguments into their own essays and oratory. In that way, James Wilson's October 6 speech became a fundamental text for the ratification debates.[38]

Rather than calm the opposition, however, Wilson's speech provoked a cascading number of refutations. The earliest answers to Wilson appeared in Philadelphia and New York, particularly in Oswald's *Independent Gazetteer*, Bailey's *Freeman's Journal*, Greenleaf's *New-York Journal*, and also the *Pennsylvania Herald*, which, under the editorship of Alexander Dallas, adopted a policy of "studied impartiality" and printed items that attacked as well as defended the Constitution. Writers such as "A Democratic Federalist," "An Old Whig," "Cincinnatus," "An Officer of the Late Continental Army," and, last but not least, the redoubtable "Centinel" answered Wilson's speech, and above all his explanation of why the Constitution had no bill of rights.

The state constitutions and the proposed federal Constitution, they said, came from the same source—the people—for the identical purpose: "framing rules by which we should be governed, and ascertaining those powers which it was necessary to vest in our rulers." The distinction Wilson drew between them was a "dictum" of his invention, a "play of words" without substance, "a distinction without a difference." If the Constitution gave Congress only those powers that it explicitly stated, why didn't it include, like the Articles of Confederation, a provision that said the states retained "every power, jurisdiction and right which is not by this Confederation expressly delegated to the United States in Congress Assembled"? Moreover, the "necessary and proper" clause gave Congress a grant of power so open-ended that it was meaningless to say its powers were carefully defined and limited.[39]

In a letter to Samuel Adams, Richard Henry Lee provided another answer to what he called Wilson's "principle Sophism . . . that bills of rights were necessary in the State Constitutions because every thing not reserved was given to the State Legislatures, but in the Federal government, every thing was reserved that was not given to the federal Legislature." He called that "a distinction without a difference," and a particularly futile one, since the Constitution in fact imposed certain reservations on Congress. It could not, for example, interfere with the slave trade for twenty years or grant titles of nobility. Those explicit limits on congressional power indicated that—whatever Wilson claimed—members of the federal Convention had assumed "that what was not reserved was given." Why, then, did the Convention refuse to impose reservations on congressional power "in favor of the Press, Rights of Conscience, Trial by Jury in Civil Cases, or Common Law securities"? In any case, as "Centinel" observed, "the lust of power is so universal, that a speculative unascertained rule of construction" provided "a *poor* security for the liberties of the people." The reasons given for omitting a bill of rights were nothing less than "an insult on the understanding of the people."[40]

Before long newspapers were "inundated" with replies to Wilson's speech, many of them by local writers, such that his argument set off a chain reaction. To be sure, there were parts of the country that had little or no access to newspapers or had newspapers that printed only essays favorable to the Constitution. Even so, the debate on the Constitution in the press, which began in Philadelphia and New York, spread so far beyond those centers of controversy by late October and early November that, despite pockets of silence, it had become national.[41]

THE STARS OF THE SHOW

Although newspaper readers across the country became caught up in the national debate, much of what they read after the initial explosion from Philadelphia was written for a surprisingly focused audience. That was true even of several series of essays that first appeared in October (or, in one case, September) and continued into the spring of 1788. Those series offered more sustained analyses of the Constitution than isolated essays or one-time publications like the address of the seceding members of the Pennsylvania assembly. They also spoke directly to the public, without the intervention of reporters like the one who wrote the *Pennsylvania Herald*'s account of James Wilson's speech at the Pennsylvania State House. The authors of newspaper series were the media stars of the ratification controversy, but their light had a limited span.

The most notable series of newspaper essays critical of the Constitution was published by the usual suspects in Philadelphia and New York. The letters of "Centinel" (eighteen essays, October 1787 to April 1788) first appeared in Oswald's *Independent Gazetteer* and Bailey's *Freeman's Journal*, "Cato" (seven essays, September 1787 to January 1788) and "Brutus" (sixteen essays, October 1787 to April 1788) in Greenleaf's *New-York Journal*.[42] Except for "Centinel," the authorship remains in dispute. People of course speculated then (and now) on who wrote under which pseudonym. Some readers probably gave the essays of "Cato" a close look because they suspected the author was New York's governor George Clinton.[43] In the end, however, the influence of serial essays on the Constitution turned far more on what they said than on who wrote them.

The sets of essays differed from each other in style and to some extent in content, although they often repeated many of the same points. "Cato," whose essays were the least powerful of the lot, made a spirited defense of the sovereign people's right to do what they wanted with the Constitution. "Centinel" was the most confrontational in his outspoken attacks on the "conspirators" who wrote the Constitution. "Brutus" appealed instead "to the candid and dispassionate part of the community" and offered tight, closely reasoned arguments in defense of what were becoming standard parts of an evolving case against the Constitution: that it violated separation of powers, provided inadequate representation for the people and insufficient protection of rights, and gave Congress excessive and dangerous powers that would destroy the states and produce an oppressive "consolidated" government. He also analyzed the proposed federal judicial system, which, again, he saw as a threat to the states. Both "Cato" and "Centinel" expressed admiration for his "masterly" arguments.[44] Even *The Federalist*, which offered a detailed, powerful case for the Constitution, recognized "Brutus" as a formidable opponent by answering him, though without acknowledging him by name.[45]

Many of the arguments of "Brutus" were also made by the "Federal Farmer," who ranks with "Brutus" for the sophistication and coherence of his essays. "Brutus," however, found the Constitution flawed in its "fundamental principles" and advocated its rejection, while the "Federal Farmer" said the proposed Constitution included "many good things" as well as "many important defects," and that "with several alterations" it could create a "tolerably good" federal system.[46] The first five letters of the "Federal Farmer," each of which carried a date between October 8 and 13, appeared in early November as a forty-page pamphlet, *Observations Leading to a Fair Examination of the System of Government Proposed by the Late Convention; and to Several Essential and Necessary Alterations in It.* The following May, Greenleaf published *An Additional Number of Letters from the Federal Farmer to the Republican . . .*, which included thirteen new "Federal Farmer" letters, dated between December 25, 1787, and January 25, 1788. Although the second pamphlet was admired, even by its opponents, the first, with the original five letters of the "Farmer," was more influential, in part because it appeared earlier in the ratification contest.[47]

These series of essays seldom circulated widely. No subsequent essays by "Cato" were reprinted as often as the first. Of the "Centinel" essays, again, the first reached the widest audience; reprintings of the second "Centinel" essay outside Pennsylvania and New York could be counted on the fingers of one hand. (By contrast, Wilson's speech was printed thirty-eight times, including some twenty-three times outside Pennsylvania and New York.) Only the Poughkeepsie, New York, *Country Journal* republished the entire set of essays by the "Federal Farmer." Even "Brutus" was seldom reprinted—although his letters were known in some states where they were not published. Critics of the Constitution circulated the writings of Brutus in New York and sent copies of the "Federal Farmer" to allies in Pennsylvania, Connecticut, Massachusetts, and Virginia.[48]

The story here is not simply one of the Constitution's supporters suppressing the circulation of essays by its critics, though that was part of the tale. The most comprehensive defense and analysis of the Constitution, *The Federalist* (eighty-five essays, October 1787 through May 1788), also had a limited circulation outside New York (and, in fact, within the state) when first published. Either John Jay or Alexander Hamilton, both New Yorkers, first came up with the idea of writing a comprehensive series of essays on the Constitution. Later, after other initiatives had failed, they recruited the help of James Madison, who was in New York City as a Virginia delegate to the Confederation Congress. All of the *Federalist* essays, regardless of author, were signed "Publius" (although the original plan was to sign them "A Citizen of N.Y.") and addressed "To the People of the State of New-York." According to Madison, their primary objective was "to promote the ratification of the new Constitution by the State of N. York where it was powerfully opposed, and where its success was deemed of critical importance."[49] The ambitious scope of the series and the authors' technique of answering opponents without acknowledging their existence (with a few exceptions) can easily mislead readers into thinking *The Federalist* is a dispassionate analysis of the Constitution, far removed from the political battleground, which was for "Publius" first and foremost New York.[50]

The first number of *The Federalist,* which appeared in the *New York Independent Journal* on October 27, promised readers a broad-based consideration of the nation's needs, a demonstration of how the Constitution fit those needs, and answers to all objections to it "that may seem to have any claim to your attention." (It also described the Constitution's critics as acting from selfish motives and said some of them supported dividing the country into separate confederacies, which signaled that "Publius" was hardly dispassionate or apolitical.) Madison and Hamilton sent copies of early *Federalist* essays to Washington, who tried to get them published in Virginia, but only a handful were republished in the *Virginia Independent Chronicle* (Richmond). In fact, a careful modern study concluded that newspapers outside the state of New York republished only twenty-four of the eighty-five *Federalist* essays during the course of the ratification controversy. Philadelphia's *Pennsylvania Gazette* reprinted eighteen and Boston's *American Herald* seven, but most non–New York newspapers published only one or two, and five at the most. Even the now-famous *Federalist* Number 10, in which Madison made a taut, ground-breaking argument that republics were more likely to survive over large than small territories, was republished only once outside New York State (in the *Pennsylvania Gazette*). The series' reach and the number of people who testified to its distinction expanded substantially after the spring of 1788, when the essays were collected and printed together in two volumes of some 600 pages (with Hamilton picking up over half the cost); the first volume appeared in March, the second in late May.[51] That, however, was very late in the game, and evidence that the essays influenced the debates in subsequent state conventions except for that of New York is sporadic at best.

In short, for all the talk about the Constitution in the newspapers, much of the debate remained local. The influence of writers such as "Brutus" and even "Publius" was felt most intensely in the ratification politics of their home states. That was also true of series published in the Massachusetts press and geared to a Massachusetts audience under pseudonyms such as "Cassius" (eleven letters, September to December 1787), "John De Witt" (four letters, October to December 1787), and "Agrippa" (sixteen letters, November 1787 to February 1788).[52]

Today virtually all the writings for and against the Constitution published over the course of the ratification contest are readily available in print, and many are also online. They were nowhere near so accessible to those who had to decide the Constitution's fate, especially if they lived outside Pennsylvania and New York, and, more specifically, outside the eastern counties of Pennsylvania and the southern counties of New York. Even there, unless someone took to clipping articles for future reference or those essays were, like the "Federal Farmer," printed together from the first or republished in anthologies, essays printed in October were no doubt long gone by December.

That helps explain the redundancy in writings on the Constitution. Different authors often made the same or similar arguments (with or without acknowledging their predecessors) for different audiences or at different times. Haste also took its toll. Madison explained that the authors of *The Federalist*, who promised to send the printer four numbers a week, had no time to show each other their essays before handing them over for printing. Sometimes they couldn't even reread their own work before it was put in type. That the series came out as well as it did was a tribute to the authors' intelligence, dedication, and deep familiarity with their subject. Under the circumstances, however, wordiness and what Madison called "an occasional repetition of . . . views" was unavoidable,[53] and it wore at readers' patience, particularly where the essays' assertions seemed groundless. When supporters of the Constitution charged its critics with advocating the creation of regional confederacies on the ruins of the union, "Centinel" could take no more. "This hobgoblin," he wrote, "appears to have sprung from the deranged brain of *Publius*, a New-York writer, who, mistaking sound for argument, has with Herculean labour accumulated myriads of unmeaning sentences, and *mechanically* endeavored to force conviction by a torrent of misplaced words." He might have "spared his readers the fatigue of wading through his long-winded disquisitions" on subjects irrelevant to his supposed subject. "This writer," he concluded, "has devoted much time" and wasted considerable paper "in combating chimeras of his own creation."[54]

Anyone today who reads "Centinel," "Brutus," and the "Federal Farmer" at a sitting might well also suffer from "fatigue" and complain about "long-winded," repetitive "disquisitions" and "chimeras" of a different sort. But at the time the essays were first published, hardly anyone read them that way. Except for the essays of the "Federal Farmer," and to some extent those of "Publius," which came out quickly, sometimes simultaneously, and were eventually collected in books, the essays in series appeared one by one, separated by many others, and their readers were more often than not within the same state where the essays were written. Moreover, their impressive theoretical achievements, as contenders continued and developed an ongoing debate about liberty and the nature of government that went back to the independence movement, are appreciated more in retrospect than they were at the time. The objectives of those who wrote both to defend and to criticize the Constitution were primarily political. They wanted to get the Constitution ratified, amended, or, in some cases, rejected. And that they would have to achieve on the local level, in the towns and counties where convention delegates were chosen, and then in one state ratifying convention after another.

THE CONVENTION'S DISSENTERS SPEAK OUT

Secretary of War Henry Knox took a few minutes on October 3 to write his old friend George Washington from New York. The burst of newspaper criticisms had not yet begun—Knox wrote on the very day that, in Philadelphia, Eleazer Oswald printed the address of the seceding members of the Pennsylvania Assembly in his *Gazetteer*—so Knox had only good news to report. "Hitherto everything promises well," he said. The Constitution would probably be ratified "in a much shorter time than I some time ago believed." He knew, however, that opposition would emerge. Its germ "originated in the convention itself. The gentlemen who refused signing it will most probably conceive themselves obliged to state their reasons publicly. The presses will groan with melancholy forebodings, and a party of some strength will be created."[55]

As Knox predicted, during the fall of 1787 and early winter of 1788, the press printed statements from those delegates who had failed to sign the Constitution, explaining why and how they differed from the majority at the federal Convention. Some of those testaments were widely republished and became points of reference in the ratification debates. Above all, they demonstrated that the reasons for opposing ratification of the Constitution differed dramatically from person to person. So did ideas of what should be done.

George Mason's objections to the Constitution exerted most of their influence soon after the federal Convention adjourned, when they circulated privately in manuscript. They were not printed until November 21, when they appeared in the *Massachusetts Centinel*, and then within a few days in two Virginia newspapers. Over the next six weeks, the objections were reprinted throughout the country in some twenty-five newspapers from New England to South Carolina, and they prompted another round of responses and counterresponses.[56] But Mason's case took so long to be published that Elbridge Gerry was able to beat him into print.

Gerry lingered in New York with his wife and her family after the federal Convention adjourned. Finally, on October 18, he wrote the Massachusetts legislature a letter explaining why he had not signed the Constitution. The state Senate read it on October 31, the lower house on November 2, and it appeared in the *Massachusetts Centinel* the next day. Gerry's statement was relatively brief: He summarized his criticisms of the Constitution—which were less wide-ranging than those he had raised in the final days of the Convention—in a single concise paragraph. The Constitution, he said, failed to provide an adequate representation for the people or to secure their right to free and fair elections; some of the powers given Congress were "ambiguous, and others indefinite and dangerous"; the executive and legislative branches were insufficiently separated; the judiciary threatened to become oppressive; treaties, which would become the supreme law of the land, could be enacted by the president and two-thirds of a quorum of the Senate, without the consent of the House of Representatives, and "the system is without the security of a bill of rights."[57] He sounded a lot like Mason.

Although Gerry said the Constitution would create a "*national* government" with "few, if any *federal* features," he granted that "in many respects" it had "great merit." Much like Washington and his political allies, Gerry understood that the preservation of the union required a more efficient government, and he feared that a rejection of the Constitution would lead to anarchy. Like Mason, he advocated ratification of the Constitution with "proper amendments" enacted prior to the Constitution's ratification, so it would serve both "the 'exigencies of government' and [the] preservation of liberty." Why "should a free people adopt a form of Government, under conviction that it wants [needs] amendment?" Certainly the people should not give "*implicit* confidence" to the respectable delegates who wrote the Constitution, as some writers urged. Even the greatest men sometimes err; a free people had to be the guardians of their liberties. And they should make sure they understood the Constitution well before deciding on it "lest they should refuse to *support* the government, having *hastily* accepted it." So long as the people had the power to amend the Constitution, Gerry saw no need for them to reject it. He assumed that they could amend the Constitution and then ratify it, unlike the Federalists who insisted that the country had to accept the Constitution exactly as it had emerged from the Convention.[58]

By November 21, when the *Massachusetts Centinel* finally printed Mason's objections, Gerry's letter had been reprinted in ten other Massachusetts papers; eventually it would appear in virtually all the state's newspapers. It caused a furor. Most previous publications on the Constitution in Massachusetts favored ratification; then, between October 23 and November 5, five newspapers reprinted the "Address of the Seceding Members of the Pennsylvania Assembly" (one fewer than published James Wilson's October 6 speech at the Pennsylvania State House). Soon the Massachusetts press would be filled with essays on both sides of the question, many of which came from local writers. But Gerry's criticisms of the Constitution were among the first that many Massachusetts readers encountered.[59]

Gerry's letter also appeared at a critical time. On October 25, the Massachusetts legislature had called a state ratifying convention, which would meet in January. Two Massachusetts delegates to the federal Convention, Rufus King and Nathaniel Gorham, had arrived in Boston five days earlier to explain why they signed the Constitution, and they were now busily at work trying to persuade members of the legislature to tell the folks back home to elect convention delegates who would vote for ratification. Everything seemed to be going smoothly: On October 28, the Boston merchant Henry Jackson happily predicted the Constitution would be ratified in Massachusetts "by a very large Majority of the People." Then the legislature read Gerry's letter—at just the wrong time for the Constitution's advocates (who would have preferred that it never appeared at all). Gerry has "done more injury to this Country," Jackson fumed on November 5, two days after Gerry's "infamous Letter" appeared in print, "than he will be able to make atonement [for] in his whole life . . . *damn him—damn him.*" Everything previously "had the most favorable appearance in this State," but "now I have my doubts."[60]

Gerry's moderation—after all, he saw the Constitution as an alternative to anarchy and wanted it ratified, although with amendments—was lost on Gorham and King. They composed a long, wordy, point-by-point refutation of Gerry's succinct list of "principal objections" to the Constitution, which they never published. Others stepped in to answer Gerry, among whom Oliver Ellsworth, a Connecticut delegate to the federal Convention, was the most prominent. His essays, signed "Landholder," first appeared in Hartford's *Connecticut Courant.* They were less notable for their arguments on behalf of the Constitution, which were also made by others in different contexts,[61] than for their personal attacks on Gerry, whose real motives for not signing the Constitution, "Landholder" charged, were "most pitifully selfish and despicable." Gerry, he suggested, might hold "dignities or emoluments" that would be threatened by the Constitution. "Landholder" also claimed that Gerry had turned against the Constitution only after the Convention refused to commit the new government to redeeming Continental currency, a measure Gerry had proposed for his personal benefit, since he held "large quantities of this species of paper."[62]

Gerry responded to these attacks in the *Massachusetts Centinel*. He said he held no public office, denied ever proposing that the new government redeem depreciated Continental currency, and insisted that he did not own more than "ten pounds in old continental money." His only motive for opposing the unamended Constitution was "a firm persuasion that it would endanger the liberties of America." No Connecticut paper reprinted his defense.[63]

———

If Mason's and Gerry's positions were much the same as they had been in the final days of the federal Convention, that of Virginia's governor Edmund Randolph shifted in the intervening weeks. On October 10 Randolph wrote—or later claimed to have written—a very long letter to the Virginia legislature explaining why he had not signed the Constitution. He did not, however, submit it to the legislature, even when he had been securely reelected as governor on October 23, nor after October 31, when both houses of the legislature agreed to call a state ratifying convention. Finally, on December 10, after four members of the Virginia Assembly asked Randolph for a statement of his objections to the Constitution, he sent them his letter with permission to publish it. The letter was printed as a sixteen-page pamphlet in late December and then immediately reprinted, sometimes in an abbreviated form, in newspapers from Virginia to Massachusetts.[64]

Randolph's views went back to those he held before the Convention, when he was a firm supporter of a stronger central government. He said the Confederation had to be "thrown aside" because it lacked "every energy, which a constitution of the United States ought to possess." The central government needed critical new powers, which "must be deposited in a new body, growing out of a consolidation of the union, as far as the circumstances of the states will allow."[65] He did not sign the Constitution because the Convention's majority insisted that the people accept it "in the whole, or reject it in the whole," with amendments "positively forbidden." No less than Mason, Randolph believed "that every citizen of America, let the crisis be what it may, ought to have a full opportunity to propose through his representatives any amendment, which in his apprehension tends to the public welfare." A constitution "ought to have the hearts of the people on its side." They should not be able to say later that it was "forced upon them" because they had either to take or to reject it altogether. Randolph also believed that "this great subject" would be "placed in new lights and attitudes by the criticism of the world," and that nobody could predict how the Constitution would work over time "until at least he has heard the observations of the people at large." He feared, moreover, that the people would reject it and so "bid a lasting farewell to the union" if they were forced to vote it up or down.[66]

Randolph said he did not sign the Constitution, in short, because he advocated amendments and also because he thought the Convention majority's "all-or-nothing" strategy would fail and do great harm to the country. Like Mason and Gerry, Randolph wanted amendments adopted prior to ratification. Like Richard Henry Lee, he thought these amendments would "remove the obstacles to an effectual government" and make ratification more likely.[67]

Randolph summarized his specific objections to the Constitution only at the end of his letter. He understood that some provisions he disliked could not be changed, such as the equality of suffrage in the Senate and Congress's capacity to regulate trade by simple majority vote. Amendments could, however, explain ambiguous terms, impose term limits on the president, define the separate jurisdictions of Congress and the states, block Congress from setting its members' salaries without limit, and redefine the power of the federal judiciary. Randolph did not mention a bill of rights. Most important, in his penultimate paragraph he said that his "most fervent prayer" was for the "establishment of a firm, energetic government," and he vowed that, even if the campaign for amendments failed, he would nonetheless accept the Constitution.[68]

Randolph sent printed copies of his letter to Washington and Madison, who received it with relief. His powerful arguments in favor of a strong national government seemed to overshadow everything else he said, including his objections to the Constitution, which, as Madison put it, seemed to come from "his particular way of thinking on the subject, in which many of the Adversaries to the Constitution do not concur." When New York critics of the Constitution republished Randolph's letter, they left out the paragraph with his pledge to support the Constitution even without amendments. If there were two sides, Randolph seemed to be somewhere between them.[69]

————

The differences between Mason and Gerry, on the one hand, and Randolph, on the other, paled beside the great gulf that divided those three contenders from Luther Martin, the attorney general of Maryland, who arrived at the federal Convention late and left on September 4, two weeks before it adjourned. In the intervening months, Martin had fought losing battles on one provision after another and, according to William Pierce, gave prolix speeches with "a very bad delivery" that tested the patience of all who heard him. On November 29, Martin presented his views orally to the Maryland legislature. He then reworked and expanded his speech, which Baltimore's *Maryland Gazette* began printing in late December. The twelfth and final installment appeared in February. Two months later, Eleazar Oswald printed the entire series in a pamphlet titled *The Genuine Information, Delivered to the Legislature of Maryland . . .*[70]

Basically, Martin wanted to make the "present *federal system*"—the Confederation—the basis of any reform. Its known defects should be repaired, and it should receive any new powers for which experience showed the need. If those changes proved inadequate, a future convention could, "with the same moderation . . . correct such errors and defects as experience . . . brought to light," and so, in an incremental manner, eventually achieve "as perfect a system of federal government, as the nature of things would admit." Instead the federal Convention had proposed to overthrow the Confederation and substitute an entirely new government. So callous a disregard for the established constitutional order was likely to be repeated and bring endemic instability to American government without any real gain, Martin said. Moreover, the Convention acted as it had because it was controlled by delegates from Virginia and other "large states" who wanted to increase their "*power* and *influence over the others*," and who, Martin charged, allied with other delegates who sought to destroy the states and establish a monarchy.[71]

The "federal government" Martin had in mind was fundamentally different from the central government proposed by the federal Convention. It would remain a government of states that acted on the states, not on individuals, and in which states, as independent sovereigns, had equal votes. By contrast, the federal government under the Constitution would be ratified by the people and, where it had authority, could act on the people as if the states did not exist.[72] Martin did not argue, like other critics of the Constitution, that the people were inadequately represented in the lower house of Congress because he saw no reason for the people to have any direct voice in the federal government. He did, however, find many other problems in the Constitution, from the fact that senators would no longer be paid by the states and could not be recalled, through Congress's extensive power to tax and to control the militia, to the creation of a federal court system and the lack of religious tests for office.[73] But no amendments to the Constitution would satisfy him since the problem lay with its organizing principles, which amendments could not fix.

Martin's position was very different than those of Mason and Gerry, from whom Martin explicitly dissociated himself. During the federal Convention, he said, on every issue "that tended to give the *large States power* over the *smaller*," Mason "could not forget he belonged to the *ancient dominion*," and Gerry could not forget "that he represented Old Massachusetts." They went over to the opposition only after they saw that the powers of the new government would lead to the destruction of the states, including their own, and even then they opposed only parts of the Constitution. By contrast, Martin felt a firm political kinship with the New York delegates Robert Yates and John Lansing, Jr., who "uniformly opposed the system" favored by the federal Convention and left in early July because, Martin suggested, they despaired of getting "a *proper one* brought forward."[74]

———

Yates and Lansing confirmed Martin's claim on December 21, when they sent New York governor George Clinton a letter that officially explained why they had left the Convention. It had become clear, they said, that the delegates would adopt a proposal at odds with their instructions, which confined them "to the sole and express purpose of revising the articles of Confederation." They had assumed that the Convention would merely devise means of giving the Confederation a sufficient source of revenue, the power to regulate commerce and to enforce provisions in foreign treaties, along with "other necessary matters of less moment." Instead, the Convention proposed a new, impractical "consolidated government" that would pervade every part of the United States and deprive New York of its "most essential rights of Sovereignty." That, they wrote, was far from the New York legislature's intention when it had appointed Convention delegates.[75]

Although Yates and Lansing disliked the Constitution, they did not complain about its lack of a bill of rights. For them, no such "cautionary provisions" could prevent the inevitable destruction of civil liberty once the United States was put under a centralized government. Nor did they argue that representation of the people would be inadequate in the new House of Representatives. In their view, a national legislature that represented the people "in the usual and true idea of representation" would be intolerably expensive and burdensome, and a smaller body would be ignorant of or ignore the interests of the greater part of the people. Their objections, like Martin's, were fundamental and could not be met by amendments to the Constitution: "We should have been equally opposed to any system, *however modified*," they said, "which had in object the consolidation of the United States into one Government."[76]

Clinton submitted the letter to the state legislature along with the report and resolution of the Constitutional Convention on January 11, 1788. Three days later, both the *New York Daily Advertiser* and Greenleaf's *New-York Journal* printed the Yates and Lansing letter. It was reprinted in another six New York papers and eleven others from New Hampshire to Georgia. It provoked relatively few responses.[77] But, with the statements by the other dissenters from the federal Convention, Yates and Lansing helped make one thing absolutely clear: Critics of the Constitution did not speak with one voice.

CALLING NAMES

Even before the federal Convention had met, the advocates of a stronger national government called those who resisted giving more powers to the Confederation "anti-federal" and suggested that such people were not altogether respectable.[78] After the Convention had adjourned, supporters of the

Constitution continued to use the term. For them, the battle was between "Federalists," who supported ratification of the Constitution as written (or "as it now stands") and "Antifederalists" who did not and whose opposition was founded on a long-standing hostility to a stronger central government. The Constitution's supporters described "Antifederalists" as state officials who feared for their jobs and so attacked the Constitution for selfish reasons. Even their commitment to the Revolution was called into question by writers who associated those who criticized the Constitution with the Loyalists who opposed independence.[79]

Most so-called "Antifederalists" contested the term and, above all, the implications of disloyalty it carried. In truth, most and perhaps all contenders—even Luther Martin—agreed on the need to strengthen the federal government in one way or another, and the critics of the Constitution were hardly confined to persons who had personal interests at stake. The way opposition to the unamended Constitution emerged in the fall of 1787 also suggests that it was a response to the Constitution itself and the hasty, strong-armed tactics of its supporters, not a simple continuation of previous divisions.

Equally important, the critics of the Constitution were no one thing. The differences among Convention dissenters mirrored those among the authors of newspaper serials. "Brutus," like Luther Martin, Yates, and Lansing, thought the Constitution was fundamentally flawed and should be rejected; the "Federal Farmer" favored amendments, and so resembled Mason, Gerry, and Lee (who have all been suspected of writing the series). "Centinel," who wanted a new federal government, although not the one proposed, was somewhere in between. Opponents of the Constitution fanned out along a spectrum: Those who preferred to keep the Confederation (though to strengthen it) were on one extreme—call it the "western" end; while those who thought the Constitution was better than the Confederation but that it should be amended before being ratified were nearer the center, adjacent to Edmund Randolph, who wanted amendments but was willing to ratify the Constitution without them.[80]

"Federalists" all supported ratification of the Constitution "as it now stands," although some wanted amendments once the new government began. Although most of them said the Constitution had flaws, they differed over what perfection would be. Judging from their pre-Convention and Convention proposals, Alexander Hamilton, Henry Knox, and John Jay wanted a government nearer to the "consolidated" form that Yates and Lansing feared. They were on the far "eastern" end of the political spectrum. Madison, who had become profoundly disillusioned with the state governments, also sought a significantly strengthened national government but understood that "a consolidation of the States into one simple republic" was both "unattainable" and "inexpedient." In April of 1787, he sought a "middle ground" that would give the central government "due supremacy" but leave the states' powers in place where they could be "subordinately useful." He hoped that the federal veto on state laws he favored would not only prevent wrongdoing by the states but create a "mutuality of dependence" between the central and state governments that would help avoid the "difficulty & awkwardness" of using force against "the collective will of a State" to enforce federal authority. Moreover, Madison agreed with several criticisms of the Constitution's provisions on representation, from the equal representation of states in the Senate through the small size of the first House of Representatives. In many ways he was more like Edmund Randolph, his old ally in Virginia, than Hamilton, although Madison and Hamilton could hide what Madison described as "a known difference in the general complexion of their political theories" under the mask of "Publius."[81]

In short, the terms "Federalist" and "Antifederalist," which were used mainly by "Federalists," oversimplify the debate over the Constitution by suggesting there were only two sides. At the end of 1787, the "Federal Farmer" argued persuasively that each of those categories included distinct sets of people whose views on the relationship of the states and the nation sometimes overlapped. Some of the Constitution's supporters, he said, were "pretended federalists" who wanted to destroy the state governments. Others were "honest federalists" who wished "to preserve *substantially* the state governments united under an efficient head." The "Federal Farmer" also claimed that some of the Constitution's critics—who often insisted that they were the only true federalists because they alone wanted to preserve the states while strengthening the central government—were "only pretended federalists" because they actually wanted "no federal government, or one merely advisory" to the states. Other critics of the Constitution were, however, "true federalists" whose position was essentially the same as those "honest federalists" among the advocates of unqualified ratification. The "Federal Farmer" also said that both the Constitution's supporters and its critics included people who had no clear position on the relationship of the states and the nation,[82] which added a significant degree of unpredictability to the contest. On the other hand, if the "honest federalists" among the Constitution's supporters and the "true federalists" among its critics were really so close in their views and, in effect, occupied positions on opposite sides of the spectrum's center, they could perhaps work out some form of mutual accommodation to save the Constitution from defeat.

In any case, the variety of views undermined—and today continues to undermine—efforts to name contending sides. If they were not "Federalists" and "Antifederalists," neither were they, as Elbridge Gerry would later suggest, "Rats" and "Anti-Rats": After all, Gerry himself feared that a rejection of the Constitution would cause chaos. Nor were they, as the "Federal Farmer" suggested, "republicans and anti-republicans," since defenders of the Constitution such as "Publius" insisted that it conformed to republican principles.[83] Who needed a category anyway? Writers went on happily writing under pseudonyms of their choosing, with critics of the Constitution taking names with "Federalist" in them—such as the "Republican Federalist," the "Democratic Federalist," and, of course, the "Federal Farmer." After all, it was they far more than the Constitution's supporters who defended the continued existence of *both* state and national governments—and so the existence of a stable *federal* system—within the United States.

How would the opinions of "We the People" and the delegations they sent to state ratifying conventions fall along the spectrum of opinion? Nobody knew. Until the elections were held and the ratifying conventions met, observers could only speculate. But by late October, Henry Knox's early confidence that the Constitution would be ratified quickly and easily had pretty much disappeared. Criticisms of it had moved from the shadows into public prominence, making the contest for the minds and hearts of voters into a real dogfight. Responsibility for that development rested in no small part with Eleazer Oswald and a rash of writers whose essays he and a handful of other newspaper editors were willing to publish.

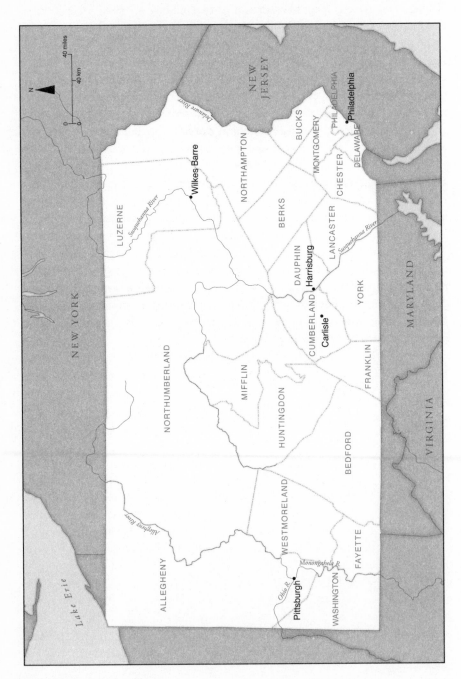

Pennsylvania, 1787–1788

FOUR

————— ★ —————

The Pennsylvania Ratifying Convention

... with Delaware, New Jersey, and Georgia

In late October of 1787, Gouverneur Morris—a wealthy and sophisticated lawyer and merchant of New York birth who had been a Pennsylvania delegate at the federal Convention—sent Washington his assessment of the Constitution's chances of being ratified. Morris wasn't altogether optimistic. All of New England except Rhode Island was unanimously in favor, he reported. So was New Jersey. In fact, support for the Constitution there was so strong "that we may count with Certainty on something more than Votes should the State of Affairs hereafter require the Application of pointed Arguments." Was he suggesting that the failure to ratify might lead to civil war?[1]

Failure was a strong possibility. New York, he reported, was deeply divided. If the legislature could decide the issue, Morris thought it would probably vote the Constitution down. "But the Legislature cannot assign to the People any good Reason for not trusting them with a Decision on their own Affairs, and must therefore agree to a Convention." And in a convention he thought those delegates who supported the Constitution might end up with a majority, but not for sure.

The outcome in Pennsylvania also remained uncertain. The Constitution had strong support in and around Philadelphia, but Morris dreaded "the cold and sower Temper of the back Counties" as well as the "wicked Industry" of people who feared losing the power and profit they were used to getting from the state government, and that of men eager to get back at their political adversaries.

Two representatives from inland Pennsylvania had, in fact, been eloquent critics of the Constitution in Pennsylvania's assembly debates. Robert

Whitehill represented Cumberland County, which lay just west of the Susquehanna River and south of the Juniata. William Findley came from Westmoreland County in the far west of the state. In the ratifying convention they would join forces with John Smilie of newly organized Fayette County, just south of Westmoreland. All were members of the Constitutionalist Party in Pennsylvania politics and were called "Antifederalists" by their opponents, although they rarely if ever used that name. Like other critics of the Constitution, they also found many ways to refer to the Constitution's supporters without using the word "Federalist."[2]

The three men were relatively obscure, provincial politicians of a sort that exerted considerable influence during the American founding era. Findley, an Irish Protestant immigrant who had arrived in America in 1763, served as a dedicated committeeman and member of the Pennsylvania Rifle Regiment during the critical years between 1776 and 1778, before the war shifted to other parts of the country. Whitehill, whose father came from Northern Ireland, was an active supporter of the Revolution who helped write Pennsylvania's 1776 constitution, which all three men supported. By 1787 Smilie, another Irish immigrant, no longer sat in the Pennsylvania assembly with Whitehill and Findley, but he was a member of the state's supreme executive council. Like so many other Irish Protestants, these men were pioneers who farmed land and raised families in parts of the state that were sometimes still claimed by Indians (the county seat of Westmoreland was attacked and burned by Indians in 1782, just before Findley arrived). Once there, they won the respect and support of their neighbors, and they proved willing to make the arduous trip eastward to represent their neighbors in Philadelphia, often at great personal cost to themselves and their wives and children. Years later, when looking back on his long political career, Findley noted that from the time he first accepted state office he had not been "but one winter with my own family," which included eleven children. His speech never ceased to reveal his origins: A later satirical attack referred to his tendency to "'Addrass the chair,' and say, 'Myster Spaker,' and avoid being 'parsenal.'" But his manner of speech was hardly unusual in eighteenth-century Pennsylvania, which was a mecca for immigrants.[3]

Like the Scottish immigrant James Wilson, these men of the west were ambitious and upwardly mobile. The comparison ends there, however, as Wilson was politically and socially worlds apart from Smilie, Whitehill, and Findley. Wilson identified with members of Pennsylvania's eastern mercantile and professional elite, who called themselves Republicans in state politics. (Samuel Bryan, the author of "Centinel," said they "were also called Aristocrats and Anticonstitutionalists.") The Constitutionalist party of Whitehill, Findley, and Smilie, whose supporters were mainly Irish Presbyterians and members of the German Reformed faith, had dominated

Pennsylvania politics from the fall of 1776, when the state's Revolutionary constitution went into effect, into the early 1780s. They lost control of the state to the rival Republicans when Pennsylvania's wartime Test Acts, which required that voters take loyalty oaths, were modified in 1786 and then repealed in March 1787. That change restored the vote to many Quakers, Anglicans, Lutherans, and other non-Calvinist sectarian nonjurors, who supported the Republican party because it had opposed the Test Acts. That swing of previously disenfranchised voters toward the Republican party gave it a popular majority and increased support for a new state constitution that, unlike the constitution of 1776, would include institutional checks on simple majority rule such as a bicameral legislature.[4]

The Republicans' victory undermined the charge that men like Findley and Smilie criticized the proposed federal Constitution for fear of losing their state jobs. The Constitutionalists had no lucrative state jobs or control over state patronage. They did, however, have grievances. They might well also have been ready to seize opportunities to regain their old political clout in one way or another. On the other hand, they had from the beginning recognized the need for a stronger federal government and admitted that the federal Constitution was an improvement over the Confederation, which might have opened the way for an accommodation of differences over the Constitution. There Findley could have played a key role: He later remembered being repelled by the "great party heats" over the state's first revolutionary constitution, and he saw himself as a moderate who worked to reconcile political differences.[5] No such reconciliation happened for reasons that were not entirely of the westerners' making.

MANAGING THE NEWS

The Constitution's proponents had done their part to "sower" the westerners' feelings. The haste and force they used to get a quorum in the assembly so it could call a state ratifying convention without delay got the politics of ratification off to a bad start in Pennsylvania, and the situation remained tense. On October 31 Philadelphia's *Freeman's Journal* printed a letter from western Pennsylvania asking what had happened to the copies of the Constitution the assembly had ordered printed and distributed throughout the state. Those copies apparently never reached the backcountry, and suspicions naturally fell on the Republicans who controlled Pennsylvania's government and supported the federal Constitution. Did they suppress—or at least not facilitate—the distribution of the Constitution in parts of the state where they feared opposition? "Much time elapses before information can reach the industrious yeomanry . . . distant from the seat of government," the letter writer noted, and if "the great body of the people" remained ignorant of what the Constitution said, how could they know how to vote in selecting convention delegates? If the Constitution "will bear the examination of the people, who are to be bound thereby, why is such precipitancy used?"[6]

Then, late on election day, November 6, a Philadelphia mob attacked Alexander Boyd's boardinghouse, where Smilie, Findley, and others with doubts about the Constitution stayed. A dozen noisy men arrived about midnight and proclaimed in loud voices that the "damned rascals" in the house "ought to be all hanged." They also threw heavy stones at the door and broke the sash before running away. The state's executive council issued a proclamation and offered a reward of $300 for apprehension of the rioters, but no one was arrested. "The Republicans could not defend the traitors tho they loved the treason," one observer commented. Not one Philadelphia newspaper reported the event.[7]

Continued efforts to prevent the circulation of arguments critical of the Constitution added to the acrimony. On November 12, about a week before the ratifying convention was scheduled to convene, Ebenezer Bowman, a Republican/Federalist politician in the inland town of Wilkes-Barre, Pennsylvania, described that strategy in an unusually open way. He was upset because a more prominent political colleague, Timothy Pickering, had sent him for distribution several copies of a four-page broadside titled *Addresses to the Citizens of Pennsylvania. Calculated to shew the Safety-Advantages—and Necessity of adopting the proposed Constitution of the United States. In which are included Answers to the Objections that have been made to it.* Bowman did not want to circulate the broadside, which included several Federalist essays. He explained that he had "carefully avoided" letting local people learn "that any objections were made to the Constitution" because they were "so prone to opposition that they would readily join in any [effort] to prevent that excellent plan from taking place." The *Addresses* included arguments "sufficient to convince any rational mind of the excellence of the proposed Constitution," he said, but, by answering objections to the Constitution, the broadside revealed that some people had criticized it and so let the cat out of the bag. As a result, Bowman predicted that it "would do more harm than good."[8]

Once the convention got underway, the Constitution's supporters suppressed news of the opposition so successfully that even today parts of the story are difficult to reconstruct. If they could keep the Constitution's critics in the west from mobilizing, they thought that Federalist strongholds in and near Philadelphia would carry the day. Their strategy affected the historical record, including the official journal of the state ratifying convention, which was published at public expense: The convention met from November 21 through December 15, 1787, but its journal is only twenty-eight pages long—and the text of the Constitution fills nine of those pages. The rest gives a summary of the convention's meeting times, motions made, and votes taken, but leaves out some important motions by the Constitution's critics.

The journal also includes brief and sometimes misleading summaries of the topics discussed.[9]

The Debates of the Convention of the State of Pennsylvania, which the shorthand reporter Thomas Lloyd published privately in February 1788, only includes speeches by James Wilson and Thomas McKean, both of whom supported ratification of the Constitution as written. A reader might think only Federalists were present, except that John Smilie made it into Lloyd's *Debates* by interrupting a speech by Wilson. Otherwise Wilson and McKean seem to be arguing with ghosts. Lloyd eliminated speeches that criticized the Constitution to satisfy Federalist benefactors who planned to circulate his account of the convention debates—as they had circulated the text of Wilson's at the Pennsylvania State House—in order to give political colleagues elsewhere arguments to use in defending the Constitution. For that reason, he included only what seemed to be the strongest orations by Federalists. Lloyd's Federalist backers of course had no reason to publicize answers to the Federalists' arguments nor, for that matter, the criticisms of the Constitution to which Wilson and McKean responded. If the incomplete *Debates* implied that the Federalists' speeches went unanswered and were perhaps unanswerable, that served their purposes perfectly.[10]

Fortunately, Alexander J. Dallas, the Jamaican-born editor of the *Pennsylvania Herald*, printed a full version of the convention debates starting with the session of November 27, a week after the convention first met. Since the transcripts were long and Dallas had other news to report, a single day's debates sometimes stretched over several issues of the *Herald*. By January 5—almost three weeks after the convention had adjourned—he had printed transcripts of the debates through the first four speeches on November 30; he had also broken his chronological order to cover the debates of December 12, when the convention concluded its main business. Then Dallas lost his job. William Spotswood, the *Herald*'s owner, fired him after a hundred Federalists, who apparently decided that his publication of "Antifederalist" speeches was increasing opposition to the Constitution, cancelled their subscriptions. The only records of speeches by Findley, Whitehill, and Smilie during the final two weeks of the convention are in newspaper summaries and fragmentary notes kept by three Federalist delegates, Anthony Wayne, Jasper Yeates, and above all, Wilson, who kept a long list of arguments raised by critics of the Constitution so he could refute them.[11]

A ROCKY START

Surviving records at least leave no doubt that the Pennsylvania ratifying convention failed to begin, as scheduled, on Tuesday, November 20, because most delegates arrived late. The next afternoon attendance jumped from the previous day's 38 to 60, which left only nine delegates still absent.

The convention elected its president, Frederick Augustus Muhlenberg, a Pennsylvania-born Lutheran minister of German descent who had served in the Continental Congress and as speaker of the Pennsylvania assembly. Over the next few days the convention appointed a secretary, a messenger, and a doorkeeper. To regulate its proceedings it adopted a set of rules that provoked no controversy, probably because the rules were fairly standard. They said, for example, that the minutes of the previous day would be read at the beginning of each day; that no member was to be referred to by name during the debates; and that no member could speak twice on a question without permission (a rule the convention later repealed).[12]

The delegates also ordered that "the doors of the Convention be left open during the session." The open-door policy followed the practice of the state legislature and seemed particularly appropriate for a convention that acted in the name of "We the People." However, the people who filled the back rows of the room in the Pennsylvania State House (now Independence Hall), divided from the delegates by only a waist-high railing, were, like most Philadelphians, ardent supporters of the Constitution who felt no obligation to hide their hostility toward speakers with whom they disagreed.[13]

In its opening days, the convention rejected a suggestion by Dr. Benjamin Rush, a somewhat quixotic Philadelphian and one of the country's best-trained physicians, that it appoint a minister to open its business with prayer. Several delegates objected: Considering the religious diversity of the state, they argued, any such appointment would offend some people. Moreover, neither the Pennsylvania legislature nor the convention that had drafted the state constitution had begun with prayer. When Rush suggested that was why the state had ever since been beset with divisions, Smilie dismissed the doctor's theory as an "absurd superstition." That ended that. It also made clear that the self-educated Irish-Americans from the west were going to speak their minds, even against their "betters."[14]

For a body of men with a historic mission, some of whom wanted Pennsylvania to be the first state to ratify the Constitution, the delegates were remarkably dilatory. On their second day in session, November 22, they broke off work to attend commencement ceremonies at the University of Pennsylvania.[15] A week later they skipped a full day of deliberations to observe an examination of "pupils in the German language, etc." on the invitation of the ministers and vestry of the German Lutheran congregation.[16] At first the convention convened at nine or nine thirty in the morning, but after a few days the delegates put the opening off until ten, and the convention apparently broke up about four hours later. Nor were the delegates eager to get going after breaking for the Christian Sabbath: The convention did meet on Saturdays, but never met before three o'clock on a Monday afternoon. In early December, as criticism of its slow pace began to mount, the delegates voted to hold both morning and afternoon sessions, beginning at nine thirty and four thirty, and some sessions stretched deep into the evening. But within a week the convention had returned to a single daily session until December 11 and 12, when, as it moved toward a decision, it again met in both morning and afternoon.[17]

Did the delegates regard the convention as in part a ceremonial occasion once its outcome seemed clear? Early reports that the delegates might be evenly divided quickly proved incorrect: By the time the convention opened, delegates who supported the Constitution outnumbered critics by almost two to one. The division generally followed old party lines, although some delegates, like McKean, who had been a member of the state's Constitutionalist Party, strongly supported the Constitution. The Republican/Federalists had solid victories in five populous counties in the eastern part of the state whose economies would benefit from a national government capable of supporting American commerce, and they picked up additional delegates further inland, including half of the four seats from Washington County in the state's distant southwest.[18] If there were any doubts about the preponderance of delegates who supported the Constitution "as it now stands," they disappeared quickly once the delegates began casting votes.

The convention finally got down to business on Saturday, November 24. After reading aloud the Constitution and letter of transmission from Congress, McKean moved "that this Convention do assent to and ratify the Constitution agreed to on the 17th of September last by the Convention of the United States of America." McKean, who had been chief justice of Pennsylvania's supreme court for a decade, was not asking for an immediate vote. He explained that he made the motion "to bring the object of our meeting fully and fairly into discussion," and he promised that "every objection that can be suggested against the work will be listened to with attention, answered, and perhaps obviated." Although the convention could "receive or reject" the Constitution, he obviously thought no case against the Constitution could stand, and he suggested—according to Lloyd's account—that a decision might be made the next week.[19]

Almost immediately James Wilson rose to give what Dallas's *Pennsylvania Herald* described as a "long and elaborate speech," and which others compared to the great orations of the ancient world. As the only member of the federal Convention present, Wilson said it was his duty to explain the challenges it had faced in designing a free government for a land as large and varied as the United States. Political theorists, he noted, said only a despotism could control a large country. The delegates knew their constituents would never submit to despotic power, so they proposed a "confederate republic" to govern this extensive land in a way that preserved freedom. No precedent existed for such a government—not in contemporary Europe, where neither the Swiss, the Dutch, nor the Germans provided an appropriate model; nor in the Achaean and Lycian Leagues or the Amphictyonic Council of ancient times. "Government . . . taken as a science may yet be considered in its infancy," Wilson said, and it had in the past been the product of "force, fraud, or accident." America, he said, offered the first instance "since the Creation of the world . . . of a people assembled to weigh deliberately and calmly, and to decide leisurely and peaceably, upon the form of government by which they will bind themselves and their posterity."[20]

The problem of allocating power within a federal republic, Wilson said, was easier to address in theory than in fact. The good of the whole had to be its object, not that of every individual or section in the union. Wilson argued that states, like individuals in a state of nature who contracted together to form governments, would gain more than the liberties lost in forming the new federal government, a concept he labeled "federal liberty." He summarized the weaknesses of the Confederation and dismissed all possible forms of government for the United States except a "confederate republic." A single centralized state risked despotism; government by thirteen sovereign states either unconnected or grouped in two or three confederacies would lead to conflict, even war, and invite foreign intervention. Finally, he emphasized that the authority of the proposed Constitution would come from the sovereign people, whose power remained "paramount to every constitution, inalienable in its nature, and indefinite in its extent"; the people could change constitutions "whenever and however they please"—but not, it seemed, before the Constitution was ratified.

Printed versions of Wilson's speech suggest that it was somewhat disjointed. The oration was also highly theoretical, and it ended not with a peroration but with an apology for trying the delegates' patience for so long a time. As the speech stretched on, at least one delegate seems to have been writhing in his seat.

The minute Wilson ended, John Smilie took the floor and attacked the motion to ratify the Constitution that McKean had made several hours earlier, before Wilson opened his mouth. McKean's motion, Smilie charged, was just another example of the "precipitancy that had uniformly prevailed" with regard "to the important subject before the Convention." Americans were continually told, he said, that they were the first people on earth to decide deliberately and calmly on a government for themselves and their posterity (obviously he had been listening to Wilson), "but we find every measure that is proposed leads to defeat those advantages and to preclude all argument and deliberation" on an issue "of the highest consequence to the happiness of a great portion of the globe." McKean's motion could only be meant "to bring on a hasty and total adoption of the Constitution." The federal Convention took four months to write the document; couldn't Pennsylvania spend "a few days" deliberating on it? "I am sensible of the expediency of giving additional strength and energy to the federal government," Smilie concluded, but the country was not so badly off that it had to accept any plan whatsoever. If the Constitution proved unworthy of adoption, he hoped the convention would have "candor and fortitude enough to reject it."[21]

McKean denied that he wanted to cut off discussion. The convention had only one question to decide, he said, "whether we will ratify and confirm, or, upon due consideration[,] reject, in the whole, the system of federal government that is submitted to us." In other words, the convention had to take or leave the Constitution; it could not propose amendments. The delegates had "no right to inquire into the power of the late Convention or to alter or amend their work," McKean said, but they could examine the Constitution's "principles in every section and sentence." In fact they had an obligation to examine the Constitution closely before deciding whether or not to ratify.[22]

Robert Whitehill gave him some unexpected support when he said Smilie had misunderstood McKean's purpose. Since the convention had an obligation to examine the Constitution carefully, Whitehill proposed that it dissolve into a committee of the whole, which would allow the delegates to debate freely, unbound by the convention's rules and without having their proceedings recorded in the convention's minutes. A committee of the whole would report to the convention (that is, the same delegates but sitting in a different capacity), which would then debate the committee's report before voting whether or not to accept its recommendation on ratification. But when the convention reconvened on Monday, November 26, it rejected Whitehill's motion by a vote of 44 to 24, which affirmed the Federalists' dominance. That vote meant the convention would go through the Constitution only once, which seemed to confirm Smilie's charge of "precipitancy."[23]

The next day Whitehill moved that "upon all questions where the yeas and nays were called, any member might insert the reason of his vote upon the Journals of the Convention." Like his previous motion, this one followed the practice of the Pennsylvania assembly. Indeed, Provision 14 of the Pennsylvania constitution of 1776 said that any member of the assembly had a right to "insert the reasons of his vote upon the minutes" whenever the "yeas and nays" were formally recorded. But again members of the majority objected. Whitehill's proposal would swell the size of the journal, of which five thousand copies in English or German were to be published at public expense. Perhaps so, Whitehill responded, if reasons were inserted on every minor vote, so he agreed to limit his motion to the final vote on whether or not to ratify the Constitution. "The people ought to be informed of the principles on which we have acted" and "to know in the clearest manner what is the nature and tendency of the government with which we have bound them," he argued. When a member of the majority claimed that the press could do that, Whitehill answered that newspapers were "transient and perishable," unlike the journal, which "will be a permanent record for posterity." The convention rejected his proposition by a vote of 44 to 22, almost the same as its previous division.[24]

John Smilie injected an ominous note into these debates. The people would not, he said, be bound by a convention vote to ratify. If "on better information and maturer deliberation" they decided the Constitution was "a bad and improper form of government," they had a right to call "another body to consult upon other measures and either in the whole, or in part, to abrogate this federal work so ratified." After all, even James Wilson had said "the people have at all times a power to alter and abolish government."[25]

If, as Wilson suggested in his opening address, those who wanted to ratify the Constitution as written thought the opposition would simply accept the majority's decision, Smilie set them straight. Nonetheless, the majority refused to concede or compromise. Every vote taken in the convention was decided by the same division, roughly 44–22, give or take a vote or two, until its very last days, after the vote on ratification had been taken and some members of the minority had left the convention.

That tells a lot about the Pennsylvania ratifying convention. It was not, as a newspaper essay signed "One of the Gallery" observed, a deliberative assembly—that is, a meeting whose members listened to each other with a willingness to learn and be persuaded, much less to work out compromises. "I believe in no one instance," the essayist wrote, "has a delegate been appointed who had not previously declared himself a Federalist or an Antifederalist," and sometimes they even had to promise that they would "absolutely vote according to the declared will of the electors." Counties, according to "One of the Gallery," sent delegates to the convention "not to debate . . . the proposed Constitution, but to announce the votes of those counties." Only in that way could "the voice of the people" decide the Constitution's fate. And "woe be to that member of this Convention who shall presume to vote contrary to . . . the will of his constituents at the time of his election."[26]

Whether or not delegates were so tightly bound by their constituents (and the record is by no means clear), they acted as if they were, holding firmly to their preconvention positions. That might explain why McKean thought the convention could wrap up its work in a week. But apparently the delegates felt obliged to discuss the Constitution, or at least to hear it discussed, before voting, and in the end the convention's debates stretched out over twenty-two increasingly tense and exhausting days. The great majority of delegates seems to have remained silent. Judging from the surviving records, only nine supporters of the Constitution gave speeches, among whom Wilson, McKean, and Rush were the most prominent, and three critics, Findley, Whitehill, and Smilie.[27] Delegates posed arguments for the record, for outside circulation to inspire and instruct delegates in subsequent state conventions, and sometimes to flaunt their erudition and rhetorical powers, all the while defending positions that they, like the great mass of their silent colleagues, had decided upon before they walked through the State House doors. Since there was no real effort to persuade, the Pennsylvania ratifying debates included a lot of showmanlike oratory, but they did not proceed according to any obvious plan or to achieve any clear purpose. That helps explain why, in the end, they tried the delegates' patience beyond endurance.

A DEBATE WITHOUT ORDER

The convention agreed to go through the Constitution article by article, then almost immediately violated that agreement. On Tuesday, November 27, McKean opened discussion of Article I, on the legislative branch.[28] Wilson, however, called the convention's attention to the preamble and its opening words: "We the people of the United States . . . do ordain and establish this Constitution." Unlike Magna Carta or the British Declaration of Rights, which were concessions from kings, the Constitution was the work of the sovereign people. A "proper attention" to that fact, Wilson said, could ease the minds of those who heard much about the necessity of a bill of rights. In effect, the people had no need to protect their liberties against themselves as they did against kings.[29]

Smilie, however, said he preferred words from the declarations of rights that opened several state constitutions, beginning with the assertion "that all men are born equally free and independent, and have certain natural, inherent and unalienable rights." Whitehill also objected to the Constitution's opening words, "We the People," which he said showed that the Constitution destroyed "the old foundation of the Union"—a confederation of states—and built on its ruins "a new unwieldy system of consolidated empire" that was "designed to abolish the independence and sovereignty of the states."[30] Two days later, after another delegate moved that the convention proceed to Article II, Smilie objected. "In his opinion," he said, the convention "had not yet got over the first six words of the Preamble."[31]

The next day McKean observed that "the gentlemen in the opposition" had abandoned their original plan "to discuss the plan minutely section after section" and jumped into "an investigation of the whole system" of government proposed by the Constitution—a direction that McKean and Wilson continued.[32] And so a torrent of issues came up almost at once. Many of them had already been discussed in the press. Never before, however, had either side been forced to defend its positions against direct attacks in face-to-face argument. As a result, on some topics the debate moved forward, although neither side was willing to concede anything to the other, and, except on a few tumultuous occasions, delegates went on giving monologues as if nothing had happened.

To explain once again why the Constitution had no bill of rights, Wilson repeated his old argument that the government under the Constitution had only those powers that were specifically given to it. To declare that it could not exercise powers it did not have, such as to interfere with freedom of speech or the press, was not just unnecessary but "preposterous and dangerous." A bill of rights "is an enumeration of the powers reserved. If we attempt an enumeration [of rights], everything that is not enumerated is presumed to be given." As a result, "an imperfect enumeration would throw all implied power into the scale of government." The idea of a bill of rights seemed so obviously "absurd" to Wilson that he claimed (incorrectly) that no member of the federal Convention had thought of the idea, much less proposed adding one to the Constitution. Moreover, he was coming to think that bills of rights were unnecessary even in the states (which departed from his October speech at the Pennsylvania State House). Were the people of South Carolina or New York, which had no declarations of rights, less free than people in states that had them?[33]

Wilson's last assertion led to a small scuffle over which states did and did not have bills or declarations of rights. He insisted that Virginia had none because no Virginia declaration of rights appeared in a standard compendium, *The Constitutions of the Several Independent States of America...*, which was first published at Philadelphia in 1781. Smilie corrected him, but Wilson waved him off. Smilie said George Mason had personally assured him that Virginia had a declaration of rights, and Smilie later produced a printed text to prove the point.[34] That was not the last time the opposition outdid the majority on a point of fact.

More important, Smilie and Whitehill attacked Wilson's argument as a whole. They pointed out that the Constitution did place some explicit limits on Congress's power: It could not suspend habeas corpus except in cases of rebellion or invasion, nor interfere with trial by jury in criminal cases. If, as Wilson insisted, it was dangerous to enumerate some rights and not others, and the Constitution enumerated a few rights, then, logically, others also needed explicit protection. Without such protection, habeas corpus and trial by jury in criminal cases might "hereafter be construed to be the only privileges reserved by the people."[35]

Richard Henry Lee had made the same argument earlier, in a private letter to Samuel Adams, and he perhaps repeated it during his meeting with prominent Pennsylvania critics of the Constitution in early November, before the start of the Pennsylvania ratifying convention.[36] The argument had also been made by several newspaper writers who attacked Wilson's October 6 speech at the State House. In any case, Smilie and Whitehill used it to great advantage. Only one member of the majority, Jasper Yeates, ventured a response. The provisions Whitehill and Smilie cited, Yeates said, were not a partial bill of rights but restrictions on "the general legislative powers of Congress." Since those powers were enumerated, it was necessary to specify any exceptions to them.[37]

But were Congress's powers so tightly enumerated as Wilson implied? Smilie found them "so loosely, so inaccurately . . . defined, that it will be impossible" without a bill of rights "to declare when government has degenerated into oppression." The Constitution, Whitehill added, gave Congress "all the powers of raising and maintaining armies, of regulating and commanding the militia, and of laying imposts and taxes of every kind" and to pass whatever laws it considered necessary to implement those powers. It was "vain" to assume that popular election would be a sufficient check on such extensive power or that the officers of the proposed government would "uniformly act for the happiness of the people." Why run a risk that could easily be avoided? To grant such "extensive and undefined power" was a "radical wrong." In framing a new government, Whitehill said, "it is our duty rather to indulge a jealousy of the human character, than an expectation of unprecedented perfection." A bill of rights, he insisted, was dangerous only to the projects of rulers aspiring to dangerous power. "Grant but this explicit criterion" for judging exercises of power "and our governors will not venture to encroach—refuse it, and the people cannot venture to complain."[38]

The majority, too, had moments of triumph. The opposition's assertion that the Constitution created a "consolidated" government that would destroy the states pushed Wilson to develop one of the great theoretical innovations of the ratification debates. From the beginning of the controversy with Britain, Americans had contended with an axiom of political thought that said sovereignty—ultimate authority—could be located in only one place within a political system. To violate that principle and create governments within a government (*imperia in imperio*) would inevitably bring conflicts of authority and, ultimately, civil war. If sovereignty could not be divided, the establishment of a sovereign nation would necessarily end state sovereignty and establish a highly centralized or, as the Constitution's critics called it, a "consolidated" government. Wilson, however, provided an alternative way of conceptualizing the problem.

On December 1—and then in subsequent speeches on December 4 and 11—he argued that sovereignty resided not in any set of governmental institutions but in the people, who "only dispensed such portions of power as were conceived necessary for the public welfare." They granted one portion to the state governments, and they could dispense another, quite different set of powers to the central government of the United States, all the while retaining their sovereignty—that is, "supreme, absolute and uncontrollable authority." In short, in the American republic only the people, the "fountain of government," were sovereign, not the governments of either the states or the nation. That resolved an old quandary and provided nothing less than an intellectual foundation for American federalism.[39]

The opposition was no more ready to acknowledge Wilson's accomplishment than he was to concede that it had destroyed his argument against a bill of rights. The minority's response to Wilson is not well documented since Dallas was fired before he could publish their speeches of early December. However, Wilson's notes on Findley's speech say "sovereignty is in the states and not in the people in its exercise." In other words, Findley didn't question the ultimate sovereignty of the people; indeed, he and his colleagues readily agreed to it. They did, however, insist that the states as a matter of actual practice were exercising sovereign powers, and also that the division of powers between the state and federal governments under the Constitution was intrinsically unstable, to the states' detriment. In specific, Findley asserted that Congress's power "for imposing internal taxation" would "necessarily destroy the state sovereignties for there cannot exist two independent sovereign taxing powers in the same community." Wilson saw no reason why not, but the *Pennsylvania Herald* reported that Findley had "established his position" that "the proposed plan of government amounted to a consolidation, and not a confederation of the states."[40] That was apparently fine with Benjamin Rush, who rejoiced at the annihilation of state sovereignties, describing the "plurality of sovereignty" in politics as a form of "idolatry" or "heathenism" like the "plurality of gods" in religion. Smilie said he had never heard anything so ridiculous except for Rush's earlier argument for opening the convention with a prayer.[41]

Obviously, tempers were fraying, and it didn't help that the opposition began questioning one provision of the Constitution after another "piecemeal," as Wilson complained, "without considering the relative connection and dependence of its parts."[42] The House of Representatives was too small, the government's treaty-making powers too great; legislators' terms of office were too long, and the interdependency of the president and Senate would breed corruption; the provision in Article I, Section 9, allowing Congress to place a tax on the importation of "such Persons as any of the States now existing shall think proper to admit" would allow taxes on white immigrants as well as slaves, and the importation of slaves should be prohibited immediately, not permitted for another twenty years. On it went.

Smilie and Findley did agree to the establishment of a bicameral legislature "as the greatest part of the states have compound legislatures." That was important: They would not insist that federal institutions take Pennsylvania's embattled constitution, with its unicameral legislature, as a model. Moreover, although the opposition questioned the right of the federal Convention to propose anything but amendments to the Articles of Confederation, Findley said he had no desire to "destroy" the Constitution that the Convention proposed. "Its outlines are well laid," he said; amendments "may answer all our wishes."[43]

Finally, on December 4, according to the convention's journal, Muhlenberg, the presiding officer, suggested that the Constitution might receive "a more full and expeditious investigation" if its critics first presented a general statement of their objections, then allowed its defenders to reply.[44] There is some evidence the convention agreed: After Findley attacked several parts of the Constitution, Wilson spoke for the rest of the morning session and most of the afternoon as well. The next day, Findley gave another long speech, then a Federalist delegate suggested they move on to Article II. But Whitehill immediately went back to attacking the powers and structure of Congress in Article I. The three opposition speakers continued to dominate debate, taking potshots at every part of the Constitution, until Saturday, December 8, when Whitehill and Findley again berated the convention for failing to secure trial by jury in civil cases as it had for criminal cases. The future of American freedom was at stake, Findley claimed: When Sweden abandoned jury trials, "the commons of that nation lost their freedom" and a "tyrannical aristocracy" took over.[45]

PANDEMONIUM

That was too much. Both Wilson and McKean jumped to their feet and demanded that Findley prove that the Swedes ever had trial by jury. Wilson said he had never come across such an idea in all his reading; McKean—who was, remember, Pennsylvania's chief justice—insisted that trial by jury never existed anywhere but in England and governments modeled on that of England. Findley promised to give his source, but McKean said "too much time" had already been spent discussing the Constitution: "The whole matter might have been dispatched in a few days." All the objections raised against the Constitution had already been discussed in the press by "Centinel," "Brutus," and other like-minded writers upon whose arguments the minority delegates drew,[46] and their objections had been answered over and over by the Constitution's defenders. Smilie was furious. McKean, he charged, had treated the opposition with contempt and condemned their arguments "*with a magisterial air.*"[47]

Pandemonium broke out. Stephen Chambers seized the floor and with "great heat" declared that Smilie's language was "indecent" and that the three minority speakers "had *abused* the *indulgence* which the other side of the house had *granted* to them in consenting to hear all their reasons." Chambers, a delegate from Lancaster, a Federalist enclave east of the Susquehanna in southern Pennsylvania, was also an immigrant from Northern Ireland, but no sense of shared ethnic origin muted his anger with Whitehill, Findley, and Smilie. He questioned their patriotism and service to the Revolution, and he recalled that Findley had received only two votes when the assembly was electing delegates to the Philadelphia Convention—which showed "the insignificance of his character" and the "wisdom of Pennsylvania" in not choosing him. Everything the opposition said in the convention was "trifling and unnecessary."[48]

How was his language "indecent," Smilie asked; he was "pleading for the Interests of his country" and intended to continue exercising his right of free speech. Findley said Chambers's speech was in keeping with his usual conduct in public bodies, which was "to discourse without reason and to talk without argument." At that "a considerable cry of order arose." But the delegates continued to taunt each other until, at Findley's request, Muhlenberg ruled that the minority members had not broken any rules of debate, although Smilie's comments on McKean were "highly improper." With that "there was a unanimous cry of adjourn," which finally ended the altercation.[49]

When, after what some delegates must have hoped would be a calming Sabbath, the delegates reassembled on Monday afternoon, December 10, William Findley produced evidence that there had, indeed, once been jury trials in Sweden. He cited a *Universal History* published at London in 1721 and, more damaging, the third volume of William Blackstone's authoritative *Commentaries on the Laws of England*. Even "the best informed men" might miss a reference in the *Universal History*, Findley said, but if his son had been studying law for six months and remained unacquainted with the passage in Blackstone "I should be justified in whipping him."[50]

Had Wilson or McKean read the section of Blackstone that Findley cited, they would have found the point hard to miss and perhaps to forget. In chapter 23, "Of the Trial by Jury," in Volume III of his *Commentaries*, which was published at Oxford in 1768 and reprinted in Philadelphia in 1772, Blackstone emphasized that trial by jury was once common in all the countries of northern Europe, and he even attributed its invention to a king of Sweden and Denmark. Juries, he said, preserved in the hands of the people "that share which they ought to have in the administration of public justice, and prevents the encroachments of the more powerful and wealthy citizens." To establish courts that did not use juries to establish facts was therefore "a step towards establishing aristocracy, the most oppressive of absolute governments." Blackstone noted "a circumstance well worthy an Englishman's observation, that in Sweden the trial by jury, that bulwark of northern liberty," which had continued in "full vigour so lately as the middle of last century, is now fallen into disuse." Consequently, in Sweden, "the liberties of the commons are extinguished, and the government is degenerated into a mere aristocracy." He ended with a peroration: It was "a duty every man owes his country, his friends, his posterity, himself . . . to guard with the utmost jealous circumspection against the introduction of new and arbitrary methods of trial, which, under a variety of plausible pretences, may in time imperceptibly undermine this best preservative of English liberty."[51] In their insistence that the Constitution explicitly confirm the use of juries in civil as well as criminal cases, Findley and his colleagues were following Blackstone's injunction.

McKean had to be as embarrassed as Wilson, who took such pride in his learning. He spoke next, but—in a prepared speech that, according to the *Pennsylvania Gazette*, was "near three hours in length" and "fully and ably answered every objection that had been made to the proposed Constitution"—McKean made no reference to Findley's statement.[52] At the first chance on Tuesday morning, however, Wilson responded to Findley. The books Findley cited convinced him, Wilson said, that he must have read the passage, "but I do not pretend to remember everything I read." He added that "those whose stock of knowledge is limited to a few items may easily remember and refer to them; but many things may be overlooked and forgotten in a magazine of literature." It could therefore be properly said, "as it was formerly said by Sir John Maynard to a petulant student who reproached him with an ignorance of a trifling point: 'Young man, I have forgotten more law than ever you learned.'"[53]

Immediately, before anyone could respond, Wilson launched into another marathon speech that consumed both morning and afternoon sessions. He went through a list of the opposition's arguments and eloquently defended the Constitution. The ratifying convention had gone on for three weeks, he said; objections to the Constitution had been fully stated and restated. Extending the debates further could have a "pernicious and destructive" effect by suggesting to other states and to opponents of the Constitution in distant parts of Pennsylvania that the delegates found the issue before them difficult, although there was good reason to think "a very considerable majority . . . do not hesitate to ratify the Constitution."[54]

Wilson ridiculed the suggestion that only three convention delegates—obviously Findley, Whitehill, and Smilie—had virtue enough to support the rights of mankind. The convention's majority was also contending for that cause, and it had been chosen "by the greater part of the people." Again he insisted that the people, not the states, were sovereign in the American republic, and that the Constitution was not a compact among the states but "an ordinance and establishment of the people." Under this system the powers of both the central and the state governments were simply "emanations of power from the people." The Constitution would not therefore create a "consolidated government," which Smilie had defined as one that transferred sovereignty from the states to a general government, because the states had no sovereignty to transfer.[55]

Wilson conceded that the proposed government was not perfect in all regards. Its parts were "not kept as distinct and independent as they ought to be," and he also regretted that states were not represented in the Senate "according to their importance." But the Constitution was an improvement on the Confederation, which made no effort to separate powers, and also on many state constitutions. "Let the experiment be made; let the system be fairly and candidly tried."[56]

He defended the size of the House of Representatives as adequate for the type of issues it would decide, and he argued that Congress's taxing and military powers were necessary for peace and national defense. He also defended Congress's much maligned power to alter "the times, places and manner of holding elections for Representatives" as necessary for "the very existence of the federal government." That power would not be misused, as critics charged; Congress would act only "to correct the improper regulations of a particular state."[57]

Wilson even discussed the Constitution's system of electing the president, although nobody in the convention seems to have questioned it. No part of the Constitution left the federal Convention more perplexed than the election of the president, he said. To have Congress make the choice would violate separation of powers. He personally preferred direct popular election, but the majority of delegates found it "impractical." The system adopted, with electors in the several states casting ballots, brought the choice of president "as nearly home to the people as is practicable" while making corruption unlikely and offering "little time or opportunity for tumult or intrigue."[58]

If the country rejected the Constitution, would a better one be framed and adopted? What objectionable provision could not "be amended more easily by the mode pointed out in the system itself, than by calling convention after convention" before establishing the new government? There was much to gain: "By adopting this system, we become a NATION; at present we are not one." And "we shall also form a national character . . . adapted to the principles and genius of our system of government." Nor, Wilson continued, were the advantages confined to the United States. By adopting the Constitution, "we shall probably lay a foundation for erecting temples of liberty in every part of the earth" and promoting "the great designs of Providence with regard to the globe; the multiplication of mankind, their improvement in knowledge, and their advancement in happiness."[59]

Presenting the speech exhausted Wilson. Its printed version remains powerful, but how closely did his fellow delegates listen to it? Much as the *Pennsylvania Gazette* noted the length of McKean's speech the previous day, Jasper Yeates recorded that Wilson began "22 minutes past 10 o'clock, A.M. . . . and ended at 1 o'clock, P.M.," then resumed at "10 minutes after 4 P.M. and spoke again 2 hours."[60] Yeates's notes on Wilson's oration are far less comprehensive than the version later published by the shorthand reporter Thomas Lloyd. Yeates, however, claimed that in the morning Wilson insisted that the Constitution did not need a bill of rights. Strangely, that issue appears neither in Lloyd's account of the speech nor in Wilson's list of objections to the Constitution that he intended to answer.[61] Could it be that the attention even of Yeates, one of Wilson's close allies, had waned? And that he wrote down what he expected Wilson to say—again—rather than what Wilson actually said? Yeates knew how he was going to vote whatever Wilson said, and Wilson's heroic oration served mainly to drag out the convention, delaying by another day its inevitable conclusion.

———

Meanwhile, civility declined in the audience as well as the convention. After McKean's long speech on Monday, a large crowd in the gallery "contrary to custom" expressed its approval by clapping, which "threw Mr. Smilie into a rage." Two days later Findley complained about a man "who has introduced himself among the members of this Convention" and laughed at everything Findley said. The culprit, William Jackson, had been secretary of the federal Convention and a member of the mob that had dragged James M'Calmont and Jacob Miley to the State House in September. Jackson "grew pale, laughed no more, and did not appear in the afternoon" after Findley's protest.[62]

Clearly the time had come for the convention to wrap up its business. There was no doubt how the vote would go, but now, in the convention's closing days, opposition members questioned whether that vote would, as Wilson claimed, represent the majority of the people. A week earlier articles in both the *Independent Gazetteer* and the *Freeman's Journal* claimed that the twenty-four minority members of the ratifying convention had in fact been elected by a thousand more Pennsylvanians than the forty-four majority delegates. In Lancaster and other counties, the *Independent Gazetteer* said, Federalists had won convention seats by very narrow margins, and in several counties the vote was pathetically low because people "declared they had not time to make up their minds on this important business." In the "very large and populous county of Chester," it claimed, only five hundred men voted, "and in Philadelphia County but 500." In Bucks, Northampton, and Montgomery counties "not one-sixth part of the people voted," and accounts from throughout the state indicated that support for the Constitution was dropping so rapidly that "in a month's time there will not remain 500 people in all Pennsylvania in favor of the new government, except those who expect offices under it." Moreover, if the unrepresentative majority in the Pennsylvania ratifying convention voted to ratify, its vote was unlikely to do much harm since "it is now reduced to a certainty" that the two Carolinas, Virginia, Maryland, New York, and Rhode Island—six of the thirteen states—were going to reject the Constitution. In short, the Constitution was a lost cause.[63]

On the morning of December 12, Findley—building no doubt on those news items—told the convention that, according to "the best information" he could get, no more than a sixth of the people had participated in the vote for convention delegates. Since a majority of the people could well be opposed to the Constitution, he proposed deferring the vote on ratification until "the general sentiments of the people could be obtained." More ominously, he said that under the circumstances the minority would not feel bound by a positive vote and had a right not only "to object to the proposed Constitution" but also, if it pleased, "to associate under another form of government."[64]

A majority delegate quickly dismissed Findley's assertion that low voter turnout brought the validity of the election into doubt. The vote was low in the city of Philadelphia and "all the large and populous counties" because the people there were so overwhelmingly in favor of the Constitution that the outcome was not in doubt. In any case, it was rare for the whole electorate to turn out. Only about six thousand votes had elected the convention that drafted and approved Pennsylvania's state constitution in 1776, he claimed, and the members of the first assembly under that constitution were chosen by a little over fifteen hundred votes.[65]

In the convention's afternoon session, John Smilie said ratification of the Constitution would bring an end to Americans' liberties "until they shall be recovered by arms," and he predicted that "discontent and opposition will arise in every quarter." Then Benjamin Rush urged the opposition to "bury the hatchet and smoke the calumet of peace," which meant that they should forget their objections to the Constitution and join the convention's majority. Rush, never afraid of going over the top, claimed that the Constitution came from the hand of God, who "proclaimed in our ears . . . 'thou shalt not reject the new federal government,'" and he predicted that "a millennium of virtue and happiness" would follow its enactment. Whitehill "regretted that so imperfect a work should have been ascribed to God," then presented petitions from 750 people in Cumberland County asking that the Constitution not be adopted without amendments, and particularly not without a bill of rights.[66]

The cry for amendments had, in fact, increased, particularly in newspaper essays, which provided a running counterpart to the convention debates. The proposal first emerged even before the election of convention delegates, in the October 27 issue of Dallas's *Pennsylvania Herald*, where a letter signed "M.C." proposed that a committee of citizens draft a bill of rights securing liberty of the press "and all other rights which the states hold sacred" and send it to the various state ratifying conventions "to be taken into consideration with the new Constitution." Everyone acknowledged, he said, that the continent needed "an efficient form of government . . . to restore America to her lost splendor, consequence, credit, and happiness." Perhaps, as the Constitution's supporters charged, some of its critics were influenced by "sinister and personal considerations," but the apprehensions of many were "patriotic and disinterested," based on a genuine fear for the liberties of posterity. A bill of rights would calm their anxiety without jeopardizing the new plan of government, which had justly attracted considerable admiration. Even if a bill of rights "does no good, it can do no possible injury" and would avoid the risk of having the Constitution voted down.[67]

The letter was widely reprinted, and by early December more commentators were endorsing what one essayist called this "middle walk" between extreme positions.[68] The federal Convention had asked that the Constitution be submitted to state ratifying conventions "for their assent and ratification," which seemed to preclude their proposing amendments. But could the federal Convention tell the sovereign people what they could and could not do, asked "An Old Whig VII" in the November 28 *Independent Gazetteer.* The sovereign people had a right to do whatever they wanted with the proposed plan of government, and "no man, reasoning upon *revolution* principles, can possibly controvert this right." In fact, the "Old Whig" observed, nobody denied the people's right to amend the Constitution. Contenders questioned only the practicality of that effort, arguing that there would be "no end" of conflicting proposals, with no hope of agreement. But that claim was demonstrably incorrect: Critics of the Constitution everywhere "speak in perfect unison," making the same objections and calling for the same amendments, "particularly in the article of a bill of rights." And so the "Old Whig" proposed a method for reconciling differences and "establishing unanimity and harmony among the people of this country." State conventions should compile objections and amendments to the Constitution and transmit them to the Confederation Congress, asking it to call another national convention to go over state returns and make what changes in the Constitution seemed appropriate, "pledging themselves to abide by whatever decision shall be made by such future convention" before putting the Constitution into effect.[69]

A pamphlet published on the same day by "A Federal Republican" made an almost identical proposal. Neither he nor the "Old Whig" was against the Constitution, which the "Federal Republican" said "was *conceived* in wisdom," and "the thanks of the United States are justly due to the members of the late Convention. But," he continued, "let their production pass again through the furnace." Let it be submitted to what another writer called the "collective wisdom of a great nation," which was necessarily superior to that of any individual—even a man of "lofty" intellect like James Wilson—and then be "revised, corrected, and amended" so ambiguous provisions were made clear, the powers delegated "accurately defined and well understood," and the rights and privileges of the people clearly stated.[70]

A few days later, on December 1, an essay in the *Independent Gazetteer* described the efforts of "a number of citizens" to define a set of amendments that were "absolutely necessary" to protect essential rights while establishing an efficient system of government. Again, it suggested that all proposed amendments be sent to the Confederation Congress, which in turn would submit them to a convention authorized to revise the Constitution before putting it into effect "without further reference to the people."[71]

These essays provide context for the Cumberland County petition that Whitehill presented to the convention on December 12, and for another from Philadelphia County that asked the ratifying convention to adjourn until the following spring so the people would have sufficient time to examine and understand the Constitution. On December 12, the *Pennsylvania Herald* also reported that "many petitions are circulating in the counties, and some in the city," asking the convention to delay voting on ratification "till April or May next."[72]

The Cumberland petition forced the ratifying convention to consider again whether it—and the people—could amend the Constitution. And again the majority refused to make any concession. McKean regretted the "improper" attempt of the petitioners and insisted again that the convention had to vote the Constitution up or down; it could not change it or even suggest amendments.[73]

Whitehill was not deterred. As "the ground of a motion for adjourning to some remote day," he proposed some fifteen "articles" that "could be taken collectively as a bill of rights or separately as amendments" to the Constitution. He then moved that the convention adjourn until an undefined future date so his amendments could be considered by the people of Pennsylvania and the delegates could learn what amendments and alterations were proposed by other states. All amendments would be submitted to the Confederation Congress for consideration "before the proposed Constitution shall be finally ratified."[74]

Whitehill's amendments had some kinship with Mason's "objections" and the amendments Richard Henry Lee had proposed to Congress in September, but they went further. They also went beyond those of newspaper essayists, such as "Many Customers" in the December 1 *Independent Gazetteer*, who tried to define a handful of amendments that were "absolutely necessary." Whitehill made no effort to find a middle way between extremes. Like Mason and Lee, he called for a more precise separation of powers by taking the task of advising the president from the Senate and giving it to an executive (or, for Whitehill, "constitutional") council. He also proposed giving explicit protection to the rights of conscience and other civil rights, including trial by jury in civil cases. Whitehill's amendments asserted the people's right to bear arms for the defense of themselves, their state, or the

United States, and "for the purpose of killing game," and said no law could disarm the people "or any of them" except "for crimes committed, or real danger of public injury from individuals." Whitehill went on to declare that "standing armies in time of peace are dangerous to liberty" and "ought not to be kept up," and that the military "shall be kept under strict subordination to . . . the civil power." A proposed amendment similar to Provision 43 of Pennsylvania's 1776 constitution—but unlike anything suggested by Mason or Lee—asserted the right of Americans to "fowl and hunt" on unenclosed land and to fish in all navigable waters not privately owned. More important, Whitehill would have had the power to organize, arm, and discipline the militia remain with the states, and his proposed articles allowed Congress to call out state militias only with a state's consent and only for a time the state determined.

Like others, Whitehill proposed enlarging the House of Representatives and electing its members annually. He would limit Congress's taxing power to "imposts and duties upon goods imported and exported, and postage on letters," eliminating entirely the power to levy any "internal" taxes other than postage, which neither Lee nor Mason had asked. He proposed to eliminate Congress's authority over the time, places, and manner of electing senators and representatives "except as to Places of chusing Senators" (in Article I, Section 4). Whitehill's amendments would also deny Congress power over inheritance laws "or the regulation of contracts in the individual states." What impact would that have on the critical provision in Article I, Section 10, prohibiting states from "impairing the Obligations of Contracts"? Could it be effective without congressional support?

If Whitehill had his way, no treaty could go into effect if it violated existing laws of the United States or the state and federal constitutions. Finally, his list of amendments included an assertion "that the sovereignty, freedom, and independency of the several states shall be retained, and every power, jurisdiction and right which is not by this Constitution expressly delegated to the United States in Congress assembled."[75] That restatement of Article II of the Articles of Confederation, complete with its affirmation of the states' separate sovereignty and independence, would have re-created the problem that undermined the Confederation's effectiveness and undone a large part of what the Constitution was designed to accomplish.

———

Wilson was livid. Whitehill's motion to adjourn the convention would "prevent the adoption of this or any other plan of confederation." He rejoiced that it "would appear upon the Journals" as evidence of the motives of those who framed and supported "so odious an attempt." But already the convention buzzed with objections by majority members to Whitehill's amendments being "officially read," which would earn them a place in the convention's journal. If the majority was sincere in affecting to refer all authority to the people, Smilie said, it would "embrace this last opportunity to evince that sincerity." In effect, he asked whether the Federalists embraced popular sovereignty as a theory but not as a political reality. Were they willing to let the people in fact debate and decide on the Constitution? Members of the majority knew the precipitancy with which the Constitution had been "pressed upon the state," he said. Now a short delay might allow canvassing the "real sentiments" of the people and prevent "future contention and animosity."[76]

His plea fell on deaf ears. Federalists rejected Whitehill's motion to adjourn by a vote of 46 to 23, then took up McKean's old motion to ratify the Constitution and adopted it by an identical tally; it was almost the same division as on November 26, when, early in its sessions, the convention defeated Whitehill's motion that it meet as a committee of the whole, with 44 opposed and 24 in favor.[77]

Moreover, when the convention reconvened the next day, December 13, Whitehill discovered that his motion and amendments were not recorded in the convention's journal. He asked that they be inserted; the majority resisted. When Wilson, who seems to have recovered from his earlier delight that Whitehill's "odious" effort would appear in the journals, persisted in opposing the request, the minority recognized there was no hope and withdrew their motion.[78] The convention's journal would record a Federalist triumph unclouded by the criticisms of dissenters.

A FEDERALIST VICTORY?

The Federalists succeeded in getting the Pennsylvania convention to ratify the Constitution, but how much did they really win?

Evidence of popular enthusiasm, even in Philadelphia, is ambiguous. Pennsylvania's supreme executive council proposed an elaborate procession at midday on December 13 to the courthouse, where officials publicly announced the state's ratification of the Constitution. The *Independent Gazetteer* and *Freeman's Journal* reported that few of the announced participants actually attended. Militia officers, the faculty of the University of Pennsylvania (where criticisms of the Constitution predominated), and ordinary people were notably absent. Even a boat dragged through the streets on a wagon, the creation of ship carpenters and sailors who went through the streets calling out "three and twenty fathoms, *foul* bottom" and "six and forty fathoms, sound bottom—safe anchorage"—recalling the convention vote on ratification—attracted only children, according to the *Freeman's Journal*. "With such astonishing indifference is this great subject treated." The Federalist *Pennsylvania Gazette*, however, spoke of "many thousand spectators."[79]

The sound of cannon fire and the bells of Christ Church echoed through the city, but in the afternoon only the forty-six delegates who voted for ratification signed the formal document by which they "assented to and ratified" the Constitution "in the name and by the Authority of the . . . PEOPLE." Smilie refused. He would never, he said, "allow his hand, in so gross a manner, to give the lie to his heart and tongue." Another member of the opposition, John Harris of Cumberland County, also refused to sign, but he said he nonetheless felt bound by the "sense of the majority." By December 15, the convention's final day, when it voted to cede a tract of land up to ten miles square for the capital of the new government, the majority of forty-six voted in favor but the minority had shrunk to sixteen.[80] The dissenting delegates, it seems, had better things to do than tend their seats in the waning convention.

Three days later the *Pennsylvania Packet* printed "The Dissent of the Minority of the Convention," which was signed by twenty-one of the twenty-three delegates who had voted against ratification (including Harris). That long, rambling statement described the questionable tactics the Constitution's supporters used to get it ratified in Pennsylvania, printed the amendments that Robert Whitehill had proposed in the convention's closing days, and explained at length the signers' reasons for voting against ratification. Its description of the dangers raised by the Constitution went beyond what opposition spokesmen had claimed during the convention's debates. Above all, it said that the Constitution would destroy the state governments and "produce one consolidated government." Congress's power to levy direct taxes would allow it to "tax land, cattle, trades, occupations, etc. to any amount," forcing the people to pay even the most oppressive taxes or have their property seized, for "all resistance will be vain." Congress would consist of "lordly and high-minded men" who had "a perfect indifference for, and contempt of" the people, "harpies of power" who would "riot on the miseries of the community," and could call upon a "standing army" to enforce their wishes. Like the earlier address of the seceding members of the assembly, this "dissent" circulated widely through the states, inspiring animated attacks and defenses.[81]

The convention vote did not end contention. Instead it opened a new, nastier phase of the ratification controversy in Pennsylvania. The harmony sought by the moderate advocates of compromise in early December quickly became a forgotten dream. On the day after Christmas, a mob opposed to the Constitution broke up a celebration of ratification in the town of Carlisle in Cumberland County, and the next day burned in effigy Chief Justice Thomas McKean and James Wilson. The "designing and artful Federalists" had realized their scheme of getting the Constitution ratified in Pennsylvania by surprise despite the fact that "the people are pretty generally convinced of their delusion," according to a writer in the January 2 *Carlisle Gazette*, "and little less than the lives of their betrayers will satiate their revenge." Federalist politics in Pennsylvania had, it seemed, provoked more of that popular "tumult" the Constitution was supposed to end.[82]

Fortunately, the violence was mostly verbal as opponents accused each other of corruption or conspiracy. Sometimes they resorted to "dirty tricks," like publishing essays falsely attributed to the other side. Rancor rose to such a height that Benjamin Franklin felt compelled to publish an essay "On the Abuse of the Press." Contemporary newspapers, he said, suggested that Pennsylvania was "peopled by . . . the most unprincipled, wicked, rascally, and quarrelsome scoundrels upon the face of the globe." Meanwhile, angry allies of the convention minority began collecting signatures on petitions asking the state legislature to nullify the convention's ratification of the Constitution.[83]

CLOSING OUT THE YEAR

To make matters worse, Pennsylvania was not, as the Federalists had hoped, the first state to ratify the Constitution. Delaware's convention met on December 3 in the town of Dover and ratified the Constitution four days later by a unanimous vote. So easy a decision was unusual for Delaware, a state deeply divided between Whig and Tory factions that went back to differences over independence. Delaware's conflicts could even become violent: Sussex County Tories used armed force to prevent their Whig enemies from voting in the 1787 elections. In neighboring Kent County, however, Whigs voluntarily stayed away from the polls when delegates to the ratifying convention were chosen, "not caring by whom the government was ratified."[84]

Both parties were of one mind on the Constitution because it so obviously served Delaware's best interests. Once the Constitution went into effect, Delaware would no longer have to pay the duties Pennsylvania levied on goods imported through Philadelphia and sold to people in Delaware with the duty built into the price. Customs revenues would be raised by the federal government for the benefit of all the states. Moreover, customs revenues, along with revenues from the sale of western lands, would eliminate the need for state taxes to support the federal government, above all in paying interest on its war debt. The new federal government would also pay members of Congress, which was previously a state obligation; that, again, would reduce Delaware's tax burden. Getting equal representation in the Senate gilded the lily, granting Delaware—a state that had only recently been totally separated from Pennsylvania—the recognition as well as the power it craved. Like Pennsylvania, Delaware offered to cede land for a new federal capital, no doubt hoping that its status as the first state to ratify the Constitution would increase its chance of hosting the new government.[85]

By mid-December, then, two states had ratified. New Jersey followed on December 18, when its ratifying convention met at the Blazing Star tavern in Trenton and approved the Constitution by a vote of 38 to nothing. Later it, too, recommended that the state cede land to Congress for the new capital. The New Jersey ratifying convention published a journal of its proceedings, but it isn't very revealing. It reported, for example, that "the Convention . . . proceeded to consider and deliberate upon the proposed Federal Constitution by sections," without providing any information on what was said. There were no published debates or newspaper accounts of the New Jersey convention, but evidence, including the final vote, suggests there was virtually no opposition to the Constitution. That's strange because the state's politics were, like nearby Delaware's, usually divided, with factions based in the eastern and western parts of the state fighting each other with gusto. The reasons for New Jersey's unanimity on the Constitution were like those in Delaware, except that New Jersey was eager to stop paying duties levied on goods imported through New York as well as Philadelphia.[86]

Together Delaware and New Jersey proved that divisions in state politics did not have to become divisions over the Constitution, as they had in Pennsylvania. There the Constitution's supporters had insisted on ramming it through, assuming losers would simply yield to a triumphant majority and ignoring indications to the contrary. They were wrong. They might have had a strong majority of voters on their side; and a knack for coalition building and support for the rights of embattled minorities might help explain their electoral strength in Pennsylvania politics.[87] That trait was, however, conspicuously absent during the September session of the state assembly and again in the Pennsylvania ratifying convention. The ham-handed politics of the Constitution's supporters left Pennsylvania in turmoil and awakened suspicions elsewhere that made ratification of the Constitution significantly more difficult to achieve.

On December 31, before the year was out and before the news from Pennsylvania had circulated broadly, the Georgia ratifying convention in Augusta voted unanimously (26–0) to ratify the Constitution after discussing it for only one day, Saturday, December 30. The state's strong consent to the Constitution stands in stark contrast to its previous disregard for the Confederation: Its delegates to Congress were notable mainly for their absence from its sessions, and Georgia never paid even the relatively small requisitions Congress levied on it. The state did, however, send delegates to the federal Convention, where they joined those from South Carolina in insisting on provisions protecting slavery and allowing the slave trade to continue for the next twenty years.[88]

The Georgia assembly empowered the state's ratifying convention "to adopt or reject any part or the whole" of the Constitution, which opened the way to a partial ratification, and an essay by "A Georgian" asking for amendments to the Constitution awoke a rancorous debate in the *Gazette of the State of Georgia*. The state convention, however, voted to ratify the Constitution with no reservations or qualifications. Its brief journals report that decision but, again, provide no explanation for it.[89]

Did Georgia ratify because it desperately needed federal help in fighting attacks by Creek Indians and defending its southern border with Spanish Florida? If a "weak state, with powerful tribes of Indians in its rear and the Spaniards on its flank, do not incline to embrace a strong general government," George Washington commented, "there must . . . be either wickedness or insanity in their conduct." But only a couple of letters by Georgians suggest a connection between the Indian wars and Georgia's unanimous ratification of the Constitution. Moreover, Georgia had some good reasons to resist increasing federal power: It did not want Congress to take title to Georgia's western lands—which extended to the Mississippi—or to negotiate with the southern Indians and perhaps come to an agreement that would keep Georgians from settling Indian lands.[90]

Whatever its reasons, Georgia's vote meant that by the end of 1787 four states had decided to ratify the Constitution, though Georgia joined the list without a day to spare. The new year had begun before the convention formally adopted and signed a ratification instrument and forwarded it to Congress along with a letter expressing hope that Georgia's quick action would "tend not only to consolidate the Union but promote the happiness of our common country."[91]

But the easy ratification victories were over. The battles in other states were going to be hard fought, and observers had a field day speculating on their outcome.[92] The conventions scheduled to meet early in 1788 would decide the Constitution's fate and the country's future. What they would do remained, however, anything but obvious.

FIVE

———— ★ ————

"We the People" of Connecticut and Massachusetts

By January 5, when the Georgia convention finally dissolved, the Connecticut convention was in its third day and the Massachusetts convention was scheduled to begin within a week. Those were the first in a string of ratifying conventions state legislatures had scheduled for the winter, spring, and summer of 1788. New Hampshire's convention would meet on February 13, Maryland's on April 21, Virginia's on June 2, and North Carolina's not until July 21. The legislatures of South Carolina, New York, and Rhode Island had yet to act.[1]

It took no genius to predict that the contest for ratification would be close. The inaction in three states—especially New York and Rhode Island, whose resistance to increased central power was well known—was hardly a good sign from a Federalist perspective. And why had Virginia and North Carolina put off their conventions until June and July? While the federal Convention was still in session, Gouverneur Morris had predicted that when the Constitution was first announced with the Convention's endorsement "the people will be favorable to it," but that as time went on "State officers, & those interested in the State Gov[ernmen]ts will intrigue & turn the popular current against it." Luther Martin agreed that as time went on the opposition would increase, though not for the reason Morris proposed. The people would not ratify the Constitution, he predicted, "unless hurried into it by surprise."[2] If so, time was on the side of the Constitution's critics. In fact, the Constitution had its easiest victories early on, and its most challenging fights at the end of the ratification process.

Poring over the news, Washington almost invariably assessed the Constitution's chances optimistically. But even he could only conclude that the effect of having the Virginia convention meet so late remained to be seen. If earlier conventions voted to ratify, he wrote a correspondent in early December, he had little doubt that Virginia would follow their example. But if some rejected it, "it is very probable that the opposers of it here will exert themselves to add this to the number." In New York, James Madison reported, "it is said . . . and I believe on good ground," that North Carolina had postponed its convention until July so it could see what Virginia did.[3]

And reports indicated that the opposition to ratification was getting stronger in Virginia day by day.[4] Patrick Henry, a powerhouse in Virginia politics, had joined forces with other critics of the Constitution, including George Mason and Richard Henry Lee. Madison understood Henry's importance: "Much will depend on Mr. Henry," he had written Washington the previous October. Madison deeply distrusted Henry. In December, he wrote Randolph that "for some time" he had thought that Henry was "driving at a Southern Confederacy" and that he had joined the movement for amending the Constitution "as he hopes to render it subservient to his real designs." If North Carolina adopted Henry's politics, which Madison found "not . . . improbable," that would "endanger the Union more than any other circumstance that could happen. My apprehensions of this danger increase every day." Indeed, before Madison heard the good news from Georgia— and so late as February 1 he still had not received confirmation of Georgia's ratification—he considered "everything . . . as problematical from Maryland southward" because the "anti-federal" inclinations of North Carolina and Virginia were likely to influence states to the south.[5]

Even with Georgia settled into the "yes" column, negative votes in five or six states—the two Carolinas, Virginia, New York, Rhode Island, and perhaps Maryland—would make the Constitution a dead letter, as the early December essayist in Philadelphia's *Independent Gazetteer* predicted. And were all of the New England states except Rhode Island "unanimously in favor" of the Constitution, as Gouverneur Morris told Washington so confidently in late October?[6] On December 11, Henry Knox wrote Washington from New York that not just Pennsylvania, New Jersey, and Delaware, but also Connecticut, Massachusetts and New Hampshire would ratify by "considerable majorities." But while Madison shared Knox's opinion about Connecticut and also New Hampshire, he foresaw "more opposition in Massachusetts," although the Constitution's supporters there remained "very sanguine of victory."[7]

Madison was sufficiently worried about Massachusetts to play the strongest card in the Federalists' hand. On December 20 he asked Washington whether he corresponded with any gentlemen in Massachusetts. If so, he suggested, Washington might seize that opportunity to express his "good wishes for the plan." That modest intervention, Madison thought, "would be attended with valuable effects." In January, as increasingly ominous reports arrived from Massachusetts, Madison could easily imagine the ratification effort unraveling. What Massachusetts did would certainly influence New

York, for better or for worse. A negative vote in the Bay State would also energize the minority in Pennsylvania, which was "very restless under their defeat" and scheming to reverse their state convention's vote to ratify.[8] To avoid giving such encouragement to the enemy, anything was worth a shot.

Washington had no objection to expressing his views of the Constitution, which were "unequivocal & decided," but, he told Madison, "I have no regu-lar corrispond[en]t in Massachusetts." Then he remembered his old fellow army officer Benjamin Lincoln. Or, to be exact, Lincoln reminded Wash-ington by sending him a long letter on January 13 with personal news and an early report on the Massachusetts ratifying convention, where, he said, it was impossible to predict how the delegates would divide.[9]

Lincoln suggested that Massachusetts Federalists had adopted an ap-proach very different from that of their colleagues in Pennsylvania. "I trust and hope," he wrote, "that the business will be conducted with moderation candor & fairness, otherwise we may bear down the opposition but we shall never smooth and quiet their minds." It would take wisdom and care not just to get the Constitution adopted but put it into effect and "avoid that confu-sion and misery which has too often masked the progress of the various gov-ernments now established in the world." Washington agreed: Moderation, candor, and fairness, he noted, were "not incompatible with firmness." The friends of the Constitution could perhaps "bear down the opposition," but "precipitate or violent measures" could never reconcile the opposition "to the exercise of the Government," which "ought as much as possible to be kept in view, & temper the proceedings."[10] The point was not just to win, but to win a victory worth having. That was the hard lesson of Pennsylvania.

Washington called Lincoln's attention to a statement of his views on the Constitution written to a correspondent in Fredericksburg, Virginia, which, he said, "I find has circulated pretty generally through the Papers." The un-authorized publication and subsequent widespread republication of his com-ments on the Constitution, casually inserted into a private letter about "Wolf dogs—Wolves—Sheep—experiments in Farming &ca &ca. &ca.," upset Washington. He would have composed his words more carefully, he said, had he known they would see print. And yet the letter could serve Madison's pur-pose. In it Washington said there was "*no Alternative* between the *Adoption*" of the Constitution "and *Anarchy*." The arguments of the Constitution's crit-ics were "addressed more to the Passions than to the Reason; and *clear I am*, if another Federal Convention is attempted . . . the Sentiments of the Members will be *more* discordant or less accommodating than the last" and so would be unable to agree on any common proposal. The country's government, he said, "is now *suspended by a Thread*," and it did not require the "Gift of Prophesy" to predict the consequences of "a fruitless Attempt to amend the one which is offered, before it is tried, or of the Delay from the Attempt."[11]

Washington had made the same point to Edmund Randolph in a letter thanking him for a copy of his letter to the Virginia legislature, explaining why he had refused to sign the Constitution. Washington also commented on Randolph's plea for amendments. Even within Virginia, the advocates of amendments differed on what they proposed, he said. What prospect, then, was there of agreement "when the different views, and jarring interests of so wide and extended an Empire," were brought together? It was "more clear than ever" to Washington that a second convention would produce not "a more perfect form" of government but "more heat, & greater confusion than can well be conceived." Adoption of the Constitution as written or "a dissolution of the Union" were "the only alternatives before us."[12]

As Washington saw it, there could be no second convention to consider amendments, and no amendments of any sort previous to ratification. That apparently was what he meant by the reference to "firmness" in his letter to Lincoln. Federalists could act with more moderation, candor, and fairness than they had in Pennsylvania, but they could make no substantial concessions to the opposition. With so much to be gained, Washington found it inconceivable that Americans would not, in the end, ratify the Constitution, even without the amendments its critics demanded. On Christmas Day in 1787—a long year after he received that fateful letter from Governor Randolph officially announcing his appointment as a Virginia delegate to the Constitutional Convention—Washington could look hopefully to a future when "the establishment of an enerjetic [sic] general Government will disappoint the hopes and expectations of those who are unfriendly to this Country—give us a national respectability—and enable us to improve those commercial and political advantages which Nature and situation have placed within our reach."[13]

If the Federalists continued to insist that the people accept or reject the Constitution without amendment, the document was going to be a very hard sell in Massachusetts. But first it would come before the ratification convention in Connecticut, where Federalists were confident of victory for reasons that can only be described as puzzling.

A ONE-SIDED "DEBATE"

Why were the Federalist prophets so confident of winning Connecticut? If, as they often insisted, the opposition to the Constitution was just a continuation of earlier opposition to strengthening the Confederation, Connecticut should have been a hothouse of what the Federalists called "Antifederalism." In the mid-1780s the state fairly exploded with anger at the Confederation Congress for granting officers of the Continental Army (but not ordinary soldiers) half-pay for life, and then, in March 1783, commuting the officers' pensions into full pay for five years after they left the army. The formation of the Society of the Cincinnati, also in 1783, seemed to confirm that army officers, including some 250 in Connecticut, aspired to become an American hereditary aristocracy. And Congress seemed more than happy to give them valuable privileges denied to others.[14]

The issue provoked so much feeling that in September 1783 a majority of Connecticut towns sent delegates to an extralegal convention in Middletown. That was remarkable in a state known for its conservatism: Connecticut reelected leaders drawn from the state's upper classes year after year and resisted changes to its government even in the midst of the Revolution. It did not, like most other states, write a new state constitution after independence; instead Connecticut kept its old colonial charter, which defined, like a constitution, its form of government.

The Middletown convention denounced "the GRATUITY made by the honorable American Congress to officers of the army for services not to be performed" and called for changes in Connecticut's government not unlike those demanded by similar conventions in western Massachusetts. Dissidents later won control of the state's lower house of assembly, where they secured a series of measures giving tax relief to farmers. That saved Connecticut from the insurrections that hit rural Massachusetts. Control of the assembly by an *"anti-federal"* party, as a 1786 newspaper writer called it, also meant that proposals to strengthen the Confederation faced an uphill battle in Connecticut.[15]

Like New Jersey, Connecticut wanted to stop paying duties to the state of New York for goods imported through New York but sold in Connecticut, and it was inclined toward giving Congress a right to tax imports. Nonetheless, the legislature at first rejected the congressional impost of 1783 and later approved it only if the proceeds would "on no account be diverted to any other use" than paying the national debt—that is, the revenue could not be used to fund pensions for army officers. The legislature also ordered the governor to tell the president of Congress "in a summary manner" that it had no money to pay requisitions but to reassure him "of the hearty attachment of the good people of this state to the Union." Then, as if to cast doubt on that assurance, the legislature put off electing delegates to the federal Convention until May 1787, about the time it was supposed to convene. Washington's correspondent David Humphreys, an ardent nationalist and also a member of the Cincinnati, supported the delay for fear that the "miserable, narrow-minded & . . . wicked Politicians" who controlled the Connecticut legislature would choose delegates who would "impede any salutary measures that might be proposed."[16] In the end, however, the delegates Connecticut sent to Philadelphia were anything but obstructionists. They threw their weight behind compromises that bridged divisions among delegates and helped the Convention succeed.

By late September 1787, Humphreys found reason to think opposition to the Constitution in Connecticut would be "less than was apprehended." For one thing, all the members of "the liberal professions"—clergymen, lawyers, merchants, and physicians—were in favor of the Constitution, and they had an extraordinary influence in Connecticut, where ordinary people tended to respect their authority. Federalists also controlled the Connecticut press far more than their counterparts in Pennsylvania, and they began preparing the public for what Humphreys called a "favorable reception" of the Constitution even before it was published. The result was almost comic, as an essayist in the *New Haven Gazette* struggled to convince citizens to support a system of government that they had not yet seen, much less examined closely. His main argument was that the delegates to the Philadelphia Convention were "men of the first character in this country for wisdom, knowledge, and patriotism," and so they could be trusted.[17] That argument would have gone nowhere with a crusty Pennsylvania critic of the Constitution like John Smilie, but Connecticut was not Pennsylvania.

Later, as the debate over the Constitution exploded in the press elsewhere, Connecticut's nine newspapers published an abundance of essays supporting the Constitution; only six pieces (one local, five from out of the state) appeared that criticized it—and two of those were printed at the request of Federalist Oliver Ellsworth so he could refute their arguments. Another "Antifederalist" essay was probably a Federalist fabrication published, again, to make way for a Federalist rejoinder. Even the newspapers' "squibs"—short items generally copied from other newspapers—favored the Constitution. They praised Federalists, claimed the Constitution's critics wanted to destroy the union, and suggested that ratification was a sure thing.[18]

There were pockets of opposition to the Constitution "as it now stands" in the state, but the newspapers generally ignored them in an effort—like the Federalists' strategy in Pennsylvania—to suggest there was no opposition. And when they did recognize the existence of opposition, they described it as disreputable, even reprehensible: For example, the *Connecticut Courant* acknowledged that there would be "some Judases" in the state ratifying convention but expressed pleasure that, in choosing delegates, most towns had fought off the "*wrong heads*" among them. How could anyone be so "lost to every principle of social compact as to militate" against the Constitution, one writer asked. Another reported that the "doings of the Convention" were "everywhere approved." What else would one expect, given "the prevailing disposition of the people" in Connecticut "to support order and good government"?[19] Under the circumstances, to question any aspect of the Constitution required extraordinary moral courage.

Roger Sherman and Oliver Ellsworth, two of Connecticut's three delegates to the federal Convention, did their part in the ratification campaign by explaining away or denying what fundamental changes the Constitution would bring. (The state's third delegate, William Samuel Johnson, was in New York, representing Connecticut in the Confederation Congress.) Their report to Governor Samuel Huntington on September 26, 1787, which was widely reprinted within the state, said that Connecticut would have the same number of representatives in the new, bicameral Congress as it had in the Confederation Congress, and that the new powers given Congress were carefully defined and concerned only "matters respecting the common interests of the Union." On all other matters, they added, "the particular states retain their *Sovereignty*." Apparently Sherman and Ellsworth did not share James Wilson's view that within the American republic only the people were sovereign, not the state or national governments (but then Wilson's speeches in the Pennsylvania ratifying convention had not yet been made, much less printed and circulated to other states).[20]

Nor were the returning delegates concerned with the broad new taxing power of Congress, which critics saw as a major threat to the authority and even the continued existence of the states. Sherman and Ellsworth said most federal revenues would come from duties on imports; if for some reason direct taxes became necessary, they would be apportioned among the states according to population. Moreover, Congress's power to collect direct taxes "need not be exercised if each state will furnish its quota." In other words, Sherman and Ellsworth said the states would get a chance to raise their share of any federal direct taxes and so to prevent the national government from collecting them. The Constitution did not, however, provide for a state option to raise taxes for federal purposes in lieu of federal direct taxes. In some states, critics of the Constitution would demand an amendment to give states that option. Sherman and Ellsworth precluded such a demand by suggesting that the Constitution already provided for it. And since Connecticut lacked a genuinely open press, nobody called them on that point.

Sherman and Ellsworth were among the most prolific contributors to the flood of Federalist literature presented to the Connecticut public. The son of a Massachusetts farmer, Roger Sherman was at first a shoemaker, and then, after moving to Milford, Connecticut, in 1743, he became the surveyor of Litchfield County, a lawyer, and soon a judge. He later settled in New Haven, becoming mayor in 1787, as well as a judge of Connecticut's superior court. He had represented the state in Congress as well as at the federal Convention (where, at age sixty-six, he was the oldest delegate except for the octogenarian Benjamin Franklin), and he won considerable respect for his intelligence, judgment, and character. By 1787 Sherman's farming days were long gone, but he signed his essays in favor of the Constitution "A Countryman." Ellsworth, a generation younger than Sherman, tall and with a commanding presence, was a prosperous Hartford lawyer who served with

Sherman on the bench of the state's Superior Court and, also like Sherman, had represented Connecticut in Congress and the Constitutional Convention. His essays, signed "A Landholder," were, like Sherman's, aimed at the Connecticut farmers who would choose the great majority of delegates to the state ratifying convention and whose hostility toward strengthening the federal government was most to be feared.[21]

The strongest arguments for the Constitution in Connecticut were economic, and there Sherman and Ellsworth had the help of "A Farmer," another newspaper essayist who argued that the Constitution was "peculiarly favorable to the agricultural part of the United States." It would shift the burden from taxes on polls and farms toward taxes on imports collected by Congress for the benefit of everyone, not by neighboring states for their own benefit. Import duties would also be paid in greater part by merchants than consumers. "A Farmer" argued that a new national government capable of retaliating against the restrictions Britain imposed on American trade might reopen the West Indian market for New England's horses, lumber, and foodstuffs. The first "Landholder" essay agreed: The new national government would open foreign markets and so assure a "generous price" for farmers' crops.[22]

From there the level of argument took a sharp turn downward as Federalists tried to discredit their (mostly unheard) opponents. Ellsworth's "Landholder" said the Constitution's critics were covert Loyalists longing for reunion with Britain, men "trembling for the liberties of poor America" for no good reason, desperate debtors incapable of honesty or industry, or self-important local politicians who could not get into public office and so spent their time sowing suspicions of those in power among their rural neighbors. Ellsworth, remember, had led the charge against Elbridge Gerry after the latter publicly explained his reasons for not signing the Constitution and accused him of acting for reasons based on "barefaced selfishness and injustice." Similarly, "A Landholder" claimed that George Mason's opposition began after the federal Convention rejected his proposal that regulations of trade require a two-thirds vote of Congress to protect Southern interests from the Northern majority. He described Mason as a man of "narrow views and local prejudices" who could "never be trusted."[23]

Ellsworth at least arranged for the publication of Gerry's October 18 letter to the Massachusetts legislature and of Mason's objections to the Constitution before criticizing them. Roger Sherman, however, attacked several essays critical of the Constitution that had not appeared in the Connecticut press, including those signed "Centinel," "Cato," "An Old Whig," and "Brutus." He even delighted in the fact that the people of Connecticut had been spared the "torrent of impertinence and folly" with which newspapers elsewhere had "overwhelmed many parts of the country."[24] Some New York opponents of ratifying the unamended Constitution tried to break through the barriers by sending to Connecticut broadsides and pamphlets with essays criticizing the Constitution as well as issues of the *New-York Journal.* Supporters of ratification managed to seize and destroy most of them but remained outraged nonetheless.[25]

Those New Yorkers campaigning against ratification of the Constitution as written, the Federalists charged, were salaried state officials whose pay depended on the New York impost, which the Constitution would bring to an end. As a result, they, like Gerry and Mason, acted out of selfishness, not principle. In fact, according to "A Landholder," no critics of the Constitution were genuinely concerned with improving the Constitution prior to its ratification. They spoke of amendments, he wrote, "of dangerous articles which must be corrected," and pretended they would readily join in a "safe plan of federal government." But "the men who oppose this Constitution are the same who have been unfederal from the beginning" and were "as unfriendly to the old Confederation as to the system now proposed." In short, their "past conduct" brought their sincerity into question. The implication was clear: Criticisms of the Constitution need not be taken seriously since they were artful efforts to dupe the public by writers moved by their own interests and "blind to the public good."[26]

But shouldn't the free people of Connecticut get to judge for themselves the quality of "antifederal" objections to the Constitution? Some observers apparently thought so. In early December, the *Connecticut Courant* reported that it had been "repeatedly accused of partiality" for refusing to print essays that criticized the Constitution. The paper replied that it was ready to publish any such essay if it was "written decently" and insisted that it had "not received a single essay upon the subject which contained the smallest objection" to the Constitution. Granted, it preferred "original essays" of Connecticut origin (although it happily reprinted Federalist essays written elsewhere) and made no secret of the paper's support for the Constitution. "But we pledge . . . to the public that we ever have and ever mean to maintain the liberty of the press, and to publish any pieces which we judge will not disgrace our paper, uninfluenced by our private opinions of the merits of any question or the wishes of any party whatsoever." Two weeks later the printers of the *Courant* and the *American Mercury* issued a joint statement acknowledging "that the press ought to be uninfluenced and that the people, the great source of power and who are to decide the momentous question, have a right to know every argument." They invited submissions critical of the Constitution and even promised to help "those who have not been educated writers" to put their views "in a dress worthy of the public view."[27]

No surge in the publication of essays critical of the Constitution followed, but the statements were important anyway. Like the response of Eleazer Oswald to efforts to prevent him from printing the work of authors who found fault with the Constitution, it suggested that liberty of the press was becoming something more than what it had been in the English past, a freedom from "prior restraint" by government censors. In the new American republic, it required that newspapers give the people access to all points of view on topics of public concern. But liberty of the press in that sense remained hard to establish. It demanded not opposing government actions, but winning over newspaper subscribers who often saw no reason why they should support the publication of arguments with which they disagreed. In Connecticut, however, most readers never saw the arguments made against ratifying the Constitution in the form proposed (though some might have seen them in New York or Massachusetts newspapers). How, then, could they know whether they agreed or disagreed with those arguments?

WHAT WAS THE ROLE OF THE PEOPLE?

On October 17, when it called a state ratifying convention, the Connecticut legislature specified that town meetings—not the smaller meetings of freemen that chose assembly representatives—would assemble on the second Monday of November and choose delegates for the purposes mentioned in the resolutions of the federal Convention and Congress, that is, "for their assent & ratification" of the Constitution. The state ratifying convention would open on the third of January in Hartford.[28]

Were the people of the town meetings supposed to debate the Constitution or leave that weighty subject to their delegates? Benjamin Gale, a contentious townsman in Killingworth, Connecticut, said that the Constitution had not been "referred back to the *people* to say whether they will adopt it or reject it," as many people believed. According to the act approved by the Connecticut assembly, he said, the people in town meetings had "no voice in the case. All our business, gentlemen, is to make choice of delegates to say whether you shall be made to submit to it or not—not whether you approve of it or not. That is not our business nor is it submitted to you." The process of ratification that the Connecticut assembly approved was, Gale charged, just "another *artful maneuver*" like that in Pennsylvania, "to hurry on matters before the people have a chance to understand it and so as to be able to make a judicious choice of delegates to act conformable to their own minds."[29]

Town records, although they are often frustratingly brief, suggest that the towns did, in fact, sometimes leave the decision on ratification to the state convention. The records of Bethlehem, for example, say that the town met, chose a moderator, elected Moses Hawley to represent it in the state ratifying convention, and dissolved—and so it apparently did no more than Gale thought it was authorized to do. Sometimes, however, the towns read and discussed the Constitution, then adjourned while a committee pondered whether the town should instruct its delegates how to vote. The town of

Windham actually adjourned twice and then, "after a very able and lengthy discussion of the subject," voted by a large majority "that, as the proposed Constitution was to be determined on by a state Convention, it was not proper for this town to pass any vote on the subject." Norfolk's committee advised the town to give its delegates no instructions but "to leave the whole matters with the delegates" and let them "act as they think best," and the town agreed. Similarly, Norwich told its delegates "to act . . . as their wisdom shall direct."[30]

That was the path of wisdom, according to a Federalist writer in the *Connecticut Courant*. Since "we are in general very unequal to the task of forming a judgment upon the Constitution," he wrote, "every man of common sense and suitable candor" would "cheerfully" leave it to the convention and acquiesce in its decision "rather than by noisy and bitter exclamations work himself and others into a ferment."[31] If, however, the subject was beyond the capacities of ordinary people to understand, what was the meaning of the statement "We the People . . . do ordain and establish this Constitution"? Was it a just a rhetorical flourish, a convenient intellectual fiction, or, as Gale proposed, part of an "artful maneuver" to bypass probable sources of opposition in the legislatures and the towns?

Some townsmen took their responsibility literally. At least fourteen of the ninety-eight towns in Connecticut that were entitled to choose convention delegates took a clear stand on the Constitution (they split equally— half for and half against). Of those, six or seven instructed their delegates in some way.[32] Federalist assurances had little impact on Simsbury, which decided that the Constitution "would institute and erect an aristocracy" that it feared "would end in despotism and tyranny," increase taxes, and destroy the townsmen's liberties and privileges. As a result, Simsbury, like Lebanon and Willington, instructed its delegates to oppose adoption of the Constitution "as it is now proposed." Greenwich also ignored the argument against instructions but, like Danbury and Ridgefield, told its delegates "to use their influence in the Convention . . . to establish and ratify the Constitution." The wording of Ridgefield's instructions is especially interesting. It "voted unanimously that this meeting do approve of the Constitution" and instructed the town's delegates "to declare the voice of the people of this meeting at their meeting . . . at Hartford."[33] The voters at the Ridgefield town meeting clearly understood they were not "We the People of the United States," but "the people of this meeting" were part of that larger whole and should make their collective voice heard.

It was, however, left to the townsmen of Preston, who considered it their right and duty to inform their convention delegates of their convictions and desires "on this important subject," to write a more balanced and thoughtful position statement than any polemic published in Connecticut, and so to bring into question assertions that the Constitution was too complex for ordinary people to understand. "It is our ardent wish," the Preston instructions began, "that an efficient government may be established over these states" and that it be so constructed "that the people may retain all liberties, privileges, and immunities usual and necessary for citizens of a free country" while providing sufficiently for the enforcement of those powers invested in the government. But how much power could the people safely yield? "'Tis much easier to give more power into the hands of government when more is necessary than to recover back where too much is already given."[34]

On that basis, the town listed several objections to accepting the Constitution "without alteration." It cited infrequent elections, inadequate representation, the six-year term of office for senators, the lack of provision for jury trials in civil cases, and "the power of direct taxation without limitation or restraint being lodged in Congress." To let a distant government tax polls and freeholds risked alienating people from their system of government and robbing the states of essential resources, Preston noted. (The townsmen were obviously not persuaded by the assurances of Sherman and Ellsworth that federal taxation posed no threat to Connecticut.) If duties on imports and other indirect taxes proved insufficient for the needs of the new federal government, it could then be given additional sources of income.

Preston thought federal judges should be elected for fixed terms, not hold office for life. The town also posed a powerful argument against Article VI of the Constitution, which allowed Congress to propose amendments to the Constitution that would go into effect when approved by three-quarters of the state legislatures, and so allowed legislators "to change the form of government . . . without ever consulting the people." Legislators, Preston said, were elected "for the purpose of making laws and not for the purpose of altering the original compact of the people." The voters of Preston understood popular sovereignty and its significance for constitutional law better than Sherman and Ellsworth, who continually spoke of the proposed government's power as coming from the sovereign states, not the sovereign people.

Given their objections, the townsmen of Preston were unwilling either to give the Constitution their unconditional support or to demand its rejection if it could not be amended. "If there be no prospect of any alterations, but it must be accepted or rejected as it now stands," they asked their delegates to "peruse these our sentiments with deliberation" and "give your assent or dissent as you shall really think will terminate for the best good of the people of these states." It would be hard to find a better way to exercise popular power without undermining the convention's capacity to deliberate.

THE CONNECTICUT CONVENTION

The convention met as scheduled at the State House in Hartford on January 3, but after electing its officers moved to the North Meeting House, where a predominantly Federalist audience observed the debates from a gallery. It resolved to consider the Constitution "by single articles, sections, paragraphs, or detached sentences as occasion might require," but to take no vote before "the one decisive, general question" on whether or not to ratify.[35] That stacked the cards against amendments.

The convention left no known journal, and all reports of debates come from newspapers, which, except for a very brief summary of a speech criticizing all federal taxation by General James Wadsworth, covered only Federalist speeches. The young Hartford lawyer Enoch Perkins, who took notes for the *Connecticut Courant* and the *American Mercury*, said the Constitution was "canvassed critically and fully," but the "exceedingly prolix" convention debates were beyond his capacity to record. "Suffice it to say," he reported, "that all the objections to the Constitution vanished before the learning and eloquence of a [William Samuel] Johnson, the genuine good sense and discernment of a Sherman, and the Demosthenian energy of an Ellsworth."[36]

With a record-keeper like that, there is reason to suspect that speeches by the Constitution's critics were not reported fairly. But even a sympathetic observer confessed that delegates who had reservations about the Constitution were relatively ineffective speakers and easily "browbeaten" by the self-styled "Ciceros" and men of "superior rank, as they called themselves," on the other side. It did not help that some spectators in the gallery coughed, talked, spat, and shuffled their feet when critics of the Constitution spoke.[37] The delegates who favored an unqualified ratification included an extraordinary number of current and past state office holders including, by one account, two governors, a lieutenant governor, six assistants (members of the upper house of the state legislature), four judges of the superior court, and an array of county court judges and justices of the peace, as well as several military officers.[38] As noted, all three Connecticut delegates to the federal Convention were also in attendance. The presence of so many dignitaries had an impact in a state where the people usually followed their leaders—and it contradicted the old Federalist chestnut about self-interested local leaders heading the attack on the Constitution.

Ellsworth and Johnson ably argued for more "energetic" national institutions and answered objections to Congress's taxing powers. Delegates were no doubt reassured when both Governor Samuel Huntington and Lieutenant Governor Oliver Wolcott said the Constitution would pose no danger to state governments or to the rights of the states. After two days, one convention member testified, the opposition's ardor declined. The same person also reported that on January 9, after the convention voted to ratify by 128 to 40, many delegates in the minority said they were satisfied and would support the new Constitution. Even a few delegates whose towns had instructed them to vote against ratification either voted to ratify or failed to vote altogether; Preston's delegates were in the majority.[39] So Connecticut ended up different from Pennsylvania in at least one critical respect: The minority did not go away mad.

Henry Knox welcomed the news of Connecticut's ratification. "It does my heart good," he told the correspondent in Hartford who informed him of the event. "Now for Massachusetts: forward all the favorable news to Mr. [Rufus] King" in Boston. How much difference would the news from Connecticut make in the Bay State? Except for a cluster of towns to the northwest and east of New Haven, opposition to the Constitution in Connecticut was strongest in towns along the state's northern border. Above the state line was Shays country, and there, Knox said, "the vile insurgents, aided by other things, will make adoption in Massachusetts more difficult than has been imagined."[40]

"WE . . . THE PEOPLE OF MASSACHUSETTS"

The heritage of Daniel Shays was only a part—the most recent and so easily remembered part—of a rich political history that raised serious obstacles for those who wanted the Constitution ratified in Massachusetts.

In Massachusetts, popular sovereignty was not just a theory; it was a reality, and it had been so long before the insurrections broke out. By the late 1780s, the sovereign people of Massachusetts were as aware and protective of their prerogatives as any king. As a result, the strategy of moderation and accommodation that Benjamin Lincoln described to Washington was more than a corrective for Federalist mistakes in Pennsylvania. Unless the Massachusetts Federalists treated critics of the Constitution with some delicacy, they were going to lose, and losing in Massachusetts would be devastating in other states whose conventions had not yet met.[41]

"Take this or nothing" had a bad history in Massachusetts. That way of getting a constitution ratified had been tried and failed there in 1778, when the state legislature submitted a draft state constitution to the towns, which were to report only whether they accepted or rejected it and the number present who voted on either side. Ratification required the approval of "at least two thirds of those [white men] who are free, and twenty-one years of age, belonging to this State, and present in the several [town] meetings." An overwhelming majority of the towns and of the participating voters rejected the document. Approval had to be unqualified by demands for amendments, which threw votes into the "no" category. Most towns, however, made their decisions clearly and unequivocally. Take the report of a Norwich (now Huntington) town meeting on May 18, 1778:

the Voters Present—41
those Voting for—00
those Voting against Said Constitution as it now Stand—41

Faced with an up-or-down vote, in short, the people of Massachusetts voted the constitution of 1778 down—but not without first discussing the document and identifying the flaws that made it unacceptable "as it now Stand."[42]

Among other problems with the proposed constitution of 1778, it was written by the state legislature. In fact, all the American state constitutions adopted in 1776 and 1777 were written and also enacted by state legislatures or their Revolutionary equivalents. By 1778, many constituencies in Massachusetts found that procedure hopelessly flawed. As the town of Concord explained, the body that forms a constitution has a right to alter it, and a constitution that can be changed by the legislature gives the people no security against legislative encroachments on their rights. The alternative, embraced by several towns throughout Massachusetts, was for the people to elect delegates to a special convention whose only purpose would be to draft a constitution, which would then be ratified directly by the people of the towns. In that way the constitution would draw its authority clearly and unequivocally from the sovereign people, which would make it superior to the ordinary laws enacted by legislatures.[43]

The idea that government received its authority from the people was not new. It was part of seventeenth-century English radical thought and had passed easily from England to America. The Declaration of Independence restated the basic precept that governments derived their "just Powers from the Consent of the Governed." In 1780, however, Massachusetts transformed popular sovereignty from a theory to a process. The creative force behind that achievement was ordinary townsmen, not prominent statesmen such as James Madison or James Wilson. To be sure, in his autobiography, written some thirty years later, John Adams claimed that on June 2, 1776, he had asked the Continental Congress to recommend that the people of the several colonies immediately call conventions "and set up Governments of their own, under their own Authority: for the People were the Source of all Authority and Original of all Power."[44] If Adams in fact made that proposal—and he failed to repeat the argument in his *Thoughts on Government* of 1776—his pleas fell on deaf ears. Constitutional conventions and direct popular ratification of constitutions entered American practice only because the townsmen of Massachusetts not only understood the prevailing theoretical assumptions of their time but found ways of reducing them to practice. In effect, the sovereign people invented the institutions through which they could exercise their sovereign power. They also refused to take "no" for an answer.

Finally, in June of 1779, after carefully soliciting the permission of its prickly constituents, the Massachusetts legislature called for the election of delegates to a convention "for the sole purpose of framing a new constitution." The draft constitution would be put before town meetings, where it would be "duly considered and approved or disapproved." The participants in the town meetings that chose convention delegates and decided whether to ratify the proposed constitution would not be limited by the usual property qualifications. The new government would therefore depend on the approval of an unusually broad electorate for the time.[45]

The state constitutional convention first met in Boston on September 1, 1779, adjourned while a committee prepared a draft constitution (John Adams did most of the writing), then reassembled between October 28 and November 12, and again in January 1780, to complete work on the document. In early March, the convention sent 1,800 copies of the proposed constitution back to the towns for their consideration "as soon as may be." This time, however, there would be no "up or down" vote. The convention instructed town meetings to discuss the document part by part and record "the Number of Votes . . . on each side of every Question." If a majority of townsmen rejected some part of the constitution, the report should "state their objections distinctly and the Reasons therefor." The convention was emphatic on the obligations of the people and the alternatives before them: "It is your *Interest* to revise [the draft constitution] with the greatest Care and Circumspection, and it is your un-doubted *Right*," it said, "either to propose such Alterations and Amendments as you shall judge proper, or, to give it your Sanction in its present Form, or, totally to reject it." In June the convention would reassemble and examine the returns. Unless the people had rejected the entire constitution, it would rewrite controversial parts so they would satisfy "two thirds of the Male Inhabitants of the Age of twenty one years and upwards, voting in the several Town and Plantation meetings," then declare the constitution ratified.[46]

A constitution created and ratified in the Massachusetts way was literally a direct act of legislation by the people, a fundamental law distinct from the ordinary laws passed by a legislature. The constitution's preamble declared that government was meant to secure the existence, tranquillity, and rights of the body-politic, which was "formed by a voluntary association of individuals," a "social compact, by which the whole people covenants with each citizen, and each citizen with the whole people, that all shall be governed by certain laws for the common good." The preamble concluded with a powerful enactment statement: "We . . . the people of Massachusetts," it said, ". . . do agree upon, ordain and establish, the following *Declaration of Rights, and Frame of Government*, AS THE CONSTITUTION of the COMMONWEALTH OF MASSACHUSETTS."[47] Later those words, with suitable adaptations, were copied into the federal Constitution. However, what the words implied with regard to the responsibilities of towns in 1787 and 1788 remained as open to debate in Massachusetts as in Connecticut.

In truth, ratification of the Massachusetts constitution of 1780 looked a lot better on paper than in reality. The returns the towns submitted were so different from one another, and they so often neglected to report critical information such as the vote on objectionable provisions, that calculating the extent of support for and against specific parts of the constitution proved almost impossible. In the end, the final session of the convention, which was poorly attended because of severe winter weather, tabulated the results in what might be called a creative way, then declared the entire document ratified—including a few provisions that probably received less than the required two-thirds popular vote.[48] Obviously, the ratification process used in Massachusetts was imperfect. It could have been fixed: A standardized return for recording town votes, for example, would have made it possible to determine more easily which parts of the constitution had won popular approval and which had not. A country that invented written constitutions could have invented standardized forms. Whether the independent townsmen of Massachusetts would have agreed to express their views by checking boxes and filling in blanks is another issue.

One thing, however, was absolutely clear: The townsmen of Massachusetts expected to be able to criticize parts of a constitution and to have their voices heard. They were the sovereign people. Nobody could tell them what they could and could not do.

THE TOWNS AND THE CONSTITUTION

Massachusetts townsmen had governed themselves through their town meetings for a century and a half. The Revolution expanded their expertise by consulting them on one issue after another whose significance went far beyond the local issues that were the town meetings' usual fare. In 1772, the Boston committee of correspondence asked their opinion on British policy and solicited their support in defending American liberty. In May of 1776, the lower house of assembly asked the inhabitants of towns whether they were prepared to support independence "with their lives and fortunes."[49] The next year the general court submitted the Articles of Confederation for the towns' consideration—and the towns identified several provisions that needed amendment.[50] In 1776, 1777, and again in 1779 the legislature asked the towns' permission to begin the process of establishing a new state constitution. After poring over the state constitutions proposed in 1778 and 1780, the adult men of Massachusetts had every reason to consider themselves experts on the subject of governance—as if, one unsympathetic historian put it, the framing of a constitution required "no higher order of intellect" than the "laying out of a county road, or . . . the formulation of rules for the pasturing of swine on the town common."[51]

Massachusetts townsmen also had a proven capacity to think in unconventional ways. In 1776, for example, the people of Ashfield in western Massachusetts said they wanted no "Goviner but the Goviner of the univarse, and under him a States Ginaral to Consult with the wrest of the united States for the Good of the whole," and they proposed a unicameral, annually elected legislature for Massachusetts whose acts with respect to towns would have to be accepted by the towns before going into effect. Two years later the townsmen of Boothbay in Maine (then still part of Massachusetts) suggested that at the war's conclusion "all distinction of Separate States" should be ended and the American union secured "by reducing the whole into one great Republick."[52] Those resolutions are especially significant since western Massachusetts and Maine were later described as centers of opposition to a strong national government. Clearly, not all the people there were die-hard localists. Some, at least, had a powerful sense of national identity.

Describing the towns of Massachusetts is one thing; explaining their peculiar traits is something else again. Perhaps the old Puritan disdain for letting priests and bishops tell believers what the Bible meant encouraged a more general free exercise of thought. The Baptists and other dissenting sects that grew spectacularly in mid-eighteenth-century Massachusetts no doubt reinforced that tendency. Or were the laying out of country roads and the regulation of swine as fine a practical preparation for understanding the subject of government as any other? Connecticut resembled Massachusetts in many ways, including its Puritan origins, but Connecticut never replaced its colonial charter, so its people had not discussed constitutions year after year, like their neighbors to the north. That probably made a big difference in how they responded to the federal Constitution.

Criticisms of the Constitution also circulated more freely in Massachusetts than in Connecticut. Boston's *American Herald* printed or reprinted a particularly large number of essays that found fault with the Constitution. That led so many Federalists to cancel their subscriptions that the publisher, Edward Powars, was forced out of business, though not until June 30, 1788, well after the Massachusetts convention had adjourned. Several other newspapers—including the *Independent Chronicle*, *Massachusetts Gazette*, and *Boston Gazette*—also printed essays critical of the Constitution. Moreover, readers responded with enthusiasm as commentaries on the Constitution began filling the newspapers in late October and November of 1787. In early November, one observer claimed that newspapers were "read more than the bible at this time," especially when they included information "about the [federal] Convention, and what people say about it."[53]

By 1787, for all these reasons, the people of Massachusetts were well prepared to give the federal Constitution a very hard look, and the state legislature gave them a full opportunity to do just that. On October 25 it called

on the towns and districts within the commonwealth "to convene as soon as
may be, the inhabitants of their several towns and districts, qualified by law
to vote in the election of Representatives, for the purpose of chusing Delegates to represent them" in a convention that would meet at the State House
in Boston on the second Wednesday in January for the purpose of "assenting
to and ratifying" the proposed federal Constitution. The state senate had
proposed that the convention meet on December 12, but the house put it
off until January 9 so the people would have sufficient time to examine the
Constitution carefully; the senate agreed.[54] There would be no rushing the
Constitution through, as in Pennsylvania.

Moreover, after William Widgery, a representative from New Gloucester,
Maine, suggested that the people simply vote on the Constitution in their
town meetings to save poor towns the cost of sending delegates to Boston,
the legislature agreed—on the motion of Federalist Nathaniel Gorham—to
pay delegates so "every town in the Commonwealth might be enabled to be
represented in the Convention."[55] That gave the Constitution a better shot at
being ratified: A convention would give educated and articulate Federalists
a chance to win over delegates from communities that, if left to themselves,
would vote the Constitution down.

The legislature also sent the towns a thirty-two-page pamphlet, printed
at public cost, that included its resolutions of October 25, copies of the Constitution, the other two documents adopted by the federal Convention in its
closing days (i.e., its letter to the president of Congress and its resolution on
ratification) and the September 28 resolution of the Confederation Congress
recommending that the states call ratifying conventions. The pamphlet was
printed in large type with descriptive subheadings, which helped readers
navigate their way through the documents. Express riders carried the pamphlets to sheriffs, who had responsibility under the legislature's orders for
distributing the pamphlets to the selectmen of towns within their counties.
Other copies went on sale to the public in early November. By the time
the convention met in January, the Constitution had been published repeatedly in Massachusetts—in five (and maybe six) pamphlets, a broadsheet,
an almanac, and at least eleven of the state's twelve newspapers. That was
dramatically different from Pennsylvania, where copies of the Constitution destined for the backcountry mysteriously disappeared.[56] The wide
distribution of materials also suggested that the towns were expected to do
something more than choose some trusted neighbors to speak for them in
the ratifying convention.

Since the selectmen were ordered to call town meetings to elect convention
delegates "as soon as may be," the elections did not all occur on the same day, as
they did in Pennsylvania and Connecticut. The first of almost three hundred
towns (246 in Massachusetts proper and another 52 in Maine) met on Novem-

ber 19, the last on January 7, only two days before the convention was scheduled to begin. That allowed some towns to influence the actions of others.

Because towns could send as many delegates to the convention as they sent representatives to the lower house of the legislature, the people of Massachusetts would be well represented in the ratifying convention. Under the 1780 constitution, incorporated towns were entitled to a representative if they had 150 ratable polls (tax-paying men over sixteen years of age), two if they had 375, three if they had 600, and an additional representative for every 225 ratable polls above that number.[57] (That helps explain why the provision that "the number of Representatives shall not exceed one for every thirty Thousand" in the federal Constitution could seem ridiculously inadequate.) All men aged twenty-one or older who had lived in the town at least a year and owned either "a freehold estate within the town of the annual income of three pounds, or any estate of the value of sixty pounds" could vote for representatives in the legislature and so also for convention delegates.[58]

Those qualifications were more restrictive than the ones used in ratifying the 1780 state constitution, but not unusual for the time. After all, they determined representation in the lower and more popular house of the state legislature. But the town of Dalton (Berkshire County), whose population was too small to qualify for a convention representative, questioned the rules' appropriateness for choosing convention delegates. Since "the forming themselves into Society and establishing a frame of Government is the common & equal Right of all Men," it said, "therefore the Idea of any other Qualification than a Competency of Understanding and common Sense in Order to be intitled to a Voice in that Business is absurd." Their exclusion from representation at the ratifying convention was "a manifest Infringement of our natural Rights as members of this Community." Then, for good measure, the good people of Dalton said that, since nobody could be bound by laws to which they had not given their consent, "the Town of Dalton . . . ought in reason and Justice to be exempted from the Burthens & Obligations of that Government the Rest of the Community may see fit to establish, without us, for themselves."[59]

Eleven towns elected more delegates than they had representatives, arguing that they were entitled to them because of growth since the last population count. A few others sent fewer than their population allowed or refused to send any delegate. The island of Nantucket, which had a large number of Quakers, apparently refused to participate in "the establishment of a Government which has a right to raise armies," so the five seats to which it was entitled went unfilled. Nonetheless, Massachusetts towns elected 370 delegates, of whom an extraordinary 364 attended the convention. That was about 100 more than the 266 members of the legislature elected in the spring of 1787, which was the largest legislature in a decade. Moreover, 99 more towns sent representatives to the convention than were represented in the

1786 legislature, an increase of some 52 percent. That dramatic rise in both overall size and town participation might have been due in part to the fact that the state would pay convention delegates, which was not the case for members of the legislature. It also suggested that the towns well understood the convention's importance.[60]

Towns met at the day and time mentioned in an official warrant issued by their selectmen. Only items included in the warrant could be taken up for discussion. Some town records tell more about their proceedings than others, but they suggest a common pattern of proceedings. When "legally warned and convened" for the purposes stated in the warrant, the towns chose a moderator and then sometimes read and discussed the Constitution. Those discussions could go on at great length. The towns of Adams (Berkshire County), Ipswich (Essex County), and Fryeburg (York County, Maine) debated the Constitution "Paragraft by Paragraft"; and the records for Ipswich add that the meeting agreed to pause after each paragraph so "Persons may have Oppertunity to Make such Observation thereon as they may think Proper." Next the towns generally voted on whether or not to send delegates to the ratifying convention and how many to send. Assuming they agreed to choose delegates, they cast ballots for candidates, each of whom needed a majority vote to be elected. Next, towns discussed whether or not to instruct their delegates. Instructions could tell delegates how to vote, or they might provide more general directions on what the town wanted its delegates to do at the convention. Unless a town immediately voted down that proposal, it usually appointed a committee to draft instructions, then adjourned to another time, sometimes several days later, when it would consider the committee's report.[61]

Some towns exercised their responsibilities with impressive rigor. Richmond (Berkshire County), for example, first met on December 7 and decided to hold no fewer than four meetings at different times and places "to consider of, and examine the Federal Constitution." Then the town meeting adjourned to December 17, when, after electing a convention delegate, it adjourned again. Finally, on December 24, the town met, rejected a motion that it read and discuss the Constitution (probably because it had already discussed it to death), and voted "That the Town think not proper to adopt the Constitution as it now stands."[62]

Was that resolution a statement of opinion or an instruction to its convention delegate to vote against the Constitution if it remained as written, without amendments? The record does not say; although towns frequently instructed their legislative representatives on matters of local interest, instructions to convention delegates were as open to question in Massachusetts as in Connecticut. The fate of the Constitution raised complex issues that affected far more than a town or group of towns. More important, if all the towns told their delegates how to vote, what was the point of the convention? There could be "no deliberation," a writer in Boston's *Massachusetts Centinel* argued, and the convention would serve "no valuable purpose"—though at substantial cost to taxpayers. The convention, another writer explained, would meet so that members could share information, hear all the arguments for and against the Constitution, and then decide "what is best." To determine the result beforehand would be like a court of justice deciding a case at law before hearing the arguments of the contenders' attorneys.[63]

And why would any man of intelligence agree to be no more than a mechanical echo of his constituents' position? When the town of Sandwich on Cape Cod (Barnstable County) voted to instruct the delegates it had already chosen to vote against ratification, one of the delegates resigned. "To place myself in a situation where conviction could be followed only by bigotted persistence in errour," he wrote his fellow townsmen, "would be extremely disagreeable to me. Under the restrictions with which your delegates are fettered, the greatest ideot might answer your purpose as well, as the greatest man."[64]

The campaign against instructions was a critical part of the Federalists' strategy for victory in Massachusetts. The ratifying conventions were for Federalists embodiments of the people, much as the British House of Commons claimed to embody the people of Britain. Representation of the people would be far fuller in the Massachusetts ratifying convention than it had ever been in the British Parliament, and Federalists thought that in general the state conventions would defend the people's interests better than the people could do themselves. Not only would the representatives be more intelligent and educated than the average citizen, but they would also have the benefit of hearing Federalist delegates explain and defend contested provisions of the Constitution. For that reason, the Constitution's supporters thought the conventions were more likely to vote for ratification than the towns acting separately and in relative isolation. For the conventions to function as the Federalists anticipated, however, delegates had to be open to persuasion, which is why Federalists roundly condemned town instructions to convention delegates—even instructions that told delegates to vote in favor of ratification.

But if town meetings could not decide whether or not the Constitution should be ratified, what, again, did it mean in saying—in words adapted from the Massachusetts constitution—that "We the People . . . do ordain and establish this Constitution for the United States of America"? And what was the point of reading and discussing the Constitution in town meetings, or of all those informational meetings in Richmond, if the only deliberations that made any difference would be in the convention? That issue had already been raised in Connecticut, but it provoked far more controversy in Massachusetts. There many more towns insisted on expressing their views and sometimes on formally instructing their convention delegates. They did so in ways that help explain why men like Benjamin Lincoln had such trouble predicting how the convention would vote.

THE TOWN RETURNS: AN EXERCISE IN SHADES OF GRAY

Surviving records indicate that the vast majority of Massachusetts towns did not instruct their delegates. That does not, however, mean that most towns favored the Constitution. Towns elected their delegates before deciding whether or not to instruct them, and if they chose delegates whose views coincided with those of most townsmen, there was little need to instruct them. Beverly (Essex County), for example, refused to elect Nathan Dane, a distinguished lawyer and recent congressman, because he opposed ratification of the Constitution as proposed by the Philadelphia Convention. Cambridge rejected Elbridge Gerry for the same reason. Neither town adopted instructions, which is unsurprising since they were Federalist. But Rehoboth (Bristol County) decided against adopting instructions after electing three delegates who opposed ratification. Probably the town saw no need to tell the delegates to do what it already knew they would do.[65]

Precisely what counted as instructions is also open for debate. The town of Ware (Hampshire County) explicitly said that its vote "not [to] approve of the Confedral Constitution" was to serve as instructions to its delegate. By contrast, on January 31, 1788, when the state ratifying convention was almost over, the town of Andover (Essex County) voted 124–115 against adoption of the Constitution "as it now stands," then defeated a proposal to instruct its convention delegates (who had been chosen almost two months earlier). Many towns, while declaring their views, failed, like Richmond, to say whether those views constituted specific instructions to their convention delegates.[66] How much difference would that make? If the delegates voted in a way that was at odds with the position their constituents adopted, they would have some explaining to do when they returned home, whether or not they had been formally instructed.

It was extremely rare, though not unknown, for a town to instruct its delegates to vote for the Constitution with no qualifications. The town of Machias in Lincoln County, Maine, debated the Constitution and then voted "that our said Representative give his Vote for Adopting the same." The towns of Sheffield and Mount Washington in Berkshire County voted 86–78 for adopting the Constitution, and Brunswick in Cumberland County, Maine, voted 23–7 to "accept . . . the proposed form of Government for the United States as it now Stands," but neither formally instructed its delegate to vote for ratification.[67]

The towns of Northampton and Easthampton, near the Connecticut River in Hampshire County, came up with another technique—one that would prove very influential—for supporting the Constitution while honoring the Federalist injunction against instructions. At a "legally warned & Assembled" meeting on November 22, 1787, the voters of those towns elected two convention delegates, then chose a committee "to prepare an Address"— not instructions—"to the Delegates Expressive of the Sentiments of the Town touching the Important business for which they were appointed." The committee, whose chairman was Samuel Henshaw, a committed Federalist, reported "soon after," which suggests the address had been prepared ahead of time, and its report, according to town records, was "Unanimously" approved by the town "(Excepting one Dissenting Vote)."[68]

The question before the town, the address began, "is of the highest magnitude in human affairs" and "too important, complicated and extensive, to be hastily decided upon." To investigate the Constitution thoroughly would require "much time and unwearied application"—more, it seems, than the towns were prepared to undertake. Instead, they told their delegates to listen patiently to the arguments presented in the ratifying convention before deciding how to vote. They should not be "unduly influenced by any local consideration," but understand "the necessity of having an equal, energetic, federal Government" and work for "the welfare and dignity of the union, as well as of Massachusetts." The townsmen said explicitly that they "mean not to give you positive instructions relative to your voting for or against the reported constitution," and expressed confidence in their delegates' capacity to form a "judicious opinion" based on the "collective wisdom of the state" as presented in the convention.[69]

The address was widely reprinted and influenced a number of other towns scattered through the state. Some, including Becket (Berkshire County) and Sherburne (Middlesex County), simply adopted the Northampton address or a close version of it as instructions to their convention delegates.[70] Two other towns adopted instructions that echoed Northampton's address in some respects, but with significant differences. Oakham (Worcester County) described the delegates' mission as being of "the greatest Importance that ever came before any Class of Men on this Earth." The Constitution appeared to be "fraught with many Inconveniences of the greatest Magnitude," although the townsmen did not "arrogate" to themselves "penetration sufficient to deside [sic] on a matter of so great Importance." Oakham instead told its delegate to consider carefully the arguments made for and against the Constitution in the ratifying convention. Then, "if convinc'd that it is well adapted to the Manners, dispositions, and Circumstances of a free People; you will give your Vote to Ratify the same;—but if not we trust you will reject it."[71]

Belchertown (Hampshire County) also mimicked Northampton, but only after what must have been a knockdown, drag-out fight. An early set of draft instructions came out powerfully against ratification of the Constitution unless it was first amended to fix several problems, which the draft instructions described in detail. The instructions the town finally adopted lifted some language from the Northampton address and "cheerfully" let the town's delegates decide how to vote on the Constitution. Unlike Northampton, however, Belchertown expressed fear that the Constitution posed a threat to "our Rights and Privalages" for reasons it explained in a passage more brief than clear: "1st. there is no bill of Right[s]. for other Reasons See artical 1 Section 2-3-4 and 8[,] artical 2d Section 1 & 2[,] artical 3d Section 1 and [Article] 6. With many other obvious Reasons."[72] Those instructions suggest that the townsmen knew the Constitution inside and out. The instructions also have all the marks of a compromise between townsmen who would have voted down the unamended Constitution and others who favored its ratification and successfully secured instructions that let the town's delegates decide how to vote.

Some towns followed the strategy of Northampton and Easthampton without adopting its language or suggesting that the people were unable to evaluate the Constitution. The town of Danvers (Essex County) "Voted not to give their Delagates any Instructions and left it with them, to assent to, and Ratify the same or otherways, as they think most Adviseable." Similarly, the town of Stoughton (Suffolk County) accepted the report of a committee appointed to draft instructions: "That it is our opinion after a mature & Deliberat consideration on the Subject that it be left descressinary with Said Delegates." Sunderland (Hampshire County) adopted a relatively long set of "instructions" that, like Northampton's address, stressed that delegates were elected to determine an issue "on which depends the existence of the United States" and, indeed, "the future happiness or misery of this new world," then essentially let the delegates decide how to vote. The Sutherland instructions also included a distinctly Federalist warning that rejecting the Constitution could lead to "Anarchy . . . with its concomitant horrors."[73]

On other occasions, towns expressed general approval of the Constitution—but not in a way calculated to warm Federalist hearts. Harpswell (Cumberland County, Maine), for example, voted "to Exsept [Accept] the federal Constitution with Amendment &c." Bristol (Lincoln County, Maine) also "Voted to Except the Constitution with ammendments" such as a town committee would propose. The instructions that Fryeburg (York County, Maine) issued to its delegate carefully stated the town's "disapprobation of some parts of the Constitution" but added "we would not wish that it should be entirely rejected, as we esteem it with proper amendments to be well calculated to promote the welfare of the Union." Bernardston and Leyden (northern Hampshire County, near Vermont) instructed their delegate "not totally, to reject the . . . Constitution, being of the opinion that by proper amendments, it may be adopted [adapted] to secure our liberties, and answer the Design of the general Union." They also told him to pay close attention to the objections to the Constitution made by Elbridge Gerry and the "Minority of the Assembly of Pensalvania, as lately published in the Springfield & Northampton papers."[74]

If, as Federalists insisted, the Constitution had to be ratified as written, with no prior amendments, a vote for ratification with "proper amendments" was essentially the same as that of Bellington (Suffolk County), whose voters decided "that they Cannot Except of the Proposd Constitution as it Now Stands."[75] Both votes implied a willingness—stronger in some towns than in others—to accept the Constitution if certain problems were fixed. In fact, at least ten towns passed resolutions or adopted formal instructions against ratification of the Constitution "as it now stands," which again suggested that with some changes the Constitution might be acceptable.

Another twenty to twenty-five towns either passed resolutions against ratification or formally instructed their delegates to vote against ratification without the modifying phrase "as it now stands." Sometimes those votes were clear and simple: Leverett (Hampshire County) "Voted we disapprove of ye. Federal Constitution"; Pownalborough (Lincoln County, Maine) "Voted unanamus not to accept of the plan for a new Constitution"; and Ludlow (Hampshire County) instructed its delegate "to use his influence that the proposed Constitution be intirely Rejected." Gardner (Worcester County) decided not to send a delegate to the convention, but five townsmen found it important nonetheless to record "that they Did not Like the perposed Constitution."[76]

One town clearly rejected the Constitution but suggested that it might have decided differently if amendments were possible. Paxton (Worcester County) condemned the Constitution as "Subversive of Liberty and Extreamly dangerous to the Civil and Religious rights of the People" and concluded that if it were ratified "all the Blessings we hold dear . . . to us as a People might be inevitably lost." And yet some clauses in the Constitution "abstractly Considered appear Plausible." However, since delegates were appointed "for the Sole purpose of acting on One Single Question, Viz. a Ratification or Rejection of the whole, we deem it our Indispensible duty to give you the following Presemptory [peremptory] Instructions . . . that you give your vote in the negative."[77] Would Paxton's renunciation have been less emphatic if it had been given the opportunity, as with the state constitution of 1780, to vote on the Constitution part by part, and so to identify those provisions that needed to be eliminated or modified while leaving the "plausible" parts in place?

———

It was by no means easy to draw conclusions about the Constitution's chances of ratification on the basis of what the towns did. For one thing, assembling a comprehensive list of town returns was all but impossible: No newspapers systematically collected and analyzed voting returns, as they do today. The Constitution's supporters in Boston had contacts in other parts of the state, but the information they received from the press or from private correspondents was haphazard at best. Even now, when surviving records of town proceedings on the Constitution have been collected and printed, attempts to categorize town responses to the Constitution are exercises in frustration: One is just a little different from another, so the categories tend to multiply, and how to classify some returns is anything but obvious. To add to the confusion, at least fifteen towns voted to instruct their delegates but left no record of what those instructions said. And many towns left no records whatsoever on their deliberations.

It is, however, clear from the surviving returns that a substantial number of towns were not simply for or against the Constitution. The towns specialized in shades of gray: There were critical but subtle differences between votes to reject the Constitution, to reject it because no amendments were possible, to reject it "as it now stands," to accept it because with a few amendments it would be just fine, and to accept it without qualifications. Several towns saw serious problems in the Constitution while expressing no fundamental objection if those defects were repaired. Only one town—Harvard, in Worcester County—said, like Luther Martin, that amendments to strengthen the Articles of Confederation would be better than the wholesale transformation of national government that the "proposed Constitution" would bring.[78] Few towns, however, listed the flaws that needed fixing, perhaps because by late 1787 the problems were, as Belchertown said, "obvious."

When towns did state their objections, the same provisions came up over and over. Towns mentioned the inadequacy of representation in the House of Representatives. They criticized the six-year term of senators and sometimes also the four-year terms of the president and vice president, which seemed excessively long in Massachusetts, where the governor and all members of the legislature were elected annually. They thought Congress's power to overrule the states on "the time and manner of holding elections for Senators and Representatives" was dangerous, and they also saw a problem with Congress's "having unlimited power of laying and collecting taxes, duties, imposts and excises." The towns questioned provisions that allowed "matters of the greatest Importanc" to be decided by the president and two-thirds of the Senate—the ratification of treaties, which became the supreme law of the land—with no participation by the House of Representatives, which would reflect the people's will most directly. One town added that "the Ligislative power is blended with the Executive, the Presidant being vested with both & having no other Council than the Senate." The towns also feared that the new federal judiciary would "greatly . . . distress the subjects, and leave their property insecure." Debtors could, for example, move across state lines to force creditors to bring cases for the recovery of even small debts in federal courts, which would often not be worth the cost. (The concern with property rights brings into question the notion that critics of the Constitution were mostly desperate debtors.) Townsmen worried about the provision in Article VI that said the Constitution, the laws of the United States made under its authority, and all treaties would be "the supreme Law of the Land . . . any Thing in the Constitution or Laws of any State to the Contrary notwithstanding," and in general they feared "that the proposed Constitution will, if adopted, effectually destroy the sovereignty of the States, and establish a National Government" that would soon become despotic. Fryeburg found it "highly absurd to propose an Oath or Affirmation to the Officers of Government, of whom no religious test is required."[79]

The towns said the Constitution should include a bill of rights and—what might seem paradoxical—also wanted religious qualifications for federal office. Townshend (Middlesex County) thought "Atheists Deists Papists or abettors of any false religion" should be kept out of office, although it "would not Exclude any Denomination of Protestants who hold the fundamentals of our religion." Above all, it seemed important to keep Catholics from exercising power since, as Belchertown explained (in draft instructions later discarded), "it has Ever been the Principale and Practice of the Papists to Persicute those of the Protestant Religion." That argument was somewhat more common in New England than in other states, although everywhere anti-Catholicism had deep roots among American Protestants who remembered the persecution of French Protestants after the revocation of the Edict of Nantes (1685) or the 1731 expulsion of Protestants from Salzburg (now part of Austria). For them, freedom of religion demanded freedom from Catholic domination. A bill of rights might solve the problem: Townshend suggested that, if religious tests for office proved impossible to enact, a bill of rights could secure the people's rights, "especially our religion." The Constitution's lack of "a clear declaration of the Rights of the people, or of the Powers of the Several State governments" was, it said, of "unspeakable importance." Issues of such significance had to be settled before the Constitution was ratified and put into effect.

————

Despite the obstacles to getting full and accurate information, Federalists tried to assess the politics of convention delegates. It didn't help that many convention delegates had not previously served in the state legislature: These men were literally unknown quantities to observers familiar with state politics. Still, Christopher Gore, a Boston lawyer, ardent Federalist, and a member of Boston's delegation to the ratifying convention, kept a list of delegates who were known to oppose the Constitution. Nathaniel Gorham, a merchant from Charlestown who had represented Massachusetts at the Philadelphia Convention and was now working hard for ratification, reported that elections in the eastern part of the state "have generally been favourable" to ratification, "but a black cloud will come down from the three Western Counties"—Berkshire, Hampshire, and Worcester, where Henry Knox had also seen much to fear. Gore added that "the Eastern delegates"—that is, those from Maine—were said to be generally against ratification for fear that the Constitution would impede their efforts to separate from Massachusetts and become an independent state.[80]

In fact, towns scattered throughout the state, not just the three western counties or the eastern counties of Maine, found fault with the unamended Constitution. Whether they controlled a majority of delegates was anyone's guess—and the mystery continued, as Benjamin Lincoln told Washington, even after the convention had begun. In the face of such widespread discomfort with the Constitution as written, could the Federalists maintain what Washington called "firmness"?

"We the people of Massachusetts" had made their state a testing ground for "take this or nothing."

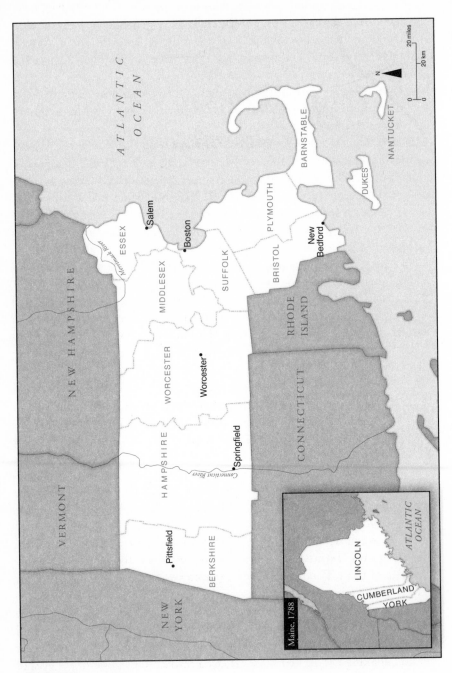

ATLANTIC
OCEAN

BARNSTABLE

NANTUCKET

DUKES

PLYMOUTH

ESSEX

Salem

Boston

SUFFOLK

BRISTOL

New
Bedford

Merrimack River

MIDDLESEX

RHODE
ISLAND

NEW HAMPSHIRE

WORCESTER

Worcester

HAMPSHIRE

CONNECTICUT

Springfield

Connecticut River

VERMONT

BERKSHIRE

Pittsfield

NEW
YORK

N

20 miles

20 km

0

0

Maine, 1788

LINCOLN

ATLANTIC
OCEAN

CUMBERLAND

YORK

Massachusetts, 1788

———— ★ ————

The Massachusetts Ratifying Convention I

The "Conversation" Begins

The excitement began building when Governor John Hancock delivered the Constitution to a joint session of the Massachusetts legislature on October 18, 1787. Six days later, when the house of representatives debated a committee report calling for the election of delegates to a state ratifying convention, crowds of people filled the galleries and spilled over onto the floor of the House.[1] Once the legislature agreed that the convention would meet on January 9 at the State House in Boston, essays on the Constitution began filling the pages of Massachusetts newspapers. Even in a remote town in Maine, according to one report, people pored over items on the proposed federal Constitution in the local *Cumberland Gazette* "with the greatest avidity." Never before was "a more interesting subject committed to the consideration of any people or nation; and never were the sons of *America* more loudly called upon to attend to the things which concern their present, and future happiness, than at this day."[2]

The Massachusetts ratifying convention was the first to meet in a state where there was significant opposition to the Constitution. If Massachusetts refused to ratify, other states—particularly New Hampshire and New York—would probably follow her example. That would all but seal the Constitution's fate since Rhode Island and now perhaps also Virginia were likely to vote "no." If, however, Massachusetts ratified, the Constitution would be well on its way toward enactment. Would that serve the country's best interests, making the United States at last a respectable nation in the eyes of the world, as Washington hoped, or would it threaten the freedom for which Americans had fought off British rule? Would ratification fulfill the Revolution or betray it?

"Little else, among us, is thought of or talked of, but the new Constitution," a correspondent in Weston, west of Boston, wrote a few days after the convention opened. A few weeks later a merchant in Maine reported that politics seemed "to engross the attention of all classes of people." That included women, whose "sphere" normally excluded politics. In a letter to George Thatcher, Silas Lee, a young law student who confessed to having doubts about the Constitution, described a friendly argument at Thatcher's home in Biddeford, Maine. (At the time, Thatcher was in New York, representing Massachusetts in Congress.) Rufus King's sister Betsy had come to visit, and she was, like her brother, "a stanch *Federalist*—and quite a politician." The dispute went on for two hours and pulled in "Mamma and Tempy"—Thatcher's niece, Temperance Hedge, whom Lee would later marry. Betsy said she "pitied me," Lee reported, "& I believe she even thought me *guilty of a crime*." Her "warmth was natural" and her "words emphatical": " 'Are you an antifederalist she began'—I laughed—'yes you are'—and [she] reasoned against me most beautifully—it was fun indeed."[3]

What was fun in Biddeford caused intense anxiety in Boston as January 9 drew near because nobody could predict with any confidence how the delegates would divide. Even Nathaniel Gorham, the onetime delegate to the federal Convention who was helping orchestrate the campaign for ratification in Massachusetts, acknowledged that "the elections have gone wrong in several places that were consider[ed] as sure" and predicted that the convention would be "tight work." Christopher Gore, a Boston Federalist who carefully kept a list of delegates, noted in late December that "many of those known to be elected, are in opposition." But just how many? One observer after another expressed an opinion, but on the day the convention met, even Gore, who was as much an expert on the subject as anyone, confessed that "I really cannot yet form any judgment of the weight of members, or which side the pros or cons will preponderate." Four days later Benjamin Lincoln wrote Washington that "I am now as much at a loss to know what will be its [the Constitution's] fate as I was the first day we met."[4]

If the Federalist election watchers had a reasonably full set of town returns—which they did not—they would have been even more bewildered. In which category, the pros or the cons, would they put a town that said it had reservations about the Constitution but let its delegates decide how to vote? Or one that voted to instruct its delegates but did not say how? And was it really necessary to place delegates whose towns told them to vote against the Constitution "as it now stands" in the cons category? Might they vote "yes" under some circumstances? In the end, the convention would have to decide whether or not to ratify the Constitution, but neither the state nor the delegates divided neatly into two categories in early January.

Nor did divisions over the Constitution follow older party lines, as in

Pennsylvania. Massachusetts politics consisted more of shifting factions than settled alignments, and what alignments existed between the supporters of ex-governor James Bowdoin and those of Governor John Hancock did not automatically translate into differences on ratification. Local writers who defended the Constitution were pretty much the only ones who used the term "antifederalist" for those who criticized it, and nobody was organizing a movement under that banner. Whether in a newspaper essay or the mouth of Betsy King, "antifederalist" was a term of opprobrium. "The proper definition of the word anti-federalism," according to a piece in the *Massachusetts Gazette*, "is anarchy, confusion, rebellion, treason, sacrilege, and rapine." Antifederalism was associated with falsehood and ignorance; "anti-federalists" were of a kind with "anti-patriots, and anti-creditors." They were, if the newspapers could be believed, bad credit risks.[5] Who would accept a label like that? "Every man who dares exercise his own judgment, is branded as an antifederalist," wrote "Candidus" in Boston's *Independent Chronicle*. "This ungenerous method of condemning characters" was inappropriate in a society that valued freedom of debate. The term was one of reproach, a stigma, that contenders were anxious to shake off.[6]

There was, in fact, good reason to question whether it made sense to group together in a single category people so different as Elbridge Gerry, who thought the Constitution should be ratified once a few problems were fixed, and the Boston newspaper writer "Agrippa," who argued for a total rejection of the Constitution and proposed strengthening the Confederation in ways that would not give Congress an exclusive right to levy duties on imports, much less let it raise direct taxes.[7] In effect, Massachusetts was divided into partisans who could overlook differences among themselves in a desperate effort to get the Constitution ratified as written and a mass of others that included rigid opponents of ratification, contenders who thought the Constitution could be fixed but insisted that critical amendments be enacted before it was ratified, and others who either had doubts about the Constitution but needed more information and time for reflection before making up their minds on ratification—or who just chose to remain silent until the dust settled a bit more. How the state—or, more important, the ratifying convention delegates—divided along that spectrum of opinion was the issue, and nobody knew for sure.

Neither Gerry nor "Agrippa"—probably James Winthrop, an ex-Harvard librarian—would, in any case, be delegates to the convention, since the town of Cambridge, where both lived, did not put them on its delegation.[8] With these two excluded, Federalists could calculate that all but a handful of the "better people" among the delegates—the educated men of ability and often wealth who could speak with practiced eloquence—were on their side. Outtalking their opponents on the convention floor would, however, not be enough; the Federalists would also need to work behind the scenes to win allies, and to manage the convention in ways that avoided giving any advantage to those who wanted to reject the Constitution or had profound doubts about it. They faced a far greater challenge than their counterparts in Pennsylvania, who had a solid majority from the start of their convention. Massachusetts was a whole new game.

To make matters worse, supporters of the Constitution in Massachusetts had come to understand, like George Washington, that victory required more than a majority vote on ratification. For a democratic government like ours "to be administered with benefit to the citizens," Gore said, "it is necessary the constitution shou[l]d be adopted with cordiality by the people—and this may be done."⁹ The question was how. How could the Constitution's advocates undercut the suspicions and hostility that so many towns expressed and persuade the people to welcome ratification "with cordiality"—or even to accept the Constitution peacefully? How, in short, could they go from so doubtful a beginning to a better outcome than that in Pennsylvania?

A COLD AND CROWDED START

It was no easy thing to get from Bath, an old shipbuilding center on the Kennebec River in Maine, to Boston in January of 1788. Dummer Sewall, a local farmer and the owner of a lumber mill, had the honor of being elected as a delegate to the Massachusetts ratifying convention and so the trouble of making that journey. He and Nathaniel Wyman, a delegate from nearby Georgetown, set out on horseback at eleven o'clock on the third morning of the month. There had been a heavy snow the day before, which made the "traviling heavy." At eight that night, Sewell noted in his journal, he and Wyman stopped at the "Widow Mitchels" in North Yarmouth, Maine, not far from Bath. They set out again at sunrise, when it was "very cold." Gradually they made their way down through Maine, stopping at inns or staying with relatives, and on an "exceeding cold" Sunday, January 6, the two men stopped to attend religious services in the town of York. Dummer also visited his four brothers who lived in York and "found them well."¹⁰

The next day, Sewall and Wyman took a ferry across the Piscataqua River to Portsmouth, New Hampshire, then rode "in pleasant Sun shine" to another ferry that carried them across the Merrimac River to Newburyport, Massachusetts. That night they stayed at Rowley, then "mounted early" the next morning, had breakfast at Ipswich, where it began to snow, and pushed on to Danvers, the onetime center of the Salem witchcraft crisis, where the snow turned to rain and the wind increased until it became a "very velolent" gale. About noon they stopped, "very wet," at an inn in Lynn, where by nightfall some twenty-five delegates had arrived and were all "Lodged comfortably." On the morning of January 9, Sewall and Wyman rose before dawn, had "brakfast by candel light," rode seven miles through new snow to a "Mr. Prats," where they arranged to have their horses boarded for the duration of the convention, and then made their way into Boston. There they took rooms at "Capt. Daggat's" (or Daggett's), a boardinghouse where several delegates, including three others from Maine, also stayed. The trip, which the convention's paymaster put at 170 miles for Sewall and 180 for Wyman, had taken them six days.[11]

The convention had already begun by the time Sewall arrived at the Massachusetts State House; it had a quorum right away on the morning of Wednesday, January 9, and so did not need to wait for stragglers. The delegates chose a temporary moderator, appointed a committee to examine the delegates' credentials, and elected its secretary, George Richards Minot, a Boston lawyer who also served as clerk of the state house of representatives, in whose chamber they were meeting. After a midday adjournment, the convention reassembled at four in the afternoon and chose Governor John Hancock as its president.[12]

That decision was carefully calculated. Hancock was popular: Without so much as leaving his home (where he was mourning the death of his nine-year-old son and only surviving child after a skating accident), he had defeated the incumbent, James Bowdoin, in the spring elections. Once in office, he helped heal the state's divisions by pardoning (with the permission of his executive council) participants in Shays's Rebellion who had not been pardoned late in the Bowdoin administration and by persuading the legislature to relieve the economic distress that lay behind the unrest. Hancock also reduced the cost of government, as the insurgents had demanded, and traveled across the state to reach out to farmers. Conservatives condemned Hancock's moderation, but it did not seriously undercut his appeal in mercantile Boston, which elected him one of its twelve delegates to the state ratifying convention with more votes than any other candidate except ex-governor Bowdoin.[13]

Hancock's views on the Constitution remained unknown. When he presented the Constitution to the general court, he avoided making any comments one way or the other. It was not within the duties of his office, he said, to "decide upon this momentous affair."[14] At the time of his election as president of the convention, however, Hancock was bedridden with a crippling case of gout and so could not attend its sessions (though Rufus King, who visited Hancock several times, thought his health would improve "as soon as a majority shews itself on either side of the convention"). In Hancock's absence, the vice president, William Cushing, a delegate from the town of Scituate and chief justice of the state's supreme judicial court, who had publicly endorsed the Constitution, would preside over the convention.[15]

Delegates from the state's central and western counties readily approved the choice of Hancock as president, and that perhaps reconciled them to giving the lesser job—but one that would, in fact, give the partisans of ratification considerable control over the convention's proceedings—to Cushing. If Hancock attended and threw his support behind ratification, he would attract many votes. From a Federalist perspective, however, the appointment was not without risk since, as King later wrote Madison, Hancock's character was "not entirely free from a portion of caprice."[16]

Other appointments early in the convention also gave signs of an effort to accommodate known opponents of ratifying the Constitution without amendments. The committee "to receive the returns of the towns"—essentially to decide on contested elections—included Dr. John Taylor from the town of Douglass, in the southern part of Worcester County, a center of Shays's Rebellion. A man who had been imprisoned for debt in 1784 (and who would die in debtors' prison a decade later), Taylor was no doubt one of the penniless no-goods whom the Constitution's supporters saw as typical "antifederalists." He and several other members of that committee were later replaced, but Taylor also served on the committee to prepare the convention's rules, along with William Widgery from New Gloucester in Maine, another critic of the Constitution from an area Federalists regularly described as a center of opposition to the Constitution. (Taylor, in fact, had connections with two regions supposedly hostile to the Constitution: He came from Shays country and had also lived in Maine during the late 1770s and no doubt still had ties there.) The five "monitors" appointed at the convention's first session to enforce the convention's rules and help count votes included Phanuel Bishop of Rehoboth in southeastern Massachusetts, a notorious critic of the Constitution who had sympathized with Shays's Rebellion; and Daniel Cooley from Amherst in Hampshire County, which had instructed Cooley to vote against ratification.[17]

It was not hard to explain why many people in the three western counties of Berkshire, Hampshire, and Worcester, which had been the center of Shays's Rebellion, were against the Constitution. Dissidents there criticized the Massachusetts constitution of 1780 for giving too much power to the wealthy, mercantile east. The proposed federal Constitution looked like more of the same. Farmers there had been pushed to desperation by the real prospect of foreclosure and prison because of debts swollen by deflation and high state taxes that had to be paid in hard money. They might well be leery of giving Congress broad taxing power or preventing the states from coining money, emitting bills of credit, making anything but gold and silver coin legal tender for the payment of debts, or interfering with the obligation of contracts. When they stated their objections to the Constitution, however, they mentioned Congress's taxing power but not the explicit restrictions on the states in Article I, Section 10.

The western part of Massachusetts did not speak with one voice. Many people there had opposed and even taken up arms against Shays's Rebellion. A correspondent in Worcester assured George Thatcher that "a considerable powerfull minority" there favored the Constitution, and the county's delegates included "good men—Not all insurgents I assure you." In the far western town of Pittsfield, Henry Van Schaack, a wealthy forty-four-year-old fur trader and onetime Loyalist from Kinderhook, New York, fought doggedly for ratification. Acceptance of "the new System," he argued, was "the only means to secure political quiet." Van Schaack exchanged information with other Federalists, including Theodore Sedgwick, a convention delegate from Stockbridge (Berkshire County), and Samuel Henshaw in Northampton (Hampshire County).[18]

Maine was more of a puzzle but no less of a problem. Supporters of the Constitution attributed opposition to the Constitution there to fears that it would make independent statehood more difficult to achieve. Article IV, Section 3, of the Constitution said Congress could admit new states into the union but that no state could be formed from a part of an existing state "without the Consent of the Legislatures of the States concerned as well as of the Congress." That at least established a process for admitting new states carved from old ones. The Articles of Confederation specified only that no "colony" other than Canada could be admitted to the union without the consent of nine states (Article XI). Perhaps the additional requirement that a "parent" state must give its consent caused discomfort. But neither the records of Maine towns nor surviving letters from people in Maine who had doubts about the Constitution mention that issue. In fact, the Maine town records are, like many others, frustratingly silent on what exactly prompted a town such as Topsham in Lincoln County to vote unanimously against accepting the Constitution after some seven hours of discussion. When Fryeburg (York County) listed its "most material objections" to the Constitution, it said nothing about Maine's prospects for separate statehood but mentioned the powers of Congress, senators' terms of office, ratification of treaties by the Senate but not the House, and the requirement of oaths by officials who were subject to no religious qualifications for office. Those complaints were much like those from other parts of Massachusetts.[19]

Whatever its reasons for doubting the wisdom of ratification, Maine was critical to the Constitution's chances. Henry Knox told Washington that "the Insurgents" in Massachusetts and their supporters represented two-sevenths of the state, Maine dissidents another two-sevenths. If so, the remaining three-sevenths, which consisted of "the Commercial part" of the state, men of property, judges, lawyers, clergymen, ex-army officers, and those in "the neighbourhood of all the great Towns" who supported ratification, desperately needed allies. And Maine's delegates seemed far more likely candidates than the resolute opponents of the Constitution from western Massachusetts.[20]

The job of recruiting Maine votes fell primarily to Rufus King, who was born in Scarborough, Maine, in 1755, and remained there until, at age twelve, he left for Dummer Academy, near the town of Newburyport in northeastern Massachusetts. After graduating from Harvard (Class of 1777), King moved to Newburyport. He was admitted to the bar in 1780 and a few years later won a seat in the state house of representatives, where his talents were quickly recognized. In 1784, the legislature chose him to represent Massachusetts in Congress and then, in 1787, at the federal Convention. Apparently his two decades living elsewhere did not seriously reduce his credentials as a man from Maine: When King returned to Massachusetts in October 1787 and worked with Gorham to persuade legislators that the Constitution was a good thing, he concentrated on those from Maine. "I am laboring in my way," he wrote Henry Knox on October 28; "last evening I spent in preaching on the Report of the Convention to the Representatives of Main[e]." They had "received some ill impressions," he said, but "I hope and believe that I removed some Difficulties."[21]

King returned briefly to Newburyport before going back to New York and his congressional duties. He had spent so much time away from Newburyport that his residency was open to question; nonetheless, the town elected him as one of its three delegates to the state ratifying convention. As the convention's opening approached and anxiety over its political complexion increased, Gorham and several other prominent Federalists urged King to return to Massachusetts. The opposition to the Constitution from the western counties would be "numerous & violent," requiring "the utmost candor & prudence" to control—but Gorham noted that "some of our friends are not good steersmen." Moreover, "most of our Eastern Members [those from Maine] are wrong," Gorham added, and "nobody can deal with them so well as you."[22]

But King stayed in New York. Like Gerry, he had married a New York woman: His wife, Mary Alsop, was the daughter of a leading Manhattan merchant. That was a risk for a state that sent some of its most eligible bachelors to Congress. Marblehead lost Gerry because of his New York wife, and now Massachusetts seemed to be losing King for the same reason. A year later he would, in fact, change his residency to New York—and resume his political career there, almost without missing a beat. For now, however, King had good reason for remaining away. His wife gave birth to their first child, a son, on the third of January. Nine days later King took his seat at the convention in Boston.[23]

And four days after that he spent the evening at Daggett's boardinghouse with three other Federalist delegates. They were paying a visit to the delegates from Maine who stayed there—Sewall and Wyman, who had traveled down the coast together; Isaac Snow from Harpswell; John Dunlap from

Brunswick; and Nathaniel Low from Berwick. The conversation, Sewall noted, was "free & open."[24]

Daggett's was also a convenient place to work on winning over another group suspected of opposing the Constitution, the Baptists, because the Reverend Isaac Backus, a prominent Baptist and a convention delegate from Middleborough in southeastern Massachusetts (Plymouth County), lodged there. In the hope that he would influence his fellow Baptists, supporters of the Constitution successfully backed the election of the Reverend Samuel Stillman, a "high Federal Man," as a Boston delegate. Stillman played his appointed role faithfully. In his journal for January 16, Sewall, who attended Baptist and Congregational religious services almost at random, noted that "Dear Mr. Stilman has paid us"—and "us," no doubt, included Backus—"2 Visits."[25]

The commercial towns along the Atlantic coast at least seemed "safe" from the perspective of those working to get the Constitution ratified in Massachusetts. Even there, however, some delegates gave reason for concern. Hancock was one, Samuel Adams another, and Adams was more of a problem than Hancock. A stocky man of medium height, Adams was in his mid-sixties in 1788, which made him a generation older than energetic young Federalists such as King and Gore, who were in their early thirties. His disregard for wealth and personal prestige, his affection for the traditions of the Puritans, whom he saw as opponents of tyranny in both church and state, even the tricornered hat he continued to wear marked Adams as a man of another era. He remained, however, a formidable figure in Massachusetts politics. He was president of the state senate; and his leadership of the resistance to Britain before 1776 gave him a powerful hold on the respect and loyalty of his Boston constituents and others throughout the commonwealth.[26]

His intense involvement in the independence movement also made Adams instinctively suspicious of any strong central government that might threaten his beloved Massachusetts and the liberties he had defended against Crown and Parliament. As early as February 1787, when the Massachusetts legislature appointed delegates to the Philadelphia Convention and drafted their instructions, Adams was "full of doubts & dif[f]iculties" and wanted to limit the delegates' powers in ways that Nathaniel Gorham thought would "exceedingly injure the business."[27] Eight months later, in early October, Adams was one of the first people to whom Richard Henry Lee sent a copy of the amendments to the Constitution he had proposed in Congress. Lee assumed, correctly, that an old colleague in the struggle with Britain would share his reservations. Adams began his reply with a devastating comment on the preamble to the Constitution: "I confess," he said, "as I enter the Building I stumble at the Threshold. I meet with a National Government, instead of a federal Union of Sovereign States."[28]

How openly Adams expressed his views in Boston remains a question. Clearly his doubts did not prevent his election as a Boston delegate to the ratifying convention. In the weeks before the town voted, contenders published no fewer than fourteen tickets of candidates; Adams was on ten of them. And on December 7, when the "Freeholders & Other Inhabitants of the Town Boston duly qualefied and legally warned" gathered in Faneuil Hall to cast their ballots, Adams won the ninth of twelve places on the delegation. Gore (the last Boston delegate chosen) said those who favored the Constitution feared the consequences of opposing him. If defeated, Adams might in "mortification" openly declare himself against ratification "and endeavor to make proselytes." If, however, he was elected by townsmen who assumed that he supported ratification, that might "damp his opposition." Adams's arguments against the Constitution could also be opposed more easily on the floor of the convention than if he remained outside, "suggesting objections to small circles of delegates."[29]

A month later, at a dinner for delegates held by James Bowdoin in his home only six days before the convention met, Adams came out "full mouthed against the Constitution." No single government could govern the United States, he said; Congress should not be able to levy "internal taxes," and the proposed representation of the people was inadequate. The Constitution should not be adopted except with amendments that Gore thought would "totally destroy it." Adams, Gore reported, supported his position with arguments "such as only . . . appear in the pieces of Brutus & [the] federal farmer." Federalists also suspected that Adams was distributing the published letters of the "Federal Farmer" in Massachusetts and writing a series of newspaper essays critical of the Constitution signed "Helvidius Priscus." His election had done nothing to dampen his opposition. In fact, rumors that Boston tradesmen opposed the Constitution might have encouraged it.[30]

Something had to be done to quiet Adams or make him change course. On January 7, some 380 Boston tradesmen met at the Green Dragon tavern and "UNANIMOUSLY" approved five resolutions that endorsed the Constitution in no uncertain terms. They said that only those Boston delegates who "would exert their utmost ability to promote the adoption of the proposed frame of government in all its parts, without any conditions, pretended amendments, or alterations whatever . . . will truly represent the feelings, wishes, and desires of their constituents." The resolutions were aimed at Adams and other delegates, including Hancock, whose stand on the Constitution remained unsettled.[31]

No doubt Adams took the resolutions seriously: Nobody respected the wisdom of the people more than Samuel Adams, and nobody was more aware, as Gore put it, that he was more dependent on the people than they were on him. The tradesmen's resolutions might well have successfully tempered his opposition, because he was anything but a "full mouthed" opponent of the Constitution during the convention. On its opening day Adams moved "that the Convention will attend morning prayers daily," and "that the Gentlemen of the clergy in Boston of every denomination be requested to officiate in turn." The motion passed with none of the altercation a similar proposal sparked in the Pennsylvania convention. Three days later he seconded a motion by Maine's William Widgery, a known critic of the Constitution, that Elbridge Gerry be invited to attend the convention. The motion failed when "a Majority appeared against it." Adams also asked that the Constitution be read aloud before the convention decided how to structure its debates, served on committees, and occasionally asked questions or made other brief interventions in the debates.[32] Otherwise, until near the convention's end, he remained silent.

Instead of speaking, he listened carefully to the debates. Having said that he was "open to conviction" on the Constitution, Adams joined a substantial group of delegates who were determined "to hear all that can be said on both sides and then vote as they shall think right."[33] Perhaps, too, his silence came from a deep sadness over the state of his thirty-seven-year-old only son and namesake, a Boston physician who died on January 17 at the family's home on Winter Street; at his invitation, members of the convention attended the funeral. When, a few days later, General Benjamin Lincoln also buried a beloved son, the convention decided against adjourning so members could attend the funeral: Its debates had reached a juncture that required keeping delegates in their seats.[34] Births and deaths nonetheless weighed on the minds and hearts of several delegates and silently left their marks on the convention.

Before turning to the Constitution, the convention had to adopt its rules of proceeding. It also had to resolve contested elections and decide what to do about a number of towns that sent more delegates than their population seemed to merit. Committees could sort through the returns, identify problems, and collect evidence on specific controversies, but the convention reserved the final decisions to itself. In the end, it allowed all sitting members to remain, which Boston's *American Herald* celebrated, along with the convention's "liberal attention" to "the great privilege of representation. . . . The body now convened," it said, "is perhaps one of the compleatest representations of the interests and sentiments of their constituents, that ever were assembled. No liberal or mechanic profession, no denomination in religion, or party in politicks" within the state was excluded. Perhaps, then, a people so fully represented at the convention would "heartily acquiesce" in its final decision on the "important subject" before it.[35]

With 364 delegates attending some or all of its sessions, the Massachusetts ratifying convention was larger than that of any other state and over five times larger than the Pennsylvania ratifying convention. It was also record-setting for Massachusetts: Theophilus Parsons (from Newburyport, in Essex County) reported that it was "by far the most numerous representation this State ever saw."[36] Just finding a space big enough for the convention was a problem. The house of representatives chamber in the State House could accommodate the delegates, but not the crowds of people who wanted to see and hear the debates. A meeting called to decide whether "We the People" would ordain and ratify the Constitution could hardly meet, like the federal Convention that wrote the document, in secret.

The ratifying convention did all it could to make its deliberations available to the people. It agreed, for example, to provide reporters from the *Massachusetts Centinel* and the *Independent Chronicle* with seats within the convention hall so they could take notes on the debates. Other newspapers in Massachusetts and a stunning fifty-one in other states reprinted accounts of the debates, sometimes almost in their entirety, for readers who understood that the Constitution's future might well be decided in Massachusetts. No other state convention received equivalent coverage. The convention also made its official journal available to any printer who requested it.[37] But what about the people who insisted on witnessing the event with their own eyes and ears?

The convention quickly accepted an invitation from the fashionable Brattle Street Church and moved there on its second day. That church was large, with galleries (or balconies) for spectators and, unlike any other church in Boston, stoves for heat. But its acoustics turned out to be terrible for a large meeting; many delegates complained that they could not hear the speakers. As a result, on Saturday, January 12, delegates and listeners crowded back into the State House, where the air was "exceedingly Noxious & disagreeable" because of the "immense Number of People" in the galleries. Some spectators scrambled into empty seats on the floor of the house to hear better. That caused confusion, so the convention voted to "exclude from the floor of the House all persons not belonging to the Convention, except such as are admitted by special order." Finally, it found a more suitable meeting place at the Congregational church on Long Lane, where the Reverend Jeremy Belknap, another Boston delegate to the convention and an avid historian, was pastor. Some "Gentlemen of the Town" volunteered to add a stove and a temporary stairway from an exterior porch to the galleries, which kept spectators from going onto the main floor; the galleries could hold as many as six to eight hundred persons. The convention moved there on the afternoon of January 17 and stayed until its deliberations had ended.[38]

Even with the additional space, however, the galleries quickly filled to capacity. By January 20, spectators had to arrive an hour before the convention began to get a seat. Most members of the audience came from Boston, but visitors from nearby states also climbed into the galleries.[39] They came to witness the convention's awesome displays of oratory and because so much seemed to turn on its decision. Later, as the convention drew toward its end, the crowding worsened because nobody—not the spectators, not even delegates supposedly "in the know"—could say for certain how the final vote would go. That meant that the anxiety among the Constitution's supporters at the convention's beginning did not fade away. Instead it grew worse, with the intensity building to fever strength as the final vote approached. After all, this convention might decide the fate of the nation.

OPENING THE DEBATES

Monday morning, January 14, a day of "*Severe* cold," perhaps the most frigid of the winter season, began in Boston with the ringing of bells to announce Connecticut's ratification of the Constitution. Federalists hoped that "pleasing intelligence" would affect delegates from the western part of the state, which bordered Connecticut. The news had first arrived the previous Friday, and, from a Federalist perspective, the timing could not have been better because on Monday, once the bells fell silent, the Massachusetts convention would finally turn to the Constitution.[40]

The delegates listened as the Constitution, Congress's resolution of September 28 transmitting the Constitution to the states, and the Massachusetts legislature's resolution of October 25, 1787, calling the state ratifying convention, were all read aloud. Then the convention adopted a plan for its proceedings. After what Dummer Sewall called "a long Debate," the delegates decided to "enter into a free Descusing or Conversation" on the Constitution "by parragrafts." That "free conversation" would continue, the convention decided, "untill every member shall have had opportunity fully to express his sentiments on the same." Then the convention would "consider and debate" whether or not to "adopt & ratify the proposed constitution, before any vote is taken expressive of the sense of the Convention, upon the whole or any part thereof." In short, the convention would go through the Constitution by paragraphs and then debate it as a whole, but there would be no votes taken except the final one, on whether to ratify or reject it.[41]

Rufus King saw that procedure as a way of avoiding proposals for amendments to one part of the Constitution or another. The long "conversation" would also allow the Federalists to outtalk everyone else. The ratifying convention included a wealth of talent: Among its members were the state's present and former governor, the chief justice and two associate justices of the supreme judicial court, two members of the governor's council, 118 members of the house of representatives, twenty state senators, nine present or former congressional delegates, and four delegates to the federal Convention (King, Gorham, Caleb Strong, who left the Philadelphia Convention early, and

Francis Dana, who did not attend). There were also large numbers of lawyers, doctors, merchants, clergymen, and men with military titles. The greater part of those "persons of influence," with the possible exception of assembly representatives and militia officers, favored the Constitution. Their ability to argue and speak would almost certainly outshine that of the many rural delegates who were farmers or the owners of small businesses like grist- or lumber mills. Whether the new and "most excellent" arguments promised by King could get the Constitution ratified was, however, unclear, even to King himself. "No question ever classed [divided] the people of this State in a more extraordinary manner," he told James Madison, "or with more apparent firmness."[42]

The Federalists also had another reason for avoiding votes. Later King wrote Henry Knox that "from motives of Policy we have not taken any Question which has divided the House, or shewn the strength of sides." In other words, the Constitution's supporters wanted to avoid showing the opposition how strong it was. That was why they favored a protracted, informal, but well-ordered "conversation" rather than a formal debate, which generally involves making decisions, and so taking votes, every once in a while. If possible, the Federalists wanted to delay the final vote until they were sure they had a majority. Their hopes turned, as Theophilus Parsons explained, not on delegates who arrived determined to fight ratification, but on those "among the opposers" who were "men of integrity and candor" and declared that they had not decided how to vote but were "ready and desirous of being informed. The effect of argument upon these will determine the fate of the Constitution."[43] The politics of the Massachusetts convention was therefore different from that of the Pennsylvania convention, where the number of delegates on each side was clear from the first and debates were carried on more for the benefit of outsiders than to persuade fellow delegates.

Before discussion of the Constitution began, its critics made another effort to invite Gerry to the convention "to answer any question of fact . . . that the convention may want to ask respecting the passing of the constitution." King, Gorham, and also Caleb Strong had attended the federal Convention; they could answer questions about its proceedings. Gerry, however, was the only Massachusetts delegate who had refused to sign—and the only one not elected to the ratifying convention. Those inclined toward his views wanted to hear his perspective. The proposal to admit a nondelegate to the convention debates was, however, irregular, and it led to a flurry of alternative motions and heated debates. Finally, as a concession to those who raised the issue (and were not, as King put it, "the most enlightened part of the convention") and to avoid making the issue "a trial of strength," some Federalists supported the original proposal to invite Gerry to come and answer questions put to him. It passed after what one delegate described as "many disputes," but, because of the Federalists' support, the vote gave no clear signal on how the delegates would divide on the Constitution. A committee of three delegates, all of whom were critics of the Constitution, presented the invitation to Gerry, who arrived at the convention on January 15.[44]

King thought that Gerry's role would provoke a controversy that would give "some Idea of our relative Strength." That did not happen, at least not in the way he had expected. Gerry sat nervously "biting the head of his Cane" until January 18, when someone finally asked him a question. At his request, it was put in writing, and he wrote a reply that was read aloud to the delegates the next day. Then, as the convention debated equal representation in the Senate, Gerry got the impression that his role at the Constitutional Convention had been misrepresented. He began scribbling away, and announced to the convention that he was preparing a statement on the subject. Francis Dana, an elected Cambridge delegate, objected since nobody had asked Gerry a question about the Senate. William Widgery proposed that the convention should forget that procedural detail, and another Maine delegate suggested that Gerry be allowed to participate in debates but not vote. Again Dana objected. Widgery tried to ask Gerry for his information, but not even that gambit ended the impasse. Finally, after the convention adjourned for the weekend without settling the issue, Gerry and Dana got into an angry "altercation." Other delegates sided with one man or the other according to their views on the Constitution, until a group of men led by King broke up the fight.[45]

Nothing like that had happened at the Philadelphia convention until its waning days. Gerry never returned to the convention, contenting himself with sending a letter to the convention justifying his actions and including "facts" on the Senate. Even that action provoked a short, heated debate. Dana, who was in any case in poor health, left the hall and sulked at home for several days, insisting that the convention come to his defense.[46] Tensions among delegates threatened to tear the convention apart before it had fairly begun.

The conflict between Gerry and Dana, both anxious to defend their honor, was only a part of the problem. Several towns had chosen as delegates men who sympathized with Shays's Rebellion and in some cases actively participated in it. Could Federalists who considered the insurgents criminals—and tended to put anyone who did not wholeheartedly support the Constitution in the same category—treat them with respect? If simple civility among delegates was a challenge, could the convention ever undercut suspicions of the Constitution and persuade the people to accept it "with cordiality," as Gore hoped? The outlook was not altogether promising.

PARAGRAPH BY PARAGRAPH

Meanwhile, the convention began discussing the Constitution paragraph by paragraph and held to that plan far more successfully than the Pennsylvania convention, though not without occasional deviations. The character of the convention was defined by those discussions and the sometimes bewildering number of delegates who participated. A dozen or so men spoke more often and more memorably than others, but in so large a convention, where "every member" was free to express his views, an unusual number of obscure people took the floor. Some delegates stated their fears clearly and openly while others—Federalists—explained parts of the Constitution in novel ways, breaking new ground almost inadvertently as they tried to argue away the opposition.

Even the records of the convention distinguish the Massachusetts convention from its predecessors, which left no published debates or reported only the speeches of Federalists. To be sure, press coverage of the convention, most of which first appeared in Benjamin Russell's *Massachusetts Centinel*, was less than ideal. The scribes and printers were so overwhelmed by the work of recording the debates and putting them into print that they missed many speeches and sometimes whole sessions of the convention. Newspaper coverage also suffered from a Federalist bias. The accounts regularly referred to Federalist speakers approvingly and on one occasion, rather than describe the debates in "minute detail," simply said that the supporters of the Constitution answered every objection, "however trivial," and that their efforts "to convince those who were in errour, were not without effect." Moreover, before March 1788, when the newspaper accounts were collected and printed in book form, some "principal speakers" revised the accounts of their speeches and the printer corrected the language of others.[47]

The convention kept an official journal that reports the motions made, the committees appointed, and the like, but says very little on the debates themselves. Fortunately, several delegates—notably the Federalists Theophilus Parsons and the Reverend Jeremy Belknap, and one resolute critic of the Constitution, Justin Dwight of Belchertown (Hampshire County)[48]—kept notes on the convention's proceedings, which add substantial (and sometimes contradictory) information to the newspaper accounts. So do the letters leading delegates and spectators sent to correspondents elsewhere, including James Madison, George Washington, Henry Knox, and Congressman George Thatcher, who both wrote and received letters from a broad range of correspondents.

Thanks to a letter Benjamin Lincoln sent Washington, we know that some delegates objected to the lack of any reference to God in the Constitution's Preamble. The delegates then turned to Article I, Section 1, which said that all legislative powers would be invested in a bicameral Congress. That aroused no objections, but there was a fierce debate over the provision in the first paragraph of Section 2 that said members of the House of Representatives would be elected every two years. In Massachusetts, all state officials were elected annually to "safeguard . . . the liberties of the people," and any deviation from that practice was bound to provoke opposition.⁴⁹

Dr. John Taylor, the debt-ridden delegate from the Shaysite town of Douglass in Worcester County, noted that under the Articles of Confederation delegates to Congress were elected annually, could serve for only a limited term (no delegate could serve "for more than three years in any term of six years"), and could be recalled by their state in midterm. None of those safeguards was in the proposed Constitution. If representatives behaved well, they would probably be reelected, "but if they behave ill, how shall we remedy the evil" without going through the cumbersome process of impeachment? For Taylor, two years was too long to let representatives stay in office without going back to the people for reelection. The issue was of considerable importance: Even the generally silent Samuel Adams asked why biennial and not annual elections had been adopted.⁵⁰

The fullest answer came from Dedham's Fisher Ames, a smart lawyer, twenty-nine years old, and, like many prominent Massachusetts Federalists, a Harvard graduate (Class of 1774) and a skilled orator. Ames conceded that he too considered frequent elections "one of the first securities for popular liberty." But representatives' terms could be too short—say, one day—or too long to keep them under the control of the people. Annual elections seemed appropriate for a state legislature, since "every citizen grows up with a knowledge of the local circumstances of the state." The business of a federal government was, however, different, and it would require "at least two years in office . . . to enable a man to judge of the trade and interests of states which he never saw." Much the same argument had been made earlier by Theodore Sedgwick, but Ames went further. Biennial elections provided "an essential security to liberty" by preventing decisions based on "faction and enthusiasm." "A democracy," Ames said, "is a volcano, which conceals the fiery materials of its own destruction. . . . The people always mean right, and if time is allowed for reflection and information, they will do right." Biennial elections provided "security that the sober, second thought of the people shall be law."⁵¹

When Ames had concluded, Adams said "he only made the inquiry for information" and had heard enough "to satisfy himself of its propriety." He knew from experience how many unfamiliar issues congressmen had to master, and Ames's assertion of the ultimate wisdom of the people corresponded with his own convictions. Perhaps Adams was also persuaded by Thomas Dawes, Jr., a judge and Boston delegate, who noted that Article I, Section 2, gave a new privilege to the people since it allowed them to vote for congressmen rather than have state legislatures choose the states' representatives, as was the practice under the Articles of Confederation. As a result,

Dawes said, the Constitution would be "in favour of the people" no matter how long congressmen served.[52]

Since not everyone had said his piece, the discussion continued. The former governor, James Bowdoin, argued that it was safe to let representatives stay in office for two years because they could make no laws or levy any taxes to which they would not also be subject. Another delegate, who insisted that terms over a year were dangerous, quoted a statement by the French writer Montesquieu, a respected authority on the nature of republican government, that great power should be held for only short periods of time. Federalist speakers questioned that principle in general and, more important, its relevance. Montesquieu had the ancient world in mind, Christopher Gore argued; the same rules did not apply to modern republics with developed systems of representation and constitutional checks on power. History could "afford little or no instruction on this subject," Rufus King added; the convention had to decide the issue "upon its own principles." Two-year terms did not seem too long to him, considering that representatives would have to consider "complicated issues" with regard to thirteen states as well as foreign relations.[53]

General Samuel Thompson, a Maine militia officer and one of the convention's most outspoken critics of the Constitution, confessed that he had never studied the history to which Federalist speakers referred, but he knew the history of his own country. Had the previous administration in Massachusetts—under James Bowdoin—gone on one more year, he said, "our liberties would have been lost, and the country involved in blood." Instead the people were able to choose a new governor, who pardoned insurgents and restored peace, and that demonstrated the value of frequent elections. Thompson's speech caused an uproar since Bowdoin and many of his supporters were present. But Thompson spoke from immediate experience and made his point well—despite a readiness to indulge in what he called a "pathetick apostrophe: 'O! my country, never give up your annual elections, young men never give up your jewell!'"[54]

The convention had discussed one paragraph—really half a paragraph—for a day and a half. At that rate the convention could go on for months. Fortunately, not all parts of the Constitution were controversial. Although the delegates discussed biennial elections at length, they said nothing about the same paragraph's provision that voting requirements for House elections be the same as those for state lower houses, which apparently seemed fine to everyone.

Meanwhile, Gilbert Dench of Hopkinton (western Middlesex County), who had strong reservations on the Constitution, was eager to jump ahead and discuss Article I, Section 4, which gave Congress the right to make or alter the times, places, and manner set by state legislatures for electing senators and representatives "except as to the Places of chusing Senators." At first Dench was called to order since the convention was discussing an earlier paragraph. But Francis Dana, who rigidly upheld the convention's procedural rules against Elbridge Gerry, moved that any member who thought another part of the Constitution was connected with the one under consideration should have "full liberty to take up such other clause or paragraph for that purpose." The convention agreed, giving another sign of a willingness to accommodate delegates who opposed or had serious reservations on the Constitution.[55]

On the morning of January 16, the convention formally moved on to the next paragraph. However, pressure to address Congress's power over elections was so overwhelming that the convention discussed Article I, Section 4, although that was *not in regular order.* Opponents feared that the provision would allow Congress to perpetuate itself indefinitely by canceling elections, or to call elections in one place inconvenient for most people—Boston, for example, or Berkshire County in western Massachusetts, or Lincoln County in Maine—in order to influence the outcome. Congress could not exercise its power over the place of elections except for that purpose, argued Charles Turner, a Harvard graduate (Class of 1752), onetime clergyman, and delegate from Scituate on the coast southeast of Boston. Congress should not be given a power that it could not use without abusing it. Ebenezer Peirce, a delegate from Partridgefield (now Peru, in Berkshire County), noted that members of the House of Representatives were "the democratical part of the general government"—that is, the one part that was directly elected by the people—and would serve as a check on the representatives of the states in the Senate, so "the utmost caution ought to be used, to have their elections as free as possible."[56]

Congress could not cancel elections altogether, Rufus King pointed out; biennial elections for members of the lower house were secured by another provision of the Constitution. Moreover, he and other Federalists explained that Congress needed the power under discussion in the event that some state, like Rhode Island, refused to call elections for members of Congress. The provision therefore served, Theophilus Parsons argued, as a way of securing the people's "equal rights of election" and also of preserving the union, since adequate state representation would be as essential to the new government as it was under the Confederation. It therefore gave Congress "a *necessary* power," added John Coffin Jones, a wealthy merchant on the Boston delegation. To say that power could be abused was a charge that could be made against any power whatsoever. Its abuse was, however, unlikely since "the federal representatives will represent *the people*—they will be *the people*—and it is not *probable* they will abuse themselves." Other speakers simply dismissed fears that Congress would call elections to some remote part of the state as absurd, like the notion "that Congress would, when chosen, act as bad as possible."[57]

If the provision was meant to assure that "refractory States may be made to do their duty," asked Phanuel Bishop, why didn't it say that? He favored "giving Congress as much power to do good as possible," but it would be far better if the Constitution allowed Congress to make or alter state provisions on the times, places, and manner of congressional elections only "*if any State shall refuse or neglect so to do.*" William Widgery agreed: Rulers "ought never to have a power which they could abuse," so Article I, Section 4, should include the limitation that Bishop proposed. As for trusting representatives to do the right thing, Abraham White, a delegate from Norton (Bristol County), said "he would not trust 'a flock of Moseses.'"[58]

Although the "conversation" on Article I, Section 4, went on through the next morning, only Francis Dana argued against Bishop's proposal, and in doing so he made an argument unique to that point in the ratification debates. It wasn't enough, he said, for a state to send its full complement of representatives to Congress. A state also had to provide for elections in which the people had an "equal influence." Suppose state legislatures did not extend representation to newly settled areas, or in some other way acted unjustly. "There may, therefore, be a case put," Dana argued, for Congress having power to make or alter state electoral provisions—even though a state had not neglected to call elections—to assure that the elections were organized and conducted in a way that respected the people's right to equal representation. However, Dr. John Taylor, one of the most cogent and articulate critics of the Constitution, said the discussion of Bishop's proposal was a waste of time since it would be "almost impossible" to amend the Constitution. Again it became clear that delegates who had reservations on the Constitution did not speak with one voice.[59]

On the afternoon of January 17—four days after substantive debates had begun—the convention finally returned to Article I, Section 2, which said that a representative had to be at least twenty-five years old, a citizen of the United States for seven years, and at the time of his election an inhabitant of the state in which he was chosen. Those qualifications seemed unobjectionable, although several delegates, including Abraham White, Ebenezer Peirce, and perhaps Samuel Thompson—who had argued earlier that people should be excluded from office when they grow old—asked why there were no property qualifications for office, as there were in the Massachusetts constitution. If men have "*nothing to lose,*" Thompson supposedly said, "they have *nothing to fear.*"[60]

Theodore Sedgwick, who harbored powerful reservations about democracy,[61] said that objection "was founded on an anti-democratical principle." He was surprised, he said, that a "gentleman [Thompson] who appeared so strenuously to advocate the rights of the people" would exclude from the federal government "a *good* man, because he was not a *rich* one." King added that he did not consider property an index to ability. "We often see men . . . who[,] though destitute of property, are superior in knowledge and rectitude," he said. "The men who have most injured the country" were "most commonly . . . rich men." Why should we "bridle the people in their elections," Francis Dana added; the people would not, in any case, choose a man with no property unless he had qualifications that offset his poverty. As for disqualifying men of advanced age, King said longevity depended a lot on climate. Men lived longer in the North than the South: "What here is the time of *ripened judgement*, is *old age* there." As a result, age disqualifications made no sense in a national constitution.[62]

The next, long paragraph—the third in Article I, Section 2—seemed sure to provoke intense dissent. It said representation and direct taxes would be apportioned according to the number of free persons, excluding "Indians not taxed" but including those bound to service and "three fifths of all other persons"; mandated a national census within three years of the new Congress's meeting and every ten years thereafter; said "the number of Representatives shall not exceed one for every thirty Thousand," and specified the number of representatives each state would have in the first federal Congress. The delegates' "conversation," however, turned in good part on the implications of apportioning taxes on the basis of population rather than land (as the Articles of Confederation specified). The adoption of population-based taxes would hurt the North, Samuel Thompson argued, because "we have more children than the luxurious inhabitants of the southern States" and also longer lives. "We live to one hundred," he claimed (apparently persuaded by Rufus King's argument against age disqualifications), "they to forty."[63]

Some delegates thought Southern lands were more fertile than those in the North; others argued that Northern lands "are worth more by the acre" and that lands cultivated by slaves were less valuable than those farmed by freemen. However, Dr. Samuel Holten of Danvers argued for expediency. Holten had a long and distinguished political career that included several terms in Congress, and he generally opposed the Constitution for fear that it would "make bad worse." Although he conceded that using population rather than land in calculating federal taxes benefited the South, he favored the provision because "it is all the rule we can get." His speech was poorly reported, but he probably meant that assessing the value of a state's lands had proven beyond Congress's capacity, so it had to depend on population in apportioning taxes.[64]

Granting representation and allocating taxes on the basis of three-fifths of a state's slaves raised some hackles. Samuel Nasson, an outspoken critic of the Constitution from Sanford in York County, Maine, complained that "this

State will pay as great a tax for three children in the cradle, as any of the southern States will for five hearty working Negro men." Dawes, however, also drew
delegates' attention to another provision, which allowed Congress to prohibit
the importation of slaves after twenty years and, in the meantime, to impose a
duty of ten dollars on each imported slave (Article I, Section 9, paragraph 1).
Congress could not simply abolish slavery "in a moment, and so destroy what
our Southern brethren consider as property," Dawes said, but those two provisions would eventually bring it to an end. As he put it, "although slavery is not
smitten by an apoplexy" that would kill it quickly, "yet it has received a mortal
wound and will die of a consumption," a lingering form of death.[65]

Nobody questioned the provision for decennial censuses, but some delegates objected to the statement that the number of representatives "shall not
exceed one for every thirty Thousand," which would allow Congress to make
the ratio even higher, and said the first House of Representatives would
be too small to represent the country's people adequately. Dana, however,
pointed out that the number of representatives under the Constitution, 65,
plus that of Senators, 26, equaled 91, precisely the maximum number of delegates the states could send to the Confederation Congress. Like other Federalists, Caleb Strong argued that representation would be adequate "because
no private local interests" would come under Congress's jurisdiction, and a
larger Congress would be too expensive. Moreover, as the country's population grew, the number of representatives would increase and become more
affordable since the costs would be spread over more taxpayers. In fifty years,
Nathaniel Gorham predicted, there would be 360 members of the House of
Representatives, "in 100 years 14 or 1500—if the constitution last so long."[66]

MAKING SENSE OF THE SENATE

By January 19, the convention had skipped over paragraphs on filling vacancies in the House of Representatives, its choice of officers, and its "sole Power
of Impeachment," and opened a discussion of Article I, Section 3, which
said each state would have two senators, each with a six-year term, and they
would vote individually, not by states. Several delegates made the predictable argument that senators' terms of office were far too long, and Samuel
Thompson questioned giving so much power to a body in which every state,
"however small, has as much influence as a great State." The colorful Amos
Singletary, a onetime gristmill owner and a delegate from Sutton in Worcester County, said that not only were six-year terms too long, but that senators
would "make themselves perpetual," move their families with them out of
the state, and have "high wages," all of which would presumably further
separate them from their constituents. Singletary, a man in his sixties whose
Protestant faith was influenced by the preaching of the revivalist Jonathan
Edwards, objected to the lack of any provision limiting eligibility to Chris-

tians, so "an Infidel" or "Papist" (whom Singletary clearly did not consider Christian) could serve. (The *New York Morning Post* published an account of the speech, apparently taken from a private letter. Singletary, "who is as remarkable for his taciturnity, as his zeal for religion," it said, first "hemmed thrice," then "wiped his face with a clean white handkerchief," which he put in "the right pocket of his great coat" before beginning: "Mr. President or Mr. Moderator, I think we are giving up all our privileges, as there is no provision in *this here* self same constitution, that men in power should have any religion.")[67]

Answers to Singletary's demand for religious qualifications for office would come later. For now, Caleb Strong explained that there had been major debates on the subject of representation at the Philadelphia Convention, which "would have broke up if it had not been agreed to allow an equal representation in the Senate." That "accommodation" to the small states, he added, was recommended by a committee of which Elbridge Gerry was a member. Strong's comment inspired Gerry's ill-fated effort to set the record straight.[68] Federalist speakers, however, were far less interested in discrediting Gerry than in making sense of the Senate as more than an unfortunate part of an unavoidable political compromise.

Fisher Ames said the Senate represented "the sovereignty of the states," the House "individuals," so the Senate served as a "federal feature" of the Constitution and a security against "a consolidation of the states." To date, the charge that the Constitution would create a "consolidated government" and destroy the states had not played a prominent role in the convention's debates. Ames, however, made a preemptive strike, cleverly portraying the "so much condemned" Senate as a critical component of the "*federal* republick" created by the Constitution, an institution that assured the continued existence of states and served as a barrier to "consolidation." If, for example, senators were chosen directly by the people rather than the state legislatures, Ames said, that would "totally obliterate the federal features of the constitution." State governments spoke for "the wishes and feelings and local interests of the people," he said; they were "the safe guard and ornament of the constitution," a "shelter against the abuse of power," and "the natural avengers of our violated rights." Without states to take charge of their internal affairs, the constitutional provisions on representation in Congress would be inadequate, Ames conceded; Congress would have too much power to entrust "to so few persons." Since senators—the "ambassadours of the states"—had so critical a place in maintaining the country's constitutional fabric, they needed "some permanency in their office." Their six-year terms, moreover, did not isolate them from the people, since a third of them would be reelected every two years, and those newly elected members, "who feel the sentiments of their states," would "awe" the third whose terms were expiring.[69] Ames's Senate, in short, was a bastion at once of democracy, liberty, and rights.

Rufus King followed Ames's lead, arguing that the Senate "preserved the equality of the States" and, again, that six-year terms were not too long given the range of their responsibilities, which included assisting the executive in making appointments to major federal offices and negotiating treaties with foreign nations. Dawes agreed: Since senators' business was more difficult than representatives', they needed a longer term of office so they could "inform themselves" on their responsibilities. Francis Dana joined the chorus, echoing Ames's argument that all states had equal representation in the Senate because it represented state sovereignty, and he noted (as Dawes had earlier) the "large gain" in adding a branch of Congress—the House of Representatives—directly elected by the people.[70]

Whether or not those speeches persuaded the doubtful, the convention pushed ahead. On January 21, it swept past several provisions in Article I, Section 3, and turned again to Section 4, on congressional power over elections, which it had already discussed at length. Now, however, Federalist speakers built on Dana's earlier argument and made the provision a critical defense of popular rights. Both Ames and Dana said they had come to the convention thinking the clause was dangerous, but now they saw it as a means of allowing Congress to remedy flawed state systems of representation. Connecticut, Rufus King noted, allocated representation to incorporated towns, with both large and small towns sending two delegates to the state legislature. Now the Rhode Island legislature had proposed a similar system, which would cut back the power of Providence and Newport. In South Carolina, Charleston had thirty of two hundred legislative seats, giving it the power to fight demands for a fairer representation of the surging population of the state's backcountry. If the same systems were used in choosing members of the federal House of Representatives, only Congress could intervene to mandate a more equal representation of the people. Would Congress abuse that power to perpetuate its members in office? Was it, Ames asked, less trustworthy than state legislators? There were, in any case, limits on what Congress could do: It could not, for example, interfere with the terms of office or the age and residence requirements set by the Constitution.[71]

That afternoon the convention skipped quickly over the next three sections of Article I. Dr. Taylor questioned the provision in that both houses of Congress would publish a journal of their proceedings "from time to time," but Rufus King said the phrase meant, in context, from session to session. Maine's William Widgery expressed his fear that the next phrase—"except such parts as may require secrecy"—would allow Congress to withhold all publications and keep the people "in ignorance of their doings." But Nathaniel Gorham said public bodies had to keep some of their proceedings secret until "brought to maturity"—the negotiation of treaties, for example.[72]

Taylor also questioned the provision in Article I, Section 6, that senators and representatives would be paid out of the Treasury of the United States. Before independence, he recalled, Parliament's effort to take the power of paying royal officials away from the provincial legislatures was a grievance because such officials would then no longer "feel their dependence on the people." On the same principle, state legislatures should remain the paymasters of senators and congressional representatives. Again Federalists answered that the situation had changed, and that the provision—like Article I, Section 4—actually protected the people's right of representation. After all, when Rhode Island refused to pay its congressmen, the people of that state lost their representation in Congress. If Congress voted its own pay, that wouldn't happen. And Congress would not give its members exorbitant salaries, Theodore Sedgwick said, because it was answerable to the people and concerned for its reputation. The Massachusetts legislature set its members' salaries and never gave themselves more than they deserved. This time even Samuel Thompson seemed mollified.[73]

THE POWER TO TAX

Many delegates were waiting to rip into Article I, Section 8, which listed the powers granted to Congress and contained, as one delegate noted, "more matter than any one yet read." On the afternoon of January 21, the convention turned to the first and most controversial paragraph of Section 8, which granted Congress "Power To lay and collect Taxes, Duties, Imposts and Excises, to pay the Debts and provide for the general Welfare of the United States." For Rufus King and other defenders of the Constitution, the provision was critical. It would remedy Congress's chronic poverty and allow it to defend the nation and pay its debts, restore its credit, and make the United States respectable in the eyes of foreign nations.[74] But the grant of such extensive taxing powers galvanized critics of the Constitution.

Abraham White said "we give up everything" in granting Congress such broad taxing powers. Amos Singletary "thought no more power could be given to a despot." The rulers might not be honest; "we may have an atheist, pagan, Mahommedan." Samuel Thompson simply said, "I totally abhor this paragraph." Other delegates chimed in. Old Revolutionary sensitivities over taxes were rekindled by recent experience, particularly in sections of Massachusetts where men had been driven to desperation by high direct taxes leveled by the state legislature. Moreover, because the Constitution granted Congress the right to levy all kinds of taxes, direct and indirect, it seemed to leave nothing for the states. Other grants of power to Congress exacerbated the problem. After the people gave the federal government all their money, established it in its own federal town of ten miles square, let it coin money and raise a "standing army," Martin Kingsley (Hardwick, Worcester County) asked, what resources would they have left for their own defense? "I cannot see any."[75]

Federalist speakers stressed the advantages to be gained by a strong federal government, which demanded that it have all the tax powers mentioned. Over and over they insisted that duties on imports, supplemented perhaps by excise taxes, would normally be sufficient to support the central government, which would resort to direct taxes only in time of war. Then the government would have to act quickly—"the operations of war are sudden and call for large sums of money"—so it needed to collect direct taxes itself, not work through the states, whose collections were "at all times slow and uncertain." If Congress were to entrust that task to the states and the states failed to act, as they had so often under the Confederation, the central government would have to coerce them with arms, introducing "all the horrors of a civil war." Tristram Dalton (Newbury, Essex County) added that power would be given "to men of our own choosing" who would use it to save us "from destruction: The danger of accepting this Constitution is not equal to the danger of refusing it." Boston merchant William Phillips said he was tempted to adopt Samuel Thompson's expression "*O! my country*" if the Constitution were not adopted since that would lead to "destruction and inevitable ruin."[76]

This time, however, the naysayers were better able to hold their own. To be sure, when Kingsley (Harvard 1778) and Samuel Willard (Harvard 1767, a delegate from Uxbridge in Worcester County) dipped into ancient history, citing Sparta, Athens, Rome, and the "Amphictionick League" to support their arguments, the Federalists quickly dismissed the relevance of their examples for a modern republic (and also questioned the accuracy of Kingsley's history). Critics of the provision were more effective when they spoke from their own experience. Ebenezer Peirce disputed claims that Congress would ordinarily depend on revenue from import duties based on his experience as a state legislator. When Massachusetts agreed to grant the Confederation Congress the right to levy duties on imports, he recalled, "gentlemen in trade" argued that duties were "an unequal tax" that bore particularly hard on them—even though they could pass most of the cost on to consumers—since "in the first instance it was paid by persons in trade," and they consumed more dutied articles than "the landed interest." The same argument would push Congress to impose direct taxes (for example, on polls or real estate) rather than rely on income from duties, particularly since Northern merchants would get support from the Southern states, which had "no manufacturers of their own" and so consumed far more imports than the Northern states.[77]

William Symmes had no such experience to draw upon. Only twenty-seven years old, he had graduated from Harvard in 1780 and studied law in

Newburyport under Theophilus Parsons, another Harvard graduate (1769), before opening a practice in rural Andover. The convention, Symmes noted, was the first representative body in which he served, and as a young man in such an assembly, examining a subject "that puzzles the oldest politicians," he confessed that it took some effort for him to speak. That he took a different position from Parsons must have added to the pressure. He continued to think the Constitution should include term limits "to prevent the . . . perpetuation of power in the same men," and he wanted a fuller representation of the people in Congress. Nor had he been persuaded that Congress should have power over the manner and place of congressional elections. Those issues, however, were minor compared with the clause on taxes, which Symmes described as the "key-stone" on which the fate of the Constitution rested, but which he thought overcompensated for the problems of the past.[78]

Symmes puzzled over the stark difference between the Confederation, which had no power to tax or to coerce states that failed to pay requisitions, and the massive grant of taxing power in the Constitution. Could it be, he asked, that members of the Philadelphia Convention, who had experienced "the impotency of Congress" while members of that body, "were rather too keenly set for an effectual increase of power"? He was ready to praise those men for inventing "a system completely consistent with itself, and pretty free from contradiction," but the provision on taxes seemed inconsistent with the rest. It was "a very good and valid conveyance of all the property in the United States" for purposes that were stated in a way that would allow Congress to authorize any expenditure it wanted to make. It could raise funds to pay the debts and provide for the "common welfare" of the United States, but the debts were not confined to those already contracted, and the term "general welfare" could cover "any expenditure whatsoever." No free people, Symmes said, should give such "universal, unbounded" power to its government.[79]

The Constitution's defenders said repeatedly that the powers granted would be used by the people's representatives for the people's welfare. In reality, Symmes argued, the power would be exercised by a public body in which "the prevalent faction *is the body.*" The Constitution's defenders must therefore mean "that the prevalent faction will always be right, and that the true patriots will always out number the men of less and selfish principles," which logically implied that "no public measure was ever wrong, because it must have been passed by the majority," which was obviously incorrect. All past governments degenerated and abused the powers given to them: Why would the proposed Congress be better than "myriads of publick bodies who have gone before them"? It would be far safer to give Congress a more limited grant of revenue "adequate to all necessary purposes," and no more. "As the poverty of individuals prevents luxury," Symmes said, "so the poverty of publick bodies . . . prevents tyranny. A nation cannot, perhaps, do a more politick thing, than to supply the purse of its sovereign with that parsimony, which results from a sense of the labour it costs." His constituents, Symmes concluded, "ardently wish for a firm, efficient continental government," but they feared the operation of the one proposed.[80]

The next morning Symmes's former teacher, Parsons, rose to answer the objections that had been made to the powers of Congress under the Constitution. The dissenters, he insisted, failed to distinguish hereditary governments, where the interest of rulers is different from their subjects, from one "administered for the common good by the servants of the people vested with delegated powers by popular elections at stated periods." To talk of keeping Congress poor, he said, "must mean depriving the people themselves of their own resources." (He said nothing about Symmes's argument that elected bodies are distinct from the people in general and do not always promote the common good.) As for rotation in office, he argued that term limits were "an abridgement of the rights of the people" that could deprive them of the services of the nation's best men "at critical seasons." Parsons also responded to Thompson's insistence on confining office to Christians. Oaths, he said, would be no barrier to "unprincipled men," and a "good life" was better proof of a man's sincere religion. Then he again went over the checks on power in the Constitution. Any usurpation of power by Congress, he said, would be resisted by the state legislatures and by the people themselves: "An act of usurpation is not obligatory, it is not law," and could be justly resisted.[81]

AN EARLY VOTE?

Dr. John Taylor had already said that the discussion of Article I, Section 8 "had taken a great deal of time"—almost two days—with many arguments repeated. The "conversation" had also wandered from the paragraph at issue to the Constitution as a whole, which Taylor and, it seems, other critics of the Constitution welcomed.[82]

That afternoon—Thursday, January 23—Samuel Nasson formally moved that the convention reconsider its decision to discuss the Constitution by paragraphs in order "to leave the subject at large open for discussion." The motion was designed to shorten the convention's deliberations and bring it to a final vote for, William Widgery said, reasons of "necessity." Delegates from the cash-poor countryside were apparently finding it difficult to pay their bills in Boston. The state of Massachusetts would pay them for their services, but only when the convention was over—assuming it could find the necessary funds somewhere. Or did Nasson and Widgery think they had enough votes to defeat the Constitution then, but perhaps not later, as more and more delegates fell under the spell of the Federalists' arguments?[83] The motion awoke "warm opposition." Nasson withdrew it, then reintroduced it the next morning. The issue was critical: The fate of the Constitution might turn on whether the motion passed or failed.

At that point Samuel Adams gave his first substantive speech of the convention. From the beginning of the controversy he had doubts about parts of the proposed Constitution, he said, and he still had difficulties with it. He had, however, chosen "rather to be an auditor, than an objector" at the convention for "particular reasons" he did not explain. Since many other delegates also wanted "a full investigation of the subject" before finally deciding on the Constitution, Adams opposed Nasson's motion. "We ought not to be stingy of our time, or the publick money, when so important an object demanded them: and the publick expect that we will not." He regretted the "necessities" of delegates who made the motion, but he would rather lend them the money they needed (though he was not a wealthy man) than "hurry so great a subject." Other delegates supported him—not just Rufus King, whose position was predictable, but John Pitts of Dunstable (northern Middlesex County), who said little else at the convention; and Jonathan Smith, a Berkshire County farmer who would later make one of the convention's most memorable speeches.[84]

The motion failed "without a return of the house"—that is, without a formal vote.[85] Thanks to Adams's intervention, the convention would not come to a precipitous end. Its orderly and probing "conversation" on the Constitution would continue. It remained to be seen, however, whether talk alone would convert enough delegates to ratify the Constitution. If not, the Federalists would have to come up with another strategy, and soon.

SEVEN

The Massachusetts Convention II

"...with Cordiality"

The convention's "conversation" had developed pretty much as the Federalists expected. Their speakers performed spectacularly day after day, and every part of the Constitution to which objections were made was "very ably defended." Rufus King "shines among the Feds with a superior Lustre," Jeremy Belknap reported; "his Speeches are clear, cool, nervous, pointed, & Conclusive." Theophilus Parsons "distinguishes accurately and reasons forcibly." Observers also singled out Nathaniel Gorham, Tristram Dalton, Caleb Strong, Theodore Sedgwick, and Fisher Ames as powerful speakers on behalf of the Constitution. They treated the spectators in the galleries to a star-studded display of oratory that "would do honour to any assembly on Earth."[1]

Francis Dana, however, seemed to steal the show. A lawyer in his mid-forties who had held many public offices—he had served in Congress and as American minister to Russia in the early 1780s and was currently an associate justice of the state's supreme judicial court—Dana had been chosen as a Massachusetts delegate to the federal Convention, but the precarious state of his health prevented him from attending. At the state ratifying convention, however, Belknap reported that Dana "thunders like Demosthenes." On January 18, when Belknap said Dana spoke with such power "that it seemed as if his feeble frame could scarcely have supported him," reporters for the *Massachusetts Centinel* were so captivated by "the fire—the pathos—the superior eloquence of his speech" that they forgot to take notes. A week later, after Dana ended his self-imposed exile from the convention because of the Gerry affair, he "drew tears into the eyes of admiring auditors before they were aware that their souls were on fire." The press gave accounts of these speeches, Belknap noted, but could not capture their "energy & pathos."[2]

Delegates on the other side were, by all accounts, less impressive. The convention was not, however, an oratory contest, and the spectators could not vote. The real question was whether the Federalist speakers could persuade enough delegates that the unamended Constitution was in the nation's best interest to win on ratification.

EVALUATING THE "OTHER SIDE"

John Forbes, who watched the convention debates from the galleries, said the position of those who found serious fault with the Constitution was "poorly advocated." There was "not a man of Education that dare speak in opposition to the Plan," he claimed. In fact, "there are but few on that side—& those few, fearing Conviction, are fortifying there [their] prejudiced minds with adamantine obstinacy." Belknap described the "Antifederal Speakers" as "very clamorous—petulant tedious & provoking." He mentioned particularly Samuel Nasson, Samuel Thompson, William Widgery, Dr. John Taylor, and Phanuel Bishop, all men, he said, "whose only force lies in noise & opposition." The opposition was so weak, King claimed, that the "Friends of the Constitution" had "the Task not only of answering, but also of stating and bringing forward, the Objections of their Opponents." Members of the opposition complained, he said, that "the Lawyers, Judges, Clergymen, Merchants and men of Education are all in Favor of the constitution" and were able "to make the worst, appear the better cause"; if the critics had such men on their side they could easily alarm the people with the Constitution's imperfections and fight down its defenders.[3]

Some members of the opposition acknowledged that there were stark differences between them and the Constitution's supporters. In mid-January Benjamin Randall, who represented Sharon, a town in Suffolk County some twenty-two miles south of Boston, observed that "*a good thing don't need praising,*" but it took "the best men in the state to gloss this Constitution." He hoped his fellow delegates would not be "biased by the best orators," who were, he seemed to acknowledge, on the other side. If "all this artillery" were "turned the other way," Randall added, "we might complete our business, and go home in 48 hours." Amos Singletary later claimed that back in 1775 the federal Constitution would have been "thrown away at once—it would not have been looked at. We contended with Great-Britain," he recalled, ". . . because they claimed a right to tax and bind us in all cases whatever. And does not this Constitution do the same?" Now, however, "these lawyers, and men of learning, and monied men . . . talk so finely and gloss over matters so smoothly, to make us poor illiterate people swallow down the pill." They expected to go to Congress, to become the "managers of this Constitution," and to "get all the power and all the money into their own hands." Then they would "swallow up all us little folks, like the great *Leviathan* . . . yes, just as the whale swallowed up *Jonah*. That is what I am afraid of."[4]

Speeches like that made a few opponents of the Constitution stand out from the others. It was easy to ridicule men like Singletary, wiping his fore-head with a handkerchief, taking about "*this here* self-same constitution," and worrying about a plague of "Papists" and "Mahommedans"; or his colleague in bombast, Samuel Thompson, with his "pathetic apostrophes." They were, however, the chosen spokesmen of constituents who probably shared the fears they expressed and even their distrust of non-Protestants (itself a step beyond an older distrust of non-Puritans) that seemed bigoted to more "en-lightened" observers.

Moreover, despite King's statement to the contrary, the dissenting del-egates needed no help in stating their objections to the Constitution. They were perfectly clear in explaining why they preferred annual elections to the longer terms proposed for members of the Senate and House of Represen-tatives, or why they feared Congress's power over the manner and place of elections and its extensive taxing powers. Nor was it true that there were, as Forbes charged, no "men of education"—which in Massachusetts gener-ally meant Harvard graduates—in the opposition. Charles Turner, Martin Kingsley, Samuel Willard, and William Symmes, all of whom spoke against parts of the Constitution, were Harvard graduates.[5] Others, like Eleazer Peirce, learned from the school of experience. Samuel Holten, who thought the country was in a bad way but feared the Constitution would "make bad worse," had a long record of public service within Massachusetts and at Congress, and he commanded obvious respect at the convention. At one point Thomas Dawes, Jr., graciously told Benjamin Randall that he "need no longer lament the want of abilities and eloquence on his side, since Dr. Holton [sic] had spoken."[6] Some delegates whom the Federalists disdained as "insurgent" sympathizers also proved to be able debaters. Taylor was in-formed and clear, and even the outspoken Phanuel Bishop helped move the debates along, as when he proposed limiting Congress's power over elections to occasions when the states failed to act. Critics of the Constitution were engaged, articulate if not eloquent, and, above all, numerous.

Some of these men spoke only rarely. Few if any had the analytical and oratorical skills of Fisher Ames and Francis Dana—or perhaps of Pennsyl-vania's William Findley and John Smilie. But on January 22, well after the debates had begun, Samuel Nasson still thought the Constitution would be voted down. He estimated that 144 delegates were for ratification and 192 against. Rufus King did not disagree: On January 23 he wrote Madison that "our prospects are gloomy." Four days later—after Nasson's motion to end the paragraph-by-paragraph "conversation" had been decisively voted down—Nathaniel Gorman was no more optimistic. "Never was there an

Assembly in this state" with "greater ability & information than the present Convention," he said, "yet I am in doubt whether they will approve the Constitution." Benjamin Lincoln told Washington that the opposition was alarmed at the Federalists' success in answering objections to the Constitution, and "the friends to it increase daily." And yet, King reported, the Federalists "were doubtful whether we exceeded them or they us in Numbers—they however say that they have a majority of Eight or twelve agt. us."[7]

The problem, King thought, and the reason the Federalists' splendid performances had no greater impact, was that the opposition was based less on specific provisions in the Constitution than on a deep fear for the liberties of the people and a distrust of the men of property or education who supported ratification—attitudes Amos Singletary expressed with remarkable directness. So far, King said, every effort to address those feelings seemed only to strengthen them. He found hope in the interest some members of the opposition took in a set of amendments proposed as a precondition for ratification by "Hampden" in the January 26 issue of the *Massachusetts Centinel.* That might at least indicate they were unsure of their strength since, King claimed, they had previously "reprobated the Suggestion of Amendments" and insisted on "a total Rejection of the Constitution."[8]

As early as January 20, King suggested privately that the convention might recommend "certain alterations" in the Constitution to members of the first Congress after its ratification. "We are now thinking of amendments to be submitted not as a condition of our assent & Ratification," he wrote James Madison three days later, "but as the opinion of the Convention subjoined to their Ratification." That might "gain a few members," but the outcome still remained "doubtful." The idea came out of desperation. "I am pretty well satisfied we shall loose [sic] the question," Gorham told Madison, "unless we can take of[f] some of the opposition by amendments."[9]

A REASONED INQUIRY

In the meantime, the convention continued to plod its way through the powers of Congress in Section 8 of Article I. Once the provision on taxes was left behind, the conversation shifted: Opposition members asked questions about constitutional provisions rather than attacking them. Taylor asked why there was to be a federal town over which Congress would have exclusive jurisdiction, which Caleb Strong explained, and then why it had to be as large as ten miles square. Dench also asked about the probable impact of the Constitution on the states. Accounts say that the debates were "desultory"[10]—that is, they wandered, jumping from one topic to another, although there were some moments of drama.

On January 25, after Amos Singletary made his memorable attack on lawyers, men of learning, and monied men for trying to get "us poor illiterate people" to swallow the Constitution, Jonathan Smith, a self-professed "plain man" who made his living "by the plough," took the floor. Although he had served in the state legislature and the Massachusetts constitutional convention, Smith, who represented Lanesborough (Berkshire County), said he was not used to speaking in public but wanted to address his "brother plough-joggers" among the delegates. He lived in a part of the country, he said, where he had learned "the worth of good government by the want of it." He spoke of the "black cloud" that had spread over the western part of the state during the previous winter, bringing anarchy and then tyranny: Shaysite insurgents "would rob you of your property, threaten to burn your houses; oblige you to be on your guard night and day." The distress was so great, Smith said, that people would have seized "anything that looked like a government for protection." When he read the Constitution, he found what he sought, "a cure for these disorders."[11]

Smith welcomed support for ratification from lawyers, educated people, and monied men, and he saw no reason to think that they intended, as Singletary charged, to get into Congress and abuse their power. They were "all embarked in the same cause with us, and we must all swim or sink together." There was "a time to sow and a time to reap," he concluded; we sowed our seed when sending delegates to the federal Convention. Now was the time of harvest, and if we did not "do it now"—that is, enact the Constitution—he feared "we shall never have another opportunity."

It was a perfect speech by a perfect delegate to address the fears and distrust that King described. From his previous service in elected bodies, Smith knew many men in the hall and they knew him, which no doubt helped him hit the mark (and reduces the likelihood that he was a Federalist "plant"). In any case, Dummer Sewall said the speech "exceeded all in favour" of the Constitution. Martin Kingsley, who had supported the Shaysites, tried to get Smith ruled out of order: What, he asked, did the events of the previous winter have to do with the Constitution? But several delegates, including Samuel Adams, said Smith was in order and called out, "Go on, go on."[12] The speech's relevance to Article I, Section 8, was, however, loose at best. After a few more speeches that further discussed the probable forms of federal taxation and the checks on power that were and were not written into the Constitution, the convention moved on to Article I, Section 9, which put certain explicit limits on Congress.

Again, despite an intemperate remark by Samuel Thompson, who said the Constitution was "a consistent piece of inconsistency," the "conversation" took the form of a reasoned inquiry. A Quaker from Maine expressed profound opposition to the clause preventing Congress from ending the slave trade for twenty years; other delegates celebrated the fact that under the Constitution, unlike the Confederation, it *could* be ended after twenty years. Dr. John

Taylor asked why there was no time limit on the suspension of habeas corpus, as there was in the Massachusetts constitution. Two members of the state's supreme judicial court, judges Dana and Increase Sumner, answered. Sumner patiently explained how the writ allowed persons who were imprisoned to force their jailers to produce the evidence that justified their incarceration or to release them. Habeas corpus was therefore "essential to freedom." On some occasions, however, it had to be suspended: Our "worst enemy may lay plans to destroy us, and so artfully as to prevent any evidence against him, and might ruin the country, without the power to suspend the writ." Given the importance of habeas corpus for freedom, both Dana and Sumner agreed that those suspensions had to be restricted. But Dana considered the clause in the Massachusetts constitution limiting suspensions by the legislature to a period "not exceeding twelve months" relatively ineffectual, since the legislature could renew the suspension "from time to time, or from year to year." By saying Congress could suspend habeas corpus only in cases of rebellion or invasion, the Constitution made it more secure. Invasions and rebellions were "facts of public notoriety," clear and indisputable. If there was no invasion or rebellion, habeas corpus could not be suspended. And it could be suspended, Sumner added, only by Congress and for persons held under its authority.[13]

On January 28, after Theophilus Parsons gave a "Loud Speach" on habeas corpus, the convention turned briefly to Article I, Section 10, which placed restrictions on the states. Most of the discussion seems to have focused on the second paragraph, which prevented the states from collecting duties on imports or exports, with Federalist speakers explaining the provision and emphasizing the benefits of uniform national commercial legislation. Surviving records suggest the delegates said nothing at all about the first paragraph, which prevented the states from coining money, emitting bills of credit, making anything but gold and silver legal tender, or impairing the obligations of contract, which could have been a red flag to onetime insurgents.[14]

In the afternoon the convention moved on to Article II, on the executive, which it debated until midway through the morning of January 29—less than a full day. Gorham justified putting executive authority in one man, and he argued that it was better to have the president chosen by electors than by Congress or "the people at large." King explained that the president would have no council because each state would insist on having at least one member, which would make it too much like the Senate.[15] Phanuel Bishop objected "as usual," as a newspaper account put it, because of "a supposed *breach of trust* & suspicion of roguery" in the president and Senate; and "Old White"—Abraham White, a longtime member of the state legislature—claimed that the president had the power of deciding life and death, and without the use of a jury. In the struggle with Britain Americans had cried out "a Jury—a Jury—a Jury," he said, but now they were "giving up this darling Privilege." That provoked "a universal laugh." Samuel Adams explained that "his friend" was mistaken; the president could only pardon a criminal or "*put him to his Jury* for trial." After a few inconclusive exchanges over whether an act of Congress or a treaty approved only by the president and Senate could oblige the militia to engage in conflicts outside the United States, the convention moved on to Article III and the judiciary.[16]

Again, the "conversation" was relatively brief. When an unidentified delegate noted that the Constitution would allow a person to bring a case in federal court against a resident of another state although only a small amount of property was in contention, Theophilus Parsons admitted that was a problem but said it "will not do to throw away a Constitution for so Small an Inconvenience." Later, after Gilbert Dench (Hopkinton, Middlesex County) asked what jurisdiction was delegated to federal courts and what was reserved to the states, Parsons simply said that only one in a hundred cases could be carried into federal courts. Meanwhile, Eleazer Brooks (Lincoln, Middlesex County) questioned the Constitution's silence about jury trials in civil cases. Caleb Strong explained that state practices were so different that the convention thought it best to let Congress find a way of settling the issue. Theodore Sedgwick claimed that references to courts implied that there would also be juries as well as judges, but Abraham White and several of his colleagues remained unconvinced.[17]

The next day, January 30, Abraham Holmes from Rochester (Plymouth County) spoke at length about the Constitution's failure to prohibit Congress from compelling men accused of crimes to furnish evidence against themselves, forcing men to prove their innocence (rather than assuming innocence until guilt is proven), or from "inventing the most cruel and unheard of punishments." Nothing in the Constitution prevented Congress from establishing judicatories like those of the Inquisition. He was not saying, Holmes explained, that Congress would do such a thing, but if it failed to act in so reprehensible a way, its restraint would be due to the goodness of its members "and not in the *least degree* owing to the GOODNESS of the CONSTITUTION." Again, Federalists answered that Congress would not do what was not in its honor and interest to do, and what would be "of no advantage" to its members.[18]

On the convention went to Article IV, including a provision for admitting new states into the union that should have been of particular interest to Maine delegates. The debates, for which there are almost no records, took up only a part of one afternoon. Rufus King claimed that under the Confederation there was no way to erect new states. He added that the establishment of new states "in the Eastern parts" of the country—Vermont and perhaps also Maine, since he spoke of "states"—would turn the balance of power in the Senate in favor of the "Eastern States."[19]

On the morning of January 31, the convention moved on to Article V and the procedures for amending the Constitution. A couple of speakers praised the provision for providing a means of peaceful political reformation unknown in any other nation. Since Article V said no amendment could affect the provision in Article I, Section 9, preventing Congress from prohibiting the slave trade before 1808, some delegates again attacked the Constitution's protection of the slave trade for twenty years and went on to condemn the institution of slavery. The argument that concessions to the slave states were necessary to save the union did not reconcile Dr. John Taylor to supporting and perhaps helping to perpetuate the slave system: We may not do evil, he said, that good might come of it. General William Heath, from Roxbury on Boston's outskirts to the west, answered that each state had authority over its internal affairs. The nonslave states could therefore do nothing about the institution of slavery in the states where it already existed. For that reason, he argued, "we are not in this case partakers of other men's sins." He did not persuade James Neal, a Quaker, who represented Kittery, Maine.[20]

In midmorning, the convention took up Article VI, whose second paragraph made the controversial assertion that the Constitution and all laws made pursuant to it and all treaties made under the authority of the United States would be "the supreme Law of the Land"; the judges in every state were bound by them, despite anything their state laws and constitution said to the contrary. Two days earlier Amos Singletary claimed that provision would allow the federal government to destroy all the laws of the states, and that if anyone had proposed such a thing ten years earlier he would have been called a Tory. On January 31, however, the delegates seem to have focused instead on the final provision of Article VI, which said no religious test would be required to hold any office or public trust under the United States. Some delegates said that clause went against the tradition of their forefathers, who came to America to preserve their religion. If "our publick men" had "a good standing in the church," a delegate from Maine insisted, "it would be happy for the United States" since "a person could not be a good man without being a good Christian." However, Daniel Shute, minister of the Second Congregational Church of Hingham (Suffolk County), said there were "worthy characters" among the followers of every denomination, including Catholics and the devotees of "natural religion," and none should be excluded from office because of their religious views.[21]

The convention skipped Article VII, which said the assent of nine states was sufficient to enact the Constitution.[22] Then, before the morning session for Thursday, January 31, had ended, the convention suddenly closed its "conversation" on the Constitution by paragraphs. Parsons moved "that this Convention do assent to and ratify this Constitution," and the convention began discussing the Constitution as a whole and whether or not it merited ratification. A vote could not be far off. Rufus King predicted that the convention would complete its business within a week—on the next Saturday or else the following Tuesday.[23]

The convention's pace had quickened once it left Article I behind. That made some sense, since everyone assumed that the powers of Congress would define those of the new government. The president would execute Congress's decisions—to impose new taxes, for example, or declare war—and the judiciary would try violators of its laws, so Article I of the Constitution, which defined the structure and powers of Congress, was the most important. Even so, the speed with which the convention tore through the last six articles, "covering" two in one morning and skipping over or saying little about provisions that must have bothered some delegates, was striking. The brakes Federalists had applied on January 24, when Nasson tried to stop the convention's discussion of the Constitution by paragraphs and bring on the final vote, were nowhere in sight. Something had changed, something that was not arranged or decided in public, on the convention floor.

A note Jeremy Belknap added to his convention notes for January 28 offers a clue. "The federalists," it said, "now seem to be sure of carrying [the] Constitut[io]n." Two days later, late in the morning on Wednesday, January 30, the convention's elected president, Governor John Hancock, rose from his sickbed and, to the great delight of the spectators crowded into the galleries as well as the delegates below, took his place at the front of the convention.[24] His arrival had everything to do with the Federalists' new confidence.

STRIKING A DEAL

Hancock, who appeared wrapped in flannel, must have made a dramatic entrance. Perhaps, as Rufus King and others suspected, his long confinement was in part political. He wanted to see in which direction the convention was moving, to avoid alienating either his constituents in Boston, who were ardent Federalists, or those in rural parts of the state who were opposed to or had strong reservations about the Constitution. Still, the man was not—or did not appear to be—in good health. He could not walk and had to be carried by his servants into the Long Lane meeting house.[25] Rising from his sickbed was an act of will. Hancock did it because a set of Federalists persuaded him that his attendance at the convention was critical. They also made it worth his while.

By late January, the convention's leading Federalists—Gorham, King, Parsons, Tristram Dalton, and perhaps others—were meeting in a caucus, trying desperately to find a way to get a positive vote on ratification.[26] They adopted the idea that King and Gorham had suggested earlier in the month: proposing a series of amendments that would be recommended in conjunction with an unconditional ratification of the Constitution. The state's representatives would be instructed to propose those amendments in the first federal Congress. The hope, as Gorham said, was to draw some delegates away from the opposition—not perhaps those who wanted the Constitution entirely rejected, but those who remained uncertain and who objected only to parts of the Constitution or to its lack of certain provisions. The proposal would be most likely to succeed, they decided, if Hancock presented it to the convention.

There had been no discussion of amendments in the convention itself aside from Phanuel Bishop's suggestion that Congress's power over elections should be limited to cases where states failed to act. The format of the convention's proceedings, consisting of an extended "conversation" on the Constitution, was, after all, designed in part to prevent delegates from proposing amendments. However, the opposition of several towns to the Constitution "as it now stands" suggested that a few changes might make it acceptable. Moreover, as noted earlier, the amendments proposed by "Hampden" in the January 26 *Massachusetts Centinel* had provoked discussion among delegates outside the convention hall. The author was probably James Sullivan, a friend of Hancock's and a member of the governor's council who supported ratification despite some reservations about the Constitution but who, to his great disappointment, had not been elected as a Boston convention delegate.[27]

Sullivan did not call for a second convention to consider amendments. Instead he proposed that Massachusetts ratify on the condition that the first Congress elected under the Constitution consider amendments proposed by Massachusetts and other states before proceeding to any other business except organizing itself and establishing its rules of procedure. It should "make such amendments" as seven states would approve, he suggested, and in considering them the Senate and House of Representatives should sit as one body and vote by states. Sullivan proposed seven amendments that would limit Congress's power over congressional elections to cases where states failed to act (as Bishop had suggested); allow state supreme court judges to issue writs of habeas corpus for persons arrested under federal laws; deny Congress a general power to tax but allow it to impose excise taxes and duties on imports; and eliminate federal courts' jurisdiction over cases between a state and a citizen of another state (Sullivan said that making a state liable to being sued violated state sovereignty) and between citizens of different states. Another three of his amendments affirmed the use of both grand juries and petit juries drawn from the vicinity in federal court proceedings.[28]

Although the Federalists in the convention refused to make amendments a condition of ratification, there is some evidence that they took the amendments Sullivan proposed into consideration. For example, William Cushing, the convention's vice president and a leading Federalist (who was not, however, clearly part of the caucus), seems to have tried rewriting three of Sullivan's amendments,[29] and the amendments the Federalists finally proposed had some similarities to Sullivan's.

First, however, the Federalists had to get Hancock on board. Their plan might well have coincided with Hancock's inclinations. Six years later, in a eulogy written after Hancock's death, James Sullivan claimed that Hancock had reservations about the Constitution and, before the state ratifying convention had even assembled, drafted a set of amendments he planned to propose.[30] That, along with uncertainty over popular sentiment, might explain why Hancock assiduously avoided endorsing the Constitution when he presented it to the legislature back in October. Getting him to attend the convention and sponsor amendments that the Federalist leaders were prepared to support would, however, require a very persuasive emissary.

Long after the fact—in the 1840s—Francis Baylies, the son of a convention delegate from Dighton (Bristol County), testified that his father told him the chosen intermediary was the Reverend Samuel West, a convention delegate from New Bedford on the south coast of Massachusetts (also Bristol County) and pastor of the First Congregational Society there. That choice made sense. West and Hancock were in many ways opposites: Hancock was wealthy, polished, not particularly intellectual but focused and politically wise, while West was poor, somewhat awkward, scholarly, and, it seems, hopelessly absentminded. They were, however, Harvard classmates (Class of 1754) and friends. West was also a strong Hancock supporter and had nothing personal to gain from the course of action he proposed. West, Baylies said, was selected to visit Hancock by "a conference among a few [convention] members." He agreed and went to the governor's home. After some chitchat on Hancock's "bodily complaints," West expressed regret that Hancock's illness was keeping him from the convention, since his presence was necessary to save his country from anarchy. He talked of Hancock's influence and his patriotism, then said heaven had given him another "glorious opportunity" to save his country and "bring imperishable honour to himself" by attending and "proposing the conciliatory plan of recommendations."[31]

Later Baylies suggested that another delegate who was also an old friend of Hancock's, Azor Orne, a convention delegate from Marblehead, joined West, and that "several others" solicited Hancock to take on the task. When Hancock pleaded his illness and lack of influence, Orne supposedly replied, "Sir, you are not aware of the extent of your influence. Your sickness, instead of impairing, will strengthen it. Even the baize which swathes your limbs, will produce an impression. If you cannot speak, you will gather many around you like birds, by a whistle."[32]

Success probably demanded more than appeals to Hancock's legendary vanity. Hancock seems to have cut a hard deal, demanding that Bowdoin's old supporters back him in the next gubernatorial election. Rufus King, at any rate, wrote Henry Knox that Hancock "will hereafter receive the universal support of Bowdoin's Friends." King and his confederates also told Hancock that if Virginia did not ratify the Constitution—and its decision remained "problematical"—then, with Washington disqualified and assuming the requisite nine states approved the Constitution, he would be "the only fair candidate for President."[33] On January 30, when Hancock made his grand entrance, Dalton, a member of the Federalist caucus, said that Hancock would support the Constitution "if he may be depended on," which suggested some agreement had been struck, and that the Constitution would then be ratified by a "large majority." Samuel Adams, he added, would also support ratification. "All this," he added, "is scarcely known out of our caucus, wherein we work as hard as in the convention."[34]

The conditional "if" in Dalton's statement about Hancock left some doubt about whether the governor would follow through. King used the same word in a letter to Madison: "If Mr. Hancock does not disappoint our present Expectations," he said, "our wishes will be gratified." It was then that King noted the "portion of caprice" in Hancock's character.[35] In the meantime, as Nathaniel Gorham reported, the caucus spent the evening after Hancock took his place in the convention busily preparing amendments that would "be ready for tomorrow," when they would be presented "if a proper pause offers." Participants had no time to drop lines to colleagues elsewhere who were desperate for news except in moments "stolen" from the caucus. "Never," Dalton said, "never were men more anxious than we are."[36]

The next morning, after Parsons moved that the convention ratify the Constitution, the convention's debate on the entire document began slowly. One delegate said he would vote against ratification unless "the article which respected the Africans" (probably preventing abolition of the slave trade before 1808) were removed; another complained again about the lack of a religious test for office. That prompted the Reverend Phillips Payson, a Congregational minister who represented the town of Chelsea, just north of Boston, to denounce all such tests as "impious encroachments upon the prerogatives of God," who alone could judge men's consciences. Then General William Heath took the floor and opened a carefully orchestrated dramatic sequence.[37]

The convention, he said, having ended a "long and painful" investigation of the Constitution by paragraphs, was "drawing nigh to the ultimate question," one "as momentous as ever invited the attention of man." It was about to decide upon a system of government not just for the people of Massachusetts and the current people of the United States but also for states that would join the federation in the future and "millions of people yet unborn." On that decision would depend "our political prosperity or infelicity, perhaps our existence as a nation. What can be more solemn? What can be more interesting?" Everything depended on the union. If it were broken, "our country, as a nation perishes," and it would then be as hard to save a particular state "as to preserve one of the fingers of a mortified hand."[38]

It would be a "happy circumstance," he went on, if only a small majority ratified the Constitution, but even happier if the decision were unanimous. He presumed that every gentleman in the hall wanted an efficient federal government with every necessary power "to shed on the people the benign influences of a good government." But many delegates seemed opposed due to certain parts of the Constitution. "Is there not a way in which their minds may be relieved from embarrassment?" He thought there was. If the convention ratified the Constitution and instructed the state's first members of Congress "to exert their utmost endeavours to have such checks, and guards provided as appears to be necessary in some of the paragraphs of the Constitution," and request the concurrence of other states in that proposal, "is there not the highest probability that every thing which we wish may be effectually secured"?[39]

When Heath had finished, Hancock rose. He was conscious, he said, of the impropriety of his joining the deliberations of the convention, given his protracted absence due to the "painful indisposition of his body." However, from the newspapers and other sources of information, he concluded that the convention was divided due to "a great dissimilarity of Sentiments." To remove some objections to the Constitution, he proposed to "hazard a proposition" for the delegates' consideration. With the convention's permission, he would present it that afternoon. Then the convention adjourned. Excitement was high. Rather than leave the hall and risk losing their seats, "hundreds continued there [through] the whole of the adjournment, and sent home & had their *dinners* brought [to] them."[40]

They were not disappointed. In the afternoon, the convention ordered its Committee on the Pay Roll to calculate its accounts through the next Tuesday, a sure sign that the end was near. Then Hancock rose again. The entire house, packed with people, went silent. The governor said he thought it was necessary to adopt the Constitution—an announcement of major significance. After frequent conversations with members of the convention, he had concluded that some general amendments to the Constitution might remove doubts and quiet certain apprehensions. He submitted his proposal with a sincere wish that it would promote a spirit of union.[41]

Hancock's proposition had two parts. The first said, without qualifications, that the convention, on behalf of the people of Massachusetts, assented to and ratified the Constitution. Then, to remove the fears of many people and "more effectively guard against an undue administration of the federal government," Hancock proposed that the convention "enjoin it upon their Representatives in Congress" to "exert all their influence" to secure nine amendments to the Constitution. The first amendment asked that a clause be inserted in the Constitution saying, like Article II of the Articles of Confederation, that all powers not expressly delegated to Congress were reserved to the states. The second specified that the number of representatives "shall be" (rather than "shall not exceed") one for every thirty thousand persons until the members of the House of Representatives reached a number that Hancock's proposal left blank. Third, Congress could not exercise its power over congressional elections "but in cases where a State shall neglect or refuse to make adequate provision for an equal representation of the people." That included Phanuel Bishop's original proposal (to let Congress intervene only when the states failed to act) and also the more expansive understanding of the provision advanced by Dana and other Federalists, who would make Congress a guardian of the people's right to equal representation against violations by the states. Fourth, Congress could not impose direct taxes except when revenue from excise and import taxes was insufficient "for the public exigencies." The fifth proposed amendment denied Congress the right to create commercial monopolies. The sixth and eighth affirmed the use by federal courts of the grand jury in criminal cases and the petit jury in civil cases. The seventh denied federal courts jurisdiction in cases between citizens of different states unless the matter in dispute was worth at least a sum that, again, was left blank. Finally, Hancock proposed removing the words "without the Consent of Congress" from the last paragraph of Article I, Section 9, so there would be an absolute prohibition on federal officeholders' accepting any emolument, office, or title from a foreign country or king.[42]

Hancock, Jeremy Belknap reported, was the "ostensible Puppet in proposing amendments" that were drafted by Federalists who thought they would be better received coming from Hancock than from anyone else. George Minot, the convention's secretary, said the text of the amendments Hancock read to the convention was in the handwriting of Theophilus Parsons, who was probably the main draftsman, except for one amendment, which was in King's hand, and a few words that Boston delegate Charles Jarvis wrote.[43] There is, however, evidence that the amendments themselves were worked out in negotiations with Hancock and also Samuel Adams, whose participation is otherwise inexplicable, since he had nothing to gain but the satisfaction of his constituents.[44] The final proposal was probably a compromise that addressed Hancock's and Adams's objections to the Constitution and honored the Federalists' insistence on an unconditional ratification by endorsing amendments that would be enacted only after the new government began to operate.[45]

In the end, all participants in the drama played their parts to perfection. Hancock "came forward in full support of adopting the Constitution" and presented the *"recommendatory* amendments," which the "Old Patriot," Samuel Adams, "seconded warmly." Adams said the amendments would help remove doubts about the Constitution among both delegates and the people. If large minorities of dissenters like that at the Pennsylvania convention developed in other states, disunion could result. However, "a proposal, of this sort, coming from Massachusetts," would have considerable weight among states whose conventions had not yet met. For that reason, he thought Hancock's recommended amendments were the most promising way of getting the Constitution amended and reuniting the country. Adams moved that the convention give Hancock's proposal precedence over Parsons's earlier motion to ratify. The delegates agreed and opened a general debate on ratification coupled with Hancock's recommended amendments.[46]

DECISION TIME

Hancock's proposal surprised most delegates and spectators. At first it seemed to backfire, allowing the Constitution's critics to take the initiative and put its supporters on the defensive. By suggesting amendments, they argued, the Federalists themselves admitted that the Constitution was imperfect. And since the amendments would never be adopted, they would not repair the problems they were meant to fix. Moreover, Dr. John Taylor insisted, nothing in its commission gave the convention authority to propose amendments; it could only "take the whole—or reject the whole." Later William Widgery took the same position: The convention, he said, could only "adopt or reject the Constitution." In effect, these determined opponents of the Constitution adopted the old Federalist position that state ratifying conventions and the people they represented had to take it or leave it. Unlike the Federalists, however, they favored leaving it—that is, rejecting the Constitution or, as Taylor suggested, adjourning without taking a vote on ratification.[47]

Over the next two days, February 1–2, the supporters of ratification defended the amendments. Adams went through them one by one, arguing that they protected the people's rights and assured the continued existence of the states. Others, such as Dalton, said they supported the amendments not as necessary responses to constitutional imperfections but as a conciliatory measure, to satisfy delegates who had doubts about the Constitution. Samuel Nasson, a prominent critic of the Constitution, gave a long speech that someone else might have written for him before Hancock made his proposal. He talked about "the Constitution at large," not Hancock's amendments, which he said he had not had time to study. It became clear, however, that the proposed amendments did not address his main objections to the Constitution: the length of representatives' and senators' terms, their capacity to be reelected indefinitely, the equal representation of states in the Senate, the assessment of direct taxes without regard to people's ability to pay, and Congress's power "to raise and support armies," which Nasson saw as threatening military rule. The delegates also discussed the chances that Hancock's amendments would be adopted. Federalists were optimistic; their opponents thought the possibility was remote at best.[48]

Hancock's proposals left blanks to be filled in. Moreover, as Adams acknowledged, the delegates were free to propose other amendments or perhaps to revise those already under consideration. On Saturday, February 2, General Josiah Whitney from the town of Harvard (Worcester County), whom Tristram Dalton described as a "half-converted *Anti*," moved that a committee consisting of two delegates from each of the state's counties consider the amendments with some additional proposals and report back to the convention. The Federalist Theodore Sedgwick seconded the motion, which the convention adopted unanimously. Representatives from twelve counties were asked to choose two delegates, one who had spoken for and one who had spoken against the Constitution. In the end, however, the Federalists had a majority because Dukes County—Martha's Vineyard—would have only one committee member, and its two delegates chose a Federalist.[49]

The "committee of twenty-five" set to work and did the unthinkable in eighteenth-century Massachusetts: It met on the Sabbath. Dummer Sewall, who generally attended religious services every few days, reported in his journal that "instead of attending Divine Worship" he attended the committee meeting in the state senate chamber. Meanwhile, the convention remained adjourned until three o'clock on Monday afternoon, when the committee was expected to present its report.[50]

The final vote was only a few days away. It would not be held before Tuesday, the convention decided, to assure that delegates who went home for the Sabbath would be back in time, and it would surely come no later than Thursday. And still nobody was confident how it would go. "The Constitutionalists say they have a majority," James Sullivan reported on Sunday, while the committee was working away. "This is denied by the anti-Constitutionalists," and "which is nearest the Truth" he couldn't say because he didn't know. The delegates were equally in the dark. "As ye day approaches & the Strength of both sides is so great that neither can *certainly* depend on a Majority," Jeremy Belknap wrote on that tense Sunday, "the anxiety of every friend to governm[en]t & Justice is increased." Christopher Gore could say no more than that there was "a fair probability of an adoption," and King wrote Madison that "the Event is not absolutely certain." The uncertainty was all the more disturbing because the decision seemed so freighted with importance for the future. " 'Life & Death are before us,'" Belknap wrote, recalling the passage from Deuteronomy that John Winthrop had put before the first shipload of passengers to Massachusetts Bay almost 160 years earlier: "I have set before you life and death . . . therefore choose life, that both thou and thy seed may live."[51]

For those in distant parts of the state, the tension became almost unbear-able. "The perturbation of mind we are in can be better conceived than described," Henry Van Schaak wrote to Stockbridge delegate Theodore Sedgwick, begging for news, on February 4. "I can bring myself to think of nothing but this important matter," which "is the last of my thought when I go to bed & the first in the morning when I wake." He added that "our friends in the State of New York are anxious beyond description," and that Stephen Van Rensselaer, the "patroon" of Rensselaer Manor, had asked him to hire an express rider to carry the hoped-for news of ratification to Albany. Rensselaer probably planned to forward the news down the Hudson River to Poughkeep-sie, where the New York legislature was discussing whether or not to call a ratifying convention. "In short," he wrote, "every thing depends on us."[52]

Under the pressure, tempers frayed. The Boston merchant Henry Jackson, who witnessed the convention from the galleries, wrote Henry Knox that "the Antis are affraid & very skittish, for they fear they may be led into a *trap*, by the proposed amendments." They were, he said, "so damnable stupid & ignorant that they cannot trust themselves." The whole opposition to the Constitution in Massachusetts came from "*that cursed spirit of Insurgency* that prevailed the last year" and would never be rooted out "but by a firm & energetic government," which is what the Constitution's opponents dreaded "because they have so much reason too." He added that "the whole race of the *Antis*" were "a set of *poor devils*, without one farthing in their pockets," who couldn't leave town unless they received their pay. They were beginning to be alarmed because the state treasurer told them he did not have "a dollar in the public Chest" and did not know where he could borrow the money. The Federalists circulated a rumor, Jackson said, that "if the Constitution is adopted, there will be no dificulty [sic] respecting the Pay—If it *is not* they must look to the Treasurer for it." In other words, if the convention voted to ratify, wealthy Bostonians would lend the state money to pay the delegates, much as they had lent it money to support the campaign against Shays's Re-bellion. If not, the delegates might well go home empty-handed.[53]

The committee reported late Monday afternoon, February 4. Most of the changes it made to Hancock's proposal were minor. It polished the language of Hancock's amendments and filled in the blanks, specifying that there would be one representative for thirty thousand people until there were two hundred members in the House of Representatives, and also stating the minimum amount in dispute between citizens of different states before federal courts would have jurisdiction. More important, it added a clause that precluded Congress from raising direct taxes, even if the revenues from excise taxes and import duties were insufficient for "the public exigencies," unless it first gave state legislatures an opportunity to raise their proportion of the general levy in whatever way they thought best. If, however, a state neglected to pay its requisition, then Congress could raise the funds itself and tack on to the original requisition six percent per year from the time the original payment was due. The committee report, moreover, was clearly a form of ratification. It ended with a resolution that "the assent and ratification aforesaid," with the recommended amendments, would be engrossed on parchment, signed by the president and vice president of the convention and countersigned by its secretary "under their hands and seals," and forwarded to "the United States in Congress assembled." A vote to accept the report would be a vote to ratify.[54]

The vote by which the committee agreed to submit the report to the convention was startling. Considering the way it had been chosen, a vote of thirteen to twelve could have been expected. Instead fifteen voted in favor and only seven against. Three of those who had criticized the Constitution in earlier debates did not vote (two were excused and one absent). Two others—Nathaniel Barrell and David Sylvester, both from Maine—were among the fifteen committee members who endorsed the report. Perhaps Hancock's proposal was already serving the Federalists' purpose by neutralizing or winning the support of some delegates who had previously opposed ratification of the unamended Constitution.[55]

The convention's debate on the report also brought some surprises. The critics of the Constitution repeated old arguments, regretting the lack of religious qualifications for office and the twenty-year ban on ending the slave trade, and insisting that the recommended amendments would never be enacted. No less prominent a man than Isaac Backus, the Baptist minister whom Samuel Stillman had courted at Daggett's, answered. Both reason and the Bible showed that religion was always a matter between God and the individual, he said. As a result, no man or men could impose religious tests without invading "the essential prerogatives of our Lord Jesus Christ." Moreover, all history showed that religious tests were "the greatest engine of tyranny in the world." As for slavery, he too hated it, but he noted that the Constitution had opened a door for the future abolition of the slave trade that was absent under the Articles of Confederation and affirmed an earlier prediction by Dawes that slavery itself was fated to die out. Backus praised the Constitution's exclusion of titles of nobility and hereditary succession as expressions of a principle basic to the "American revolution . . . that all men are born with an equal right to liberty and property, and that officers have no right to any power but what is fairly given them by the consent of the people." The people could constitutionally reduce to a "private station" any officer who invaded their rights or abused his power. "Such a door is now opened, for the establishment of righteous government, and for securing equal liberty," Backus concluded, "as never was before opened at any people on earth."[56] Backus was on board. Would other Baptists follow him?

Then Dr. Charles Jarvis from Boston—another delegate whose convictions on the Constitution were once in some doubt—delivered a powerful
answer to those who said the convention had no power to propose amendments. "If we have a right . . . to receive, or reject the Constitution," he said,
"surely we have an equal authority to determine in what way this right shall
be exercised." The convention derived its authority not from the "late federal
Convention" or Congress or the state legislature, but from the people who
authorized their delegates "to execute the most important trust which it is
possible to receive." Those who said the convention could not recommend
changes in the Constitution "must have ideas strangely derogatory to the
influence and authority of our constituents," whose "aggregate sense . . . can
only be determined by the voices of the majority of this Convention." Fisher
Ames took the same position. "Have we no right to propose amendments?"
he asked. "This is the fullest representation of the people ever known—and
if we may not declare their opinion, and upon a point for which we have
been elected, how shall it ever be known?"[57]

First opponents of the Constitution like John Taylor and William Widgery took over the Federalist position that conventions had to "take this or
nothing," to vote the Constitution up or down and do nothing else; and now
Jarvis and Ames, the latter at least a committed Federalist, became defenders of the people's right to propose amendments. The convention's strange
transformations were like those in a story Abraham Lincoln would later tell
about a fight between two drunks: At the end of the brawl, each contender
had somehow fought his way into the other man's overcoat.

The ratification for which Federalists argued was, of course, unconditional: The convention's vote would not turn on the enactment of the amendments it recommended. Jarvis argued against conditional amendments not
as beyond the authority of the convention and the people for whom it spoke,
but as unwise. Five states had already ratified without demanding amendments. Under the circumstances, a vote to ratify on the condition that certain
amendments were accepted would be tantamount to a rejection, which risked
losing all the advantages a strengthened federal government would bring.
Moreover, if another four states ratified like the first five—that is, without
amendments—Massachusetts would either have to give in or stay outside
the union. If outside, it would have no voice in the debate over amendments
in the first federal Congress, which Ames described as "too absurd to need
any further discussion." The ratifying convention could, however, hope to
influence states that had not yet met. The amendments Massachusetts would
hopefully propose were not for the benefit of Massachusetts alone; they were
general and suitable to the circumstances of people, as Jarvis put it, "on the
banks of the Savannah" as well as those along the Kennebec in Maine. "Why
then they should not be adopted," he said, "I confess I cannot conceive."[58]

In his notes for the day, Jeremy Belknap reported that the speakers had won "many Proselytes . . . to [the] federal Side." A week earlier a delegate from Stoughton (Suffolk County), Elijah Dunbar, announced that he had changed his position on the Constitution and would vote for ratification. That provoked an attack by Samuel Thompson, who claimed that Stoughton had instructed its delegates to oppose ratification. Then the Reverend Samuel West of New Bedford, the Federalist emissary to Hancock, responded to Thompson by denouncing instructions and urging delegates to act on principle. If they had promised to vote against the Constitution but had been persuaded "it was right," West said, they should "*repent of their wicked* promise & vote accord[in]g to their Judgment." Dunbar also defended himself, which was easy since his town had in fact voted to let its delegates decide for themselves how to vote.[59] Not all of his wavering colleagues had that advantage. If their towns had instructed them to vote "no" for reasons Federalist speakers had persuasively explained away, what were they to do? Follow their convictions or their instructions? If at an earlier time their constituents opposed the Constitution "as it now stands," did the recommended amendments sufficiently change the situation that they could vote "yea"?

The delegates' sense of responsibility to their constituents was strong. The consequences of ignoring instructions—or even a nonbinding resolution that the Constitution "as it now stands" was unacceptable—could be devastating. The delegates' constituents were their neighbors, the people they would have to face day after day once they went home: at religious services, in town meetings, taverns, the local store, or chance encounters along the road. Moreover, coming to a reasoned judgment after hearing the convention's debate was no simple thing. It required weighing complex considerations against each other. Nobody—not even Fisher Ames—argued that the Constitution was perfect, only that it was "good and happy . . . upon the whole," and that its rejection would threaten disunion and anarchy while giving up the economic advantages a strong federal government would bring.[60] How would delegates balance the threats raised by its imperfections against the gains it promised? And how could they justify a vote to ratify to the folks back home who thought differently?

In one of the convention's final days, Nathaniel Barrell expressed the dilemmas that many other delegates also faced. He was, he said, a "plain husbandman" whose talents did not equal those of the convention's "giants of rhetoric," but his constituents expected something more from him than a "silent vote." Barrell had been a member of the committee of twenty-five and voted for its report. He nonetheless had several objections to the Constitution: senators' six-year terms, congressmen's setting their own salaries, Congress's extensive taxing power, the probable cost of the new government, the fact that the Constitution was often "obscure and ambiguous" (although a frame of government should be "so simple and explicit, that the most illiterate may understand it"). Some of his objections had been removed "by the ingenious reasonings" of its defenders, he said, but not all of them. He thought amendments to the Constitution were necessary to secure "that liberty, without which life is a burden," and he would prefer to have the changes made before it went into effect. The proceedings in Pennsylvania also gave him pause. He wished the Constitution had not been "in some parts of the continent hurried on like the driving of Jehu very furiously," since such deliberations demanded "cool deliberation." Still, he wanted the Constitution ratified because he feared anarchy and thought it was "the best Constitution we can now obtain." His deepest wish, he said, was for an adjournment so he could lay before his constituents "the arguments . . . used in the debates" that had "eased" his mind. That, he thought, would bring them "heartily to join me in ratifying the same." If he could not first speak with his constituents, however, he was "almost tempted to risque their displeasure and adopt it without their consent."[61] *Almost*, not more.

Late in the morning of February 5—the day some thought the final vote would come—Gilbert Dench, a critic of the Constitution, moved that the convention "adjourn to a future day" for the purpose of informing the people "of the principles of the proposed Federal Constitution" and the amendments proposed by Hancock and modified by the committee of twenty-five. Henry Jackson—who, as a spectator, could indulge in harsh judgments that Federalist delegates worked hard to suppress—said the motion was made by "Rascals" for the purpose of "*damning* this business" because the "*Antis*" had "discovered their weakness." Perhaps. Isaac Backus, however, described the effort as "earnest"—that is, a sincere effort on the part of men like Barrell to consult their constituents. The motion, however, raised more problems than it solved. How far off was "a future time"? Would the towns send new delegates, perhaps with new instructions, to the reconvened convention? Would it need to go over all its debates a second time? What about the cost to the commonwealth? Federalists, fearful of losing the gains they had made, opposed the motion, but so did others for different reasons. The convention debated the proposition for the better part of the day, then voted it down, with 115 in favor, 214 against. The convention had finally counted heads on a formal proposition and, despite the complex considerations that explain the majority, the result discouraged the opposition.[62]

The convention planned to vote on the committee report—and so on ratification—the next morning, Wednesday, February 6. Then Samuel Adams threw a wrench into the plan: He moved to amend the committee report by adding explicit provisions barring Congress from interfering with a long list of civil liberties. The effort was paradoxical; he himself had said earlier that the amendment reserving to the states all powers not expressly granted to Congress was "a summary of a bill of rights," and, moreover, that any federal laws that went beyond that limit would be "adjudged by the courts of law to be void." Adams's proposal was a mistake, particularly if he intended to ease the delegates' fears. Instead it heightened them by suggesting that he thought the Constitution still posed a serious threat to civil liberties. Once he saw the confusion he had caused, Adams tried to withdraw the motion, but critics of the Constitution renewed it. In the end, he voted against his own motion, which failed "by a very large general Vote." Jeremy Belknap thought the maneuver "lost the Constitution several Votes," votes that it could not easily spare.[63]

The convention put off its final decision to the afternoon, which left time for Samuel Stillman to present a lengthy address over which he had labored long and hard. Stillman quoted at length Governor Edmund Randolph's letter to the Virginia assembly, including his statement that he would support ratification even if the effort to amend the Constitution failed. In that spirit, Stillman called on the delegates to unite behind the Constitution "as a band of brothers." He stressed the importance of the decision before them for Massachusetts and the union, and he explained at length how the powers granted Congress under the Constitution were defined and limited. He was willing, he said, "to submit my life, my liberty, my family, my property, and . . . the interest of my constituents, to this general government." One observer called it an "elegant speech."[64]

The convention took its midday adjournment, but the galleries again remained full. Henry Jackson sent a boy to buy him a dinner of ginger bread and cheese in a neighboring shop rather than risk losing his seat. Dummer Sewall noted that spectators filled not just the usual galleries but the "Sellar . . . and part of the upper Loft" of the Long Lane church. Nobody wanted to miss hearing the vote called.[65]

When the convention reconvened at three o'clock, another set of speeches added to the drama. Charles Turner, who had spoken ably against the Constitution early in the convention, had been absent for almost two weeks and remained silent even longer because of ill health. He was one of a few men of "practiced eloquence" among the Constitution's critics: He had been a minister in the coastal town of Duxbury for twenty years before retiring in 1775, probably because of ill health, to his family's ancestral home in nearby Scituate. After his retirement, Turner represented Scituate in the state house of representatives and then the senate. He was probably best known for an election day sermon that he presented in 1773 before the royal governor, Thomas Hutchinson, that questioned whether the colonists should be under the *"absolute* disposal" of Parliament and asserted the people's "unalienable right" to alter their constitution of government "at pleasure." Now he again took the floor—not, as in 1773, to ruffle feathers, but to smooth them.[66]

He had been against the Constitution in its original form, Turner said, but the recommendation of amendments reconciled him to it. Although even with the proposed amendments the Constitution would be imperfect, Turner despaired of getting a better one "at present," and he thought the needs of the country made the abandonment of the powerless Confederation and ratification of the Constitution compelling. Captain Jedidiah Southworth, a delegate from Stoughton (Suffolk County), argued for rejection but was too ill to complete his speech. Then William Symmes, the Andover lawyer who had so impressively answered Federalist defenses of the taxing powers entrusted to Congress, announced that the recommended amendments had also reconciled him to ratification. He had no doubt they would be enacted since they were "equally beneficial to all the citizens of America," not just to those of Massachusetts.[67]

Speakers who favored ratification did not monopolize the day's debates, as the published debates suggest. The brief, incomplete notes kept by Justin Dwight, a resolute critic of the Constitution, report that Abraham White called the recommended amendments a piece of sugar "to make the Constitution go down" and hoped "that people will not be taken in." Meanwhile Samuel Thompson said the convention had only "to adopt or reject the Constitution"; Thompson no doubt favored rejection.[68]

Finally, Governor Hancock took the floor. All the arguments against as well as for the Constitution, he said, "have been debated upon with so much learning and ability, that the subject is quite exhausted." Everyone agreed that a general system of government was essential to keep the country from ruin and that the one under consideration had defects. Hancock was confident that the proposed amendments would be enacted, and that the amended Constitution would "give the people of the United States, a greater degree of political freedom, and eventually as much national dignity, as falls to the lot of any nation on earth." But however the convention's vote went, he said there should be "no triumph on one side, or chagrin on the other." Everyone who loved his country should cultivate a spirit of conciliation both in- and outside the convention. "The people of this Commonwealth," he said, are a people "of great intelligence in public business." They knew "we must all rise or fall together" and would abide by the decision of the majority. If the proposed government were rejected, they would propose another; if the Constitution were ratified, they would acquiesce and, if they saw "a want of perfection in it," work for its amendment in "a constitutional way." The question before them, he told the delegates, "is such as no nation on earth . . . have ever had the privilege of deciding upon." Since the "Supreme Ruler of the Universe" had bestowed upon them that "glorious opportunity," "let us decide upon it . . . in humble confidence that he will yet continue to bless and save our country."[69]

The question was put at four o'clock. Would the convention accept the report of the committee of twenty-five and approve both ratification of the Constitution and the nine recommended amendments? The names of 364 delegates were called out, one by one, according to the counties and towns they represented, and they answered with a "yea" or a "nay." The roll must have gone at a fast clip—some six votes a minute—if it was finished by five, as Dummer Sewall reported. We can only imagine Christopher Gore and other practiced scorekeepers checking the votes against their lists of those they expected to vote for or against. Meanwhile, Sewall noted, the crowded hall fell into a deep quiet except for the litany of names and votes. "You might have heard a Copper fall on the Gallery floor," William Widgery remembered, there was "Such a profound Silence."[70]

When the voting was complete, 187 delegates had voted for ratification and 168 against; 9 delegates were absent. Massachusetts had ratified the Constitution with a majority of only 19 out of 355 votes. Soon bells all over Boston began to ring, and the city's people poured into the streets, shouting "huzza" and celebrating what was for them a glorious victory.[71]

"WITH CORDIALITY . . ."

Dummer Sewall voted "yea." So did his travel companion, Nathaniel Wyman, and another Maine delegate, Isaac Snow, who stayed at Daggett's and would join Sewall and Wyman on the trip home. In fact, all but one of the delegates from Maine at Daggett's voted to ratify. Maine delegates in general favored the Constitution by the close vote of 25 to 21. Another lodger at Daggett's, Isaac Backus, also voted for ratification, but of the five Baptist ministers at the convention, only he and Stillman supported the Constitution; Backus estimated that two-thirds of roughly twenty Baptist delegates opposed ratification.[72] The reason is not entirely clear, although the men might have been troubled, like Baptists in Virginia, by what they considered the Constitution's inadequate provision for liberty of conscience.[73] Massachusetts Baptists had suffered enough from the state to make them wary of a strong new government, even under a Constitution that explicitly precluded a religious test for office.

Central and western Massachusetts were also opposed: Worcester County delegates split 7–43, Hampshire County 19–33, Berkshire 7–15. Those three counties together cast 91 of the convention's 168 votes against ratification. Aside from the 21 "nay" votes from Maine, the other 56—a fair proportion—came from rural parts of eastern Massachusetts: Middlesex County, with a narrow eastern side along the Atlantic and a long western border with Worcester County, voted 17 for and 25 against ratification. Bristol County, in the state's southeast, bordering Rhode Island, cast 10 votes for and 12 against. Coastal counties' votes were generally lopsided the other way, but even they had some "nay" votes, usually cast—as in Middlesex County—by inland towns.[74]

Some Federalists remained convinced that the "nay" votes came from Maine separatists as well as "Insurgents & some of the most atrocious Characters in existence," men with no property and deeply in debt who wanted no obstacle to tender acts and paper money so they could defraud their creditors.[75] If so, why did the opposition say so little about the provision for admitting new states to the union and the fiscally conservative provisions in Article I, Section 10, of the Constitution? The final vote did, however, suggest that discomfort with a strong, distant government—or a commitment to liberty as they understood it—was alive and well among the people of rural Massachusetts. Not surprisingly, their understanding of liberty put great emphasis on maintaining a full and free representation of the people and allowing only representatives with direct knowledge of the people's circumstances to levy taxes. Both their Revolutionary past and their most recent history underscored the critical importance of those issues.

"It is now no secret that on the opening of the convention, a majority were prejudiced against" the Constitution, Henry Knox told Washington after the vote was in. Federalists liked to say that (and historians tend to repeat their conclusion) because it made their triumph seem all the greater.[76] They forgot that they were unable to calculate the number of delegates against ratification when the convention opened, in good part because many delegates were undecided and, indeed, had often been told by their towns to listen to the convention's debates before drawing conclusions. Nothing that came later could change that well-founded initial uncertainty.

The proposed amendments had pulled some delegates with doubts into the "yea" category, as Charles Turner and William Symmes testified. They also gave delegates leaning toward adoption a justification to offer their constituents who found fault with the Constitution in its unamended form. The debates, too, changed some delegates' convictions, though probably not enough to get the Constitution ratified without the recommended amendments. Nathaniel Barrell said that the Federalists' arguments had removed many of his objections to the Constitution. So did Isaac Backus: The debates, he said, gave him more "light" on the country's affairs, the Constitution, and the security of the people's rights under it than he had when he left home, and he "therefore voted for it." The Federalists' visits to Daggett's and other similar places also had an impact, if only in dissolving the rural delegates' sense of distance between themselves and more educated and wealthy delegates. "We are not idle by Night or Day," Federalist caucus member Tristram Dalton said in late January, "and sacrifice everything but moral Honesty to carry our point."[77]

Sometimes they might have pushed "moral Honesty" beyond the breaking point. Theophilus Parsons loved to tell the people in his law office, including the young John Quincy Adams, about the "maneouveres" he and his colleagues used "in and out of the convention" to outwit the *antifederalists*." Adams was unimpressed; he thought many of those maneuvers showed a "meanness" that made them a strange basis for boasting.[78] Still, each convert that the Constitution's advocates won added a vote to their side while subtracting a vote from the other.

Even delegates who voted "nay" were changed by the convention. After the vote was taken, one after another rose to say that he would abide by the majority's decision and try to persuade his constituents to do the same. First Abraham White spoke. Although he opposed adoption of the Constitution for fear it would endanger the country's liberties, he promised to "use his utmost exertions to induce his constituents to live in peace under, and chearfully submit to it." Then William Widgery, a leader of the opposition, said that he had been overruled "by a majority of wise and understanding men" and would try to "sow the seeds of union and peace among the people he represented." He thanked the people of Boston for the civility they had shown the delegates. General Josiah Whitney, a Shaysite sympathizer who represented the town of Harvard, said much the same thing; and Daniel Cooley, whose Amherst constituents had instructed him to vote "nay" and who did so, he said, in keeping with "the dictates of his own conscience," announced that he accepted the majority's decision and would try to "convince his constituents of the propriety of its adoption." Even Dr. John Taylor, who, again, had played a conspicuous part in the opposition, said he found himself "fairly beaten" and would try to "infuse a spirit of harmony and love" among the people when he returned home.[79]

Others wanted to speak, but the hour was late so the convention adjourned. The next morning Samuel Nasson, Benjamin Randall, and Benjamin Sawin of Marlborough (in the far west of Middlesex County), all of whom had voted "nay," promised they would try to persuade their constituents to submit to the majority "that we may all live in peace." Sawin added that there had not to his knowledge been any "undue influence exercised to obtain in its favour," and, like Barrell, he testified that many of his doubts about the Constitution had been removed in the course of the convention debates. He would "support the Constitution as cheerfully and as heartily as though he had voted on the other side of the question."[80]

Boston's *Independent Chronicle* contrasted the "manly and honorable conduct" of many members of the Massachusetts minority with "that of the turbulent opposers of the Constitution in Pennsylvania," who not only issued an "odious protest against its adoption" but were "endeavouring to involve their country in all the horrors of a civil war, by exciting tumult and insurrection."[81] The difference owed a lot to the Massachusetts Federalists, who listened to delegates with objections to the Constitution, addressed their concerns and answered their questions with seriousness, and, in general, treated them publicly with the respect their power demanded—even if they were uneducated, had no wealth to speak of, and had supported Shays's Rebellion. The Constitution's supporters were well rewarded for their efforts with a vote for ratification, an acceptance of that victory by several members of the minority, and the prospect that dissenting delegates would go home and urge their fellow townsmen to accept the Constitution, as Christopher Gore had prayed, "with cordiality."

The convention had changed the Federalists too. Under pressure they developed new understandings of the Constitution. Dana and King interpreted Congress's power over elections as a way of correcting unjust state voting systems and defending the people's right to equal voting power; Ames made the Senate a bastion of state sovereignty and a barrier against national consolidation instead of a regrettable concession to small-state demands; Jarvis asserted the right of a convention that spoke for the sovereign people to recommend amendments to the Constitution, a position that had previously been made only by the Constitution's critics. Over and over, Federalist speakers emphasized that the new federal government would be directed by men chosen by the people for limited terms of office and who would share in the results of their actions, and that to grant power to such a government was to empower the people themselves. The argument responded effectively to traditional fears of power inherited from America's monarchical colonial past, but it sometimes rode roughshod over the way elected institutions actually worked, as William Symmes pointed out. Occasionally the Federalists' arguments might have been disingenuous, as when Sedgwick, no friend of democracy, attacked property qualifications for office as antidemocratic, or when King argued that wealth was no measure of worth. But they had learned to talk the talk and to play the game of American democratic politics.

On its last day, the convention accepted the report of its committee on the payroll and asked the governor, with the consent of his council, to draw £4499.2.0 from the treasury to pay the delegates, thanked its officers and others, including the proprietors of the Long Lane church where the convention met for most of its duration, and authorized a committee to prepare an address to the people. That address would explain the principles of the Constitution, answer objections to it, and demonstrate the necessity of its adoption for the preservation of the union. The convention formally asked the legislature to provide for its printing and distribution to the towns. Strangely, that further effort to get the people to accept the Constitution "with cordiality" seems never to have been written, probably because the state house of representatives, where hostility to the Constitution remained strong, refused to authorize its publication.[82]

On completing these housekeeping tasks, the delegates retired from the church on Long Lane—which was already being called Federal Street in honor of the convention[83]—to the State House. Hancock made the short journey, despite his protests, in an "elegant vehicle" pulled by thirteen brawny mechanics as an expression of their high regard for him. After the procession arrived, the governor, other convention officers, the high sheriff of Suffolk County, and some additional "respectable characters" crowded onto the balcony where the Declaration of Independence had been read twelve years before. Hancock gave a short speech, then the sheriff declared the Constitution adopted and ratified by the commonwealth of Massachusetts. There were more shouts of "huzza"; Hancock officially dissolved the convention, and the delegates retired to the senate chamber for an "elegant repast" provided by a group of Bostonians.[84] There was punch and good Madeira to drink with thirteen toasts—including one that hoped the "candour" and "liberality" of the Massachusetts minority would prevail in every state of the union. William Widgery was "really elated" by the honor he received for his promise to support the decision of the majority. Despite their differences on the Constitution, he recalled with surprise, "I was never Treated with So much politeness in my Life as I was afterwards by the Treadsmen of Boston[,] Merchents & every other Gentleman."[85] Boston was trying hard not to be Philadelphia.

There were holdouts, of course. Neither Amos Singletary, Samuel Thompson, nor Phanuel Bishop pledged to support the Constitution. But later, when Bishop tried to get the state house of representatives to denounce the convention, he had to contend not just with mainline Federalists but onetime allies like Widgery and Nasson.[86] Thompson "is roaring about like the old Dragon to devour the *Child now it is born* and breathes forth fire, arrows, and Death," an observer reported a week after the convention adjourned, "but his Hosts are almost fled . . . the old Serpent is beaten down," and the "republican Angel and his Hosts are proclaiming Peace, wealth, Honor, Liberty and Independence." He had lost the epic battle, and his old allies were gone. Jeremy Belknap said Thompson had "a kind of a distraction about him"; he seemed a bit unbalanced, but the man did not lack wit. At the end of the convention, Belknap reported, Theophilus Parsons warned Thompson that he should be careful about continuing his opposition now that the Constitution had been ratified "& reminded him of the danger of being punished for Treason." Thompson replied that he had no fear of being hanged if he could hire Parsons as his lawyer.[87]

The Federalists still had debts to pay for their victory. That to Hancock they honored: The old supporters of Bowdoin switched their allegiance to Hancock in return for his services at the convention. But if they had promised to loan money to the state for paying the delegates if the convention voted to ratify, as Henry Jackson claimed (and that tactic might have been an example of the "meanness" John Quincy Adams found in the Federalist maneuvers Parson described), they seem not to have followed through. The convention's committee on the payroll dutifully listed the 364 delegates who had attended the convention and, in separate columns, the approximate number of miles each had traveled, the amount due for travel at seven shillings per mile, the number of days he attended, the pay that warranted, and the total sum owed to each man. But Justin Dwight received only £4, 10 shillings of the £13, 13 shillings coming to him—leaving, he carefully noted, £9, 3 shillings "yet due." When Isaac Backus went to collect his money on February 8, the day after the convention adjourned, he too was given only a third of what he was owed, which was not quite enough to pay his debts for staying at Daggett's, laundry, seven shaves at a barber, and the care of his horse. He had hoped to do some shopping for his wife before leaving Boston, but there was no money left for that.[88]

Dummer Sewall's journal says nothing about collecting his pay. He was still in Boston on Friday, February 8, however, because he witnessed the "Grand Procession" organized by the committee of mechanics to celebrate ratification. Unlike most earlier processions, where the people watched dignitaries march, this one put the people, organized by their crafts, at the center of attention. That "very great perade," Sewall noted, included "Husband Men & every Sort of Macanaks with their Utenticls decorated." There were farmers along with blacksmiths, shipwrights, makers of rope, masts, and sails, ship joiners, coopers, bakers, carvers, riggers, plumbers, hatters, tailors, carpenters, printers, goldsmiths and jewelers, button and comb makers—a living catalog of the occupations of a preindustrial world in the age of sail, all with their tools (or "Utenticls").[89]

Another delegate, William Heath, recalled that the parade include a ship called the "new Constitution" on a sledge pulled by thirteen horses, with men on board who represented "a flourishing commerce," and another boat "representing the old Confederation, very leaky and irrepairable." The participants marched through town "in great order," Sewall said, "& Sang Huszass at every Delicates [delegate's] Door." There were bands for music, cannon firing, bells ringing, and, finally, a huge feast with three pipes of wine, two huge hogsheads of punch, bread, cheese, and more at Faneuil Hall. Only about a third of the participants could get in—although the hall could hold fifteen hundred people.[90]

———

Sewall must have arrived at the party early. The parade began at eleven o'clock and ended at Faneuil Hall five hours later, about the time he left town with his old traveling companion, Nathaniel Wyman, and now also

Isaac Snow. It was sunset before he retrieved his horse, who then fell, injuring Sewall's knee and causing such pain that he could hardly sleep that night. But he continued, and the three travelers arrived in Newburyport, then took the ferry to New Hampshire on Saturday. They "Crost Portsmouth Ferry" on Sunday and made it to York, Maine, in time for afternoon services. Sewall was "importuned to tarry till Monday" by relatives, and "with some Dificulty" he talked his companions into staying with him.[91]

After rising early and having breakfast with Sewall's brother, Moses, who lived in York, the three men pushed on to Falmouth, overtaking along the way four other delegates who had followed another route. On February 12, the companions began splitting off in different directions. Sewall, Wyman, and Snow were probably together at Harraseeket ("Harriski" for Sewall)—now Freeport, Maine—but soon afterward Snow would have turned southeast toward Harpswell and Sewall northeast toward Bath, while Wyman rode alone to Georgetown. The men were blessed: The weather was cold, but Sewall reported no snowstorms, no driving rain. And so, between seven and eight in the evening, after only a little over four days on the road, Dummer Sewall arrived home, "with Joy."[92]

EIGHT

— ★ —

A Rough Road to Richmond

New Hampshire, Rhode Island, Maryland, and South Carolina

"We are locked fast in Ice," George Washington wrote John Jay on January 20. The weather added to his self-imposed isolation. Since returning from Philadelphia, Washington had not gone more than ten miles from his home. He had a powerful aversion, he once explained, to sleeping in a bed other than his own if he could possibly avoid it. His information on the world outside Mount Vernon still came from visitors, letters, and newspapers, all in short supply for the moment. Once the weather broke, he would, he thought, learn what the conventions of Connecticut and Massachusetts had decided.[1] The eternal optimist in him no doubt expected the news to be good.

It wasn't. That very day in January Madison wrote from New York that "the intelligence from Massachusetts begins to be very ominous." Letters from Boston gave reason to fear the convention would vote against ratification. Given the importance of Massachusetts, Madison sent Washington regular updates, but the news, as he put it a week later, "rather increases than removes the anxiety produced by the last." He kept watching for some information that could defuse the tension, but on February 1 Madison had to report that "another mail has arrived from Boston without terminating the conflict between our hopes and fears."[2]

Washington was as anxious as anyone. A rejection in Massachusetts, he feared, would invigorate the opposition not only in New York but also the other states whose conventions had not yet met. It would also allow the minority in states that had already voted to ratify—he was clearly thinking of Pennsylvania—"to blow the Trumpet of discord more loudly." Even "acceptance by a *bare* majority, tho' preferable to rejection," would cause trouble.[3]

When, finally, Madison learned that Massachusetts had ratified—and it took a week for the news to get from Boston to New York—he should have been both relieved and delighted. His reaction was, however, begrudging at best. "The amendments are a blemish," he said, although they were "in the least offensive form," and the minority was "disagreeably large," although its good temper perhaps compensated somewhat. Washington, however, realized how the "good sense, sound reasoning," and above all the "moderation and temper" of the Constitution's supporters had wrested victory from defeat in Massachusetts. No doubt it would have been better if the majority were larger and the convention had not recommended amendments. Still, the outcome in Massachusetts along with "the favorable determinations of the States which have gone before" was, he thought, "a severe stroke" to the opponents of the Constitution in Virginia, who were very much on Washington's mind. He also predicted that the result in Massachusetts would have a happy effect on those opponents who were moved, not by "disappointment, passion and resentment," but "moderation, prudence & candor."[4]

The number of states in the "yes" column had doubled: By the time the news from Massachusetts arrived at Mount Vernon, Washington knew that Georgia and Connecticut had also ratified.[5] That made six states altogether. New Hampshire's convention was scheduled to meet on February 13, and it seemed sure to ratify. One of Washington's Boston correspondents reported that John Langdon, an ex-president (governor) of New Hampshire who had attended the Massachusetts convention for a few days, said that if Massachusetts voted to ratify, New Hampshire would do so within a week. On February 14, when Henry Knox wrote Washington that Massachusetts had ratified, he added that he expected to send the good news of New Hampshire's approval within twenty days. "There seems to be no question," Madison said, that New Hampshire would add a "*seventh* pillar, as the phrase now is, to the federal Temple."[6]

It was easy to think the game was almost over. Once Massachusetts had ratified, Washington wrote Knox, he had no doubt that the next two states scheduled to convene—New Hampshire and then Maryland, whose convention would meet on April 21—would ratify. Then South Carolina, whose convention was to begin on May 12, would join the list; after all, Madison had assured him that the news from South Carolina was very good. That would make nine states—the number needed for ratification—"without a dissentient." In this delirium of optimism, it was even possible to imagine that Rhode Island, which had so far refused even to call a convention, would fall in line. Washington's Boston correspondent—the same one who reported John Langdon's prediction on New Hampshire—told him that some "principal Gentlemen" from Newport and Providence who attended the Massachusetts convention had predicted that Rhode Island would "immediately" call a convention once Massachusetts ratified, and they had "no doubt but the Constitution would be ratified."[7]

New York was still a problem. So was Virginia, whose convention would assemble at Richmond on the second of June. Virginia's decision would probably determine the outcome in neighboring North Carolina, which had scheduled its convention to meet very late, on July 21—probably, the speculation went, so it could see what Virginia did before acting. Washington was sufficiently worried about the outcome in Virginia that he made one of his rare interventions in the ratification contest. He tactfully let Madison know that he, Madison, had to attend the Virginia ratifying convention. "Many have asked me with anxious sollicitude," he wrote, "if you did not mean to get into the Convention, conceiving it of indispensable necessity."[8]

Madison at first thought the final decision on the Constitution should be made by men who had no hand in writing it. However, after seeing that other delegates to the federal Convention were attending their state ratifying conventions, he wrote his brother in November 1787 that he would "not decline the representation of the County if I should be honoured with its appointment." Unfortunately, opposition to the Constitution was sufficiently strong in Orange County that one correspondent after another—Henry Lee, Edmund Randolph, Madison's father, and several others—wrote him with increasing urgency that he would have to come home from Congress to secure his election. Washington's letter settled the issue; Madison gave in. But he wasn't happy. The convention would involve him in "very laborious and irksome discussions," and he did not look forward to "a journey of such length"—from New York to Richmond—"at a very unpleasant Season." But if his presence at the county election was "indispensable," he would come.[9] Washington replied that Madison's decision "will give pleasure to your friends" and added that "the consciousness of having discharged that duty which we owe to our Country, is superior to all other considerations, and will place smaller matters in a secondary point of view." That was the philosophy by which Washington lived, and it had cost him far more than a few weeks of "irksome" debates and a trip from New York to Virginia in March.[10]

Madison's participation would add intellectual heft to an already illustrious set of men who would defend and explain the Constitution at the Richmond convention. If, moreover, nine states—and maybe ten if Rhode Island came to its senses—had already ratified the Constitution when the Virginia and New York conventions met in June, the odds of their voting to ratify would improve. The question for those two critical conventions would be not what they thought of the Constitution, but whether or not their states would remain part of the United States. It seemed for the moment possible that all thirteen states would be in the new-formed nation by late July or early August.

Then, suddenly, all dreams of a rapid and smooth resolution of the conflict disappeared. Stunningly, on February 22, after meeting for only nine days, the New Hampshire convention voted to adjourn without ratifying. The future once again become uncertain.

A COLD WIND FROM THE NORTH

By 1787, New Hampshire's townsmen, like their kinsmen in Massachusetts, were experienced constitutionalists. The state's Revolutionary provincial congress adopted its first written constitution in January 1776. From the first that constitution provoked criticism, but revisions were slow in coming, though not for lack of trying. New Hampshire's towns voted down a new constitution proposed by a convention that met in the summer of 1778. Three years later another convention met and proposed two more constitutions that the towns rejected before they finally ratified what became New Hampshire's second state constitution in 1784. Meanwhile, the state legislature also submitted the Articles of Confederation to the towns for comment. Most of them approved the document, but some found various provisions objectionable, especially those that seemed to threaten New Hampshire's sovereignty.[11]

New Hampshire's townsmen might have been even more strong-willed and independent than their neighbors in Massachusetts. For several years a group of towns along the eastern side of the Connecticut River had tried to secede from New Hampshire and join Vermont. Moreover, during the depression of the mid-1780s, many towns met in extralegal conventions and demanded tax relief and paper money. They also took to giving their assembly representatives binding instructions to support such measures. And in the fall of 1786 a raucous mob, infuriated by efforts to repeal laws that violated the 1783 peace treaty by impeding the collection of debts by British subjects, surrounded the meeting house in Exeter where the legislature was in session. The siege continued until a militia company restored order.[12]

There was strong support for the Constitution in Portsmouth, as in other Atlantic port cities. New Hampshire's merchant community predicted that the stronger national government created under the Constitution would protect and expand American commerce, bring prosperity to New Hampshire, and end civil disorder. However, New Hampshire had far fewer commercial towns than Massachusetts. Its Atlantic coastline was relatively short; the great mass of the state extended inland to the west and north. And a substantial part of the people in those inland areas did not expect to benefit from a revival of commerce; they distrusted merchants, and once they read the Constitution, they saw a lot they didn't like. Hostility toward the Constitution was particularly strong among communities in central New Hampshire along the Merrimack River. Federalists, centered in the east, told correspondents elsewhere that New Hampshire would easily ratify the Constitution and only later discovered that, in fact, they had an uphill battle. From the first, however, they devised strategies to assure their victory.[13]

Rather than wait for the next regular meeting of the legislature, John Sullivan, the president of New Hampshire, an ex-officer of the Continental Army and a strong supporter of the Constitution, called a special legislative session to authorize a state ratifying convention. It would meet not in the fall, when travel was relatively easy, but on December 5, in Exeter, on the eastern side of the state, which was Federalist territory. Attendance was predictably sparse: It took six days to get a quorum, and then fewer than half of the state's towns sent representatives, although supporters of the Constitution made it a point to be present. The legislature readily agreed to call a convention, also at Exeter, on the second Wednesday in February "for the Investigation, Discussion, and Decision of the Federal Constitution." By then, the Federalists hoped, six states, including Massachusetts, would have ratified. The legislature also ordered four hundred copies of the Constitution distributed to the towns. Representation at the convention would be the same as in the state legislature, although towns that did not qualify for independent representation (like Dalton in Massachusetts) could each send a delegate, and the state, not the towns, would pay the delegates' expenses. Other qualifications—including stiff property requirements—would be the same as for legislative representatives, except that the restrictions on plural officeholding would not apply. That allowed prominent state officials, most of whom supported the Constitution, to serve as delegates. The state house of representatives easily voted down a proposal to double the size of the convention, which was meant to dilute the influence of eastern delegates who favored the Constitution.[14]

New Hampshire's five newspapers printed almost nothing critical of the Constitution and, like Federalists elsewhere, argued that for towns to instruct their delegates how to vote would undercut the deliberative purpose of the convention. The circulation of those newspapers was largely confined to the area near Portsmouth, but New Hampshire towns along the Connecticut River often got their information from the equally one-sided *Connecticut Courant*. Meanwhile, clergymen throughout the state gave sermons supporting ratification. Nonetheless, opposition to the Constitution remained strong. Later John Langdon wrote Washington that "designing men" had circulated "rumors" that the Constitution threatened liberty and was designed for the benefit of "the great men," that Massachusetts would refuse to ratify, and "a thousand other absurdities," which succeeded in frightening the people "almost out of what *little* senses they had."[15] Or did the townsmen just read the Constitution and come to their own conclusions?

Those who knew what happened in Massachusetts might well also have decided to make their delegates vote as their constituents wanted. In the end, twenty-six of the roughly one hundred towns in New Hampshire not only decided the Constitution was seriously flawed but gave their delegates firm instructions to vote "no" on ratification; only four instructed their delegates to vote "yes." Another group of towns left their delegates free to decide how to vote after hearing the convention's debates, but they probably also made it clear that the townsmen were less than enthusiastic about the Constitution. In the end, a majority of convention delegates arrived in Exeter intending to vote against ratification.[16] Federalists might well have first learned how strong the opposition to the Constitution would be in conversations with town representatives during the legislative session at Portsmouth immediately before the convention met. They were in serious trouble and needed a way to avoid disaster.

The Constitution's supporters arrived early on February 13, when the convention first assembled. A few of them had slipped away from Portsmouth, where President Sullivan kept the legislature in session an extra day, debating an issue of particular interest to legislators (who were often also convention delegates) from the Merrimack River valley, where many towns opposed ratification of the Constitution. Right away—before the other legislator/delegates arrived—the convention elected a temporary president and appointed a committee of three strong supporters of the Constitution to examine delegates' credentials and prepare rules for the convention's proceedings. The next day, when attendance doubled, in part because more legislators had arrived from Portsmouth, the convention elected Sullivan its president and approved the rules proposed by the committee.[17]

Those rules looked innocuous, but they served the Federalists' purposes. One said that "on the question for adopting the federal Constitution, and on that only, the yeas and nays may be taken if desired by a member." In other words, no record of votes would be taken except on ratification. Also, a motion to postpone consideration of a question or to adjourn would take precedence over every other motion. That would allow Federalists to avoid a final vote on ratification if it looked like the vote might go the wrong way by moving to adjourn. And no vote could be reconsidered unless there were as many delegates present as when it was first passed, so delegates could prevent reconsideration of a vote simply by ducking out the door. With the rules settled, the convention approved a motion to discuss the Constitution by paragraphs, and the delegates turned to Article I.[18]

The records for the New Hampshire convention give only glimpses of its proceedings. The official journal for the February meeting of the convention consists of only four printed pages in the *New Hampshire Provincial and State Papers*. Newspaper accounts are brief and incomplete. A reliable record survives of only one speech, a defense of the proposed federal judiciary. The official journal does, however, say how much time the convention devoted to debating various parts of the Constitution, which suggests which provisions the delegates found troublesome. They were, it seems, no more happy with biennial rather than annual elections for members of the House of Representatives than their neighbors in Massachusetts: The convention gave that provision (Article I, Section 2) "much debate" starting on February 14 and continuing through the next morning. The delegates moved quickly through Article I, Sections 2, 3, 4, 5, 6, and 7. However, the convention devoted a day and a half to Section 8, on the powers of Congress, including the controversial grant of broad taxing powers that provoked controversy in virtually every convention.[19]

It briefly considered Article I, Section 9, which put limits on Congress, and also Section 10, which took certain powers from the states, including the power to issue paper money, to make anything but gold and silver legal tender, or to interfere with the obligation of contracts. Article II, on the executive, got less than a morning, but the convention went carefully over Article III, on the federal judiciary, which John Sullivan vigorously defended. The delegates then flew through Articles IV, V, and VI, except for the last provision in Article VI, banning a religious test for federal officeholders. That awoke substantial opposition in New Hampshire, whose 1784 constitution explicitly required that members of the legislature, the president, executive council, and delegates to Congress be Protestants.[20]

Judging from the bits of information in the press, the debates followed a pattern like those in Massachusetts, but they came to a very different end. The *New-Hampshire Spy* informed its readers that "the gentlemen opposed to the proposed new form of government" raised "every objection that could possibly be invented" but were "ably answered by gentlemen in favor of it."[21] After a week of debate, Federalist orators seem to have persuaded some delegates that their fears of the Constitution were misplaced.

As Langdon told Washington, a number of such delegates approached him and said they wanted to vote for ratification but could not do so without first consulting their constituents. Without those delegates' support, the Federalists calculated, they would lose the vote on ratification. As a result, on February 22 Langdon moved "that the Convention adjourn to some future day"—the same proposal Federalists had vigorously beaten down in the Pennsylvania and Massachusetts conventions. The convention set that "future day" as the third Wednesday in June and agreed to reconvene at Concord, where the state legislature was already scheduled to meet. It then adopted the motion to adjourn by a vote of 56–51, according to the *New-Hampshire Spy* (there was, by the rules of the convention, no official count), although the adjournment was "greatly opposed" by delegates convinced that ratification of the Constitution would lead to "tyranny in the extreme and despotism with a vengeance." According to the best modern analysis, the majority consisted of forty-five hard-core Federalists and another eleven delegates, at least eight of whom had been bound by their constituents to vote "no" on ratification.[22]

New Hampshire's Federalists did their best to make that vote look like a victory, but as they had already told anyone who would listen that the convention was certain to ratify, that required some ingenuity. When the convention first assembled, John Langdon wrote Washington, "contrary to the expectation of almost ev'ry thinking man, a small majority of (say four persons) appeared against the system." Sullivan, however, said there were at first seventy delegates against and only thirty for ratification.[23] Given the chance to gather information about town politics at the recent legislative session, New Hampshire's Federalists might well have had more reliable preconvention information than their colleagues in Massachusetts. Why, then, were their retrospective descriptions of the original division among delegates so different? Langdon was perhaps trying to suggest the gap was so small and developed so quickly that Federalists could have missed it, Sullivan to make the vote to adjourn look like a triumph. In either case, the reliability of their numbers was and remains open to question.

For now, the best they could do was reassure supporters of the Constitution elsewhere that the story would have a happy ending. Langdon told Washington that he had no doubt New Hampshire would ratify in June. Henry Knox delayed sending Washington the news from New Hampshire because it was "so contrary to the expectations of every person who conceived themselves informed of the dispositions of that State, that I knew not what to write." He put pen to paper only after receiving a letter from John Sullivan that, he claimed (and both he and Sullivan were given to overstatements), predicted that New Hampshire would finally give three votes in favor of ratification for every one against.[24]

The Federalist press both in and outside New Hampshire took the same tack, pretending that the Constitution had suffered no serious setback and the bandwagon was still rolling. On February 27, five days after the adjournment, the *Massachusetts Centinel* reported that New Hampshire towns had chosen and instructed their delegates based on information from "factious demagogues who rode through the State, inflaming and prejudicing the people's minds" against the Constitution. Now, with better information, they would reverse their position. The towns would allow delegates persuaded by Federalist arguments in the convention to vote for ratification, and their votes, with those of the Constitution's old supporters, would constitute a "considerable majority." Two days later the *New Hampshire Recorder* picked up that story and added reports from New York that said, "notwithstanding reports to the contrary," only "a small group" of men whose salaries were threatened by ratification stood opposed to ratification there. All the states except Rhode Island had called conventions, and after the next meeting of the Rhode Island assembly "it is expected that she will not remain an exception," and, "as saith the scripture, 'there is more joy over one sinner that repenteth, than, &c.'"

In truth, the outcome in New Hampshire was anything but certain. Building a majority for ratification would take extensive political maneuvering, starting at the town level. Moreover, as one Federalist after another acknowledged in private, the vote to adjourn had done tremendous damage to their cause. In late March, New Hampshire congressman Nicholas Gilman wrote Sullivan that it was hard to imagine "what pernicious effects our Convention business has produced in a number of the States." Both friends and foes of the Constitution had considered New Hampshire "perfectly federal," so the surprising news that it had adjourned without voting to ratify gave new life to "opposers" who had been profoundly discouraged by the positive vote in Massachusetts. New York's governor George Clinton had become "open and indefatigable in the opposition," and the "Antis" in Pennsylvania were forming associations, holding county conventions, and in general acting "in the stile of the Massachusetts rebellion." In Virginia too, the opposition was growing, and there was reason to think North Carolina was "too highly tinctured with the same spirit."[25]

Whatever the newspapers claimed, Gilman and other defenders of the Constitution knew that ratification was doubtful in New York, Virginia, North Carolina, and Rhode Island. If New Hampshire joined that list, ratification was uncertain (or worse) in five of the thirteen states, enough to prevent the Constitution's ratification by the nine states required for its enactment. The situation was "truly alarming." Even if New Hampshire ended up in the "yes" column, Madison said, the "mischief" caused in the meantime by its decision to adjourn was "of a serious nature" and "no small check to the progress of the business."[26]

Washington particularly regretted what he called the "extreme malapropos" effect on Virginia, where the bad news from New Hampshire arrived in March just as delegates to the state ratifying convention were being chosen. "Were it not for this unfortunate event," Washington complained, "the opposition in this State would have proved entirely unavailing," but now he could not say with any certainty how the election would play out. Like Madison, he asked whether New Hampshire had purposely scheduled the next meeting of its convention at a time when the convention of Virginia (and also New York) would be in session. Sources from New Hampshire assured them that the state had set the date for the convenience of the delegates: Since many of them were also members of the state legislature, back-to-back meetings of the legislature and convention reduced their travel time. Nonetheless, Washington reported, opponents of ratification in Virginia claimed that New Hampshire, like North Carolina, wanted to see what Virginia did before making a decision on the Constitution. If Virginia voted against ratification, Washington feared that "all those which follow will do the same; & consequently, the Constitution cannot obtain [pass], as there will be only eight states in favor of the measure."[27]

In the most literal sense, the New Hampshire convention's decision to adjourn "baffled all calculation," as Washington said.[28] It destroyed optimistic predictions of a fast and untroubled road to ratification and, incidentally, suggested a new reading of a popular Federalist illustration that portrayed the ratifying states as "pillars" of a "federal edifice." On January 16 for the first time, Benjamin Russell's *Massachusetts Centinel* printed an illustration of "THE FEDERAL PILLARS" with five up and a sixth, labeled "MASSA.," being put in place by two hands from a cloud. In February the Massachusetts pillar took its appointed place in the expanding colonnade, which Russell renamed the "GRAND REPUBLICAN SUPERSTRUCTURE" (or sometimes "The GLORIOUS FABRICK"). When the *Centinel* announced New Hampshire's decision to adjourn, it added to the cartoon a "N. HAMP." pillar leaning away from the others, resting on a short support, while a finger in the sky pointed to an assertion that "It WILL yet rise."[29] But an illustration of a pillar neither up nor down is necessarily ambiguous. In which direction was it going? Was the "federal edifice" being raised or taken down?

"ROGUE ISLAND"

The next piece of major news ended forever dreams of ratification without a single dissenting vote. The Rhode Island assembly met, as scheduled, in February of 1788. Four months earlier it had authorized the distribution of a thousand copies of the Constitution so the state's freemen would have "an opportunity of forming their sentiments" upon it. Now, after every other state had acted, Federalist hopefuls thought Rhode Island would surely call a state ratifying convention. However, the assembly—dominated by a "Country Party" that had swept into power on a paper money platform in 1786—voted down a motion for a convention. Instead it authorized a statewide referendum on the fourth Monday of March "at such Place where the Town-Meetings are usually holden." That was consistent with the policies of the Country Party, which had a partiality for referenda. It would also deny Federalists, centered in the commercial towns of Newport and Providence, an opportunity to talk other delegates into supporting the Constitution (or to "decoy" them, in the words of a Rhode Island assemblyman), as they had done with some success in Massachusetts and New Hampshire.[30]

The referendum decisively voted down the Constitution, with 2,708 against and only 237 for ratification. Supporters of the Constitution in Newport and Providence boycotted the election, but those towns together had only between 825 and 900 freemen, far too few to have changed the outcome even with the support of Federalists in other towns who also chose not to vote. Only two towns voted "yes," and they were badly split—Bristol on Mount Hope Bay (26–23) and Little Compton, on the Atlantic and lower Sakonnet River (63–57). Several others cast their votes unanimously against ratification. And then, at its late March session, the legislature again rejected a motion to call a state convention.[31]

The main cause of Rhode Island's opposition was probably the paper money it had issued in 1786 to address a complex set of economic problems. The state's Revolutionary War debt, much of which had fallen into the hands of speculators, was extremely burdensome. Annual interest alone was over £10,500, an enormous sum at the time: Before independence, the total annual revenue collected by the state was rarely over £2,000. Most property owners found it virtually impossible to pay their taxes, especially after the postwar balance-of-payments crisis had drained the state of its hard money. The resulting deflation also made it difficult to retire private debts, which often required that debtors pay back a principal greater in real terms than the amount they originally borrowed. The situation called for (in modern terms) an increase in the money supply. Paper money was an obvious way to do that, one that Rhode Island had used successfully for that purpose before independence.[32]

The new state-issued currency was meant to allow people to pay their taxes and support economic development, not to defraud creditors. The state issued much of it in the form of loans secured by the borrower's land, and borrowers paid the state an annual interest of four percent on the loans. But the paper was legal tender for the payment of all debts, and it depreciated badly compared to hard money (7:1 by late 1787). The legislature passed draconian laws to force creditors to accept its paper money, one of which specified that accused violators of the law would be tried without juries and could not appeal verdicts that went against them. The legislature also refused to let out-of-state debtors use the depreciated money to pay off Rhode Island creditors, which violated the "privileges and immunities" provision in the Articles of Confederation. Eventually, however, the paper money would allow Rhode Island to redeem its public debts without widening the gap in wealth between a few speculators and everyone else. It would also end the state's need to make massive annual interest payments, reduce its tax burden, and put it back on a reasonably sound fiscal basis.[33]

In the meantime, while Rhode Island's paper money remained in circulation, the provisions in Article I, Section 10, of the proposed Constitution, forbidding states from making anything but gold and silver a legal tender, threatened to throw the state into financial chaos. Would ratification force Rhode Island to recall its paper currency and abandon its program for retiring its public debt? Or would the paper currency no longer be considered legal tender for the payment of debts? Nobody knew for sure. Opposition to the Constitution was, however, stronger than support for the Country Party, which suggests that Rhode Islanders' objections to the Constitution went beyond the threat it posed to the state's outstanding paper money.

They probably shared other New Englanders' fear of federal direct taxes and hostility toward the two- and six-year terms, respectively, of representatives and senators. (Members of Rhode Island's lower house were elected twice a year, in April and August; the upper house, as well as the governor and deputy governor, annually in April.) The Constitution's provisions on slavery and the slave trade particularly offended Rhode Island's substantial Quaker population. Moreover, Federalists continually condemned the wickedness and folly of "Rogue Island," and they made it a prime example of the damage an "excess of democracy" could do. That confirmed Rhode Islanders' sense that the Constitution was at odds with their radical democratic traditions and hardened their determination to go their own way.[34] Why should Rhode Islanders link arms with people who habitually denigrated them? There was, to be sure, a handful of men in the state, centered in the Providence and Newport mercantile communities, who dissented from the majority and favored ratification. But the prodigal son was not coming home soon.

Federalists could take consolation in the fact that other states were unlikely to follow Rhode Island's example, which was considered too disreputable. That was not true of Virginia, however, and a negative vote there could derail the ratification process for good.

"MUCH WILL DEPEND ON MR. HENRY"

It was not easy for Madison to get out of New York. He felt compelled to be in Congress when issues that involved Virginia came up, and in early March Congress received Virginia's claim for expenses in maintaining control of the Northwest Territory. Finally, on March 3, he thought he could leave the next day, if not that afternoon.[35]

Winter was not giving way to spring easily. The early days of the month brought snow, strong winds, and low temperatures, and the continued "uncommon badness of the winter," as Richard Henry Lee described it, persisted for weeks. The weather, along with the "badness of the roads," further delayed Madison, who arrived home in Orange County, in the Piedmont section of Virginia to the west and south of Fredericksburg, only on March 23, the day before the election of convention delegates. He had stopped for two days at Mount Vernon and probably also took time along the way, as one of his supporters suggested, to meet and try to mollify the Reverend John Leland, a Baptist minister with some strong objections to the Constitution. The Baptists were a worry for supporters of the Constitution in Virginia, as in Massachusetts. Nobody could better calm their fears for religious freedom than Madison, who had seen the Virginia Statute of Religious Freedom, which his friend Thomas Jefferson had drafted, through the Virginia legislature despite Patrick Henry's powerful opposition. The Baptists were, however, not the main reason the Constitution's supporters were so desperate to get Madison back in Virginia so he could secure his seat in the state ratifying convention. As Washington's secretary, Tobias Lear, explained, Madison was "the only man in this State who can effectually combat the influence of Mason & Henery."[36]

Of the two, Henry was the greater danger; Mason lacked Henry's political power. After Mason's constituents in Fairfax County learned that he had not signed the Constitution, they instructed him, as their representative in the state legislature, to vote for the calling of a state ratifying convention. In fact, Mason had no intention of opposing that measure, but the instructions suggested strongly that Fairfax County's position on the Constitution was not the same as his, and that it would not choose him as one of its convention delegates. As if to leave no doubt on that score, Mason made himself more unpopular by an ill-timed, "illiberal" attack on the local turnpike commissioners. Some "characters of influence" in neighboring Stafford County who shared his views asked Mason to stand for election there, according to Edward Carrington, a strong supporter of the Constitution, "but it is supposed he will not succeed in the election."[37]

Next to Henry, however, Mason looked downright moderate. George Nicholas, a Virginia Federalist who sat in the house of delegates with Mason, wrote Madison that, after his return from the federal Convention, Mason said he would accept the Constitution "as it was rather than lose it altogether" despite his objections to parts of it. But Nicholas suspected that Mason's views had changed since then, in part because of irritation over the "hard things" said about him. Henry, however, was "almost avowedly an enemy to the union, and therefore will oppose every plan that would cement it." Nicholas, like Madison, thought Henry "industriously concealed" his "real sentiments," and he spoke about amendments to the Constitution to mislead "friends of the union" who would not follow him for a moment if they knew, as somehow Nicholas and Madison did, "his real design."[38]

Madison and Washington had held some slim hope that Henry might support the Constitution back in September and early October of 1787, when Madison wrote Washington that "much will depend on Mr. Henry," and it seemed as if his "favorable decision . . . may yet be hoped for." Those hopes sank after October 19, when Henry acknowledged receipt of a copy of the Constitution from Washington. He graciously thanked Washington for the "great Fatigue" involved in attending the Convention but said he could not support ratification. "The Concern I feel on this Account," Henry said, "is really greater than I am able to express." Clearly the Constitution was far different from anything he had anticipated, and it filled him with apprehension. Perhaps, he politely suggested, "mature Reflection" would give him reason to agree with persons (such as Washington) for whom he had "the highest Reverence."[39] Henry did not, however, change his mind. That became clear on October 25, 1787, when the Virginia house of delegates debated how exactly to call the state ratifying convention.

Francis Corbin, from Middlesex County on the lower Rappahannock River, moved "that a Convention should be called, according to the recommendation of Congress." Corbin was in his late twenties, having been born in Caroline County in 1759 to wealthy Loyalist parents. He had attended Cambridge University in England and studied law at the Inner Temple before returning to Virginia after the war. Corbin seemed fated by his personal history and his own ambition to cross swords with Henry, a firm supporter of the Revolution who was a generation older and a more capable combatant. Now, right away, Henry objected to Corbin's motion. Since Congress, following the recommendation of the Philadelphia Convention, said the Constitution should be sent to state ratifying conventions for their "assent and ratification," he said Corbin's resolution would prevent the convention from proposing amendments. Henry proposed an amendment to Corbin's motion that would explicitly allow the convention to propose amendments. Both Corbin and Nicholas opposed Henry's amendment. Nicholas said it would suggest that the legislature thought the Constitution needed to be amended, which Nicholas did not think was the majority's view. He added that neither he nor Corbin "denied the right of the Convention to propose amendments." Then Mason seconded Henry's motion to amend and took the occasion to declare "that no man was more completely federal in his principles than he was" or "more fully convinced of the necessity of establishing some general government." For him, "our perfect union was the rock of our political salvation." Mason thought, however, that some articles in the Constitution were "repugnant to our highest interests."[40]

John Marshall, a thirty-two-year-old Richmond lawyer who represented Henrico County, settled the dispute. Marshall, a future chief justice of the United States, had been born in a cabin on the Virginia frontier. The bookish boy was carefully tutored under his father's supervision, and he fought in the Revolutionary War, first as a Virginia militiaman and then in the Continental Army under Washington, who was an old family friend. Tall and slender, with a round face, thick black hair, and piercing dark eyes, Marshall was good humored and smart. He studied law briefly under George Wythe at William and Mary and in 1780 entered the bar. Two years later, his constituents sent him to the Virginia house of delegates where now, "with his usual perspicuity," as a contemporary newspaper put it, he dismissed both previous motions as improper and suggested instead that the Constitution "be submitted to a Convention of the people for their full and free investigation, discussion, and decision." Both the house and senate agreed.[41]

The final resolutions of the legislature, which were approved on October 31, specified that the election of delegates would occur in each county on the first day of the county court meeting in March. That meant the elections would be spread through the month, from March 3 through March 27, not all on one day, as in Pennsylvania, or over several months, as in Massachusetts. Each of the state's eighty-four counties could choose two delegates, and each "city, town, or corporation" entitled to send a delegate to the legislature—of which there were two, Williamsburg and Norfolk—could each send one. With 170 delegates, the convention would be about half the size of the Massachusetts convention. Every freeholder in the commonwealth qualified for a seat, with none of the other "legal or Constitutional restrictions" that limited the people's choice of legislators, so all of the state's officeholders from the governor and delegates in Congress through county sheriffs and clerks were eligible. Not even the residence requirements included in Virginia's 1776 constitution applied, which is why Mason could stand for election in Stafford County although he lived in Fairfax. However, only men qualified to choose members of the house of delegates could vote, which meant that they, like the candidates, had to be freeholders—that is, adult white men who owned twenty-five acres of land with a house or fifty unimproved acres (though there were special provisions for voters in Williamsburg and Norfolk). The convention would meet in Richmond on June 2, the first Monday of the month. The general assembly also ordered two thousand copies of its resolutions distributed within Virginia and to members of Congress and the legislatures and executives of the other states.[42]

The legislature did not decide on the delegates' privileges or pay, which gave Henry and other advocates of amendments another chance. In December, as expected, they proposed to give members of the convention all the privileges exercised by the general assembly and to recompense delegates for attendance and travel to and from Virginia's June ratifying convention. They also proposed to compensate delegates to a second federal convention if that became necessary to consider amendments to the Constitution, and to support any expenses the ratifying convention incurred by conferring with other state conventions.[43]

Federalists fought down explicit references to amendments and a second federal convention, but the final resolutions, which were adopted by both houses on December 12, went beyond providing for the privileges and pay of delegates and officers of the June convention. To foster "the most friendly sentiments" between "the people of this and other states in the union" and unanimity on the great issues before them at that time, the general assembly promised to pay from the state treasury whatever "reasonable expenses" might be incurred if the convention found it necessary to communicate with other state conventions or in collecting in some other way "the sentiments of the union respecting the proposed Federal Constitution." Archibald Stuart, a Federalist lawyer and member of the house of delegates, wrote Madison that the resolution, which passed with a sixteen-vote margin, showed that a majority of the legislature was against the Constitution "as it now stands." Stuart feared that the Constitution's critics, having discovered their strength, would adopt other measures to its prejudice.[44] Henry and his allies seemed to have the upper hand.

Henry's main political base lay in counties of the Virginia backcounty south of the James River, including his own Prince Edward County. But Henry was no outsider—no Virginia equivalent of Pennsylvania's John Smilie or William Findley. He was well off and well connected. His father, John Henry, was a Scot who attended Aberdeen University before emigrating to America in 1727 and settling in Virginia's Hanover County. After a few years, he moved up the social ladder in the classic Virginia way: He married a rich widow, Sarah Syme, who brought not just a substantial estate but, through her parents, ties to the prominent Winston and Dabney families. Patrick Henry, born in 1736, was the second of the couple's eleven children. As adults, his many brothers and sisters and their spouses brought him more useful family connections.[45]

Henry had little formal education. He left school—or what passed for school—at age ten and never attended college. Instead his father placed him at age fifteen as a clerk with a small merchant in Hanover County and a year later put him and his older brother into business for themselves. At age eighteen, Henry married Sarah Shelton, whose father was able to set them up on a three-hundred-acre plantation with six slaves. Within a year he became the father of the first of six children with Sarah. (After her death he married Dorothy Dandridge, with whom he had another ten children.) But the mercantile business failed and the plantation house burned down; for a time he worked at his father-in-law's tavern, where his conviviality was put to good use. Only when Henry took up the law did he begin his path toward fortune and fame.[46]

Thomas Jefferson, who was Henry's junior by seven years but whose political career ran parallel to Henry's for two decades, had no respect for his legal competence. After what Jefferson claimed was only six weeks of preparation, Henry arrived in Williamsburg in 1760, a man of twenty-four seeking a license to practice law. The panel of distinguished lawyers who examined him, Jefferson said, signed his license only with extreme reluctance; and one, George Wythe, the most distinguished legal scholar in Virginia and the teacher of both Jefferson and Marshall, refused. Later, as a legislator, Henry "could not draw a bill on the most simple subject which would bear legal criticism, or even the ordinary criticism which looks to correctness of stile & idea." And yet he built a thriving practice in Hanover and adjacent counties, which he left only for a less strenuous and more lucrative practice before the state high court (called the general court). Henry did so well that he was able to speculate in land and government securities. He regularly moved his growing family from one plantation to another with a larger and more impressive mansion house—which, like the scarlet cloak, black clothes, and dressed wig he wore, advertised his wealth and respectability. His skill was especially notable before juries in criminal cases for the same reasons that also brought him political power. Patrick Henry was "the best humored man in society I almost ever knew," Jefferson recalled, "and the greatest orator that ever lived." He had "a consumate kno[w]ledge of the human heart," which, with his eloquence, "enabled him to attain a degree of popularity with the people at large never perhaps equaled."[47]

Others affirmed Jefferson's assessment of Henry's oratorical power. They said he was stirringly theatrical, although controlled and "decorous," not emphatic or intemperate, and he had an ability to captivate his listeners' feelings in a way "that baffled all descriptions." Even the opposing attorney in the landmark Parson's Cause (1763), where Henry defeated the Anglican clergy's claim for greater compensation, testified to Henry's capacity to command the attention of everyone in earshot and hold it until he was finished. The struggle with Britain gave Henry many occasions to exercise his oratorical powers in the house of burgesses, Virginia's Revolutionary conventions, and, after 1776, the house of delegates, where he represented Louisa, Hanover, Henry, and Prince Edward counties, changing his constituency as easily as he changed his residence. In 1774 and 1775 Henry was also a Virginia delegate to the Continental Congress, where Jefferson claimed Henry felt out of place when mundane issues of governance commanded attention rather than the "general grievances" that gave occasion for his "bold and splendid eloquence." He nonetheless served as Virginia's governor from 1776 to 1779 and again from 1784 to 1786, when Edmund Randolph succeeded him.[48]

It was no good thing to be on the opposite side of an issue from Patrick Henry, but Madison and Jefferson, who were friends and close political collaborators, repeatedly found themselves in that unenviable position once the Revolutionary War ended. Madison defeated Henry's effort to get state support for religion when he secured the passage of Jefferson's Statute of Religious Freedom (1786), which essentially put religion outside the province of the state. But he and Jefferson lost on other issues: Henry had successfully fought Jefferson's earlier efforts to revise the state's laws, and also Madison's campaign to repeal Virginia statutes that violated the Paris peace treaty of 1783 by obstructing the payment of old debts owed to British creditors. Henry's power was undeniable. In 1784, when he raised objections to a proposed revision of the flawed state constitution of 1776, Jefferson told Madison that they should just abandon the project. "While Henry lives another bad constitution would be formed and saddled forever on us. What we have to do I think is devoutly pray for his death."[49]

Now, in 1788, Henry, who was still standing, set himself against ratifying the Constitution, at least without amendments. Jefferson also had strong reservations about the Constitution when he first read it in Paris. He was appalled by the lack of a bill of rights and term limits for the president, thought Federalist fears of imminent anarchy were ridiculously exaggerated, and even suggested, like Mason, that a second convention should be held after the people made their will known. Then long letters from Madison muted his opposition.[50]

Maybe, too, Jefferson was horrified by the idea of taking the same position as Patrick Henry, for whom his antipathy was deep and lasting. His dislike for the man dated from 1781, when Jefferson suspected Henry of prompting a legislative inquiry into his conduct as governor when the British invaded Virginia. Henry sided with the legislative majority that absolved Jefferson of wrongdoing, but Jefferson's rancor persisted. So late as 1805, when Henry was six years in the grave, Jefferson described Henry to his grandson and biographer as "avaritious & rotten hearted." Henry's two great passions, he said, were "love of money & of fame," and if they competed, money won. Jefferson's opinion that Henry was "the greatest orator that ever lived" is all the more striking considering how profoundly Jefferson disliked him.[51]

Madison continued to do battle with Henry on one issue after another after Jefferson had left for France, but he was more guarded in his language than Jefferson. Nonetheless, Madison could think of no dastardly act—not even disunion and the formation of a Southern confederacy under Henry's leadership—that was beyond the man. He stated his suspicion that Henry was working to found a Southern confederacy in a letter to Edmund Randolph on January 10, 1788. Tobias Lear, who picked up his information from conversations at Mount Vernon, suggested much the same thing in early December: Lear thought Henry wanted "to divide the Southern States from the others." In that new confederacy, "Virginia would hold the first place," and "he [Henry] the first place in Virginia—But this," Lear candidly confessed, "is conjecture."[52]

The closest surviving evidence for that conjecture came from Edward Carrington, who wrote Madison from Richmond on January 18 that "it is said" Henry was determined to amend the Constitution and leave it to the other states to conform to what Virginia did. "His language," Carrington claimed, "is that the other States cannot do without us," so Virginia could dictate the terms on which it would enter the newly formed union. If, however, that proved untrue, "we may alone enter into foreign alliances—the Value of our Staple is such that any Nation will be ready to treat with us separately." If in fact those were Henry's words, they suggested that Virginia might be a separate nation, not part of a Southern confederacy. On April 24, however, Carrington wrote Jefferson that, although Henry did not "openly" call for breaking up the union, his arguments against the Constitution "go directly to that issue—He says that three Confederacies would be practicable & better suited to the good of America than one." But where did Henry say that, and when? Carrington never said, and Henry's surviving papers are too few to confirm or disprove the charge.[53]

In any case, simple distrust of Henry played a critical role in Madison's understanding of Virginia's divisions over the Constitution. "My information leads me to suppose there must be three parties in Virginia," he wrote Jefferson on the ninth of December. The first was for "adopting the Constitution without attempting amendments," a party that included Washington, those Virginia delegates who signed the Constitution, Edmund Pendleton, George Nicholas, probably John Marshall, Francis Corbin, and several others. The second, "which urges amendments," included Governor Edmund Randolph and George Mason. "These," Madison said, "do not object to the substance of the Govern[men]t but contend for a few additional Guards in favor of the Rights of the States and of the people." He found it difficult to distinguish delegates in the second from those in a third group, headed by Patrick Henry, who also professed to want amendments. Henry and his followers would, however, probably contend for amendments that, Madison predicted, "strike at the essence of the System" and would lead toward either a union based on the principle of confederation, which had been proven unworkable, or "a partition of the Union into several Confederacies." Henry, Madison said, was "the great adversary" who made the Constitution's chances of being ratified in Virginia precarious.[54]

Madison's classification suggests that attitudes toward the Constitution in Virginia, as in Massachusetts, did not fall into a simple for or against dichotomy.[55] In another way, however, his division of prominent Virginians among three groups identified a major difference between the politics of ratification in Virginia and in most states to its north. In Virginia, Madison observed, "the men of intelligence, patriotism, property, and independent circumstances" were divided. In New England, however, "the men of abilities, of property, of character, with every judge, lawyer of eminence, and the Clergy of all Sects" with hardly any exceptions supported ratification without amendments. Much the same was true in "most of the Middle States."[56]

That meant the dynamics of Virginia's ratifying convention would be different from any before it. There would be educated men of ability both for and against ratifying the Constitution "as it now stands," and, with Henry in the opposition, the opponents of unconditional ratification might well be more persuasive than its supporters. Even an observer who thought the "great weight of abilities, of talents & virtue" was with the Constitution's supporters had to concede that "the powers of Henry in a large assembly are incalculable." If Richard Henry Lee, another powerful orator, also attended the convention, the advantage would swing even more toward the Constitution's critics. In the end, Lee decided not to go to Richmond for health reasons. Even without him, however, supporters of the Constitution feared that any conversions of delegates as a result of arguments made in the convention would go in the "wrong" direction.[57]

For that reason, they sometimes took a stand on instructions directly opposite that of their colleagues in Massachusetts. There, Federalists firmly and uniformly condemned constituents' instructing their convention delegates to vote either for or against ratification because instructions would undermine the deliberative character of the convention—and so the Federalists' capacity to persuade delegates to vote for ratification. In Virginia, however, Edward Carrington favored having counties instruct their delegates, particularly when the freeholders favored ratification. Each delegate instructed by his constituents to vote "yes" was one less in danger of falling under Henry's spell.[58]

"WE THE PEOPLE" OF VIRGINIA

There were many reasons why Madison hesitated to go home for the election of convention delegates. The rough-and-tumble of Virginia county elections was not to his taste. They were often much like a carnival, with crowds of people milling around, drinking and sometimes fighting, while the sheriff presided over the casting of votes for members of the general assembly. To be sure, not all elections were mob scenes. In many counties, incumbent legislators were reelected year after year, and if there were no more than two candidates for two positions, or if the support for a third candidate was obviously insufficient to win a seat, the sheriff could conclude the election after taking a "view" or rough headcount of the assembled freeholders. If, however, there were more candidates than places or if one of the candidates demanded it, the sheriff took a formal poll from a table, either in the courthouse or outside on the courthouse green. There the sheriff sat with several justices of the peace, "clerks" who kept count for the candidates, and the candidates themselves.[59]

One by one the voters came up, gave their names, and announced their votes, which were recorded on official poll sheets—and no doubt on many unofficial ones as observers calculated who was likely to win. Successful candidates for the legislative seats filled in county elections were almost always wealthy planters with experience as justices of the peace and in other local offices. But there, at the polling place, the vote of a poor farmer with twenty-five acres and a hutlike house was equal to that of the richest planter in the county. Failure awaited any candidate who did not treat the freeholders with respect, sometimes by offering them hospitality at their homes as voters traveled to the election, or by buying them—friend and foe alike—drinks, though by law they could not do that between the time the sheriff issued writs for the election and when the polls closed. The promise of free and abundant rum punch, and maybe also ginger cakes and barbecued pork, was enough to keep freeholders and other odd characters hanging around, amusing themselves in one way or another, until the sheriff declared the election over.

The elections of March 1788 did not promise to be of the quiet variety. Divisions over the Constitution had raised voter interest to a fever pitch in many counties, and the electorate was unusually assertive. In Virginia, Madison observed, the "mass of the people" were "accustomed to be guided by their rulers on all new and intricate questions," but on the Constitution, which he considered beyond most people's capacity to understand and judge, the people "not only go before, but contrary to, their most popular leaders." The elections would also be lively since there were no incumbents up for reelection. The state constitutional convention was a one-time event; each member had to be elected. And thanks to the suspension of the restrictions on eligibility that governed legislative elections, there would be an abundance of star-studded candidates, which in itself encouraged small planters to make the often fairly long trip to the county seat to share in the excitement.[60]

The surviving records of the elections are relatively meager but revealing nonetheless. They say precious little about the rum and other treats common at legislative elections, but they indicate that campaigning for and against the Constitution went on well before election day. In early February, Edward Carrington, who supported ratification, traveled through Chesterfield, Powhatan, and Cumberland counties, three adjacent counties on the south side of the James River. Those counties lay just above Patrick Henry's own Prince Edward County and were part of what Carrington described as Henry's "neighborhood." He reported that Henry had "pretty well prepared the people for being his blind followers—his demagogues are loud in their clamours against the Constitution, professing a determination to reject unless amendments can be had even at the hazard of [Virginia's] standing alone." Carrington did what he could to counter Henry's influence and "fix the minds of the people upon the preservation of the Union."[61] Meanwhile, to the northeast in Fairfax County, two men, John Pope and Richard Chichester, a justice of the peace whose daughter had married one of Mason's sons, were "very active in alarming the people." Chichester, according to a report Washington received, traveled with his pockets full of Mason's objections to the Constitution, "which he leaves wherever he calls"—and he called, it seems, at "every house."[62]

There are also intriguing accounts of freeholder meetings surprisingly reminiscent of New England town meetings. Most of them came early in the ratification process. On October 2, 1787, for example, a meeting of "a

Number of the Freeholders of Fairfax County, at Price's Old-Fields," met, read, and "unanimously approved of" the Constitution, and they instructed their representatives in the state legislature, George Mason and David Stuart, to secure "the immediate Convocation" of a state convention to ratify the Constitution. All the freeholders present at the meeting signed the instructions, and a substantial committee of some twenty-nine members tried to get other freeholders in their neighborhoods to sign.[63] Another meeting "of the Freeholders and other Inhabitants of the City of Williamsburg" met at the city's courthouse on October 6 and called on the legislature to summon a ratifying convention, adding that it should also "be empowered to revise and amend the Constitution of this Commonwealth." Williamsburg's resolutions took the form not of instructions but of a memorial to the legislature that would be published in the *Virginia Gazette*. Similar meetings of freeholders in Frederick and Henrico counties and of the inhabitants of the town of Fredericksburg instructed their representatives to support a convention and also endorsed ratification of the Constitution.[64]

There are some traces of efforts to instruct delegates to the ratifying convention, and not always to vote "yes." On March 13, 1788, while the election of delegates was underway in Warwick County, according to a sworn deposition, a freeholder moved that the delegates about to be chosen should be instructed how to vote. He was talked out of the idea with assurances that at least one of the candidates opposed ratification of the Constitution without previous amendments and did not need to be instructed.[65] An unsigned, undated manuscript among the papers of James Monroe, who opposed unqualified ratification, is also clearly a draft of instructions to delegates from Monroe's Spotsylvania County. It expresses grave reservations about the Constitution: The Senate and the judiciary were too powerful; the president needed a council of advisors answerable for their advice; the states should be given a first chance at raising federal requisitions; and trial by jury should be more firmly secured. But "we mean not . . . to break the Union," it ends. The draft instructions would have authorized the delegates to vote for ratification if nine states ratified before the Virginia convention took its final vote, but to do so "protesting ag[ains]t or declaring our dissent to such parts" as a majority thought objectionable and pressing on the first Congress "an early consideration and adoption of [amendments] into the System."[66]

It seems unlikely that those instructions or any others were adopted in March 1788 because they were generally unnecessary. Candidates were expected to make their opinions on the Constitution known to the voters, which they often did with public addresses to the assembled electorate. Edmund Randolph said that on the election day in Henrico County, March 3, "it being incumbent upon him to give his opinion, he told the respectable freeholders of that county his sentiments." The next day, when Spotsylvania

County voted, John Dawson, one of the candidates for election, explained the Constitution's "fatal tendency in so masterly a Manner," according to a newspaper report, "that his Countrymen were fully convinced of the impending Danger, and consequently were almost unanimous" in choosing him. The other candidate, James Monroe, seems to have been less open regarding his reservations about the Constitution before his election, but later explained his views at length in a pamphlet addressed to his constituents that was, however, never widely circulated, in part because of problems with the printed text.[67]

George Mason also made a short speech "on the election ground" in Stafford County on March 10. If the published reports are correct, he "expressly informed" the voters that he intended to vote against the Constitution and cast some nasty aspersions on other members of the Philadelphia Convention. And in Orange County on March 24, James Madison mounted a rostrum before a large crowd and launched into a "harangue of some length on a very windy day" in an effort to answer the "absurd and groundless prejudices against the federal Constitution" among the voters. Madison said it was the first time in his life—despite several terms in the assembly—that he had given such a speech. He also acknowledged that the election would probably have come out badly had he not been present. Another supporter of the Constitution spoke a full hour and a half in Gloucester County—and then lost by a considerable margin to other candidates whose views were not so different from his own.[68]

And in Powhatan County, where Patrick Henry's influence was supposed to be so strong, the two candidates who were chosen (one of whom had started "in the opposition") spoke in favor of ratification and were "elected under that declaration," so the county went "from being *anti*" to being "entirely federal." Patrick Henry also addressed his constituents in Prince Edward County before being elected, and in Prince William County, between Fairfax and Stafford counties in northern Virginia, William Grayson "harangued the People at the Court House" holding a small snuff box. Perhaps, he said (according to a private letter), "you may think it of Consequence that some other States have accepted the new Constitution," but "what are they? when compared to Virginia they are no more than this snuff Box is to the Size of a Man." He was later reported as saying he could risk making such an assertion, which suggested Virginia did not need the union, because there was no "short-Hand-man present"—that is, his speech would not be reported in the newspapers.[69]

Constituents expected delegates to hold true to the position they took at the time of their election, much as if they had been instructed. On at least one occasion, however, taking a firm stand on the Constitution might have backfired. An 1823 account of the election in York County claimed that before the voting began, when the poll takers had already made out their sheets with two candidates for ratification and two against, and those four candidates were seated "on the bench as is customary," an old man named Charles Lewis stepped forward. He had examined the Constitution, he said, but could not decide whether he favored its adoption or rejection and so considered it improper to vote for candidates who had already declared how they would vote. Instead he favored persons who had formed no opinion so far as he knew but were still "open to conviction" and whose judgment he trusted. The men whom he thought best fit that description were George Wythe and John Blair. Immediately the two Federalist candidates supposedly said they agreed entirely and cast their ballots for Wythe and Blair, who were "elected by unanimous vote." Then the crowd of voters agreed "by acclamation" to go as a body to tell the surprised victors of their election and persuade them to accept.[70] Like many often-told tales, the story has a problem. Wythe and Blair had been delegates to the Federal Convention and were hardly without opinions on the Constitution. Blair had signed it on the Convention's final day; Wythe did not because his wife's illness had forced him to leave early. In part for that reason, his position on the Constitution was unknown to the public.

In most counties, in any case, freeholders cast their votes for candidates whose position on the Constitution corresponded with their own convictions, which made the election something akin to a referendum on ratification. That made it easier to predict the division of delegates at the convention. Newspapers facilitated the nose-counting by printing the names of the delegates elected in almost all of Virginia's counties. Many interested observers constructed their own lists of delegates, distinguishing those for or against ratifying the Constitution without amendments. The results were reassuring to nobody. In early April, George Nicholas thought the Constitution's supporters had a small majority, but Governor Randolph, after assessing information arriving in Richmond, suspected the majority was actually against the Constitution, at least without amendments prior to ratification. Another observer in Richmond, Charles Lee, the brother of Henry "Light Horse Harry" Lee, thought there was a majority of ten or twelve for ratification, although he also said that "the best information yet had" on the delegates' sentiments left the outcome "very uncertain." On April 20, almost a month after elections had ended, Washington concluded that information on the known or presumed opinions of convention members showed that the sides were "pretty equally balanced. The one in favor of the Constitution p[r]eponderates at present— but a small matter cast into the opposite scale may make it the heaviest."[71]

THE PROBLEM OF KENTUCKY

The most important unknown was the district of Kentucky, which was still part of Virginia although it aspired to separate statehood. Its seven counties would have fourteen votes in the Virginia ratifying convention. Suddenly, given the close division in the rest of the state, it seemed that those fourteen votes might decide the outcome in Virginia and so the future of the union. And Kentucky had no warm feelings toward the federal government for one of the reasons Patrick Henry's support for it had gone sour—the failure of the Confederation Congress to defend Americans' right to navigate the Mississippi River.

In 1786, John Jay, the Congress's secretary for foreign affairs, asked Congress to change his instructions to give him permission to conclude a treaty with Spain that would give up navigation on the Mississippi River (which Spain had closed to Americans in 1784) for twenty-five or thirty years in return for receiving certain commercial privileges. The future economic development of the South, and certainly of Kentucky, which extended to the Mississippi in the west and whose northern border followed the Ohio River, which flows into the Mississippi, would depend on trade down the Mississippi. After the war, settlers had rushed into Kentucky and also the western part of North Carolina, which would become Tennessee and also extended to the Mississippi. If Americans lost access to that river for so long a period, migration to Kentucky and Tennessee would slow to a trickle, and the value of western lands would drop precipitously. The Northern states, however, saw the promised commercial concessions as a way to revive trade and breathe new life into their ailing economies. After a bitter debate in Congress, seven Northern states voted in favor of changing Jay's instructions while the five states from Maryland through Georgia stood resolutely opposed.[72]

Since nine states had to approve treaties under the Articles of Confederation, that close sectional vote doomed Jay's proposed treaty with Spain. The episode nonetheless left many in the South, and certainly in Kentucky, disillusioned and uncomfortable being linked to Northern states ready to advance their interests while brazenly sacrificing those of the South and southwest. Moreover, because closing off the Mississippi would reduce migration to the southwest, it was possible to see the Northern states' vote as an effort to assure that their superiority in population and power would continue into the future. Northerners, however, considered the South unreasonable for opposing an opportunity that could have immediate consequences for the commercial states while insisting on a right to navigate the Mississippi that would be important mainly in the future. Sectional tensions and talk of separate confederacies had added urgency to the movement for constitutional reform in 1786, but now, two years later, reverberations from the fight over Jay's proposed treaty threatened its success. The greatest danger for ratification in Virginia, Nicholas wrote Madison on April 5, came from the Kentucky delegates, "and one consideration only has any weight with them: a fear that if the new government should take place . . . their navigation [of the Mississippi] would be given up."[73]

George Washington attended the federal Convention and then followed the ratification closely from Mount Vernon.

1

2

The west front of Mount Vernon, the home Washington hated to leave.

Henry Knox, a onetime
Boston bookseller and
general in the Continental
Army, was one of
Washington's most trusted
correspondents.

3

James Madison
represented Virginia
in the Confederation
Congress and also the
federal Convention.
He worked tirelessly
for the Constitution's
ratification.

4

George Mason drafted Virginia's landmark Constitution and Declaration of Rights, attended the federal Convention and helped create the Constitution, but refused to sign the document and wrote a list of objections to it.

5

Governor Edmund Randolph was a member of Virginia's delegation to the federal Convention and favored strengthening the national government. Nonetheless, like Mason, he refused to sign the Constitution.

Elbridge Gerry, a federal
Convention delegate from
Massachusetts, also declined
to sign the Constitution.
The town of Cambridge
then refused to elect him to
the Massachusetts ratifying
convention.

7

8

Nathan Dane was a
member of Congress
from Massachusetts.
When he first saw the
Constitution, he found
a lot in it that he did not
like. He was a friend
and political confidant of
New York's Melancton
Smith.

Richard Henry Lee of Virginia, a friend and correspondent of George Mason, led a failed effort to amend the Constitution in the Confederation Congress before it sent the document to the states.

9

10

The Pennsylvania State House, now Independence Hall, where both the Federal Convention and the Pennsylvania ratifying convention met.

James Wilson,
Pennsylvania's
leading advocate
of ratification,
spoke long and
often at the state's
ratifying convention.

11

Benjamin Rush,
another Pennsylvania
Federalist, tended to
take extreme positions
in the convention
debates.

12

William Findley, an Irish Protestant immigrant from western Pennsylvania, was a leading critic of the Constitution in the Pennsylvania ratifying convention.

13

FEDERAL STREET CHURCH, BOSTON

The Congregational Church on Long Lane in Boston, later the Federal Street Church, where the Massachusetts ratifying convention met.

14

Rufus King, a member of Congress and leading Federalist at the Massachusetts ratifying convention.

15

Francis Dana, member of Congress, American emissary to Russia and state Supreme Court justice, was one of the most spectacular orators at the Massachusetts ratifying convention.

16

Governor John Hancock was a Boston delegate to the Massachusetts ratifying convention, which elected him as its president although he was home suffering from an attack of gout. Some thought his illness was more political than physical.

17

18

John Hancock's spectacular home on Beacon Hill, overlooking the Boston Common. He was convalescing here when carefully selected emissaries persuaded him to get up from his sickbed and play a critical role at the Massachusetts ratifying convention.

Samuel Adams, whose patriotism was unquestioned, had powerful doubts about the Constitution, but listened to the Massachusetts convention debates with an open mind.

19

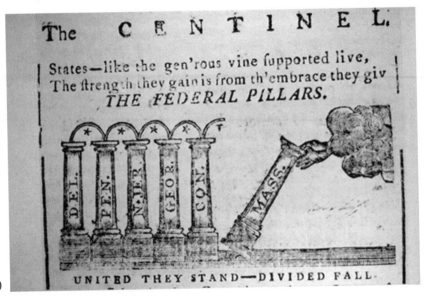

20

The Federal Pillars—one by one the building rose, guided by mysterious hands from the clouds.

Edmund Pendleton was president of the Virginia ratifying convention. When it met as a committee of the whole, he helped defend the Constitution against its critics.

21

John Marshall, the future Chief Justice, demonstrated his promise at the Richmond convention.

22

Patrick Henry. Thomas Jefferson, who disliked him, called him "the greatest orator that ever lived." He dominated the opening debates at the Virginia ratifying convention.

23

AN OLD VIEW OF POUGHKEEPSIE

24

The town of Poughkeepsie on the Hudson River, where the New York ratifying convention met.

25

Chancellor Robert R. Livingston was a leading Federalist speaker at the New York ratifying convention.

Alexander Hamilton, a New York City lawyer and former officer in the Continental Army, joined Livingston in defending the Constitution.

26

John Jay, the Confederation's Secretary for Foreign Affairs and an author of *The Federalist*, used his diplomatic skills very effectively in the Poughkeepsie convention.

27

28

Governor George Clinton, Hamilton's nemesis but an old friend of Washington, attended the New York ratifying convention as a delegate from Ulster County. He had profound doubts about the Constitution.

Melancton Smith, a top adviser to Governor Clinton and recent member of the Confederation Congress, led the Antifederalist/Republicans at Poughkeepsie.

29

30

John Lansing, Jr., who had left the Federal Convention early because he disagreed with the direction it was taking, joined Smith as lead speakers for the Antifederalist/Republican majority at the New York ratifying convention.

31

The "Ship Hamilton," a float in New York City's massive parade celebrating ratification of the Constitution by ten states on July 23, 1788.

James Iredell defended the Constitution brilliantly— but hopelessly—at the North Carolina convention in Hillsborough.

32

The Mississippi was not the only issue on Kentuckians' minds. In October 1786 the Virginia legislature passed an act "concerning the erection of the District of Kentucky into an Independent State" that imposed some conditions on Kentucky's independence from Virginia. One required that Congress consent by July 4, 1788, to the organization of Kentucky as an independent state, release Virginia from all federal obligations related to the district, and agree that Kentucky would be admitted to the union as an independent state at some time in the future. An elected convention in Kentucky during the fall of 1787 agreed to Virginia's terms, made arrangements for another convention to draft a state constitution, and successfully petitioned the Virginia legislature to designate one of Kentucky's leaders, John Brown, as a member of the Virginia delegation to the Congress.[74]

Brown, who was barely thirty years old, had attended Princeton before joining the Continental Army during the Revolution, graduated from William and Mary, and studied law under Thomas Jefferson. When in New York, he lived in the same house as his old friend James Madison. Finally, in February 1788, he presented Kentucky's petition for statehood to Congress. Madison tried to help: He waited as long as he could before leaving for Virginia in early March in the hope of seeing something done on the petition, but nothing happened. Congress, crippled for long periods of time by quorum problems, put off consideration of the issue until May 30, and then, on June 2, the day the Virginia ratifying convention met, resolved that it was "expedient" to make Kentucky into a state and appointed a committee to prepare an act for receiving Kentucky into the union. The committee was later discharged after doing nothing. The delays raised suspicion that the Northern states were dragging their feet to prevent another Southern state from weakening their majority in Congress. On May 12, Brown wrote Madison that his anxiety "daily increases" that, if Congress did not act before July 4, "the consequences may be unfavorable to the union especially as that District [Kentucky] entertains such prejudices against the new Constitution."[75]

Brown was an important link with Kentucky's leaders, many of whom were, like Brown, members of the influential Political Club of Danville, which met regularly in Danville, the de facto capital of Kentucky, to discuss such issues as the proposed federal Constitution. The record of their discussions shows that they found a lot to dislike in the Constitution: They thought the Senate should be able to choose its own presiding officer, for example, that the states should have complete control over congressional elections, and that the Constitution should be preceded by a bill of rights.[76]

On April 9, Madison sent Brown the Virginia election returns "as far as they are published" and observed that "a good deal may depend on the vote of Kentucky." Madison had already written to several gentlemen in Kentucky explaining that the Constitution included strong impediments to "improper measures relating to the Mississippi." In fact, the requirement of a two-thirds vote in the Senate to ratify treaties had been added to the Constitution with the Mississippi in mind. The proposed new government would also, Madison argued, be more likely to get the British out of their old posts in the Northwest, which he thought was an issue of consequence for Kentucky. He wrote to Brown again on April 21, and on May 17 he sent George Nicholas, who planned to move to Kentucky and had contacts there, a very long letter arguing in great detail that the Constitution would establish a nation with sufficient energy to protect the interests of all parts of the union and that ratification would "have several consequences extremely favorable to the rights and interests of the Western Country."[77]

Brown at first had doubts about the Constitution, but he came out in favor of ratification. He would not, however, be a delegate to the convention. From Madison's perspective, Brown's support was about the only good news from Kentucky. On May 12, Brown wrote Madison that letters from George Muter and Harry Innes—Muter was chief justice, Innes an associate justice of the district court of Kentucky—reported that the Constitution had "few or no Supporters in that Country." The interests of the western and eastern states were so opposite, Muter explained, that there was not a "ray of hope" that the west would get justice under the new government. Adoption of the Constitution "would be the destruction of our young and flourishing country"—by which he meant Kentucky. Innes and Muter also sent Brown a list of Kentucky delegates to the ratifying convention and told him that a convention would meet at Danville "expressly to take into consideration the new Constitution & instruct & charge their representatives with the Sentiments of the District upon that Subject." That meant, Brown concluded, that no good would come from his writing the delegates. He was willing to "hazard the Attempt," but the delegates would hold themselves "religiously bound to observe Instructions framed and given with such Solemnity."[78]

Madison could only hope the Danville convention would not meet and that Kentucky's delegates would bring to the ratifying convention "no other fetters than those of prejudice" against the Constitution: Attitudes, unlike instructions, could be reversed in the course of the ratifying convention's debates. In fact, the Danville convention never met. Moreover, by the time Madison received Brown's bad news, the most up-to-date calculation of delegates seemed more favorable for the Constitution. Not counting Kentucky, there were 85 to 88 votes for ratification, 66 against, and 3 neutral. Even if all 14 of Kentucky's votes and one or two of the neutrals were added to the other side, there would remain what Madison called a "very minute" majority for ratification. "But the issue must be somewhat uncertain," he acknowledged, "where the data are so far from being clear & precise, and the calculations so nice & tickleish."[79]

The preconvention delegate count was probably the work of George Nicholas and a few other leading Virginia Federalists. Madison referred to Nicholas on April 10 as one of "those who have more data for their calculations than I have" and listed him "among the best judges" of the election returns.[80] However, Edward Carrington, one of Nicholas's colleagues, suggested that divisions within the categories remained critical. There were, he thought, only a few "truly antifederal" delegates who followed Henry. Back in December, Madison had distinguished Henry, who was adamantly against the Constitution, from Mason and Randolph, who generally favored the Constitution but wanted amendments before its ratification. Carrington's concern lay with a group Madison had not mentioned, "federalists who are for amendments" and who might "be drawn into steps favouring the antifederal scheme."[81]

The concerns of several "federalists who were for amendments" were probably influenced by the same event that upset the Kentuckians. The Northern vote in the Confederation Congress on Jay's instructions, and so the future of the Mississippi, made them hesitant to let the new Congress, which the populous North would dominate, pass commercial laws by a simple majority. They wanted, like Mason and other Southern critics of the Constitution, amendments that would protect the rights and also the interests of the South, including an amendment requiring a two-thirds majority to enact commercial regulations.[82]

Carrington's concern suggests that the delegates to watch in the convention were grouped near the center of a broad spectrum of opinion. They thought the Constitution would benefit from amendments, but differed on when and how they should be passed, and were hidden within both the "for" and the "against" categories. To add to the problem, a number of delegates were unknown to the set of wealthy planters who normally controlled Virginia's government and politics. Those "weak and obscure men" would be "subjects for Management," Edward Carrington feared, "and the popular talents of Mr. H[enry] is to be dreaded amongst them."[83]

LOOKING NORTH TO MARYLAND

With the vote so close, supporters of the Constitution in Virginia feared that developments outside the state could throw the balance of power toward their opponents. The adjournment of New Hampshire's convention meant that nine states would not ratify before the Virginia convention met. However, having eight states in the "yes" column would also increase the pressure on Virginia to ratify. Six were already committed, and the Maryland and South Carolina conventions were scheduled to meet before Virginia's. Nicholas predicted both would be "favorable to the plan," but he warned Madison that "great efforts will be made to induce them to adjourn" until after the Virginia convention met. Moreover, he warned that "if this can be brought about, depend on it Sir, it will have great influence in this country," encouraging the critics of the Constitution in Virginia to persist in the hope of influencing enough states to get their demands met.[84]

Madison followed Nicholas's advice to impress upon his friends in Maryland and South Carolina the importance of having those states ratify the Constitution before the Virginia convention met. He wrote to Daniel Carroll and James McHenry, both of whom had been Maryland delegates to the Constitutional Convention, and a "friend" in South Carolina, perhaps Charles Pinckney, another veteran of the Philadelphia Convention. Writing letters and having letters written was, however, all he could do, and he couldn't even mail his letters directly to their recipients. Madison sent the Carroll letter to Washington, who he hoped knew whether Carroll was in Annapolis or Georgetown, and mailed the letter to South Carolina via New York, where Cyrus Griffin, a Virginia delegate and current president of Congress, forwarded it to Charleston "by a proper conveyance."[85]

Madison was so concerned that Maryland would follow the example of New Hampshire and derail the ratification effort in Virginia that he managed to get Washington involved. "The difference between even a postponement and adoption in Maryland," he wrote Washington on April 10, could, given the close balance of parties in Virginia, "possibly give a fatal advantage to that which opposes the Constitution." Ten days later—the day before the Maryland convention met—Washington wrote Thomas Johnson, a Baltimore lawyer. Based on a letter from the previous December, Washington said, he concluded that Johnson favored ratification and so took the liberty of expressing "a *single* sentiment": that a vote by the Maryland convention to adjourn to a time after the Virginia convention met would be tantamount to rejecting the Constitution. A vote to adjourn would influence South Carolina and encourage the opposition in Virginia, which was already claiming that the New Hampshire convention had adjourned so it could see what Virginia did before voting on ratification. If his modest intervention in Maryland's politics was improper, Washington apologized. He had, he said, only one remaining public wish, "that in *peace* and *retirement*, I may see this Country rescued from the danger which is pending, & rise into respectability."[86]

Strangely, on the same day, April 20, James McHenry, a onetime army surgeon who had served on Washington's staff during the war and had been a Maryland delegate at the federal Convention, wrote Washington from Baltimore. He asked what impact Washington thought an adjournment of the Maryland ratifying convention would have. "Our opposition intend to push for an adjournment under the pretext of a conference with yours respecting amendments," he explained. McHenry knew the answer to his question—adjournment would be, in effect, a rejection of the Constitution by

Maryland and would lead to its rejection in Virginia—and was doing all he could to prevent it. In that effort, he thought a written statement of Washington's thoughts would be useful. Because he hadn't sent to Alexandria for his mail for several days, Washington didn't receive McHenry's letter until April 26, then quickly affirmed his conviction that a Maryland adjournment was tantamount to a rejection of the Constitution. Moreover, the opponents of ratification understood it that way, he said, but "to adduce arguments in support of this opinion is as unnecessary as they would be prolix—They are obvious."[87]

Worries over an adjournment of the Maryland convention proved misplaced. As elsewhere, amendments were the main issue there. In November 1787, while making arrangements for a state ratifying convention, Maryland's house of delegates managed to fight off an effort by the Federalist state senate to call elections quickly, require a stiff £500 property qualification for delegates, and submit the Constitution to the convention for its "assent and ratification" only. In the end, the legislature called elections for early April, leaving several months for debate, imposed no property qualification for delegates, and submitted the Constitution to the convention for its "full and free investigation and decision." Each of Maryland's eighteen counties could send four delegates to the convention, and the cities of Annapolis and Baltimore would each have two. The electorate would be the same as for members of the Maryland lower house: All freemen who owned fifty acres of land in the county where they voted, or property in the state of any kind worth £30, could vote.[88]

Despite a rash of pamphlets and newspaper essays over the next four months, the electorate in Maryland was, by all accounts, surprisingly uninterested in the contest over the Constitution. Newspaper accounts tell of lively battles for convention seats in a few constituencies, with candidates declaring themselves for or against unqualified ratification, and with both voters and candidates brazenly ignoring inconvenient details such as residence requirements. In three quarters of the constituencies, however, Federalist candidates ran unopposed, and less than a fourth of the qualified voters seem to have participated in the election of convention delegates. The results, as Daniel of St. Thomas Jenifer wrote Washington, were generally "in favor of the New Constitution." Only three counties—Anne Arundel, Baltimore, and Harford—had elected "Antifederal" delegates, though that was enough, as Edmund Randolph learned, to leave the prominent Carroll family, including Madison's correspondent Daniel Carroll, a Maryland delegate to the federal Convention, without seats in the ratifying convention. On April 30, the *Pennsylvania Gazette* reported that if delegates held true to the positions they took on the hustings, "sixty-four Federalists are elected out of a total of seventy-six."[89]

That meant supporters of ratification in Maryland went into the convention with a majority substantially larger even than in Pennsylvania, and they used their strength in a distinctive way. On April 21, before the convention assembled in Annapolis, members of the majority met and agreed that, since the "main question" had already been decided by the people in county elections and the delegates were "under a sacred obligation" to vote according to the sentiments of their constituents, they would move toward a vote on ratification "as speedily as was consistent with decorum," avoiding debates that were unlikely to throw new light on the subject.[90] To save time, the majority apparently also decided not to contest the elections of four critics of the Constitution who were not residents of the counties that elected them; the Federalists could spare those votes. Then on Wednesday, April 23, when it had elected officers, established rules of debate, and settled its membership, the convention decided to debate the Constitution as a whole rather than go through it clause by clause. After the Constitution had been "fully debated and considered," the convention would vote whether to "assent to and ratify" it.[91]

The three leading members of the opposition raised no objection because, amazingly, they had not yet arrived. Samuel Chase, a prominent Annapolis lawyer, and Luther Martin, the disgruntled delegate who had left the federal Convention early, took their seats only on Thursday morning, about halfway through the convention's short life and after the rules of procedure were settled. Martin had laryngitis and said nothing; Chase explained some of his objections to the Constitution, then said he was exhausted and would continue the next day. In the afternoon, William Paca arrived. A respected and wealthy lawyer who had, with the less polished Chase, led Maryland's opposition to Britain and signed the Declaration of Independence, Paca had been Maryland's governor and chief justice of its supreme court. He told the convention that he had several objections to the Constitution and wanted to propose a set of amendments, which, he made clear, would not be a condition of ratification. Like those from Massachusetts, they would be "standing instructions" to Maryland's representatives in the first federal Congress. Paca had not, however, finished preparing the amendments, so he "requested indulgence, until the morning, for that purpose." Thomas Johnson, Washington's correspondent and a strong supporter of ratification who nonetheless favored some changes in the Constitution, called the request "candid and reasonable" and moved to adjourn. The convention agreed "without a division."[92]

The "indulgence" ended the next day. When Paca tried to introduce his amendments, a delegate from each of eleven counties and from Annapolis and Baltimore rose, one by one, and declared that they were obliged to vote for ratification and could propose no amendments since their constituents had given them no directions on that issue. Paca was then ruled out of order because—as the majority insisted—the question before the convention was whether it would "assent to and ratify the proposed constitution," not whether it would propose amendments. The opposition continued to raise objections to the Constitution, all of which were, the Federalist Alexander Condee Hanson observed, "familiar to almost every auditor," but the majority resolutely refused to respond. Finally, on the afternoon of Saturday, April 26, the convention voted to ratify, with 63 in favor, 11 against. Four days later Washington received the news, which he happily tacked on to the end of a long letter to the Marquis de Chastellux.[93]

The Maryland convention was not over, however. Once the main issue was decided, Paca again laid his propositions before the convention. He had voted for ratification, he said, assuming "that such amendments would be peaceably obtained so as to enable the people to live happy under the new government." A "general murmur of approbation seemed to arise from all parts of the house," supporters recalled, and the convention agreed by a vote of 66–7 to appoint a committee to consider and draft amendments that would be "recommended to the consideration of the people of this state, if approved by this Convention." The committee met and agreed to thirteen amendments, either unanimously or by a substantive majority. Some of those amendments protected basic rights such as trial by jury and freedom of the press. Others declared that Congress could exercise no power that was not "expressly delegated" by the Constitution, limited federal jurisdiction in cases involving small amounts of property, protected the jurisdiction and so the existence of state courts, and imposed limits on Congress's power to raise an army except in time of war "and then only during the war."[94]

However, the committee rejected another fifteen amendments proposed by the committee's minority. When some members of the majority insisted that no amendments other than those the committee had approved should be presented to the convention, Paca and his colleagues proposed a compromise. They would submit only the first three of the rejected amendments to the convention, and, if the convention rejected those amendments, they would accept the majority's decision and cease all further opposition to the Constitution. The first three amendments would require the consent of a state's legislature or executive before its militia could be marched beyond the limits of an adjoining state; limit Congress's power over congressional elections under Article I, Section 4, to instances where states failed to call or to hold elections; and require Congress to give state legislatures an opportunity to raise their states' portions of federal direct taxes before the federal government collected them itself. Those amendments were too extreme for members of the committee's majority, which, Hanson claimed, had agreed to the other amendments not because they thought the Constitution needed perfecting but to accommodate the opposition. The committee turned down Paca's proposition by a vote of 5–8. Moreover, since the opposition seemed determined to persist and push for more radical amendments on the floor of the convention, the majority decided—without, it seems, taking a formal vote—to propose no amendments whatsoever. The committee members simply went back to the convention, which had repeatedly called for their return, without approving any recommendations.[95]

That, for all practical purposes, settled the issue. While waiting impatiently for the committee to report, the convention had decided that it would consider only amendments that the committee recommended. Since the committee proposed no amendments, the convention refused to consider even those less objectionable amendments to which the committee had previously agreed. Moreover, the convention ordered that its vote on that issue—and of course the text of the proposed amendments—would not appear in its official journal. Finally it voted to adjourn, with 47 delegates in favor, 27 against. Several members who had voted for ratification joined the minority on adjournment. They probably thought, like Thomas Johnson, that the Constitution would be better with some amendments, though not all of those that had been proposed, and regretted that the convention had come to so precipitous an end.[96]

Later members of the Maryland minority, following the example of their colleagues in Pennsylvania, issued an address to the people that described the convention's proceedings and included the texts of the proposed amendments. "We consider the proposed form of national government as very defective," it said, "and that the liberty and happiness of the people will be endangered if the system be not greatly changed and altered." The address's impact, however, fell far short of its Pennsylvania predecessor. In fact, it made so small an impression on the people that the majority lost interest in issuing an answer to it.[97] The address came too late in the ratification process; and most of the people in Maryland, or at least the elite that dominated its affairs, were pleased with the Constitution. Congress's failure to defend American navigation of the Mississippi sparked no profound feelings in Maryland, which had no western lands and whose hopes for the future focused on the Potomac. The concerns over ownership of western lands that had led Maryland to delay ratification of the Articles of Confederation for three years were gone: Virginia and other states had yielded large parts of their land claims to Congress. A stronger national government could defend and control its expanding domain, protect Maryland's booming sale of wheat at home and abroad, and end the tumultuous conflicts over paper money that had recently wracked Maryland as well as other states. The equal representation in the Senate of small states like Maryland with others that were in some cases twice its size added to the Constitution's appeal.[98]

Some prominent leaders in the fight against unconditional ratification of the Constitution had also fought for paper money in Maryland. Those affluent freeholders were often also debtors, having borrowed money to buy confiscated Loyalist property. They had sometimes tried to pay off debts to British creditors with depreciated money, a practice the Constitution and a strict regard to the 1783 peace treaty would bring into serious question. But support for paper money and opposition to the Constitution among individuals and counties did not correlate closely, and the amendments Paca and his colleagues proposed said nothing at all about paper money or any other part of the Constitution that threatened their financial welfare except perhaps the provision on taxes. They did talk about rights, which were more than abstractions to men who had fought a revolution in the name of liberty. The split vote on adjournment suggested that other delegates who had voted for unconditional ratification shared some of the minority's reservations on the Constitution.[99] As in Virginia, the Constitution's supporters in Maryland were not entirely of one mind.

Whatever the causes of Maryland's divisions, the outcome of the convention was glorious from the perspective of Virginia's Federalists. It had not adjourned precipitously but voted to ratify by a solid majority and without recommending amendments. Maryland's ratification would be "a thorn . . . in the sides of the leaders of opposition in this State," Washington wrote Madison with delight. "Should South Carolina give as unequivocal [an] approbation of the system," the opposition in Virginia would "become feeble," since ratification by eight states "without a negative [Washington had conveniently forgotten the Rhode Island referendum] carries the weight of argument, if not of eloquence along with it, which might cause even the unerring sister to hesitate."[100]

THE EIGHTH PILLAR?

The probability that South Carolina would approve the Constitution was high, but its approval was unlikely to be as "unequivocal" as Maryland's. There was opposition to the Constitution in the state: That became clear in January 1788, when, in the course of calling a state ratifying convention, the South Carolina house of representatives debated the Constitution. A full-fledged legislative debate on that topic was unusual since, as everyone acknowledged, another body—the state convention—would decide South Carolina's position on the Constitution. The debates, which went on from January 16 to 19, were held on the Federalists' initiative, according to one participant, "for the sake of informing the country members" who came from constituencies where suspicion of the Constitution was high. But the legislative debates gave one particularly articulate delegate, Rawlins Lowndes, an opportunity to express some profound reservations about both the Constitution and the union.[101]

Lowndes, a Charleston lawyer who had once been governor of South Carolina, claimed to speak not only for himself but also for others less accustomed to public speaking. He found the Constitution inferior in several regards to the Articles of Confederation. The requirement of a two-thirds vote in the Senate to approve treaties was not, he said, equivalent to the current requirement that nine of the thirteen states approve treaties. The problem was made worse by Article VI, which made the Constitution, all laws made pursuant to it, and treaties enacted under its authority the "supreme law of the land." He feared for the future of the South in a nation dominated by a Northern majority. In the federal Convention, he argued, the North had carefully protected its commercial interests but, by providing for the end of the slave trade after twenty years, violated those of the South. "Without negroes," he said, "this state would degenerate into one of the most contemptible in the Union." Moreover, once Northern shippers monopolized trade with the South, as they would under regulations adopted by a Congress dominated by the North, they would charge "whatever freightage they thought proper to impose. It was their interest to do so, and no person could doubt but they would promote it by every means in their power." He saw no "reciprocal bargain" in a Constitution that "took all from one party, to bestow it on the other!"[102] Lowndes also objected to the transfer of taxing power from the states to Congress and to the prohibition on state-issued paper money in Article I, Section 10. "What evils had we ever experienced by issuing a little paper money to relieve ourselves from any exigency that pressed us?"[103]

Other members of the house—who included all four members of South Carolina's formidable delegation to the Constitutional Convention—answered Lowndes point by point. Treaties, they argued with a raft of learned references, were always the law of the land. Lowndes's reference to the South was specious, one representative observed, since only Georgia and the two Carolinas—not Virginia nor Maryland—allowed the importation of slaves. And the "Eastern States"—by which he meant Pennsylvania and those to its north and northeast—had been generous in allowing representation for three-fifths of the slave population, "a species of property which they have not among them." Slaveholders also received assurance in the Constitution that runaway slaves would be returned from other parts of the union, an advantage they did not have before. If, moreover, the "immense" flow of people into the South—particularly Kentucky and Tennessee—continued, the Northern majority in Congress would cease "in the course of a few years." Competition of the commercial states with each other and with foreign shippers would keep freight costs down. Nor was it certain the slave trade would end after twenty years. If Northern ships carried Southern exports that required slave labor, why would they "dam up the sources from whence their profit is derived"? One house member recalled the support of Northern troops during the British occupation of South Carolina to counteract Lowndes's aspersions on the Northern states: The "shackles of the south," he said, "were broken apart by the arms of the north."[104]

There was no talk, as in Virginia, of South Carolina's standing alone. Instead speakers argued that South Carolina's weakness required union for its security. Charles Cotesworth Pinckney went so far as to describe the assertion that the Declaration of Independence had made each state "separately and individually independent" as a "species of political heresy." The Declaration, which never mentioned the states by name, was meant, he argued, to impress on America the maxim that "our freedom and independence arose from our union, and that without it we could neither be free nor independent."[105]

Pinckney also insisted that it was essential that the general government be able to levy "internal taxes" since "requisitions had been in vain tried every year since the ratification of the old Confederation, and not a single state had paid the quota required of her." To Lowndes's question about the harm done by paper money, Pinckney recalled that "he had lost fifteen thousand guineas by depreciation." Paper money also "corrupted the morals of the people," turned them from "the paths of honest industry to the ways of ruinous speculation," destroyed "both public and private credit," and "brought total ruin on numberless widows and orphans."[106] There Pinckney spoke more for himself than for other members of the South Carolina elite: Low country debtors with substantial resources, not less propertied debtors, much less the poor, were the main beneficiaries of the debtor relief laws and limited issue of paper money approved by the state legislature. Now, it seemed, the wealthy beneficiaries of South Carolina's debtor relief laws were willing to give up those benefits for the greater advantages they expected the federal Constitution to provide.[107]

With so formidable an array of talent against him, Lowndes acknowledged that the prevailing opinion favored the Constitution. Only three other members of the house, all from the Ninety-Six district in the western part of the state, questioned or attacked the Constitution: Two asked about Congress's power over religion, and the third, James Lincoln, raised objections only after expressing the greatest deference to the Federalist majority, "whose abilities would do honor to the senate of ancient Rome." He alone asked why the Constitution did not begin, like many state constitutions (though not that of South Carolina), with a bill of rights. Charles Cotesworth Pinckney answered. Most state bills of rights, he observed, began by declaring that all men are by nature free, and "we should make that declaration with a very bad grace, when a large part of our property consists in men who are actually born slaves."[108]

Finally, on January 19, the House unanimously agreed to hold elections on April 11–12, a Friday and Saturday, for delegates to a convention that would meet on May 12, "for the purpose of Considering and of *Ratifying* or *rejecting* the Constitution." Those who were "intitl'd to Vote for Representatives to the

General Assembly" could participate, which confined the electorate to free, white adult males twenty-one years of age or more, who had lived in the state at least a year, acknowledged the existence of a God, believed in "a future state of rewards and punishments," had owned a freehold of at least fifty acres or a town lot for at least six months, or had paid taxes within the past year (or been subject to such taxes for at least six months) equivalent to those on a fifty-acre freehold. Qualified men could cast ballots in the parish or district where they lived or in any other where they had "the like freehold."[109]

The distribution of seats in the convention was much the same as for the legislature, which meant the backcountry would be significantly underrepresented. Newly organized sections in the west received six extra delegates, but that was nowhere near enough to offset the dominance of delegates from the low country. The coastal districts of Charleston, Georgetown, and Beaufort, with under 29,000 people, had 143 delegates, but the backcountry, with almost four times as many people, had only 93 delegates. Finally, by a majority of only one vote, the legislature decided to hold the convention in Charleston, where the press and, according to Aedanus Burke, a judge and convention delegate who opposed ratification, the vast majority of the population supported the Constitution. That was enough to persuade several men, including Lowndes, that there was no point in going to the convention since its outcome was already determined.[110]

Only a handful of miscellaneous speeches survive from the convention, which met from May 12 to 24. Its official journal says that, after adjourning for a day so more delegates could arrive, the convention elected its officers, set up a committee on elections, adopted rules of procedure, and then began debating the Constitution by paragraphs. It spent two to three days on Article I, roughly two on Article II, then moved quickly to Article VII.[111] Delegates probably did not object to biennial congressional terms, since members of the state's house of representatives had two-year terms; nor were they likely to complain about the lack of a bill of rights, since South Carolina's 1778 constitution had none, though the rights themselves were of concern. The one recorded convention speech by a critic of the Constitution said his constituents were willing to give Congress "ample and sufficient powers" but not to give up their liberty, and they feared the Constitution would "promote the ambitious views of a few able and designing men, and enslave the rest." His constituents were not only generally against the Constitution; "they say they will resist against it," and "that they will not accept of it unless compelled by force of arms."[112]

Aedanus Burke later recalled that the Constitution's critics were disorganized while "its friends and abettors left no expedient untried to push it forward." Charleston's "merchants and leading men kept open houses for the back and low country members during the whole time the Convention sat." Moreover, on the sixth day of the convention's proceedings, news arrived that Maryland had ratified. That was a "severe blow" to the opposition, Burke said; thereafter it was "every day losing ground and numbers going over to the enemy," thinking "further opposition was useless."[113]

As a last-ditch effort, on May 21 General Thomas Sumter made the motion dreaded by Virginia Federalists: that the convention adjourn until October 20 so it could know what the Virginia convention had decided. After spending "considerable time" debating the motion, the convention rejected it, with 89 votes in favor, 135 against. That vote was understood at the time, according to Dr. David Ramsay, a historian and Federalist convention delegate, as decisively "in favor of the constitution." When the count was announced, "strong and involuntary expressions of joy burst forth from the numerous-transported spectators," which Ramsay said was "unexampled in the annals of Carolina." The minority complained of disrespect, but members of the majority joined "in clearing the house, and in the most delicate manner soothed their feelings."[114]

However, on the next day, May 22, Edward Rutledge, a Charleston Federalist, moved that a committee be appointed to draw up amendments to the Constitution that would be recommended for adoption to the first federal Congress. Early in its proceedings the convention "received and read" a letter from John Hancock with a copy of the Massachusetts convention's proceedings; now it seemed to be following that precedent.[115] In Massachusetts, Federalists had recommended amendments to win votes essential for ratification. That was not the case in South Carolina, where a clear majority of the convention supported adoption of the Constitution. There the amendments had another purpose: to reconcile an opposition to the ratification of the Constitution that was more powerful outside than inside the convention, thanks to the severe underrepresentation of inland districts.

The committee was appointed and reported the same day, obviously having done its work beforehand. The convention, which devoted most of May 23 to the report, rejected several proposed amendments and also a separate motion that a committee be appointed "to draw up a Bill of Rights to be proposed as an amendment to the Constitution." However, it agreed to recommend four amendments. One would confine congressional control over the elections of senators and representatives under Article I, Section 4, to cases where states "refuse or neglect" to make the necessary arrangements. Another said no part of the Constitution warranted a construction "that the States do not retain every power, not expressly relinquished by them" to the "General Government of the Union." The third would preclude Congress from levying direct taxes unless revenues from duties, imposts, and excises was insufficient for the public needs, "nor then" until the states had been given an opportunity to "assess, levy, and pay" their proportion of the tax. If, however, a state neglected or refused to act, then Congress could "assess and

levy" the amount owed by the state with interest of six percent a year from
the time the original requisition fell due. The final amendment would have
added "other" to Article VI, so, after prescribing that both state and federal
officeholders take oaths to support the Constitution, it would say that "no
other religious test" would be required, understanding that an oath is a form
of religious test. These amendments would be a "standing instruction" to
future South Carolina congressmen, who were to exert "their utmost Abilities and influence to effect an alteration of the Constitution conformably to
the foregoing Resolutions."[116]

At the end of that long day, the convention ratified the Constitution by
a vote of 149 to 73—roughly two to one—with most "no" votes cast by delegates from inland constituencies. Another nine of the 222 delegates who
attended the convention—out of 236 who were elected—did not vote. Once
that decision was made, the convention ordered the printing of 1,200 copies
of the Constitution with its recommended amendments for distribution to
the convention's members.[117] Other states had distributed copies of the Constitution before the election of delegates to the ratifying conventions, for the
information of voters. South Carolina distributed them with the convention's
recommended amendments to persuade the people to accept the Constitution, which, Burke claimed, 80 percent of South Carolinians detested. That
figure was probably too high, but a modern study concludes that the convention's majority spoke for only 39 percent and the minority for 52.2 percent of
South Carolina's nonslave population. (Delegates who were elected but did
not attend or attended but did not vote account for the remaining 8.8 percent.)[118] That meant the Federalists still had some proselytizing to do if the
state was to accept the Constitution willingly, and the recommended amendments were part of that effort.

The vote to ratify was, however, unconditional and final. By consenting to
engage with their opponents, mollifying resentments, and recommending a
few amendments, South Carolina's Federalists had managed to avoid another
"dissent of the minority" like those in Pennsylvania and Maryland.

———

Information traveled slowly in the eighteenth century. If Burke's account was
correct, it took about three weeks for the news of Maryland's ratification to
reach Charleston. News of South Carolina's ratification was unlikely to reach
Richmond before the Virginia ratifying convention met a little over a week
later. But when it arrived, Federalists would be overjoyed despite the amendments that South Carolina recommended. The majority vote was convinc-
ingly large and South Carolina's decision to stay in the union undercut fears
of a Southern confederacy. Best of all, the fact that eight states had approved
the Constitution meant that Virginia, the state more responsible than any
other for getting the Philadelphia Convention to meet, could now round out

its glory by giving the Constitution the final vote it needed to go into effect.

On the other hand, Patrick Henry could argue with some persuasiveness that Virginia could go it alone. It was the largest state in the Confederation, with a sixth of the population of the United States and no less than a fifth of its territory.[119] The union might get along for a time without Rhode Island and North Carolina, but if Virginia decided to go its separate way, and if New York also rejected the Constitution, the United States would be a most peculiar country: a broken string of states stretched along the Atlantic coast interrupted by big chunks of alien territory. Could such a nation survive?

The fate of the Constitution and the country's future would be decided, for all practical purposes, in June, when for a time three ratifying conventions—Virginia, New Hampshire, and New York—would meet simultaneously. Virginia was the first to convene, but, as the delegates began arriving in Richmond, nobody could say with absolute confidence which side would win. Nowhere else were the supporters and critics of the Constitution so balanced in numbers and talent. The Virginia convention promised to be like none before it. And its outcome would have reverberations far beyond the capacious borders of Virginia.

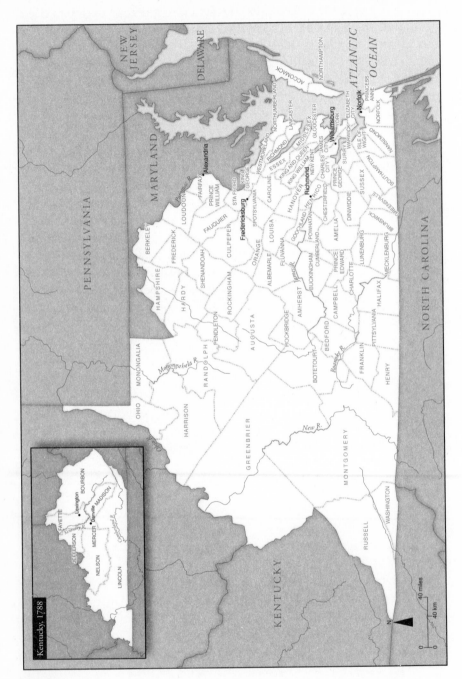

Virginia, 1788

NINE

The Virginia Convention I

A Battle of Giants

The ice of January and March was long gone when delegates hit the road to Richmond; they had to worry more about the heat and drenching rains of early summer. Some took the stagecoach, which would conveniently arrive on Sunday, June 1, the day before the convention was scheduled to meet, instead of the usual Monday. The stagecoach company promised to put extra coaches into service from Williamsburg and Fredericksburg if needed. The trip was seldom easy: The relatively uncomplicated fifty-mile trip by stage from Williamsburg to Richmond could take fifteen hours after a heavy rain. Delegates from western Virginia and Kentucky had many times that distance to travel and mountains to cross.[1]

Richmond, their destination, was different from Philadelphia, Boston, Charleston, or even Annapolis, where previous state conventions had met. The people of those old port cities were almost all in favor of a quick, unqualified ratification of the Constitution, which they hoped would bring a much-needed boost for American commerce and breathe new life into their economies. Richmond, however, was on the upper reaches of the James River, in Virginia's Piedmont, just below where water flowing down from the Appalachian Mountains broke into rapids that blocked navigation farther inland. It had become Virginia's capital in 1779, during the Revolutionary War, when the old capital, Williamsburg, seemed too close to the sea and vulnerable to naval attacks, and the surging population in interior parts of Virginia argued for moving the state's government to a more central location. The legislature chose Richmond because it was "more safe and central than any other town situated on navigable water."[2]

The fledgling city had trouble enough accommodating members of the legislature; now the arrival of some 170 convention delegates and a "prodigious number of People from all parts of the Country" who wanted to witness the convention made the capital "exceedingly crowded." Many of those visitors were what an unsympathetic witness called "Anti Federalists," who were "clamorous in their opposition out of Doors" and ready to follow their leaders on the convention floor in any "desperate step."[3]

Spread out on two hills along the river, Richmond remained a small town in 1788 with about two thousand residents and fewer than three hundred wooden houses, mostly small with heavy shutters and chimneys built of short logs, along with taverns, shops, and tobacco warehouses. Goats and hogs wandered through its dirty streets, and yet as early as 1781 the Marquis de Chastellux could find there what he considered a magnificent meal and decent lodgings. For diversion, elegantly dressed gentlemen and women could go dancing to the music of black fiddlers and banjo players. In 1788 the town even had a new "Academy," otherwise known as the "New Theatre on Shockoe Hill," a "Spacious and Airy Building" first conceived as a school for dancing, drawing, and foreign languages that was sometimes rented out for theater performances. The convention would put it to good use, moving there on its second day from the old wooden statehouse, because it had space for both the convention itself and the throngs of people who wanted to get in.[4]

There was no mystery why the spectators were crowding into Richmond. The convention promised to be a contest of epic proportions. The sides were almost equally strong, though the opposition perhaps had an edge in oratorical strength. The delegates included many stars of Virginia politics. Patrick Henry alone was a big draw, and George Mason would be at his side, opposing ratification of the Constitution in its current form. So would William Grayson, a fifty-two-year-old lawyer and former member of the Continental Army from Prince William County who had been a member of Virginia's house of delegates and the Confederation Congress; and the handsome, dark-haired James Monroe, only thirty years old but already an experienced public servant. Monroe had cut short his studies at William and Mary to fight in the Revolutionary War, then studied law with Jefferson, served in Virginia's house of delegates as well as its council of state, and between 1783 and 1786 was a Virginia delegate in Congress.[5]

Another, more senior delegate, Edmund Pendleton, came from a poor family and had little formal education, but he had nonetheless become one of the most respected jurists in a state where almost every prominent public figure seemed to be a lawyer by profession or avocation. In his late sixties in 1788, Pendleton was president of Virginia's high court of chancery and supreme court of appeals. His health was frail: He struggled with asthma and had walked with crutches since 1777, after a fall from a horse. Given his infirmities, Pendleton was allowed to sit while presiding over the convention.[6] Governor Edmund Randolph would also be there, along with the up-and-coming John Marshall; George Nicholas, with whom James Madison had conferred on the Kentucky situation, and Madison himself. There were some notable absentees: Jefferson remained in Paris, Washington at Mount Vernon, and Richard Henry Lee at Chantilly, his home in northern Virginia. But even *in absentia* they would play a role in the debates, and on different sides. The convention promised to be a battle of giants.

But was there anything left for these distinguished statesmen to say by June of 1788? Two months earlier, the majority in the Maryland convention refused to debate the Constitution because, it said, nothing new remained to be said. At the start of the South Carolina convention in May, Charles Cotesworth Pinckney also suggested that there was no need to discuss the Constitution in detail because it had already been "thoroughly investigated," with every topic "sufficiently explored."[7]

The publication of *The Federalist* in book form during the spring of 1788—volume I in March, volume II in late May—added to the problem. The first volume included thirty-six essays, the second forty-nine, eight of which had not been previously published, and the volumes' publication increased the series' influence outside New York. The writings of "Publius" had little if any impact on the Massachusetts ratifying convention: Some three months after it had adjourned, the Federalist delegate George Cabot said he had seen only a few essays from the series, all of which were sent to him by another supporter of ratification. In April of 1788, however, copies of volume I of *The Federalist* were advertised in the *Norfolk and Portsmouth Journal*, and John Marshall was among the purchasers. By June, several Virginians owned the first volume, of which Hamilton, on Madison's request, had sent fifty-two copies to Edmund Randolph in May. "Publius" was on his way to becoming the preeminent defender of the Constitution. Nonetheless, most delegates to the Virginia convention had probably never seen *The Federalist*—or, for that matter, many other essays on the Constitution. In early April, George Nicholas had urged Madison to send him thirty or forty copies of "*Publius of the federalist* if it is published in a pamphlet" so he could distribute them because the "greater part of the members will go to the meeting without information on the subject." At least one critical Kentucky delegate found it impossible to locate a copy of *The Federalist* before leaving for the convention.[8]

The Virginia convention managed to avoid the fate of spending its days tediously restating arguments that had already been made, thanks in no small part to Patrick Henry. For better or worse, he forced it to confront big questions that were not on its formal agenda and that had not been explored, certainly not with equal rhetorical flare, in any previous ratifying convention.

ORGANIZING THE DEBATES

Madison assumed that the convention would start late, like most eighteenth-century meetings, and arrived only in the evening of the day it was supposed to convene. He was wrong; the convention had a "very full house" already on Monday, June 2. It proceeded to choose its president, Pendleton, and several other officers, appoint a committee on privileges and elections, order copies of basic documents printed for the use of delegates, and—without apparent controversy—select a chaplain to offer a prayer each morning, all before Madison walked in the door. It also decided to move from the statehouse to "the New Academy, on Shockoe Hill."⁹

Virginia's weekly newspapers gave surprisingly little space to the convention, but they reported one other development on the convention's first day. George Nicholas asked the convention to allow a "short hand gentleman," David Robertson, to record its debates, but the proposal met rough treatment from Mason and other critics of the Constitution. Mason had seen Thomas Lloyd's truncated, Federalist version of the Pennsylvania debates and had no intention of giving official sanction to an account of the Virginia debates that he expected to be similarly "garbled" since Robertson was a "*federal Partizan*." In the end, Nicholas withdrew his motion, but the convention gave Robertson (who was also a prominent Petersburg lawyer) a seat in the galleries where he could take notes on the debates. He eventually published the fullest account of debates for any state ratifying convention—over six hundred pages in three volumes.¹⁰

Robertson's *Debates and Other Proceedings of the Convention of Virginia* was imperfect, as he himself acknowledged. The problem, however, came less from his politics—he recorded speakers on all sides of the debate without the obvious bias in some other convention accounts—than from the difficulty he had hearing speakers from a distance while nearby spectators were, as he said, "constantly going out and coming in." His *Debates* are peppered with notes that he could not hear some parts of a speech. Many years later, in 1832, John Marshall said Robertson did best with speakers like William Grayson and James Monroe, who wrote out their speeches beforehand, or George Mason, who spoke slowly and distinctly from "very copious notes." Randolph, "whose elocution was good," was also "pretty well reported." However, Robertson did a bad job with the soft-spoken Madison (indeed, Robertson's *Debates* frequently say Madison spoke "too low to be understood") and even worse with Henry, whom "no reporter could Correctly report." As for his own speeches, Marshall said that "if my name had not been prefixed to the speaches I never should have recognized them."¹¹ And yet Robertson succeeded to a remarkable extent in capturing the speakers' eloquence, their reasoning, and even occasionally their incoherence. Used carefully along with contemporary letters and newspaper reports, his *Debates* preserve for posterity a record of the convention that would otherwise have slipped silently into the unrecorded past.

———

On its second day, settled into its new quarters and with Madison in his seat, the convention made decisions that shaped its future debates. To save time, Governor Randolph proposed that the convention adopt the house of delegates' rules of debate insofar as they were applicable to its proceedings. The delegates agreed, but then Mason argued that no rules should interfere with the delegates' full and free discussion of the Constitution. Another delegate suggested that the convention debate the Constitution as a committee of the whole, in which the rules were normally suspended. Mason agreed that a committee of the whole was "the most proper mode of proceeding," and the convention adopted the proposal. As a result, each morning from June 4 through June 25—nineteen of the twenty-three days it was in session—the convention quickly decided any business issues that came before it, most of which had to do with contested elections, and then resolved itself into a committee of the whole. Pendleton passed the gavel to George Wythe or, on June 24 and 25, two other delegates, who, as chairmen of the committee, had very little power. They could not, for example, stop a delegate from speaking more than once on an issue or even call a delegate out of order. The fact that the convention spent most of its time sitting as a committee of the whole meant that Pendleton could participate in its discussions. It also meant that the convention's official journal, which did not cover the committee's proceedings, is even less informative than those of most other conventions, which makes Robertson's *Debates* all the more important.[12]

Mason moved that no question or vote would be taken on the Constitution or on any part of it until it had been discussed "clause by clause, through all its parts." The supporters of ratification quickly agreed and the motion passed unanimously. Federalists in the Massachusetts convention had proposed that slow, methodical way of proceeding so they would have time to persuade wavering delegates and to discourage their opponents from proposing amendments. In Virginia, however, Mason and members of the opposition such as William Grayson thought the rule favored their side. Several weeks before the convention met, Richard Henry Lee had, in fact, written Mason that the convention should have "a thorough, particular, and careful examination" of all parts of the Constitution before calling any question. That would allow critics of the Constitution to assess the views of the other delegates and propose amendments in a form that they were likely to accept.[13]

The actual debates began on the convention's third day, June 4, with a brief scuffle after Henry proposed that the acts of the Virginia assembly appointing delegates to the Annapolis and Philadelphia conventions be read. Pendleton objected: Henry, he said, obviously wanted to show that the federal Convention had exceeded its powers. To be sure, the Convention had been asked to revise the Articles of Confederation, but it found the old system defective beyond remedy and instead proposed a new one that the people of Virginia had appointed the ratifying convention to evaluate. The documents Henry wanted read were irrelevant to that task. Henry withdrew his motion without, it seems, another word. Then the convention's clerk read the Constitution's Preamble and the first two sections of Article I, and George Nicholas opened the debates on the Constitution with a long speech defending the structure and powers of Congress.[14]

Next Henry took the floor and effectively redefined the questions for debate. The public was "extremely uneasy" over the proposed change in government, he claimed. The people were secure before the Constitutional Convention met, but its proposal had destroyed that security and put the republic in "extreme danger." The Constitution would set up a new government of nine states (the number required for ratification), annihilate treaties with foreign nations, and pose a grave threat to American liberty. He asked why the members of the Convention proposed a "consolidated Government, instead of a confederation." And what right had they to found its authority on "We, the People" instead of "We, the States"? Even Washington, Henry suggested, was answerable for his actions in Philadelphia, although he posed his questions to those delegates to the federal Convention who were present. He insisted that there had been "no dangers, no insurrection or tumult" in Virginia and no danger of sufficient magnitude to justify that "perilous innovation," the Constitution. The federal Convention should have amended the Confederation, as instructed. It was necessary "to be extremely cautious, watchful, jealous of your liberty; for instead of securing your rights you may lose them forever."[15]

Governor Randolph was the obvious person to answer Henry. He had opened the debates at Philadelphia with a speech on behalf of the Virginia delegation that assumed the existence of a crisis, explained in detail the defects of the Confederation, called for a thorough restructuring of the national government to prevent an "American downfal[l]," and proposed to submit the new plan of government to bodies "expressly chosen by the people, to consider and decide upon."[16] Now, in a speech of two and a half or three hours, he again argued that the Confederation had proven "totally inadequate." When the federal Convention found it beyond repair, what should the delegates have done? Return without proposing "some scheme to relieve their distressed country?" And why not found the authority of the Constitution on the consent of the people who would be bound by it? Treaties with other nations would be unaffected by ratification of the Constitution, as Article VI made clear. How many states did Henry think should be obliged to ratify the Constitution before it went into effect? Requiring unanimous consent would allow "any one State to dissolve the Union" and a simple majority of states seemed "too few," so nine seemed about right.[17]

Randolph explained that he had refused to sign the Constitution because he thought the federal Convention's demand that state conventions either accept or reject the Constitution as written was too severe and would lead to its rejection. If the state conventions rejected it "because the chance for amendments was cut off, the Union would have been irredeemably lost." Randolph supported the establishment of a strong, energetic government and would, he said, concur in "any practical scheme of amendments" that addressed his reservations about the Constitution. The only question, he said, was whether the amendments should be made previous to or after ratification. But he feared that to insist on prior amendments now, in so late a convention, after several other states had ratified the Constitution without insisting on amendments before it went into effect, would mean "inevitable ruin to the Union." In short, Randolph had made his peace with recommending amendments that would be enacted under Article V of the Constitution once the new government had begun. He also made clear that he wanted the Constitution ratified in the name of the union, which was, he said, "the anchor of our political salvation."[18]

"The Governor has declared the day of previous amendments passed, and thrown himself fully into the federal scale," Madison wrote Washington that evening with obvious delight. Members of the opposition were not so happy about Randolph's stand, and periodically in the course of the convention they would make comments about Randolph's inconsistency that provoked brief, emotional flare-ups. They were also unhappy about another "unlucky circumstance" of the day: the arrival of news that South Carolina had ratified the Constitution. Washington, however, took heart from the strong majority for ratification in South Carolina. That, he predicted, along with "the almost absolute certainty of its adoption in New Hampshire," would help dispel "the mist" that "blinded the eyes of the wavering" and "turn them into the right road."[19]

The fact that there were eight states in the "yes" column also seemed to confirm Randolph's conviction that the possibility of prior amendments had passed. Getting the ratifying states to reconsider their decisions would be difficult, and a second convention, called to sort through the proposed amendments, might be shackled by state instructions that prevented compromises like those made at Philadelphia. And would the enactment of such a convention's recommendations, assuming it came to an agreement, require calling another round of state conventions? At best the demand for prior amendments would delay implementation of the Constitution, which Randolph and many Federalists considered urgently necessary.

Strangely, Richard Henry Lee seems to have come to much the same conclusion on prior amendments. He too recognized the Constitution as a step forward and privately counseled Mason to watch carefully so "the foes of union, order, and good government" did not "prevent our acceptance of the good part of the plan proposed." After extensive reflection, he proposed that Virginia should ratify the Constitution but demand "such amendments as can be agreed upon" as statements of "their undoubted rights and liberties which they mean not to part with." The amendments would be proposed and adopted using the procedures in Article V. However, if the amendments still had not been enacted two years after the new government began, Virginia would "be considered as disengaged from this ratification." That "friendly and reasonable" method, Lee said, would allow the new Congress to amend the Constitution "without risking the convulsion of conventions," gratify critics of the Constitution and also those Federalists who thought amendments were needed, harmonize the undetermined states, and quiet the "formidable minorities" in states that had already ratified. Lee recommended his plan for Mason's "serious and patriotic attention."[20]

Mason took the floor after Randolph. At first he seemed to echo Henry, observing that the Constitution created a national government, not a confederation. But Mason's objection was grounded on Congress's ability to lay direct taxes, which, he said, was "at discretion, unconfined, and without any kind of controul." Would the people "submit to be individually taxed by two different and distinct powers? Will they suffer themselves to be doubly harrassed?" Since the "General Government" was superior to and more powerful than the states, the latter "must give way to the former," transforming "the confederation of States into one consolidated Government." But no extensive territory could be governed by a single government without destroying the people's liberty.[21]

Mason did not, however, want to revert to the Confederation, whose "inefficacy" he, unlike Henry, readily acknowledged. Instead he proposed an amendment like those already recommended by Massachusetts and South Carolina that would let state legislatures, where the people were more fully represented, levy their portion of federal direct taxes. Only if a state failed to act could the federal government collect those taxes itself. Mason acknowledged that the people could not be represented fully and adequately in the general government; that would be "too expensive and too unweildy." Only powers "absolutely necessary" should be granted a government that was unavoidably defective in that way. He wanted the Constitution amended to define more sharply the line between the general and state governments and so prevent "that dangerous clashing of interest and power, which must, as it now stands, terminate in the destruction of one or the other." The problem was not confined to the provision on taxation; the judiciary, Mason suggested, also threatened the state governments. But with amendments that protected the states, he would "most gladly" put his hand to the Constitution. The amendments, he implied, would have to come before its adoption.²² Mason clearly did not entirely agree with Richard Henry Lee, and he seemed out of step with Henry too.

At the end of the day, Madison wrote Washington that Henry and Mason "appeared to take different & awkward ground," and "the federalists are a good deal elated by the existing prospect." The convention's outcome, however, remained uncertain. The opposition was privately using "every piece of address . . . to work on the local interests and prejudices" of delegates from Kentucky and "other quarters."²³ Meanwhile, Grayson, who had "just come from a meeting," said the opposition was "alarmed but we do not despond." Kentucky was "with us," and if the Constitution's critics could win over four counties beyond the Appalachians on the Ohio River, "the day is ours."²⁴

The meeting Grayson mentioned might well also have addressed the apparent differences between Mason and Henry. In any case, like Mason, Henry later argued for amending the Constitution before ratifying it. But reigning in Henry was probably impossible. He was and would remain a one-man show. It also proved impossible to keep speakers focused on the first two sections of Article I, which were supposedly the topic of discussion. Madison tried to get the debates back on track in the late afternoon of June 4, immediately after Mason spoke. The levying of direct taxes would be more properly discussed when the delegates came to Article I, Section 8, which gave Congress taxing power, he said; delegates should respect the resolution they passed and proceed through the Constitution clause by clause.²⁵ He failed. The next day Pendleton went back to hammering away at Henry and then, with only a slight nod to the clauses supposedly under debate, took a few whacks at Mason.

If the public mind was at ease before the federal Convention, Pendleton said, it must have been in an "inactive unaccountable stupor" because the Confederation had proven "totally inadequate." Commerce was decayed, finances deranged, "and public credit destroyed." There was "no quarrel between Government and liberty; the former is the shield and protector of the latter." The real conflict, he said, was "between Government and licentiousness, faction, turbulence, and other violations of the rules of society" that "preserve liberty." The people, "possessing all power," had every right to form a government they thought would serve their happiness; if that expectation proved wrong, the amendment process specified in the Constitution provided "an easy and quiet method of reforming what may be found amiss." The Constitution did not create a "consolidated government" since its power extended only to the "general purposes of the Union" and did not meddle with "the local particular affairs of the States." Moreover, in several regards, such as the election of senators, the central government was "absolutely dependent on the State Governments."²⁶

As for Mason's proposal to let the state legislatures raise their portion of a federal requisition before Congress could levy direct taxes, it would waste precious time. Congress might lay requisitions in December, but Virginia's legislature wouldn't meet to consider the issue until the following October. And what if the legislature refused to comply? Wouldn't there be resistance to federal tax collectors, which would lead to confusion and even the dissolution of the union? Pendleton saw no reason why both the states and federal government couldn't raise direct taxes since the taxes were for different purposes. Federal direct taxes, in any case, were likely to be minor since most of the central government's revenue would come from duties on imports. As for the provision in Article I, Section 2, that said "the number of Representatives shall not exceed one for every thirty Thousand," Pendleton found that limit on representation perfectly satisfactory given the limited sphere of authority delegated to Congress.[27]

Henry "Light Horse Harry" Lee followed Pendleton and repeated his points on the "imbecility" of the Confederation, the adequacy of representation under the Constitution, and the propriety of founding its authority on the consent of "We, the People" who would be bound by it. Lee also testified to the power of Henry's oratory, though he questioned the propriety of his appeals to fear. That was enough to bring Henry again to the floor, which he held through the rest of the day. His marathon speech on June 5, long even in comparison with the other lengthy orations in the convention's opening days, was more an eruption than a structured argument. At its end Henry confessed that his mind "hurried on from subject to subject," ranging over topics he had not come prepared to discuss, and yet he covered not "one hundred thousandth" of what he had on his mind. Robertson struggled to keep up with the flow of words, stumbling at times, but continuing page after page, trying desperately to capture one of Henry's greatest performances.[28]

Nothing less than the fate of America, Henry insisted, turned on "that poor little thing—the expression, *We, the people*," with which the Constitution began, instead of "we the States." The people in their collective capacity were not the proper agents for entering leagues, alliances, or confederations; that was the work of "states and sovereign powers." Founding the Constitution on the people transformed a confederation into a consolidated government. "Here is a revolution as radical as that which separated us from Britain," Henry said, since it endangered "our rights and privileges" and relinquished the states' sovereignty. It was wrong to ask "how your trade may be increased" or "how you are to become a great and powerful people." The only appropriate question was "how your liberties can be secured; for liberty ought to be the direct end of your Government. . . . Liberty the greatest of all earthly blessings—give us that precious jewel, and you may take everything else."[29]

Again and again Henry charged that those who proposed and supported the Constitution wanted "a great" and "splendid" government. "Some way or other we must be a great and mighty empire; we must have an army, and a navy, and a number of things." That ambition was new. "When the American spirit was in its youth, the language of America was different: Liberty, Sir, was then the primary object." But now "the American spirit, assisted by the ropes and chains of consolidation, is about to convert this country [in]to a powerful and mighty empire," which was "incompatible with the genius of republicanism." If the United States could "make nations tremble," would that "constitute happiness or secure liberty"? What men of modest wealth, who made up the mass of Americans, wanted was not national power and glory, but to enjoy the fruits of their labor and the company of their families "in peace and security."[30]

A veteran of the independence movement from the very beginning, Henry, now fifty-two years of age, played the old man. "I am fearful I have lived long enough to become an old fashioned fellow," he said. He was sarcastic: "Perhaps an invincible attachment to the dearest rights of man, may, in these refined enlightened days, be deemed old fashioned: If so, I am contented to be so." Some called him suspicious for saying Americans' rights and privileges were in danger, but "suspicion is a virtue, as long as its object is the preservation of the public good, and as long as it stays within proper bounds." It was right to "guard with jealous attention the public liberty" and "suspect every one who approaches that jewel." Perhaps his fears were "the result of my age; they may be feelings natural to a man of my years, when . . . his mental powers, like the members of the body, are decayed."[31] But clearly he believed that, as in 1776, the danger to liberty was real.

Henry granted Pendleton's point that licentiousness was dangerous and that the proposed government would guard against it, but he said the government would also effectually "oppress and ruin the people." In the course of his speech Henry attacked one part of the Constitution after another in a scattershot manner, as they came to mind. Why didn't the Constitution say in clear and unambiguous language that there would be one representative for every thirty thousand people rather than that the number of representatives "shall not exceed" that proportion? The clause giving Congress power over the time, place, and manner of congressional elections would discourage voters' participation and destroy confidence in the "democratic branch" of the legislature. The "very indefinite and indeterminate" provision requiring Congress to publish "from time to time . . . the receipts and expenditures of public money" (Article I, Section 9, paragraph 7) would allow it to delay publication for a century, hiding ruinous misappropriations of revenue. The "unbounded and unlimited" taxing power given to Congress violated a principle in the Virginia declaration of rights that said people could not be "*taxed* or *deprived* of *their property* for public uses, without their own consent, or that of their Representatives," since the people would be taxed "by people who have no connection" with them.[32]

Henry did not, like Mason or Richard Henry Lee, concede that the Constitution had some good parts. He saw only "deformities," including "an awful squinting . . . toward monarchy." The president could easily become a king, he said, and, according to Robertson, Henry "strongly and pathetically expatiated on the probability of the President's enslaving America." The Senate was so "imperfectly constructed that your dearest rights may be sacrificed . . . by a small minority." The president and a two-thirds vote of those senators present could enact "ruinous treaties" that would become "the supreme law of the land." The judiciary would not help since it was "oppressively constructed." There were no real checks or balances in the Constitution, Henry insisted; even the British government was far superior in that regard. Worse yet, the people would have no means of defending their rights. Pendleton had said the people would meet in convention and recall powers that were abused and punish officeholders for violating their trust, but "we should have fine times indeed, if to punish tyrants, it were only sufficient to assemble the people." The federal government would have a "standing army" and control the militia. "Will your Macebearer be a match for a disciplined regiment?"[33]

None of this had to be. The crisis Randolph and his colleagues cited was "imaginary." There had been no uprisings against the law in Virginia; nor was there any real danger from Europe. The haste with which the Constitution's supporters pushed for ratification in the name of that supposed crisis did, however, cause serious danger. Pennsylvania, Henry said, had perhaps been "tricked" into ratifying; other states were, if not tricked, at least "too much hurried into its adoption." In several of them "respectable minorities" voted against ratification; "and if reports be true," Henry said, "a clear majority of the people are averse to [the Constitution]." Surely it did not command the people's affection, which was essential for a republican government. "Take longer time in reckoning things," Henry advised; "revolutions like this have happened in almost every country in Europe" where the people lost their liberty "by their own carelessness and the ambition of a few."[34]

It was no easy thing defining what exactly Henry proposed. To him it made no difference that eight states had already ratified the Constitution. If twelve and a half had ratified, he said, he would "with manly firmness, and in spite of an erring world, reject it." Later he said that unless the new plan of government was amended "we can never accept it." No amendment, however, was likely to address his fundamental criticism of the Constitution: that its authority came from the people instead of the states. In any case, Henry dismissed the possibility of amendments under Article V after the Constitution went into effect. The requirement that three-quarters of the states agree to amendments meant that a bare majority in four small states could block even the most pressing changes. Only prior amendments would do. If the new government went into effect without essential amendments and Virginia stayed out because of "scruples," its decision would not destroy the union. Virginia could jog along with the new government, supplying its requisitions of money and soldiers, and the states that formally ratified the Constitution would not object since, Henry said, they could "hardly stand on their own legs" without her. Virginia could just "stand by a while" and see how the Constitution worked out in the ratifying states, remaining in an "amicable alliance" with them. In Switzerland, he said, dissimilar governments had been confederated like that for over four hundred years.[35]

The galleries perhaps found Henry's oratory deeply moving: One spectator recalled that he had "involuntarily felt his wrists to assure himself that the fetters were not already pressing his flesh" when Henry spoke. Many delegates, however, were moved mainly to exasperation. "If we go on in this irregular manner, contrary to our resolution," Randolph complained, "instead of three or six weeks, it will take us six months to decide this question." Henry countered that not only he but many delegates had spoken "out of order" and that, "instead of discussing the system regularly, a variety of points" had been "promiscuously debated in order to make temporary impressions" on fellow delegates. The "disorder" lasted another nine days: Not until June 14, some ten days after the debates began, would the committee of the whole move on to Article I, Section 3. Henry had made too many assertions; he had raised too many big issues—the reality of the "crisis" that led to the Constitution, the nature of the Constitution and its consonance with the Revolution of 1776, the future of the United States, the place of Virginia in the union—for the delegates to go on as if nothing had happened. Even those who expressed dismay at the course the debates had taken went on to ignore the convention's decision to go through the Constitution methodically because, as Randolph put it, "the Honorable Gentleman ought to be answered."[36]

Patrick Henry had, in effect, hijacked the debates. By doing that, he provoked one of the most probing—and chaotic—debates in any state ratifying convention.

ANSWERING HENRY

"Mr. Chairman," Edmund Randolph began the committee of the whole's debates on the morning of June 6, the day after Henry's startling speech, "I am a child of the revolution." That response to Henry's play on age was true to Randolph's life. Born in 1753, Randolph was seventeen years—almost a generation—younger than Henry. But he was no less a patriot. In 1775 Randolph had gone off to join the American army in Cambridge, and the next year he was a member of the Revolutionary assembly that enacted Virginia's first state constitution. By then he was also a child of the Revolution in another sense: His Loyalist father, John Randolph, had gone into exile in England with his wife and two daughters, leaving Edmund behind to follow his very different convictions. "My country very early indeed took me under its protection," Randolph told the convention, and at a time when he most needed it. "I feel the highest gratitude and attachment to my country—her felicity is the most fervent prayer of my heart."[37]

Henry's dramatic appeals to age called attention to the generational differences in the ratification conflict. He and others prominent in the independence movement, such as Richard Henry Lee and Samuel Adams, had been born in the 1720s or 1730s and had learned their politics as colonists under a distant monarchy, where suspicion of power made good sense. Their politics required moving slowly: They waited until the people were of a mind on independence before acting, conscious that without popular support they would fail. In 1787 and 1788, they instinctively turned to each other, seeing in the Constitution a reincarnation of all they had rejected in 1776. "'Tis really astonishing," Lee wrote the old New York Son of Liberty John Lamb in June 1788, "that the same people, who have just emerged from a long and cruel war in defence of liberty, should agree to fix an elective despotism upon themselves and posterity!"[38]

Several leading proponents and defenders of the Constitution—Madison, Hamilton, Jay—were, by contrast, young men of the Revolution. Born in the 1740s and 1750s, they had learned their politics during the resistance to Britain, which was founded on popular support, and under the republic formally established with independence. Consequently, they were less burdened with the fears and scruples of their elders. There were of course older patriots who supported the Constitution, including Washington (born in 1732) and Franklin (1706), while some young men like James Monroe (1758) opposed it. Randolph's point, however, was that he and others like him, young or old, were no less committed to the Revolution than their opponents. Later Henry Lee said the same thing more directly: The friends of the Constitution were "true republicans, and by no means less attached to liberty, than those who oppose it."[39]

Nor did they long to be "a grand, splendid, and magnificent people. . . . The magnificence of a royal court is not our object. We want Government, Sir," Randolph said, "—A Government that will have stability, and give us security." Madison also insisted that "national splendor and glory are not our objects." To be "respectable abroad" was, however, perfectly consistent with security and happiness at home; indeed, security and happiness at home would win the United States respectability abroad.[40] How, one speaker after another asked, could Henry deny that the Constitution was a response to real and urgent dangers? Why else did all the states but Rhode Island send delegates to the federal Convention? Had Henry never heard of the insurrections in Massachusetts and other states? Perhaps there had been none in Virginia, George Nicholas said, but "had it been attempted here by an enterprising adventurer, I believe he could hardly been prevented by the laws" given their "want of energy." Commerce was languishing; creditors complained that the courts gave them no justice; state legislatures ignored both their own constitutions and their obligations under the Articles of Confederation. "There is no peace, Sir, in this land," Randolph insisted. "Can peace exist with injustice, licentiousness, insecurity, and oppression?"[41]

Danger also loomed from abroad. The country's substantial debts to France and Holland had gone unpaid. So had those to British creditors despite the fourth provision of the Treaty of Paris, which promised there would be no legal obstacles to the collection of old debts. What if those creditor countries demanded payment? The Confederation had not punctually paid the interest on the French debt, and "not a shilling is discharged of the principal." Requisitions on the states yielded so little to the federal treasury that the Confederation had to take the "ruinous and most disgraceful expedient" of borrowing money to pay interest on its debts. Claims that the Confederation had brought the country through the Revolutionary War were unfounded: The Articles were not ratified until 1781, and immediately their feebleness became clear. George Washington had pointed out the need for strengthening the powers of Congress and paying the nation's debts in 1783, when he resigned his military commission. Since then the problems had only become worse.[42]

Madison reviewed the history of confederations: the Amphictyonic and Achaean leagues of ancient times; those of the Germans, Dutch, and Swiss. None of them worked. In every instance they were "productive of anarchy and confusion, ineffectual for the preservation of harmony, and a prey to their own dissentions and foreign invasions." Americans needed a government sufficient to protect them against attacks that, under current circumstances, would inevitably end with "the catastrophe of a dismemberment" as foreign countries nibbled away one piece of territory or another. No confederation would do. A government had to operate on individuals, not states, to be efficient.[43]

What kind of government did the Constitution propose? A republic, of course, since all power came from the people and it would have no hereditary offices. But Madison said the proposed government was of a "mixed nature" and "unprecedented" in the history of the world. In some ways it was federal; in others it had a "consolidated nature." The people formed it—not the people as a single body but "the people as composing thirteen sovereignties" since the people of each state chose representatives who met in convention to decide on ratification and no state was bound until its people gave their consent. Even so, the Constitution was dramatically different from the Articles of Confederation, whose authority came from the state legislatures. The Constitution rested on "the superior power of the people." Members of the House of Representatives would be chosen by the people, senators by the state legislatures. If the government were completely consolidated, senators would also be chosen by the people. A consolidated government would have comprehensive powers, but the Constitution enumerated Congress's powers and made clear that its power could "only operate in certain cases." Just naming so strange a government was a problem. Francis Corbin said some referred to it as a federal and others as a consolidated Government, but he proposed to call it "a Representative Federal Republic."[44]

With one voice, the Constitution's supporters dismissed what Corbin called "the old worn out idea" that a republic and the liberty that was its hallmark could survive only over a small area. That "some of the most illustrious and distinguished authors" had endorsed that idea made no difference to Randolph, who said "the force of reasoning" had more weight with him than "the dignity of names." The idea that only small countries could be republics, John Marshall added, was based on studies of governments "where representation did not exist" and so did not apply to the United States. And just how small did a country have to be "to suit the genius of republicanism"? If too small, Corbin said, it would be weak and vulnerable. Liberty would be on a "precarious footing" in such a "petty state" since it depended on the "philanthropy and good nature of its neighbors." If a republic were too large, it would become subject to "confusion and tyranny." But geographical extent was irrelevant for the proposed government, which could act only on matters of a general nature and left all internal administration to the state legislatures, which would exercise the powers of small republics while escaping their weaknesses and vulnerabilities.[45]

The new government would, moreover, avoid faction and threats to minority rights from the "caprice and arbitrary decisions of the majority." Factions—groups of contentious, self-interested delegates—were a greater threat in large than in small bodies, Corbin argued, and so would be far easier to control in Congress than in the larger state legislatures. A government constructed according to the Constitution was "of all others" the best for an extensive country: It could "extend to all the Western world" and even "ad infinitum." Corbin added that all the states except Delaware and Rhode Island had too much territory to qualify for republican governments under the rule Mason cited, so "its absurdity is demonstrated by our own experience."[46]

Madison had made a more comprehensive argument on the issue of size in the tenth essay of The Federalist. Contrary to prevailing belief, he said, republics were better suited to large than small territories. The multiplication of interests in large republics would make it more difficult for any one interest to command a majority and oppress the minority. Moreover, popular opinion did not feed directly into legislation in large republics; instead it was refined through high-minded legislators with vast, complex constituencies before being translated into law. At Richmond, however, Madison did little more than hint at that landmark argument. Throughout history, he said on June 6, majoritarian abuses of power, which led to "factions and commotions," had posed a greater threat to freedom in republics than the usurpations of power by public officials that Henry feared. "Perhaps in the progress of this discussion it will appear," Madison said, "that the only possible remedy for those evils, and means of preserving and protecting the principles of republicanism," is "in that very system which is now exclaimed against as the parent of oppression." Then he shifted to another subject and never returned to make the argument he forecast.[47]

Madison probably failed to present the argument he promised because he fell sick. An oppressive heat that set in during the convention's first week and the tension he was under took him out of action for a few days and left him weak and tired. On Monday, June 9, when Henry again spoke for a good part of the day, Madison wrote Rufus King that "I have been for two days & still am laid up with a bilious attack" that made even writing "scarcely practicable." Although "extremely feeble," he struggled back to the convention on the following day but suffered a relapse within a week. "My health is not good," he wrote Hamilton on June 16, "and the business is wearisome beyond expression." His "indisposition" gave considerable uneasiness to friends of the Constitution elsewhere who understood how critical the Virginia convention was and how much of a difference Madison in top form could make.[48] They had no idea how effectively others—Randolph in particular—would take up the slack.

Madison's silence made Henry's comments on the size issue in his long speech on June 9 all the more remarkable. He might well have read the tenth number of *The Federalist*, since Henry seemed to respond as much to Madison's printed argument as to Corbin's spoken one. First he attacked the contempt for democratic state legislatures that ran through the private writings of Madison and other Federalists. The Constitution "reflects in the most degrading and mortifying manner on the virtue, integrity, and wisdom of the State Legislatures," Henry said. "It presupposes that the chosen few who go to Congress will have more upright hearts, and more enlightened minds, than those who are members of the individual Legislatures." He expressed outrage at the notion that the 180 representatives in the Virginia legislature were "a mobbish suspected *herd*" that "cannot be trusted" with the interests of their constituents. Then he struck at Madison's, and to some extent Corbin's, argument by pushing it ad absurdum. "If ten men be better than 170"—that is, if the ten men Virginia would send to the proposed Congress were preferable to the 170 in its state legislature (Henry's numbers were not altogether consistent)—"it follows of necessity," he continued, "that one is better than 10—The choice is more refined."[49] In other words, Madison's argument that filtering public opinion through a relatively few members of Congress would protect the liberties of the people better than could be done by large state legislatures led logically toward filtering opinion still further by entrusting all power to one person, such as—what else?—a king.

Henry's clever argument, briefly stated within another long and rambling speech, suggests why Federalists found him so exasperating. The showman had a sharp mind. He also had a way, as Henry Lee complained, of throwing out "bolts" in a "desultory" or random way, one after another and in great profusion,[50] which made him hard to answer in a systematic way. That explains why the responses to Henry were often also "desultory" as well as long and repetitive. While the heat wore at people's patience, and spectators in the gallery, as Robertson reported, kept shuffling in and out, the debates became, as Madison put it, "wearisome." That does not, however, mean that nothing was said worth remembering.

Federalist speakers spent little time answering Henry's scattershot attacks on specific provisions in the Constitution. They said a "standing army" was essential for defense and preferable to depending on the militia, and they argued that the Constitution's provisions on representation were adequate and also economical.[51] Those issues had already been thoroughly discussed elsewhere.

So had the issue of federal taxing power, to which—as always—one speaker after another returned, although Virginia's Federalists brought to the discussion a more sophisticated understanding of national finance than characterized most previous debates. For the first time, moreover, they considered in detail the amendment proposed by Massachusetts and South Carolina—and now also by Mason—that would give state legislatures a chance to pay a federal requisition before the federal government imposed a direct tax on their people. Pendleton had already criticized the proposal; now other Federalists repeated and added to his arguments. They too said duties on imports would normally be sufficient for federal needs. Congress would resort to direct taxes only in "great emergencies" such as in times of war, when revenue from imports would decline. Every country, even the oldest and wealthiest, resorted to loans to finance wars, which require good credit. For Congress to be able to borrow easily, both Randolph and Madison argued, Congress had to have "full scope, and complete command over the resources of the nation." Then it would be able to "borrow with ease." If it lacked that power—if its capacity to command the resources of the nation were compromised—lenders would have no confidence in its ability to repay loans. The power of imposing direct taxes without the proposed limit was therefore "essential to the very existence of the Union."[52]

The proposed amendment would also cause endless trouble. If asked to raise money for the federal government, the states would refuse. Suppose the state of Virginia had humbly to supplicate counties for tax revenue, Randolph asked, "what would be the result of such applications for voluntary contributions? You would be laughed at for your folly." People do not pay taxes voluntarily. The proposed system of requisitioning the states would be no more successful than the current one, which produced very little revenue for the Confederation's treasury. States would continue to cite "the probable delinquency of other States" as a pretext for not paying their requisitions. Once a state refused to pay, there was little chance the federal government could collect direct taxes peacefully. Its attempts would provoke resistance that could be overcome only with military coercion, which raised the threat of civil war. The only distinction of the proposed system was that it would give "a little more time to a refractory State to provide itself with arms and foreign alliance, to enable it to . . . resist federal collectors." What, moreover, could the federal government do if a state paid only a part of its requisition? The answer was by no means clear, which opened the way to more disputes. In short, the proposed amendment would "leave the country exposed and open to those who should choose to invade us" and provoke "such sedition and confusion among ourselves, as must subvert and destroy every object of human society."[53]

For the Federalists, in short, comprehensive federal taxing power was a sine qua non of an effective national government. Henry and his colleagues—Mason, Grayson, and also Monroe—questioned its wisdom and necessity, but they saw the entrusting of direct taxes to Congress first and foremost as a rights issue. Given the inadequacies of representation under the Constitution, for Congress to levy direct taxes would, as Henry insisted, violate the right of the people to be taxed only with their consent or that of representatives who knew their circumstances and so imposed taxes in ways they could bear.

The Federalists, all of whom were, like Randolph, children of the Revolution, did not dispute the principle of "no taxation without representation." They simply said it did not apply. Whether taxes were levied by Congress or the state legislators, they would be imposed by "our own Representatives, freely chosen." Couldn't members of Congress "derive information from every source from which the State Representatives get theirs, so as to enable them to impose taxes judiciously?" Would Virginia's ten congressmen have no "fellow feeling for their constituents"? Wouldn't the people choose "men of integrity, and of similar circumstances with themselves, to represent them"? Election to Congress would require "greater talents, and a more extensive reputation" than election to a state legislature, so congressmen would have to be well known for their integrity and knowledge of the country they represented. What would they gain by making the collection of taxes oppressive to the people? They would be "out of their senses" to do that. Considering the convenience of the people would cost them nothing "and in many respects will be advantageous to them." George Nicholas also noted that by allowing more public obligations to be met from duties on imports, an indirect and so relatively unoppressive form of taxation that currently produced little revenue, the Constitution would reduce the burden of direct taxes, to the people's great benefit.[54]

Above all, Federalist delegates dismissed out of hand Henry's idea that Virginia could somehow jog along with the new government of the United States even if it did not ratify the Constitution. A decision by Virginia not to ratify or to ratify with conditions would dissolve the union, Randolph said, and "that dissolution will destroy our political happiness." Henry's Swiss analogy was crazy: The Swiss cantons held together because they were surrounded by powerful, aggressive neighbors, which the United States was not. Their territory, moreover, was small and the soil "not very fertile" and so relatively unattractive to invaders, again unlike the United States. Henry had asserted that the United States could not survive without Virginia, but Randolph said he had the relationship exactly backwards: Virginia and the Southern states could not survive without the union. With a huge, thinly populated land mass, a long coastline, and an extensive "Western Country" inhabited by "cruel savages," Southern states were vulnerable to attacks by enemies but lacked the means of defense without help from other states. Virginia's "immense proportion" of slaves added to its weakness: It held, by Randolph's calculations, 236,000 slaves to 352,000 whites, a proportion large enough to alarm "gentlemen who have been long accustomed to the contemplation of the subject." The other states had over 330,000 men capable of bearing arms; the Virginia militia consisted of 50,000 men, too few to mount an effective defense against attacks by foreign enemies, Indians, or insurgent slaves.[55]

Even if Virginia's white population continued to grow, the governor went on, it would need a navy "in time of peace as well as war" to guard the coast. The state could not afford it, as it already had a heavy load of war debt to retire. Confederating with North Carolina, which was also burdened with debt and slaves, wouldn't help. As he reflected on the subject, Randolph saw one problem after another that disunion would bring. An independent Virginia could be denied access to neighboring states that remained part of the United States. Would commercial rivalry generate new hatreds? Would old border disputes and quarrels over the backcountry be reopened? The people of Virginia's Northern Neck would probably secede from the state and join Maryland. Since Maryland's original charter gave it control of the Potomac, it could deny Virginians access to that river, on which their dreams for future commercial prosperity were so dependent. And "upon what footing would our navigation of the Mississippi be"? Union was, in short, essential to Virginia's safety and well-being.[56]

So was Congress's capacity to collect direct taxes for defense in times of danger. Under the proposed requisition system, interior states would probably hold back on paying their shares, shifting the burden to states along the coast that were in greater danger, including those in the South. A uniform national tax system would assure that all parts of the union shouldered the burden. The opportunity to save the union and the advantages it brought were, however, fleeting. If the union were lost now, Madison feared that it would be lost forever. Governor Randolph agreed. When I "maturely weigh the advantages of the Union, and dreadful consequences of its dissolution; when I see safety on my right, and destruction on my left; when I behold re-spectability and happiness acquired by the one, but annihilated by the other," he said, "I cannot hesitate to decide in favor of the former."[57]

Nothing persuaded Henry, who took the floor time and again. One report claimed that he spoke all day on Thursday, June 5, "all Friday, Saturday, Monday, Tuesday, and Wednesday, and was still speaking on Thursday," June 12.[58] That was an exaggeration: Henry spoke on June 5, 7, 9, intervened briefly on June 11, and spoke again the next day—but others who were no less prone to go on for hours also took the floor. Like Monroe and Grayson, Henry continued to insist that the dangers Federalists cited were imaginary while those posed by the Constitution were real and present. He had a talent for attacking his opponents where their arguments were weakest, as when he dismissed their talk of imminent danger from abroad since "it is little usual for nations to send armies to collect old debts," and in any case, European nations had more pressing issues to think about. In support of his position, he cited Thomas Jefferson, now American minister to France, whose reports indicated that the French were less interested in hostilities than in nego-tiating commercial agreements with the United States. For good measure, Henry added that Jefferson—his old enemy, now transformed into a distin-guished servant of the republic—recommended rejection of the Constitution until it was amended.[59]

Somehow Henry had seen a letter Jefferson wrote on February 7 to Alex-ander Donald, a Richmond tobacco merchant, in which Jefferson expressed hope that nine states would ratify the Constitution and so "secure to us the good it contains," but that four states would hold out until a bill of rights was attached to it. (By late May, however, Jefferson had changed his mind and decided that it would be better if states followed Massachusetts and ratified the Constitution while recommending amendments—a fact not yet known to anyone in Virginia.) Jefferson's close friend James Madison objected to Henry's invoking an outside authority and countered that the Federal-ists could cite "a character equally great on our side," obviously Washing-ton. Madison added, with good reason, that he "was in some measure acquainted" with Jefferson's "sentiments" and that if Jefferson were in the convention he would vote for ratification, but he hesitated to say more from "considerations of personal delicacy." Pendleton also considered Henry's use of Jefferson's letter improper. He, however, had seen the letter to Donald, and he now read relevant sections of it to the convention. Jefferson, he noted, wanted the Constitution ratified. Moreover, Jefferson said that neither the amendments he favored nor any other objections to the Constitution should be allowed to divide the union, which he said "would be an incurable evil; because friends falling out never cordially re-unite."[60]

What, if anything, did this haggling accomplish? Already on June 10 Nicholas complained that "although we have sat eight days, so little has been done, that we have hardly begun to discuss the question regularly." The next day Madison also urged the delegates to resume discussing the Constitution clause by clause. That, Robertson reported, opened a discussion on how to proceed that was itself "desultory." Henry thought it would be better to discuss the Constitution "at large"—that is, as a whole; Madison preferred "a regular progressive discussion" over the "unconnected irregular method which they had hitherto pursued." Then Mason entered into another speech that wandered from point to point, like so many before it.[61] The convention seemed unable to break the pattern.

"THE BUSINESS OF THE MISSISSIPPI"

When the convention met on Friday, June 13, Nicholas insisted that it either follow its original plan to go through the Constitution systematically or rescind that plan. Henry again objected since so many topics remained to be discussed. Many previous speakers had referred to "the business of the Mississippi," and he thought the delegates should take up that topic and, in specific, that "the transactions of Congress relative to the navigation of that river should be communicated to the Convention" so the delegates could draw conclusions "from the best source." This time Nicholas, the debate disciplinarian, raised no objection, although he hoped that afterward the delegates "would confine themselves to the order of the House." Madison, who had more than once bemoaned the course of the debates, also said he had no objection. As a result, the convention again resolved itself into a committee of the whole "to take into further consideration the proposed Constitution, and more particularly" to receive information "concerning the transactions of Congress relative to the Mississippi."[62]

Henry had again defined the agenda, this time with the overt consent of prominent Federalists. On the face of it, that was strange: Congress's record on the "business of the Mississippi" seemed no more relevant to evaluating the Constitution than the instructions Virginia had given its delegates to the federal Convention. The difference was political. The division in the convention remained so close, Madison wrote Washington on June 13, that "the majority will certainly be small on whatever side it may finally lie." The situation was "in the most ticklish state that can be imagined," and the outcome could well depend on the "Kentucky members." The Federalists had nothing to lose and something to gain in discussing "the business of the Mississippi." The Kentucky delegates had "arrived generally under an adverse bias" to the Constitution, Madison noted; winning over even a delegate or two could make all the difference. The importance of a positive vote in Virginia became all the greater thanks to another piece of bad news Madison forwarded to Washington: The convention elections in New York had "proved adverse to the Constitution." Within a week, Madison would get a letter from Alexander Hamilton that reaffirmed what he already knew, that Virginia's decision would have a "vast influence" on New York.[63]

The debate on the Mississippi was at least focused. First several resolutions of the Virginia house of delegates on the issue were read aloud. Henry Lee said Congress never intended to yield access to the river. Then Monroe and Grayson, both of whom had served in Congress, summarized in detail its proceedings relative to Jay's negotiations with the Spanish and, in particular, his request for permission to yield navigation of the Mississippi in return for commercial concessions. The Articles of Confederation, both noted, required the consent of nine states to ratify treaties; under the Constitution, a treaty could have the approval of as few as seven states. As a result, they argued, the interests in the Mississippi of the "Western country" would be less secure under the Constitution. Northern states were ready to concede access to the river in order to stem Southern population growth, which threatened their power. If the Constitution were ratified, Henry said, seven states would give up navigation of the Mississippi "forever. . . . The thing is so obviously big with danger, that the blind man himself might see it."[64]

Madison, however, said the weakness of the Confederation explained why Jay had been forced to propose temporarily yielding access to the Mississippi. "A weak system produced this project. A strong system will remove the inducement." Moreover, the North had no settled disposition to give up navigation of the Mississippi; after all, it stood to profit from improved access to the produce of western states, which its merchants would sell in foreign markets. Madison also noted that Monroe's statement that seven senators could vote away navigation on the Mississippi assumed that all Southern senators would be absent for a vote of immense interest to their constituents, leaving the Senate free to approve a treaty with only a minimal quorum present. Under the Constitution, "two-thirds of the Senators present (which will be nine States, if all attend to their duty) and the President, must concur in every treaty which can be made." The president would be chosen by the nation—and the South's population, including its new settlements in the west, was growing quickly enough to insure that the president would regard their interests.[65]

Randolph restated Madison's calculations, counting probable state votes to refute the opposition's claims. The arguments of George Nicholas, a superb debater whose plans to move to Kentucky were well known, were probably even more effective. The much execrated vote of seven states to allow Jay to give up access to the Mississippi had been taken in Congress "under the existing system," Nicholas noted—that is, by Henry's "favorite confederation. Is this an argument to continue that confederation?" Kentucky, he concluded, "can expect support and succour alone from a strong efficient Government, which can command the resources of the Union when necessary. . . . That country contains all my wishes and prospects. There is my property, and there I intend to reside." He would oppose any system that threatened its interests, but he was confident that the proposed government would secure Kentucky's "happiness and liberty."[66]

The debate ended with a bang. A violent summer storm with wind, hail, and rain interrupted a speech by Francis Corbin, blew the windows open, and left the hall so "wet & uncomfortable" that the convention adjourned. Edmund Pendleton stayed home the next day because his health could not endure the "extream dampness."[67] Efforts to reopen the discussion in the morning failed: The delegates had had enough of the Mississippi, and perhaps of water in general, at least for the moment. The "scuffling for Kentucky votes" might, however, have had an impact of considerable importance. Five days later Grayson wrote Nathan Dane in Massachusetts that the opposition to unqualified ratification had "ten out of 13. of the Kentucki members, but we wanted the whole," and he wasn't sure that they had won over even one of the four "upper counties" on the Ohio River beyond the mountains whose votes seemed open to recruitment. Madison also noted that the Kentucky delegates were mostly but "not unanimously" against ratification. Perhaps the Federalists had persuaded a few Kentucky delegates that their fears of the Constitution were misplaced.[68]

A spectator who heard the debates on the Mississippi said they exceeded his expectations. They were "elaborate, elegant, eloquent, & consequently entertaining and instructive."[69] Not everyone who sat through the debates over a longer period of time was so entranced. The New Yorker-become-Pennsylvanian Gouverneur Morris, one of a handful of "Founding Fathers" with a keen sense of humor, passed his time among the visitors in the gallery composing a rough chronicle of the convention in verse. "The State's determined Resolution," it began, "Was to discuss the Constitution."

> For this the Members come together
> Melting with Zeal and sultry Weather
> And here to their eternal Praise
> To find it's Hist'ry spend three Days
> The next three Days they nobly roam
> Thro ev'ry Region far from Home

Call in the Grecian Swiss Italian
The Roman [Russian?] Dutch Rapscallion
Fellows who Freedom never knew
To tell us what we ought to do
The next three Days they kindly dip yee
Deep in the River Mississippi

Since that made nine days "eer they begin"—that is, after the first two, which were devoted to procedural matters—"Let us suppose them fairly in. And then resolve me gentle Friend," Morris concluded, raising the question in everybody's minds, "How many months before they End"?[70]

BACK TO BUSINESS

The sprawling debates made Madison nervous. He knew that Eleazer Oswald, publisher of Philadelphia's *Independent Gazetteer*, had arrived in Richmond on Saturday, June 7, and met privately with "the leaders of the Opposition." His mission, Henry Lee said, was to open "a correspondence" among the "Malecontents" in Pennsylvania, New York, and Virginia. Virginia Federalists speculated that opposition delegates were purposely trying to "spin out" the debates until the Virginia convention could coordinate a demand for amendments with the New York convention, which would begin on June 17 in Poughkeepsie. If that failed, and if the opposition members decided they could not get the Virginia convention to demand amendments as a condition of ratification, they would try to "weary the members into a[n] adjournment without making any decision."[71] To add to the pressure, Governor Randolph had called a special meeting of the Virginia legislature for June 23 to deal with a state constitutional crisis. Many convention members were also legislators, and they could not attend both meetings simultaneously. If the opposition members kept the convention "disputing" until then, some observers thought the convention would be forced to break up without coming to a decision. In the opening days of the convention, in fact, Henry Lee had warned delegates that if they did not complete their business by June 22 they would be "compelled to adjourn."[72]

The idea of coordinating action with other conventions was not new. The Virginia legislature had suggested the convention might do that the previous December, when it agreed to pay any "reasonable expenses" incurred by the convention in communicating with sister states or with conventions that were simultaneously in session. On the legislature's request, Governor Randolph sent copies of that act to the executives and legislatures of other states. For reasons that remain unclear, New York's governor George Clinton received the letter only on March 7, some six weeks after other states received theirs. He quickly informed the New York legislature about the letter, but the legislature did nothing about it before adjourning two weeks later. On May 8, Clinton nonetheless wrote Randolph that he was certain the New York convention would "with great Cordiality hold a Communication with any Sister State" on the Constitution, but he assumed that the Virginia convention would take the lead since it was meeting first. Although Clinton had said that he was not writing under the instructions of the New York legislature and spoke only for himself, Randolph asked Virginia's council of state whether the letter was public or private. It decided it was public, which gave Randolph a pretext for not presenting Clinton's letter to the convention. Instead he waited until he could give it to the legislature—on June 23.[73]

That failed effort at interstate cooperation led directly to Oswald's mission. The Federal Republican Committee of New York, a group in and near New York City whose members wanted the Constitution amended before being ratified, took up the slack. Its leader, John Lamb, had been prominent in New York's resistance to Britain and a brigadier general in the Continental Army. After the war, Lamb became a supporter of Clinton in New York politics and collector of the port of New York. Between May 18 and 20, Lamb, on behalf of the Federal Republican Committee, wrote to several men in other states whose politics committee members had reason to think coincided with their own. To avoid the distrusted postal system and insure confidentiality, Oswald personally carried Lamb's letters to Henry, Mason, Grayson, and also Richard Henry Lee, whom the New Yorkers incorrectly assumed was a convention delegate. Oswald also brought them some pamphlets, including the letters of the "Federal Farmer," which, Lamb said, provided a good statement of the Federal Republican Committee's objections to the Constitution.[74]

Lamb proposed that the conventions of Virginia, New Hampshire, and New York correspond with each other to coordinate efforts to amend the Constitution prior to its ratification. "A number of the leading and influential Characters who will compose the Opposition in our Convention are associated with us," he noted. The committee did not favor amendments that benefited local interests. It insisted only on those that "affect the Cause of general Liberty, and are drawn from those genuine Republican Principles and Maxims, which we consider as the Glory of our Country, and which gave rise to the late glorious Revolution."[75]

When Oswald left Richmond on June 9, he carried responses from Grayson and Henry as well as Mason, who had agreed to lead what Grayson called the Virginians' "Commee. of Opposition" and Henry called their "republican society." The group had "not taken any particular form," Mason explained, "being composed only of Members of the Convention who meet to prepare such Amendments as they deem necessary to be offered to the Convention." The amendments proposed by Massachusetts were a start,

Mason said, but others were also necessary: The executive branch, for example, should include a council that would take over the Senate's responsibility for giving the president advice. Members of his committee, Mason said, were about to begin discussing the judiciary, "the exclusive Legislative Power over the ten Miles Square," and the milita. He enclosed a draft list of amendments that the committee had already approved. Like Grayson and Henry, Mason said that the division in the convention was very close. If, however, their side had a majority, he did not doubt that "an official Communication will immediately take place between the Conventions of this State and yours."[76]

According to Lamb, Oswald said the Virginians also thought it would help "fix some of the doubtful Characters" in the Virginia convention if the New York convention took the lead and appointed a committee to meet with another appointed by the Virginia convention "to agree on the necessary Amendments." Nowhere, however, was there talk of dragging out the debates or calling for an adjournment of the Virginia convention to facilitate coordinating action with New York.[77]

Without access to the information Oswald received, Virginia Federalists could only speculate on their opponents' strategy. Fear that Henry and his colleagues would try to adjourn the convention made it imperative that the delegates stop wandering and get back to the business at hand. On June 14, Federalists fought off Grayson's effort to continue the debate on the Mississippi. Then, ten days after it formally took up Article I, Sections 1 and 2, the committee of the whole moved on to Article I, Section 3. Before the day was out it had covered Sections 4 through 7, and begun discussing Section 8, on the powers of Congress.[78] When speakers wandered from the topic under discussion, some Federalist—often Nicholas or Madison—chastised them. "If we depart from regularity," Madison said, "we will never be able to reach a decision."[79] Compliance was voluntary since the debates remained within the committee of the whole and so without governing rules. Nonetheless, shorter, more focused speeches suddenly replaced the previous grand displays of oratory. Soon the debates fell into a pattern: Members of the opposition raised questions or objections, then Madison, with some solid support from his colleagues, answered them.

Monroe asked why Article I, Section 4, gave Congress residual power over the election of its members. Madison responded that it was necessary to assure that members of Congress were chosen even if the states failed to act. Congress also needed that power to protect the people's right of suffrage. He assured Henry that Congress's right to set its members' salaries under Article I, Section 6, paragraph 1, could not be abused "without rousing universal attention and indignation." The restrictions on federal officeholding by congressmen and ex-congressmen in Article I, Section 6, paragraph

2, were, Madison argued, sufficient to avoid the corruption that Grayson predicted. When Grayson questioned the power of the Senate to "propose or concur with Amendments" to bills for raising revenue (Article I, Section 7, paragraph 1), Madison defended the provision by citing experience under comparable provisions in the state constitutions, which he knew well. When state legislatures could not amend money bills to which they had objections, he said, they were forced to reject them altogether. Randolph had, of course, forecast the same fate for the Constitution if state conventions were precluded from offering amendments. If Madison recognized that similarity of argument, he gave no sign of it. He simply argued that the Senate's power to propose amendments did not violate the House of Representatives' primary responsibility for revenue bills since no amendments would go into effect without the House's consent.[80]

So it went, clause after clause, day after day. Nobody rivaled Madison's skill at a line-by-line analysis of the Constitution, but the task must have put enormous strain on him given that he had not entirely recovered from his illness. Some arguments had already been made in other states, but not all of them, and even relatively familiar discussions sometimes took novel turns in the Virginia debates. Henry and Mason came down particularly hard on Congress's powers under Article I, Section 8, "to raise and support armies," to organize, arm, and discipline state militias, and to call up the militia "to execute the Laws of the Union, suppress and repel Invasions." When a country establishes a professional "standing army," Mason said, "the people lose their liberty." It was better to rely on the militia, which was more connected with the people; but Congress could destroy the militia by making service odious or failing to supply it with sufficient arms. Mason wanted to require the consent of state legislatures before Congress could take a state's militia farther than a neighboring state. He also said militiamen should not be subject to martial law except in time of war.[81]

Madison agreed "that a standing army is one of the greatest mischiefs that can happen." The best way to avoid it was "to render it unnecessary" by giving the general government authority to call up the militia instead. The power of arming the militia, he said, was "concurrent, and not exclusive," so the states could act if Congress failed to fulfill its duties. Mason's suggestion would enhance the security of states whose borders touched several other states, leaving those on the extremes—New Hampshire and Georgia—relatively vulnerable. And the notion that Congress would unnecessarily drag the militia from one end of the continent to the other, as Mason feared, was "preposterous." What would be gained by so irrational a move?[82]

Nicholas added that making Congress's use of the militia subject to the "caprice" of state legislatures would undermine its power to provide for the general defense and, ironically, force it to turn from the militia to a regular army, which the opposition wanted to avoid. Mason's proposed restrictions on the militia would also work against the interest of the Southern states, which "from their situation" were most likely to need help from the militias from other states. Whose militia was most likely to come to their aid? "The Eastern States from their strength," so putting it in the power of individual states to prevent Congress from raising their militias "would operate against ourselves." Nicholas also emphasized—as did Madison—that the president could not raise the militia. "God forbid we should ever see a public man in this country who should have this power," he said. Only Congress could call up the militia, and then only to execute the laws of the union, suppress insurrections, or repel invasion. In all other instances, John Marshall added, the states retained control over their militias. Nor was Congress's power to raise the militia exclusive even in the cases cited. The Constitution, Madison said, simply gave the states a "supplementary security" by allowing Congress to enlist the help of other states in suppressing insurrections (including slave uprisings) or resisting invasions.[83]

Henry Lee said the opposition continually objected to possibilities with no consideration of probabilities. Worse yet, they moved into the realm of impossibilities when they described as one of the most dangerous in the Constitution a provision that gave Congress power "to exercise exclusive legislation in all Cases whatsoever" over a district "not exceeding ten Miles square" that would "become the seat of the Government of the United States" (Article I, Section 8, paragraph 17). Such unchecked legislative authority would become oppressive, Mason said. The ten-miles-square district would become "the sanctuary of the blackest crimes," a haven for felons and also, Grayson added, runaway slaves, since under Article IV such persons could only be returned to their owners if they escaped into another state, and the district would not be a state. Like Lee, Madison found it hard to imagine how the clause could threaten such horrors; there would be more danger to the system without the provision than with it. Congress had to have exclusive authority over the home of the federal government, Madison explained, to make it independent of the state in which it was located. And if the district was "crowded with rogues," Henry Lee asked, would it be "an agreeable place of residence to Members of the General Government"? Mason's objections were so far-fetched that they implied no government was possible because any law whatsoever could be abused.[84]

On June 17 (when the New York convention opened), the committee finally turned to Article I, Section 9, paragraph 1, which Mason called a "fatal section." By allowing the slave trade to continue another twenty years, he said, it "created more dangers than any other." The trade was "diabolical in itself, and disgraceful to mankind," and by increasing the number of slaves it "weakens the States." Moreover, the Constitution gave no security for property rights in those slaves already present. Congress, he charged, could "lay such a tax as will amount to manumission." Henry also suggested that some dark design lay behind the omission of any clause protecting slave property.[85]

Madison explained that "the Southern States," by which in this instance he meant Georgia and South Carolina, would not agree to the Constitution without that temporary continuation of the slave trade. Mason was ready to leave those states out of the Union unless they agreed to discontinue "this disgraceful trade," but Madison disagreed. "Great as the evil is," he said, "a dismemberment of the Union would be worse." Since the Constitution allowed Congress to end the slave trade after twenty years, which it could not do under the Articles of Confederation, it was a step forward; and the provision providing for the return of fugitive slaves (Article IV, Section 2, paragraph 3) also gave a new security to slaveholders. Nor did Congress's taxing powers threaten slavery: Direct taxes would be proportional to population, counting only three-fifths of the slaves, and raised "in the most convenient manner for the people." There had to be "some degree of confidence" in our representatives, Madison said, or "we must reject a state of civil society altogether." He left it for George Nicholas to point out the inconsistency in attacks on the Constitution for both continuing the slave trade and threatening the manumission of slaves. "At the same moment it is opposed for being promotive and destructive of slavery!"[86]

Federalist tolerance for frivolous arguments seemed to be running thin. When Mason charged that the provision requiring Congress to publish a "regular Statement and Account of the Receipts and Expenditures of all public Money . . . from time to time" (Article I, Section 9, paragraph 7) was so ambiguous that Congress could conceal misappropriations of money and shelter the guilty for long periods of time, Henry Lee refused to take his objection seriously. The common understanding of "from time to time" was "short convenient periods," and since the state's general assembly was scheduled to meet the next week he wished the gentlemen in the opposition would "confine themselves to the investigation of the principal parts of the Constitution."[87]

Henry's persistent demands that the Constitution needed a bill of rights could not be dismissed so easily. Article I, Section 9, he observed, included "express restrictions" on Congress: It could not, for example, suspend habeas corpus "except when in Cases of Rebellion or Invasion the public Safety may require it," or pass bills of attainder and ex post facto laws (paragraphs 2 and 3). Henry found those restrictions "so feeble and few" that he thought "it would have been infinitely better to have said nothing about it." The clauses implied that Congress "can do every thing they are not forbidden to do," undermining the argument of the Constitution's friends (and, above all, James Wilson) that "everything is retained which is not given up." The people's "dearest privileges will depend on the consent of Congress: For these are not within the restrictions of the ninth section."[88]

The Constitution's defenders pulled out the standard answers to pleas for a bill of rights and added a few others. Nicholas used a simply analogy to make James Wilson's old argument that all powers not granted to Congress were reserved without Wilson's bewildering language. If he had a thousand acres of land and sold half of it, Nicholas asked, did he need to declare that he kept the rest? "Do I grant the whole thousand acres when I grant five hundred, unless I declare that the five hundred I do not give, belongs to me still?" The situation with the Constitution was the same, he insisted: "After granting some powers, the rest must rest with the people."[89]

Randolph added that the restrictions in Article I, Section 9, did not prove, as Henry suggested, that Congress had powers "by implication" because they were exceptions "not from general powers, but from the particular powers therein vested." For example, the restriction on ending the slave trade was an exception to Congress's power to regulate commerce, and that on suspending habeas corpus was an exception to its power "to regulate courts."[90] Moreover, experience showed that bills or declarations of rights were ineffective. The five or six states that had no separate bill of rights were as free as Virginia, Nicholas said, and "their liberties as secure as ours." Virginia's declaration of rights "gave no security"; it was only "a paper check" on power and had "been violated in many instances."[91]

None of these arguments persuaded Henry, who knew that here, at least, he had a winning argument. A bill of rights was "a favorite thing" among Virginians as well as the people of the other states. "It may be their prejudice, but the Government ought to suit their geniuses" or "its operation will be unhappy." Even if the effectiveness of bills of rights was open to doubt, they would "exclude the possibility of dispute, and with great submission," he said, it was best to have no disputes. "A bill of rights may be summed up in a few words," he concluded. "What do they tell us?—That our rights are reserved.—Why not say so? Is it because it will consume too much paper?" He did not give an inch. "My mind will not be quieted," he insisted, "till I see something substantial come forth in the shape of a Bill of Rights."[92]

The delegates looked briefly at restrictions on the states in Article I, Section 10. Henry and Mason expressed fear that Virginia would be forced to pay its share of the continental debt at face value, "shilling for shilling," enriching Northern speculators. Madison and Nicholas answered that the continental debt would be the obligation of Congress, not the states, and in that regard its responsibilities would be precisely the same under the Constitution as under the Confederation. Randolph also described the provision preventing states from impairing the obligation of contracts and precluding the states from issuing paper money as "a great favourite" of his "because it is essential to justice."[93]

Then the delegates turned to Article II, on the executive, to which Henry, Mason, Monroe, and Grayson raised one objection after another. The president's term was too long and, given the lack of term limits, he could be re-elected indefinitely. An executive council should advise the president in place of the Senate, whose advisory function violated the separation of powers between the executive and legislative branches and added to the already excessive powers of the Senate. The office of vice president was unnecessary; the Senate should elect its own presiding officer, and the head of the executive council could succeed the president in case of disaster. Grayson also attacked the system by which the president and vice president would be chosen, particularly the provision that inconclusive presidential elections would be decided by the House of Representatives, where each state would have one vote. He threw out a flurry of numbers to show that five small Northern states plus Georgia and North Carolina could choose a president although they represented a distinct minority of congressmen. The president had too much power, which would make it worth the while of foreign countries to interfere in his election—as they had done when Poland chose a new king in the early 1760s. The Senate, moreover, was an improper agency for trying impeachments: Since it was also charged with advising the president, it would be his partner in crime.[94]

The Constitution's supporters defended the presidential electoral system as the best alternative to direct popular election, which Madison said might well be "impractical" given "the extent and population of the States." The president would be the choice of the people, Madison and Nicholas insisted, since the people would choose the electors (although in fact the Constitution let the state legislatures decide how electors would be chosen). As for the suggestion that seven states could carry a presidential election over the opposition of the larger states, Madison noted that in his "extravagant calculation" Grayson had associated North Carolina and Georgia with the five smallest Northern states, which were unlikely to vote alike given their different interests and geographical separation. He justified having the House of Representatives vote by states in deciding presidential elections as a compromise that guarded the rights of small states. Federalists, however, made no concerted effort to answer all the objections raised against the Constitution, in part because the delegates soon went back to discussing the way treaties were to be negotiated and approved (Article II, Section 2, paragraph 2) and the implications for the Mississippi, which Nicholas said was the opposition's "favorite business," the "scuffle for Kentucky votes."[95]

DISCUSSING THE JUDICIARY

On Thursday, June 19, the delegates turned to Article III, on the judiciary, which remained the subject of debate for the rest of the week and most of the following Monday. No previous convention had discussed the judiciary at such length or brought such distinguished legal talent to the task. The debates on the judiciary took a somewhat different form from those that preceded it in the convention. Pendleton, not a member of the opposition, opened the discussion with a general survey of the provisions on the judiciary. Madison made significant contributions to the discussion, but other Federalist delegates who, unlike Madison, were formally trained in law, such as John Marshall, also had a lot to say.

Pendleton began by asserting that the judiciary needed to be an integral part of the government, and that its responsibilities required both a Supreme Court and inferior courts. He predicted that Congress would give the state courts inferior federal jurisdiction rather than create a set of entirely new courts. That would save money and "give general satisfaction," in part, no doubt, by affirming the importance, quality, and continuing existence of state courts. The Constitution secured judges' independence by giving them tenure in office and fixing their salaries, although Pendleton wished that increases in pay had been precluded as well as reductions. Under Article III, Section 2, he noted, the Constitution defined eleven areas of jurisdiction for federal courts, all of which were in his opinion "cases of general and not local concern." The Supreme Court's original jurisdiction, however, was confined to cases involving ambassadors, ministers, and consuls, and those in which a state was a party.[96]

It also had appellate jurisdiction, which was "undoubtedly proper" and might have raised no objections if that jurisdiction did not unfortunately extend "both to law and fact," words Pendleton wished "had been buried in oblivion." Except for chancery and admiralty cases, he explained, issues of fact were normally decided by juries in inferior courts. He was confident that Congress would adopt regulations making "appeals as to law and fact proper and perfectly inoffensive," and would also avoid having too many cases go into federal courts, for example by specifying that the amount at issue had to be above a certain sum. Congress could also fill out those details on jury trials in criminal cases that the Constitution left unstated. From there on Pendleton spoke "too low" for Robertson to hear him.[97]

Since he was not a lawyer, Mason answered with, he said, reluctance. He declared that the judicial branch was "so constructed as to destroy the dearest rights of the community." Its jurisdiction was so broad that it left no business for state courts, which would be wiped out. Federal courts would try all cases under the laws of Congress, whose power was essentially unlimited. He also questioned federal court jurisdiction in cases between a state and private citizens, whether drawn from its own people or those of another state. "Is the sovereignty of the State to be arraigned like a culprit, or private offender?" he asked. "Will the States undergo this mortification?" And what if they lost? A state's body could not be put in jail, and "a power which cannot be executed, ought not to be granted." Conflicts between citizens of different states should be left to state courts, which were more convenient and whose members had the community's confidence. Since federal appellate courts had jurisdiction as to both fact and law, the problem was compounded. Even if a poor man who had suffered some serious injury received justice in an inferior court, what chance did he have on appeal? He might have to travel hundreds of miles at his own expense, and bring his witnesses "where he is not known, where new evidence may be brought against him, of which he never heard before, and which he cannot contradict."[98]

Pendleton had hoped that Congress would remedy the various problems with the judiciary that he identified, but Mason said "mere hope" was insufficient. He wanted amendments that would reduce the jurisdiction of federal courts, confine their appellate jurisdiction "to matters of law only, in common law controversies," and secure the "sacred right" of trial by jury in civil cases. Moving to specifics, Mason claimed that members of the old Indiana Company, which once held claim to three or four counties in western parts of Virginia, could bring cases in federal courts against the current possessors of farms on those lands, producing "a scene of distress and confusion never heard of before." Federal courts could also make people in Virginia's Northern Neck pay quitrents to the heirs of Lord Fairfax, who had held title to that area. To avoid those contingencies, Mason proposed another amendment that would deny federal courts jurisdiction where the cause of action predated ratification of the Constitution in all but a few types of cases.[99]

Madison found Mason's fears groundless, but he acknowledged that parts of Article III could have been "better expressed." Designing the judiciary was, like designing the executive, particularly challenging, and precision in technical terms proved more difficult to achieve than might be imagined. With regard to jurisdictional issues, Madison said, objections to putting cases involving states and private citizens into federal courts were "perhaps without reason." The provision would apply only where the state brought a case against a citizen or, if citizens of other states were the complainants, where "a State should condescend to be a party." States could not therefore be forced into federal courts. Madison agreed that cases between citizens of different states might have been left to state courts. He did not, however, think the problem of great significance and could imagine situations where plaintiffs would face prejudice in the courts of another state and were more likely to receive justice in federal courts. Certainly the future of state courts was not imperiled by that or by any other provision: "In the ordinary state of things," he thought "the far greater number of cases—ninety-nine out of an hundred, will remain with the State Judiciaries."[100]

The major objection to the proposed organization of federal courts concerned their "appellate cognizance, as well of fact as law." Madison noted that Article III, Section 2, gave the Supreme Court "appellate Jurisdiction, both as to Law and Fact, with such Exceptions, and under such Regulations as Congress shall make," so Congress clearly had power to secure the privilege of juries on issues of fact. He also thought it improbable that the Supreme Court would remain in one place, forcing litigants to travel long distances. Congress was more likely to "fix it in different parts of the Continent, to render it more convenient." Congress would also provide for trial by jury where appropriate in civil cases. Even the provision preventing Congress from reducing but not raising judges' salaries was defensible. If the federal courts' business increased substantially, the judges' salary should be adjusted so their pay was not reduced over the course of their long terms in office (far longer, he noted, than the president's) "to a most trivial consideration." The opposition presumed that Congress would "do every mischief they possibly can, and . . . omit to do every good which they are authorized to do." Madison found it more reasonable to assume that congressmen "will as readily do their duty, as deviate from it." Since they were chosen by the people, to distrust them was nothing less than to distrust the people themselves. Madison preferred to proceed "on this great republican principle, that the people will have virtue and intelligence to select men of virtue and wisdom."[101]

Again, Henry ceded nothing. Here once more, he said, the Constitution demanded "the surrender of our great rights." The Virginia judiciary was "one of the best barriers against strides of power." If, as Pendleton predicted, the state courts would serve as inferior courts for federal cases, that advantage would be taken away; state judges would "combine against us with the General Government," since the Constitution declared federal law superior to that of the states. Henry was unconvinced by the argument that states would appear in federal courts only as plaintiffs; the Constitution gave federal courts jurisdiction in cases between a state and citizens of another state, he noted, "without discriminating between plaintiff or defendant."[102]

Henry also denied that Congress could modify the constitutional provision giving federal appellate courts jurisdiction over questions of both fact and law. That, he said, would be to rewrite the Constitution, and "laws in opposition to the Constitution, would be void." Was it Congress's duty to "new model" the Constitution? "Is that their duty, or ours? . . . It is our duty to rest our rights on a certain foundation, and not to trust to future contingencies." He read the passage on the importance of jury trials from Blackstone's *Commentaries* that William Findley had cited in the Pennsylvania convention: If a people lost their right to trial by jury, it said, all others would follow. The Constitution not only failed to provide for jury trials in civil cases, Henry said, but it provided for them so poorly in criminal cases—not assuring a defendant's right to challenge jurors, for example—that it would have been better to leave that provision out altogether. America had once refused to depend on Parliament for its rights; now it was asked to depend on Congress. "Old as I am," Henry said, "it is probable I may yet have the appellation of rebel.—I trust that I shall see Congressional oppressions crushed in embryo. As this Government stands, I despise and abhor it."[103]

That was enough to bring Pendleton and then John Marshall to their feet. After hearing Henry, Pendleton said, any member of the audience who had not read the Constitution would be surprised to learn that it does not exclude juries in civil cases and explicitly provides for them in criminal ones. And when it says trial will be by jury, "every incident will go along with it"—that juries will be drawn from the neighborhood, for example, and jurors can be challenged. Marshall added that neither the Magna Carta, the English Bill of Rights, nor the Virginia constitution provided for jury trial with the detail Henry demanded. "If we are secure in Virginia" although the right of challenging jurors went unmentioned in the constitution, he asked, "why should not this security be found in the Federal Court?"[104]

Marshall described the Constitution's provisions for a federal judiciary as a "great improvement" over the current system, since it established tribunals to decide controversies that were previously provided for improperly or not at all. The federal judiciary decided cases of a "general and national" character, Pendleton said, leaving local issues to state courts, and they "act in cooperation to secure our liberty." Marshall also insisted that the state courts were in no danger: Nothing took from them the jurisdiction they already had, and the state courts had more business than they could easily handle. He affirmed Madison's argument that states would not be "called at the bar of the Federal Court . . . It is not rational to suppose," he said, "that the sovereign power shall be dragged before a Court. The intent is, to enable States to recover claims of individuals resident in other States." He thought the words of the Constitution—interpreted, it seems, with the light of reason—warranted that interpretation.[105]

Marshall also denied Mason's claim that the jurisdiction of federal courts would expand because they had jurisdiction over cases under the laws of Congress and Congress's power was essentially unlimited. Once again Marshall—like so many other Federalists—stressed that Congress's powers were enumerated and so limited. If Congress tried to make a law outside those powers, Marshall said, judges would consider it an infringement of the Constitution that they were pledged to defend and "declare it void." But among the powers explicitly given Congress (in Article III, Section 2, paragraph 2) was that "to make exceptions"—that is, Marshall explained, alterations or diminutions—"to the appellate jurisdiction, as to law and fact, of the Supreme Court." Those exceptions "certainly go as far as the Legislature may think proper, for the interest and liberty of the people." Was there any reason to trust federal judges less than state judges? Or to think, as Pendleton put it, that "the Representatives of any twelve States" would "sacrifice their own interest, and that of their citizens, to answer no purpose?"[106]

Before the day was out, Governor Randolph assured delegates from the Northern Neck that federal courts would never force them to pay quitrents: The Virginia legislature had laid that issue to rest forever. Moreover, the Indiana Company's claim to land within Virginia was dormant and unlikely to be revived—and if it were, it would take the form of a suit for compensation against the State of Virginia, not the settlers who had "an indefeasible title" to their land. Like other Federalists, he saw flaws in Article III, particularly in the appellate jurisdiction as to fact and the possibility that litigants in different states could bring cases into federal court for trivial sums. It was not, however, worth rejecting the Constitution "for faults which can be corrected."[107]

———

When the committee of the whole reconvened on Monday, June 23, Benjamin Harrison, a member of the opposition from Charles City County, presided in place of George Wythe. He had intervened in the debates once—to defuse an angry exchange between Henry and Nicholas. The end of the convention was in sight, and the delegates' patience was in ever shorter supply. After spending some time repeating old arguments on the judiciary, they moved on to Article IV. The records of debate for the day include a brief, spirited exchange over the prospect for the admission of new Southern states into the union (Article IV, Section 3) and some dour predictions by Mason of popular resistance to the Constitution if it were ratified. Then the published *Debates* ends with an unusual, sweeping summary statement: "The remainder of the Constitution was then read," it says, "and the several objectionable parts noticed by the opposition," particularly with regard to the process for amendments. Finally, after discussing that issue fully, the committee of the whole deferred further discussion and the convention adjourned until the morning.[108]

David Robertson, the note-taker, was unable to attend that day. That was the reason for what the account of the debates on June 23 describes as "the incomplete and inaccurate state in which the speeches of this day appear." Robertson's printer, William Prentis, stepped in and tried to provide the public with as full an account as possible "without the aid of stenography," but the challenge proved beyond his ability.[109] Nothing testifies more powerfully to Robertson's achievement than the spare summary of debates on the one day he was absent—as it happened, the day when delegates to the Virginia ratifying convention concluded their examination of the Constitution.

That brought the delegates face to face with the questions that lay behind all their deliberations: Would Virginia ratify the Constitution? And, if so, with what stipulations?

TEN

The Virginia Convention II

Under the Eyes of Heaven

The special session of the state legislature on June 23 did not, as some
delegates feared, force the convention to adjourn. To accommodate the
sixty-two members who belonged to both bodies, the general assembly met
for relatively short sessions in the morning, the convention an hour or two
later.[1] The inconvenience was unlikely to last more than a few days because
the convention was almost over. For James Madison, however, the arrival of
legislators from all over the state at so critical a time was unfortunate. The
legislators, he said, included "a considerable majority of antifederal members." Since those who were not convention delegates came "immediately
from the people at large," they could "give any colour they please to the
popular sentiments at this moment" to influence members of the convention,
who had been separated from their constituents for several weeks.[2]

Anything that could possibly strengthen the opposition awoke concern
because the division among delegates remained very close. On June 20,
Madison wrote his father that no vote had yet been taken that could measure
"the strength of parties," and the calculations made by the different sides
were at odds, with each predicting a small majority. He was inclined to think
"the friends of the Constitution" were more confident and could well have
a majority of three or four, and maybe more. But, as Madison explained
to both Alexander Hamilton and Rufus King two days later, in so large a
convention—with some 170 members—it was possible to make mistakes in
assessing some delegates' convictions, and the probable majority was so small
that "ordinary casualties" could tip the outcome the other way.[3]

The opposition, Madison predicted, would propose a bill of rights "with
sundry other amendments" as a condition of ratification. If that failed, they
would probably move for an adjournment. Some feared "a secession," with
opposition delegates stalking out of the convention, but Madison thought

there were "too many moderate and respectable characters" among the dissenters for that to happen. The "friends of the Constitution" nonetheless found it prudent to practice an exemplary fairness and even sometimes "to give way to unreasonable pretensions" to avoid giving any pretext for "so rash a step." They planned to "preface the ratification with some plain and general truths that can not affect the validity of the Act" and to recommend—like Massachusetts and South Carolina—amendments that would be enacted later "in the constitutional mode." That expedient, which Madison had regretted when Massachusetts first adopted it, was necessary in Virginia, he explained to King, to conciliate delegates who were inclined to vote for ratification but had "scruples drawn from their own reflexions, or from the temper of their Constituents."[4] That was precisely the situation the Constitution's supporters had faced in Massachusetts.

Even with "recommendatory" amendments, victory was no sure thing. The convention's decision would probably be made within a week, Madison wrote King on June 22, but how the final vote would go "I dare not positively decide." The next day he was a bit more optimistic. The discussion on the judiciary had gone better than expected, and on June 23—the day Robertson was absent—the opposition "seemed to betray despair." Madison saw no other way to interpret George Mason's predictions of "civil convulsions" if the Constitution were ratified or Patrick Henry's statement that, despite "his aversion to the Constitution," he would "remain in peaceable submission to the result." The Constitution's supporters "calculate on a majority," Madison told Washington, "but a bare one," and "adverse circumstances" could still intervene.[5]

If the Constitution went down in Virginia, New York and North Carolina, to say nothing of Rhode Island, would almost certainly follow suit. Then, if New Hampshire became the ninth state to ratify—as almost all the "friends of the Constitution" expected—the Constitution would go into effect over a "United States" that had lost a third of its states and a considerable part of its territory. Whether so impoverished a nation would be "respectable" in the eyes of the world, as Washington hoped, or even continue to exist as a nation, was open to question. From a Federalist perspective, the future of the United States seemed to turn on a handful of votes that might well be cast by delegates from Kentucky and a few counties in the far western reaches of Virginia.

DEFINING THE ALTERNATIVES
The event played out much as Madison predicted. On Tuesday, June 24, the convention again resolved itself into a committee of the whole, this time with Thomas Mathews of Norfolk presiding. George Wythe quickly took the floor. After a brief speech, he moved that the committee recommend ratification of the Constitution. His complex motion was almost certainly

the work of several "friends of the Constitution" since not only Madison had predicted its form but also Randolph in a speech he gave several days earlier, near the end of the debates on the judiciary.[6]

Wythe's motion included a preamble that said the powers granted to the federal government under the Constitution were a gift of the people, and the people could reclaim those powers if they were misused to cause oppression. Every power not specifically granted remained with the people and could not be cancelled, abridged, restrained, or modified by Congress, the president, or any other officer of the United States except where the Constitution gave them power to do that. Among other essential rights, liberty of conscience and of the press as well as the right of trial by jury could not be cancelled, abridged, or restrained by anyone holding authority under the Constitution of the United States. Wythe's preamble also said that any imperfections in the Constitution should be addressed through the amending process it prescribed rather than endanger the union by seeking previous amendments.[7]

Wythe then moved his main resolutions: that, in the opinion of the committee of the whole, the Constitution should be ratified, and that the convention should recommend amendments to the first federal Congress. He perhaps asked that another committee draw up those amendments. According to Patrick Henry, the text of Wythe's motion—which Robertson did not include in his *Debates*—also said that Virginia's ratification would "cease to be obligatory" if the amendments the convention proposed were not enacted. If so, his motion had some similarity to what Richard Henry Lee had recommended to Mason in early May.[8]

To nobody's surprise, Henry objected. Early in the convention, he had denounced "the absurdity" of ratifying the Constitution "and relying on the chance of getting it amended afterwards." He would consider anyone a "lunatic" who advised him to adopt a government "avowedly defective, in hopes of having it amended afterwards. Were I about to give away the meanest particle of my own property," Henry said, "I would act with more prudence and discretion." Now, after hearing Wythe's motion, he again asked whether it made sense to "enter into a compact of Government first, and afterwards settle the terms of the Government." If you adopt the Constitution "unaltered," he told the delegates, you "endanger the tranquility of your country—you stab its repose."[9]

Wythe's motion specifically reserved only three basic rights. Henry asked about the others. Unless a statement that the people retained all rights not specifically granted was part of the Constitution at the time it was ratified, "inevitable destruction" would follow. The members of Congress would construe the Constitution "as they please." Among the ten thousand implied powers they could assume, "they may, if we be engaged in war, liberate every one of your slaves" and enlist them into the army under Congress's power to provide "for the general defence and welfare." "As much as I deplore slavery," Henry said, "I see that prudence forbids its abolition. I deny that the General Government ought to set them free, because a decided majority of the States have not the ties of sympathy and fellow-feeling for those whose interest would be affected by their emancipation." As if his meaning weren't already clear, he explained that "the majority of Congress is to the North, and the slaves are to the South," which would suffer the "dreadful and ruinous consequences" of emancipation.[10]

The "great body of the yeomanry" was, Henry claimed, "in decided opposition" to the Constitution. He knew from personal experience that nine-tenths of the people in nineteen contiguous counties (probably those south of the James River) were "conscientiously" against ratification. The promise of subsequent amendments would not reconcile such men, who held tightly to their rights. There was a majority of only nineteen in the Massachusetts convention, and he heard that only ten thousand of seventy thousand qualified voters were represented in the Pennsylvania convention. Could there be a tranquil and lasting union under such circumstances? New York and North Carolina would never ratify unless the Constitution was amended first, so if Wythe and his fellow "friends of the Constitution" dreaded disunion, "the very thing they advocate will inevitably produce it."[11]

Henry proposed an alternative motion to Wythe's: that the convention "refer a declaration of rights, with certain amendments to the most exceptionable parts of the Constitution, to the other States in the Confederacy [i.e., the Confederation], for their consideration, previous to its ratification." He assured the delegates that his amendments would leave "the arm of power . . . sufficiently strong for national purposes" while securing the rights of the people. "The Government unaltered may be terrible to America; but can never be loved, till it be amended." Amendments that confirmed "the privileges of the people" would give the new government a firmer hold on the affections of the people, and so make it stronger than without those amendments.[12]

By defining himself as an advocate of union and strong national government, Henry cleverly moved onto critical territory his opponents had claimed. Then he made another brilliant play by appealing to a pride in Virginia that bound all delegates regardless of their stand on the Constitution. What, he asked, prevented Virginia from offering these amendments to the other states? Virginia had proposed the convention that met at Annapolis; it had proposed that which met in Philadelphia. "Have we not a right to say, *hear our propositions?*" The amendments were designed not to dictate to the other states or to give Virginia a preeminence, but to assure that the people received what they most wanted—"to sit down in peace and security under their own fig trees." Every state would agree, since they all wanted "to banish discord from the American soil."[13]

As with Wythe's motion, Robertson failed to include Henry's amendments in his *Debates*. In both cases he referred readers to later resolutions and amendments that were supposedly—as he said with regard to Henry's proposal—"nearly the same." In the course of debating the Wythe and Henry motions, however, members of the convention provided considerable information on their contents. Madison said Henry's proposal consisted of "no less than forty amendments—a bill of rights which contains twenty amendments, and twenty other alterations, some of which," he added, "are improper and inadmissible." Randolph set out to show the bill of rights was unnecessary, then ripped into one of the "other alterations" after another, revealing as he went along what Henry had proposed.[14]

Henry's motion seems to have been a fuller and more finished version of the draft amendments that Mason had sent to New York with Eleazer Oswald. If so, the bill of rights was closely patterned on Virginia's 1776 declaration of rights, which Mason had drafted. The set of "other alterations" began with a clause that reserved to the states all powers not expressly granted to Congress, which echoed Article II of the Articles of Confederation. The next specified that there "shall be" one representative for every thirty thousand people until the House of Representatives had two hundred members. A third was the much-discussed amendment on taxes that said Congress could raise no direct taxes or excises unless the revenue from import duties was insufficient for public needs, and then only after requisitions on the states had been tried and failed. Henry's long list of amendments seems to have given no new protection to the property rights of slaveholders. It did, however, include provisions that required a two-thirds vote of the members present in both houses of Congress to approve laws regulating commerce or to raise an army, and a *three-quarters* vote of both houses to approve "treaties ceding or restraining territorial rights." In the end, concern for Southern trade and fear of federal treaty-making power—and, ultimately, of losing access to the Mississippi—weighed more heavily on the opposition than fear of a possible abolition-minded federal Congress.[15]

Henry said that if the convention chose to ratify the Constitution without previous amendments, he would have nothing to do with it; he would "go home" and "act as I think my duty requires." That set off Randolph's fears. Was Henry threatening to secede from the convention if he didn't get his way? Henry said he had no such thing in mind. That didn't stop Randolph from conjuring any opposition delegates who were thinking about seceding from the convention to think carefully first, since "refusing to submit to the decision of the majority, is destructive of every Republican principle. It will kindle a civil war, and reduce everything to anarchy, uncertainty, and confusion." He regretted that Henry had raised the topic of emancipation: It seemed "dishonorable to Virginia" to suggest that, at the moment Virginians were trying to secure their own rights, they objected to even "a spark of hope, that those unfortunate men now held in bondage, may, by the operation of the General Government, be made *free*." However, Randolph also noted that nothing in the Constitution gave Congress power to free slaves. The clause Henry cited—referring to Congress's responsibility to "provide for the common defence and general welfare"—applied only to its power to raise taxes and other revenue measures; it would "violate every rule of construction and common sense" to separate it from the power of raising money and apply it to anything else.[16]

The bill of rights Henry proposed was unnecessary, Randolph argued, while other amendments on his list were useless or downright dangerous. Randolph personally favored requiring more than a simple majority vote in Congress for commercial regulations, but the federal Convention had given that up as a sine qua non of union. Nothing in the Constitution gave Congress the right to give away territory, but the proposed restriction on its power to do that through treaties would imply that, except for that restriction on treaties, Congress had a right to "dismember the union" in the "fullest latitude." Randolph favored some amendments with regard to the jurisdiction of federal courts, but not those Henry proposed. On the whole, Randolph thought Henry's proposed amendments were perhaps "fraught with . . . more defects than the Constitution itself." And whatever Henry said, previous amendments amounted to a rejection of the Constitution. They would "throw Virginia out of the Union" and, with the union dissolved, "the dogs of war will break out and anarchy and discord will complete the ruin of this country."[17]

Madison continued the attack. He saw in Henry's amendments evidence of "a great contrariety of opinions among the Gentlemen in the opposition" that had long been evident in their writings. The published debates from earlier conventions also showed that there was "no sort of uniformity in the grounds of the opposition." Like Randolph, Madison objected to several specific amendments that Henry proposed. Some violated agreements negotiated in the Convention that, by enlisting Northern support for the defense of the South, were in Virginia's interest; others enabled congressional minorities to block measures for the common good. Madison insisted again that the proposed bill of rights was unnecessary because "the General Government had no power but what was given it"—and dangerous, because "an enumeration which is not complete, is not safe." No complete enumeration of rights could be made "within any compass of time" that would do the job as well as Wythe's proposal, which simply said the people retained all rights and powers they had not specifically given away and could resume the powers they had granted if those powers were used for their injury and oppression.[18]

But would Wythe's preamble have the power and authority Madison attributed to it? George Nicholas told the committee of the whole that the preamble, if adopted by the convention, would secure everything Henry wanted because it would be "part of the contract. The Constitution cannot be binding on Virginia, but with these conditions." Privately, however, Madison told Rufus King that the preface would declare "a few obvious truths which can not affect the validity of the act." In short, the preface was politically but not legally significant; only the resolution ratifying the Constitution would be binding. However, Madison also said that the principles in the Wythe resolution were "obviously and self-evidently the case, without the declaration. Can the General Government exercise any power not delegated?" he asked. "If an enumeration be made of our rights, will it not be implied, that every thing omitted, is given to the General Government?" Wythe's opening principles would therefore constrain the new government whether or not the convention adopted his preamble, but an imperfect enumeration of rights—like Henry's proposal—could cause far more problems than it solved.[19]

There was no denying the Constitution was imperfect: Madison acknowledged that its firmest supporters said it had defects. They did not, however, think those flaws were so dangerous that they had to be rectified before the Constitution went into effect, and before experience showed that amendments were in fact necessary. Madison was willing to support those of Henry's amendments that were "not objectionable, or unsafe" because they might "gratify some Gentlemen's wishes." But he would never agree to previous amendments because they were "pregnant with dreadful dangers." If nine states voted to ratify, having "freely and fully considered the subject," would they, "on the demand of a single State, agree that they acted wrong, and could not see its defects . . . ?" They would tell Virginia that "it is more reasonable that you should yield to us, than we to you. You cannot exist without us. You must be a member of the Union." It was "a most awful thing that depends on our decision," he said, "no less than whether the thirteen States shall Unite freely, peaceably, and unanimously, for the security of their common happiness and liberty, or whether every thing is to be put in confusion and disorder!"[20]

The opposition, however, thought a demand for amendments previous to ratifying the Constitution could succeed. William Grayson argued that Virginia's wealth and geographical location gave it leverage over the other states, particularly if it joined forces with North Carolina and perhaps also New York. If those states did not ratify, they would leave the United States "topographically separated, though politically connected." The "carrying states"—those with merchant communities and major ports—wanted not only the protection of a stronger federal government under the Constitution but also access to the produce of North Carolina and Virginia. As a result, "tobacco will always make our peace with them." In short, with the support of North Carolina, Virginia could "command such amendments" as it thought necessary "for the happiness of the people." By contrast, "the idea of subsequent amendments is preposterous," Grayson said, because the small states, which gained so much by the Constitution, would consent to no changes. Henry also insisted that the states that had already adopted the Constitution would not make a "respectable appearance" without Virginia. Why would they turn down her proposal? "We have nothing local to ask. We ask rights which concern the general happiness. Must not justice bring them into the concession of these?" Under his proposal, Virginia would not reject a connection with the other states. It would declare its willingness to adopt the Constitution "if they will but consent to the security of rights essential to the general happiness."[21]

Contenders had come to agree on the need for a stronger central government (though not so much as to make it "great and powerful"[22]) and the value of the union. Nobody questioned the country's republican form of government, the importance of rights, or the significance of the American Revolution, to which so many delegates, young and old, had contributed in one way or another. Almost everyone said that the Constitution was flawed. They disagreed over what its defects were and whether they should be repaired before or after the Constitution was ratified. But immense consequences seemed to follow from that difference.

The "Honorable Gentleman"—James Madison—"tells you of important blessings which he imagines will result to us and mankind . . . from the adoption of this system," Henry told the delegates in beginning what might well have been the high point of his rhetorical performance at the convention. He saw instead "the awful immensity of the dangers with which it is pregnant. I see it. I feel it." He could even see "*beings* of a higher order, anxious concerning our decision." When he looked "beyond the horrison that binds human eyes . . . at the final consummation of all human things," and saw "those intelligent beings which inhabit the aetherial mansions, reviewing the political decisions and revolutions which in the progress of time will happen in America" and the "consequent happiness or misery of mankind," he understood how much would depend "on what we now decide." More than the future of America was at stake. "All nations" were concerned in Virginia's decision. "We have it in our power," he said, "to secure the happiness of one half of the human race." The adoption of the Constitution "may involve the misery of the other hemispheres."[23]

At that point a violent storm shook the hall and forced Henry to stop. It was as if the "*beings* of a higher order" in their "aetherial mansions" screamed out to support Henry's thunder. But the convention did not adjourn in disarray, as some later accounts of Henry's "thunderstorm speech" suggest. The debates continued for a time before the delegates went off to their suppers and their beds,[24] conscious that on the next day they would decide among the alternatives before them and determine, if Henry was right, the future of not just America but "all nations."

UNDER THE EYES OF HEAVEN

The Virginia convention resolved itself into a committee of the whole one last time on Wednesday, June 25, again with Thomas Mathews presiding. George Nicholas and the Federalists saw no purpose in further debate. They wanted the Constitution ratified and were willing to recommend "such amendments as may be thought necessary" to the first federal Congress for enactment under the process described in the Constitution itself. "The amendments contained in this paper," he said, "are those we wish," but the Constitution's advocates would consider any others that would better secure liberty and not destroy the spirit of the Constitution. The specific amendments he proposed are again missing from Robertson's debates, and this time subsequent speeches reveal more of what Nicholas's list omitted than what it included.[25]

Finally, Nicholas moved that the clerk read Wythe's motion so the delegates could vote on it. John Tyler, an opposition delegate from Charles City County, asked that Henry's amendments and bill of rights also be read for the same purpose. The delegates then debated the alternatives before them. That debate was different from earlier ones, which were dominated by a small number of delegates. The most prominent speakers to that point in the convention could be counted on the fingers of two hands: Madison, Randolph, Nicholas, Edmund Pendleton, and sometimes Francis Corbin and John Marshall defended the Constitution; Henry, Mason, William Grayson, and occasionally James Monroe took the other side. Now, in what everyone knew were the meeting's final days, a handful of backbenchers took the floor. Sometimes, as in the Massachusetts convention, they spoke because their constituents expected something more of them than to listen and vote, sometimes simply from a conviction that they had something worth adding to the discussions, or, in one case, to lodge a demand. A few speakers in a large convention could hardly indicate how the vote would go, but they suggested how men who had sat through the debates day after day made sense of what they had heard. Clearly they did not all draw the same conclusions.

The backbenchers had begun to break their silence the day before, when William Ronald from Powhatan County insisted that the supporters of the Constitution state what amendments they proposed to recommend, much as Henry had done, before any vote was taken. He said that unless he saw amendments introduced that would "secure the happiness of the people and prevent their privileges from being endangered," he would have to vote "against this Constitution," although that was "much against" his inclination. Ronald's demand probably explains why Nicholas showed the committee of the whole a list of amendments that he and his colleagues could support. The Federalists could not afford to lose even a single vote because of their inaction.[26]

John Dawson, a thirty-six-year-old lawyer and planter who represented Spotsylvania County, made his maiden speech on the same day Ronald spoke. He had remained silent from a sense of the inferiority of his talents, he said, and a desire "to acquire every information which might assist my judgment . . . on a question of such magnitude." He saw the problems with the Confederation, respected the federal Convention, and favored "a firm, federal, energetic Government," which initially made him favor ratification. But he had become convinced that adoption of the Constitution "as it now stands" would threaten the liberties of America in general and the property of Virginia in particular. His reservations, he said, had been confirmed by the debates.[27]

Dawson objected to Congress's military powers and its capacity to levy direct taxes, to the links between the executive and the Senate that violated separation of powers, and above all to the capacity of the president and two-thirds of the Senate to make treaties "by which any territory may be ceded or the navigation of any river surrendered." To his mind, the objections to the federal judiciary had gone "unanswered." There was no bill of rights. The Constitution, he charged, created a "consolidated Government" that could not govern an area as large as the United States without sacrificing its freedom. Ten years earlier, "when the *American spirit* shone forth in the meridian of glory," the country would have rejected it as "incompatible with republican liberty." He planned to vote for "previous amendments."[28]

Now, after the opposing motions had been read, Benjamin Harrison, who had chaired the committee of the whole for a day but made only two brief earlier contributions to the debates, spoke on behalf of Henry's proposal. By his calculations, seven states wanted amendments: Massachusetts and South Carolina as well as Maryland, where several members of the state convention supported amendments, plus Virginia, North Carolina, New York, and New Hampshire. The argument for prior amendments was therefore far from hopeless. "I call Heaven to witness that I am a friend to the Union," he said, but the proposal to adopt without prior amendments was "unwarrantably precipitate, and dangerously impolitic."[29]

James Monroe supported Harrison. Disunion was less to be feared as a result of proposing prior amendments to the Constitution, he said, than from "the adoption of a system reprobated by some, and allowed by all to be defective."[30] Harrison's fellow Charles City County delegate, John Tyler, also predicted that prior amendments would "reconcile all the States" to the

Constitution. Harrison had described the amendments presented by Nicholas as "inherently good," except that they were "put in the wrong place—subsequent instead of previous." Tyler, however, complained that they said nothing about direct taxes, nor would they limit federal courts' jurisdiction. Indeed, they would not alter a single dangerous part of the Constitution. "Little did I think matters would come to this," Tyler said, "when we separated from the mother country." Americans "ought to have been unanimous" on changes to their national government "and gone side by side, as we went through the revolution." Instead, Tyler said, the Constitution had produced "a general diversity of opinions, which may terminate in the most unhappy consequences." Even British tyranny would be more tolerable than the arbitrary government that was certain to follow ratification of the unamended Constitution.[31]

Those who allied with Nicholas and Madison took a predictably different stand, sometimes with an unpredictably novel twist. James Innes, a Williamsburg delegate and the state's attorney general, had missed part of the debates because he had to be in court. His brother Harry Innes was a judge and a critic of the Constitution in Kentucky, but James Innes said he had come to the Virginia convention inclined toward ratification, although with a mind "open to conviction." Now he argued that the convention had no power to insist on prior amendments because that would "transcend and violate the commission of the people," who had never seen Henry's proposed amendments, much less authorized their delegates to insist upon them. The convention could, however, recommend amendments that would not go into effect until the people had a chance to consider and possibly alter them by instructions to their congressmen. Innes also thought that it would be far better to have Congress propose amendments according to "the mode pointed out in the Constitution" than to call a new convention. He had heard "such a variety of contradictory objections" to the Constitution that a new federal convention was likely to bring "great discord, and no good effect at all." We look in vain for a perfect constitution, Innes said; he doubted that a document more perfect than the one in hand could be had at that time. "Let us try it," he said. "Experience is the best test." The Constitution would act equally on all the states, and if the "spirit of America" called for amendments, they would certainly take place. Congress was, after all, nothing but a set of fellow citizens with a "fellow feeling for us" no less than in the state legislatures, and Congress would not forget "that this Government is that of the people."[32]

Innes reprobated fears of Northern oppression. Why would the North act in ways that alienated Southern affections and adopt measures that would dissolve a union "as necessary to their happiness as ours"? He hoped for a government "respectable and happy," one that had political and civil liberty and yet was "formidable, terrible, and dignified in war"—or at least able to protect its people against petty enemies like those on the Barbary Coast of North Africa who were seizing American ships and seamen. The question before the convention was "as important as the revolution which severed us from the British empire." It would determine "whether America has in reality gained by that change which has been thought so glorious—and whether those hecatombs of American heroes, whose blood so freely shed at the shrine of liberty, fell in vain."[33]

Before the day was out, even Patrick Henry testified to Innes's "great eloquence." But it was rivaled by the more personal and commonsensical eloquence of Zachariah Johnston, a respected planter in his mid-forties, longtime member of Virginia's house of delegates, and ardent proponent of religious freedom who represented the backcountry county of Augusta in the Shenandoah Valley. Johnston said he had arrived at the convention anxious to hear the most complicated parts of the Constitution discussed "by Gentlemen of great abilities" and had listened carefully to the arguments of both sides. Now that he was "called upon to decide the greatest of all questions," he considered it his duty to declare the conclusion he drew "after an attentive and mature consideration of the subject," which he did, as he promised, "without erudition or eloquence, but with firmness and candour."[34]

From the first he was inclined to support ratification, Johnston said, but, like Innes, he was prepared to go the other way if persuaded that his convictions were "ill founded." Now, when he compared the "satisfactory and liberal manner" with which Pendleton and others explained the Constitution with the "strained construction" the other side put on "every word and syllable, in endeavouring to prove oppressions which can never possibly happen," he felt assured of the "safety and propriety of this system." Had the delegates held to the "plain and obvious meaning of the words, without twisting and torturing their natural signification," he said, they "would have come to a decision long ago."[35]

Johnston saw nothing fundamentally dangerous about the Constitution. The people at large elected the lower house of Congress, the states the upper house; the people also chose the president "in a secondary degree." Terms of office were short but proportioned to their difficulty and responsibility. Officeholders under the United States could not serve in Congress. All of those considerations persuaded him that the provisions on representation were well designed and would secure the country's liberty. Fears over state control of the militia were vastly exaggerated; Congress's powers were limited to arming and disciplining the militia, which would be subject to federal command only when actually called into the service of the United States. Moreover, the people were not being disarmed; they would remain in full possession of their weapons. Johnston liked the provision in Article VI prohibiting a religious test for office, which critics of the Constitution had attacked on June 23, when Robertson wasn't present to record their words. It would "strongly tend to establish religious freedom" in a country with so many different religious sects and opinions. He also saw nothing wrong with a "strong and energetic" government, nor did he see why such a government should oppress the poor more than the rich. Proportioning direct taxes among the states seemed to him reasonable, and he assumed Congress would raise those taxes in "the most equitable manner," according to the people's ability to pay. As for the emancipation of slaves, do what we will, Johnston said, that was going to happen. "Slavery has been the foundation of that impiety and dissipation which have been so much disseminated among our countrymen. If it were totally abolished, it would do much good."[36]

"It is my lot to be among the poor people," Johnston said. At best he was "of the middle rank," and he wished no more. He had a large family (eleven children were still at home in 1788), and if the Constitution proved oppressive it would bear as hard on him as on anyone and also on his children, "who are as dear to me, as any man's children can be to him." With their happiness in mind, he was prepared to vote for the Constitution but not for Henry's amendments, which he found flawed. Of course, the Constitution also had defects; no human institution was perfect. He was not about to see the blood and treasure lost during the Revolution shed in vain "and permit anarchy and misery to complete the ruin of this country." For those reasons he was "for adopting the Constitution without previous amendments." To reconcile those "gentlemen" with greater qualms than his, Johnston was willing to have Virginia propose subsequent amendments as the "great and wise State of Massachusetts" had done, and to rest his future happiness and that of his posterity on that footing.[37]

Johnston did not have the last say. Before the vote, Henry said the amendments Nicholas proposed had confirmed his fears. They weren't serious; "the proposition of subsequent amendments is only to lull our apprehensions." Many "essential and vital rights" were not even on the list. Nicholas's "paper" said nothing about "the power of direct taxation" and the "invaluable right" that was at stake. It said nothing about allowing the states to arm the militia if Congress failed to do so. It proposed nothing to "guard against the temporary suspension of our great national rights" by modifying the power of the President and Senate to enact treaties. Nothing about trial by jury. The "proposed subsequent amendments" did "not secure one single right." They would never be enacted, and if they were they would do no good.[38]

But Henry sensed that his side was losing. He apologized for having "taken up more time than came to my share" and thanked the delegates "for the patience and polite attention with which I have been heard." If he proved to be in the minority, he would have "those painful sensations, which arise from a conviction of being overpowered in a good cause," but he would be a "peaceful citizen." He would continue to work "to retrieve the loss of liberty, and remove the defects" of the Constitution "in a constitutional way." He had no intention of advocating violence but would wait with hopes that "the spirit which predominated in the revolution" was "not yet lost," and it would make the new government "compatible with the safety, liberty and happiness of the people."[39] He did not talk of an adjournment or threaten to secede from the convention: Either Federalist fears that the opposition would adopt those tactics in the face of defeat were based on fantasy, or the strategy of treating their opponents with patience and courtesy had worked again. Virginia would not repeat the disastrous postconvention divisions of Pennsylvania.

Governor Randolph claimed "one parting word," to explain again that he had refused to sign the Constitution because he had, and continued to have, objections to it; but ratification by eight states had reduced Virginia's decision to "Union or no Union." Then the committee of the whole finally came to an end. Edmund Pendleton resumed the chair, and Thomas Mathews reported that the committee of the whole had, "according to order," gone through the Constitution and come to several resolutions on it, which he read "in place" and then delivered to the clerk's table. Those resolutions, which Wythe had originally moved in the committee of the whole, were then read again. Attention turned to his first resolution, *"That it is the opinion of this Committee,* That the said Constitution be ratified."[40]

At that point "a motion was made to amend the same" by substituting for the "said resolution and its preamble" the motion Henry had presented: that, previous to ratification of the Constitution, a declaration of rights and other amendments "to the most exceptionable parts of the said Constitution . . . ought to be referred by this Convention to the other States . . . for their consideration." It lost by eight votes: 80 delegates voted for it, 88 against. That was the critical vote. The Constitution's "friends" had won. On Henry's request, the names of delegates on each side were taken and recorded in the convention's official journal.[41]

Nobody then moved for the convention to adjourn, as some still predicted.[42] Instead, between two and three o'clock in the afternoon, the convention turned to the main question, Wythe's resolution that the Constitution "be ratified." It passed by ten votes, 89 for and 79 against. This time George Mason asked that the names be taken down. Two delegates out of the convention's 170 were absent, and one—David Patteson of Chesterfield—had voted for both resolutions: that is, for recommending previous amendments to the other states and, after that had failed, for ratification. One of the absentees and three "aye" votes came from Kentucky, whose remaining ten votes went against ratification. Had all of Kentucky's votes been in the negative, the Constitution would still have been ratified, but by only three votes—about the margin Madison had predicted. No description has survived of the casting of votes, but one witness said "the scene was truly awful & solemn." Another reported that over a thousand spectators were present, "with minds agitated by contending and opposite opinions." The "dignified humility of the majority," the "tempered patience, manly firmness and virtuous demeanor of the minority," along with its honorable declarations of acquiescence and support for the government, completed the "grand and solemn" scene.[43]

The convention went on to the second resolution recommended by the committee of the whole—that whatever amendments seemed necessary would be recommended to the first federal Congress "to be acted upon according to the mode prescribed in the fifth article thereof"—after removing some unnecessary prefatory comments about relieving the fears of those who were "solicitous for amendments."[44] The convention also appointed two committees, one to prepare a form of ratification and another to bring in a list of amendments that would be recommended to the new Congress. The first consisted exclusively of delegates who supported ratification without previous amendments: Randolph, Nicholas, Madison, Marshall, and Corbin. The second, which would be chaired by Wythe, included all of those on the other committee except Corbin, another seven supporters of ratification, and nine critics of the Constitution including Henry, Mason, Grayson, Tyler, and Monroe. The effort at conciliation continued.[45]

Within the day the first committee reported a form of ratification that was firm and unqualified. "In the name and in behalf of the People of Virginia," it declared, the delegates "assent to, and ratify the Constitution," which was "binding upon the said People . . . in the words following." A copy of the Constitution was then included. A preamble to that declaration said that "the powers granted under this Constitution, being derived from the people of the United States may be resumed by them whensoever the same shall be perverted to their injury or oppression," and that all powers not granted remained with the people "and at their will." (It was, however, the "people of the United States" who gave and might reclaim the powers granted to the United States, not "the people of Virginia" alone.) No rights could be "cancelled, abridged, restrained or modified" by any officers of the United States unless the Constitution specifically gave them power for those purposes; and "among other essential rights, the liberty of conscience and of the press" were sacrosanct. The ratification document also said that any imperfections in the Constitution should be "examined in the mode prescribed therein," rather than endanger the union by delaying ratification with a hope of getting amendments first. The convention approved the proposed form. President Pendleton signed an engrossed copy on behalf of the convention at a short session the next day—Thursday, June 26—and the convention ordered it sent to the Confederation Congress.[46]

Finally, on June 27, the Wythe committee recommended a bill of rights and an additional twenty amendments to the Constitution that the convention, in the name of the people of the commonwealth, would "enjoin" on their representatives in Congress to "exert all their influence and use all reasonable and legal methods" to have enacted. Until then, all laws were to "conform to the spirit of these amendments as far as the said Constitution will admit." The bill of rights, which the convention approved without dissent, was a revised version of the 1776 Virginia declaration of rights, including its affirmation of the right of trial by jury but without its opening statement "that all men are by nature equal" and have "certain inherent rights."[47]

The other amendments were much like those proposed to the committee of the whole by Patrick Henry. They began by declaring that each state would retain every power, jurisdiction, and right that was not granted by the Constitution to Congress or the other departments of the federal government. Several amendments addressed ambiguities in the Constitution that its critics feared. They said, for example, that "there shall be one Representative for every thirty thousand" people rather than "the number of Representatives shall not exceed" that proportion; once the House of Representatives had two hundred members, Congress could revise the proportion to keep it that size or, if it chose, to increase it. Other amendments would limit Congress's power over the elections of senators and representatives under Article I, Section 4, to cases where the states neglected, refused, or were unable to act because of rebellions or invasions; require Congress to publish its proceedings (except for necessarily secret business) and reports on public finance every year, not "from time to time," and assure that the states could organize, arm, and discipline their militias if Congress failed to act.[48]

Congress would be unable to collect direct taxes in any state where the legislature, after being informed of its quota, raised the requisite sum by itself. (The proposed bill of rights also included a provision that "no aid, charge, tax or fee can be set, rated, or levied upon the people without their own consent, or that of their Representatives, so elected.") The amendments would require a two-thirds vote of the entire membership of the Senate to approve commercial treaties, and no less than a three-quarters vote of all members of the Senate and of the House to approve any treaty that yielded the territorial rights or claims of the United States, the rights to fish "in the American seas," or the rights to navigate American rivers. Others would require a two-thirds vote of the members present in both houses of Congress to approve any "navigation act or act regulating commerce" or to raise or maintain a standing army in time of peace. Moreover, Virginia proposed an amendment that said no clause denying Congress certain powers was to be interpreted so as to increase its power, but should be "construed either as making exceptions to the specified powers" or "as inserted merely for greater caution." It proposed to preclude presidents from holding office more than eight years in sixteen, and to prevent laws for increasing the salaries of congressmen from going into effect until after the next election for the House of Representatives. The amendments also sought to limit the appellate jurisdiction of federal courts "to matters of law only," not law and fact, except in equity or admiralty cases, and federal courts would have jurisdiction "in no case where the cause of action shall have originated before the ratification of this Constitution" except for certain disputes over land "and suits for debts due to the United States."[49]

The amendments suggested that "some tribunal other than the Senate be provided for trying impeachments of Senators." However, they asked for no major structural changes such as the establishment of an executive council to advise the president instead of the Senate, or the elimination of the office of vice president. Critics of the Constitution had pulled back on those demands, understanding perhaps that the time had passed for so substantial a revision of the Constitution's institutional design.[50] The Wythe committee did, however, propose amendments on direct taxes, control of the militia, and the jurisdiction of federal courts that were notably absent from the list of amendments that George Nicholas had presented to the committee of the whole. Henry and his allies could not have won that victory alone, since they had nine votes to the Federalists' eleven on the Wythe committee. The additional votes could only have come from the Constitution's "friends," among whom there was obviously more support for amendments—even for amendments Madison found "improper and inadmissible"—than Nicholas or Madison understood.

Only the provision on direct taxes provoked opposition in the convention, but a motion by Nicholas to strike it out lost by a vote of 65–85, a larger margin than on ratification, and not just because some delegates had left or for some other reason did not vote. The opposition to eliminating the tax amendment attracted six more votes than did the "nay"s on ratification—including that of Edmund Pendleton, who voted with Henry and Mason and against Madison, Nicholas, Randolph, and Marshall.[51] Again, support for amendments made what might seem like strange bedfellows once the issue of "prior" versus "recommended" was settled. Pendleton's views on amendments were, however, not so far from those that his friend and correspondent Richard Henry Lee had come to embrace by the spring of 1788. Both men favored amendments, thought those recommended by Massachusetts did not go far enough, and proposed to start the process of enacting them with the first federal Congress, not a new convention. Pendleton, however, found the need less urgent than Lee, and he questioned the wisdom and utility of a bill of rights. Declaring that the people retained all rights they did not specifically give up would be a lot safer, he thought, than trying to enumerate the rights they held.[52]

After rejecting the attempt to strike out the amendment on taxes, the convention approved the entire slate of amendments proposed by the Wythe committee, ordered them engrossed on parchment, signed by the convention's president on behalf of the convention, and sent by him with the form of ratification to Congress and to the executives or legislatures of the other states in the union. The convention had already arranged for the payment of its officers; unlike in Massachusetts, delegates had no trouble collecting their ten shillings a day for attending the convention plus travel allowance. Virginia had even issued advance payments to those who requested them. And so, after entrusting its journal to the archives of the state's privy council, ordering copies of the ratification and recommended amendments printed and sent to the counties (the people, after all, deserved to know what had been done in their name), and thanking the president for his services, the convention adjourned twenty-five days after it first met, *sine die*.[53]

———

Several leading Federalists left Richmond profoundly distressed with the amendments the convention had endorsed. Francis Corbin described the "whole business" as "ludicrous" and "absurd in the Extreme." He wished his friend Madison hadn't been on the committee that drew up the amendments; "I am sure he blushes when it is talked of." Madison himself wrote Hamilton that many of the "recommendatory alterations" were "highly objectionable," above all "an article prohibiting direct taxes where effectual laws shall be passed by the States for the purpose." He had carefully explained to the convention why that amendment would cripple the new government, but "it was impossible to prevent this error." The objectionable amendments, he told Washington, "could not be parried."[54]

Not at the Richmond convention, anyway. What happened later was another issue. Perhaps it was necessary to recommend amendments, even bad ones, to get the Constitution ratified in Virginia. As Henry fully understood, "recommendatory" amendments were binding on nobody. His doubts that the "friends of the Constitution" took them seriously except as a way of lulling the opposition's fears was probably right, at least for men like Madison and Corbin (though perhaps not Pendleton). Henry knew that Madison opposed amendments that, in Henry's opinion, were essential to protect the rights of the people and of the states. He had, after all, heard Madison condemn those amendments in the convention. Knowing the enemy was important; it defined the lines of future battles.[55]

UPSTAGED

It had been a great show. When witnesses looked back, they remembered Henry's "popular Eloquence" with awe and no apparent annoyance at his having talked on and on, day after day. Henry had "made a most noble stand in Defence of the Liberties of the People." He "was always attacked, but never conquered." He was "indefatigable," growing "more & more able day by day, for near three weeks." He gave "exemplary proofs of his Greatness, & in the opinion of many, of his Virtue," Henry's son-in-law Spencer Roane concluded, adding to the opinions of other, less biased, observers. "I have heard some Touches of Eloquence from him," Roane added, that would "almost disgrace Cicero or Demosthenes." Henry's response to defeat, promising to carry on his cause peacefully, without violence or disorder, added to his honor—except with Madison, who expected a continued, determined effort by Henry to "undo" the Constitution, whether through the state legislatures or the new federal Congress.[56]

On the other side, George Nicholas "was thought more equal to answering Henry, than any other person." Pendleton, "tho much impaired in health" and "in the decline of life," showed "as much zeal . . . as if he had been a young man," although one account said his weak voice deprived three-quarters of the delegates of hearing his "solid and persuasive Arguments." Randolph "amazed everyone" by the warmth with which he argued for ratification: "He spoke often and eloquently," and he contributed "in no small way to the favorable outcome." John Marshall's "perspicuity & force were greater than ever."[57]

But Madison stood out among the Constitution's supporters. He was "the one who, among all the delegates, carried the vote of the two parties," one observer claimed. Madison "was always clear, precise and consistent in his reasoning, and always methodical and pure in his Language." Another account of the "many shining characters" at the Virginia convention described his performance with a bit of poetry:

> Maddison among the rest,
> Pouring from his narrow chest,
> More than Greek or Roman sense,
> Boundless tides of eloquence.

William Nelson, Jr., had missed the convention, but he listened attentively as others discussed at length the various speakers' performances. In the end, he regretted most not hearing Madison and also James Innes, whose one speech at the end of the debates had a powerful impact. "By the unanimous voice of all whom I have heard speak on the subject, except one coxcomb, who did not like Madison," Nelson said, those two men were "astonishingly great in their respective ways." Zachariah Johnston also "surprized every body." Although Johnston had a reputation for being "very sensible & clear-headed," his speech at the end of the convention astounded listeners. Nelson heard one "man of judgement" declare that Johnston's speech was the best of any in the entire convention.[58]

Only one delegate left the convention with a tarnished reputation: George Mason, who, according to Nelson, was said to have behaved with less good temper than Henry. Unlike Henry, Mason had no political ambitions to mute his resentments; he was now sixty-two, eleven years Henry's senior, afflicted with periodic bouts of bad health and, as always, more than happy to stay home. On the evening after the convention adjourned, he assembled a substantial number of delegates who had voted against ratification on the pretense of issuing an address that would reconcile their constituents to the Constitution. Instead he proposed an inflammatory address to the public that prompted some men to leave the hall immediately. Others sat in stunned silence until, finally, Benjamin Harrison suggested that the meeting adjourn without doing anything. The opposition members had lost; now it was their duty as good citizens to submit to the majority. When other speakers supported Harrison, Mason withdrew his address and the meeting dissolved.[59] The Virginia minority was as determined as the majority to avoid replicating the postconvention history of Pennsylvania.

That's not to say the minority had no cause for resentment. Governor Randolph's failure to show the convention the letter he had received from New York's governor George Clinton, suggesting the Virginia convention take the lead in coordinating a response to the Constitution, was particularly upsetting. Randolph presented the letter to the house of delegates on June 24, when the special session of the legislature first had a quorum, as the last in a packet of five public documents. It was "partially read," then tabled and taken under consideration only on June 26, when the convention had already voted to ratify and the Wythe committee was busily compiling amendments to recommend with no consideration of what New York might do. Mason was so angry that, although he was not a member of the legislature, he drafted a legislative resolution saying Randolph should have presented Clinton's letter to the convention when it first convened and another resolution calling for the appointment of a committee to question Randolph about his conduct. There is no mention of those resolutions in the house's journal, despite what Madison called the "antifederal" character of the legislators. Six months later, Mason referred to Randolph as "young A[rnol]d," comparing him with Benedict Arnold, the archtraitor of the Revolution.[60] Randolph's questionable maneuver was, however, successful: It prevented any serious effort by the Virginia convention to coordinate its actions with New York. That could not be undone.

The opposition's efforts to open a correspondence with like-minded men in New York had also failed. On June 17, the day after Eleazer Oswald delivered the letters from Mason, Grayson, and Henry, John Lamb forwarded them "by a special messenger" to Governor George Clinton in Poughkeepsie, where the New York convention was gathering. Clinton quickly turned the letters over to a special committee of correspondence created by what Clinton called the "Republican Members" of the New York convention, who opposed "the Adoption of the new Constitution without previous Amendments." Its chairman, Robert Yates, a judge and one of the two New York delegates to the federal Convention who had left it in disgust, immediately wrote Mason. He expressed delight that the Virginians' views on amendments coincided so closely with those of their counterparts in New York. Yates and his committee were willing to open a correspondence with Mason's committee, but they feared that the Virginia opposition had only a slim chance of getting a majority and, moreover, that the New York convention would complete its work "before we could avail ourselves of your Advice." The New Yorkers had no committee to draft amendments, but Yates sent along a copy of some that had been agreed upon by several individuals. "We shall not adopt the present Constitution without previous Amendments," he promised. Yates sent the letter on June 21 "under Cover to Mr. George Flemming Merchant in Richmond," as Mason had suggested, to avoid interference from the postal system, which was supposedly controlled by Federalists. The letter arrived after Virginia had already voted to ratify.[61]

That wasn't necessarily the end of intercolonial cooperation among those who saw the Constitution as a threat to all the Revolution had won. Earlier in June, Henry suggested to Lamb that a grass-roots movement might well be needed if the Virginia convention ratified the Constitution without insisting on prior amendments. In that circumstance, with the Constitution already ratified by the necessary nine states, societies dispersed through Virginia and also North Carolina, all committed to securing amendments, might be "the only remaining Chance for securing a Remnant of those invaluable Rights" that would otherwise be lost. Madison feared some such scheme was afoot. To be sure, he wrote Jefferson, the opposition agreed to abide by the decision of the convention's majority and opposed popular violence. That did not mean that it would positively support the Constitution. Indeed, Henry and Mason had explicitly refused to do that.[62]

Supporters of the Constitution could at least try to avoid provoking bitter resentments among the members of the minority. "The federalists behave with moderation and do not exult in their Success," Spencer Roane reported. There were no celebrations of ratification in Richmond out of consideration for the feelings of the opposition delegates.[63]

Richmond, however, was not Virginia. After all, since—as they assumed—Virginia was the ninth state to ratify, the "friends of the Constitution" could rejoice at a general as well as a local victory. The celebrations were sometimes put off until July 4, when independence was also celebrated, but Norfolk, a port down the James River from Richmond, could not wait that long. The booming of guns from both the shore and ships in the harbor announced the news of Virginia's ratification on June 27. That evening houses were illuminated with candles, and finally, at about nine o'clock, "a Balloon . . . ascended, amid the acclamation of a numerous groupe of spectators," who closed the festivities "with every demonstration of joy."[64]

That evening the mail brought the news of Virginia's ratification to Alexandria, the town on the Potomac near Mason's and Washington's plantations, where Washington described the citizens as "federal to a man." Then, two hours before dawn on Saturday, June 28, an express rider—David Henley, hired by Virginia's congressional delegates—arrived from New York with another piece of startling news. The New Hampshire convention had voted to ratify on June 21. In Alexandria, Henley learned that Virginia had also ratified. Rather than go on to Richmond, he forwarded the news from New Hampshire to Madison, who received it on June 29, eight days after the New Hampshire vote. That same day, after having joined the celebrations in Alexandria the night before, Henley turned around and rode through Philadelphia back to New York City, where he arrived early in the morning of July 2. Another express rider, William Smith Livingston, quickly set off for Poughkeepsie to bring the news of Virginia's ratification to the New York ratifying convention.[65]

Virginia been upstaged: It had not put the Constitution into effect. It would have to be content as the tenth, not the ninth, pillar of the new federal edifice. Rather than detract from the celebration, however, the news increased the celebrants' joy. Alexandria, Washington noted, became "the first public company of America" that could drink to the prosperity of the ten states that had adopted the Constitution. Its festivities on June 28 included the shooting of cannon, illuminations, and a splendid men-only dinner at John Wise's Fountain Tavern. The following Monday—when the town of Winchester also celebrated—Alexandria finished its festivities "with fiddling & Dancing, for the amusement, & benefit of the Ladies."[66]

Washington and his current house guest, David Humphreys, attended the stag dinner. A party of gentlemen on horseback met the general outside town and accompanied him to the tavern, where the deafening fire of ten cannon announced his arrival. The drinking of ten toasts was a high point of the evening. The party drank to the convention of Virginia, the ten ratifying states, the king of France, the dead of the Revolutionary War, Lafayette, Alexandria's delegates to the state ratifying convention, and the Potomac, "may its navigation be improved to its sources, and its trade flourish to the degree bountiful nature intended." There were three toasts to go, including "the learning, agriculture, manufactures, and commerce of America" (there was no regional bias there); and "the majesty of the people of America: Let the nations of the world look to them as an example, where, on mature deliberation, and with one accord, they have laid down one form of Government and accepted another." Last but not least, the revelers toasted "Union and harmony among the members of the federal empire."[67]

Washington realized that June 28, when he heard the "flood of good news," was memorable for more reasons than one. It was the anniversary of the 1776 battle at Sullivan's Island, where Americans successfully kept British invaders out of Charleston harbor, and also the Battle of Monmouth two years later, when Washington narrowly prevented an action against British troops leaving Philadelphia from turning into a debacle. The confluence of events might seem minor in themselves, he said, but they suggested "we may rationally indulge the pleasing hope that the Union will now be established upon a durable basis," and that Providence would continue to favor its members "with unequalled opportunities for political happiness."[68]

NEW HAMPSHIRE, AGAIN

Washington never worried about New Hampshire. His correspondents assured him that when the state convention met for a second session in June it was sure to ratify the Constitution. He believed them, although the same sources—John Langdon and John Sullivan—had also predicted victory in February, when Federalists ended up having to propose an adjournment to avoid having the Constitution voted down. Were their predictions of victory in June any more reliable than those for February? They assumed that delegates bound by instructions to vote "no" but who had been persuaded by Federalist arguments at the first session of the state ratifying convention would go home, get their instructions cancelled, and come back ready and able to vote for ratification.[69] But how easy would it be to change their constituents' minds and the balance of power among delegates?

Evidence suggests that there was, in fact, substantial political maneuvering on the local level between February and June. Only one town—Hopkinton—released its delegate from instructions against ratification, although two others fought off efforts to bind delegates who supported the Constitution with similar instructions. Federalists challenged the election of two delegates opposed to ratifying the unamended Constitution as replacements for delegates who, unlike their constituents, favored ratification. Moreover, three communities that went unrepresented at the earlier meeting of the convention at Exeter sent delegates to the June session in Concord. One of those delegates, from Lincoln/Franconia, actually lived in the town of

Piermont and had never been elected by his supposed constituents. The Federalists managed nonetheless to get him through the credentials committee. Altogether they picked up about six new votes. As for those delegates who could not convince their constituents to release them from instructions to vote against ratification, Federalist leaders suggested they could just stay away from the convention. News of Maryland's and now also South Carolina's ratification also seemed to tip the scales toward an affirmative result. It meant that, if it acted quickly, New Hampshire could become the ninth state to ratify and have the honor of putting the new Constitution into effect.[70]

Finally, on June 18, when the Virginia convention had already been at work some two weeks and the New York convention was in its second day, the New Hampshire ratifying convention began its second session in Concord's old North Meeting House. One hundred and thirteen delegates had been elected, of whom only ninety were present on that first day; the majority of the missing members were from towns hostile to ratification. Federalists took advantage of the situation by settling two contested elections in their favor. Meanwhile, the rules committee approved the credentials of new delegates, including the one who had never been elected by his "constituents" in Lincoln/Franconia. The next day, when all but six delegates had arrived and the convention began discussing the Constitution, Pierce Long, a delegate from Portsmouth, recalled that the "dry arguments gone over again" left "both sides . . . quite tired out." The Federalists "determined to take the question" once they saw the chance of winning perhaps "by a majority of one only."[71]

That one vote, Major Joseph Kimball of Plainfield, arrived on June 20, when only five delegates remained absent—one known supporter of ratification without prior amendments and four probable opponents. The convention appointed a committee under John Langdon to propose "such articles as they shall think proper to be proposed as amendments to the Federal Constitution." That afternoon the committee reported twelve amendments, which the convention approved. At that point Joshua Atherton, a leading member of the opposition, moved that the convention ratify both the Constitution and the amendments, "but that the said Constitution do not operate in the State of New Hampshire without said amendments." The convention journal reports that, "after some debate," Samuel Livermore, a Federalist, moved to postpone Atherton's motion and consider in its place another—that if the Constitution were adopted, the amendments would be recommended to Congress for adoption.[72]

That set the alternatives for Saturday, June 21, the convention's fourth and final day. First the convention adopted Livermore's motion, which meant that the amendments would not be a condition of ratification. At that point Atherton made the dreaded proposal that the convention "adjourn to some future day," but it lost. Then the "yea"s and "nay"s were called on the main question: whether or not to ratify the Constitution. It passed, 57–47, to the Federalists' surprise and delight. Pierce Long said the margin was greater than they expected because "three of the opposition were excused from voting and one left the house." There were also "three or four whom we did not expect" who "voted in favor." The outcome was less obvious than the ten-vote spread in the final vote suggested. The struggle had continued until the very end, and then the division was far from the three-to-one victory that John Sullivan supposedly predicted in March.[73] The Federalists won because of their dogged political management in both the towns and the convention itself. They were counting noses all the time and, to make their victory more secure, had agreed to recommend amendments for enactment after the Constitution was ratified. Those amendments might well have helped win over the surprise "yea"s and perhaps persuaded some delegates not to vote at all rather than oppose ratification.

The strategy of recommending amendments to get an unqualified vote for ratification of the Constitution came from Massachusetts, and the first nine of New Hampshire's amendments were either identical with or closely modeled on those of its neighbor. They said all powers not expressly granted under the Constitution were reserved to the states, declared that there "shall be one Representative to every Thirty thousand" persons, limited Congress's power over elections under Article I, Section 4, and denied Congress the right to raise direct taxes unless revenue from other sources was insufficient for the "Public Exigencies"—and in that contingency required it to ask the state legislatures to "Assess, Levy, & pay" their proportion of the federal direct tax "in such way & manner" as the legislatures thought best. Like Massachusetts, New Hampshire also proposed to prevent Congress from creating commercial monopolies, to assure indictments by grand juries in cases that threatened "an Infamous Punishment, or loss of Life," to deny federal courts jurisdiction in suits between citizens of different states where less than $3000 was at issue, to assure trial by jury in civil actions "if the Parties, or either of them request it," and to preclude federal officers from accepting titles from foreign countries.[74]

New Hampshire also added three amendments of its own. One would prevent the quartering of soldiers in private houses without the owners' consent and require the consent of three-fourths of the members of both branches of Congress to raise a "standing Army" in peacetime. That was similar to an amendment Virginia suggested, but Virginia had asked for only a two-thirds vote. New Hampshire's last two proposed amendments said that "Congress shall make no Laws touching Religion, or to infringe the rights of Conscience," nor could it "disarm any Citizen unless such as are or have been in Actual Rebellion."

Virginia proposed far more amendments than any previous state convention, but its list included the first four amendments on both the Massachusetts and New Hampshire lists. Three of those—on direct taxes, reserving undelegated powers to the states, and limiting Congress's power over state elections of senators and representatives—were also on South Carolina's very brief list. Even without formally coordinating their actions, the states were coming to agree on a core set of changes to the Constitution.

The question was whether those amendments had any serious chance of enactment. Throughout the Virginia convention, Patrick Henry insisted that recommending critical amendments for enactment after the Constitution went into effect was idiotic: The time to negotiate the terms of a contract was before signing it. For Henry, American liberty—the most important consideration of all—was at stake. Although New Hampshire did not demand, like Virginia, a bill of rights, its amendments were also designed to protect rights: the right to free and equal elections, to be taxed only by bodies in which the people were adequately represented, to trial by jury, to be free from vexatious lawsuits and military rule, to the "rights of Conscience." But if Washington's secretary, Tobias Lear, was right, New Hampshire Federalists understood the amendments as a way to get votes for ratification and not much more. "I take the liberty to enclose a copy of the amendments recommended by this Convention," he wrote Washington from Portsmouth, New Hampshire, on June 22, 1788; "they were drawn up more with a view of softening & conciliating the adoption to some who were moderate in their opposition than from an expectation that they would ever be engrafted in the Constitution."[75]

That was precisely what Henry charged in Virginia. When he agreed not to fight the majority decision in the Virginia ratifying convention, he also pledged that he would continue to work, though in a constitutional way, for amending the Constitution. Henry remained a very powerful man in Virginia and, above all, in its legislature; he had not, like Mason, squandered his political influence. Judging by the amendments proposed by other states, his cause had substantial support. The Constitution had been ratified, but the ratification controversy was not over. The battle lines had, however, been redefined. The next fight would be over the future of those amendments that, it seemed, a substantial part of "We the People" wanted.

———

There were a few other remaining issues of some significance. New York, North Carolina, and Rhode Island had still not ratified. Washington was sure there would be no problem rounding out the union. Ratification by both Virginia and New Hampshire meant there were "ten affirmatives without a negative." (Somehow the decisive vote against the Constitution in Rhode Island's March referendum still did not count as a "negative" for Washington.) With so powerful a track record, the Constitution seemed sure to triumph everywhere. There was "little or no question . . . of North Carolinas treading in the steps of Virginia," and it was "hardly to be conceived that New York will reject it." That left Rhode Island, which had so far "baffled all calculation." Even in the surge of confidence that came with the good news of late June, Washington understood that predictions about Rhode Island were foolhardy. "He must be a hardy man, indeed," he wrote, "who will undertake to declare what *will be* the choice of the majority of *that* State, lest he should be suspected of having participated in *their phrensy*."[76]

Washington was no passive witness to the ratification of the Constitution. Among other strategic interventions, he had nudged Madison to attend the Virginia convention, which contributed to the Federalist victory in his home state. Now he had "real concern" about the impact on Madison's health of the services he had urged him to provide. While visiting his mother in Fredericksburg, Washington heard that Madison planned to go from Richmond directly to New York after the convention adjourned. On June 23 he wrote Madison, urging him to rethink his plans. Some time away from business was "indispensably necessary" for Madison's recovery. He should take a few days off before returning to Congress, and spend some of them at Mount Vernon as Washington's guest. "Moderate exercise, and books occasionally, with the mind unbent, will be your best restoratives." Madison accepted the invitation and stayed with Washington for two or three days in early July. He probably spent less time reading books than talking with the general, adding details to the brief but regular reports on the convention's proceedings that he had sent Washington from Richmond and thinking through the event's probable consequences. They could well also have discussed plans for the new government and its location, which would appear on the Congress's agenda soon after Madison returned.[77]

Washington's support for ratification was everywhere a point of persuasion for Americans who idolized him. Those who disagreed with his position often repeated, like John Dawson in the closing days of the Virginia convention, the "melancholy truth, 'that the greatest men may err,' and that their errors are sometimes of the greatest magnitude." William Grayson gave more direct tribute to Washington. "I think that were it not for one great character in America," he told the convention, "so many men would not be for this Government. . . . We do not fear while he lives: But we can only expect his *fame* to be immortal." Washington's leadership—perhaps, as many assumed, as the first president under the new Constitution—would end one day, and who else could "concentrate the confidence and affections of all America"? "Be assured," James Monroe wrote Jefferson after Virginia had voted to ratify, Washington's influence "carried this government."[78]

Washington was not about to take the credit. He rejoiced at the steps taken "by the People of this great Country to preserve the Union—establish good order & government—and render the Nation happy at home & respected abroad." No other country in the world had it more in its power to achieve those blessings than "United America." How strange and regrettable it would be if the country strayed "from the road to which the finger of Providence has so manifestly pointed. I cannot believe it will ever come to pass!" he said. "The great Author of all good has not conducted us so far on the Road to happiness and glory to withdraw from us, in the hour of need, his beneficent support."[79]

For Washington no less than Henry, the heavens were watching over the United States. Unfortunately, as so often happens when God and politics are brought together, each man's God pointed toward a different route and a somewhat different future: One focused on happiness and freedom at home without forgetting respectability abroad, the other on respectability and glory in the company of nations without forsaking—and perhaps promoting—happiness and freedom at home. In retrospect, the difference might seem like points of emphasis in the arguments of men who agreed on far more than they disagreed. At the time, however, the division seemed like that between right and wrong, good and evil. For Henry and others in the minority, the battle had been lost—the Constitution had been ratified—but the war over the nature and governing principles of the new government was far from over.

ELEVEN

★

On to Poughkeepsie

The number-one enemy for those who fought for the Constitution—the man who defined the meaning of "antifederalist"—was not Patrick Henry but New York's governor George Clinton. There was a time when James Madison dreamed that Henry might support the Constitution. No Federalist ever had that illusion about Clinton. His opposition seemed so certain that Alexander Hamilton started attacking him even before the Federal Convention adjourned.

In an unsigned piece in New York's *Daily Advertiser* for July 21, 1787, Hamilton charged that the governor had publicly attacked the Federal Convention "without reserve" and had predicted that it would have a "mischievous" outcome. According to Hamilton, Clinton said the Confederation was adequate for the "purposes of the Union," and the Convention would frighten people over evils that did not exist. For the governor to try to prejudice the public against the proposal of a body to which America had "entrusted its future fate," Hamilton said, showed that Clinton was more attached "to his *own power* than the *public good*." A "free and enlightened people" should watch such a man "with a jealous eye" and, when he "sounds the alarm of danger from another quarter," ask whether they "have not more to apprehend from *himself*."[1]

The attack provoked a burst of responses that continued on into the fall and became increasingly nasty. One critic described Hamilton—who admitted responsibility for the initial attack on Clinton—as a low-born, "upstart attorney" from the West Indies who had "palmed" himself off on Washington during the Revolutionary War and then been summarily dismissed from the general's staff. Upset by that slur on his honor, Hamilton asked Washington to state that the charges were false. Washington agreed, but he also expressed regret that such a dispute had broken out between two men, Clinton and Hamilton, for whom he had "the highest esteem and respect."[2]

Washington and Clinton first met at the Second Continental Congress in 1775, before Washington became head of the Continental Army, and their friendship solidified through the early years of the war. But Washington had a way of breaking his ties with men who took a different stand from his on the Constitution. His relationship with George Mason, for example, never returned to what it had been before the federal Convention met. Washington's friendship with Clinton was much warmer than that with Mason, and it continued until Washington's death. Clinton's affection for the general was so strong that he named a son George Washington and a daughter Martha Washington.[3] The persistence of their friendship raises some question about Hamilton's claims. Had Clinton gone from being a committed nationalist—which he clearly was during the war years—to an extreme defender of state power? From a supporter to an enemy of all that Washington believed in—and managed to remain Washington's friend nonetheless?

Clinton and Washington were both muscular, tall men—over six feet—who looked the parts they were destined to play as leaders in the new republic. Neither had much formal education. Although Clinton loved books (as a soldier in the French and Indian War, he carried with him a book of poetry and a two-volume history of England), he was, like Washington, more a man of action than a man of ideas.[4] Clinton, again like Washington, first won renown as a military leader. His main claim to fame came, however, primarily from his record in elective office.

The son of an Irish Presbyterian immigrant who had settled in the town of New Britain in New York's Ulster County, Clinton was born in July 1739. He studied law with the respected lawyer (and future Loyalist) William Smith, Jr., in New York City, and while there he became an ardent supporter of the American cause against Britain. Clinton won a seat in the state legislature in 1768 and, in 1775, became a New York delegate in the Continental Congress. That December the New York committee of safety appointed him brigadier general of the militias of Ulster and Orange counties on the west bank of the Hudson, and later added to his command the militias of Westchester and Dutchess counties on the river's east bank, where, with nearby Albany County, most of the state's great landed estates were found. Clinton was so successful in controlling the large population of Loyalists and securing the upper reaches of the Hudson River against the British that New York's provincial congress recommended him for a commission as a brigadier general in the Continental Army, which he received in March of 1777. He preferred "a more retired Life than that of the Army," he told Washington, but had taken it as a maxim in the "present Contest . . . not to refuse my (but tho poor) Services to my Country in any way they should think proper to appoint me."[5] Washington's position was exactly the same.

Within months of receiving his commission in the Continental Army, Clinton was elected by voters as the first governor under New York's new state constitution. Most of the Revolutionary state constitutions concentrated power in their legislatures, but the New York constitution of 1777 gave significant power to a governor elected every three years by voters who owned land (or occupied it on a twenty-one-year lease) worth "one hundred pounds, over and above all debts charged thereon." The state's wealthy upper classes, which had controlled New York before 1776, assumed the office would go to Philip Schuyler, a forty-three-year-old, well-connected (his mother was a Van Cortlandt, his wife a Van Rensselaer) Albany County "manor lord" and major general in the Continental Army. When the votes were counted, however, Clinton had defeated Schuyler 1,828–1,199 thanks to the solid support of small, independent farmers and a set of last-minute votes from soldiers who knew his leadership skills first-hand.[6] The wealthy Livingston family's inability to deliver the votes of their tenants to Schuyler also contributed to Clinton's victory. In the spring of 1777, the Livingstons had faced another of the region's endemic uprisings by tenants desperate to throw off their dependent status and secure title to the land they worked. This time the insurgents expected an intervention on their behalf by British troops; instead, Revolutionary militiamen crushed their uprising. A month later, when the election occurred, the Livingstons' tenants chose not to vote.[7]

Schuyler promised the new governor his support although, as he wrote John Jay, Clinton's "family + Connections do not Entitle him to so distinguished a preeminence."[8] No doubt the upstart's victory would be reversed at the next election. But Clinton was reelected (unopposed) in 1780, then in 1783, and again in 1786. His popularity was firmly rooted among small farmers and an array of other "new men"—middle-class shopkeepers, mill owners, schoolteachers, country lawyers, and the like—who entered politics in the wake of independence. Clinton held the loyalty of his constituents by an unswerving commitment to their interests and an astute use of the broad patronage power he held: The state constitution allowed the governor (with a generally sympathetic council) to appoint not just state officials but the mayors of Albany and New York City and an array of county officials including judges, sheriffs, clerks, justices of the peace, and militia officers. Clinton's affable, unpretentious "plain republican manner" and commonsense approach also appealed to voters who saw no reason that coming from a "good family" and having the right social connections should confer a claim to high office in Revolutionary America.[9]

After becoming governor, Clinton asked Washington to be relieved of his military responsibilities with "a Degree of Pain." Lieutenant-Colonel Hamilton, Washington's chief aide at the time, regretted "that so useful an officer is obliged to leave the posts under his superintendency" at such a critical point in the war. Clinton, however, promised Washington he would return to the army until the current campaign was over if "the Business of my new appointm't admit of it." In the fall of 1777, when the British tried to seize control of the Hudson, Clinton led a heroic but hopeless effort to hold Forts Clinton and Montgomery in Orange County against much larger British forces. There he had the help of Captain John Lamb, a prosperous wine merchant and onetime secretary of New York's Sons of Liberty, who would remain one of Clinton's loyal political supporters.[10]

While the British army occupied the southern part of his state, Governor Clinton gave Washington all the support he could. He also championed efforts to strengthen Congress so it could more effectively help the army win the war. In 1781, for example, New York was the very first state to approve a proposal allowing Congress to levy a 5 percent tariff on imports (the 1781 impost), which never went into effect thanks to Rhode Island's opposition. Washington remembered his friends from those bleak years: After resigning his commission in December 1783, he wrote Clinton that he felt a keen sense of obligation for the "spirited & able assistance" he had received from New York under Clinton's leadership. After Yorktown, Clinton remained a strong advocate of union. Above all, he wanted Congress to have power to fight British restrictions on American trade.[11]

Once the war ended, however, New York conflicted with Congress on one issue after another. It protested the size of the requisitions Congress leveled on it and argued over the future garrisoning of British forts in western portions of the state, as well as claims by Massachusetts to land within New York's borders and the future of Vermont, which wanted to break off from New York and become an independent state. More important, it questioned New York's obligations to compensate Loyalists for property the state had confiscated. New York had seized the lands of major Loyalist families, then divided and sold those lands, often to former tenants, which increased the number of small freehold farms. The seizure and sale of Loyalist lands also provided the state with over $3,600,000 by the end of 1782. Clinton saw no reason to restore the "estates, rights, and properties" of Loyalists, which would require refunding the price subsequent purchasers paid for confiscated property, or to compensate Loyalists for their losses, as Congress recommended under Article V of the 1783 peace treaty. Would New York be compensated for the wanton damage the British and their Loyalist supporters had done in the course of the war?[12] To restore Loyalist property would undermine the state's financial stability and turn back the clock, undoing a small social revolution that increased the number of small, owner-occupied farms while cutting the size of the old landed elite and weakening its political power.

But the main issue between Congress and the government of New York— and the reason critics charged Clinton and his supporters with "antifederal" convictions—was the New York legislature's refusal in 1785, 1786, and again in early 1787 to approve a 1783 impost proposal in a form Congress would accept. Since 1784, New York had levied its own duties on imports, part of which was paid by the final purchasers of goods imported through New York but sold in nearby states. New York's impost funded a third to a half of the state's annual expenses, which, with the revenue from confiscated Loyalist estates, helped keep New York's real estate taxes relatively low.[13]

In 1786, the state legislature also approved a limited issue of paper money, a quarter of which was used to pay interest on the state's outstanding debt and to take over that portion of the national debt owed to New Yorkers. The state issued the rest of its paper money as loans on real estate, for which recipients paid 5 percent annual interest. The currency was not legal tender for all debts, but it could be used to pay taxes—and then was destroyed, so the amount outstanding declined over time, which helps explain why New York's paper money did not lose value. In fact, it traded on a par with gold and silver. The availability of a circulating medium helped farmers pay their bills, which, with the state's modest real-estate taxes, saved New York from the rural discontent that afflicted other states. Paper money also gave a much-needed stimulus to commerce and allowed the state to acquire by late 1788 almost $3 million in federal interest-bearing securities. In short, New York's economy pulled out of the depression of the mid-1780s and began to prosper—with no help from Congress.[14] That the governor would resist giving Congress a right to tax imports, which was at the time an exclusive right of New York, was not hard to imagine.

Governor Clinton did not, however, personally lead New York's opposition to the federal impost. Two legislators took on that job: in the state senate, Abraham Yates, Jr., a onetime shoemaker, lawyer, and wine merchant from Albany who was a prolific newspaper writer with principled objections to giving Congress revenue without state control, and his counterpart in the lower house of assembly, John Lansing, Jr., a lawyer and mayor of Albany who later became one of New York's delegates to the federal Convention. The legislature technically accepted the congressional impost but insisted that New York customs officers collect the duties, which would prevent the creation of a vast federal bureaucracy. It also reserved the right to use New York's paper currency when transferring revenue from the impost to the federal treasury. Congress refused to accept those conditions. Meanwhile, Clinton remained above the fray.[15]

To be sure, in 1786, when Congress insisted—twice—that the governor call a special meeting of the legislature so it could reconsider the unacceptable requirements attached to its approval of the congressional impost, Clinton refused. The New York constitution allowed him to call the legislature outside its regular meeting time only on extraordinary occasions, and the current situation, he said, was not extraordinary. As the New York congressman Melancton Smith predicted, Congress's demand that Clinton reconvene the legislature despite his constitutional scruples bred only resentment. When the legislature finally met in January 1787, it endorsed the governor's decision by a vote of 39 to 9. Finally, in February, despite Hamilton's impassioned pleas for the federal impost, the legislature reaffirmed its earlier position, killing the measure for good.[16]

By then Hamilton, who married Philip Schuyler's daughter Elizabeth in 1780, had become New York's most prominent nationalist and a spokesman for the state's increasingly nationalist landed elite, which was dead set against Clinton and the policies of his administration. Those "manor lords" who had sided with the Revolution (and so still held their vast estates) saw the confiscation of Loyalist lands much as Henry Knox and Benjamin Lincoln saw Shays's Rebellion—as a threat to all property rights by persons of the "leveling kind." They thought the time had come to end New York's anti-Loyalist laws, despite their popularity, in the interest of reconciliation, stability, and a respect for both the spirit and the letter of the 1783 Treaty of Paris.[17] Hamilton and his allies wanted to create a stronger national government in part to counter the power of states like Clinton's New York; and when the impost proposal failed, they supported a more radical restructuring of national institutions. To succeed, they built an electoral base with coerced tenant votes and formed alliances with merchants, urban mechanics, lawyers, and tradesmen who wanted a national government that could revive foreign commerce and breathe new life into the economy.[18]

Clinton's critics assumed that he had orchestrated opposition to the congressional impost behind closed doors. Publicly, however, the governor carefully watched his words: In presenting Congress's request to the legislature that it reconsider the impost of 1783, he said he would "forbear making remarks" on the subject since the legislature had already discussed it repeatedly.[19] Similarly, in the summer of 1787, despite Hamilton's charge, he said nothing in the press or before a public body about the federal Convention. The governor might have made some unguarded comments to Robert Yates and John Lansing, the New York delegates who left the Convention on July 10 and stopped to give Clinton a report on their way home,[20] but that was a private conversation that Yates and Lansing were unlikely to have described to Hamilton. The public, in any case, had no idea what Clinton did or did not say about the federal Convention until Hamilton broadcast his charges in the New York *Daily Advertiser.*

After Hamilton's attack, the governor was even more careful to hold his tongue in public.[21] His circumspection did not calm Federalist suspicions. "Notwithstanding his reserve," Madison reported to Jefferson's private secretary in Paris on October 24, 1787, when the controversy over Hamilton's charges had about burned out, the governor was considered "a decided adversary" to the Constitution. The next June, when John Adams's daughter,

Abigail Adams Smith, had dinner at the governor's home, she reported that the members of his family—which included five daughters and a son—were "all politicians," and his fourteen-year-old daughter, Cornelia, "as smart and sensible a girl as I ever knew," was a particularly "zealous politician, and a high anti-Federalist." Smith added that the governor did not "conceal his sentiments, but I have not heard that he has given any reasons for them."[22]

Federalists, however, had no problem explaining his politics as founded upon a "selfish spirit." Critics of the Constitution in New York consisted "only of a small group of salary-men," a widely reprinted newspaper essay claimed. That is, they were paid by the state with revenue that came in part from the state impost, so their livelihoods were supposedly threatened by the Constitution. The prime example was Clinton's old subordinate officer John Lamb, whom Clinton had appointed collector of customs for New York and who also was also head of New York's Federal Republican Committee, which opposed ratification of the unamended Constitution.[23]

It was never altogether clear how Governor Clinton or Abraham Yates were personally threatened by the Constitution. And what about the significant number of state officeholders—Chancellor Robert R. Livingston, for example—who favored ratification? Federalist essayists suggested their support for the Constitution went against their interest and so showed that they preferred "the *public good* to their own *consequence*."[24] "Antifederalist" officeholders were, by contrast, selfish and provincial almost by definition. And many Federalists seemed to assume that what was true in George Clinton's New York was true everywhere.

LET THE PEOPLE DECIDE

Clinton waited until the regular meeting of the state legislature in January of 1788 to send it the Constitution and a raft of related documents, including the December 21 letter from Robert Yates and John Lansing explaining their early departure from the Convention in Philadelphia. "From the Nature of my Office," the governor told the legislature on January 11, "you will easily perceive it would be improper for me to have any other agency in the Business than that of laying the Papers respecting it before you."[25]

Three weeks passed before the legislature took up the question of calling a convention. Madison predicted that there would be a close fight in New York over whether or not to submit the Constitution to a state convention. Most senators seemed opposed, he wrote Washington on January 20, but the assembly was more friendly to the document. Madison thought that the outcome of the Massachusetts ratifying convention would determine what the New York legislature did. Others agreed.[26]

In fact, there was very little opposition to calling a convention, which the New York legislature did on the first of February, five days before the Massachusetts convention voted to ratify. The only argument turned over how to phrase the call. A couple of assemblymen wanted to preface the house resolution calling a convention with a statement that the federal Convention, "instead of revising and reporting alterations and provisions in the Articles of Confederation," as instructed, had proposed "a new Constitution for the United States" that, if adopted, would "materially alter" New York's constitution and "greatly affect" New Yorkers' rights and privileges. Supporters of the preface said it "was a simple detail of facts, which no one could deny." Opponents saw it as an inappropriate effort to influence the people. In the end, the assembly voted down the proposal, 27–25, then considered another motion to submit the Constitution to the ratifying convention delegates "for their free investigation, discussion and consideration." That also lost (28–23) because the words seemed to open the way to amendments. There would no doubt have been a firestorm had anyone proposed to say the convention would meet, as the federal Convention had put it, to give the Constitution its assent and ratification. The resolution that the house sent to the senate for its concurrence called a convention and laid out the rules for electing delegates but said nothing about what the convention was supposed to do.[27]

Everyone in the senate agreed that the legislature had no right to withhold the Constitution from the people. James Duane, the Federalist mayor of New York City (a Clinton appointment) as well as a state senator, said it would be "a high stretch of arbitrary power" for the legislature to refuse to call a convention. Abraham Yates, however, argued for postponing the convention until far into the future. More time was needed, he said, to inform the people, many of whom, as a colleague observed, were too poor to buy newspapers and "too remote from the common opportunities of information." A people who knew little about the Constitution, Yates said, "might easily be deceived." The senate, however, defeated his motion and approved the house proposal 11–8.[28]

In the end, the New York legislature called a convention that would meet at Poughkeepsie on June 17. The election of delegates would begin "on the last Tuesday in April" at the place where elections for assemblymen were normally held and continue "from day to day until . . . completed, not exceeding five days." That meant the voting could continue from April 29 through May 3. Members of the assembly and a third of the state senators would be elected at the same time. The state's cities and counties would have as many convention delegates as they had members in the lower house of the legislature. However, the electorate for convention delegates was not subject to the property requirements that the 1777 state constitution imposed for legislative elections—i.e., a £20 freehold or "renting a tenement to the yearly value of forty shillings." Any free white male who was twenty-one years of age or older could vote. As in all state elections after 1787, voting would be by secret ballot. Moreover, once the voting was over, as in assembly elections, all the ballots and poll books would be packed up, bound with tape, sealed and signed by the election inspectors, and delivered to the county clerk for safekeeping. The packets would be opened and the ballots counted some four weeks later, on May 27.[29]

The state agreed to pay delegates at the same rate as assemblymen (although they would have to wait until a subsequent assembly acted to get their money). On February 2, the house ordered five hundred copies of its resolution with the senate's concurrence—but not the Constitution—printed and distributed to "the several counties of this State."[30]

THE FIGHT FOR VOTES

Although the elections were almost three months away, contenders quickly went into action. The contest for delegates in New York was distinctive. More than in any other state, the fight was between two organized parties. Moreover, in New York, again to an extent unequaled in any other state, both groups of contenders—not just those who supported ratification of the Constitution "as it now stands"—used the terms "Federalists" and "Antifederalists" (or, more simply, "Antis").

Even in New York, however, some critics of the Constitution, particularly those in southern parts of the state, avoided the "Antifederalist" label. New York City's Federal Republican Committee, which opposed ratifying the Constitution without amendments, did not use the term, and writers in Thomas Greenleaf's *New-York Journal* tended to call the Constitution's critics "republicans" and referred to its supporters as "anti-republican."[31] Governor Clinton, whose personal politics were increasingly beyond question as the ratification fight went on (he "does not oppose the Constitution in his legislative capacity," an observer reported, "yet is open and diligent against it"), referred to his allies in a variety of ways. He spoke of them as "Friends to the Liberties of our Country" and "Friends to the Rights of Mankind" (as opposed to "the Advocates for Despotism"), "the Gentlemen opposed to the Adoption of the new Constitution without previous Amendment," or, in June, the "Republican Members of the Convention."[32]

In Albany, however, an organized political group issued broadsides as "the ANTI-FEDERAL COMMITTEE." Its opponents formed a "FEDERAL COMMITTEE."[33] Those precocious political organizations emerged from deep historical roots in New York. Before independence, two political alliances, the Livingstons and the De Lanceys, had fought for power; later a new division developed among the supporters of Clinton and those of Schuyler or his son-in-law, Alexander Hamilton, and solidified over the Constitution.[34] What those parties called themselves, according to an "Anti-Federal Committee" circular, made little difference: "Terms of distinction, on a difference in political sentiments, are frequently arbitrary, and often, in their origin, without a precise meaning affixed to them."[35] Essentially, the committee waved off the assumptions Federalists associated with the word "antifederalist" and denied that the term had any more substantive meaning than, say, those of modern baseball teams. Once stripped of those implications, "Anti-Federalist" was as good a name as any. Of course, the Federalists had no objection, as they had invented the terms.

Albany Antifederalists were (with the possible exception of their colleagues in neighboring Ulster County) the first to organize and take action. They met on February 12 and appointed a committee to nominate candidates for the ratifying convention. The next day an Albany Federalist reported that "the opposers to the new Constitution here are indefatigable in endeavouring to excite the People against it." Members of the committee were visiting the various electoral districts to consult on appropriate persons to represent Albany County at the ratifying convention "and to sow the seed of opposition & dissention." Another Albany Federalist wrote Henry Knox that "the Antifed[erali]sts . . . use every art, & strain every nerve to gain their points," and warned that if the Federalists did not exert themselves in a similar way "they will be beaten."[36]

Not all Federalists were so impressed with their opponents' activity. Writing in the *Albany Journal*, "Fabius" called the city's "antifederal party" a "junto" whose members were "despicable for their attachment to self-interest, self-consequence, and an unbounded popular influence" that made them well suited to become "leaders of a gang of Shaysites." Another hostile writer compared them to "the witches in Macbeth, dancing round the chaldron of sedition, each throwing in his proportion of spells, for the confusion of his country." In mid-March, an Antifederalist essayist used the same reference against the Federalists.[37] Overt, organized politics were not yet fully accepted even in New York. Each side considered itself profoundly patriotic and its enemies a seditious threat to law, order, and the public welfare.

Choosing the right candidates was the Albany Anti-Federal Committee's first task, and for that purpose it called a public meeting of district representatives from the city and county of Albany—essentially a county nominating convention—on March 13 at the house of an Albany tavernkeeper. Two days later, the committee issued a circular with the names of people "unanimously nominated" for election to the state ratifying convention and the legislature. In nominating convention delegates, the circular explained, people who had or were closely connected with persons who had "very large possessions" were excluded from consideration for fear that they might expect to benefit if "the government became invested in the hands of a few." It was also "injurious and dangerous" for a free people to choose a representative whose situation would make him "little affected by any changes in government, which may abridge the liberties of his fellow citizens." That would seem to rule out members of the great landed families as convention delegates (though the list of assembly candidates included a few Van Rensselaers) and appealed to their tenants, who could in theory (though not necessarily in fact) vote for Antifederal candidates without fear of retaliation now that New York used the secret ballot. The circular also ruled out other categories of candidates, including persons determined "first to adopt a defective Constitution, and afterwards . . . affect to depend on a precarious recommendation for future amendments."[38]

The Anti-Federal Committee's nominees for the convention, according to the March 15 circular, considered the Constitution "dangerous to the Liberties of the People," but they were "not averse to the cultivation of a spirit of conciliation" so long as it did not require depending upon a recommendation of future amendments. The circular granted that the Confederation had its defects, but that was no reason to adopt a Constitution with additional defects or to deprive the states "of their most important rights of sovereignty." Nor was the previous consent of six states (by March) of any significance. Whatever the people of other states decided, "we are to judge for ourselves."[39]

On March 14, Albany County Federalists also issued a circular with nominees for the convention and the state legislature who had been chosen by a fifteen-member "Federal Committee" after canvassing opinion in the county's electoral districts. Its list of convention candidates avoided "any Person enjoying an Office of Profit under this State or the United States" for fear they would act from "private Motives." (That consideration, if followed strictly, would have eliminated some of the state's most distinguished defenders of the Constitution such as Hamilton, who had recently been elected to Congress, and the secretary of foreign affairs, John Jay. But then neither of them would stand for election to the convention from Albany County.) It also claimed to have eliminated anyone who had "officially determined on the proposed Plan of Government." And yet the committee itself advocated ratification of the Constitution "in its present Form" while recommending the amendments proposed by Massachusetts and any others that might "be found requisite." For Federalists, the previous ratification by six states—including four adjacent to New York—argued strongly for New York's ratification.[40]

In another circular issued on March 26, Albany County Federalists said the issue had come to this: "*Shall we continue to be* UNITED *with the other* STATES? or, *Shall we rashly oppose them?*" No "thinking Man" would hesitate to "*go Hand in Hand with the other States*, with whom we have fought and conquered." The committee strongly advised electors to vote for "*every Individual*" on the Federalist ticket, "for if we omit *one* Man, it will open a Door for one of another List to go in" and undermine the cause of "NATIONAL

UNION." The broadside included the names of committee members and twenty-four other prominent citizens of Albany who endorsed the circular and asked their "Friends in the Country" to comply with its request.[41]

"With respect to Politicks in this Quarter," the Antifederalist farmer and legislator Henry Oothoudt wrote from Albany on April 3, "I am at a Loss where to Begin. . . . I Do believe Since the Settlement of America Such Exertions have not been made upon a Question of any Kind" as at present over the new Constitution. Its supporters were "Engaged from Morning until Evening," and travel "both night and Day to proselyte the unbelieving Antifederals." Philip Schuyler would have agreed; he commended Albany's Federal Committee, noting that it had extended its attention to Montgomery County, where his nephew, Peter Schuyler, was helping coordinate the Federalist campaign. The Albany Anti-Federalist Committee also extended its activities westward into Montgomery County, as well as northward into Washington and Clinton counties (which acted together in electing delegates and legislators in 1788).[42]

Separate committees nominated Federalist and Antifederalist slates and navigated the complex politics of Columbia County to the immediate southeast of Albany County and in all the other counties along the Hudson River to the north of New York City.[43] Occasionally they confronted issues that required broader consultation. Ulster County Antifederalists organized early and well: On February 7 they held a rally in the town of Montgomery; later a county committee organized meetings within towns. Finally, representatives from ten districts met at New Paltz on February 28 to settle the Antifederalist convention ticket. The question arose whether Governor Clinton should be on the ticket for Ulster, where he was sure of being elected. Perhaps the popular governor could win a seat in one of the state's southern counties, such as Kings (Brooklyn) or New York (Manhattan), where the Federalists were strong and let other Antifederalists take all six of Ulster's convention seats.[44]

The Ulster Antifederalist leader Peter Van Gaasbeek raised that issue at a meeting in Poughkeepsie with members of the legislature from Ulster and other leading Antifederalists, including Samuel Jones from Queens County, Melancton Smith, a New York merchant and lawyer who was one of Governor Clinton's top advisors, and perhaps Clinton himself. Later that caucus of Antifederalist leaders in Poughkeepsie established a central committee of correspondence to inform the people about "the Combinations and Measures that are pursued to Cajole them out of some of their most inestimable Rights." The caucus wanted Clinton on the Ulster ticket at first, then reversed itself. In the end, Melancton Smith investigated the situation in Kings County and decided "it would not be prudent to hazard his Election" there. It would be better, Smith concluded, to have Clinton elected in two places than "not to be elected at all."[45]

The City and County of New York, along with neighboring Richmond (Staten Island) and Kings County, were a different political world from the upper Hudson Valley. All three counties were dominated by Federalists. Moreover, no well-organized "Federal" and "Antifederal" committees like those in the upper Hudson Valley faced each other in those three counties, nor, for that matter, to their east in Queens and Suffolk counties, which, like King's County, were on Long Island. The "Spirit of Electioneering" there was nonetheless sometimes "at a very high pitch."[46] In Suffolk County, a group of Federalists circulated a slate of candidates in early April. Antifederalists moved into action only after a former resident chided the assemblyman John Smith, who was a bit annoyed at having been left off the Federalist ticket because he was considered an "anti." Smith should stir himself, his correspondent suggested, meet his friends somewhere, and put up a "good list." Within a few weeks members of the opposition were campaigning for their candidates. That, however, was relatively late in the electoral contest.[47]

Less is known about the politics of Kings County, but there did seem to be opposing "Federalist" and "Antifederalist" candidates for its convention seats. In New York City and County, however, many self-appointed nominators proposed candidates for the upcoming elections to the readers of whatever newspaper would print their tickets. New York's Germans issued a slate of candidates for the convention; so did the city's master carpenters and "a large number of respectable Mechanics and Tradesmen." There was also a "Federal Ticket" of candidates for the convention and state legislature, all of whom were "unequivocally attached to the establishment of a firm national government." The group that proposed those candidates *To the Citizens of New-York* identified itself only as "A number of your fellow Citizens," not a "Federal Committee." An opposing ticket appeared ten days later, on April 19, in Greenleaf's *New-York Journal*, which again identified the nominators only as "a number of your fellow Citizens." Governor Clinton was at the top of the list, which also included several prominent Federalists, as if the nominators were trying to sneak Clinton in among others of a different political persuasion.[48]

The relatively organized electoral politics in the state of New York—stronger in some counties than others, but in general far more developed than in other states—meant that key people had to choose their constituencies carefully to be sure of a seat at the convention. The "Anti" Melancton Smith ran in Dutchess County, where he had lived most of his life and owned property, not New York City, his home since 1785. Similarly, the Federalist Robert R. Livingston ran in New York City and County, where he owned substantial property, not his home county, Columbia, where the members of his party were divided into factions.[49]

The closely fought election brought accusations that Clinton appointees were campaigning for Antifederalist candidates, and even allegations of outright bribery.[50] Contenders sometimes resorted to dirty tricks. In Ulster County, a group of Federalists met at Newburgh on March 10 and nominated a slate of Antifederalist convention candidates different from those on the "official" Antifederalist ticket in an effort to confuse and divide voters hostile to the proposed Constitution and so to diffuse their electoral power.[51]

All that political activity got people's attention. "All we hear here," remarked an ex-army officer in Columbia County in early April, "is a Constitution talk." The *Hudson Weekly Gazette* also testified to the intense interest the campaign attracted and its impact. "One excellent effect produced by the constitution," it observed, is "that almost every man is now a politician, and can judge for himself" upon that "great and important question," and "without the aid of itinerant teachers, true or false."[52]

A WAR OF PRINTED WORDS, CONTINUED

The press was a major battleground in the fight for convention seats. At the time, New York State had twelve newspapers, seven of which were printed in New York City. Of those seven, only one, Thomas Greenleaf's *New-York Journal*, published a substantial number of Antifederalist essays. Although the "Antis" were stronger outside than within the city of New York and its immediate vicinity, all five newspapers published outside of Manhattan (in Poughkeepsie, Hudson, Albany, and Lansingburgh) were Federalist. Antifederalists were so eager to get an "impartial paper" in Albany that on January 31 they tried to get Greenleaf to send one of his journeymen to start a new printing office there. Later they renewed their request and promised to advance the printer "a sum of Money on Account, immediately on his Arrival." Finally, on March 23, "despairing of receiving any Aid from New York," the Albany Antifederalists cancelled their request, having made an alternative arrangement, probably with Charles Webster, the owner or co-owner of both the *Albany Gazette* and the *Albany Journal*.[53]

Webster probably printed one of the most important Antifederalist broadsides produced upstate: a circular issued by the Albany Anti-Federal Committee on April 10, 1788, that included over thirty objections to the Constitution and answers to five common Federalist assertions. Most of the objections—to the powers of Congress, the president, and the courts; the long terms of federal officers; counting slaves in apportioning representation; the lack of a bill of rights; the supremacy clause in Article VI—had already been raised time and again, though not with such force and together in one place. Since they thought the proposed government would be "more arbitrary and despotic" than that of Britain, Albany Anti-Federalists opposed ratification of the Constitution "in its present form." Their circular dismissed out of hand the idea of ratifying while recommending amendments for enactment later. That was "*First* to make a *surrender* and *afterwards* ask for terms of *ca-*

pitulation." The circular was issued "by order of the Committee" and signed by its chairman and clerk. It also listed the names of another twenty-six subscribers who endorsed its position and the slate of Antifederalist candidates for both the convention and the state legislature.[54]

About ten days later, Webster published a twenty-eight-page pamphlet, *An Impartial Address, to the Citizens of the City and County of Albany*, for the local Federal Committee. It gave a point-by-point answer to the Anti-Federalist circular. Webster included his name on a list of seventy-eight subscribers who said the pamphlet's refutation of the Anti-Federalists' objections was "fully satisfactory to us."[55] That didn't stop him from printing an Anti-Federalist circular that responded to the *Impartial Address*. He probably also published another Anti-Federalist circular a few days later and a Federalist broadside, "To the Inhabitants of the District of Schenectady."[56] Webster's willingness to print treatises on both sides of the question increased his claim to be an "impartial" printer whose press was free. He must also have enjoyed the surge of business the ratification controversy brought.

Thanks to the presence of printer Thomas Greenleaf in New York City, Anti-Federalists had access to a wealth of literature that supported their cause, and they made full use of that advantage. An Albany Federalist, William North, complained to Henry Knox in mid-February that "The Centinel, the farmers letters, & every other publication against the Constitution are scattered all over the County, while the federalist remains at New York, & not a single Piece (of which there are many more intelligible to the common people) is sent abroad." For months the Federal Republican Committee in New York City had sent packets of writings critical of the Constitution, including the letters of the "Federal Farmer" (North's "farmers letters"), to places within and outside New York where they might have a political impact. Now, in early April, after Greenleaf republished a pamphlet from Massachusetts titled *Observations on the Constitution* and signed "A Columbian Patriot," the committee sent some 1,700 copies to Antifederal committees throughout New York State.[57]

"A Columbian Patriot" was Mercy Otis Warren, a writer and militant patriot from Milton, Massachusetts. She was the devoted sister of James Otis and wife of James Warren, both well-known leaders in the fight against Britain. Her pamphlet was the most prominent contribution to the ratification debates by a woman, although of course Warren's use of a pseudonym hid her gender. Some people thought Elbridge Gerry had written the pamphlet, which first appeared in late February, after the Massachusetts ratifying convention adjourned.

Warren was outraged by that convention's outcome. To her, the Constitution violated everything the Americans of 1776 had stood for; to ratify it was equivalent to fixing "shackles on our own necks" while depending on "a precarious hope of amendments" for redress. The pamphlet listed fifteen numbered objections to the Constitution—many of which, she noted, had close links to issues in the fight with Britain. Warren hoped that New York and several other states would reject the Constitution, and that the country would adopt "the wise measure of another federal convention" where "more skilful and discreet architects" could design a government better suited to American freedom. Like "Centinel," in short, she wanted the convention to start over from scratch, not, like Richard Henry Lee and many others, to repair the Constitution's most egregious shortcomings.[58]

Warren had a tendency to indulge in overlong, complex sentences. The opening part of the pamphlet was particularly turgid and sprinkled with literary allusions that could put readers off. The Albany Anti-Federal Committee acknowledged receipt of the pamphlet on April 12; it was "a well composed piece," it said, "but in a Stile too sublime & florid for the common people in this Part of the Country." The committee had, as requested, forwarded copies to Montgomery County, planned to send others to Washington County, and would distribute the rest in Albany County, but it was not about to pay the cost of printing them, as the New York committee proposed: It said it already had considerable expenses.[59]

The New York Federal Republican Committee also sent out 225 copies of an anthology that included the "Dissent of the Minority of the Pennsylvania Convention," Governor Edmund Randolph's letter of October 10 explaining why he had refused to sign the Constitution (but without the paragraph in which Randolph said he would support ratification even without prior amendments), and the first nine essays of "Centinel." It seems that "vast quantities" of the anthology circulated through Dutchess County, but Albany County's copies failed to arrive in time to be of service before the election. In any case, the Albany Anti-Federal Committee said it preferred the pamphlet version of Luther Martin's speech to the Maryland assembly, which would have helped "open the Eyes of our Country more than any Thing yet published."[60] Perhaps, like Martin, the Committee would have preferred to keep the Confederation rather than suffer the dangers raised by the Constitution: In its circular of April 23, the Albany committee described an "ANTI-FEDERALIST" as "one who is for preserving" the Confederation—not, as an earlier circular suggested, one who favored amending the proposed Constitution previous to its ratification.[61]

The Federalists had no program for distributing pamphlet literature like that of the New York Federal Republican Committee. Still, the complaint that no copies of *The Federalist* could be found outside New York City became outmoded once the book version of "Publius" became available. On April 10 the publisher, Archibald M'Lean, sent Stephen Van Rensselaer sixty copies of volume I, most of which were for subscribers in Montgomery and

Albany counties who had agreed to pay the advertised price of five shillings
for a 200-page volume or six shillings for one of 250 pages or more. However,
the lawyer James Kent said he received a "large number of the volumes" in
Poughkeepsie for "gratuitous distribution." Kent helped give them out at a
meeting to nominate Federalist candidates for Dutchess County's convention
seats.[62] How giving Federalists free copies of *The Federalist* would win over
members of the opposition was not obvious. Perhaps "Publius" was supposed
to help the already converted explain their convictions more persuasively. In
any case, *The Federalist* was probably no more effective among the people of
rural New York than Mercy Warren's "Columbian Patriot." Even William
North, who had complained back in February about the lack of Federalist
literature in Albany County, suggested that other Federalist writings were
"more intelligible to the common people" than those of "Publius."[63]

The most effective Federalist pamphlet distributed during the New York
electoral campaign first appeared on April 15 and was signed "A Citizen
of New York"—the same pseudonym that the authors of *The Federalist*
had planned to use before Madison, a noncitizen of New York, joined the
team.[64] The nineteen-page pamphlet, *An Address to the People of New-York,
on the Subject of the Constitution*, was written by John Jay, a genuine citizen
of New York and the author of five essays in *The Federalist*. As its title suggests, the pamphlet was aimed at a New York audience, and it appeared two
weeks before the election of delegates to the New York ratifying convention.
Written in a direct, clear style, in a spirit of inquiry without the stridency
or polemics of "A Columbian Patriot," Jay's *Address* began by describing the
problems that made constitutional reform necessary: a central government
"destitute of power, and so constructed as to be very unfit to be trusted with
it," so that "almost every national object . . . is at this day unprovided for."
The members of the federal Convention were "excellent and tried men" who
had faced and resolved problems of immense complexity, often through compromise, which explained why so many people objected to one or another
part of the Constitution.[65]

Jay said he could not discuss the entire Constitution and the objections
made to it. "Such a task would require a volume," he said, thinking perhaps
of the book version of *The Federalist*, and "few men have leisure or inclination
to read volumes on any subject." He did, however, make a few quick points.
Critics of the Constitution claimed "among other strange things" that it left
liberty of the press insecure, although, like New York's state constitution, it
said nothing on that issue. They also asserted that the Constitution abolished trial by jury, which it actually protected in some cases "and takes . . .
away in none." It was "absurd" to construe the silence of either the state or
proposed federal Constitution on rights as an extinction of them, since "silence and blank paper neither grant nor take away anything." As for a bill of

rights, the New York constitution also included none. The traditional function of bills of rights, to mark the limits of a king's prerogative, made them irrelevant in republics, where the people ruled. "The Constitution," he said, "only serves to point out that part of the people's business, which they think proper by it to refer to the management of the persons therein designated" and who were to exercise the powers they received "not for themselves . . . but as agents and overseers for the people to whom they are constantly responsible, and by whom only they are to be appointed."[66]

Jay was halfway into the *Address* before he came to his main argument, one peculiarly appropriate to New York voters in the spring of 1788. "Let it be admitted" that the Constitution, "like every thing else devised by man," had imperfections. It then became a question "of great moment . . . whether the probability of our being able seasonably to obtain a better, is such as to render it prudent and adviseable to reject this, and run the risque." Jay's *Address* discussed that issue through three subsidiary questions: Was it probable that a better constitution could be devised? If so, was that likely to happen within a reasonable time? And "what would be our situation if after rejecting this, all our efforts to obtain a better should prove fruitless?"[67]

If the Constitution were rejected, some critics (like "Centinel" and "A Columbian Patriot") argued that a second federal convention, informed by the extensive public debate over the proposed Constitution, would design a better plan of government. Jay acknowledged that "this reasoning is fair, and as far as it goes has weight," but he questioned whether a second convention, although better informed, would be as "*disposed to agree*" as the first, which was characterized by a distinctive spirit of candor, mutual respect, and accommodation. That seemed improbable since "we have unhappily become divided into parties," which were likely to send their most extreme members to another federal convention. The fact that several states had ratified the Constitution of 1787 and were "content with it as it is" would also complicate the work of another convention, as would the supposed determination of "a sect of politicians" to divide the United States into two or three separate confederacies. ("Publius" had also raised that threat, which "Centinel" dismissed as a "chimera" of his own creation.) Moreover, foreign countries would try to influence a new convention. In short, "new divisions, new parties, and new distractions" made it unlikely that another convention would be able to agree on a better plan of government or, with reasonable unanimity, on any plan at all.[68]

The design and ratification of an alternative constitution would take time, which itself had a cost when "our affairs are going on from bad to worse, and . . . our distresses are accumulating like compound interest." And what if the new convention could come to no agreement? The Confederation would probably not survive, so "every band of Union would be severed." Each state would become "a little nation, jealous of its neighbours, and anxious to strengthen itself by foreign alliances, against its former friends." In that situation, New York had a lot to lose. It was surrounded by states that had adopted the Constitution and thought New York's opposition to it came from a desire to keep the proceeds of its impost. "They cannot, they will not love you." Vermont would combine with others against New York, and the people of Long Island, "whom you cannot protect," would resent their exposure to "the depredations of every invader." Was the risk worth taking? Any problems that proved serious in practice once the Constitution was put into effect could be fixed through constitutional amendments.[69]

Suppose, finally, that New York rejected the Constitution, but nine other states ratified it. "Would you not in that case be obliged either to separate from the Union" and suffer all the problems Jay mentioned, "or rescind your dissent"? The path of wisdom was clear. The people of America—and especially of New York—should take "the safe and easy path of Union," continue to act as "a *Band of Brothers*" with "confidence in themselves and in one another," give the proposed Constitution "a fair trial, and to mend it as time, occasion and experience may dictate." If the American union dissolved in "licentiousness, disorder and confusion," men everywhere would look with suspicion on republican forms of government and prefer others that, "though less friendly to liberty, afford more peace and security."[70] In short, the state's decision would have serious implications for the future of not only New Yorkers, but mankind.

———

Federalists understood that Jay's pamphlet was a winner and quickly moved to get it out to voters. On April 23, Robert R. Livingston sent copies to his estate in Columbia County "to distribute . . . as soon as possible." The pamphlet circulated freely in Dutchess and Suffolk counties, where it seems to have had an impact on voters, and presumably elsewhere. In New York City, where the Federalist cause was in no trouble, a correspondent reported on April 27 that "a small Pamphlet written by John Jay . . . has had a most astonishing influence in converting Antifederalists, to a knowledge and belief that the New Constitution was their only political Salvation."[71]

Although the *Address* was republished in other states, particularly those whose decisions had not yet been made, there were few rejoinders.[72] That was perhaps because it was so clearly meant to influence the New York electorate and appeared only two weeks before New York voted. In fact, the one direct response came in a quickly composed postscript to another *Address to the People of the State of New-York*, this one signed "A Plebeian," a pseudonym that made clear that the author did not identify with the state's "better sort." That pamphlet of twenty-six pages was already in print when Jay's *Address* appeared and was published two days later, on April 17, when the elections were still twelve days off. The author was probably Melancton Smith, who may also have written the letters of the "Federal Farmer" and, in the opinion of at least one modern scholar, the newspaper essays signed "Brutus." The arguments of "A Plebeian" were closer to those of the "Federal Farmer" and to those Smith would later make at the New York ratifying convention than to those of "Brutus." More to the point, both the postscript of the pamphlet signed "A Plebeian" and the main body of its argument, which had been composed before the author saw Jay's *Address*, answered several parts of Jay's argument.[73]

Since everyone, including Federalists, agreed that the Constitution was imperfect, "A Plebeian" said its flaws should be repaired before it was ratified. And there was plenty of time for that. The nation was in no dire crisis, as Federalists such as Jay insisted. Sure, there were problems, as there always were after a long, expensive war, but the United States was "at peace with all the world" and its internal situation was no worse than it had been for several years past. The public debt had actually been reduced, and the sale of western lands, which were finally being brought to market, would reduce it more. The notion that states might go to war with each other was "abhorrent to the principles and feelings of almost every man of every rank in the union"—and that of one or more states attacking another "more extravagant still." That wasn't to say the current political system was without problems: "A Plebeian" agreed that the Confederation in its current form was inadequate. Nor was he against adopting the Constitution if its most serious problems were repaired first, which was "consistent with our ideas of prudence in the ordinary concerns of life." Changes would also be easier to get before the ambitious Federalists held the federal offices they sought and opposed efforts to curb their power. Now, before the Constitution was ratified, such men were more likely to give in to the popular will rather than see the Constitution and their dreams go down together.[74]

Federalists said the Constitution's critics did not agree on which amendments were necessary. If so, "A Plebeian" said, that would be as much a problem after the Constitution was ratified as before. More important, the assertion was untrue. There was "a remarkable uniformity in the objections made to the constitution, on the most important points." The "opposers" wanted a statement that the government's powers were confined to those expressly granted; a fuller representation of the people in Congress; and restrictions on Congress's "unlimited power of taxation," its power to create a "standing army," and its capacity to overrule state provisions for congressional elections. They also agreed on the need to impose some limits on federal court jurisdiction, to secure trial by jury in civil cases, and to repair the unhealthy confusion of judicial, executive, and legislative powers in the Senate. They disagreed only over "matters of small importance." "A Plebeian" suggested that differences among the Constitution's "principal advocates" were greater than those among its critics with regard to what amendments were necessary.[75]

Nor was he concerned about the previous ratification of the Constitution by six states or the likelihood that nine would ultimately ratify it. He saw every reason to think those states—apparently on New York's insistence—would readily reconsider the subject. The strong majorities on behalf of ratification in New Jersey and Connecticut were based on a vast overestimate of the amount of revenue New York got from its impost. Their estimates were as high as £80,000 lawful money, and some said New Jersey paid a third of that sum and Connecticut another third, all of which went for the use of New York alone. In fact, the impost revenue for the past two years did not exceed £50,000, and New York had paid that amount "and more" to the federal treasury while the complaining states paid nothing. The expectation of lower taxes under the Constitution in New Jersey and Connecticut was therefore a "mere delusion." When that became clear, those states too would advocate amendments. In fact, the glittering promises of the Federalists would lead only to disappointment and higher taxes. How could it be otherwise given the hordes of new federal officers and the cost of a new federal city?[76]

The pamphlet's postscript took issue with Jay's argument that the Constitution's silence posed no threat to liberty of the press, which remained at risk given the "indefinite powers" granted to the government. The Constitution not only left trial by jury in civil cases to the discretion of Congress, but directly threatened the role of juries by giving federal courts appellate jurisdiction over both law and fact. "A Plebeian" also questioned Jay's euphoric description of the Constitution's framers. It would not be hard, he suggested, to assemble twenty assemblies of men "equally respectable" for their "ability, integrity, and patriotism." He revered some members of the federal Convention, but regarded others as "of small consequence" and "a number" were suspected "of notorious peculation and fraud, with regard to public property in the hour of our distress." The Constitution should be judged "on its own merits," he said. "If it be good, it stands not in need of great men's names to support it. If it be bad, their names ought not to sanction it."[77]

THE VOTE

There is no evidence the Federal Republican Committee shipped out bundles of "A Plebeian" for distribution, although the pamphlet did apparently circulate through Suffolk County, and about half of it was reprinted upstate in the *American Herald*. Clearly, however, New York's voters were able to know and evaluate the alternative arguments on ratification before April 29, when they began casting their written ballots for convention delegates. Then the state settled down to a relative quiet for four weeks. Hamilton, who finally found time to answer his mail, was anything but confident about the outcome. "In this state, so far as we can judge," he wrote Gouverneur Morris on May 19, "the elections have gone wrong."[78]

Finally, in late May, the ballots were counted. Thanks to the advanced partisan politics of New York, the results had none of the ambiguity so pronounced in preconvention Massachusetts and even in Virginia. They were precise and unambiguous. The Antifederalists had won forty-six seats, the Federalists nineteen. No county split its delegation: The delegations were entirely Federalist or Antifederalist/Republican. All of the Federalists' delegates came from four counties—New York, Kings, Richmond, and Westchester, on the east bank of the Hudson north of New York City. The Antifederalists, however, took all the counties north and west of Westchester, as well as Queens and Suffolk Counties on Long Island.[79]

Because the election of convention delegates was on the basis of adult white manhood suffrage, it brought out a substantial number of voters who lacked the property required to vote for members of the lower house of the legislature. In heavily tenanted Albany County, 7,300 voters cast ballots for convention delegates, roughly half again as many as the 4,900 who voted for assemblymen. There, as in other Hudson Valley counties and in parts of Long Island, the Antifederalist vote depended primarily on small, independent farmers. In New York City, almost twice as many people voted for convention members as voted for assemblymen. There the new voters—unpropertied workers of one sort or another—voted Federalist. And the Federalist ticket in New York City included a heavy concentration of men who by birth or marriage were tied to the state's landed gentry: Hamilton, James Duane, John Jay, and Robert R. Livingston. In 1788 every great Hudson Valley family would have one or more Federalist delegates at the ratifying convention, but most of those men were chosen by New York City and County, the remainder by Westchester County.[80]

As in Virginia, both sides would have formidable spokesmen at the ratifying convention. Governor Clinton would be there. He was no orator, but Melancton Smith, a delegate from Dutchess County, could fill in on that score. All of the state's delegates to the federal Convention were in attendance: state supreme court justice Robert Yates and Albany mayor John Lansing, Jr., both of whom opposed ratification of the Constitution as it stood, and, on the other side, Alexander Hamilton. John Jay received Congress's permission to be excused from his duties as secretary of foreign affairs to attend the ratifying convention as a delegate. Chancellor Robert R. Livingston, whose position as head of the state's court of chancery made him one of New York's highest-ranking officials, would attend along with another state supreme court chief justice, Richard Morris; an associate justice, John Sloss Hobart, and eleven past or present members of the Confederation Congress.

Like many other state legislators, Jonathan Havens and John Smith, members of the state assembly from Suffolk County, would also be delegates. Havens once said he cared "not a fig" about going to the convention, but he dreaded the "ridicule" he and Smith would suffer for being left off the Federalist ticket because they were thought to be "antifederalists." Smith and Havens got the last laugh by being elected—on an "anti" ticket.[81]

HOPES AND STRATEGIES

If the numbers were against them, the timing of the convention gave New York Federalists some hope. News had arrived in early May that Maryland ratified the Constitution. A month later, New Yorkers learned that South Carolina had also ratified. That made eight states. If Federalist delegates could drag out the convention debates until news that New Hampshire or Virginia had ratified, that would tip the odds in their favor. After all, once nine states had ratified, the Constitution would go into effect among the ratifying states. New York's only decision would be whether or not to remain within the union.

Or so it seemed to Federalist strategists. In early June, Alexander Hamilton and Rufus King arranged for an express rider to bring news of New Hampshire's final vote to Springfield, Massachusetts, where another rider—appointed by Henry Knox—would carry the information to Hamilton at the New York convention in Poughkeepsie. Hamilton and King would pay the cost. Hamilton had already made a similar arrangement with Madison to assure that he received word of any "*decisive*" and "favourable" action in Richmond as quickly as possible. "Our only chances," he said, lie in a previous ratification by nine states, which might "shake the firmness" of Governor Clinton's followers, "and a change in the sentiments of the people which have been for some time travelling toward the Constitution." As a French observer reported, the "partisans of the new Government" were "left with no other expedient than to draw out the deliberations until the moment when the sentiments of Virginia is known, which, if favorable," could make their opponents shrink from the possibility of leaving the Union along with Rhode Island, "which is generally despised."[82]

There was from the beginning reason to question whether the strategy would work. "A Plebeian," after all, said it didn't matter what other states did; New Yorkers had to think for themselves. The probable author of the "Plebeian" pamphlet, Melancton Smith, would be a leader of the Antifederal/Republican convention delegates. Hamilton himself reported that "the language of the Antifederalists is that if all the other states adopt, New York ought still to hold out." He added that he had "the most direct intelligence," received in a way that "forbids a public use being made of it, that Clinton has in several conversations declared his opinion of the *inutility* of the UNION."[83] If so, Clinton and his "party" might just shrug off news that New Hampshire or Virginia had ratified. In that case, Federalists could only hope that the convention would vote to adjourn rather than reject the Constitution.[84] An adjournment would, however, keep New York out of the union as effectively as a vote against ratification. Moreover, unless the state's political climate changed dramatically, another meeting of the convention was as unlikely as the first to ratify the Constitution "as it now stands."

Federalists would not control the Poughkeepsie convention. Power lay clearly with their opponents, which made the New York convention unique at that point in the ratification process. John Jay suspected that the leaders of the opposition wanted to reject the Constitution "with as little Debate and as much Speed as may be"—a strategy like that of the majority in the Maryland convention, but for the opposite outcome. Jay, however, questioned how much the "principal Leaders" of the majority controlled the rank and file. Many members of the opposition, Jay said, were, unlike their leaders, "Friends to Union and mean well"; and despite the published election results, it was by no means clear that the Antifederalist delegates were all "equally decided, or rather equally desperate." Moreover, "an Idea has taken Air," Jay wrote Washington, that "the Southern part of the State will at all Events adhere to the Union, and if necessary to that End seek a Separation from the northern." And that "idea," he added, "has Influence on the Fears of the Party," although in general he thought the opposition had failed to consider the "contingent Events" should New York vote down the Constitution. Those considerations, however, didn't make Jay an optimist. As he hurried to finish leftover business matters before leaving New York for Poughkeepsie, he wrote Jefferson that there was reason to think that a majority of the convention was "decidedly opposed to the Constitution," and it remained uncertain whether they would reject it or "adjourn and postpone a Decision."[85]

For the moment, however, members of the opposition seemed of one mind. Perhaps some—as one of the Albany Anti-Federal Committee's circulars suggested—would have preferred simply to keep the old Confederation. If so, they seemed to understand that there was no hope of that anymore and concentrated on repairing the problems with the new Constitution before ratifying it. Even Abraham Yates, Jr., as dogged an Antifederalist as any, was talking about previous amendments rather than simply rejecting the Constitution. Yates had championed the fight against the federal impost of 1783 in New York, and then, writing as "Sydney," he argued that the Constitution was the result of a longstanding plot to destroy the Confederation and establish a government that would absorb all the powers of the states. By late May, however, he was urging Antifederalist delegates who were in New

York City to prepare amendments for use at the ratifying convention. A correspondent in Albany, Abraham G. Lansing, promised to urge his brother, convention delegate John Lansing, Jr., to do the same. He also suggested that news of the New York elections might invigorate what he called the "Republicans" in New Hampshire. On April 6, in something of a countermeasure to Hamilton's express system, the Federal Republican Committee of New York sent news of the Antifederalist/Republican victory in New York's election to its counterparts in other state conventions and renewed its effort at coordinating their attempts to obtain amendments.[86]

On June 15, when Governor Clinton and "a number of the anti-Members of the Convention" quietly set out from Manhattan for Poughkeepsie on a Hudson River sloop, Yates reported that they carried "the Notes for Amendments." He added that the group was determined not to adopt the Constitution without previous amendments "tho all the others Should." The same day Lansing reported from Albany that all the persons with whom he spoke thought "that the Constitution will be effectually amended previous to its adoption—or that it will be Totally rejected."[87] Nowhere had the Constitution faced worse odds against ratification "as it now stands" than it would face at the New York convention in Poughkeepsie.

TWELVE

★

The New York Convention I

A Failure of Oratory

The New York ratifying convention would meet, like Virginia's, away from the Federalist Atlantic coast. Poughkeepsie was in Antifederalist Ulster County, about a mile east of the Hudson River, the "highway" on which many delegates traveled, and almost halfway between New York City and Albany. The state legislature occasionally met in Poughkeepsie, which had about 2,500 residents (including 199 slaves), a couple of churches (Presbyterian and Episcopal), an academy, and a newspaper, the *Country Journal*, published by Nicholas Power. Although Power's sympathies were Federalist, he readily printed criticisms of the Constitution. His was the only newspaper in the country that published, piece by piece, the entire *Letters from the Federal Farmer to the Republican*.[1]

Those considerations made the town a convenient and admirably neutral site for the Antifederalist/Republican majority. There was no Federalist mob in Poughkeepsie, as in Philadelphia, and no wealthy Federalist grandees to woo delegates with their hospitality, as in Charleston. Nor were the hundred or two hundred spectators who crowded into the courthouse to hear the state's "first geniuses" all on one side. They seem to have taken pleasure in the arguments and performances of speakers in both parties indiscriminately.[2]

As in some other conventions, only a handful of delegates—six on one side, seven on the other—spoke during the debates, and an even smaller group did most of the talking. Melancton Smith, the lawyer, merchant, congressman, and pamphleteer who represented Dutchess County, and the Albany lawyer John Lansing, Jr., one of the two New York delegates who had left the federal Convention early, were the lead speakers for the majority. The fiery, dapper, thirty-three-year-old Alexander Hamilton and the tall, elegant, forty-one-year-old Chancellor Robert R. Livingston, from one of

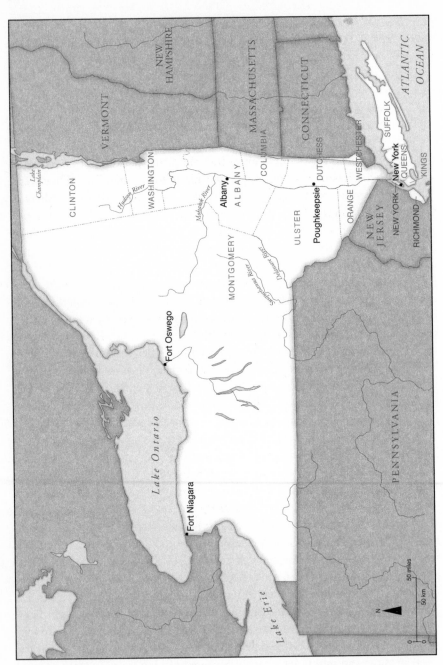

New York, 1788

New York's elite landed families, carried the burden for the Federalist minority. Both were dazzling orators. Even Smith conceded that the Federalists had "the advantage of Abilities and habit of public Speaking."[3]

Differences in speaking style were as striking as those in politics. Hamilton's passionate oratory delighted his supporters, but sometimes confirmed his opponents' suspicions and fears. He could also run on at length while off the subject. Livingston, a graduate (like Hamilton) of King's College (now Columbia) and a lawyer who had served as the Confederation's first secretary for foreign affairs, was a fluent and often eloquent speaker, but he indulged in bursts of sarcasm that, again, pleased his fellow Federalists. They were, however, more likely to alienate than convert the rank-and-file members of the majority, the middle-class yeoman farmers Clinton would later describe as "men of sound Judgment" who were "not used to public speaking."[4] John Jay, another graduate of King's College and about a year older than Livingston, was tall, thin, and pale, with fierce convictions hidden behind a gentle exterior. He was a less polished speaker and far more conciliatory than Hamilton and Livingston. By the end of the convention he would come into his own, but he spoke only rarely in the convention's opening weeks.

Smith, the most active speaker for the Antifederalist/Republican side, lacked the oratorical skills of the two leading Federalists. He was a plain man and plainspoken, forty-four years old, from an undistinguished family, and not particularly handsome, with a thick neck and unruly hair. His speeches were focused, consistent, sometimes eloquent; they alienated nobody and won the admiration even of some opponents. One Federalist called him a "good and able man" and a "true republican"; another, the future chancellor James Kent, described Smith as "a man of remarkable simplicity, and of the most gentle, liberal, and amiable disposition."[5]

John Lansing, Jr., a tall, dignified man with dark, well-disciplined hair, seemed less likely to hold his own with the Federalist "Ciceros." His federal Convention colleague William Pierce said he had "a hesitation in his speech, that will prevent his being an Orator of any eminence." Although Lansing was mayor of Albany and a practicing attorney, Pierce heard that his knowledge of the law was "not extensive, nor his education a good one." With more authority, Pierce described Lansing as "a Man of good sense, plain in his manners, and sincere in his friendships," which underscored some similarities with Smith. He had been General Philip Schuyler's military secretary early in the war, served several terms in the New York legislature (he was speaker of the assembly twice), and represented his state in Congress. Pierce estimated that Lansing was "about thirty-two years of age," which was a couple of years off: He was born in 1754, ten years after Melancton Smith, with whom he worked closely in the opening stages of the Poughkeepsie convention. By its end, Lansing would play a more independent and forceful role than anyone could have predicted on the basis of Pierce's description. He was "often upon the floor," the Poughkeepsie *Country Journal* reported, and was "heard with attention."[6]

Most of the convention's debates on the Constitution occurred in the first two weeks of the five to six weeks it met. Then, at a point where Federalists thought a decision to ratify would be possible and even likely, the convention moved into a new, uncharted stage whose outcome was anything but clear. Oratory and argument seemed to have accomplished little except to fill time while entertaining some spectators and alienating others. If anything, the ratifying convention seemed further from a decision than at its opening.

SETTING THE RULES

Some 53 of the 65 delegates were present in Poughkeepsie's Dutch-style, two-story stone courthouse at noon on June 17, when the convention first met. The Antifederalist/Republicans arrived promptly: They understood that decisions made in the opening sessions of a convention could affect its outcome. The convention unanimously chose Governor George Clinton as its president, perhaps, as John Lansing suggested, because the Federalists understood there was no hope in opposing him. Then it went on to choose its secretaries, doorkeeper, and messenger, and to appoint Nicholas Power as its official printer. Before adjourning for the day, the convention also decided without apparent controversy to open every day with a prayer, and it chose a committee of five, three "Antis" and two Federalists, to propose rules and regulations for the convention.[7]

The rules committee worked quickly. The next morning the convention began going over its report, paragraph by paragraph, occasionally making changes as it went along. In the end, most of the rules it adopted were standard. At the start of each day, the convention would read and correct the minutes of the previous day; motions (except to adjourn) had to be made in writing and addressed, while standing, to the president; "yea"s and "nay"s would be recorded when requested by two members; the president would decide disputes over who had the right to speak; committee members would be chosen by ballot. The rules also specified "that no member be referred to by name in any debate." Speakers referred to one another as "the gentleman," sometimes adding the constituency for which he sat, saying, for example, "the gentleman from Orange."[8]

More striking, the list ended by specifying "that the preceding rules shall be observed when the Convention resolve itself into a committee of the whole." That was important since later that day (June 18), after hearing the documents issued by the federal Convention and Congress's resolution of the previous September read aloud and ordering copies printed for the use of delegates, the convention resolved to open its debates the next day as a committee of the whole. Federalists wanted Chief Justice Richard Morris to preside over the committee, but the majority insisted that Henry Oothoudt, an Antifederalist delegate from Albany County, have that position. The minority yielded; Oothoudt was elected "without opposition." Finally, the convention voted that its secretaries deliver a copy of the journal for printing every day. That way no surprising omissions would be discovered when it was too late to do anything about them.[9]

Although Lansing formally moved that the delegates discuss the Constitution as a committee of the whole, his colleague Robert Yates said the idea originally came from the Federalists. That made sense: The Federalists wanted to delay the proceedings in the hope of glad tidings from New Hampshire or Virginia. The majority agreed, Yates explained, "to prevent the Opposition [the Federalists] from charging us with Precipitation"—that is, to avoid the sin the Federalist majority had committed in the Pennsylvania ratifying convention.[10]

On the next day, June 19, Chancellor Livingston opened the debates of the committee of the whole with some "general observations." He stressed the historic importance of the occasion and the necessity of union, above all for the state of New York. Livingston also described the defects of the Confederation in an effort to prevent the delegates from considering reform of the Confederation a viable plan for the future. They should focus their attention on the Constitution, which he urged them to consider carefully and with open minds. "Many of us, Sir," he said, facing Clinton, "are officers of government, many of us have seats in the Senate and Assembly" and "may be unwilling to sacrifice any portion of the power of the State." But on this "solemn occasion," he urged, "let us consider ourselves as simple citizens assembled to consult on measures . . . to promote the happiness of our fellow citizens."[11]

Livingston then moved that the committee of the whole take no vote until it had gone through the entire Constitution, clause by clause. Elsewhere Federalists adopted that strategy in an effort to avoid amendments. At Poughkeepsie, however, the Antifederalist majority agreed only on the condition that delegates could propose amendments, although, again, no votes would be taken on those amendments until the committee had gone through the entire Constitution. "Fully relying on the Steadiness of our Friends," Robert Yates said, "we see no Danger in this Mode."[12]

Not every "Anti" was so sanguine. Abraham G. Lansing, after receiving the convention's news from his brother John, feared that an extended discussion of the Constitution, paragraph by paragraph (and, as it turned out, amendment by amendment), would disappoint country members for whom early summer was "the Busy Season." Unless the issue was decided quickly, he feared, those delegates would go home to their farms, reducing the Antifederalist/Republican majority. Delay would also give the Federalists more time to "operate upon the Hopes and Fears of some." The outcome in Massachusetts, he said, "has shewn us what Federal Chicanery can Effect." His words echoed those of his brother, who also anticipated "some Injury from a long Delay by diminishing our Numbers and perhaps from [Federalist] Operations on the Hopes or Fears of a few."[13]

In short, the majority leaders' agreement to discuss the Constitution at length in a committee of the whole would test its capacity to hold their followers together over an extended period of time. It meant they would not use their strong majority to vote down the Constitution quickly and without debate, following the example of Maryland's Federalist majority but to reject, not ratify, the Constitution. If, however, New York's Antifederalist/Republican majority wanted not to reject the Constitution but to ratify it with amendments, as the evidence suggests—including the appointment by Antifederalist/Republican delegates of a committee to correspond with members of other state conventions who also favored amending the Constitution—the process fit its purposes well. The formulation of amendments, to say nothing of coordinating action with other states, would take time, but hopefully not so much that it would wear out the patience of "Anti" backbenchers.[14]

Since the rules of debate for the New York convention bound its committee of the whole, the committee's presiding officer would have more power than his counterparts at other state ratifying conventions. And since the New York convention held most of its deliberations as a committee of the whole, George Clinton could contribute to its debates, much as Edmund Pendleton, president of the Virginia convention, was able to speak at Richmond.

Unfortunately, holding its debates as a committee of the whole made the convention's official journal unusually uninformative and bizarrely repetitious. For day after day until late July, the journal says the same thing in almost the exact same words: "The order of the day being read, the Convention accordingly resolved itself into a committee of the whole. . . ." After "some time" the president—Clinton—resumed the chair, and "Mr Oothoudt reported, that the committee had made some progress, and had directed him to move for leave to sit again." After giving the committee of the whole permission to meet again, the convention would adjourn until ten o'clock the next morning except for a few days in early July, when it met at noon.[15]

Fortunately, Francis Childs, publisher of New York's *Daily Advertiser*, went to Poughkeepsie to take shorthand notes of the debates, which he printed, day by day, in his newspaper, and later in book form.[16] Childs's record is best for the early weeks of the ratifying convention, when its debates were relatively conventional. The story thereafter has to be pieced together from newspaper accounts; the official journal for the convention's final days, after the committee of the whole had reported; the fragmentary notes kept by some delegates and by John McKesson, one of the convention's two secretaries, and private letters from delegates or their close political allies.[17] To reconstruct the complicated, dramatic development of the New York convention is like putting together a jigsaw puzzle with many pieces, not all of which fit together neatly.

A "SECOND EDITION OF PUBLIUS"

John Lansing answered Livingston's opening speech on Friday, June 20. Like many speakers on both sides, Lansing said that he, like Livingston, was committed to the union and agreed that the Confederation was flawed. However, like most critics of the Constitution, Lansing thought that power was more safely entrusted to the states than the central government because the states "will always possess a better representation of the feelings and interests of the people at large." Again, like several (but not all) critics of the Constitution, Lansing attributed the country's economic problems to Americans' penchant for buying luxury goods they could not pay for, not to flaws in the country's "system of Government." The Confederation could have been made adequate to the country's needs if it were simply amended to give it more power, including that of collecting taxes from individuals in states that failed to pay their congressional requisitions. Lansing, however, did not propose to stick with the Confederation. In keeping with the wishes of his constituents (and, it seemed, of most Antifederalist delegates), he promised to support amendments to the Constitution that would "lessen the danger of invasion of civil liberty by the general Government."[18]

Lansing attacked Livingston's suggestion that state officeholders in New York opposed the Constitution out of self-interest, which seemed especially disturbing from a man "distinguished for his liberal turn of thinking" who held "one of the most lucrative offices of the state." Were New York officeholders "warped by apprehensions of loss" more than their counterparts in neighboring states, who were "among the warmest advocates of the new system"? New York officials were "perhaps more divided in sentiment than any other class of men whatsoever," Lansing said, not grouped together on one side.[19]

After a brief reply by Livingston, the delegates—on Melancton Smith's insistence—finally turned to the Constitution, starting with the first section of Article I. They raised no objections until the clerk read Article I, Section 2, paragraph 3, which brought Smith to his feet. To count three-fifths of a state's slave population in allocating seats in the House of Representatives was "absurd," he said; it would serve only to enhance the power of "persons who were so wicked as to keep slaves." Perhaps the provision was unavoidable "if we mean to be in union with the Southern states"—and Smith, like Lansing, insisted he was no less committed to union than Livingston so long as it was compatible with "the liberties of his country"—but it was "utterly repugnant to his feelings." Smith could not, however, make his peace with the next provision, which gave Congress control over the number of representatives so long as each state had at least one and the total did not "exceed one for every thirty Thousand." Even at that proportion, Smith said, the number of representatives would be incompetent for "the great purposes of representation." That failure was dangerous, since Congress's power "extended to every thing dear to human nature."[20]

Nowhere in the world through all of history were the people represented in government as fully as in the American states since the Revolution, Smith said, and the Constitution could move the country "a great way towards perfection" if the number of representatives in Congress were increased and its powers clearly "confined to great national objects." As a step in that direction, Smith proposed an amendment, the convention's first. It would fix the number of representatives at one for every twenty thousand inhabitants, "ascertained on the principles mentioned in the second section of the first article of the Constitution" (that is, the provision counting all free persons and three-fifths of a state's slaves would remain) until the number reached three hundred. After that, representatives would be apportioned among states relative to their population. Smith's amendment would also double the number of representatives in the first federal Congress.[21]

The next speaker, Alexander Hamilton, seemed at first to ignore Smith's amendment. His speech was long; witnesses said he spoke for as long as an hour and a half. It had obviously been prepared ahead of time (or, in the contemporary phrase, it "smelt of the lamp") to answer not Smith but Lansing's earlier suggestion that the Confederation with a few more powers could have solved the nation's problems. That was a common problem with the most carefully prepared convention speeches: When presented, they often seemed off the subject, or on a subject the delegates had left behind. Hamilton insisted that the Confederation was fundamentally defective because the laws of the union applied only to the states in their corporate capacities, not to individuals. That allowed "thirteen different bodies to judge of the measures of Congress" and decide whether to comply or to ignore them. Moreover, the same "false and impracticable principle ran through most of the ancient governments," including the Amphyctionic League, the Dutch republics, and the German confederacy. Hamilton went through those confederations one by one, sparing his audience a discussion of other examples although they would, he said, prove that the principle was destructive "even as far back as the Lycian and Achaean leagues."[22]

That history had been discussed before—in *The Federalist* among other places. That was why Governor Clinton wrote the next day that "the most that has been said by the new Government Men, has been only a second Edition of Publius, well delivered." Similarly, James Kent said Chancellor

Livingston's opening oration "only gave a summary of the arguments of Publius when treating . . . the defects of the confederation," and one that was "neither so perfect nor so instinctive by a vast difference as the Original."[23] What, then, was the point of these Federalist orations? Were the speakers repeating familiar arguments for the benefit of delegates who had never read "Publius"? Or were they just filling time until news from New Hampshire or Virginia arrived? Whatever their reasons, Melancton Smith was not impressed with the Federalist main guard. He later described Livingston as a "wretched reasoner, very frequently." Hamilton, he said, spoke "frequently, very long, and very vehemently," and, "like publius," had "much to say" that was "not very applicable to the subject" at hand.[24]

Halfway through the speech, Hamilton finally turned to "the question immediately before the committee." The country, he said, was divided into different "classes"—navigating and nonnavigating states, small and large ones—and any future convention, like the one in Philadelphia, would have to find ways to reconcile those competing interests. For that purpose he justified giving the South additional representation for its slave population: It would allow the South to protect its exports, which had benefits for the entire union. Moreover, since slaves would be considered in assessing taxes, it was only just that they be counted in allocating representatives. Hamilton also denied that the Constitution would allow Congress to reduce the number of representatives, as Smith claimed. The proportion of one representative for thirty thousand people was "fixed as the standard of increase" and would bring a steady increase in the size of the House of Representatives as the country's population grew. But how big was too big? The size of state legislatures varied widely and so gave no guidance. Since experience alone could decide the issue, it could be safely left "to the discretion of the legislature." He added that the size of the first Congress—that is, ninety-one members, with sixty-five in the House and twenty-six in the Senate—was "fully adequate to our present exigencies," but then he left off the subject because he felt "not a little exhausted."[25]

Discussion of representation continued another two days. Meanwhile, there was a lot of activity off the convention floor. Charles Tillinghast, the secretary of New York's Federal Republican Committee and John Lamb's son-in-law, reported that Livingston, Hamilton, and John Jay were "continually singling out the Members in Opposition" outside the courthouse. Jay, the most polite of the three, was also the most effective: His "manners and mode of address would probably do much mischief," Tillinghast said, "were the members not as firm as they are."[26] At about the same time, the "Republican Members" of the convention, as Clinton called them, appointed a "special Committee of Correspondence with the neighbouring Conventions" under the chairmanship of Judge Robert Yates.[27]

The public debates were, however, neither unimportant nor uninteresting. Since the delegates often discussed specific amendments offered by members of the majority, the debates did not always replay discussions of the Constitution in other state conventions or restate arguments already made in print. Moreover, since the critics of the Constitution were on the whole more able than those in Massachusetts and less given to oratorical excursions than in Virginia, the critical issues of representation and taxation, on which the New York debates focused, received a particularly thorough examination. Speakers also revealed attitudes that, for the Federalists at least, might have been better left unsaid.

REPRESENTATION

On Saturday, June 21, Melancton Smith opened one of the most probing examinations of the nature of representation in any state convention. Smith was not a man to waste time. He did not bother to answer Hamilton's defense of slave representation, though he thought it could be "easily refuted," because he considered that provision an unavoidable concession to the Southern states. He was, however, determined—as his amendment proposed—to increase the number of representatives and fix the rules for determining the future size of the House of Representatives, which, he said, should not be left to the discretion of Congress because it was "essential to liberty." He proceeded to explain why, which demanded describing the nature and function of representation in a republican government as he saw it.[28]

Representatives, Smith argued, should together be a microcosm of their constituents. They should "be a true picture of the people; possess the knowledge of their circumstances and their wants; sympathize in all their distresses, and be disposed to seek their true interests." That concrete knowledge of the people's needs and circumstances was better known by "men of the middling class of life . . . than those of a superior class" from which, he feared, the members of Congress would all be drawn. Smith described that "superior" or "first class in the community" as its "natural aristocracy," even though he knew his opponents would deny that any such class existed in the American republic. In every society, Smith explained, "birth, education, talents and wealth, create distinctions among men as visible and of as much influence as titles, stars and garters." Men so distinguished naturally command respect. They could also organize themselves more readily than the people at large. As a result, where the number of representatives was small and the districts large, elected offices would seldom go to substantial yeomen "of sense and discernment." A government controlled by the "few and great" would be, for the masses, "a government of oppression."[29]

Smith denied suggesting that "the great" lacked honesty or principles. All men hold the same passions and prejudices, but the circumstances of their lives "give a cast to the human character." Men in "middling circumstances" had fewer temptations and were less able to gratify those they had. As a result, they tended to be "more temperate, of better morals and less ambition than the great," who consider themselves above the common people, demand respect, and have many of the same feelings as hereditary aristocrats. "Will any one say," Smith asked, "that there does not exist in this country the pride of family, of wealth, of talents; and that they do not command influence and respect among the common people?" He did not propose to exclude such "natural aristocrats" from office, since "they would be more dangerous out of power than in it." Smith also conceded that they were more capable of grasping "extensive political and commercial information, such as is acquired by men of refined education." A government should be "so framed" to admit such men "together with a sufficient number of the middling class to controul them." He thought a representative body "composed principally of the respectable yeomanry"—like the ratifying convention—was "the best possible security to liberty" because the body of every nation consisted of that class, and when its interest was pursued "the public good is pursued."[30]

Smith's position was the direct opposite of James Madison's in the tenth number of *The Federalist*. Madison saw the threat of majoritarian tyranny in the direct representation of a community's various interests. He put his faith in a large republic and, by inference, large electoral districts because they would elect men of superior talents—Smith's "natural aristocrats"—"whose wisdom may best discern the true interest of their country" rather than yield to the "temporary or partial considerations" of the people. To Madison, rule by the talented, disinterested few was most likely to serve the public good. To Smith, the people themselves—that is, the mass of ordinary, middle-class Americans—were more likely to pursue the public good because they *were* the public, so whatever served their interests served the good of the public.[31]

In answering Smith, Hamilton did not, however, repeat what "Publius" had said. Instead he played the democrat. In some cases it might be "necessary and proper" for representatives to disregard the opinions of the majority, he said, but "in the general course of things," they would follow "popular views and even prejudices" because they were dependent upon the will of the people for their offices. In any case, it was "the true principle of a republic . . . that the people should choose whom they please to govern them." If the people chose to elect "their most meritorious men," should the Constitution oppose their wishes and "abridge their most valuable privilege?"[32] (Charles Tillinghast, in describing the day's debates for John Lamb, said, "You would be surprised . . . what an *amazing Republican* Hamilton wishes to make himself be considered—*But he is known*."[33])

Hamilton denied that all of a community's interests should be represented in the legislature. "No idea is more erroneous than this," he said. "Only such interests are proper to be represented, as are involved in the powers of the General Government," such as commerce, taxation, and the like; and they could be understood as well by five men as by fifty. Nor was the people's confidence in government dependent upon a "numerous representation." The Massachusetts legislature, he noted, had three hundred members, that of New York sixty-five. "Have the people in this state less confidence in their representation, than the people of that?"[34]

As Smith anticipated, Hamilton, whose closest associates were with New York's rich and well-born, denied the existence of an American aristocracy. "I hardly know the meaning of this word as it is applied," he said. For Smith, as Hamilton observed, in the writings of the "Federal Farmer" "every distinguished man is an aristocrat," which was "ridiculous." After denying the existence of such a class, Hamilton defended its morality. It was a "harsh doctrine," unjustified by experience, he said, "that men grow wicked in proportion as they improve and enlighten their minds." Rich and poor, learned and ignorant were distinguished by the kind rather than the quantity of their vices, "and here the advantage of character belongs to the wealthy," whose vices were "probably more favorable to the prosperity of the state, than those of the indigent; and partake less of moral depravity."[35]

Hamilton also argued, this time like "Publius," for large electoral districts rather than the small ones that Smith preferred, but because they were more difficult to corrupt. Nor was there any reason to fear infringements of the people's rights by the federal government because the state governments would stand guard on their behalf. A firm union was as necessary "to perpetuate our liberties, as it is to make us respectable," Hamilton said, and he predicted "that the national government will be as natural a guardian of our freedom, as the state legislatures themselves."[36]

Later in the day, Governor Clinton intervened, not as a partisan but for information that would help him decide "on which side of this important question truth rests." Since each state was small compared to the United States, he observed, the components of its economy were familiar in some degree to all members of its legislature. Representatives from a state's "minute districts" could provide information on the circumstances of their constituents, which helped prevent legislative errors. By contrast, members of Congress would be "totally unacquainted with the local circumstances of any particular state, which mark the proper objects of laws, and especially of taxation." A law suitable for Georgia might operate "most disadvantageously and cruelly" upon New York. Although those considerations inclined him to think the House of Representatives should be larger, Clinton said he was "open to conviction." If his objections were answered satisfactorily, he was ready to "acknowledge their weakness."[37]

In response, Hamilton repeated the stock Federalist argument that the powers of Congress extended only to the "aggregate interests of the Union," which did not require detailed knowledge of local circumstances throughout the nation. He conceded (and the concession was critical) that the argument for a larger representation was "most plausibly used" with regard to taxation, particularly the levying of direct taxes. But the United States was not as diverse as Clinton suggested; the interests and manners of Americans were as alike as those in any European nation. He added that the differences among Americans were a "favorite theme" with those who argued that no general government was possible, and "who are disposed for a division of our empire."[38]

In short, Hamilton answered Clinton's gentlemanly request for information with an accusation of disloyalty to the union, which was consistent with charges that Hamilton had made against the governor in private correspondence.[39] Clinton emphatically denied the charge: "The dissolution of the Union is, of all events, the remotest from my wishes," he said. "That gentleman"—Hamilton—"may wish for a consolidation—I wish for a federal republic. The object of both of us is a firm energetic government: and we may both have the good of our country in view" and disagree only "as to the means of procuring it."[40]

The highlight of the remaining debates on Article I, Section 2, was a sarcastic attack on Smith by Robert Livingston. In his person and his family, Livingston embodied New York's landed aristocracy, but he dismissed Smith's "recourse to the phantom aristocracy" as the "bugbear of party." Who, he asked in a torrent of words that held the audience transfixed, would Smith have as representatives? Not the rich, the learned, the wise, the virtuous, "for they are all aristocrats. Who then? Why, those who are not virtuous; those who are not wise; those who are not learned." He "must go out into the highways, and pick up the rogue and the robber," to the "hedges and ditches and bring in the poor, the blind and the lame." Livingston apparently mesmerized the audience with his theatrical performance. But even a sympathetic newspaper reported that Livingston's version of Smith's position was "more *fanciful* than *solid*." Smith protested that Livingston distorted and then made fun of his arguments rather than answer them, and "to irritate is not the way to conciliate."[41]

The Federalist conciliator was John Jay, who spoke against Smith's amendment. In marked contrast to Livingston, Jay stopped in the course of his speech to ask Smith if he had described his position accurately. Jay said that he, like Smith, favored "large representations" of the people, but there was so much disagreement on how large the House of Representatives should be—Massachusetts said two hundred members, Smith three hundred—that he thought it best to leave the Constitution unchanged, confident that in time representation would increase enough "to answer the wishes of the most zealous advocates for liberty." His speech was brief (it took only fifteen minutes), his position reasonable, his demeanor courteous. The *Daily Advertiser* noted that Jay had none of the attributes of a polished orator, "yet none who hear but are pleased with him, and captivated beyond expression."[42]

On June 24, the committee finally turned to Article I, Section 3, on the Senate, which Gilbert Livingston, an Antifederalist lawyer from Dutchess County who came from an undistinguished branch of the Livingston family,[43] described as a "dangerous body" with judicial, executive, and legislative powers. He had an unfortunate penchant for overstatement: The delegates let out a "great laugh" after he described a future scene in which senators, elected for life, luxuriated in the new federal capital, cut off from the people by "an impenetrable wall" of gold and "adamant" (which turned out to mean diamonds), as the wealth of the country flowed in. The speaker sounded over the top, but he was dead serious. He proposed an amendment—the second to date—that would limit senators' service to six years in any twelve and give state legislatures the power to recall and replace senators before their terms of office had expired.[44]

Robert R. Livingston could not contain himself. Rotation in office was "an absurd species of ostracism—a mode of proscribing eminent merit, and banishing from stations of trust those who have filled them with the greatest faithfulness." Like Hamilton, he played the democrat: The people, he said, were the best judges of who should represent them, and mandatory rotation in office was "an absolute abridgement of the people's rights."[45] On the other hand, Livingston had no fondness for popularly controlled state legislatures. Recall, he said, would subject senators "to all the caprices, the parties, the narrow views and illiberal politics of the state governments."[46] The next speaker, Federalist Richard Morris, also referred to "the contracted views and prevailing factions of the state governments."[47] That was unlikely to calm delegates who believed, like Lansing, that the people's interests and feelings were best represented in the state legislatures, were often legislators themselves, and feared for the states' future under the Constitution. Livingston's and Morris's comments also undermined Hamilton's earlier effort to portray the state legislatures as "the most powerful obstacle to the members of Congress betraying the interests of their constituents." The legislatures, he said, were "standing bodies of observation, possessing the confidence of the people, jealous of federal encroachments, and armed with every power to check the first essays of treachery."[48]

Hamilton, who couldn't play the democrat forever, soon revealed his reservations about the capacities of the people and their elected representatives. The body of the people wants the country to prosper, he said, but lacks "the discernment and stability necessary for systematic government" and was "frequently led into the grossest errors by misinformation and passion." Since representatives reflected their constituents, there had to be in every republic "some permanent body to correct the prejudices, check the intemperate passions, and regulate the fluctuations of a popular assembly." The federal Convention had created the Senate for that purpose. But the proposed amendment would take away the Senate's stability, permanency, and independence by putting its members under the control of state legislatures and making them "subject to the same weakness and prejudices" that the Senate was "instituted to correct."[49]

John Lansing said Hamilton's fears were exaggerated (a claim the Federalists more often made about the "Antis"). The proposed amendment would only give the states "a constitutional and peaceable mode of checking maladministration by recalling their senators" and so not force the people "into hostilities" to get redress. The states enjoyed the power of recall under the Confederation but had never once used it. Powers rarely or never invoked could hardly have the devastating effects Hamilton anticipated.[50]

Similarly, Melancton Smith predicted that the power of recall would be used only for "notoriously wicked" conduct, and probably not as often as it ought to be. Since senators represented the state legislatures, it was "reasonable that they should be under their controul." The proposed amendment would not rob the Senate of the stability it needed but put it in a "proper medium between a fluctuating and a perpetual body." It was inconsistent with republican principles for the Senate to be "a fixed and unchangeable body of men," which was likely to happen if its members could serve indefinitely. Smith went on to defend state legislators, who, he said, did not act on impulse or passion like "the multitude," and rarely made decisions "hastily and without consideration." Hamilton's effort to sever the close connection between the state legislatures and the Senate would "root out the last vestige of state sovereignty" in the proposed Constitution.[51]

The sparring over the relationship between the Senate and the state legislatures went on for several days. Speaker after speaker acknowledged that the contenders agreed on many things: the need for a stronger national government, the inadequacy of the Confederation, the wisdom of a bicameral legislature. They expressed radically different attitudes toward state legislatures, but both majority and minority spokesmen said that the states would and should remain a part of American government under the Constitution. Hamilton, however, feared that the central government would be too dependent on the state legislatures and that the states, "with every power in their hands," would encroach on national authority "till the union is weakened and dissolved." Lansing thought that improbable since the new central government would have an army and "unlimited power of taxation." The states would soon be found "unnecessary and useless, and would be gradually extinguished." How long, Smith asked, would the people be willing to pay thousands of state legislators who met once a year only to make laws regulating the height of fences or repairing roads? They would say, "We had better get rid of the useless burthen." And then, without the states to intervene on their behalf, the people would lose their liberties and be reduced from citizens to subjects. Like Mason in Virginia, Smith wanted to define the line between state and national powers so clearly that there would be "no room for jealous apprehensions or violent contests."[52] The committee had, however, not yet reached Article I, Section 8, on the powers of Congress.

The delegates were moving through the Constitution very slowly because the issues were complex, and also because the committee of the whole met only four hours a day, between ten and two. (Later in June, they would add another session to their days.) But were the debates accomplishing anything? The Federalists took great pride in their debating skills, but in early July Hamilton wrote Madison that "our arguments confound, but do not convince." He was half right. The Federalists were not winning converts; on that Jay confirmed Hamilton's judgment.[53] But they were hardly confounding their opponents. Smith and Lansing held up their end of the arguments very well; nobody in New York claimed, like the Federalists in Massachusetts, that the Constitution's supporters were arguing circles around its critics.

Jay, who was no orator but took a moderate stand and showed respect for his opponents, seems to have been more effective both off the convention floor and on it, though he seldom spoke in the convention's opening weeks. Hamilton's and Livingston's "well delivered" speeches with their denigrating comments on the people and their legislators and, above all, Livingston's clever but blatantly unfair dismissal of Smith's "natural aristocracy" probably scored few points with the bulk of the Antifederalist/Republican delegates. Those small, independent farmers were no strangers to the manor system of the Hudson Valley, and they knew what aristocracy meant in a practical sense. Before 1776 they had themselves lived under the domination of New York's landed gentry either politically or, sometimes, more immediately, and they did not want to see the clock turned back. Denials that such a thing as aristocracy existed by the likes of Robert R. Livingston could not fool them. Nor did Hamilton's and Livingston's efforts to play the democrat mislead anyone. Their own words betrayed them.

Later, when the convention was nearing its end, DeWitt Clinton observed in his journal that Livingston's "ridicule and terror" did "more harm than Good to the feds. I like to hear him speak," he added; "he does it so impolitically."[54] That observation was even more apt in the convention's opening weeks, when oratory, the Federalists' pride, proved a positive disadvantage to their cause. Perhaps they were not seriously trying to convert delegates by their arguments, like their colleagues in the Massachusetts ratifying convention. Instead they may have been talking to keep the convention going until news arrived that would make a vote to ratify the Constitution unavoidable. If so, they were about to suffer a major disappointment.

A CHANGE OF CIRCUMSTANCE?

The news arrived on June 24, a Tuesday, just a week after the convention opened. New Hampshire had ratified the Constitution three days earlier, bringing the number of ratifying states to nine. That was what the Federalists were waiting for. It meant the Constitution would go into effect. Now, they assumed, what the convention thought of the Constitution was beside the point. The only issue was whether New York would stay in the union or leave it, and that would be easy to decide.

Their expectations proved wrong. Governor Clinton said the news from New Hampshire did not have "the least Effect" on the Antifederalist/Republican members of the convention, who remained "Firm & I hope and believe," he added, "will remain so to the End." One observer after another confirmed Clinton's observation. Melancton Smith said the news had "no effect" except perhaps in prompting the convention "to consider what is proper to be done in the present situation of things," and he wasn't even sure that would happen.[55] So Smith and Hamilton returned to their fight. Hamilton denied that the function of the Senate was to represent the states, as Smith and many Federalists (such as Massachusetts's Fisher Ames) argued. Instead he insisted it should "be so formed, as in some measure to check the state governments," particularly those whose legislatures were no more than "the image and echo of the multitude," which was precisely what Smith thought a representative assembly should be.[56]

The return to business as usual seemed unreal to Robert Livingston. Perhaps, he began on June 25, it would not be "altogether impertinent" to remind the committee of the whole that "since the intelligence of yesterday . . . the circumstances of the country were greatly altered, and the ground of the present debate changed. The confederation . . . was *dissolved*." Now the only question before the delegates was one "of policy and expediency. . . . He supposed, however, that some might contemplate disunion without pain." Smith responded that the "change of circumstances" had not affected his feeling or wishes since he had "long been convinced" that nine states would ratify the Constitution. Lansing denied even that New York's circumstances had changed in any significant way. True, a ninth state had ratified the Constitution, "but . . . no such event ought to influence our deliberations." It was still "our duty to maintain our rights." Nobody in the convention supported disunion, as Livingston suggested. But if nine states agreed to the new government, Lansing said, "let them make the experiment." Whatever other states did, "we ought not . . . to suffer our fears to force us to adopt a system, which is dangerous to liberty."[57]

So the debates continued, though their pace picked up. The committee of the whole skipped the rest of Article I, Section 3, on the composition of the Senate, and turned to Section 4, which gave Congress the right to "make or alter" state regulations of the "Times, Places, and Manner" of electing senators and representatives "except as to the Places of chusing Senators." Samuel Jones, an Antifederal/Republican delegate from Queens County, proposed an amendment that would limit Congress's exercise of those powers to instances where the state legislatures refused or were incapable of making the necessary regulations. The next day Melancton Smith proposed an addition to Jones's amendment, which, after being modified in response to other delegates' objections, affirmed the right of states to divide themselves into districts for the election of representatives. Smith wanted to avoid statewide elections since they would lead to the election of "natural aristocrats." In the end, rather than dictate to the states, he settled for protecting their capacity to hold district elections from congressional interference.[58]

The committee went over several succeeding paragraphs without debate until it reached Article I, Section 6, paragraph 2, which precluded members of Congress from being appointed to certain civil offices under the United States and, in turn, said those officers could not be members of Congress. Lansing proposed an amendment that changed the paragraph's wording to include all offices. Then the committee, still on a roll, passed over Section 7 and arrived at Section 8, on the powers of Congress, and the critical first paragraph on federal taxing power.[59]

TAXATION

John Williams, an Antifederalist delegate from Washington and Clinton counties who occasionally took a part in the debates, immediately objected to the extent of power granted Congress in general and specifically its power "to lay and collect taxes, duties, imposts, and excises, to pay the debts and provide for the common defense and general welfare of the United States." He proposed an amendment—the fifth so far—similar to those recommended by Massachusetts and South Carolina (and later also by Virginia and New Hampshire). It said Congress could raise direct taxes only when revenue from impost and excise taxes was insufficient, and then it would have to requisition the states to "assess, levy and pay" their portion of the tax in whatever way the states judged best. If, however, a state neglected or refused to pay its portion, Congress could collect that state's portion plus interest of 6 percent per year from the time the original payment was due. Williams's amendment would also deny Congress the power to impose any excise tax on articles that were grown or manufactured in the United States.[60]

The committee of the whole spent much of the next five days discussing Congress's power to tax and the proposed amendment. That it devoted so much energy to debating first representation and then taxation testified again to the importance of those issues for a people whose movement toward independent nationhood began with an argument over "no taxation without representation." In 1788, when contenders referred, like Lansing, to protecting rights, they included, often at the top of their lists, the right to be taxed only with the consent of representatives who, as Melancton Smith explained (and Hamilton came close to conceding), knew the circumstances of the people and their capacities to pay. That was why, as Robert R. Livingston noted, the issue had taken up a disproportionate amount of time in earlier ratifying conventions.[61] The debates on federal taxing powers in the New York convention necessarily restated arguments that had been said before but, given the strength of the opposition, explored the topic with particular thoroughness and some new twists.

The issue, Melancton Smith began, required the delegates' "utmost attention, and most careful investigation." Like John Williams, he complained that the clause reserved no source of revenue to the states. Congress was also given authority to make all laws necessary and proper to carry out its stated powers. Nothing was left to construction; its powers were "express." Disputes, moreover, would be settled in federal courts. As a result, those provisions would gradually undermine the state governments and, with them, "the liberties of America," and particularly the right of the people to be taxed only by legislatures in which they were fully and adequately represented. Williams's amendment addressed that problem by forcing Congress to requisition the states for direct taxes.[62]

Congressional requisitions, Smith claimed, had an undeserved bad reputation, since two-thirds of the money Congress requisitioned from the states over the previous decade had been paid. (In fact, only New York paid that high a percentage of its requisitions.) The "difficult circumstances" of the war and postwar periods explained the shortfall, and, as prosperity returned, the states would find it easier to pay congressional requisitions. He argued for the retention of strong state governments not because political theorists such as Montesquieu said republics worked only over small areas: He acknowledged that the applicability of those arguments to governments established after the development of representation was subject to dispute. Instead, Smith depended on reason and experience. Could a single body legislate justly for people some 1,200 miles distant? Could it "frame a system of taxation that will operate with uniform advantage?" he asked. Could it execute such a system without "an innumerable swarm of officers" who would "infest our country and consume our substance?"[63]

Livingston readily conceded that the size of the country prevented a representation of the people "upon principles, in any degree, democratic," but that, he said, was irrelevant to the points in dispute. Experience showed that requisitions were nothing but "pompous petitions for public charity" that caused a lot of noise but brought little cash into the treasury. Smith's argument that wartime troubles kept states from paying their requisitions was simply wrong: Those states that suffered most during the war, like New York, felt the most need of federal support and paid the most. Others that were barely touched by war, like New Hampshire, were the most derelict. Direct taxes would be needed mainly in times of emergency, but the requisition system mandated by the proposed amendment would delay their collection. Probably only half the legislatures—and maybe none of them—would be in session when the money was needed. Once assembled, they might refuse to pay, which would provoke resistance to federal tax collectors and cause internal wars. Those difficulties would undermine federal credit. "What hopes have we of borrowing," he asked, "unless we have something to pledge for repayment?" The returns from direct taxes were "the only positive fund" that could be pledged against the "extraordinary expenses" of "future wars." New York, as a likely "theatre of war," would be the first to suffer if the new federal government was incapable of defending its people. In short, like many other Federalists, Livingston wanted to secure the new government's capacity to borrow so it could support an army, like other contemporary nation states.[64]

Neither Livingston nor Hamilton saw federal taxing powers as a threat to the state governments. The only taxes exclusive to the federal government were on imports; for all others, the states and the central government, they said, would have "concurrent jurisdiction." Livingston noted that New Yorkers had state, county, and city taxes, which were often collected by the same men. Concurrent tax jurisdiction, Hamilton added, was preferable to a rigorous division of sources between the states and the federal government. In the future, some of those sources might dwindle and others flourish, so one level of government would become destitute of revenue while the other had an "unnecessary abundance."[65]

John Williams had anticipated that argument. The Constitution, he noted, did not clearly grant the states concurrent taxing power, which depended upon interpretations or "constructions" of the Constitution. "Ingenious men may assign ingenious reasons for opposite constructions of the same clause." He favored "certainty" in a constitution that would operate on "millions yet unborn" rather than leaving critical issues open to "the sophistical constructions of men, who may be interested in betraying the rights of the people."[66] Samuel Jones and Governor Clinton agreed.[67]

Hamilton took a broad view in answering the opposition's fears. There was no danger in giving the new government ample powers, he said, "when we have given a proper balance to the different branches of administration, and fixed representation upon pure and equal principles." His concept of separation or balance of powers was, however, hardly conventional. Executive authority, he said, was divided between two branches, supposedly the president and the Senate; legislative authority rested in "three distinct branches properly balanced," no doubt the president and the two houses of Congress, and the judicial was "reserved for an independent body" whose members held office on good behavior.[68]

"An assembly constituted for general purposes," Hamilton said, could be competent for "every federal regulation, without being too numerous for deliberative conduct." The issue, however, was not regulations but taxes, for which even he had conceded that the opposition's position had some plausibility. Hamilton also dismissed Melancton Smith's argument over the practical problems of a large republic as taken from a "celebrated writer," Montesquieu, whose arguments, he claimed, referred only to simple democracies, not representative republics. Hamilton ignored Smith's anticipation of that objection, and he ended by expressing confidence that he had presented "abundant reasons" to prove "the entire safety of the state governments and of the people" under the Constitution. "Bravo," his fellow Federalist Richard Harison wrote after hearing Hamilton give what he described as "one of the most excellent energetic Speeches that ever I heard."[69]

From there the substantive debates soon gave way to personal wrangling. On Saturday, June 28, Hamilton introduced a set of official state papers dated from 1780 to 1782, supposedly to demonstrate that New York was once "on the verge of destruction, for want of an energetic government," that is, Congress was unable to protect it against the British Army. Why, another delegate asked, was he trying to prove a point that nobody questioned? And why, Clinton asked, hadn't Hamilton exercised the simple courtesy of telling him beforehand that the papers—which included some Clinton had written—would be brought into the debates? He suspected they were meant to show an inconsistency in his policies during the war and now, when he was accused—incorrectly, he again insisted—of opposing "an energetic government. I declare solemnly," he said, "that I am a friend to a strong and efficient government. But . . . we may err in this extreme: We may erect a system, that will destroy the liberties of the people."[70]

Hamilton answered that the papers he introduced were meant to show "that requisitions have been the cause of a principal part of our calamities," and that "defective and rotten" system "ought forever to be banished from our government." He also questioned Clinton's commitment to a strong government: The conditions added to New York's ratification of the 1783 federal impost amounted to a "positive rejection." As for the amendment under discussion, it would be both harmful and unnecessary. Federal direct taxes would not be oppressive: "It has been proved," Hamilton said, "as far as probabilities can go," that the federal government would follow state practices and so raise those taxes in the way to which the people were accustomed. Why go through "the empty ceremony of a requisition" on the states since, in the end, the people would pay, whether through the states or directly to federal collectors? The burden would be the same: "Why play the ridiculous farce?"[71]

Like Livingston before him, Hamilton objected to the amendment's provision outlawing excise taxes on articles grown or manufactured within the United States. He said it would prevent the states from seizing a source of revenue that could compensate New York for the loss of taxes on imports. Livingston, by contrast, emphasized the provision's impact on the federal government. As the country's manufactures increased, he said, the returns from import duties would decline and other sources of revenue would become necessary. Taxes on "wines, brandy, spirits, malt liquors, &c." of domestic manufacture were "proper objects of taxation" because they would be both productive and "favorable to the morals of the citizens." The Williams amendment would preclude such taxes, which would eventually force the federal government to levy the despised "direct taxes, that is," Livingston explained, "taxes on land, and specific duties."[72]

Having defended federal taxing to the extent of his power, Hamilton was exhausted. But before ending he made an unusual apology. He feared that from a warmth of feeling he had "uttered expressions, which were too vehement." If so, his language came "from the habit of using strong expressions" and from the "interesting nature of the subject." He had always condemned "those cold, unfeeling hearts, which no object can animate." Hamilton denied that ambition and self-interest had any part in his politics. "If the gentlemen reckon me among the obnoxious few," he said, if they imagined that he sought the "immediate honors of the government" at the cost of the country's freedom, they should remember that he had close friends and children who would be "among the oppressed many." It could not be the wish of any "reasonable man, to establish a government unfriendly to the liberties of the people."[73]

That apologia did not keep Lansing from coming down hard on Hamilton. Nobody contended for requisitions as they existed under the Confederation, he said. As a result, much that Hamilton said was irrelevant. The proposed amendment would produce "an entire change" in the operation of requisitions by allowing Congress to collect taxes from individuals if the states refused to do so. Would requisitions delay the collection of money in times of emergency? Governments always had trouble raising money by taxes "on the spur of the moment," Lansing said. In commercial countries, however, people could always be found who were ready to lend money to the government "and to wait the regular operation of the revenue laws."

Their readiness depends on the security of the taxes and so of the lenders' being repaid, which the proposed amendment did not affect. "The certainty of repayment is as well established, as if the government could levy the taxes originally on individuals." But why go through what Hamilton called the "farce" of asking the state to collect taxes that, in the end, the people would have to pay in one way or another? Yet again Lansing explained that "the state legislatures are more nearly connected with the people, and more acquainted with their situation and wants. They better know, when to enforce, or relax their laws; to embrace objects, or relinquish them according to changes of circumstances." The national Congress would lack that advantage.[74]

There was no disagreement over the need to make the United States fiscally responsible, only over how to do that. The "Antis" insisted that the revenue needs of the states—and, indeed, their future existence—had to be assured to protect the liberties of the people, and above all their right to be taxed by representatives who understood their circumstances. Lansing was infuriated by Hamilton's earlier claim that fears of conflict between the states and central government were chimerical and that the states would serve as protectors of popular rights. Those assurances were insincere: He had been at the federal Convention where Hamilton argued "with much decision and great plausibility, that the state governments ought to be subverted"—or, more exactly, reduced to exercising "corporate rights," but even in that weakened situation Hamilton had considered them a danger to the federal government. Perhaps, Lansing concluded, subsequent reflections had led Hamilton to "correct" his earlier views.[75]

Hamilton was furious. He was not inconsistent; he did not want to subvert the states, and it was "highly improper and uncandid" for Lansing to bring up arguments he had made in Philadelphia (though he apparently found it perfectly acceptable to bring up those Clinton had made years earlier). Lansing answered that there was nothing wrong with revealing arguments made at the federal Convention since its rule of secrecy ceased with the publication of the Constitution. The "warm personal altercation" lasted the rest of the day, until finally Judge Robert Yates—Lansing's ally at the federal Convention—called for an adjournment to end the "ferment."[76]

The fight began again on Monday, June 30, when the committee of the whole met from nine to noon and then again at three in the afternoon. To verify what Hamilton had said at Philadelphia, Lansing called on Yates, but the good judge seemed intensely uncomfortable under Hamilton's aggressive cross-questioning. He confirmed that many leading members of the federal Convention thought the states would be unfriendly to the national government, but he wasn't sure that was a "general sentiment." Yes, Hamilton wanted the states reduced to "mere corporations," but perhaps not to a status as weak as the incorporated City of New York. In answer to a question from Jay, Yates said Hamilton sought not to destroy the states but to prevent them from "impeding the operation of the Union." Lansing wanted Yates to read the notes he had taken on Hamilton's proposals during the federal Convention debates, but Lansing declined to make a formal motion to that effect, which the rules required. That ended the altercation; the delegates went back to discussing Williams's proposed amendment and Congress's taxing powers under the Constitution.[77]

There was not much more to say. Smith insisted that requisitions were the most efficient way for the federal government to raise taxes and would produce more revenue than if the federal government collected the taxes itself. The people would more readily obey the states, which would levy taxes "more judiciously" and in "less Burthensome" ways.[78] Otherwise speakers generally went over arguments already made, so Clinton suggested the convention take up the next clause. Jay objected: The committee hadn't finished the provision under debate. What was the rush? Lansing supported Clinton, but his colleague Samuel Jones agreed with Jay. The provision on taxes was "of great Importance," Jones said, and the proposed amendment left "ample Room" for further discussion. The amendment's purpose, as he saw it, was to give the state governments more power and stability. Jones, however, made a major concession. He would be willing to amend the proposed amendment by making an exception for "*Time of War*."[79]

Then Jay asked a critical question: "What are direct taxes?"[80] Everyone agreed that the category included poll taxes, that is, taxes levied on adult men. Robert R. Livingston included taxes on land and also "specific duties," which he did not define.[81] The only subsequent speaker who attempted to answer Jay's question, which would be of importance for future American jurisprudence, was Jay himself. On July 1, he said that "direct taxes were of two kinds, general and specific." The only possible problem was with direct taxes of a general sort "upon all property." Even there Jay thought Congress could easily collect information on the states' preferred ways of raising revenue and design "a general system as perfect as the nature of things would admit." Direct taxes of the specific variety required no "particular, minute knowledge" of the people and their circumstances. Congress could, for example, tax "articles of luxury" like coaches that were the same throughout the country without "difficulty or partiality."[82] If, however, a carriage tax was a direct tax, it would have to be levied among the states according to their population regardless of the number of luxurious carriages its people could afford. That meant that the tax per carriage would be substantially higher in a poorer state like North Carolina than in a wealthy one like New York. Was that fair? Strangely, even in the New York convention, which discussed the proposed federal tax system at length, that problem never came up.[83]

Meanwhile, Robert R. Livingston contented himself with making fun of the supposed inconsistencies in the arguments of his opponents who, he claimed, differed not only with the Constitution's supporters but with each other. They said direct taxes were "odious and useless," but in the proposed amendment such taxes were "necessary and proper." They said it was "impracticable" for the federal government to collect direct taxes, and yet that the taxing power of Congress, which could not "realize a farthing," would destroy the state governments and rob the people of their property. He compared the "Anti" arguments to "children making bubbles with a pipe." Could he "pick out something that looks like reasoning" for "all this rubbish"? He was "embarrassed by their mode of reasoning." If, with the proposed amendment, states had to supply all the funds Congress called for without limitation, the only issue was how the taxes would be levied, not how heavy they would be. "Is this the almighty matter about which we differ?" Other arguments of the opposition were also "very confused."[84]

The *Daily Advertiser* reported that Livingston's "fine vein of humor" brought "bursts of applause . . . from every side," which "seemed to add energy to his genius," and that the "whole speech was a stream of delicate satire and truly Attic eloquence." Even a determined "Antifederalist" delegate from Ulster County, Cornelius Schoonmaker, referred to Livingston's speech as "a Masterly piece of Redicule."[85] Probably after probing the intricacies of federal taxing power the delegates needed a good laugh. However, the next day, July 2, Gilbert Livingston, John Williams, and Melancton Smith protested Livingston's distortion of their arguments. Smith showed how Livingston's technique could be used to demonstrate that he too contradicted himself. Livingston didn't back down. Surely the house would confirm that the opposition had said "the powers of Congress would be dangerous, and yet impracticable. If they will speak such nonsense, they must be exposed. Their other arguments are equally ridiculous." His comments again provoked delight in the Federalist press,[86] but they stood in stark contrast with the more patient, respectful, and effective arguments of Federalists at the Massachusetts ratifying convention. Making fun of your opponents is no way to win them over, as Melancton Smith himself had warned Livingston earlier in the debates.

A CHANGE OF PACE

The flap over Livingston's comments at least pushed the delegates on to the rest of Article I, Section 8. Lansing proposed to amend the provision giving Congress power "to borrow Money on the credit of the United States" by requiring a two-thirds vote of the members present in both houses of Congress. Jay said that amendment would allow a minority faction to block loans needed for the public good and Hamilton found it an unwise "fetter" on the government.[87]

At midday, the sudden appearance of a messenger interrupted a speech on behalf of the amendment by Governor Clinton. An express rider—Colonel William Livingston—had arrived from New York City in a little over nine hours with the news from Richmond: Virginia had ratified the Constitution. There was a buzz through the house. The elated Federalists cheered. They had pinned their hopes on Virginia: On June 27, after New Hampshire's ratification seemed to have had no effect on the "Antis," Hamilton wrote Madison that "our only chance of success depends on you." And on July 2 before the express arrived, when Hamilton still thought the outcome in Virginia was in doubt, he again wrote Madison that there was "more and more reason to believe that our conduct will be influenced by yours."[88] The opposition might shrug off ratification by New Hampshire, but Virginia was the most powerful state in the union. North Carolina would surely follow its example in short order. If New York still held out, it would be left in the company of the despicable Rhode Island. Even the Antifederalist Abraham Lansing anticipated that ratification in Virginia would have a "more serious effect" than New Hampshire on the "Spirits and determinations" of his political friends.[89]

The Antifederalist/Republican delegates seemed, however, to be no more moved by the news from Virginia than they were by that from New Hampshire. They "took no more notice of it," one observer said, "than if the most trifling occurrence had been mentioned."[90] The news and its failure to have the expected impact did, however, bring a major change in the Federalists. They stopped debating. If they had engaged in the discussions to keep the convention from coming to a decision until the hoped-for good news from New Hampshire and Virginia arrived, they had met their objective. Their arguments had, as best they could tell, done nothing to chip away at the "Anti" majority. Why continue?[91]

The change came rapidly. Later on July 2, Samuel Jones moved another amendment that would prevent Congress's power to establish post offices and post roads (Article I, Section 8, paragraph 7) from being construed to allow "the laying out, making, altering or repairing high ways, in any state" without the consent of its legislature. The *Daily Advertiser* reported that "instead of a debate," the amendment "created much laughter" (preventing Congress from repairing its roads apparently struck many delegates as ridiculous).[92] The committee of the whole then finished Article I, Section 8, went through Sections 9 and 10, and began Article II, on the executive, "with little or no debate."[93]

As the secretary read parts of the Constitution, majority delegates continued to propose amendments, eight of them on July 3 alone, more than in all previous sessions together. They would require a two-thirds vote of both houses to raise a standing army in time of peace; restrict the federal government's use of state militias without a state's consent; confine Congress to powers expressly granted and reserve all other powers to the states; restrict suspensions of habeas corpus to a six-month period or until the next meeting of Congress; provide that the restriction on "*ex post facto* laws shall not be construed, to prevent calling public defaulters to account," but should "extend only to crime"; outlaw poll taxes; make the new government publish its accounts at least once a year and send its reports to the states for consideration by their legislatures, and prevent Congress from allowing federal officeholders to accept titles of nobility.[94]

The next day, July 4, the committee of the whole met despite the holiday, and the flow of amendments resumed at a quick pace, uninterrupted by Federalist objections. Antifederalist/Republican delegates proposed to confine the president to a single, seven-year, nonrenewable term (an option the federal Convention had rejected) and to prevent him from commanding the army, militia, or navy in person or granting pardons for treason without Congress's consent. Another amendment would create an executive council to assist the president in making appointments, taking that responsibility from the Senate, and defining the qualifications for council members (at least age thirty-five and a citizen by birth or before July 4, 1776).[95] The "Anti" delegates were not trying to define a limited number of essential requirements. They were rewriting the Constitution. How could they do that after it had been ratified by more than the required nine states?

The delegates were making up for lost time, moving rapidly through Article II on Saturday, July 5, and beginning Article III the next Monday. By the end of that day, July 7, they had gone through the entire Constitution. And day by day the pile of amendments increased. On July 5, Samuel Jones proposed no fewer than seven that defined and restricted the jurisdiction of federal courts and barred judges from all other public offices. On July 7, he added two more amendments to Article III, one of which would allow appeals from Supreme Court decisions to special, presidentially appointed commissions.[96]

Articles IV and V escaped unscathed, but not the next, with its "supreme law of the land" provision. Lansing proposed an amendment that said no treaty could abrogate the Constitution of any state or any law of the union. Then Smith introduced an amendment to the next clause, which required that state and federal officers swear to support the Constitution. It would require officers of the United States to swear not to infringe the constitutions or rights of the respective states. Melancton Smith also criticized Article VII, which said ratification of the Constitution by nine states would be sufficient to establish the Constitution for the states "so ratifying the same." It was a terrible breach of the Confederation, he said. But what could he do? It was obviously way too late to change that provision.[97]

Even then, after the committee of the whole had completed its consideration of the Constitution's last article, the amendments didn't stop. "Anti" delegates proposed a few more restrictions on Congress's powers in Article I, Section 8. One would require a two-thirds vote of both houses to declare war; another—a long and complex amendment proposed by Smith—would restrict Congress's legislative power over the federal district that would become the new government's home. Still another would prevent Congress from creating monopolies. Finally, John Lansing presented a bill of rights, with some fifteen paragraphs, that he wanted "prefixed" to the Constitution. That proposal, John Jay noted, was to be "incorporated in the *Ratification*," which implied that the idea of rejecting the Constitution had been "entirely deserted."[98]

Something would have to be done with all of the amendments that had been presented to the committee before it came to a decision on the Constitution. The first five, which the delegates had discussed at some length, read like amendments to the Constitution. The first of them began, for example: "*Resolved*, That it is proper, that the number of representatives be fixed at the rate of one for every 20,000 inhabitants. . . ." The most recent, however, was more ambiguous: It began "Resolved, as the opinion of this committee, that . . ."[99] Was it a statement of interpretative judgment or a demand that the Constitution be so amended? Clearly not all the proposed amendments were the same. Some, Governor Clinton observed, were "merely declaratory, others of a different nature." He moved that the committee of the whole adjourn so the proposers could arrange them in a way appropriate for the delegates' consideration.[100]

And so the meeting ended until the next day, when Robert Yates reported that the group of delegates arranging the proposed amendments needed more time. The same thing happened on July 9. The delegates finally presented their report the next day, July 10.[101] The interim was precious. It gave both sides time to consult, define their positions, and come up with new plans for achieving what they hoped to accomplish.

MEETINGS, FIGHTS, AND CELEBRATIONS

The delegates didn't spend all of July 4 at work. The day began in Poughkeepsie with a discharge of cannon. At noon, a detachment of militiamen fired thirteen guns and "the citizens assembled to congratulate each other on the DAY, under an elegant and fanciful arbor." The members of the convention, those "gentlemen whose curiosity led them to attend to hear their debates," militia officers, and other citizens were "politely and elegantly entertained" at the quarters of "his Excellency the Commander in Chief," Governor George Clinton. Later members of the Antifederalist/Republican party held a celebratory dinner at Hendrickson's Tavern, the Federalists at

Poole's, but a deputation from each dined with the other. John Jay wrote his wife, Sarah (the daughter of New Jersey's governor William Livingston, who was by birth a New York Livingston), that "the two Parties mingled at each table" and joined in thirteen toasts, all carefully prepared beforehand (they were written out, and each celebrant had a copy), and accompanied by thirteen cannon shots.[102]

The toasts were a model of accommodation. The delegates raised their glasses to the United States, Congress, the allies of America, the memory of departed patriots, "science, agriculture, commerce and manufactures." They toasted the governor and the state of New York, General Washington, the convention, with a hope for "wisdom and unanimity in their councils," "public faith and private credit," a federal government that united "energy with liberty," "happiness at home and respectability abroad." They ended with "the American Fair"—the country's women—and "The Day." There was no reference to the fact that the Constitution had been ratified by ten states. That was the price of having the day pass, as an observer put it, "in pretty good humour" with all parties united.[103]

Elsewhere, Antifederalists and Federalists often held separate celebrations, with little or no effort to accommodate the other side. In Brooklyn, a group of Federalists celebrating the holiday at Dawson's Tavern wished "continual disappointment and never-ending remorse, pain, poverty and contempt" to "those antifederalists who, thro' motives of interest, stand opposed to a government, formed for the good of their country." The last of their thirteen toasts prayed that "the United States, cemented by the New Constitution," would "rise beautiful as a Phoenix from the ashes of contempt," and that "Commerce, in all its branches, flourish unrestricted under its auspices, as long as America has a name amongst the nations." Did the celebrants consider that "motives of interest" might have had some role in the politics of Federalists, so many of whom lived in areas whose economies were tied to commerce? The shoe was always on the other foot. Even a "FEDERAL SONG" composed for the occasion called for stopping

> those antis . . . in their daring career,
> Who for gain wou'd their country undo.[104]

New York City hoped to celebrate Independence Day along with the ratification of the Constitution by the requisite nine states plus Virginia. Its Federalist leaders planned a grand federal procession like that in Boston after Massachusetts voted to ratify. The slow progress at Poughkeepsie forced them to put off the event and celebrate independence only, which they did in the usual manner by holding festive dinners, ringing bells, and shooting guns, some from the deck of "the FEDERAL SHIP HAMILTON," a vessel built for use in the federal procession (but not yet entirely finished), and the firing of rockets at night on Long Island, across from Manhattan.[105] The toasts offered at a Federalist dinner in Jamaica, Queens County, included "The Ten adopting States of the New Constitution."[106] Antifederalist celebrants in Fredericksburg, Dutchess County, instead toasted a wish that "the Constitution now offered to our consideration, be so amended to secure freedom to the citizens of the United States, and give sufficient energy to government." They concluded, "May the genius of America ever guard her sons against Tyranny." Similarly, the toasts at Kingston, Ulster County, ended ominously: *"That our liberty and independence may not be impaired in its thirteenth year."*[107]

Harmony failed entirely at Albany, a Federalist enclave in a predominantly Antifederalist county, where news of Virginia's ratification arrived on the afternoon of July 3. Federalists fired guns to celebrate and rang the city's bells until sundown. The next morning they welcomed the Fourth of July with ten gunshots in honor of the ten ratifying states. That so infuriated the local Antifederalists that they marched from their headquarters—Hilton's Tavern—to a vacant lot at the former site of Fort Frederick, a British stockade. There they ceremoniously burned the Constitution along with a broadside announcing Virginia's ratification, gave three cheers, and returned to their favorite drinking place.[108]

Later in the afternoon, the Federalists organized a counterprocession. The participants, who numbered in the hundreds, returned to the site of Fort Frederick, raised a thirty-six-foot pine tree with the Constitution at its top on the very spot where the "Antis" had burned it that morning, played music, shouted huzzas, shot more cannon, then took the tree and the Constitution down and paraded them through the town. As the procession neared Hilton's, a set of Antifederalists attacked it with clubs, stones, bricks, and other weapons. The Federalists won the ensuing "fracas," trashed Hilton's Tavern, and took some Antifederalist prisoners, including Abraham Lansing. Several men were hurt but none killed; the prisoners were later released, and the civil magistrates managed to restore order.[109]

For Albany's Antifederalists and many others, including some in the convention at Poughkeepsie, burning the Constitution was a perfectly appropriate way to celebrate Independence Day. For them, the document threatened all that Americans had won in their fight against Britain. The Fourth of July toasts of Antifederalists in Kingston and Fredericksburg suggested the same conviction. It was stated with absolute clarity by Cornelius Schoonmaker, the staunch Antifederalist delegate from Ulster County, in a letter to William Smith, a man of like sentiments on Long Island. Schoonmaker took "Singular pleasure" in his friend's "Studious Attachment to preserve and Support the freedom and Independence of the United States" against both internal and external efforts "to Wrest from the People any of those Valuable and inestimable Rights" for which they recently fought the British crown. For him, the Constitution was a "Plan of Despotism" whose opponents, he hoped, would remain "firm and United" despite its supporters' "power of Oratory and Deception." In that way they could "be the Means of saving the Liberties of the people of this state" and "probably of the United States, with the aid and direction of an over Ruling Providence."[110]

The principled opposition to the Constitution by delegates like Schoonmaker would be a problem for Melancton Smith, who led the Antifederalist/ Republican party at the convention. His troops, as he no doubt fully understood, were not truly of one mind, although they all opposed ratifying the Constitution without changes. His personal views were at some odds even with those of Governor Clinton, for whom any government that derived its authority from and acted directly upon the people was a "consolidated government,"[111] and who probably would have preferred a strengthened Confederation to the Constitution. There Clinton's preference was like that of John Lansing and those members of the Albany Anti-Federal Committee who expressed a fondness for the position of Maryland's Luther Martin. Smith also differed from Lansing in his willingness to acknowledge that the decisions to ratify by New Hampshire and then Virginia had implications for New York. His great fear, Smith wrote his old colleague in the Confederation Congress, Massachusetts's Nathan Dane, was that there would not be sufficient moderation "in some of our most influential men, calmly to consider the circumstances in which we are, and to accommodate our decisions to those circumstances."[112] Smith's views were even further from Schoonmaker's. He feared the Constitution would, over time, eat away at the foundations of American liberty, but he stopped short of calling it a "Plan of Despotism" and thought its defects could be repaired.

His great object, Smith told Dane, was "to procure such amendments . . . as to prevent [the Constitution's] attaining the ends, for which it appears to me, and to you calculated"—that is, amendments were required to prevent the destruction of Americans' freedom. He would also "rather recommend substantial amendments, than adopt it conditionally with unimportant ones." As early as June 28, when he wrote Dane, Smith was ready "to make the condition, a subsequent one, that is," the required amendments would have to "take place in one or two Years after adoption" or the state's ratification would become void. In that way, he thought, Antifederalists could "accommodate with the advocates of the constitution" and get them to accept "more substantial amendm[en]ts."[113] Whether he could persuade the Schoonmakers of the convention to ratify without amendments already firmly in place was, however, doubtful at best.

The "Antis" recognized the emerging differences among their numbers, which was why one after another emphasized the importance of keeping their side united. Nonetheless, the seams linking the members of the convention's majority began to open during a series of meetings in early July. Those sessions, according to one anonymous report, were filled with "warm debate." Some delegates wanted to reject the Constitution, but "the majority, more moderate, insisted on an adoption, with certain conditions," which was "at length . . . agreed on, as the extreme point of concession." John Jay, who spent considerable time talking with other delegates, also heard that the majority party "begins to divide." Some members insisted on *previous* conditional amendments," although a greater number would be satisfied with "*subsequent* conditional amendments"—that is (as Smith suggested to Dane), amendments that would have to be ratified within a certain time. Those circumstances, Jay said, "afford Room for Hope."[114]

For Abraham Lansing, still in Albany and smarting from the violent confrontation on July 4 (which never would have happened, he said, had both sides not been "heated with Liquor"), the news from his friends in Poughkeepsie was profoundly discouraging. It suggested the Antifederalist/Republicans were divided "respecting the mode of introducing the Amendments." He had from the first seen the protracted debates as full of peril, and now his predictions seemed to be coming true: The "length of the Business" could well lead to a "total disappointment, to our Friends who wish to promote the True Interests of our Country." The confident, postelection days were gone; the convention's outcome had become "exceedingly doubtful." What was needed, he said, was a set of amendments so interwoven with the Constitution when it was adopted that it could not function without them.[115]

Was that still possible? Could the Federalists prevent New York from ratifying on condition that amendments were first—or at least soon—made to the Constitution? Federalist delegates had stopped debating the Constitution, but they did not plan to remain silent forever. "We shall close the whole business with a strong pathetic [moving] address to their [the Antifederalist/Republicans'] fears and their feelings," an anonymous delegate wrote in Childs's *Daily Advertiser.* The Federalists would emphasize "the new situation of the State, if placed out of the Union, and the dreadful consequences that must ensue." In the meantime, they were "waiting with great impatience for the *Act of Congress*, to put [the new] Government in motion." That would "add much energy to our arguments, will change the nature of the ground, and will beget a new relative situation betwixt the representatives and their constituents" that was not in place when the delegates were elected.[116]

Always, it seemed, the Federalists hoped that news from elsewhere would save them. This time they would not get the news they wanted. On July 2, after receiving news of both New Hampshire's and Virginia's ratification of the Constitution, the Confederation Congress submitted all state ratification forms to a committee "to examine the same and report an Act to Congress for putting the said constitution into operation." Six days later the committee recommended that presidential electors be chosen on the first Wednesday in December and that the electors cast their votes on the first Wednesday in January. The new government, it proposed, should begin on the first Wednesday in February—but where?[117]

Those who wanted it to meet in New York, Madison wrote Washington on July 21, were working for delay, hoping the convention in Poughkeepsie would keep New York in the union. Others without interest in having New York continue as the federal capital were also dragging their feet until as many states as possible had decided on the Constitution—or, more exactly, until as many state legislatures as possible were newly elected. At present everywhere, Madison said, the state legislatures were "less federal than their successors hereafter to be elected will probably be." And since the legislatures would elect senators, make arrangements for the election of representatives, and decide how presidential electors were chosen, they would have considerable influence on the new government. Congress therefore delayed action on its committee's report.[118] That meant there would not be more good news from Congress in time to shore up the minority's case in the New York convention.

On Monday, July 7, Jay told his wife that the convention would probably conclude in another week. Another Federalist delegate, whose comments appeared in the *Daily Advertiser* that same day, also predicted that "next week will probably terminate our labor."[119] That was optimistic given what one observer—John Swann, who was in New York as a member of Congress from North Carolina—described as the convention's "extreme indecision." To him, the convention's inability to come to a conclusion was astonishing since the delegates knew that ten states had already voted to ratify. The Constitution was "ably supported" at Poughkeepsie by "Gentlemen of great literary Merit," he said, "but the Opposition[,] who are by no means contemptible, seem determined to dispute the ground intch by intch." What did the Antifederalist/Republican members hope to gain? Given the situation and "the disposition of a great part of the State . . . they will find their concurrence sooner or later not only expedient but unavoidable."[120]

But could the convention be kept in session long enough for the majority to crumble—or to come to its senses? Was expediency likely to persuade delegates who remembered when time and again expediency had argued for a surrender to Britain, and yet their countrymen fought on to victory? And what, in any case, could be "expedient" for men at war with a "Plan of Despotism"?

THIRTEEN

★

The New York Convention II

In or Out?

So far as George Washington was concerned, the ratification contest was over for all practical intents once New Hampshire and Virginia voted to ratify. Now that the new government would go into effect no matter what the other states did, there seemed to be no question what those states would in fact do.

On June 28, when the heady celebrations in Alexandria were still fresh in his mind, Washington wrote Charles Cotesworth Pinckney that he would be "truly astonished" if North Carolina decided to leave the union. He was even optimistic about a certain determinedly recalcitrant small state: It was *"universally believed,"* he reported, *"that the scales are ready to drop from the eyes and the infatuation to be removed from the heart of Rhode Island."* There was some doubt about New York, where there seemed to be a majority in the convention against adopting "the New federal System." Still, it was hard to think the New Yorkers would reject the new government once "the point in debate" had "shifted from policy to expediency." That is, discussions of the Constitution itself had given way to deliberations on how best to proceed now that the new government had been formally ratified. Perhaps, Washington suggested, the wisest course would be for the New York convention to adjourn until the people of "some parts of the State" could coolly and deliberately consider "the magnitude of the decision" and its consequences.[1]

Expediency—the practical advantages of remaining in the union and the cost of leaving it—had also become the main consideration for the Federalist minority in Poughkeepsie. Could it make the majority recognize how much the issue had changed? For the moment, however, the Constitution's supporters had a few more immediate problems to deal with, including the mass of amendments their opponents had proposed and, on July 10, presented, divided into three categories, for the consideration of the New York convention's committee of the whole. That report seemed to bring the delegates' deliberations to a dead stop.

A PERFECT CRISIS

John Lansing explained that the Antifederalist/Republican delegates charged with arranging the proposed amendments had categorized some as explanatory, others conditional, and the rest "recommendatory." It had also made "material alterations" in the wording of some amendments. The amendment on representation now asked that the number of representatives be fixed at one for every thirty thousand inhabitants (not, as Melancton Smith originally proposed, twenty thousand) until the House of Representatives had two hundred (not three hundred) members, and the committee eliminated entirely the provision for doubling the size of the first House of Representatives.[2]

Perhaps the most important change was in the bill of rights, which, having been renamed a "Declaration of Rights," was placed among the "explanatory" amendments. The text Lansing had proposed on July 7 included a provision "that no Freeman ought to be taken imprisoned or deseised of his Freehold or be exiled or deprived of his previledges, Franchises[,] Life, Liberty or property but by the Law of the Land." The committee substituted for the final phrase "by Due Process of Law," which had been used in "An Act Concerning the Rights of the Citizens of this State" approved by the New York legislature in early 1787. At that time Hamilton explained that "due process of law" referred more clearly to the courts alone; "the law of the land" could imply the legislature as well. Both phrases came from England, but "due process of law" made its way via New York into American law, where it was destined to have a glorious future.[3]

The proposal from the committee was, like so much during the final weeks of the New York ratifying convention, complicated. It said New York would "assent to & ratify" the Constitution "with a firm Reliance and on the express Condition that the Rights aforesaid" would not be "lost abridged or violated" and that the Constitution would "receive the Constructions herein before expressed"—that is, by the "explanatory" amendments. More important, its ratification was "upon Condition" that Congress would not exercise certain powers within New York State until amendments with reference to those powers were "submitted to and determined upon" by a convention "called in the Mode prescribed by the said Constitution." Specifically, Congress could not keep New York's militia in service over six weeks without the consent of the state legislature, make provisions for congressional elections in New York under Article I, Section 4, unless the state failed to do so, levy excise taxes within New York on items of American manufacture, or impose any direct taxes on New Yorkers without first giving the state legislature an opportunity to raise those taxes itself in whatever manner it preferred.[4]

"Now, in the name of Common Sense," asked Abraham Bancker, a Federalist delegate from Staten Island, "will this be considered and treated as an Adoption"? Federalists opposed the proposal because, they said, Congress could not accept a conditional form of ratification. But the Antifederalist/ Republican delegates said the committee recommendation was their "ultimatum" and they would not go "a Step beyond it."[5] That brought the delegates to an impasse. Lansing asked for a bipartisan committee to consider the report, but when the bipartisan committee met, Jay said that unless all forms of the word "conditional" were removed there could be no discussion of amendments. The committee dissolved after about an hour of sometimes angry debate without accomplishing anything.[6]

The next day, July 11, Jay moved an alternative to Lansing's motion. It would ratify the Constitution without conditions, but said that "such parts of the said constitution as may be thought doubtful, ought to be explained, and that whatever amendments may be deemed useful, or expedient, ought to be recommended." The motion did not, however, specify what those amendments might be. Lansing's original proposal, Jay said, was "inadmissible." It made New York's ratification conditional on Congress's calling a new convention and giving up the exercise of certain powers until the convention met, which the Constitution did not authorize it to do. Unless New York ratified in an acceptable way, it would remain outside the union and would have no hand in drafting amendments or in organizing the new government. Moreover, New York City could no longer be the capital of the United States, and it would lose some $100,000 a year in business directly attributable to government spending. "All the Hard Money in the City of New York" came from Congress's meeting there. Were the delegates ready to give that up?[7]

Melancton Smith said Jay went too far: The "conditional amendments" only asked Congress to refrain from exercising certain powers that it was unlikely to exercise right away in any case. Would it levy excise taxes on New York manufactures, of which there were hardly any? Would it immediately start raising direct taxes? The convention's majority was dictating nothing; it asked only for a "fair consideration" of its proposals by a convention called by the other states.[8]

When Jay again insisted that Congress had no power under the Constitution to accept the restrictions specified by the "conditional" amendments, Governor Clinton asked where Congress had received power to change the original Confederation or, for that matter, to organize the new government. Jay responded that it was "a fine way of Answering difficult Questions" by asking other questions, but in 1788 the issue of who had authority to decide what others could or could not do was real. Lansing said the people had given Congress no power to organize the new government or, presumably, to decide what did and did not constitute an acceptable form of ratification. Its exercise of that responsibility was "a mere assumption of Power" based on a suggestion of the federal Convention, which itself had acted beyond the authority granted to it by the states. Only the New York legislature could say what the state ratifying convention could and could not do, and it had not precluded the convention from putting conditions on its ratification.[9]

Robert R. Livingston jumped in. He too insisted that Congress had no power to accept a conditional form of ratification. If New York refused to ratify in an acceptable way it would, as Jay said, remain outside the union and lose a hand in making new laws, forfeit all the money Congress spent within the state, and make it less likely that nine states would call another convention, as the Constitution required. There was another consideration that, Livingston said, pained him to mention. Wouldn't the southern part of the state—with New York City at its center—secede from the northern part if the convention failed to ratify? And could the people of frontier Montgomery County, which faced unorganized territory to the west, resist the British who remained in their old western posts or the "Slaughter of the Savages" without federal help?[10] If early in the convention debates the Federalists began by quoting "Publius," they now sounded more like Jay's "Citizen of New York," counting out the practical benefits New York enjoyed from being part of the union and the problems it would face outside its bounds. In Washington's terms, they had moved from policy to expediency.

This time Livingston was powerful, eloquent, and perhaps even persuasive. But the convention had come, as his colleague, Abraham Bancker, recognized, to a perfect crisis, with two opposing proposals on the table, each rigidly supported by one party or the other. The young DeWitt Clinton, the governor's nephew, agreed that the convention had "wound up to a Crisis," and he said that Lansing's motion was "the ne plus ultra of anti concession." Many members of the majority thought "they had conceded too much."[11] They had, after all, softened their demands substantially. Many of the "Antis" went to Poughkeepsie insisting that the Constitution would have to be amended before New York ratified; some wanted outright rejection. Now they were asking Congress only to forbear exercising a few of its powers in their state until a new convention considered the proposed amendments. They didn't even insist that Congress give up the exercise of those powers until the convention or the requisite number of states approved the amendments.

Some leaders of the Antifederalist/Republican majority, including Smith and perhaps Lansing, thought their proposal went a long way to accommodate the Federalist minority and that the Federalists might even welcome it.

That didn't happen. The question, however, is why Smith, the leader of a party with a two-to-one majority, was so eager to reach out to members of the minority. The answer is that Smith could not count on getting all, or perhaps even most, of the forty-six Antifederalist/Republican votes for a form of ratification that he considered reasonable under current circumstances. Had the Federalists "been friendly instead of being inimical to the proposal," DeWitt Clinton reported, there was reason to think "a majority of antis" would have voted against it when the question was called. However, he thought the Federalists' opposition had reestablished and hardened the majority's resolve. "I have no doubt that the antis will keep together now," he wrote.[12]

Bancker seemed to agree. If the "general Question" was called the next week, Bancker feared that he (and the other Federalists) would be on the losing side.[13] But would the vote be called so soon? Given the complicated divisions among the delegates and the majority leadership's apparent unwillingness—or inability—to push through its form of ratification over the objections of the minority, that seemed unlikely.

A QUESTION OF CIRCUMSTANCES

The "Anti" delegates might deny that the ratification by New Hampshire and Virginia had any effect on them, but in fact it had made a tremendous difference. The entire "ground of argument" on the Constitution shifted once nine and then ten states had ratified. The *New York Packet* summarized that transformation on July 15. "*Then*," before the accession of nine states, it said, there was hope of getting amendments before the Constitution went into operation; "*Now*, all hope of that sort has vanished." "*Then*" the old Confederation was "entire and unimpaired," but now ten states had seceded from the old union, leaving the others "to shift for themselves." "*Then*, those who voted against the New Constitution, only preferred the old one, or a chance for another," but "*Now*, those who vote against the New Constitution, vote themselves out of the New Federal Union."[14]

Critics of the Constitution understood that their options had changed profoundly. Melancton Smith had befriended one of them, Nathan Dane, when the two men served together in the Confederation Congress. A Harvard graduate (Class of 1778) and a lawyer in his mid-thirties from the town of Beverly on the Massachusetts coast north of Boston, Dane had already served in both houses of his state legislature and represented Massachusetts in Congress from 1785 to 1788, when Smith was a New York congressman. The two men had worked together on the Northwest Ordinance, which defined how the territory north and west of the Ohio River would be organized.[15]

Dane's views on the Constitution were set in September 1787, as he watched its defenders try to push it through the Confederation Congress.

In earlier times he had supported strengthening the national government, but after the spectacle in Congress his reservations were strong enough to keep his constituents, who favored the Constitution, from sending him to the Massachusetts ratifying convention.[16] Now, in the early summer of 1788, Smith asked Dane for his opinion on several questions. Those questions have been lost; only the answers survive. Dane wrote them out at length on July 3; by then he had heard the news from both New Hampshire and Virginia.

The big question, Dane understood, was what the remaining three states (New York, North Carolina, and Rhode Island) should do. Since the Constitution had already been ratified, Dane said, "there can be no previous amendments"—that is, no amendments that would have to go into effect before the new government began operations. Now a state with reservations on the Constitution had only two choices: It could vote to ratify and recommend amendments, or it could make amendments a condition of its participation in the new government. Dane favored the former as more likely to serve his objective and Smith's: "the peaceable establishment of a general Government on genuine federal and republican principles." The alternative was likely to cause a lasting division in the union and raised the real possibility of serious and ultimately violent conflicts between the ratifying and nonratifying states.[17]

The idea of retaining the Confederation, he noted, had attracted "few or no advocates" since it was "more difficult to mould the Confederation to the wishes of the people than the Constitution." As a result, "the Community in fact consists of two parties": the Constitution's advocates, who wanted to establish the Constitution as the federal Convention wrote it, and its opposers, who considered the Constitution a "tolerable basis" of a new government but "as an imperfect and unguarded system unless amended." Using those definitions, Dane was an opposer. His objective and, he assumed, Smith's was to "improve the plan proposed" by strengthening the Constitution's democratic features, securing equal liberty with stipulations that would prevent "any undue exercise of power" and putting it "beyond the power of faction" to make the new government anything but "a genuine federal republic."

What was the best way to accomplish those objectives? The answer, Dane said, began to change when a few states ratified without asking for amendments; and now, in early July of 1788, the ground had "totally shifted" in a way that made change more likely to be achieved from within the system. Like John Jay and Robert R. Livingston, Dane noted the obvious point that only representatives of those states that had already ratified would be in the first Congress, where laws critical for the character of the new government would be adopted and "essential amendments" recommended. Experience suggested that staying out of the action was a mistake. If Rhode Island had sent delegates to the federal Convention, they could have helped prevent some objectionable provisions from being included in the Constitution, provisions that the federal Convention accepted only after considerable controversy. The same was true of individuals who were appointed as delegates to the federal Convention but did not attend and now argued against its proposals. For any state to stay out of the new government would repeat the error.

Nobody, Dane assumed, wanted to separate the states or to form separate confederacies: "In all our late political discussions," those options were not to his knowledge mentioned as serious options. Past history suggested that the three states still undecided on the Constitution wanted to remain part of the American nation. They had all readily taken part in the Revolution, acceded to the Articles of Confederation, and supported the union. They should now join those men in other states who wanted to make "the best of the Constitution now established." Dane's position, in short, was identical to the recommendation the Federalist *New York Packet* would make twelve days later: that it was better to "adopt the New Constitution, with its defects, under a prospect of future corrections, than hazard the consequences of being repudiated from the Grand American Confederacy," and contenders should adopt that stand "whatever part they may have taken *heretofore*."[18]

Dane added that no Constitution could give the people so much security that they could sit back and stop watching what their government did. He had faith in the country and its people: In the past, efforts to pass off "vice for virtue, the mere show of talents for real abilities, and the arts and pulls of party for a well earned reputation have generally failed." All it took to defeat such efforts was "to excite the attention of this intelligent people." Although "the system may be abused by bad men . . . the road to lasting fame in this Country has generally been Justice, and Integrity, prudence and moderation, political information and industry," and there was "more than an equal chance that this will continue to be the case." Nathan Dane was a man of faith.

Smith replied that his opinions were in complete accord with Dane's, but it would take "time and patience" to bring his party to agree. He had, in fact, long inclined toward Dane's position. Already on June 28, Smith had written Dane that he wanted to amend the Constitution in ways that would "prevent its attaining the ends, for which it appears to me, and to you calculated." He was not, however, rigidly committed to making amendments a condition of ratification. He was ready "to consider the circumstances they were in" and fit decisions to those circumstances, but he feared "some of our most influential men" were not.[19]

Circumstances, however, involved more than what other states had done; and there Smith had sources of information and advice beyond Dane. On July 11, Samuel Osgood, who had represented Massachusetts in Congress and now served as a member of the Confederation's three-man board of treasury in New York, sent Smith and his fellow delegate Samuel Jones a report on the current state of affairs. Congress had postponed taking steps to organize the new federal government because it had heard the convention in Poughkeepsie was likely to reach a decision on the Constitution within a few days. Once it learned what the convention decided, Congress could "more properly" choose a place for the new government to meet. If the ratifying convention voted not to ratify, Osgood said, "the Opposition will have all the Blame laid at their Door for forcing Congress to leave this City." Moreover, if the convention voted against ratification, Smith was unlikely to receive a "Cordial" reception when he returned to his home in Manhattan. There might even be rioting by a people who "when rowzed exhibit some of the Obstinate & ungovernable Passions of their Ancestors."[20] Osgood said nothing about New York's seceding from the rest of the state and the violence that might provoke. There was no need for him to do that. Rumors that the state might split had been in the newspapers long before delegates had raised the possibility at the Poughkeepsie convention.

Was it worth those risks to secure amendments if, as Osgood also indicated, amendments were already a sure thing? "Those who have been deemed antifederal" had already done "a great deal of good," he said, and had "very nearly accomplished their Views." Osgood was convinced that, "in the present State of the Business," those who had "well founded Objections" to parts of the Constitution "will succeed in their laudable Endeavors of getting those Objections fairly removed." In fact, there was "little Danger in assenting to the Plan now," and whatever danger remained of not getting amendments would, in his Opinion, "be greatly enhanced by the Absence of New York" in the new government.

Smith had told Dane that "the principal labor of managing the Controversy lies upon me." His one wish was "to support the party with whom I am connected as far as is consistent with propriety," which suggested that, despite his position of leadership, he might break with his party under some circumstances. Osgood understood. Smith, he predicted, would decide what to do "conscientiously" according to what he thought would be "for the best Interest" of his "State & Country." He knew Melancton Smith's priorities, and those priorities would shape his complicated role in the concluding weeks of the New York ratifying convention.[21]

A MAZE OF MOTIONS

Two motions were before the committee of the whole on Monday, July 14: Lansing's, which would ratify the Constitution on certain conditions; and Jay's, which would ratify the Constitution with explanatory and "recommendatory" amendments but no conditions. The delegates were getting impatient for a decision. William Harper, an Antifederalist from Montgomery

County, said they had done nothing but talk for three days, and a colleague from Columbia County added that arguments were being repeated over and over. Harper called for a vote. Alexander Hamilton, however, wanted the question put off since "he supposed it would amount to a rejection." Like Jay, he said Lansing's motion asked Congress to do what it had no power to do. Congress would have to reject so flawed a form of ratification. Rather than act hastily, Hamilton urged the delegates to sleep on the question before voting. The "Anti" Gilbert Livingston supported him.[22]

The vote did not, however, come up at the beginning of the next day, Tuesday, which instead brought the beginning of a flurry of motions. First Melancton Smith moved to amend Jay's motion so that, like Lansing's, it would make New York's ratification of the Constitution conditional upon Congress's not exercising several powers (the same that Lansing's motion listed) "until a Convention shall be called and convened for proposing amendments to the said Constitution." That reconciled Gilbert Livingston, who thought Smith's motion was more compatible with Article V of the Constitution than Lansing's.[23]

Then Hamilton proposed still another form of ratification without conditions but with a number of "recommendatory & explanatory" amendments. His motion echoed Jay's but included the text of amendments, and more of them than Lansing had proposed. Several were cleverly modeled on those recommended by the Virginia ratifying convention. Hamilton said the Federalists were "ready to go as far as they thought safe" to secure ratification of the Constitution, and they pledged to work for the adoption of the amendments they proposed "as far as they can." Philip Schuyler reported that Hamilton's proposal "so evidently deranged and embarrassed" the opponents of unqualified ratification that the Federalists suddenly had new hope that the convention might end in a way they could approve.[24]

Lansing admitted that some of Hamilton's amendments were valuable; they could be added to the list of those already proposed. First, however, the convention had to decide whether to ratify with or without conditions. Jay tried to put off that vote, which he knew would go the wrong way. Couldn't the conditional amendments be "pared down so that we may agree," he asked? The Federalists were willing to go far toward a position on which both sides could agree, but they honestly believed that Congress would have to reject a ratification in the forms Lansing and Smith had proposed. John Williams, an Antifederalist from Washington and Clinton Counties, disagreed: Congress would accept New York's ratification, conditions and all, he said, because it wanted its impost and its assistance. Meanwhile, Harper again called for a vote, and again the delegates agreed to put off a decision for another day.[25]

When the convention met on Wednesday, but before it went into a committee of the whole, John Sloss Hobart, a Federalist from New York City, moved that it adjourn until September 2. He presented the motion as a way to let delegates consult their constituents' wishes on what to do under current circumstances, which had changed substantially since the election of convention delegates. In fact, as everyone understood, Hobart (like the Federalists at the February session of the New Hampshire convention) saw adjournment as a way of avoiding a vote that the Federalists considered a de facto rejection of the Constitution.[26]

The convention debated the motion all day and again on Thursday, July 17, when Hamilton gave a speech that the *Daily Advertiser* said "drew tears from most of the audience." He objected to the notion that critics of the Constitution were carrying on "our spirit in 76." Britain had given the colonists no share in representation and claimed absolute power over them. That was not the case with the Constitution, which was built on the principle of representation and offered securities—"beauties"—that its critics overlooked when seeking out its defects. If a conditional form of ratification were adopted, Congress would refuse it and New York would be out of the union. With the greater part of the country against it, New York could not subsist without an alliance with Britain, which would risk bringing New York once again under British domination.[27]

Lansing interrupted: Hamilton was out of order, since the issue before the house was adjournment. Harper agreed, but Jay said Hamilton was explaining that he wanted to adjourn to avoid a form of ratification he considered injurious. After Smith and Samuel Jones both said he should go on, Hamilton continued to portray the dire consequences of rejecting the Constitution, or, which was for him the same thing, adopting a conditional form of ratification. The southern part of the state would secede from the northern and the union would support its secession since it wanted access to the port of New York. That would leave the northern part of the state to support and defend itself. Nor would the union be anxious to receive it back into the fold once it had "our port—the chief source of wealth." There were distinguished patriots on both sides, Hamilton said, but most were for the Constitution: John Hancock, John Adams, John Dickinson, Benjamin Frankin, that "old great headed patriot looking into the Grave," and Washington himself. Would those great heroes endorse a government dangerous to the liberties of their country? The other states, which were as jealous of their liberty as New York, were inviting New York to join them. There was more safety in accepting the invitation than in rejecting it. Even if on the "verge of eternity," Hamilton said he would exhort his countrymen to maintain the union.[28]

If Hamilton wanted to persuade the convention to adjourn, he failed. After he finished, the convention voted down the motion to adjourn, with 22 votes in favor, 40 against. However, three Antifederalist/Republican delegates had joined the Federalists in voting for the motion: Samuel Jones and John Schenck from Queens County and Jonathan Havens from Suffolk. The convention's president, George Clinton, did not vote (as was customary for presiding officers), nor did two other members of the majority, David Hedges from Suffolk County and Ezra Thompson from Dutchess County. Thompson, DeWitt Clinton recorded in his personal journal on the day of the vote, "went hastily home this morning—thro' fear it is Supposed."[29] Fear of what? Reprisals from his fellow "Antis" for breaking rank? For angering his constituents? For voting against his conscience? Clinton didn't say.

The Antifederalist/Republican majority, though still formidable, had split, and there were more signs that the bonds among them were weakening. Even the stalwart "Anti" John Williams wondered if there wasn't some "middle line" between the two sides' conflicting positions, something, it seemed, different from his party's previous "ne plus ultra." He could vote neither to reject the Constitution nor to ratify it without conditions, but he found the consequences of disunion "dreadful."[30] Perhaps Hamilton's speech had affected Williams, although Jay and Livingston had also stressed the dire consequences of New York's leaving the union.

Immediately after the vote on adjournment had lost, the convention again resolved itself into a committee of the whole. It began by reading Jay's motion for an unconditional adoption of the Constitution and a full version of Smith's proposed amendment to Jay's motion, which included a series of prefatory amendments as well as a conditional form of ratification. One newspaper, the *Daily Advertiser*, said the committee of the whole also read Hamilton's motion, which it described as an amendment to Smith's motion to amend Jay's motion.[31] The maze of motions was becoming mind-boggling.

While the delegates pondered how to proceed through that parliamentarian's nightmare, James Duane, the Federalist mayor of New York, moved that the committee of the whole postpone consideration of Smith's propositions to consider Hamilton's (parts of which were in Jay's handwriting). Hamilton's proposal used some strong language: It said, for example, that "no right of any kind . . . can be cancelled, abridged, restrained or modified by Congress, or by an Officer or Department of the United States, except in conformity to the powers given by the said Constitution." It recommended that New York ratify the Constitution "with a full confidence"—not on condition—that the amendments proposed by the convention would receive "an early and mature consideration" and that those that "may in any degree tend to the real security and permanent advantage of the people will be adopted." Rather than impose restrictions on what Congress could do in the interim, Hamilton's motion said Congress "ought not to interfere" with state provisions for the election of senators and representatives. It also eliminated the demand that states be given an opportunity to raise direct taxes for the federal government, which many Federalists found especially objectionable. Instead it declared that, except for duties on imports and exports, tonnage, and post office fees, "the United States, and the States respectively, have concurrent and co-equal authority to lay and collect all taxes whatsoever." That would at least assure the states a means of supporting themselves once the Constitution was ratified.[32]

The delegates began to cut through the maze by voting down Duane's motion to postpone consideration of Smith's proposal, with 41 votes against it and 20 in favor. This time two of the three absconding "Antis"—Havens and Schenck—returned to vote with their colleagues on the negative; Henry Oouthoudt, the chairman of the committee of the whole, and Henry Wisner, an "Anti" from Orange County, did not vote. George Clinton cast a vote this time around, since he was not presiding, but not Hedges and Thompson; they were apparently gone for good.[33]

For a moment the agenda seemed clear. The convention would turn next to Smith's motion with the Antifederalist/Republican majority still mostly intact. But then, in one of the strangest turns in that most complex convention, Smith announced that he no longer supported his own proposal because he had come to think that Congress would not accept it. Its objective, he said, was "to bring the question of amendments before the people of America, as soon as possible." The restrictions on Congress's exercise of power, which the Federalists said Congress could not accept, were meant as "an inducement to call a Convention." Perhaps there was a better way to achieve that purpose, one free of the objections raised against his previous proposal.[34]

Smith then moved a substitute proposal. It began by stating seven general problems with the Constitution. Because of those problems, it went on, New York would not have agreed to the Constitution except from a strong attachment to its sister states. New York agreed to the Constitution "in the firmest confidence that an opportunity will speedily be given to revise and amend the Constitution" in the manner specified in Article V. However, the state reserved the right "to recede and withdraw from the said Constitution, in case such opportunity be not given within ___ years." The idea of including an escape clause in the state's form of ratification wasn't new: Smith had mentioned it to Dane in late June. In Virginia, Richard Henry Lee had proposed a very similar form of ratification after the acceptance of the Constitution by several other states complicated the demand for prior amendments. Smith's new proposal also recommended that the state legislature ask Congress to call a second general convention and that "a circular letter" be sent to the other states asking them to join in calling a convention to consider the amendments proposed by the states.[35]

Smith had good reason to fear for the worst. He had not attended the convention session on July 16, perhaps so he could work on his new proposal. That evening, according to DeWitt Clinton, Smith circulated copies of the

proposal among members of his party. It was "received with indignation &
Suspicion by many,"[36] but he presented it to the committee of the whole the
next day anyway. He knew, he said, that he stood on "ticklish ground" and
that his proposal would not get the entire approval of either side. However,
he believed in his "conscience" that it would achieve the objectives of both
sides in the convention, and he presented it "from the sincerest desire to
accommodate."[37]

Smith had not won over his old partner in battle John Lansing, who immediately said he preferred Smith's first proposal and would reintroduce it if
Smith withdrew it from consideration. Before anything else happened, the
committee of the whole ended its session and the convention adjourned for the
night. July 17 had been a very long day, and it ended in considerable confusion.
The *New-York Journal* announced that it was unable to predict how "these momentous debates" would end and could only print a "faithful narration, leaving
our readers to judge for themselves." DeWitt Clinton was equally mystified.
"What will be the result of all these propositions I cannot determine," he
wrote. "I look forward with anxiety. The Scylla and Charybdis I would wish
to avoid are non-conditional adoption & a disunion of the opposition." And
yet "the political sky" was "so frequently overcast and so variable to appearance
that I am oftentimes at a loss what to think or what to say."[38]

At least Bancker was cheered by Smith's motion, which he thought could
be "So Amended" that Congress would accept it. In fact, Smith's fondest
admirers seemed to be on the Federalist side of the house. When the committee of the whole resumed its deliberations on Friday, July 18, Zephaniah
Platt, Smith's Antifederalist colleague from Dutchess County, seconded
his motion, but both John Lansing and John Williams said they could not
support Smith's new proposal. Jay found it "less evil" than Smith's earlier
motion and said he would vote for making it the basis of future deliberations.
Mainly, however, a protracted silence greeted Smith's motion, and after
about an hour the committee of the whole adjourned. Jay wrote Washington
that the "opposers" of the Constitution seemed embarrassed—that is, perplexed and confused—by Smith's proposal. Many were "very averse to the
new Plan" but wanted desperately to avoid dividing against each other.[39]

The "Antis" met that evening. After failing to come to an agreement,
they called another meeting the next morning. "Some are much enraged at
it [Smith's new proposal] and its author," DeWitt Clinton reported. Cornelius Schoonmaker was no doubt among them. He considered the form of
ratification Smith suggested as "very little short of an absolute Adoption."
Rather than agree to it or see their party split, some "Antis" now wanted
the convention to adjourn. On the other hand, Samuel Jones, who had
already voted twice with the Federalists, declared openly that "We must
join the union sooner or later and We might as well now and trust to future

amend[men]ts." If the party fell apart, DeWitt Clinton was ready to blame Smith and Jones. Smith, he said, "goes so much among the fed[eralist]s that he has raised jealousies against him." Some members of his party had even come to detest him "as much as Hamilton."[40]

CREEPING TOWARD A DECISION

With Smith's leadership in disarray, John Lansing took charge. On Saturday, July 19, the beginning of what would be the convention's last week, he moved that the committee of the whole set aside all the other propositions and consider a draft ratification and amendments based on Smith's first proposal but with some provisions rewritten and a few new ones added to Smith's list. Among other changes, "due process of law" reappeared. Those words were in the set of amendments Lansing proposed on July 10, but Smith's motion said freemen could not be taken, imprisoned, exiled, or deprived of their privileges, life, or property "but by the law of the land." Other critical words remained the same. Both Lansing's motion of July 19 and Smith's first proposal would ratify the Constitution only "on the express condition" that the rights previously stated would not be "lost, abridged, or violated," that ambiguous clauses would be construed as the ratifying convention explained them, and also "upon condition" that Congress would not exercise certain powers in New York until a convention met to consider amendments to the Constitution.[41]

That was the position Governor Clinton had come to favor, though he thought it fell short of what the delegates' constituents wanted. It was apparently the only proposal on which members of the Antifederalist/Republican party could agree. The committee of the whole accepted Lansing's motion, 41 to 18, voting on strict party lines, with even Jones and Smith, who were perhaps chastened by the party caucus, in the majority.[42]

Rather than decide whether the ratification would be with or without conditions—the issue on which Lansing had earlier pushed for a decision—the delegates proceeded, on Governor Clinton's motion, to go through the text by paragraphs. As a result, the proposed amendments were discussed carefully and occasionally compared with equivalent provisions recommended by the Virginia convention. Where items were controversial, votes were taken. At the end of the day, the delegates had gone through the first set of amendments and submitted them to an "informal committee" of four (two "Antis," Melancton Smith and Robert Yates, and two Federalists, James Duane and Richard Harrison), to arrange in proper order and correct their language.[43]

The committee of the whole returned to its task on both Monday and Tuesday of the next week. It approved provisions limiting Congress's taxing power, 38 to 16, again on party lines; in fact, most amendments passed despite Federalist opposition. However, the provision recommending the creation of a council of appointment to approve the appointment of officeholders failed, 46 to 10, with "Antis" on both sides. Party members split again over an amendment that would require a two-thirds vote of the senators and representatives present in both houses to declare war, which nonetheless passed, 32 to 25.[44] Pressure to bring the convention to an end was growing: The *Poughkeepsie Journal* reported that some delegates were anxious to go home and gather their harvests,[45] and the total vote on propositions consistently fell short of 65, the number of delegates originally sent to the convention. The quicker the delegates finished their business, the more members would remain.

Finally, on Wednesday, July 23, the delegates confronted the big question of how to ratify. The informal committee appointed four days earlier submitted its report, which included not just a more finished form of the "explanatory" amendments, but also a form of ratification, which went beyond its charge. Lansing moved that the committee of the whole consider not the form of ratification proposed by the informal committee, but instead the conditional form of ratification in Melancton Smith's first proposal. The delegates agreed and turned to the critical statement in Smith's proposal that New York ratified "on the express condition, that the rights aforesaid will not, and shall not be lost, abridged or violated, and that the said Constitution shall in the cases above particularized, receive the constructions herein before expressed." Smith, of course, had already decided that the words "on the express condition" would probably keep Congress from accepting New York's ratification. He moved that the paragraph be "expunged" for another that replaced the objectionable words with "in confidence that." His motion passed, amazingly, by 40 to 19, with a substantial number of "Antis" in the majority, including John Lansing, Robert Yates, Gilbert Livingston, John Williams, and even George Clinton.[46]

The committee of the whole then turned to the next section, the enacting clause:

> We the said Delegates, in the name and in the behalf of the People of the State of New-York, do by these presents assent to and ratify the said Constitution: UPON CONDITION NEVERTHELESS, That until a Convention shall be called and convened for proposing amendments . . .

That passage introduced the list of powers Congress could not exercise in New York before a convention met.[47]

This time Samuel Jones moved to remove the words "upon condition" and substitute "in full confidence." Immediately Smith explained why he would vote for Jones's amendment. He had become convinced "from the reasonings of gentlemen in opposition to it, and whose opinions alone would . . . have great weight in the national councils," and from "the sentiments of people abroad" that Congress would not accept a conditional ratification. He believed as firmly as ever that the Constitution was "radically defective," but he would work for amendments in a "practicable way." Before Virginia had ratified, he had reason to believe amendments could be "obtained previous to the operation of the Government. He was now satisfied that they could not," and that amendments could only be achieved "in the mode prescribed by the Constitution." He also dreaded the state's situation if it ratified the Constitution in a way that Congress could not accept, with "convulsions in the northern part" of the state and "factions and discord in the rest." Zephaniah Platt said that he too would vote in favor because he thought it would "tend to the happiness of the people."[48]

The amendment passed, 31 to 29, with Yates, Lansing, and Governor Clinton in the negative along with many other "Antis," including the redoubtable Cornelius Schoonmaker. Twelve of their political colleagues were with the majority. As a letter in the *New York Independent Journal* put it, all but one of the delegates from counties in the southern part of the state, "four of the Dutches County members, and Mr. Williams from Washington voted in the affirmative." Had any of them voted on the other side the motion would have failed. The vote was still in the committee of the whole; a final decision would have to be made by the delegates sitting officially as a convention, and Jay expected the opposition "to rally their forces" and attempt to regain the ground it had lost.[49] For the moment, however, the delegates had decided to ratify the Constitution without conditions.

NEW YORK'S "GRAND FEDERAL PROCESSION"

New York City held its spectacular celebration of the Constitution's enactment on Wednesday, July 23, the same day the delegates in Poughkeepsie seemed to overcome the main barrier to ratifying the Constitution in a way that Congress would accept. The event had been postponed repeatedly—so the ship *Hamilton*, a prominent part of the festivities, could be finished; to avoid July 22, a Jewish holiday, and in the hope that the convention in Poughkeepsie would come to a decision that would add to the causes of celebration. Finally the city could wait no longer. The festivities began with a grand procession designed to outshine a similar parade in Philadelphia on July 4, which itself was greater than the one held in Boston on February 8 to celebrate Massachusetts's ratification of the Constitution.[50] The competition among cities was stiff.

The New York procession was a mile and a half long and divided into ten "divisions" in honor of the ten ratifying states. The *Hamilton* was in the seventh division: A miniature but water-worthy thirty-two-gun frigate, twenty-seven feet long and ten high, with over thirty seamen inside and canvas waves slapping its sides, it was seated on a platform and pulled through the streets by ten horses. The seventh division, which included both mariners and people in the printing trade, had a "Federal Printing Press" that produced and handed out broadside copies of two celebratory odes written for the occasion. Other divisions included farmers, tailors, bakers, brewers, and manufacturers of chocolate, wigs, and mathematical instruments, along with the representatives of several other trades, as in Boston's parade. The participants were not, however, confined to craftsmen: They included lawyers, members of the Philological Society, the president and students of Columbia College, merchants and traders, all of whom were in the ninth division. Physicians and clergymen of various creeds, including a rabbi, all "walking hand-in-hand," were in the tenth division. Meanwhile, according to a witness, "several of the richest and most important Persons of the town" mingled with the various tradesmen to show they did not "look upon them with contempt."[51] They too had learned to play the game of democratic politics.

The parade began at eight o'clock in the "the Fields" (now City Hall Park), wound down Broadway and through the city at a "slow and majestic pace," and finally arrived at the farm of Alderman Nicholas Bayard (now between the Bowery and Broadway). There the marchers joined members of Congress, foreign dignitaries, and others to feast on beef, mutton, and ham in an enormous banquet hall designed for the occasion by Pierre Charles L'Enfant, a French-born architect, and constructed, according to one account, in five days. The fan-shaped structure consisted of several connected pavilions and included ten 440-foot tables, spread out like the spokes of a wheel, with space to serve six thousand people. There were the inevitable toasts: the United States; the ten ratifying states; may the New York convention "soon add an eleventh pillar to the Federal Edifice"; Washington; America's allies; "may the Union of the States be perpetual."[52]

Finally, at four in the afternoon, thirteen shots from the *Hamilton* summoned the marchers back to their places in the procession. They marched to the Fields where they had begun and dispersed by half past five. Accounts remarked that there was no disorder of any kind all day. Even the procession, with the large crowds it attracted, produced "an unexpected silence," with "no sound heard but the deep rumbling of carriage wheels, with the necessary salutes and signals," which gave "a solemnity to the whole transaction suited to the singular importance of its cause."[53]

The massive and costly celebration was designed in part to persuade the members of Congress, whose president sat at the center of the banquet hall,[54] that New York City would be a welcoming home for the new federal government. It also sent a strong signal to Poughkeepsie. The City of New York was powerfully committed to the union and would not be easily reconciled to any form of ratification that kept it outside the federal fold. Federalist convention delegates had already made that point, but the City of New York itself made it more powerfully, not with words, but with a ritual celebration larger in scale than anything seen before in America (though some Philadelphians questioned its preeminence) or, some proud souls dared to suggest, in the great cities of Europe.

DECISION

Meanwhile, convention delegates moved step by step toward a final decision. On Thursday, July 24, the committee of the whole turned to what had once been the conditional amendments—the restrictions on Congress's exercise of certain powers until a convention met. That business ended quickly since they were no longer conditions, only statements of the delegates' expectations. The committee debated the provision limiting the time the New York militia could be deployed outside the state without its permission to six weeks. It passed, 32–22, with Hamilton, Jay, and Robert R. Livingston in the majority. The other former conditions, including the one that asked Congress to requisition the state for any direct taxes, were approved unanimously. Jay went out of his way to emphasize the extent to which Federalists and Antifederalists shared the same objectives. "Let us be Unanimous in pursuing the Object—to get a convention—to reconsider the constitution." He too wanted "*some* amendments," he said, and the delegates were more likely to get them by working hand-in-hand.[55]

Then, in yet another turn in the delegates' tortuous course, Lansing destroyed the unnatural harmony by reintroducing a provision, taken from Melancton Smith's controversial second proposal, that would reserve New York's right to "recede and withdraw" from its ratification if no convention were called to consider amendments after a certain number of years, which his motion left undefined. Federalists who once found that proposal preferable to a form of ratification with conditions now decided they didn't like it anymore. After all, the delegates' rejection of a conditional form of ratification meant that ratification with an escape clause was no longer a lesser form of evil.

Hamilton said Lansing's proposal would keep New York out of the union as effectively as a conditional ratification. To prove his point, he read a letter from James Madison, whom he had asked for advice on the issue. "My opinion," Madison said, "is that a reservation of a right to withdraw if amendments be not decided on under the form of the Constitution within a certain time, is a *conditional* ratification," and so it would not make New York "a member of the New Union." The Constitution, he explained, had to be adopted "*in toto*, and *for ever*," as it had been by the other states, and "any *condition* whatsoever must viciate the ratification." Madison spoke for himself and perhaps expressed the prevailing sentiment of the Confederation Congress, of which he was a member, but he admitted that he could say nothing of "what the new Congress by virtue of the power to admit new States, may be able & disposed to do in such a case."[56]

Madison's letter might have influenced Smith, who sat strangely silent through the day's debates, but it did not settle the issue. Lansing said Madison expressed only "an Impression of the Moment," or "an opinion." He claimed that he had agreed to the elimination of conditional clauses in the proposed form of ratification only on the assumption that an escape clause would be included, and he seemed as devoted to that proposal as he was before he heard Madison's letter read. Other delegates said they had to act according to the wishes of their constituents, who opposed an unconditional ratification. A new concern over the peace treaty with Britain was probably more persuasive than the Madison letter: Would the treaty remain in force in New York if the state was no longer part of the United States? The question had serious implications for those forts in unsettled sections of western New York that the British still held, but which they were committed to abandon under the terms of the treaty. Would the British have a right to remain if the treaty no longer bound New York? Was it worth taking that risk in return for a provision in the ratification document that New Yorkers would probably never act upon? On July 25, the committee of the whole voted down Lansing's motion, again by 28 to 31, with Smith (and several other "Antis") voting with the Federalists against what had once been his own proposal.[57]

The work of the committee of the whole was almost done. After making one change to the statement on rights, it adopted explanatory amendments that included a declaration of rights, and a form of ratification, again by a vote of 31–28, and on July 25 officially submitted those items to the convention. Henry Oothoudt read the committee of the whole's report out loud, then delivered it to the convention officials, who read it again. The convention voted 30–25 to accept the report, then had a copy put in a finished form for signing.[58] It also appointed a committee, consisting of Jay, Lansing, and Smith, to prepare a circular letter to the other states. Smith had first raised the idea of a circular letter, which was later picked up by Jay and Hamilton as a way of reconciling disgruntled delegates to an unconditional ratification. Finally, the delegates once again went into a committee of the whole to go over the list of "recommendatory" amendments, which it then presented to the convention. After accepting one amendment proposed by Jay that restricted major offices to freeholders, the convention unanimously accepted the list, ordered it engrossed, and adjourned until the next day.[59]

Finally, on Saturday, July 26, the convention formally adopted the entire package—the explanatory amendments, ratification form, and recommended amendments—by a vote of 30 to 27. At that point the convention president Governor George Clinton addressed the convention "very politely." The body of the people, who opposed the Constitution, would probably be dissatisfied with the convention's outcome, he said, but he pledged to use all of his influence to maintain peace and order. The Poughkeepsie *Country Journal* reported that both delegates and spectators were "very attentive."[60]

The delegates also agreed unanimously to the text of a circular letter to the other states urging them to join in calling for a new general convention to consider amendments, and they asked the governor to sign it and send it to the executives of the other states. Forty-six delegates signed the copy of the letter that is bound into the convention's manuscript journal. The convention also sent its proceedings to the state legislature, which was "earnestly requested" to cooperate in calling a general convention, ordered copies of its journal distributed throughout the state, voted the customary thanks, and, at long last, adjourned.[61]

NEW YORK'S RATIFICATION

The document approved by the New York convention in ratifying the Constitution was longer and, like the convention itself, more complicated than that of any other state. It opened with a declaration of rights and explanations or interpretations of several constitutional provisions that included twenty-five paragraphs, some of which spoke to more than one point. Then came the actual form of ratification, buried in another barrage of words. "Under these impressions and declaring that the rights aforesaid cannot be abridged or violated," and that the aforesaid explanations were consistent with the Constitution, and also with confidence that the amendments "which shall have been proposed" would receive "an early and mature Consideration," the delegates assented to and ratified the Constitution "in the behalf of the People of the State of the New York." The delegates also expressed their "full confidence" that, until a convention met to consider amendments to the Constitution, Congress would not keep the New York militia outside the state for over six months without the legislature's permission, alter state regulations of congressional elections, tax items in New York State that were of American growth or manufacture except "Ardent Spirits," or raise direct taxes without first giving the state legislature an opportunity to levy them itself. The signature of George Clinton, as the convention's president, and its two secretaries followed.[62]

Next, the convention asked the state's representatives in the new Congress to exert all their influence and use "all reasonable means" to secure ratification of no less than thirty-two recommended amendments, which did *not* include a bill of rights. Some of those amendments were brief ("That no Person shall be eligible to the Office of President of the United States a third time"); others, like one that proposed a new court for trying impeachments, were long and detailed. This document was also signed by Clinton and the convention's secretaries.[63]

The circular letter adopted by the convention was an equally remarkable document. It said that a majority of the convention's members found some parts of the Constitution so exceptionable that they never would have agreed to ratify it without demanding previous amendments, except from a confidence that it would be revised by a general convention and "an invincible reluctance" to separate from their sister states. Several other states had also called for amendments, and the "Apprehensions and Discontents" behind those recommendations could be allayed only if the new Congress called another general convention as one of its first acts. For that purpose, the letter asked the other state legislatures to join in calling for a new convention under the procedure described in Article V of the Constitution. John Jay drafted most of the circular letter, although John Lansing was responsible for a final paragraph that said New York's amendments showed that the state did not act on "local views" since the problems it addressed "equally affect every State in the Union."[64]

WHO WON?

New York City welcomed the good news from Poughkeepsie, which arrived on the evening of July 26, by firing several "salutes" from Fort George and the ship *Hamilton*, now safely "docked" on the Bowling Green. Merchants at coffeehouses celebrated and crowds visited the homes of Federalist convention members, giving three cheers in recognition of their "united, unremitted, and toilsome Exertions" on behalf of the Constitution. In short, according to a *Supplement Extraordinary to the Independent Journal* published on July 28, a "general joy" ran through the whole city. Even people who were "of different Sentiments drank freely of the *Federal Bowl*, and declared that they were now perfectly reconciled to the New Constitution."[65]

Some supporters of the Constitution marked the occasion in another way. Between one and three in the morning, some five hundred men attacked the home and print shop of Thomas Greenleaf, publisher of the *New-York Journal*. They smashed the windows and threw his type and other printing materials into the street. The ostensible reason was a deprecatory description of the potters' display in an account of the "Grand Federal Procession" that Greenleaf had published. Greenleaf explained that the remarks were given "in a vein of innocent humor." That didn't satisfy enemies who, he understood, had other reasons for attacking his press. They wanted to silence the one newspaper in New York City that regularly published essays critical of the Constitution. When better to do so than in the moment of Federalist triumph?[66]

The mob also visited the homes of Governor Clinton and John Lamb but did no damage there. Clinton wasn't home; Lamb was present, but he had barred his doors and windows, barricaded the stairway with furniture, extinguished all lights, and sat with relatives on the second floor with arms in hand, which persuaded the mob to go away. Greenleaf, who had escaped the attackers through a back door, was able to resume publishing the *New-York Journal* five days later. From then on, however, he published the newspaper, formerly a daily, only once a week. God save us, Eleazer Oswald commented in his *Independent Gazetteer*, "if these be *the dawnings* of the new federal government."[67]

If not all their forms of celebration were admirable, the Federalists at least had reason to celebrate. Despite the fact that they had gone into the convention outnumbered by more than two to one, they—and above all Jay, whose negotiating skills served his cause extremely well in the final weeks of the convention—had secured an unconditional ratification of the Constitution. The radical "Anti" Cornelius Schoonmaker concluded that the Federalists had "outmaneuvered" the majority and, moreover, "fought and beat us from our own ground with our own weapons." He probably meant that they had argued, like the "Antis" on other occasions, that Congress could do only what the Constitution expressly gave it the power to do. Schoonmaker did not, however, think the Federalists had won a great victory since they "very freely declare that they will join with us in applying to Congress, immediately after the organization of the government, to call a convention" that would consider the amendments proposed by New York and the other states.[68] From that perspective, perhaps the "Antis" had won if they had, in fact, gained new and influential proponents for the amendments they sought.

Far from thinking they had lost, some members of the Antifederalist/Republican party said that they had taken the only course possible to achieve their original objective—amending the Constitution—given the fact that by the time they voted the Constitution had been ratified by the requisite number of states and would go into operation with or without New York. That was Melancton Smith's position. Zephaniah Platt said he supported the convention's form of ratification "not from a conviction that the Constitution was a good one or that the Liberties of men were well Secured," but "as a Choice of evils in our own present Situation." The delegates "desided on what we Supposed was for the Intrest and peace of our State under present Curcumstances."[69]

More surprising, Gilbert Livingston, the committed "Anti" whose over-the-top image of lifelong senators hiding behind a wall of gold and diamonds in a corrupt new national capital once provoked laughter from convention delegates, ended up perfectly happy with how the convention ended. In a moving speech before the final vote, Livingston said he had come to the convention "as fully determined on previous amendments" as any other delegates, and he would not have changed his position in a way that put him at odds with many friends except from a conviction that he was serving his country's best interests. Sometime soon after the convention assembled, he revealed, the Antifederalist/Republican delegates had met and discovered that a majority was against simply rejecting the Constitution. The only issue then was how best to insure that a general convention of the states would meet and graft onto the Constitution those amendments necessary to make it safe. Now, after careful reflection, he had decided that "the adoption on the table, with the bill of rights and amendments contained in it, and the circular letter to the different States accompanying it," was, "considering our *present* situation with respect to our sister States, the wisest and best measure, we can possibly pursue." He would vote for it, and he was willing to stand before God having made that decision on "this most *important* transaction of my life." Like Platt, he promised to continue, with all true friends of his country, seeking by all possible means "to procure this desirable object, a revision of the Constitution."[70]

Once Livingston had finished, Henry Wisner, an Antifederalist from Orange County, said that he had come to the convention determined to reject the Constitution, then watched as the delegates moved, "from one step to another," toward a conclusion for which, after careful reflection, he could not vote. If the convention adopted its unconditional form of ratification, he would, however, "aid it all he can."[71]

Not all the Antifederalists who voted against the convention's ratification were so generous. They focused their anger on Smith, who later lost a seat in the new Senate because, Governor Clinton explained, he had "disgusted many of the Antifeds. by acceding to the Ratification of the Constitution."[72] Certainly Smith knew what risks he took. Although he had tried to find a position that would keep the members of his party from being, as he put it, using the language of Scripture, "dispersed like sheep on a mountain,"[73] he finally voted not for the interest of his party but for the good of his state and his country as he understood it.

Such a decision is rarely without cost, but it also brought some personal gain. The convention's decision to ratify saved Smith from the riotous reception on his return to Manhattan that Samuel Osgood predicted in the event of a negative vote. The city was still not entirely safe for the "Antis," as the attack on Greenleaf and the threat to Lamb demonstrated. However, a broadside *Supplement Extraordinary to the Independent Journal* for Monday, July 28, described in detail for New York City readers how Smith had fought for a form of ratification that would keep New York in the union.[74] He would not make it to the United States Senate, but Melancton Smith could at least go home again.

———— ★ ————

FOURTEEN

Some Final Twists

The North Carolina Convention, a Meeting in Pennsylvania,

and the Ratification Story Draws to an End

The news from Poughkeepsie delighted Henry Knox, and he was quick to give credit where it was due. It went to "Messrs Jay Hamilton and the rest of the federalists," who "derived great honor from their temperate and wise conduct during the tedious debates" at the New York ratifying convention, and also "those Gentlemen who were opposed to the constitution in the first instance, but afterwards voted for its adoption . . . when it became apparent," as he saw it, "that a perseverance in opposition would most probably terminate in Civil War."[1]

James Madison was neither so delighted nor so gracious. New York's Federalists had given up too much to bring their state into the union. New York's circular letter had "a most pestilent tendency. If an Early General Convention cannot be parried, it is seriously to be feared that the System which has resisted so many direct attacks may be at last successfully undermined by its enemies." Federalists could have consented to the circular letter only "to purchase an immediate ratification in any form and at any price" rather than lose New York City's chance of becoming the new government's meeting place. He might even have preferred to have New York reject the Constitution than to ratify and adopt the circular letter. A rejection would have alarmed "well meaning antifederalists elsewhere," done no harm to the Federalists, raised the indignation of neighboring states, and led to a "speedy reconsideration of the subject."[2]

Was he unaware that John Jay, a fellow author of *The Federalist*, had drafted much of the circular letter? Jay had no second thoughts about his role. Opposition to the Constitution in New York had decreased and become more moderate since the convention adjourned, he wrote Washington in Septem-

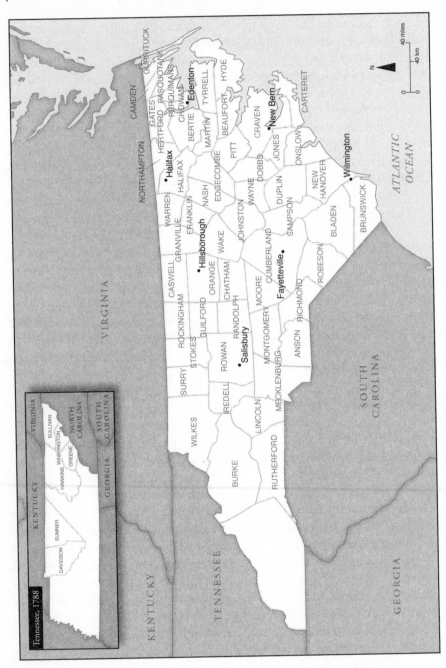

North Carolina, 1788

ber. New Yorkers had no expectation that a general convention would approve all the amendments their convention recommended; they assumed that some would be enacted, others rejected. He hoped New York's call for a second convention to consider amendments to the Constitution would be accepted "with a good Grace, and without Delay or Hesitation." Jay did not, however, think the convention had to meet quickly. The circular letter called for the second convention to convene "at a period not far remote," but Jay suggested that it could be put off for as much as three or four years without opposition. By then it would be of no danger if, as Jay expected, the new government recommended itself to the people "by the wisdom of its Proceedings."[3]

Madison considered the circular letter a far more immediate threat. And if developments in New York caused him concern, he would soon get worse news from a place he least expected to receive it. Like Washington, Madison assumed that North Carolina would ratify the Constitution once Virginia showed the way. North Carolina did not, however, follow Virginia's example. In fact, although North Carolina's ratifying convention was the twelfth to meet, it managed to be different from any of its predecessors in the course, character, and to some extent the contents of its debates—and, above all, its outcome.

As the ratification contest drew to an end, Madison and even Washington, the eternal optimist, found more reasons for concern than for celebration.

NORTH CAROLINA: THE END OF THE ROAD?

The ratification struggle began early in North Carolina and seemed to go on forever. In the summer of 1787, before the federal Convention had completed its work, Federalists began working for the election of state legislators who would be sympathetic to a significantly stronger national government. The elections were often literally hard fought (in Orange County, one prominent Federalist had "his eyes blackened" by an opponent), and when the general assembly met on November 17, 1787, critics of the Constitution controlled both houses. They had, however, no intention of departing from the prescribed way of considering the Constitution, like their counterparts in Rhode Island. In early December, the general assembly set the last Friday and Saturday of March, 1788, for the election of delegates to a state ratifying convention that would convene in the town of Hillsborough on Monday, July 21, "for the purpose of deliberating and determining on" the proposed Constitution. Each of the state's fifty-eight counties could send five delegates, and its six borough towns could send one each, so the convention, with just under three hundred members if every constituency were fully represented, would be one of the country's largest. Any inhabitant qualified to vote for members of the lower house of the state legislature (freemen of at least twenty-one years of age who had lived in some county for twelve months and paid public taxes) could vote, but only freeholders—land owners—could serve as delegates. Since there were no residency requirements for delegates, they could sit for any county or borough that chose them.[4]

The date of the convention, some seven and a half months in the future, was late; North Carolina's convention would be the last to meet before the new government began. The nearly four-month gap between the election of delegates and the meeting of the convention was especially curious. Some observers, particularly Virginians, thought that North Carolina had delayed the meeting of its convention so it could see what Virginia did before making its decision on the Constitution, but that was not the case. North Carolinians learned when the Virginia convention would meet only after their convention had already been scheduled.[5] Some other states where opposition to the Constitution was strong also scheduled their conventions relatively late, perhaps assuming—incorrectly, as it turned out—that time was on their side.

In North Carolina, geography also argued for leaving a healthy length of time between the assembly's December vote and the elections in March. In the late eighteenth century, the state was enormous. It stretched some five hundred miles from the Atlantic to the Appalachians; then it continued another four hundred miles beyond the mountains to the Mississippi, including what would become the state of Tennessee, much of which remained in the possession of Indians. By the census of 1790, North Carolina had the country's fourth-highest population—almost 430,000 ethnically and religiously diverse people. All but about 36,000 of them lived east of the mountains, where rivers, creeks, and bays cut the land into pieces, making communication slow and difficult. Bridges were welcome but rare, and the ferries that crossed coastal sounds and bays were slow and often out of service. Then there were the long stretches of forest, the swamps, the primitive roads that made it easy to get lost. Stagecoaches began offering service in North Carolina during the mid-1780s, but they remained, like the postal system they served, notoriously unreliable. It would take time for the people of such a state to get the information they needed to make an intelligent decision on the Constitution. The legislature did its best: It ordered three hundred copies of its resolutions calling a convention and 1,500 copies of the Constitution and asked its members, who would be going home anyway, to circulate them among their constituents.[6]

The state had a handful of towns, including Wilmington, New Bern, and Edenton, on bays along the ragged eastern edge of the mainland. Most of the state's newspapers were published there, but their reach was modest. Before 1790, they sold at best about 150 copies. (By comparison, by 1776 newspapers in Philadelphia had circulations as high as 3,000 copies.)[7] Many of the state's largest estates and the greatest concentration of its slaves were also in counties in the eastern side of the state, or Tidewater. However, North Carolina had no major port because barrier islands—the Outer Banks—separated its coast from the Atlantic, and the occasional inlets were too shallow for ocean-going ships; most of the state's external trade was carried through South Carolina or Virginia. As elsewhere, North Carolinians who were involved in commerce favored the Constitution, even those in inland towns such as Halifax or Hillsborough, but there were fewer of such people than in many other states. North Carolina also had relatively few of those "better people"—men of wealth and education—who tended to be Federalist. Most North Carolinians lived on isolated and scattered small farms.[8]

Particularly if they lived in the Piedmont, a region in the western reaches of North Carolina proper, they saw more dangers than benefits in the proposed federal Constitution for reasons buried in their own experiences. Between 1766 and 1771, the residents of Orange, Anson, Rowan, and adjacent counties had waged a vigorous fight against corrupt county officials who were appointed by the royal governor and his council and whose "highest Study," critics charged, was "the Promotion of their Wealth." The county officials collected illegal taxes and fees, pocketed the proceeds, and sometimes auctioned off the property of poor farmers who couldn't pay—in part because of a lack of currency, as in Massachusetts during the 1780s—for less than the property's real value. The "Regulators" at first petitioned for help from the legislature, which was badly malapportioned in favor of the Tidewater, and tried other peaceful means of redressing their grievances, including actions in court, without success. When, as they saw it, all the alternatives had failed, they used force to protect their rights and property, closing courts and intimidating appointed officials including court officers, sheriffs, and tax collectors. Their resistance had some parallels with that of the Sons of Liberty who opposed British "oppression," but it came out badly. On May 16, 1771, the royal governor, William Tryon, and a body of 1,185 militiamen, drawn predominantly from the Tidewater, crushed some two or three thousand untrained and poorly armed Regulators at the Battle of Alamance in Orange County.[9] Strangely, North Carolinians prominent in the resistance to Britain supported the repression of the Regulators, whom they said had turned to force prematurely and without cause, while their counterparts in others states cheered on the Regulators.[10]

North Carolina's relatively democratic 1776 state constitution did much to address the insurgents' demands for greater control over those who ruled them, and its declaration of rights affirmed the right of the people "to assemble together, to consult for their common good, to instruct their Representatives . . . to apply to the Legislature, for redress of grievances"; it said the people "ought not to be taxed, or made subject to the payment of any impost or duty, without the consent of themselves, or their Representatives in General Assembly, freely given."[11] Still, memories of the Regulation—or, more exactly, the grievances that prompted it—made many North Carolinians acutely conscious of how much their welfare depended on being governed by officials who were accountable to the people, under laws written by legislators who knew the circumstances of their constituents and who might even be, as the Regulators had insisted, farmers themselves. Having suffered from the twin scourges of corruption and collusion, the people of the Piedmont understood with particular force the need to prevent them in the future. And having had more than enough experience with litigation, they also grasped the importance of juries drawn from the local population and a ready access to the courts. The Regulators had managed to secure the creation of four new western counties mainly to make trips to county courts less long and onerous.[12] The Constitution too often ran up against those sensitivities.

Western North Carolinians had other tangible reasons to connect the Constitution with their painful past. Governor Samuel Johnston, a strong Federalist, had sponsored a draconian riot act used against the Regulators seventeen years earlier. The convention would also meet in Hillsborough, the county seat of Orange County, where, on June 19, 1771, six Regulators were publicly hanged on a carefully cleared hilltop before a crowd of onlookers that included the condemned men's wives, children, and sympathizers.[13] Regulator ghosts roamed freely through Hillsborough.

North Carolinians discussed the Constitution with passion in taverns, at militia musters, on court days, and wherever else the people gathered. Grand jury presentments were one way they could make their views known: On November 12, 1787, the grand jury of the Edenton district praised the Constitution and called on the state legislature to call a ratifying convention "on as early a day as possible." The statement was drafted by James Iredell, a thirty-six-year-old lawyer who would be a star speaker at the Hillsborough convention.[14] Voters could also instruct their elected delegates how to vote: Two convention delegates, one from Wilkes County in the far northwest and another from inland Franklin County, said their constituents had instructed them to oppose the Constitution.[15] In most places, however, electors probably cast their ballots for men who thought as they did and expected them to vote accordingly at the state convention.

An account of a particularly raucous election in Dobbs County in late March 1788 from New Bern's *North Carolina Gazette* allows us to "see" the scene at the courthouse in Kinston, the county seat. The sheriff, election inspectors, and clerks sat at a bench, perhaps where judges sat during trials, watching as the county's 372 voters cast ballots into a box. There were five candidates "supposed to be in favor of the Federal Constitution," including an ex-governor and other prominent North Carolinians, and five who were "supposed to be" opposed to it, most of whom were obscure men without political experience. How the candidates had been chosen went unsaid, but they apparently did not sit together on a platform or "husting," as in Virginia. The balloting went on until sunset, and, as the natural light waned, people lit candles, which they apparently held in their hands. Then the polls closed and the sheriff began "calling out" the "tickets"—pulling ballots from the box and reading them out loud while the other officials and the spectators kept count.[16]

He made it through 282 ballots. The lowest "Antifederalist" had 155, the highest "Federalist" only 121; and, as the tickets were "coming out fast in favor of the Antifederalists," the "other party," and in particular one Federalist candidate, Colonel Benjamin Sheppard, seeing that he was going to lose, became "exasperated." First he started verbally abusing the other candidates; then he went to the bench and threatened to beat one of the inspectors. Suddenly the Federalists—at least twelve or fifteen of them—pulled out a set of clubs they had hidden and knocked or pulled down all the candle holders, throwing the hall into darkness. "Many blows with clubs were heard to pass," the *Gazette* reported, but most were said to land on fellow Federalists since the "Antifederalists," who came unprepared to defend themselves, "expecting better treatment" from opponents who considered themselves "gentlemen," fled for their lives. One blow, however, hit the sheriff. Then "the ticket box was violently taken away," which effectively ended the election with no official result.[17]

Colonel Sheppard (or "Shepherd"), whom a contemporary described as "a man of considerable property and great influence in Dobbs County," apparently had no monopoly on violence. The following July he got into a scrape with some local "antifederalists" who attacked him with axes and left him "on the ground, almost void of speech, and insensible," with blood pouring from his mouth, nose, and ears "in considerable quantities." However, his bad conduct at the Dobbs County courthouse might well have denied critics of the Constitution five seats in the convention. In going over the record, the convention's elections committee invalidated the results because enough ballots remained uncounted to give the election to candidates other than those who had a majority when the ballot box was taken away "by violence." The committee also invalidated a second election, held on the recommendation of the governor, because the people of the county opposed it (only eighty-five Federalists showed up). Dobbs County would go unrepresented at the ratifying convention in Hillsborough.[18]

The account of the Dobbs County election gives no sign of organized parties like those in New York's Hudson Valley. The candidates who were "supposed" to be for or against the Constitution do not seem to have been nominated by county "Federalist" or "Antifederalist" committees. (The "Antis," however, voted only for the five men who shared their views, which indicated a discipline the Federalists lacked.) It isn't even clear whether candidates "supposed to be opposers" of the Constitution called themselves "Antifederalists" or whether the newspaper writer threw in that name. Neither Timothy Bloodworth, an ardent opponent of ratification, nor his political colleague Thomas Person used the term in letters to John Lamb in New York. Bloodworth wrote "In behalf of the Committee of Correspondence," with no more specific name attached to a group that pledged to fight the unamended Constitution "with pure melting ardor."[19]

Despite the lack of conspicuous party organizations, there seems to have been little doubt over where candidates for the convention stood. When the elections were over, those against unqualified ratification outnumbered supporters by over two to one, roughly the same division as at Poughkeepsie when the New York ratifying convention began.

THE "DEBATES" AT HILLSBOROUGH

New York's ratifying convention met for thirty-five days, that of North Carolina for only thirteen, between Monday, July 21, when some two hundred delegates gathered at St. Matthew's Church in the town of Hillsborough, through August 4, when the meeting adjourned. Other delegates arrived, in clumps or trickles, on succeeding days: Their names and times of arrival were carefully recorded in the convention's journal. As usual, the delegates spent the first few days electing officers (Governor Samuel Johnston became president of the convention), settling rules, and examining delegates' credentials.[20]

Next, on a motion by James Galloway, a Scottish immigrant and critic of the Constitution from Rockingham County in the Piedmont, a set of documents was read aloud, including the North Carolina constitution and bill of rights, the Articles of Confederation, the proposed federal Constitution, the resolution of the Confederation Congress asking the states to call ratifying conventions, and the act of the state legislature that had brought the delegates to Hillsborough. The president also "laid before the Convention" official accounts of the ratification of the Constitution by Massachusetts and South Carolina.[21]

The *Journal of the Convention of North Carolina*, which was published in late 1788, after the convention adjourned, tells the story to that point. Like most official journals, it reports the motions made in the convention when it sat as a convention, but no speeches. Fortunately, two leading supporters of the Constitution, James Iredell and William R. Davie, hired a man named Robinson to take shorthand notes of the North Carolina convention's debates with the intention of publishing them later. Unfortunately, the relationship went sour. Robinson apparently remained at work through North Carolina's relatively short convention, then lost interest in the project.

Rather than make a "fair copy" of the debates and check it again against his "short-hand manuscript," he hired a "little boy, the son of Mr. Turnbull," to copy all but a few pages, sent the result to Davie, and then stopped answering Davie's letters. "We have been grossly used in this business," Davie wrote Iredell; "the money was all he was interested in"—that is, the money Robinson received in advance—and the reporter was unwilling to see the debates through the press. The boy's copy—not, Davie suspected, Robinson's original notes—made such a mess of some speeches that Davie had to copy them over, "making no alterations except where [the] sense was entirely perverted." He figured purchasers of the book were unlikely to be concerned about those corrections, but they would expect "grammatical English at least," assuming that was "the business of the Stenographer."[22] He and Iredell managed to get the manuscript published the next year as *The Proceedings and Debates of the Convention of North Carolina, Convened at Hillsborough on Monday, the 21st day of July, 1788*. . . . It carried a note on its final page explaining that the unnamed person who took the notes had a "very inconvenient seat in the gallery" and was "frequently molested by the noise" in the gallery and below. Consequently, he feared that his account might include some inaccuracies and omissions, but he assured the delegates and the public that he was motivated only by a strict attention to "justice and impartiality."[23]

As records go, *The Proceedings and Debates* is less than ideal. Federalists published it to support their cause. Davie, and possibly Iredell, might also have revised the accounts of their speeches more than Davie admitted,[24] though Davie seems to have had some respect for the integrity of the record, such as it was. Unlike the Federalist-sponsored published debates of the Pennsylvania convention, *The Proceedings and Debates* includes speeches and other interventions by critics of the Constitution, even when they argued well, and describes the course of a convention that, despite a similar political division, developed in a different way from that of New York and, in fact, from all of its predecessors.

According to the *Proceedings and Debates*, once the convention had heard the Constitution and other documents read aloud, Galloway moved that the Constitution should be discussed clause by clause. Then his political colleague Willie (pronounced "Wylie") Jones moved an alternative motion: that the question should be put immediately. The Constitution had been discussed for so long, Jones said, that everyone in the convention was ready to vote, and a short convention would save the state a lot of money.[25]

Jones, who represented inland Halifax County and was a leading critic of the Constitution, had a reputation as a radical democrat, but he was no common man. Born in Surry County, Virginia, Jones moved to North Carolina with his parents and siblings in the 1750s. He was educated in England and, after returning to America in the 1760s, became a part of the elite circle around North Carolina's royal governors. He served as William Tryon's aide-de-camp when he marched against the Regulators in May 1771. Soon, however, Jones embraced the Revolution and began an active political career in the state legislature and the Continental Congress. He also served on the state's Revolutionary council of safety and its council of state. He was elected a North Carolina delegate to the federal Convention, but (like Patrick Henry) he declined the appointment, being uncertain, as he explained, that he could be present at the appointed time. Jones would not have been out of place among the gentlemen gathered at Philadelphia in the summer of 1787: He was a wealthy planter with some 120 slaves and so was one of North Carolina's largest slaveholders, as well as a man with a sense of style and a taste for life's luxuries.[26]

Jones had clearly not coordinated action with Galloway. However, Thomas Person quickly seconded Jones's motion. A supporter of the Regulators (he narrowly escaped the gallows in 1771), brigadier general in the Revolutionary War, longtime member of the state house of commons, and large landholder, Person represented Granville County, which was in the Piedmont, northeast of Orange County. He too questioned whether any delegate had come to Hillsborough undecided on the Constitution. It looked like the delegates might go home before they had so much as unpacked.[27] But Iredell objected: He was astonished at the suggestion that delegates decide "without the least deliberation" a question that was "perhaps the greatest that ever was submitted to any body of men." He had come to the convention inclined to vote for ratification, and his constituents had probably chosen him because their views were like his. He would, however, have refused to attend if they instructed him how to vote, and he was ready to oppose ratification if convinced that his present opinion was wrong. No doubt it was necessary to conserve public funds, but not when the question could well involve "the safety or ruin of our country."[28]

Iredell had an unlikely career. He came to Edenton at age seventeen as a British customs officer, about as unpopular a job as any man could hold in America, and had the additional bad luck of arriving in 1768, when the colonists' opposition to Britain's Townshend Acts, which attempted to raise revenue through import duties, was in full swing. Most British officials became Loyalists, but not Iredell. He studied law under Samuel Johnston (who later became the state's governor and president of the ratifying convention), married Johnston's sister, Hannah, in 1773, and supported the Revolution even at the risk of losing a legacy from a rich and intensely patriotic British relative in Jamaica.[29]

Iredell's income from the customs service disappeared with independence, but, having cast his lot with the Americans, he became a state superior court judge and then state attorney general. He returned to private practice in 1781, riding from place to place to serve his clients, who included several Loyalists, laboriously scratching out a living to support his wife and family. The couple had gone childless for over a decade before 1784, when their first child, a son, was born—and then died after only two days. Other children, all the more precious for their parents' waiting, followed: A daughter, Annie, was born in 1785, and a son, James Jr., in late 1788, after the Hillsborough convention had adjourned. Later, in 1792, they had a second daughter, Helen.[30]

Iredell became one of the state's most respected lawyers. He often contributed to the local newspapers and, in early 1788, wrote an extended essay, later published as a pamphlet, that answered each of George Mason's objections to the Constitution. However, Iredell had never served in an elected body before Edenton chose him as its delegate to the Hillsborough convention. There his courtroom experience served him well. Iredell did not, like James Wilson in Pennsylvania, try to win a place in history as a great orator. He argued as if he were speaking to a jury, staying close to the point and taking care to alienate no possible ally. He could be eloquent, but his eloquence was always part of an effort to persuade. His achievement was all the more striking because he struggled with a speech impediment of some kind that "would have abashed and discouraged weaker minds."[31]

Iredell's first convention speech prevented a precipitous vote and fast end to the convention: Jones and Person agreed to a debate on the Constitution. After some circuitous discussion on how to proceed, the convention resolved itself into a committee of the whole on Thursday, July 24, and began to discuss the document, paragraph by paragraph.[32] That is, the Federalists discussed the Constitution. Jones and all but a handful his colleagues remained silent, letting long sections go by without comment. The Constitution's defenders filled the silence, offering a knowledgeable and relatively succinct running explication and defense of one provision of the Constitution after another.

Iredell took the lead. Davie gave him substantial support, particularly in explaining and defending the federal Convention, which Davie had attended (though he left before signing the Constitution) along with another ratifying convention delegate, Richard Dobbs Spaight. Davie, who was thirty-two in 1788, five years younger than Iredell, had come to America from Scotland with his parents at age eight in 1764, finished the College of New Jersey (later Princeton) in 1776, joined the nasty fight against the British and Loyalist partisans in the southern Piedmont, and later became a lawyer in Halifax, North Carolina, with an avid interest in politics and horse racing. Spaight, two years younger than Davie, was a native Carolinian who had attended the University of Glasgow in Scotland. He returned to North Carolina in 1778, fought in the Revolutionary War, and held seats in the state legislature and the Confederation Congress before winning places at the federal Convention and the state ratifying convention, where he sat for New Bern. Spaight corresponded with

Iredell, and, like Davie, probably talked with him at length about the convention in Philadelphia. For a man who had not been at the federal Convention, Iredell became amazingly knowledgeable about its proceedings.[33]

Archibald Maclaine, a crotchety, fifty-nine-year-old lawyer, planter, and Scots-Irish immigrant who represented the town of Wilmington, also spoke frequently and intelligently at the North Carolina ratifying convention, but often, like Robert R. Livingston in New York, "impolitically." Where Iredell urged fellow delegates to state their qualms about the Constitution and treated their arguments with respect, Maclaine dismissed opponents' objections as "very trifling," "silly," or founded on "horrid ignorance" and "advanced by persons who ought to know better." That was no way to get the other side to speak out or to win them over. At least Maclaine was consistent: The essays signed "Publicola," which he had published the previous March, treated those who criticized the Constitution in much the same way.[34]

Carrying on a debate with tight-lipped opponents was no easy thing, so the Federalists sometimes answered objections that had been made in print but not at the convention. That caused some flak. After Maclaine defended biennial elections for congressmen, another delegate questioned the propriety of the Constitution's supporters "making objections, when none were urged by its opposers." It was "very uncommon," he observed, for a man "to make objections and answer them himself," and it would take an immense amount of time to answer every argument against the Constitution raised anywhere in the country. What else could the Constitution's supporters do? Willie Jones had a tongue-in-cheek answer: "Let one of them . . . make objections and another answer them."[35] Consenting to holding a debate on the Constitution and agreeing to participate were, it seems, entirely different things.

About half a dozen critics of the Constitution were willing to speak, but they felt no obligation to mount a comprehensive attack on the Constitution, like their counterparts at the Virginia convention. They made only objections that seemed to them "necessary to be made," as Judge Samuel Spencer put it.[36] There they argued hard and stood their ground. The issues that provoked something akin to a normal, two-sided debate often involved the familiar, connected issues of representation and taxation.

Spencer, a native of Connecticut, where he was born in January 1734, was, like his opponent Davie, a graduate of the College of New Jersey (1759); he held substantial land in Anson County, old Regulator country, which he represented at the convention. In 1771 he had stood beside Governor Tryon at the Alamance and against the Regulators, whom he considered a licentious mob. At the ratifying convention, however, Spencer's arguments were in keeping with the sensitivities of his constituents and coincided well with those of Person, who had supported the Regulators. Now a state superior court judge with whom Iredell had served briefly, Spencer took strong exception to

Congress's power under Article I, Section 4, to lay aside state decisions on the times, places, and manner of choosing members of Congress. He said that "reprehensible clause" would undermine the representation system, destroy the power of the states, and lead toward a consolidation of government.[37]

Iredell, like Federalists elsewhere, explained that the provision was meant for occasions when the states did not or could not provide for elections, such as in the event of an invasion, and that in no case could Congress override the provision that representatives must be chosen every second year. Spencer remained unconvinced. Iredell read the provision that way, but others could interpret it differently. Its "vague and uncertain" words would ultimately "destroy the whole liberty of the United States." Timothy Bloodworth agreed. A native North Carolinian from a poor family with no formal education who had scratched out a living in one trade after another (innkeeper, blacksmith, wheelwright, ferryman, preacher, farmer, even doctor), longtime state legislator and ardent democrat, Bloodworth represented New Hanover County in the Cape Fear region of the Tidewater. He said the clause would allow Congress to "make the time of election so long, the place so inconvenient, and the manner so oppressive, that it will entirely destroy representation." Then other opponents of an unqualified ratification joined in. If the Constitution's framers intended Congress to exercise its power over elections only when the states failed to act, why didn't they say that? If adopted in its current state, the Constitution would lead, as Bloodworth said, to "the subversion of our liberties."[38]

Several critics of the Constitution took the floor again when Article I, Section 8, came up for discussion. Spencer immediately said that Congress's taxing power was "too extensive" because it included every form of taxation, leaving no source of revenue for the states. Moreover, "every power is given over our money to those over whom we have no immediate control." Spencer said he was all for the creation of an efficient federal government that could enforce its powers on individuals, not states. He was willing to let the federal government collect taxes on imports and also, more reluctantly, excise taxes, which he described as "odious to a free people." But direct taxes, which for him included poll taxes and "assessments on land or other property," were both inconvenient and oppressive. If the state legislatures, which were more aware than Congress of the people's ability to pay, were allowed to levy a state's share of direct taxes, the problem would be solved.[39]

Spencer's fears—and, as became clear, those of many other North Carolinians—were not theoretical but immediate. There was, he said, "no hard money" in North Carolina. If the federal government levied taxes payable in gold or silver, the people could not pay and would see their lands, slaves, animals, and furniture seized for nonpayment of taxes and auctioned off for a tenth of their real value, causing "great distresses." The state legislature could tailor a tax to their situation, for example by accepting farm produce suitable for export in place of hard money. Having the state levy taxes to meet a federal quota would also reaffirm the importance of state legislatures. If the state did not pay its quota punctually, however, Spencer—like John Lansing in New York—was willing to let Congress collect direct taxes itself, because "this power is absolutely necessary for the support of the general government."[40]

Governor Johnston answered that taxes in kind like those Spencer suggested were tried during the war and proved to be the most oppressive and least productive taxes ever known in North Carolina. Moreover, if the states were charged with levying direct taxes, they would have to collect the entire outstanding amount, but Congress could borrow the sum needed and collect only the interest on the debt, which would be far less burdensome. Nor would the requisition system reaffirm the states' importance. Past experience showed that the states would not pay the requisitions and so would "be disgraced." Then the people would resist federal tax collectors, causing "insurrections and confusion."[41] He sounded just like his counterparts in earlier conventions.

Again, Spencer would not yield. "The most certain criterion of happiness that any people can have, is to be taxed . . . by those representatives who intermix with them, and know their circumstances. . . . Our federal representatives cannot sufficiently know our situation and circumstances." In case of war, he would be willing to let Congress collect direct taxes before waiting for the states to act. But he believed that if the state legislatures paid requisitions promptly, as they would if inaction brought federal tax collectors into the state, the system would not damage Congress's capacity to borrow. Between the two systems—letting the states normally collect federal direct taxes versus having Congress levy them itself—there was "an immense difference. The one will produce the happiness, ease, and prosperity of the people; the other will destroy them, and produce insurrections."[42]

No Federalist effort to defend congressional power "to lay and collect taxes" was any more successful. Joseph McDowell, one of three McDowells (two brothers and a second cousin, who was also Joseph McDowell's brother-in-law) on the delegation from Burke County in western North Carolina, where the hills of the Piedmont meet the Blue Ridge Mountains, was adamant. "Mr. Chairman," he said, "this is a power I will never agree to give up from the hands of the people of this country." The income from duties on trade would be trifling and the taxes high given the "very great" expenses of the new government. He knew the situation of the people. "They have no money." If Congress levied a tax of "two shillings per hundred" acres of land, how would they pay it? They might, with industry and frugality, help pay requisitions through moderate taxes levied by people who knew their situation and had "a feeling for them." But federal tax collectors would, "like the locusts of old, destroy us."[43] McDowell's colleague William Goudy from Guilford County in central North Carolina said he couldn't follow "these learned gentlemen" who defended the Constitution "through all the laby-rinths of their oratory," but he didn't have to. The issue was simple: "Whether it be proper to give any man, or any set of men, an unlimited power over our purse, without any kind of control." The people had "no gold or silver, no sub-stantial money, to pay taxes with." The clause on taxes along with that giving Congress power over elections "will totally destroy our liberties."[44]

Anxiety over federal taxes and the men who would collect them also lay behind a handful of earlier objections to the final provision in Article I, Sec-tion 2, which said the House of Representatives "shall have the sole power of impeachment." Some delegates feared they would have to go "to Congress, at an immense distance," to get relief from federal tax collectors who abused their powers. That prompted one of Maclaine's outbursts: Impeachment was re-served for "high crimes and misdemeanors," not lesser injuries to property that could be redressed through suits at law. "I never heard, in my life, of such a silly objection. A poor, insignificant, petty officer amenable to impeachment!"[45]

No other powers of Congress provoked a debate equivalent to that on taxes. In fact, the rest of Article I inspired very little discussion. Two crit-ics of the Constitution objected to the provision in Article I, Section 9, that assured that the slave trade could continue for another twenty years. They thought that "abominable trade" should be ended—but not slavery itself. "If we must manumit our slaves," Galloway asked, "what country shall we send them to? It is impossible for us to be happy, if, after manumission, they are to stay with us."[46] Section 10, which prohibited the states from emitting bills of credit, making anything but gold and silver legal tender, or impairing the obligation of contracts seems to have gone by without comment. That was strange: North Carolina had twice issued highly controversial legal-tender paper money that depreciated, like that of Rhode Island (though to a lesser extent). It later became clear that delegates wondered what would come of the state's outstanding currency under the Constitution and whether state taxpayers would have to redeem old, depreciated obligations at face value and with hard money.[47] For the moment, however, they seem to have said nothing.

As the delegates turned to Article II, Section 1, and the majority members again held their tongues, Davie expressed alarm at the speed with which the delegates were hurrying through the Constitution. "We are assembled here to deliberate for our own common welfare, and to decide upon a question of infinite importance to our country." Why were the "gentlemen of the opposi-tion" so silent? Joseph Taylor, who had been born in Virginia and represented Granville County, along the Virginia border, said it would be a "useless waste of time" to dwell on passages that had already been considered "in some degree," and he would object only when an "essential defect" of the Constitu-tion came before the house. Later in the day he attacked Congress's power to set dates for choosing presidential electors, but no one supported him.[48]

When nobody else took the floor, Iredell spoke, explaining the meaning and significance of provision after provision, answering common objections along the way. Often he restated standard Federalist positions, but sometimes his arguments came at a familiar issue from a new angle. He argued, for example, that the clause in Article II, Section 2, which said the president "may require the Opinion, in writing, of the principal Officer in each of the Executive departments," was an appropriate substitute for the executive or privy council that "many gentlemen" advocated. The idea of an executive council, he argued, came from the British past and showed how difficult it was for Americans to disengage themselves from familiar British institutions. Since the British king holds office by hereditary claim and "can do no wrong"—that is, he cannot be tried for crimes or constitutionally removed from office—it was essential that he have advisers who were answerable for his policies. But "if the President does a single act by which the people are prejudiced, he is punishable himself," with no other men to screen him. He could be impeached, removed from office, and made incapable of holding other public offices for "high crimes and misdemeanors," or tried in the courts of the land for more ordinary crimes. There was therefore no reason for an executive council on the British model. If the president needed advice, the principal officers of his government would be "on the spot." In the end, the president would have to exercise his own judgment because he would "have the credit of good, or the censure of bad measures." A formal council risked diluting that personal responsibility. Iredell had made the argument before in answering George Mason's objections to the Constitution, but his comments in the convention were shorter and clearer. Together his convention speeches remain among the best glosses on the Constitution, particularly on the powers of the president and the limitations on those powers, anywhere in the ratification debates.[49]

If Iredell did not convince the majority members, he at least broke their silence. One delegate conceded that Iredell had "obviated some objections" but still insisted that the president had too much power, particularly over the military. Congress should be entrusted not only with declaring war, but given power "to direct the motions of the army." Another delegate objected to the power of the president, with two-thirds of the Senate, to negotiate and ratify treaties that would be "the supreme law of the land." That power could be used to "sacrifice the most valuable interests of the community," even to "give up the rivers and territory of the Southern States," since a quorum of senators might all be drawn from "the small, pitiful states to the north." And how would the malefactors be brought to account? An impeached president would be tried by the Senate, which might have advised the actions that led to his impeachment, and there was no provision for trying senators. Spencer also argued, despite Iredell's earlier comments on the inappropriateness of an executive council, that the proposed government "would have been infinitely better and more secure" if the president had a standing council made up of one member from each state. Giving the task of advising the President to a council rather than to the Senate would more effectively separate the legislative and executive branches. It would also end the "farce" of having an impeached president tried by the same men who had advised him.[50]

The delegates then zipped through the rest of Article II with only one speech by Maclaine, who answered objections nobody had made. It was still Monday, July 28, the delegates' fourth day deliberating the Constitution, when the convention turned to Article III and the judiciary. Spencer said the broad jurisdiction of federal courts would leave the state judiciaries with so "very little to do" that it would become "almost useless to keep them up," which would lead toward an oppressive consolidation or centralization of American government. People would also be forced to go to "far-distant tribunals" to settle issues that could easily be handled in state courts. Spencer was a state judge, but he insisted that his objections were not based on self-interest because the changes were unlikely to affect him personally. It would take time to establish federal courts, and even more for their jurisdiction to "materially affect the state judiciaries." He was moved only by a desire that the new government would be "so constructed as to promote the happiness, harmony, and liberty, of every individual at home, and render us respectable as a nation abroad."[51]

Spencer introduced another objection to the Constitution: "There is no declaration of rights, to secure to every member of the society those unalienable rights which ought not to be given up to any government." The Federalists, he knew, argued that the states retained all power not formally granted to the new government. The Articles of Confederation made that point explicitly, but the Constitution did not. Spencer suggested that such a provision might have made a declaration of rights unnecessary. Now, however, since there was no such clause, he argued powerfully for a declaration or bill of rights "ascertaining and securing the great rights of the states and the people" as a way to keep the government within bounds and "keep the states from being swallowed up by a consolidated government." The Articles of Confederation did not need to include specific protections of individual rights since they operated on the states. The Constitution, however, would act on individuals, which meant that their "great essential rights," which government was founded to protect, had to be carefully secured. With regard to basic human rights, "no latitude ought to be left. They are the most inestimable gifts of the great Creator."[52]

The Federalists quickly answered Spencer's attack on federal court jurisdiction. State courts, Governor Johnston said, would have the same jurisdiction as before, which brought them "a vast deal of business." Moreover, the federal courts' jurisdiction in "all cases in law and equity arising under the Constitution and laws of the United States" was concurrent—that is, shared with the state courts, not exclusive. Iredell had no doubt that Congress would keep their constituents from the inconvenience of frequent trips to distant federal courts by allowing appeals to the Supreme Court only in very important cases "where the object may be adequate to the expense" and perhaps having the court sit in different places at different times.[53]

The Constitution's advocates also repeated the standard argument that no bill of rights was needed under the Constitution "because the powers of Congress are expressly defined." For Iredell, bills of rights were another old English institution that made sense in a country "where no written constitution is to be found," but not in the United States, where, under the Constitution, the people "expressly declare how much power they do give, and consequently retain all they do not." A bill of rights would, moreover, be dangerous because not all rights could be listed, which might imply that those not mentioned did not exist. When Spencer persisted, Maclaine—Mr. Maladroit—said simply "the gentleman's objections to the want [lack] of a bill of rights had been sufficiently answered."[54]

Nothing dented the opposition. Instead, Johnston's defense of federal courts prompted Timothy Bloodworth to ask whether cases brought into federal courts would be tried with juries. He had listened to the many words spoken on behalf of the Constitution, Bloodworth said. They took up a "long time" by his reckoning, but "they have gone in at one ear, and out the other," by which he meant, he later explained, that he found them unconvincing. Joseph McDowell also said that none of the objections to Article III had been answered to his satisfaction, and trial by a jury of the vicinage (or neighborhood), which the Constitution failed to secure in civil cases, "is one of the greatest securities for property." If cases were to be tried far from people's homes, the poor would be oppressed and wealthy suitors would prevail. What man of ordinary circumstances could stand "the expense and trouble of going from Georgia to Philadelphia . . . to have a suit tried?" And to be tried without the benefit of a jury! The Constitution assured that there would be jury trials in criminal cases, but even that provision raised concern because it failed to specify that the juries would be of the "vicinage."[55]

When the Constitution's supporters said once again that the federal Convention included no provision for jury trials in civil cases because state practices were different, Spencer begged to differ. The federal Convention "might have provided that all those cases which are now triable by a jury should be tried in each state by a jury, according to the mode usually practiced in such state," he said. "This would have been easily done, if they had been at the trouble of writing five or six lines." As for Iredell's argument that bills of rights were outmoded throwbacks to Britain, again Spencer dis-

agreed. Their need came "from the nature of human societies" and the pro-
clivity of men to oppress others, so they were not confined to any one time or
place. Federalists effused confidence in people elected to office and responsible to their constituents; their opponents argued instead that "the depravity
of mankind militates against such a degree of confidence." The rights of the
people, including trial by jury, needed to be "fixed." Unless subject to "the
most express restrictions, Congress may trample on your rights."[56]

Once that debate was over, the committee of the whole reverted to its
old ways. The rest of Article III was read, then Article IV and Article V,
without provoking comment except for an occasional Federalist speech
explaining why some provision—providing for future amendments of the
Constitution, for example—was important.[57] When the committee of the
whole reached Article VI, Section 2, and the clause stating that the Constitution and both the laws of the United States and treaties enacted under
its authority were "the supreme law of the Land," Iredell explained that it
meant nothing more than that they had to be obeyed. That again smoked
out the opposition. Bloodworth said the provision that "the judges in every
State" were bound by the supremacy clause, "any Thing in the Constitution
or Laws of any State to the Contrary notwithstanding," would repeal state
laws and constitutions and "produce an abolition of the state governments."[58]

Bloodworth and his colleagues were especially concerned with the provision's impact on the state's paper money. Iredell and Davie explained that it
would prevent further issues of legal-tender paper currency but have no effect
on past issues except, Maclaine suggested, to raise their value by prohibiting
future emissions. Paper money had made people hide their gold and silver,
which would again go into circulation as paper money gradually disappeared,
so a more reliable circulating medium would become available to the people.
Federal taxes, Maclaine conceded, would have to be paid in gold or silver,
"not in imaginary money," but he said informed people expected that "there
will be no taxes laid immediately, or, if any, that they will be very inconsider-
able." Taxes on imports would bring the new government "very large sums
of money," and soon the sale of western lands would add to its income. He
predicted, moreover, that the new government would borrow what additional
funds it needed and charge taxpayers only for the interest on its debt. After
Galloway asked whether the Constitution would force North Carolina to
pay off depreciated state-issued securities in hard money at face value, Davie
said no. The prohibition in Article I, Section 10, on states' passing laws
"impairing the Obligation of Contracts" applied only to contracts among
individuals. The general government would not and could not interfere with
state securities. Moreover, Article I, Section 10, was "the Best in the Constitution" because it was founded "on the strongest principles of justice." Davie
thought it "would have endeared the Constitution to this country."[59]

Bloodworth raised another sore point by claiming that Southern interests would be at the mercy of a Northern majority in Congress. Iredell answered that there would be twenty-seven representatives from states north of Pennsylvania and thirty to its south. Pennsylvania's eight votes could go either way, so there would be no obvious Northern majority. Moreover, interests did not always follow a North/South division: For example, New Jersey and Connecticut, like North Carolina, received their imports through other states, so those three states had common interests despite their different geographical locations. Finally, as people filled the large spans of uncultivated land in the South, the number of Southern representatives would rise. That would make little difference, Bloodworth responded, because the North would still have a majority in the Senate.[60]

Always the response was the same. The Constitution's critics were sometimes informed by their more learned colleagues who supported ratification, but they were never convinced that the Constitution was safe in its current form. The "supreme law of the land" provision was for them obviously too broad; it would "be the destruction of every law which will come in competition with the laws of the United States." Its extent had to be "limited and defined." Bloodworth supposed "every reasonable man" would see that some amendments to the Constitution were necessary.[61]

The delegates crossed swords one more time over the last part of Article VI, Section 3, which prohibited religious tests "as a Qualification for any Office or public Trust under the United States." Henry Abbot, a delegate from Camden County in the predominantly Federalist northeastern part of the state, said some people feared that "pagans, deists, and Mahometans might obtain offices among us" and were concerned for their own religious freedom. Iredell responded with a powerful speech that attacked all religious tests as violations of religious freedom. "America has set an example to mankind," he said, ". . . that a man may be of different religious sentiments from our own, without being a bad member of society." How was it possible "to exclude any set of men" from public office without "taking away that religious freedom which we ourselves so warmly contend for"? The provision excluding religious tests for office was "calculated to secure religious liberty, by putting all sects on a level—the only way to prevent persecution."[62]

For once Judge Spencer sided with Iredell and against the Reverend David Caldwell, a Presbyterian minister, onetime supporter of the Regulators, and delegate from Guilford County who said it was a mistake to invite "Jews and pagans of every kind to come among us." The "Christian religion," Caldwell explained, was "best calculated, of all religions, to make good members of society, on account of its morality" and so should, by implication, be given legal protection. The prohibition of religious tests for office, Spencer said, "leaves religion on the solid foundation of its own inherent validity, without any connection with temporal authority; and no kind of oppression can take place." He found no reason to object to that provision and wished only that "every other part was as good and proper." The apparent agreement of many delegates on that point was especially striking since the North Carolina state constitution excluded from state offices persons who denied "the being of God or the truth of the Protestant religion," the divine authority of either the Old or New Testament, or who held religious convictions "incompatible with the freedom and safety of the state."[63]

The delegates raised no objections to Article VII. The committee of the whole's clause-by-clause discussion of the Constitution was over. It was Wednesday, July 30, and the delegates had gone through the entire document in a little over five days.

DEFINING THE INEVITABLE

Governor Johnston immediately moved a form of ratification that the delegates were unlikely to accept. The committee of the whole, Johnston proposed, should recommend "that the Convention do ratify the Constitution, and at the same time propose amendments, to take place in one of the modes prescribed by the Constitution." He wanted North Carolina to follow the examples of Massachusetts and South Carolina, whose forms of ratification he had presented to the delegates in the convention's opening days.[64]

After a discussion that went over much that had already been said, Jones moved the previous question to make way for another proposal calling for amendments prior to North Carolina's ratification of the Constitution. His motion would have closed debate and brought Johnston's motion to a vote, which would kill it. Iredell urged Jones to withdraw his motion. Any alternative to Johnston's unconditional ratification would leave North Carolina out of the union, increase Northern influence, and bar North Carolina's participation in the first federal Congress. Jones refused. He had listened attentively to all the previous debates, he said, but believed that they had persuaded no delegate to change his mind. Person agreed; the other side "had all the debating to themselves, and would probably have it again, if they insisted on further argument." When the vote was taken, Jones's motion carried, 183 to 84.[65]

At that point Jones probably made his alternative motion. It said that a bill of rights and amendments to various "ambiguous and exceptionable" parts of the Constitution ought to be laid before Congress and "the convention of states that shall or may be called" for amending the Constitution "previous to the ratification of the Constitution . . . on the part of the state of North Carolina." In short, North Carolina would not ratify before amendments to the Constitution were considered by either Congress or a new convention. The motion also included a twenty-point bill of rights and another twenty-six proposed amendments to the Constitution.[66]

On the morning of July 31, Governor Johnston attacked Jones's motion. If it passed, Johnston said, North Carolina would be out of the union until another federal convention met, which could be eighteen months or two years away. That prospect did not bother Jones in the least. North Carolina could rejoin the United States whenever it wanted to. His amendments were modeled on those of Virginia, and Virginia would "not oppose our admission" since the two states had a "common cause." In fact, by his calculations a majority of states wanted amendments and would, he assumed, support North Carolina. He also cited the letter in which Jefferson said he wished that nine states would ratify the Constitution so it would go into effect and the other four would reject it to assure the enactment of necessary amendments. Jones's information was not entirely correct: The letter he mentioned did not go to Madison, as Jones claimed, and Jefferson had later changed his mind and endorsed the Massachusetts form of ratification. In any case, Jones thought Congress would do nothing of significance until another federal convention met, which could take about eighteen months. He said he "would rather be eighteen years out of the Union than adopt it in its present defective form."[67]

Nothing the Federalists argued made the slightest difference. At the end of the day the committee of the whole adopted Jones's motion "by a great majority" and that same day reported its recommendation to the convention, which deferred consideration of the report until the next day, Friday, August 1. Then, after the majority report was read into the record, Iredell moved an amendment to it that he knew would be "instantly rejected." The Constitution's supporters wanted something on the permanent record, he explained, so their constituents could know what position they had taken in the convention. His motion, a slightly reworked version of the one Johnston had moved in the committee of the whole, would ratify the Constitution without conditions but recommend that as soon as possible a list of six amendments "be proposed for the consideration and adoption of the several states in the Union, in one of the modes prescribed" in Article V of the Constitution. The convention swiftly voted it down, 84 to 184.[68]

Then, on Saturday, August 2, it adopted the report of the committee of the whole—the resolution Jones had submitted, which was essentially not to ratify at present—with an almost exactly reversed vote, 184 for and 83 against. The "Federalist" counties that voted against the motion were clustered together in the northeastern part of the state (the Albemarle Sound region). With only a few exceptions, all others, from the Pamlico Sound and Cape Fear region in the southeast to the Piedmont in the west and northwest, voted in favor and so against immediate ratification. Of the six borough towns represented at the convention, only Hillsborough voted "yea."[69] But by far the greater part of rural North Carolina, and so of the state, voted against ratifying the Constitution in its current state without amendments. That vote would keep North Carolina outside the new government of the United States, at least until a declaration of rights and other amendments were laid before Congress or a new convention.

The declaration of rights and additional amendments proposed by North Carolina were, as Jones said, almost identical to those proposed by Virginia. The main differences were in six additional amendments. The first, which was number twelve on the North Carolina list, would require a two-thirds vote of all members present in both houses of Congress to declare a state in rebellion. The others said Congress could "erect no company of merchants with exclusive advantages of commerce"; insisted that no treaty could violate the Constitution or the laws of Congress until those laws were repealed by Congress; provided a more emphatic bar on states' levying duties on goods bound for another state or obliging ships from another state to clear in its ports; required a two-thirds vote of Congress to introduce foreign troops into the United States, and said that neither Congress nor the federal courts could interfere with state paper money "already emitted and now in circulation, or in liquidating the public securities" of a state.[70] As in Virginia, the list was prepared off the convention floor and adopted as a whole, without debating its specific provisions.

The delegates had no intention of staying out of the union forever. Their decision, in Willie Jones's words, "neither to ratify nor reject the Constitution" was a strategy for getting the new government to give serious attention to the amendments that it and other states proposed. To avoid unnecessary friction with the new government, the ratifying convention agreed, on Jones's motion, to ask the state legislature to collect an impost on imports like those the first federal Congress was likely to enact, and to appropriate the proceeds "to the use of Congress." The convention also asked the state legislature to retire the state's paper money as quickly as possible "consistent with the situation and circumstances of the people of this state." Finally, it sent copies of its report, with the attached declaration of rights and other amendments, not only to Congress but to all the other states.[71]

The convention remained in session one more day, only to finish an unusual piece of business delegated to it by the legislature: to decide where the new state capital should be located; it had acquitted its main business in twelve days. "We are . . . for the present out of the Union," James Iredell wrote his wife, "and God knows when we shall get in to it again."[72] Not, it seemed, until Congress or a new federal convention took up the proposed amendments to the Constitution, or until there was a revolution in North Carolina's politics. Or both.

PENNSYLVANIA, AGAIN

Meanwhile, the opposition to ratification of the unamended Constitution in Pennsylvania took a new turn. On July 3, 1788, a circular went out from Cumberland County to societies or individuals who opposed unqualified ratification of the Constitution in counties throughout Pennsylvania. Since ten states had "already, unexpectedly, without amending, ratified the Constitution," it said, the new government would be organized with all its "foreseen and consequent dangers" still in place. Unless the "friends to amendments" found a way to act together, American liberty would "lie at the discretion of Congress" and posterity would probably become "slaves to the officers of government." The circular asked recipients to help get townships to send representatives to county meetings that, in turn, would send delegates to a "general conference of the counties of this commonwealth" at Harrisburg on the third of September "to devise such amendments, and such mode of obtaining them, as in the wisdom of the delegates shall be judged most satisfactory and expedient." That general meeting could also nominate candidates for Pennsylvania's eight seats in the first federal House of Representatives.[73]

The circular's recognition that the Constitution had been ratified and its willingness to work within the new order marked a new stage in Pennsylvania's opposition to the Constitution. Five months earlier, the chairman of the Cumberland County committee that issued the circular, a farmer named Benjamin Blyth, thought ratification by nine states would not calm Pennsylvania's "Mealcontents," who would instead support "Such Stat or Stats as may have warmness anough to apose the Mishure." But by July no state except Rhode Island had set itself against the Constitution. By then, too, a campaign to persuade the state legislature to set aside the recommendation of the Pennsylvania ratifying convention had failed. By the end of March the legislature had received petitions from six counties, with over six thousand signatures, asking that it set aside the state convention's ratification of the Constitution. The legislature tabled them all, and then, after reading a letter from Governor John Hancock and Massachusetts's ratification of the Constitution with its recommended amendments, adjourned until the first Tuesday of September.[74] Rather than retire from the field, the "friends of amendments" adopted a new strategy, one that led to Harrisburg.

Delegates from thirteen counties and the city of Philadelphia attended the unofficial convention. They included Robert Whitehill and John Smilie, who had argued for the minority in the Pennsylvania ratifying convention, and the young Albert Gallatin, a future secretary of the Treasury for the new nation. William Findley was absent: His home county, Westmoreland, had met, resolved to work for amendments to the Constitution, and appointed a committee of correspondence, but it sent no delegates to Harrisburg.

Whether the meeting in Harrisburg nominated candidates for Congress during its regular proceedings remains uncertain (although a "Harrisburg" ticket later circulated through the state). More significant, the Harrisburg meeting did not advocate reversing Pennsylvania's ratification of the Constitution. Instead it resolved that the people of Pennsylvania should "acquiesce" in the organization of government under the Constitution but continue to work for "very considerable amendments and alterations" and, specifically, for "a speedy revision of said Constitution by a general convention." It also petitioned the state legislature to ask the first federal Congress at "the earliest opportunity" to call "a general convention of representatives from the several states in the Union."[75]

The petitioners said they were "well apprized of the necessity of devolving extensive powers to Congress" and accepted the "general system of government framed by the late federal Convention," but "in full confidence"—a phrase clearly taken from New York's form of ratification—"that the same will be revised without delay." Many people had agreed to ratify the Constitution more from "fear of the dangers that might arise from delays than by a conviction of its being perfect." They, too, might now concur in calling for amendments to conciliate their fellow Americans and "prevent the total defection of some of the members of the Union."[76]

The petition included twelve amendments that were "essentially necessary" for consideration by the United States. Most of them were familiar. Although the Harrisburg convention described the amendments it proposed as essential to protect the rights and privileges of the states and the people, it did not call for a separate bill of rights. Neither did any of the state conventions that recommended amendments except Virginia and North Carolina. The Harrisburg convention did, however, propose to declare that all protections of individual rights in the state constitutions would "remain inviolate, except so far as they are expressly and manifestly yielded or narrowed by the national Constitution." Otherwise, the threats to rights that concerned it and most official state conventions were in the body of the Constitution: above all in its provisions on representation and taxation; in the military powers of Congress and the extended jurisdiction of federal courts, and in the lack of any assurance that the states would continue to be able to exercise those "rights of sovereignty which are not by the said Constitution expressly and plainly vested in the Congress."[77]

A SECOND CONVENTION?

As if the news from North Carolina and Harrisburg weren't enough, Madison learned that the Virginia legislature would give the New York circular letter a hearty welcome. That was no surprise: Patrick Henry's influence remained powerful in the Virginia legislature, and Madison was not a man to underestimate Henry's power. In fact, Madison attributed North Carolina's refusal to ratify to the influence of the Virginia minority, which was particularly strong in southern parts of the state along the North Carolina border, "and to the management of its leader," Henry. The New York circular letter, Madison told Jefferson, had also "given fresh hopes" to those who "opposed the Constitution. The object with them now will be to effect an early Convention composed of men who will essentially mutilate the system."[78]

Henry was not the only problem: Governor Edmund Randolph thought well of the New York circular letter. Randolph favored a second convention during the federal Convention and had not changed his mind on that issue. A second convention, he said, would reaffirm the idea that the Constitution rested firmly on the authority and wishes of the people and "give contentment to many, who are now dissatisfied." Like the critic of the Constitution he once was, Randolph also saw good reason for certain amendments. He wanted to constrain the power of some men who were likely to have important positions in the new government and who were, he feared, "capable of making a wicked use of its defects. Do not charge me with undue suspicion," he wrote Madison; "the management in some stages of the [federal] convention created a disgustful apprehension of the views of some particular characters" who did not openly acknowledge their preference for a highly centralized government. Hamilton at least was "honest and open in his views." To be sure, there was reason to fear that "the constitution may be enervated, if some states prevail in all their amendments; but if such be the will of America, who can withstand it?"[79]

Madison was not surprised that the circular letter was being warmly received in Virginia; it had become "a signal of concord & hope to the enemies of the Constitution every where" and would, he feared, prove "extremely dangerous." An early convention, he told Randolph, would be driven by "party & passion," and the amendments it proposed would not reflect "the deliberate sense of the people." They would be won "by management, or extorted by menaces, and will be a real sacrifice of the public will as well as of the public good, to the views of individuals & perhaps the ambition of the State legislatures." To Jefferson, too, he argued that "an early Convention" was "in every view to be dreaded in the present temper of America." Even a short delay would diminish the warmth and increase the light of all contenders, and a year of experience was likely to suggest "more real amendments"— that is, amendments that were genuinely needed—"than all the antecedent speculations of our most sagacious politicians." Efforts to change the Constitution before it was firmly established, and while the public mind remained in a "feverish state," would cause only division and instability.[80]

The greatest danger of an early convention lay, however, in what it might do. There was a chance it would do nothing: Madison had long argued that the proposed amendments were too diverse and contradictory for a convention to agree on anything. The proposals of the Harrisburg convention did not "rhyme very well" with Southern advocates of a convention in that "the objects most eagerly pursued by the latter"—requiring a supermajority in Congress for laws regulating commerce, for example—were "unnoticed in the Harrisburg proceedings."[81] In truth, proposed amendments that were of primarily sectional interest or simply idiosyncratic were unlikely to survive a general convention of the states. Similarly, only three ratifying states (New Hampshire, Virginia, and New York) recommended an amendment that would require a two-thirds (or, for New Hampshire, a three-quarters) vote of Congress to authorize a regular or "standing" army in time of peace, which suggested such an amendment would have trouble getting the consent of three-quarters of the states.

There remained, however, several amendments that were supported by both the state ratifying conventions and the extralegal Harrisburg convention. Many of these, as Nathan Dane had sagely observed in early July, were unlikely to make much of a difference. How would the new government be hurt by untangling the Constitution's language and assuring there would be one representative for every thirty thousand people until the House of Representatives reached a certain size, or putting limits on Congress's ability to set aside state decisions on the time, places, and manner of holding elections for senators and representatives? Or even eliminating the federal courts' jurisdiction over cases involving small amounts of property? If Congress could exercise only those powers expressly given to it, as Federalists insisted time and again, why not say that to calm people's fears?

There was, however, another amendment on which the Harrisburg convention and every state that proposed amendments, including North Carolina, agreed, but that the Federalists feared. It would require Congress to requisition the states for their portion of a federal direct tax, and let the federal government raise those taxes itself only after a state failed to act. That was the only amendment Federalists had tried—unsuccessfully—to remove from the list recommended by the Virginia convention. When Randolph expressed a concern that amendments might "enervate" the Constitution, he mentioned in particular that federal "direct taxation may be too much weakened." The object of those who supported the New York circular letter, Madison wrote Jefferson, was to "mutilate the system, particularly in the article of taxation, without which in my opinion the system cannot answer the purposes for which it was intended." In August 1788, Washington went so far as to say that he had no strong objections to *any* of the proposed amendments "except that wh[i]ch goes to the prevention of direct taxation," and that amendment, he supposed, would be advocated more strongly than any other. He had expected that the new government would be capable of doing "justice to the public creditors and retrieve the National character. But if no means are to be employed but requisitions, that expectation was vain and we may as well recur to the old Confederation."[82]

The state ratifying conventions had discussed the issue at length. Federalists insisted that import duties and proceeds from the sale of western lands would be the primary sources of federal revenue. Direct taxes would be needed only in crises such as wars, when the delays caused by requisitioning the states could be fatal. Moreover, if the state legislatures refused or neglected to pay their requisitions, that would encourage the people to resist federal tax collectors. Above all, any restriction on federal taxing power would undercut the federal government's capacity to borrow, which was critical in time of war, and keep it in the disreputable financial state that had prompted the federal Convention in the first place. Proponents of the amendment sometimes said there could be an exception for wartime. They also insisted that the failure of requisitions under the Confederation was irrelevant in judging the amendment's probability of success; the state legislatures would pay requisitions if inaction would bring federal tax collectors into their states and force their constituents to pay both the original requisition and an interest penalty. Supporters of the amendment even argued that the readiness of people to pay, and so the yields from a federal direct tax, would increase if it were levied by the trusted state legislatures rather than a distant Congress.

Nobody denied that the new government needed a steady revenue stream for the United States to become a "respectable nation." Contenders differed over how to get the necessary funds and over what constituted adequate representation for the purpose of levying direct taxes, which were impossible for individuals to avoid and could be ruinous. Critics of the Constitution were, however, adamant on the tax amendment. They insisted that the people had a right to be taxed only with the consent of representatives who knew them and understood their circumstances in a way that would be impossible for federal congressmen with some thirty thousand constituents. In Pennsylvania, an informant told Madison in July 1788, the "most sensible, cautious and artful" members of the "late opposition" were disposed to "acquiesce" in the establishment of a new government under the Constitution, but they still talked about amendments: And the amendment they "*constantly*" mentioned was "the resumption of the power of direct taxation." That was the issue "most dear" to members of the opposition, and "no other is much felt."[83] Their sensitivity made sense for a people who had fought the strongest nation in the world on the principle of "no taxation without representation," which was for them a critical rights issue.

The question for the Federalists was how an early convention and the dreaded tax amendment could, as Madison put it, be "parried." North Carolina's refusal to ratify made it easier to fight off the threat: Without North

Carolina in the union, it was less likely that two-thirds of the states would ask the first federal Congress to call a convention for proposing amendments to the Constitution or that three-quarters of the state legislatures would approve amendments proposed either by a new federal convention or by Congress, as Article V of the Constitution required. Perhaps, Madison suggested, it was just as well that Rhode Island remained outside the union "till this new crisis of danger is over." Its vote would go to the wrong side.[84]

PUTTING THE CONSTITUTION INTO EFFECT

In the meantime, the withdrawal of Rhode Island's and North Carolina's delegates from active participation in Congress complicated efforts to implement the Constitution. Scheduling elections was no problem, but deciding where the new government would sit kept Congress deadlocked for weeks. No place could get the required seven votes, and that became particularly difficult after the two nonratifying states stopped voting on the issue. Baltimore briefly had seven votes, but "it was not difficult to foresee that such a vote could not stand." Soon New York moved to the lead thanks to the support of Rhode Island's delegates, who then decided to go home. Efforts to place the new government in Wilmington, Delaware, in Lancaster or Philadelphia, Pennsylvania, or in some other place "to the southward of New York" all failed.[85]

New York, Madison insisted, was too "excentric" a location, too far from the center of population, and particularly inconvenient for people in the South and West. People from interior Georgia, South Carolina, North Carolina, Virginia, and Kentucky "will never patiently repeat their trips to this remote situation," he said, "especially as the legislative sessions will be held in the winter season." The best solution, Madison thought, was to place the capital on the Potomac, which he, like Washington and Jefferson, considered the best route to the West.[86] Reasons of state so sensitive he could not discuss them openly also affected his insistence on a location that accommodated the South and West. Madison had reason to think that Spain was trying to take advantage of Kentucky's disaffection from Congress by promising favorable trade concessions if Kentucky seceded from both Virginia and the union.[87] But July went by, then August, without Congress coming to a decision. The deadlock was becoming an embarrassment to Congress and a threat to the new government.

Finally, on September 13, Congress formally announced that the Constitution had been ratified by the required number of states and set the first Wednesday of January, 1789, for appointing presidential electors in states that had ratified it, the first Wednesday in February for the electors to assemble within their states to vote for a president, and the first Wednesday in March as the time "and the present seat of Congress"—New York—"the place for commencing proceedings under the said constitution." Nine states voted in favor, none against. Maryland was so angry, Madison reported, that its delegates left the hall before the vote was taken; and Delaware, which also failed to vote, was "equally inflexible." Madison voted in favor only because the alternative was to "strangle the Gov[ernmen]t in its birth."[88]

LOOKING BACKWARD

Congress's vote of September 13 marked a conclusion to the ratification contest. Two states remained out of the Union, and there the struggle would continue, but the main issue had been settled: The Constitution had officially been ratified and would go into effect. It had been about a year since divisions over the Constitution began in the waning days of the federal Convention, when a majority of delegates insisted that the sovereign people would have to vote the Constitution up or down as written—to "take this or nothing," as George Mason put it. Those differences began to spread and harden in late September 1787, during debates in Congress on the proposed Constitution, and in October, thanks to the Federalists' strong-armed tactics in the Pennsylvania assembly and the beginning of a vigorous debate in the press.

Although the divisions within the states sometimes followed older party lines, there were no national "Federalist" and "Antifederalist" parties in the modern sense during the ratification fight. The Federal Republican Committee in New York, which distributed essays by critics of the Constitution and attempted to coordinate state support for amendments, was the only prominent organized group that worked across state lines. More often individuals on both "sides" wrote to men of similar convictions in other states, then sometimes waited months for answers. When Alexander Hamilton wanted to get the news of ratification in New Hampshire or Virginia to the New York convention in Poughkeepsie as fast as possible, he, with the help of some political friends, arranged for an express rider to bring the news—and helped pay for the rider himself. He also paid over half the cost of publishing The Federalist in book form. There was no party treasury to pick up the bills. The opprobrium Federalists associated with the term "antifederalist" itself signaled that the day of a loyal opposition and so of modern party conflict, in which each side accepts the legitimacy of the other, had not yet arrived.

In retrospect, it is surprising how readily contestants accepted the Constitution as the basis of reform. Only a minority of the Constitution's critics, including Maryland's Luther Martin, literally opposed the Constitution. They argued that the federal Convention had exceeded its authority and that amending the Articles of Confederation would be a more prudent way to strengthen federal authority. However, amendments to the Articles required the unanimous consent of the states, which had proved impossible to get. In part for that reason, over time some allies of Martin, such as John Lansing, Jr., came to advocate amending the Constitution rather than rejecting it.

Other critics of the Constitution, from Richard Henry Lee in the Continental Congress to the majority at the Harrisburg convention, conceded that the Constitution was better than the Confederation, which (as the Harrisburg convention said) was "so weak as to deprive us of some of the greatest advantages we had a right to expect from it."[89] They insisted, however, that the Constitution was dangerous as written and had to be amended before it went into effect—not, as the Federalists said, after it was ratified, using the provision for amendment in Article V.

At first, the edge of reason and experience was probably with those who wanted amendments before ratification. As Patrick Henry argued in the Virginia ratifying convention, only a madman signs a contract thinking he can renegotiate its terms later. However, as more and more states ratified without requiring amendments, the argument for prior amendments became increasingly impractical. Once nine states had ratified, the argument approached impossibility: How could a state demand amendments prior to something that had already happened? At that point, the question became whether a state would join the new-formed United States or leave the union and become, in effect, an independent nation. And would its influence on behalf of amendments be greater inside the new government or outside it, making amendments the price of its future participation?

As a result of that change, a critical contingent of those who had serious reservations about the Constitution started to shift toward advocating amendments that would be enacted once the new government began. The device of linking amendments of the Constitution with recommended amendments, which Massachusetts invented, facilitated that development: It allowed some delegates from constituencies opposed to the Constitution "as it now stands" to vote for ratification. In Virginia, Edmund Randolph and even Richard Henry Lee came to think that recommending amendments for later ratification made sense (although Lee would have made Virginia's ratification conditional on the adoption of amendments within two years of the new government's inauguration). In effect, they crossed the center line of the political spectrum that divided the more moderate critics of the Constitution from those Federalists who also favored amendments, but only after ratification. Without such a migration by Melancton Smith and eleven other Antifederalist/Republican delegates, the Constitution would not have been ratified in New York.

Once the Constitution had been ratified, Federalists who favored amendments occasionally moved in the opposite direction. Edmund Pendleton, one of the Virginia convention's most effective defenders of the Constitution, broke with his old Federalist colleagues and voted for an amendment that would have limited federal power to levy direct taxes. Before the year was out, Edmund Randolph, a powerful Federalist speaker in the Virginia convention, had moved back toward where he began, looking at the possibility of a second convention to propose amendments to the Constitution without Madison's or Washington's fear of what it might do.[90] Those cases suggest that—despite the intense, emotional fights in one state after another—the division between the Constitution's supporters and its critics was porous at the center. After all, the views of most critics of the Constitution were closer to those of the "Federalists for amendments" than to those of Luther Martin and his dwindling allies. And those Federalists who genuinely wanted to enhance the protection of rights in the Constitution and to protect the states had more in common with moderate critics of the Constitution than with more extreme Federalists who, like Hamilton, voted for recommending amendments only to get the Constitution ratified and still dreamed of creating a more centralized nation.

Ratification of the Constitution did not end the fight over amendments. The battle moved to another field: either the first federal Congress or a convention called to propose amendments, as specified in Article V of the Constitution. From the perspective of some Federalists, that meant it was too early to declare victory. Washington regarded the New York circular letter's call for a second convention to consider the amendments recommended by the states—including the direct tax amendment—as nothing less than a covert attempt to "undo all that has been done." The creation of a stronger new national government was not, he insisted, to achieve glory but to assure the survival of the United States as an independent republic and prevent its decline into "insignificant & wretched fragments of Empire." The ratification of the Constitution by so many states and the acquiescence of minorities seemed to promise success—until the New York circular letter raised a new standard for the "disaffected." The Constitution's supporters still faced, it seemed to him, a real and painful possibility of being "shipwrecked in sight of the Port."[91]

LOOKING FORWARD

Washington proved to be wrong. Once the ratification game was over, the score was tallied, and the crowds went home, a surprising quiet set over the land. After Congress declared the Constitution ratified and called the first federal elections, the country rallied behind the new Constitution.

Even some of the Constitution's leading critics fell in line. Elbridge Gerry, who had refused to sign the Constitution in Philadelphia, cheered New York's decision to ratify. Like Nathan Dane, who also had reservations about the Constitution, Gerry considered ratification "the wisest policy under the circumstances" and one that would allow New York "to cooperate with the other states for amendments." In January 1789, he publicly proclaimed that opposition to the new government would be "highly criminal." Later he said that "the salvation of America depends upon the establishment of this government, whether amended or not." If the people did not support the Constitution they had ratified, he said, "I despair of having a Government of these United States."[92]

More surprising, a few days after the New York convention, Judge Robert Yates, who had left the federal Convention in disgust, said that "it was now his and every other man's duty" to support the Constitution. And on August 3, 1788, Abraham Lansing wrote Abraham Yates, Jr., from Albany that "our Friends are much better pleased" with the news of New York's ratification "than we had reason to expect. The Bill of Rights which is intervowed with the Adoption is considered by the Majority of those to whom I have shewn it as a security against the Encroachment of the Gen[era]l Government."[93]

In fact, the mass of evidence supports John Jay's statement that opposition to the Constitution in New York decreased and became more moderate after the state ratifying convention. In October, Aaron Burr, a former member of the New York legislature and future Vice President of the United States, said "political strife" was "still high" in Albany, but that was "the only part of the state where the spirit of party is . . . thoroughly alive." There, however, differences between "adopting" and "non-adopting" segments of the Antifederalist/Republican party and a fight between the lower house of the New York legislature and the Federalist-dominated senate prevented the election of senators until July, four months after the new Congress began. Then the legislature chose two Federalists, Philip Schuyler and, of all people, Rufus King, a leading supporter of ratification in the Massachusetts convention who had since become a New York resident. New York also sent four Federalists and only two "Antis" to the House of Representatives, an amazing return for a state that had been a stronghold of opposition to ratifying the Constitution in its original form.[94]

The same was true elsewhere. Opposition to the Constitution ceased in places where it had once been strong, like the New Hampshire General Assembly. There and, it seems, throughout the country, the new attitude was, "It is adopted, let us try it." All but two members of the new Senate, all of whom were chosen by the state legislatures, were Federalists. The House of Representatives, whose members were chosen in elections held between late November 1788 and the spring of 1789 (with some run-off elections continuing into early summer), would be almost as lopsided. In the end, Federalists won an overwhelming majority: forty-eight of the fifty-nine seats. Onetime critics of the Constitution won only eleven seats in four states—Massachusetts, New York, Virginia, and South Carolina.[95]

To be sure, Federalist legislatures organized elections for the House of Representatives in ways that favored Federalist candidates. They avoided district elections in Pennsylvania, for example, because western districts would elect critics of the Constitution, and avoided at-large elections in South Carolina for fear that voters hostile to the Constitution in the back-country, where 80 percent of the population lived, would overwhelm the pro-Constitution Tidewater. Sometimes Federalist candidates had to prom-ise—or at least indicate, even disingenuously—that they favored amend-ments. Voters might have been persuaded by the Federalists' claim that their education and experience made them especially well qualified to complete the work of the federal Convention by filling in the gaps in the Constitu-tion—designing the federal judiciary system, for example—and establishing the new government. In many states, moreover, Federalists had learned to talk the talk of democratic politics, maybe even enough to win the trust of the electorate.[96]

Because congressional elections were held over so long a period, it took time before the Federalist electoral victory became certain. The Federalist majority in the first federal Congress meant, however, that the Constitution would not be "shipwrecked in sight of the Port." Washington's ship of state would be carefully brought into harbor under the control of its most commit-ted friends.

EPILOGUE

———— ★ ————

"Playing the After Game"

Amendments, Rights, and the Future of the Republic

This time the news did not sit in Alexandria waiting for someone to pick up the general's mail, like the notice of Washington's election as a Virginia delegate to the federal Convention. It was hand-delivered.

Charles Thomson, an old Philadelphia Revolutionary and longtime secretary of the Continental Congress, arrived at Mount Vernon at midday on Tuesday, April 14, 1789, after seven days on the road from New York. Washington greeted him and, after the men exchanged a few pleasantries, Thomson pulled out a formal address he had written to inform Washington of his election as president of the United States. Because the general had given so much proof of his "readiness to sacrifice domestic ease & private enjoyments to preserve the liberty & promote the happiness" of his country, Thomson said, Congress had no doubt that he would accept an office to which he was called "not only by the unanimous vote of the Electors but by the voice of America." As a result, the Senate had commissioned Thomson to inform Washington of his election and also to accompany him to New York, "where the Senate & house of Representatives of the United States are convened for the dispatch of public business."[1]

Washington pulled out a reply he had prepared beforehand. "Whatever may have been my private feelings and sentiments," he said in that strangely formal private ceremony, he could give no greater evidence of his sense of honor from receiving the unanimous support of his fellow citizens than by accepting the position. He understood the arduous nature of the task ahead of him and feared that his abilities would fall short of the challenge, but he promised to perform his duties with "an honest zeal." He would be ready to leave in two days.[2]

Thomson's arrival was no surprise: Henry Knox had told Washington that Thomson was coming. The news Thompson brought was even less surprising. Washington's correspondents had long since predicted that he would be the first president if the Constitution were ratified. Nobody else had so firm a hold on the confidence and affections of the people. The promise of his presence had made the federal Convention an event worth attending, and his support had helped get the Constitution ratified. Of course, his endorsement was not enough. The people of the United States had to take their measure of the document state by state, convention by convention. And yet, as Gouverneur Morris put it in late October 1787, if Washington had not gone to the federal Convention or had no connection with the Constitution, "it would have met with a colder Reception, with fewer and weaker Advocates, and with more and more strenuous opponents." Morris added that "should the Idea prevail that you would not accept of the Presidency it would prove fatal in many Parts."[3]

In January 1788, when the Constitution's fate still remained in doubt, Washington's old comrade Lafayette urged him to accept the presidency. "You only Can settle that political Machine," he said. On July 4, 1788, after the Constitution had the required consent of nine states, celebrants in Wilmington, Delaware, toasted "Farmer Washington—may he like a second Cincinnatus, be called from the plow to rule a great people." And on July 23, the tallow chandlers' flag in New York's grand federal procession carried a picture of Washington with the line "may he be the first President of the United States."[4]

The pleas that Washington consent to serve became more urgent after the Continental Congress set the date for choosing presidential electors. "Without you," Henry Lee, Jr., wrote from New York, the new government would "have but little chance of success." Hamilton told him the same thing. Benjamin Lincoln was so sure Washington would be the first president that in late September 1788, he urged him to support John Adams for the vice presidency.[5]

That was too much. Just to talk about accepting an office that he had not yet been offered seemed inappropriate to Washington; endorsing a vice-presidential candidate was out of the question. Assuming the person elected as vice president was a "true Federalist," he told Lincoln, he would let the electors decide who should fill that office. Still, the requirement that the vice president be a "true Federalist" ruled out Washington's old friend George Clinton, another candidate for the position. As for the presidency, Washington said he most heartily wished that the electors would choose someone else. He had assumed that his 1783 renunciation of future offices would put him out of the running for another public position, and he clung to that hope "as a last anchor of worldly happiness in old age." If, in the end, he saw that his services were absolutely necessary and a refusal would suggest that he preferred his personal reputation and private ease to the good of his country, he would accept. But "I call Heaven to witness," he told Lincoln, that to accept the presidency "would be the greatest sacrifice of my personal feelings & wishes that ever I have been called on to make."[6]

As in the spring of 1787, when Washington agonized over whether or not to attend the federal Convention, he feared being charged with ambition and inconsistency if he accepted the presidency after having renounced public life. He desperately wanted to live out his life at home in Virginia. But to refuse an office before it was offered, he told Lee, might make him seem like the fox in a fable who disparaged grapes he could not reach. In strict confidence, Washington said that he wanted above all "to remain as I am."[7] The thought that he would soon have to make a decision cast "a kind of gloom" over his mind, he told Hamilton. He would accept the office "with more diffidence and reluctance than ever I experienced before in my life." And he would do it hoping that his services could soon be dispensed with so he could retire again and "pass an unclouded evening, after the stormy day of life, in the bosom of domestic tranquility." In the meantime, he even imagined that he might lose the election thanks to the machinations of evil men who affected moderation to "lull and deceive" as they worked to undermine the new government.[8]

———

Early in 1789, as Washington began to accept the inevitable, he asked his old aide-de-camp David Humphreys, who had been living at Mount Vernon since 1787, to draft an inaugural address. He never used the long, rambling draft that Humphreys produced, probably after long conversations between them, and that Washington carefully copied, perhaps making adjustments along the way. He once showed the text to Madison, who later described it as a strange production, and it has an equally strange history. The first editor of Washington's papers, Jared Sparks, received permission to bring the papers to his office in Boston. After beginning work on them in 1829, he came across the draft speech, saw that it had no obvious impact on the inaugural speech Washington actually gave, and apparently thought it so worthless— and perhaps even an embarrassment to Washington and so better destroyed than published—that he cut it into pieces for people who wanted samples of Washington's handwriting. The dedicated editors of the modern *Papers of George Washington* located many of those fragments (Americans don't throw away Washington relics) and put them together, like a giant puzzle, in what seems like their probable order with gaps for missing pieces.[9]

The draft address went on at an unseemly length about Washington's desire for retirement and love of agriculture and his distress at being pulled back into public life. It also suggested that, once the Constitution had been in place for a reasonable time, it might make sense to "remove all the redundanc[i]es or supply all the defects, which shall be discovered" in that "complicated machine." In the meantime, the address asked whether it might be "practicable for this Congress (if their proceedings shall meet the approbation of three fourths of the Legislatures) . . . to secure to the people all their justly—"

The fragment ends there, probably with a call on the first federal Congress to propose amendments that secured the people's rights.[10]

———

Presidential electors were scheduled to cast their votes "within their respective States" on the fourth of February, then send the results "to the Seat of the Government of the United States, directed to the President of the Senate." On February 16, Henry Knox, almost as an afterthought in a brief letter on another topic, told Washington that the returns of states from Maryland north were unanimous for him as president. When it became clear that Virginia's electors—including Patrick Henry—had also voted for Washington, his election was assured. But the ballots had to be counted before both houses of Congress, which were supposed to meet on the fourth of March but did not get the requisite quorums until April. The delay was a familiar annoyance for congressmen who came on time, but Washington regarded it as a reprieve.[11]

He used the time to make a last visit to his difficult, eighty-year-old mother, Mary Ball Washington, who was dying of breast cancer in Fredericksburg, to settle some personal affairs, and to instruct George Augustine Washington, who would manage Mount Vernon in Washington's absence, as he had when Washington attended the federal Convention. There was so much to explain: the importance of manuring the fields, how best to do that, what to plant and when to harvest crops (as fast as possible to avoid waste and embezzlement), the importance of saving clover and timothy seed, and also honey locust seed ("in the fall plant them on the Ditches . . . about 6 Inches apart"), and of making sure the seeds in the case in his study were planted on time in his botanical garden "& proper memos kept of the times & places." Would Washington learn to avoid such micromanaging as president? Frugality and economy were commendable, he told his nephew, and also necessary since "my means are not adequate to the expense at which I have lived in my retirement to what is called private life." In truth, his prized domestic tranquillity was riddled with financial worries. After being forced to purchase corn thanks to a crop failure and finding it difficult both to sell western lands at an acceptable price and to collect rents, Washington had trouble paying his taxes. He was forced to borrow money to pay urgent debts and to finance his imminent trip to New York.[12]

Washington turned down an offer from Governor Clinton to stay at his house in New York City until the new president could move into more permanent accommodations; his presence would be too burdensome on a family, Washington said. In 1787 he had at first refused a similar offer from Robert Morris in Philadelphia for the same reason before acquiescing, but this time he was unlikely to change his mind. To stay with an old friend who had signed the New York circular letter involved political complications beyond the private burdens it would impose. Having declined an invitation from the governor, Washington could not accept any of the other invitations he received. He asked James Madison to find rented lodgings for him, even rooms in a good tavern, until Congress provided a house appropriate for the president (as it did soon, at Number 3 Cherry Street). In early April, before Thomson's arrival, Washington also sent his secretary, Tobias Lear, and his personal servant, Will (William Lee, a slave), to New York to help prepare for his arrival; and he began to ask that purchases be delivered to him or, in his absence, to his nephew.[13] He would make the trip to the seat of the new government with Thomson but with feelings, he told Henry Knox, "not unlike those of a culprit who is going to the place of his execution," so unwilling was he "in the evening of a life nearly consumed in public cares, to quit a peaceful abode for an Ocean of difficulties."[14]

———

Chancellor Robert R. Livingston, who had spoken so eloquently but "impolitically" for ratification of the Constitution at the New York ratifying convention, administered the oath of office at Washington's inauguration on April 30. (The chief justice and other members of the Supreme Court had not, of course, yet been appointed.) Fisher Ames, one of the stars at the Massachusetts ratifying convention and now a member of the House of Representatives, found the scene "very touching." Washington, he said, seemed "grave, almost to sadness."[15]

His inaugural address was much shorter than the old, discarded draft by Humphreys. Nothing could have filled him with greater anxiety, Washington said, than the notification he received two weeks before, when his country summoned him from "a retreat which I had chosen . . . as the asylum of my declining years." Every step in the American people's advance to independence had been "distinguished by some token of providential agency." He hoped the new government would remain under its influence since "the sacred fire of liberty, and the destiny of the Republican model of Government" were deeply and perhaps finally staked "on the experiment entrusted to the hands of the American people."[16]

The new president referred to only one issue facing Congress: how far "an exercise of the occasional power delegated by the Fifth article of the Constitution" was expedient at the present time due to the objections made to the Constitution and "the degree of inquietude which has given birth to them." He was confident that Congress would recommend no amendments that might "endanger the benefits" of a united and effective government, or that should not be made without the "lessons of experience." A "reverence for the . . . rights of freemen, and a regard for the public harmony," he told the members of Congress, would "sufficiently influence your deliberations on . . . how far the former can be impregnably fortified, or the latter be safely and advantageously promoted."[17]

The fact that a majority of congressmen were "true Federalists" had helped reconcile Washington to accepting the presidency. Perhaps by recommending amendments to protect the people's rights, they could promote public harmony and, implicitly, fend off those dissidents who wanted a second federal convention and amendments—or, more exactly, one amendment on direct taxes that, in his opinion, would undermine the government's strength and respectability. But what Congress would do was for Congress to decide. And the task of getting it to do anything would rest on the man who had drafted Washington's inaugural address: James Madison.

MADISON'S DILEMMA

Reports from Richmond, where the Virginia assembly met on October 20, 1788, were "very unpropitious to federal measures," Washington reported in November. Patrick Henry was in control: As Washington put it, "He has only to say let this be Law—and it is Law."[18] The legislature had to choose Virginia's senators, and for those positions Henry favored two old critics of the Constitution, Richard Henry Lee and William Grayson. The Federalists nominated James Madison, the only supporter of ratification with a prayer of winning a seat. Henry did not fault Madison's talent and integrity but said he was "not to be trusted with *amendments*" since he had declared in the ratifying convention "that not a letter of the Constitution cou'd be spared." On November 8, a joint meeting of the state senate and house of delegates sent Lee and Grayson to the Senate, though Madison came in a strong third.[19]

His defeat was probably neither a surprise nor a disappointment. Madison had already expressed a preference for a seat in the House of Representatives, in part because he feared senators would have to maintain a style of life beyond what their salaries could support. He also thought the arrangements for House elections might save him from a competition that would require a "spirit of electioneering which I despise."[20] That turned out to be an impossible dream. The legislature divided Virginia into ten districts for the election of representatives and, in an early example of "gerrymandering," set up his district in a way that favored Madison's opponent, James Monroe, whose convictions on the Constitution were nearer Henry's than Madison's. The district included Madison's home county, Orange, as well as seven other counties. Of those eight counties, the delegates of only two had voted for and five against ratification of the Constitution at the state ratifying convention, while another, Louisa, split, one delegate voting for and the other against.

The legislature required candidates to be residents of the district in which they ran, which prevented Madison from running in a more solidly Federalist constituency. Finally, the legislature reelected him to the lame duck Confederation Congress, perhaps hoping that would keep him in New York, where, in fact, he wanted to remain.[21]

Again, as in 1787, Madison's supporters urged him to return to Virginia or forfeit all hope of winning the election. If he failed at the polls he would probably receive an appointed position in the Washington administration, but the most important action in the next few years was likely to be in Congress, which would pass legislation fleshing out the new government and fending off those who supposedly wanted to cripple it before it had fairly begun. As a result, Madison dutifully went home in late 1788, stopping along the way to spend Christmas at Mount Vernon before mounting his five-week campaign. In the end, he again proved very effective at the distasteful work of "electioneering." He probably visited only three counties: Orange, where he lived; Louisa, where Henry once lived, and Culpepper, a critical, relatively populous county where he had to answer "multiplied falsehoods" circulated by his enemies. Personal appearances were less effective than usual since the rigorous winter weather—with snow, ice, rain, and even hail—kept attendance at county court days unusually low. Guided by the advice of George Nicholas, his old convention colleague, Madison also made extensive use of the written word. He sent several carefully composed letters to constituents that explained his position on amendments, the election's number-one issue. Recipients were supposed to circulate the letters privately or have them published in the press for an even broader circulation. Four of those letters survive.[22]

Three were essentially the same. Madison said he never considered the Constitution perfect, but he did not think its imperfections were as dangerous as others claimed. He opposed amendments before ratification because he feared they would cause serious contention among the states and help those who wanted to dissolve the union. However, now that the Constitution was ratified, he supported such amendments as would "serve the double purpose of satisfying the minds of well meaning opponents, and of providing additional guards in favour of liberty." In particular, he endorsed amendments to protect "the rights of Conscience in the fullest latitude, the freedom of the press, trials by jury, security against general warrants &c.," to mandate an increase in the number of representatives until the House reached a size "entirely satisfactory," and to put "the judiciary department into such a form as will render vexatious appeals impossible. There are sundry other alterations," he added, that "are either eligible in themselves, or being at least safe, are recommended by the respect due to such as wish for them."[23]

He insisted, however, that the first federal Congress, not a general convention, recommend the amendments. (Article V said either could recommend amendments, which, in any case, required the consent of three-quarters of the state legislatures or of conventions in three-quarters of the states before going into effect.) Congress could act quickly, perhaps as early as March, when it was scheduled to meet. A convention could not be called until two-thirds of the states applied to Congress and then would take more time to meet and make its recommendations. Moreover, Congress, which was "appointed to execute as well as to amend the Government, will probably be careful not to destroy or endanger it." A convention, given the current "ferment of parties" and the likelihood that it would include "insidious characters from different parts of America" (think Patrick Henry), was likely "to turn every thing into confusion and uncertainty."[24]

There was, however, one amendment he could not support, as he explained in the fourth letter, written on January 29 to a supporter in Fluvanna County. Forcing Congress to requisition the states for direct taxes, he argued, would lead to an unequal distribution of the tax burden since not all states would comply completely. States that furnished more revenue would complain about those that supplied less; from the quarrels would come wars, and from wars "a long catalogue of evils including . . . disunion and a general confusion." Restrictions on the federal government's capacity to collect direct taxes would also invite attacks by foreign countries "by shewing the inability of the Union to repel them." Finally, nations financed their defense either by taxes "within the year equal to the public expences" or by borrowing "on the credit of taxes pledged for the future repayment" of the loans. The first was "chimerical" for the United States, which would be largely dependent on revenue from import duties that would dry up in time of war, and the amendment would make borrowing all but impossible. Who would lend to a government dependent "on the punctuality of a dozen or more Governments" for the means of meeting even interest payments? Loans, if available at all, could only be obtained from "usurers" who would charge outrageous rates to compensate "for the risk & disappointment apprehended." The provision giving Congress general taxing power was therefore "absolutely necessary" to preserve domestic justice and tranquility and to prevent or repel foreign wars, and it had to remain as written, with no crippling amendment.[25]

Madison added that it was particularly counterproductive for Virginia to weaken the federal government's capacity to levy direct taxes since that would increase its dependence on import duties. "Now who is it that pays duties on imports?" he asked. "Those only who consume them. What parts of the Continent manufacture least and consume imported manufactures most? The Southern parts," including Virginia, so it was in their interest "that trade should not be overburdened." Direct taxes "tend to equalize the general burden on every part of the Continent." Moreover, direct taxes would mainly be needed for wars and other emergencies. And who was most likely to be attacked? The Southern states, especially Virginia, "whose long navigable rivers open a great part of her Country to surprise and devastation whenever an enemy powerful at Sea chuses to invade her." In short, restrictions on the federal government's capacity to raise direct taxes went against Virginia's best interests.[26]

Later, when the election was over, Madison acknowledged that without his active campaigning he would not have beaten the odds and won 1,308 votes to James Monroe's 972 on February 2, 1789, a snowy, frigid election day when most of the district's 5,189 voters stayed home. Observers also testified that Madison's letters did "much good."[27] The new congressman stood pledged to work for amendments to the Constitution and would be held accountable on that issue, for which he had declared his position in no uncertain terms.

A CHANGE OF CONVICTION?

Except on direct taxes, the position Madison took during his electoral campaign seemed at odds with the one he had taken at the Virginia ratifying convention, where he said "a solemn declaration of our essential rights" would be "unnecessary and dangerous." Even then, however, he suggested that he was open to amendments that were "without danger" if they "would give satisfaction to any Gentleman"—that is, if they would calm discontent.[28] He had not changed his mind: He still supported rights amendments to quiet the fears of the discontented, not because he thought they would secure the people's rights. That became clear in the course of his extended correspondence with Thomas Jefferson, who in December of 1787 had said he saw two glaring defects in the proposed Constitution: It imposed no term limits for the president and did not include a bill of rights, which "the people are entitled to against every government on earth . . . and what no just government should refuse, or rest on inference."[29]

Madison received Jefferson's letter only in July 1788 and did not immediately respond to his arguments. In August he sent Jefferson a copy of the New York circular letter, which, he said, had given "fresh hopes" and new energy "to those who opposed the Constitution" and wanted an early convention to "mutilate the system, particularly in the article of taxation, without which in my opinion the system cannot answer the purposes for which it was intended." Some who opposed a second convention opposed all amendments. Others favored them but thought they should be proposed by Congress and considered it "most expedient at present" to introduce "supplemental safeguards to liberty against which no objections can be raised."[30]

Then on October 17, he sent Jefferson a thirty-two-page pamphlet that included the amendments recommended by the various states, including

North Carolina. He conceded that "not a few" critics of the Constitution, "particularly in Virginia," argued for amendments "from the most honorable and patriotic motives" and that some of the Constitution's advocates also wanted "further guards to public liberty and individual rights." On the other hand, the Constitution's critics had not made a bill of rights central to their demands. There was "scarce any point on which the party in opposition is so much divided as to its importance and its propriety," he said.[31]

He had a point: Despite the attention paid to a bill of rights, only the Virginia and North Carolina conventions had formally asked that one be added to the Constitution; however, every state that recommended amendments demanded the direct tax amendment. Jefferson agreed that the people had a right to be taxed only with their consent or that of their representatives ("no taxation without representation"), but he disagreed with those who said the Constitution violated that right. Since the House of Representatives would be "chosen by the people directly," he said, the Constitution preserved "inviolate the fundamental principle that the people are not to be taxed but by representatives chosen immediately by themselves." That the people were more fully represented in the state legislatures apparently made no difference to him. The bill of rights he had in mind would provide "clearly and without the aid of sophisms for freedom of religion, freedom of the press, protection against standing armies, restrictions against monopolies, the eternal and unremitting force of the habeas corpus laws, and trials by jury in all matters of fact triable by the laws of the land."[32]

Now in October, almost midway between the Virginia ratifying convention and congressional elections, Madison claimed that he had "always been in favor of a bill of rights" if it was "so framed as not to imply powers not meant to be included in the enumeration." "Always been in favor" was an exaggeration, since he still thought that such a document was unimportant, unnecessary, and dangerous for several reasons. First, the people's rights were already reserved ("though not in the extent argued by Mr. Wilson"), since Congress was confined to the powers explicitly granted to it, which included no power to interfere with basic rights. Madison also argued that a statement of certain essential rights, above all the rights of conscience, "could not be obtained in the requisite latitude": Some New Englanders, Madison noted, feared that the lack of religious qualifications for office under the Constitution would open a door "for Jews Turks and infidels." (He forgot that some Virginians had made the same or a similar objection.[33]) Madison added that the vigilance of state governments would check federal wrongdoing effectively. Finally, "experience proves the inefficacy of a bill of rights on those occasions when its controul is most needed." Overbearing majorities had violated those "parchment barriers" in every state.[34]

The power of the majority was the greatest threat to rights in the American republic, he argued. Danger therefore lay not in government's acting against the people "but from acts in which the Government is the mere instrument of the major number of its constituents." If so, Jefferson's declaration that the people were entitled to a bill of rights "against every government on earth" missed the point entirely: The government was not the problem in America except as the agent of a popular majority. Then what possible use could a bill of rights serve in a republic? Madison suggested two: Insofar as the political truths they declared became "fundamental maxims" incorporated into the "national sentiment," bills of rights might moderate the majority's tendency to act according to its interests and passions. A bill of rights could also be used against the government in the unlikely event that it became the source of oppression.[35] That was hardly a compelling argument. The negatives still outweighed the positives.

Jefferson's reply, dated March 15, 1789, reached Madison in late May, when the new Congress was already in session, and within weeks of when Madison would propose amendments in the House of Representatives. Jefferson answered each of Madison's arguments against a bill of rights. Perhaps it was possible to write a Constitution in such a way that no bill of rights was needed. However, the federal Constitution left "some precious articles unnoticed" and raised "implications against others," so it needed a bill of rights "by way of supplement." If rights could not be stated with the requisite latitude, "half a loaf is better than no bread. If we cannot secure all our rights, let us secure what we can." A bill of rights would also help the states guard against federal abuses of power. And if experience showed the inefficacy of bills of rights, it also showed they were "rarely inefficacious" and better than nothing. "A brace the more will often keep up the building which would have fallen with that brace the less."[36]

Jefferson agreed that the "tyranny of the legislatures," where majorities ruled, "is the most formidable dread at present, and will be for long years." But not forever. "That of the executive will come in it's turn . . . at a remote period," so the usefulness of a bill of rights against the government would increase with time.[37] He also added another item to Madison's list of ways in which a written bill of rights might be of use in a republic: "the legal check which it puts in the hands of the judiciary." An independent judiciary composed of men like George Wythe, John Blair, and Edmund Pendleton could give a bill of rights teeth. He admitted that declarations of rights might sometimes "cramp government in it's useful exertions," but that was "shortlived, moderate, and reparable," while the disadvantages of having none were "permanent, afflicting, and irreparable" and moved inexorably from bad to worse. Moreover, a bill of rights could be written in a way that posed no danger to the frame of the new government "or any essential part of it." There were also more immediate political considerations at stake. Jefferson had already reminded Madison that the minorities within the states were "too respectable not to be entitled to some sacrifice of opinion in the majority," particularly when "a great proportion of them would be contented with a bill of rights."[38]

The two men's positions were close, but Madison lacked Jefferson's enthusiasm. He was no less ardent a believer in rights. On the rights of conscience, he stood second to nobody except perhaps Jefferson himself. However, Madison put less faith in constitutional guarantees to safeguard rights than in structural limits on power built into the new government and the size of the territory it served, which, as he argued in the tenth *Federalist*, would discourage the formation of oppressive majorities. He hoped and expected that the new Congress would make "some conciliatory sacrifices," he wrote Jefferson on March 29, 1789, just before the first House of Representatives had a quorum, but the purpose would be less to secure rights than "to extinguish opposition" to the Constitution, "or at least break the force of it, by detaching the deluded opponents from their designing leaders." The leaders he had in mind were those "who urge a second Convention with the insidious hope of throwing all things into Confusion" to subvert the new government and perhaps "the Union itself."[39]

UPHILL

Its Federalist majority made the first federal Congress far less likely than a convention to propose amendments that would weaken the new government. However, the Congress had so many urgent issues on its agenda that Madison had a miserable time getting his colleagues to consider any amendments at all. Even members of the House of Representatives such as Massachusetts's Elbridge Gerry and South Carolina's Aedanus Burke, who had long argued for amendments, thought Congress had more pressing issues to settle first. It had to design and establish a federal revenue system, give concrete form to the federal judiciary, set up executive departments and decide the extent of the president's power over department heads—in short, to get the government up and going. Everything took an inordinate amount of time, Madison reported, thanks to "incorrect draughts of Committees," the tendency toward a "prolixity of discussion" in public bodies, and, above all, the "novelty and complexity" of actually creating a functioning government from the plan in the Constitution. "We are in a wilderness without a single footstep to guide us," he wrote Jefferson in late June 1789. "Our successors will have an easier task, and by degrees the way will become smooth short and certain."[40]

In early May he moved that the House of Representatives take up the subject of amendments in three weeks, but other business pushed off discussion of the issue until June 8. Then several members of the House wanted a further delay until the government was organized and fully operating. James Jackson of Georgia, whose ratifying convention had not recommended amendments, thought the subject could easily be put off until March 1790, when Congress had more experience under the new government. The Constitution was like "a ship that has never yet put to sea. . . . Upon experiment she may prove faultless, or her defects might be very obvious." It was too early to change anything.[41]

Madison answered that he wanted only to introduce the topic so "our constituents may see we pay a proper attention to a subject they have very much at heart" and "to quiet that anxiety which prevails in the public mind." Echoing Jefferson, he noted that "the applications for amendments come from a very respectable number of our constituents." If Congress took up the subject for even one day, then put off action because of urgent public business, it would undercut suspicion and make the public more receptive to other congressional measures. The prospect of amendments might also help bring the two states that had not seen fit to ratify the Constitution back into the union. Since he could not fulfill his duty to himself and his constituents by letting the subject "pass over in silence," Madison begged a patient hearing for his arguments and the specific amendments he proposed.[42] His fellow Virginian John Page understood: If Congress kept postponing the subject, Page said, the advocates of amendments "will clamor for a new convention."[43]

Madison emphasized that he did not want to change the structure of the government or to bring into question any of its critical powers. He proposed only "to incorporate those provisions for the security of rights" against which no serious objection had been made and that were also likely to secure the requisite consent of two-thirds of each house of Congress and three-quarters of the states. "We have in this way something to gain," he said, "and, if we proceed with caution, nothing to lose." The great mass of the people who opposed the Constitution did so, he argued, because it did not provide against encroachments on particular rights. That meant it was possible "to satisfy the public mind that their liberties will be perpetual . . . without endangering any part of the constitution" that its supporters considered essential to the new government.[44]

———

Madison proposed nine amendments of differing length and complexity, all of which would be added to or incorporated within the body of the Constitution:

First. That there be prefixed to the Constitution a declaration. That all power is originally vested in, and consequently derived from the people. That government is instituted, and ought to be exercised for the benefit of the people; which consists in the enjoyment of life and liberty, with the right of acquiring and using property, and generally of pursuing and obtaining happiness and safety.

That the people have an indubitable, unalienable, and indefeasible right to reform or change their government, whenever it be found adverse or inadequate to the purposes of its institution.[45]

Those provisions were essentially a watered-down, condensed, rearranged version of the first three provisions of the Virginia Declaration of Rights (1776), without its opening assertion that "all men are by nature equally free and independent." A similar assertion in the Massachusetts declaration of rights had been used in court to argue against the legality of slavery, which probably increased the discomfort of South Carolina and other slave states with constitutional statements of universal human equality. Under the circumstances, to include such an assertion in an amendment to the Constitution would make it more difficult to get the required support of three-quarters of the states. Madison, however, said only that, although "the perfect equality of mankind" was "an absolute truth," it was "not absolutely necessary . . . at the head of a constitution."[46] He also modified the more radical assertion in the Virginia declaration of the people's right to "reform, alter, or abolish" a government that failed to serve the people's happiness and safety; by his formulation, they could only "reform or change" it.

Next, Madison proposed to change the language in Article I, Section 2, paragraph 3, so it said that "there shall be one representative for every thirty Thousand" until the House reached a certain size (unspecified), after which Congress would regulate the proportion so it fell within certain (undefined) proportions, although each state was guaranteed at least two representatives. Madison explained that he "always thought this part of the constitution defective."[47]

He proposed no change to Article I, Section 4, which had provoked considerable fear that Congress's power to set aside state provisions on the times, places, and manner of electing congressmen would subvert the people's right to a free and full representation. All of the states that recommended amendments asked for a modification of that provision so Congress could regulate congressional elections only when the states themselves did not or could not call elections. Massachusetts and New Hampshire also proposed to add a statement that would allow Congress to use its power over elections against state electoral rules that were "subversive of the rights of the People to a free & equal representation in Congress agreeably to the Constitution." In the Virginia ratifying convention, Madison had defended the provision as it stood and suggested that it already gave Congress the power that Massachusetts and New Hampshire wanted to make explicit. Apparently he saw no need to change Article I, Section 4, even to remedy the discontent it had caused in many state conventions.[48]

Madison's third amendment would add to Article I, Section 6, a provision preventing members of Congress from increasing their compensation until after an intervening election of representatives. Although he thought Congress was unlikely to abuse its power to set its members' pay, there was an impropriety or "indecorum" in allowing "any set of men without controul to put their hand into the public coffers, to take out money to put in their pockets."[49]

His fourth amendment would add several clauses to the restrictions on Congress in Article I, Section 9, to protect freedom of conscience, speech, the press, petition, and assembly, and the right to bear arms; to assure that persons with religious objections would not be "compelled to render military service in person"; to prevent "unreasonable searches and seizures," and to establish several rights of the accused in judicial proceedings. Although the amendments' place in the Constitution suggested they imposed limits on Congress, Madison declared the rights of the people in general terms, avoiding the pusillanimous "ought" common in state declarations or bills of rights and in those recommended by Virginia and North Carolina. He said, for example, "The people shall not be deprived or abridged of their right to speak, to write, or to publish their sentiments." And where the bill of rights recommended by the Virginia ratifying convention said "the freedom of the press is one of the greatest bulwarks of liberty and ought not to be violated," Madison wrote that "the freedom of the press, as one of the great bulwarks of liberty, shall be inviolable." He also adopted the language proposed by New York in saying that no person could be deprived of life, liberty, or property "without due process of law"—not "but by the law of the land," as the Virginia ratifying convention suggested. Madison's last proposed change to Article I, Section 9, asserted that "the exceptions here or elsewhere in the constitution . . . in favor of particular rights" were not to be construed to "diminish the just importance of other rights retained by the people" or "to enlarge the powers delegated by the constitution," but as actual limits on those powers or provisions "inserted merely for greater caution."[50]

Since they feared the federal government, not the states, no state ratifying convention requested the next of Madison's proposals, a provision to be added to Article I, Section 10: "No state shall violate the equal rights of conscience, or the freedom of the press, or the trial by jury in criminal cases." There was "more danger of those powers being abused by the state governments," he told the House, "than by the government of the United States," so that provision was "of equal if not greater importance" than those already mentioned. Not all states had declarations of rights that protected those rights, and the states that did would benefit from a "double security on those points." He called on those who "opposed this constitution" to prove their attachment to rights by supporting the provision.[51]

Madison's sixth proposal addressed the issue of vexatious appeals to federal courts by adding to Article III, Section 2, paragraph 2, a provision preventing appeals to federal courts in cases where the property at issue was worth less than a certain sum, which he left unspecified.[52] The seventh amendment would eliminate a relatively brief statement assuring trial by jury in criminal cases within the state where the crime was committed (Article III, Section 2, paragraph 3) and substitute a more detailed provision that responded to the concerns expressed in several state ratifying conventions. Trials, it said, "shall be by an impartial jury of freeholders of the vicinage, with the requisite of unanimity for conviction, of the right of challenge, and other accustomed requisites." It also declared that "in suits at common law, between man and man, the trial by jury, as one of the best securities to the rights of the people, ought to remain inviolable."[53] That answered the charge that the Constitution had "abolished" trial by jury in civil cases.

Madison wanted to insert into the Constitution a new Article VII: "The legislative department shall never exercise the powers vested in the executive or judicial; nor the executive exercise the powers vested in the legislative or judicial; nor the judicial exercise the powers vested in the legislative or executive departments." The new Article VII would also include a statement that "the powers not delegated by this constitution, nor prohibited by it to the states, are reserved to the States respectively." That was weaker than the parallel provision in the Articles of Confederation, which said that each state retained "its sovereignty, freedom and independence" as well as "every Power, Jurisdiction and right" that the Articles of Confederation did not "expressly" delegate to the United States in Congress Assembled. Similar amendments proposed by Massachusetts, South Carolina, and New Hampshire (though not Virginia and North Carolina) included the word "expressly"; New York instead referred to powers "clearly" delegated to Congress.[54]

Finally, after renumbering the old Article VII so it became Article VIII, Madison explained and justified his amendments beginning with the first, which he said "relates to what may be called a bill of rights," as if that title applied only to his "prefix." His comments suggest, however, that the designation included the rights amendments he proposed to insert in Article I, Section 9 (though not, it seems, the restrictions on the states that he wanted added to Article I, Section 10, which he discussed separately): In late May he had written Jefferson that a bill of rights "incorporated perhaps into the Constitution"—not just tacked on to its beginning—would be proposed along with "a few other alterations most called for by the opponents of the Government and least objectionable to its friends."[55]

Now, having proposed amendments, Madison had to answer the objections that he and other Federalists had made to bills of rights during the ratification debates and that were "likely to be made by gentlemen on this floor."

Some of the dangers Federalists had seen in bills of rights were addressed by the proposed amendment that said the people's rights were not confined to those specifically mentioned and that provisions on rights were not to be interpreted in ways that enlarged the powers of government specified in the Constitution. As for James Wilson's old argument that a bill of rights was unnecessary because the powers of the federal government were enumerated, Madison said it was neither "entirely without foundation" nor conclusive because the government had discretionary powers that could be abused. Congress might, for example, pass a law for collecting revenue, which would be a "necessary and proper" exercise of its power to tax, but that allowed the use of oppressive general warrants. If there was reason for the state bills of rights to preclude state governments from issuing general warrants, the same was true for the federal government.[56]

Moreover, if provisions protecting rights were incorporated into the Constitution, "independent tribunals of justice will consider themselves . . . the guardians of those rights" and will become "an impenetrable bulwark" against unlawful assumptions of power by the executive and legislative branches, resisting "every encroachment upon rights expressly stipulated . . . in the constitution by the declaration of rights." That was Jefferson's point. Madison, however, put more emphasis on the state legislatures, which, with a bill of rights to assist them in jealously watching the federal government, would be "able to resist . . . every assumption of power" more effectively "than any other power on earth can do."[57]

His argument was not without loose ends. Although he asserted rights in general terms, his location of those provisions in Article I, Section 9, suggested they were limits on Congress. "In our government," he said, it was perhaps least necessary to guard against abuses in the executive department because "it is not the stronger branch of the system, but the weaker." Restrictions should be "leveled against the legislative" branch because it was "the most powerful, and most likely to be abused." And yet he specifically said the courts could use a federal bill of rights against assumptions of power by both the legislative and executive branches. In the American republic, however, he thought that the greatest power and so the greatest danger lay "in the body of the people, operating by the majority against the minority." Although a "paper barrier" was notoriously ineffective against "the power of the community," insofar as a bill of rights commanded respect and favor it could "be one means to controul the majority from those acts to which they might be otherwise inclined."[58]

After moving more quickly through the other amendments, Madison insisted again that nothing he proposed would "endanger the beauty of the government . . . even in the eyes of its most sanguine admirers." If the Constitution could be made more satisfactory to its critics without weakening its frame or usefulness, "we act the part of wise and liberal men." With that, he said, he had fulfilled his duty. "The subject will not be taken up till the revenue and Department bills are passed," he told Jefferson three weeks later.[59]

Getting the amendments on Congress's agenda was only part of the problem. What Congress did with them was more discouraging, even to Madison.

CONGRESS

In July, the House of Representatives submitted Madison's proposed amendments along with those of the states to a select committee on which each state had one member. That committee, which included Madison, reduced Madison's "prefix" to a single phrase: "Government being intended for the benefit of the people, and the rightful establishment thereof being derived from their authority alone," which would precede "We the people . . ." It tightened some of Madison's language, filled in blanks, and rearranged some of his provisions but generally stayed close to what he had proposed. According to its chairman, John Vining of Delaware, the committee also went through the other amendments recommended by the states but found them superfluous, dangerous, or "so contradictory that it was impossible to make anything of them." Madison thought some of the changes made by the committee were "perhaps for the better, others for the worse," but at last he had confidence that something would be done with his proposal, at least in the House of Representatives.[60]

It took a few more weeks before the House agreed to take up the select committee's report. The House spent six days debating the report as a committee of the whole (August 13–18) and then discussed the report of the committee of the whole as the House of Representatives (August 19–24). In the course of these extended debates, critics insisted that the proposed amendments would never satisfy their constituents. Rather than "those solid and substantial amendments which the people expect," Aedanus Burke said, the select committee's proposals were "whip-syllabub," an eighteenth-century dessert that was "frothy and full of wind, formed only to please the palate," not the stomach; or "like a tub thrown out to a whale" by sailors to divert it from attacking their ship.[61]

Burke proposed to limit Congress's power over elections under Article I, Section 4, by allowing it to alter, modify, or interfere in the times, places, or manner of holding elections for representatives and senators "only when any state shall refuse or neglect, or be unable, by invasion or rebellion" to make such regulations itself. That responded to a widespread demand that Madison had chosen to ignore. New Hampshire's Samuel Livermore said the provision had taken up more time in the New Hampshire convention than any other whatsoever; Gerry considered the change critical to the people's right "even to elect their own representatives." Later South Carolina's Thomas Tudor Tucker introduced the amendment Madison dreaded most. It would allow Congress to raise direct taxes only after requisitions on the states had failed. Livermore pronounced that amendment "more important than all that has been agreed to." Without it the people would regard the amendments "as a mere musketo bite," he said; they wouldn't "give a pinch of snuff for them all." Both motions failed. So did several others, including one to require a two-thirds vote of both houses to raise or maintain "a standing army of regular troops in time of peace," which was "dangerous to public liberty," and another that would reserve to the states all powers not "expressly" delegated to Congress by the Constitution (rejected twice).[62]

The House made some minor changes in the amendments proposed by the committee of the whole, and some not so minor. It entirely eliminated the remnant of Madison's "prefix." More important, it accepted Roger Sherman's motion, which the committee of the whole had rejected, to list the amendments at the end of the Constitution rather than work them into its text. Sherman insisted that the original form of the Constitution had to remain "inviolate" because it had been ratified by the people; his supporters said that the Constitution in its original form was "sacred." Moreover, adding changes to the text would give the impression that Washington and other members of the federal Convention had signed the revised text, which was not the case. Madison explained that the House had to accept Sherman's demand to satisfy a handful of delegates whose consent was needed to get the required two-thirds vote for amendments to the Constitution.[63]

Finally, on August 24, the House of Representatives agreed to a list of seventeen amendments and sent them off to the Senate, where they received a cold reception. All Senate debates were behind closed doors, and no running account of its debate on amendments exists. However, Virginia's Senators Richard Henry Lee and William Grayson said they introduced all the amendments recommended by the Virginia ratifying convention that were not already in the House proposal. The Senate rejected them all. Then, on September 14, it approved a revised and compressed list of twelve amendments. It grouped the House's second amendment, which said Congress could make no law "establishing religion or prohibiting the exercise thereof, nor shall the rights of Conscience be infringed," with its third, which said freedom of speech, of assembly, of the press, and to petition the government for redress of grievances "shall not be infringed," into a single amendment that began: "Congress shall make no law . . ." The Senate also eliminated the House version of Madison's amendment that ruled out state infringements of basic rights. Several other "rights" provisions also disappeared, including those asserting separation of powers, giving persons with religious scruples exemption from military service, and requiring that criminal trials be in the "vicinage" of the crime. The Senate threw out the minimum value of property at issue for appeals to federal courts. It also altered the final House amendment, which said, "The powers not delegated by the Constitution, nor prohibited by it, to the States, are reserved to the States respectively," by adding the words "to the United States" after "delegated" and "or to the people" at the end of the sentence. Those final four words acknowledged that the people retained certain powers—or rights—that they delegated to neither level of government.[64]

The House agreed to most of the Senate's changes; it apparently had little interest in fighting for amendments it had adopted only reluctantly. A conference committee set out to reconcile the remaining differences. Five of its six members—all but Madison—came from states whose ratifying conventions had not recommended amendments. The conference committee proposed two changes of note. The Senate began its third amendment "Congress shall make no law establishing articles of faith, or prohibiting the free exercise of religion," which the committee changed to "Congress shall make no law respecting an establishment of Religion, or prohibiting the free exercise thereof . . ." It also added the words "by an impartial jury of the district wherein the crime shall have been committed, as the district shall have been previously ascertained by law" to the Senate's amendment that assured the accused in criminal prosecutions a speedy and public trial.[65]

Once the House consented to those changes and a few other adjustments, the amendments went to the president. Washington forwarded them to the states without comment on October 2, 1789, a few days after Congress ended its historic first session and began a three-month recess. At the request of the House, the amendments went not only to current members of the union but also to "the executives of the states of Rhode-Island and North-Carolina."[66]

"PLAYING THE AFTER GAME"

Richard Henry Lee was outraged at how the Senate had weakened the amendments proposed by the House, which themselves fell far short of what the Virginia convention recommended. In retrospect, he decided, the idea of proposing amendments for enactment after ratification to the Constitution was a "delusion" that had all along been understood as such "by the greater part of those who arrogated to themselves the name of Federalists." It was "little better than putting oneself to death" with an expectation that "the doctor, who wished our destruction, would afterwards restore us to life." How could Congress be so miserly with the rights of the people? "The great points of free election, Jury trial in criminal cases" were "much loosened," and "the unlimited right of Taxation, and Standing Armies in peace" were "as they were. Some valuable Rights are indeed declared, but the powers that remain are very sufficient to render them nugatory." Lee's colleague William

Grayson said the outcome was what he had long feared would be the result of "playing the after game" rather than insisting on amendments before ratifying the Constitution. Despite his and Lee's best efforts, the final amendments were "so mutilated & gutted that . . . they are good for nothing." He and "many others" thought "that they will do more harm than benefit."[67]

Madison was also disappointed. The Senate's changes struck "at the most salutary articles." Above all, it threw out his amendment prohibiting the states from violating the rights of conscience, freedom of the press, or trial by jury in criminal cases, which he considered the most important of all. "The difficulty of uniting the minds of men accustomed to think differently," Madison wrote Edmund Pendleton, "can only be conceived by those who have witnessed it."[68]

But then Madison never fought for amendments as essential protections of Americans' rights. He hoped, as he put it in mid-August of 1789, that "the nauseous project of amendments" would "kill the opposition every where," and by "putting an end to the disaffection to the Gov[ernmen]t itself, enable the administration to venture on measures not otherwise safe."[69] Would the amendments that Congress proposed serve that purpose? More important, did they need to?

"MALADIES IMAGINAIRES"

Some congressmen thought that Madison exaggerated the danger posed by enemies of the Constitution, particularly outside his home state. Theodore Sedgwick, a Federalist representative from western Massachusetts, said Madison was "constantly haunted with the ghost of Patrick Henry." Pennsylvania senator Robert Morris thought that Madison "got so Cursedly frightened in Virginia" that he "dreamed of amendments ever since." Even an admirer suggested that, like a "sensible physician," Madison was treating "maladies imaginaires" in an appropriate way, with "bread pills powder of paste & neutral mixtures" that would have no real effect. His amendments, in short, were a placebo administered in response to a nonexistent problem.[70]

Madison's critics had a point: The victory he sought had probably been won before the first federal Congress met. By the spring of 1789, the New York circular letter was in little need of being "parried," as Madison had put it. Only Patrick Henry's Virginia readily agreed to ask Congress to call a new convention, as the New York letter proposed. A Federalist majority in New York's newly elected Senate managed to keep that state from submitting its request for a second convention to Congress until February, three months after Virginia acted. By then the issue was all but dead since the other states failed or refused to act on the issue. The House of Representatives filed the Virginia and New York requests without debate. After all, Congress could not call a new convention until two-thirds of the states joined in the demand, which seemed unlikely to happen.[71] In an effort to get action on his amendments proposal, Madison and some supporters suggested that the movement for a second convention might revive if Congress continued dragging its feet. Or, as Richard Henry Lee said in September 1789, the disappointing amendments Congress sent to the states might mean that "e'er long" the required number of state legislatures would demand a convention. He understood there was no hope of that "at present."[72] The political climate had changed dramatically from a year earlier.

The Federalist majority in Congress was one sign of that change. So was the demise of New York's Federal Republican Society, which had attempted without success to coordinate state efforts to amend the Constitution before ratification. Some of its members, including John Lamb and Melancton Smith, tried to reorganize the group in the fall of 1788 "for the purpose of procuring a general convention to revise the Constitution," but attendance at its meetings declined and by the end of the year the organization disappeared. All of a sudden, Smith commented, it seemed as if everyone in New York City considered the Constitution to be of divine origin. The Constitution was on its way to becoming a sacred text. Under the circumstances, New York Federalists felt no obligation to honor their convention pledges to join the fight for amendments. Those promises were "mere illusions," Smith wrote Gilbert Livingston as 1789 began. The Federalists "intend to urge the execution of the plan in its present form," and "no reliance can be placed in any of them."[73]

Washington's acceptance of the presidency reinforced the people's confidence in the new government, and the amendments Madison proposed added to the already well-established trend. In September 1789, Edward Carrington, fresh from a visit to several counties in southern Virginia along the North Carolina border, where support for Patrick Henry's politics had been strong, reported that people there were "perfectly quiet & reconciled to the government." They asked Carrington what Congress was doing, seemed content with his answers, and honored Madison as "the patron of amendments." Equally important, they seemed to think about direct taxes seldom if at all. A leader of the Baptists, who had been leery of the Constitution, also sent Madison word "that the amendments had entirely satisfied" members of that group. Even Massachusetts's Mercy Otis Warren, as outspoken a critic of the Constitution as any, later recalled that "the amendments and amelioration of the constitution" after its ratification "united all parties in the vigorous support of it." By November 1789, Madison could tell Washington that, so far as he could tell, "the late opponents are entirely at rest, and more likely to censure a further opposition to the Gov[ernmen]t as now Administered than the Government itself."[74]

NORTH CAROLINA AND RHODE ISLAND

Before 1789 was over, North Carolina had joined the union. The state had experienced the same swing toward acceptance of the Constitution as other parts of the nation. It also needed federal help with Indians in the west and feared suffering commercial discrimination as an independent state once a short-term congressional exemption from tonnage fees expired in January 1790. Being associated with Rhode Island, the only other nonratifying state, pleased nobody in North Carolina.[75]

Federalists began their campaign almost immediately after the Hillsborough convention adjourned, filling the newspapers with the case for union. They won more seats in the state legislature during the annual elections in August 1788 and took control of the senate but not the lower house that met in November. The legislature finally called a second convention, but delayed it until November 16, 1789, long after the new federal government began. It would convene, like the legislature, in Fayetteville, on the Cape Fear River at the foothills of the Piedmont in Cumberland County. Once it met, the convention took only five and a half days to ratify the Constitution, with 194 votes in favor and 77 against.[76]

No record survives of the debates at Fayetteville, but the amendments recommended by Congress undoubtedly contributed to the convention's final decision. In late June Madison had sent Governor Samuel Johnston copies of the amendments he proposed to the House. A month later he forwarded a copy of the select committee's report with an optimistic prognosis of the amendments' chance of getting through both houses in the current session.[77] North Carolina Federalist William Davie had assured Madison that the "farrago of Amendments borrowed from Virginia" by the Hillsborough convention did not represent "the sense of this Country," and he listed eight changes that were genuinely important to "the honest and serious." Madison's proposal included most of the amendments on Davie's list, and the twelve amendments recommended by Congress came only a bit less close. On its third day the Fayetteville convention ordered, with bipartisan support, three hundred printed copies of the Constitution and the amendments proposed by Congress, a sure sign that the amendments were considered significant.[78]

The convention did not stop with its vote to ratify. On its final day—Monday, November 23—it asked the state's representatives in Congress to "endeavor to obtain" another eight amendments to the Constitution and requested the governor to send the other states copies of those amendments. Ratification would not, however, be conditional on the adoption of those amendments; the convention decisively defeated a motion to that effect. Even that failed motion acknowledged that "in some measure" the amendments already proposed by Congress, when adopted, would fulfill "the object

that this State had in view" when the last convention requested a bill of
rights and other amendments to the Constitution.[79]

The amendments that the convention recommended included no restriction on Congress's power to levy direct taxes, although that amendment had
been proposed. They were essentially a toothless concession to the minority
and an example of the spirit of compromise in which North Carolina's Federalists took great pride. In the end, the opposition members seem to have been
moved by the same spirit. The minority appeared "perfectly Satisfied" after
the decision to ratify, William Dawson reported to James Iredell, not because
their "doubts and fears" were entirely removed, but because they, like so many
other Americans, had "determined chearfully to acquiesce in every measure
which meets the approbation of the Majority of their Country men."[80]

————

It took another six months and a lot more pressure to bring Rhode Island
back into the union. The state's legislature repeatedly turned down calls for
a convention. Much of the opposition to the Constitution came from Rhode
Islanders opposed to slavery and the slave trade and also from a concern over
the state's paper money and its program for retiring Rhode Island's debt from
the Revolutionary War. But by September 1789 the debt had been repaid or
forfeited, and the state's insistent independence from the rest of the union
became less pressing and more dangerous. Rather than call a convention,
however, the legislature asked Congress not to impose impediments on its
commerce. The proposed amendments, it said, had already "afforded some
relief and satisfaction to the . . . people of this state," and Rhode Island
looked forward to a time when it could "be again united with the sister
states." Rhode Islanders were disappointed in the fall of 1789 when, on a trip
through New England, President Washington conspicuously refused to visit
their state. Nonetheless, on October 26 the Rhode Island legislature refused
to call a convention.[81]

The situation was becoming desperate. Congress had delayed the impo-
sition of tonnage charges on Rhode Island's ships until mid-January 1790.
As the deadline came and went, the legislature deadlocked. Its lower house
approved but the upper house rejected a resolution calling for a convention.
Finally, at an emergency Sunday session on January 17, after a member who
opposed the proposition had gone to church, the upper house voted four in
favor and four against the convention. That allowed the governor to break
with his party and cast a heroic, tie-breaking "yea" vote. The convention met
at the town of South Kingston on March 1, 1790—and five days later voted
to adjourn without deciding on the Constitution.[82]

That action pushed the United States Senate over the edge. In response
to Rhode Island's petition, Congress in February had put off commercial restrictions on the state until April 1 but "no longer." Now, on May 13, 1790, an

exasperated Senate passed a bill that prohibited all trade with Rhode Island by land or by sea. Violators would face the confiscation of their ships, fines up to $500, and six months of imprisonment. The Senate bill also demanded that Rhode Island pay its share of the old government's debt, some $25,000, a fair sum at the time, by December 1. Rather than see its economy destroyed, the Providence town meeting voted to open negotiations with Newport and other commercial towns over seceding from the state and joining the union. Finally, on May 29, five days after it had reconvened in Newport, the convention voted by a grudging 34–32 to ratify the Constitution. Four opposition members were absent: Had they voted, Rhode Island would have remained outside the United States.[83]

A "BILL OF RIGHTS"?

After they ratified the Constitution, both North Carolina and Rhode Island quickly approved all or, in Rhode Island's case, all but one of the twelve amendments Congress sent to the states in September 1789. That was insufficient to make them the law of the land. To be ratified, each amendment had to be approved by three-quarters of the states, that is, ten of the thirteen. By the end of 1790, only four states had approved all twelve of the proposed amendments. Three other states had approved all but the second, which would preclude members of Congress from giving themselves a pay raise that took effect before an intervening election to the House. Delaware approved all but the first amendment, which set a procedure for increasing membership in the House of Representatives as population grew. However, amendments three through twelve had been approved by eight states.

Then, in May 1791, when Vermont became the fourteenth state, the consent of eleven states became necessary. By the end of that year, Vermont, Pennsylvania, and, finally, Virginia had approved all twelve amendments (Vermont) or all but the second (Pennsylvania and Virginia), so the ten amendments numbered three through twelve went into effect. The first proposed amendment narrowly failed. It had emerged from Congress in a more complex form than Madison proposed and without his assurance that every state would have at least two representatives. That provoked Delaware's opposition, so it received the approval of only ten states, one too few. Delaware and five other states (New Hampshire, Rhode Island, New Jersey, Pennsylvania, and Virginia) also failed to approve the second amendment. The three states that did nothing officially at the time—Massachusetts, Connecticut, and Georgia—finally ratified the first ten amendments to the Constitution in 1939, one hundred and fifty years after Congress had submitted them to the states.[84]

What, however, had the states ratified? Between September 1789 and early 1792, nobody seems to have referred to either the twelve amendments proposed by Congress in September 1789 or the ten that were ratified by the end of 1791 as a "bill of rights." Washington's letter transmitting the amendments to the states for their consideration referred only to "the amendments proposed to be added to the Constitution of the United States." And on March 1, 1792, Secretary of State Thomas Jefferson, the great champion of bills of rights, sent state governors official notice of "the ratifications by three fourths of the Legislatures of the Several States, of certain articles in addition and amendment of the Constitution of the United States, proposed by Congress to the said Legislatures." He could have saved a lot of words by calling those amendments a bill of rights, but he did not.[85]

The amendments did not satisfy George Mason, who had asked the federal Convention to add a bill of rights to the Constitution. On March 16, 1790, he wrote Jefferson that "unless some Material Amendments" to the Constitution took place—and not, it seems, those that Congress had already proposed—he "apprehended great Danger to the Rights & Liberty of our Country." Jefferson replied that he too wished "to see some amendments, further than those which have been proposed" to fix the new government "more surely on a republican basis," and he hoped they would be "obtained before the want of them will do any harm." Madison, who referred to some of the amendments he proposed on June 8, 1789, as "what may be called a bill of rights," did not use that term for the amendments Congress sent out for enactment. In late 1789, at least, he referred to them as "the plan of amendments" or "the amendments proposed by Congress" or simply "the amendments." His correspondents used similar language.[86]

Five state legislatures (Maryland, North Carolina, Rhode Island, South Carolina, and Vermont) seemed to consider the twelve proposed amendments as a package and ratified them all (without, however, calling them a bill of rights). The other state legislatures apparently thought they were considering a series of separate amendments, among which they could pick and choose. In submitting Congress's "propositions for amendments in the constitution of the United States" to the Massachusetts legislature, Governor John Hancock recommended "the adoption of some of the proposed amendments," including, above all, the seventh, eighth, and ninth. The Massachusetts legislature rejected not just the first and second proposed amendments, but also the twelfth—and then neglected to finalize its ratification of the others.[87] At one point, Virginia's senate refused to approve the third, eighth, eleventh, and twelfth proposed amendments (the future First, Sixth, Ninth, and Tenth Amendments) because they fell "far short of affording the same security to personal rights, or of so effectually guarding against the apprehended mischief of the government" as the amendments proposed by the Virginia ratifying convention.[88] One report from Richmond in late 1789 predicted that, regardless of what it did with regard to Congress's amendments, the Virginia legislature would propose additional ones since Congress had not addressed the single most important problem for the Constitution's critics, "the power of direct taxation." Patrick Henry said the direct tax amendment was alone worth more than all of the amendments Congress approved.[89]

The press included surprisingly little discussion of the proposed amendments, but then it too referred to "The AMENDMENTS, agreed on by Congress, to be laid before the Legislatures of the several States," "the amendments in the Constitution of the United States, proposed by Congress," or the like. When newspapers spoke of a "declaration of rights" or "bill of rights," they were referring to the documents appended to several state constitutions, not the proposed amendments to the federal Constitution.[90]

Rhode Island gave no evidence that it considered the proposed amendments a bill of rights. In 1790 the Newport convention decided to open its instrument of ratification with a declaration of rights, much as the Virginia ratifying convention had done two years earlier. It began by asserting that men had "certain natural rights" including "the enjoyments of life and liberty, with the means of acquiring, possessing and protecting property, and pursuing and obtaining happiness and safety," that all power was derived from the people and magistrates were their "trustees and agents . . . at all times, amenable to them," and that the people could resume their powers "whensoever it shall become necessary for their happiness." It also declared that "the rights of the states . . . to nominate and appoint all state officers" and to exercise every other "power, jurisdiction and right" not clearly delegated to the new government by the Constitution remained with "the people of the several states, or their respective state governments."[91]

Then it listed specific rights that Congress's proposed amendments promised to protect along with others that Congress left unmentioned. Rhode Island declared, for example, that "the people have a right peaceably to assemble . . . to consult for their common good," that "the people have a right to freedom of speech," that "all men have an equal, natural and unalienable right to the free exercise of religion, according to the dictates of conscience," and "that standing armies in time of peace are dangerous to liberty, and ought not to be kept up, except in case of necessity." Like New York, Rhode Island also ratified "in confidence" that a long list of recommended amendments, including the familiar one on direct taxes and another calling for an immediate end to the slave trade, would receive "an early and mature consideration," as if Congress had only begun the work of making the Constitution fit for a free people.[92]

Similarly, in October 1791 a federal grand jury in Augusta, Georgia, protested "the want of a Bill of rights clearly defining the reserved rights of the several States." The next year, when the first ten amendments had become the law of the land, Georgia's federal grand jury again presented "as a very great greviance [sic], that a bill of Rights was not formed, and executed prior

to the adoption of the Federal Constitution, as the true principles of Freedom cannot [securely] exist long without," as if the country was still in need
of such a document.[93]

The proposed amendments did not, in fact, look like a bill or declaration
of rights as Americans of the late eighteenth century knew them. Thanks
to Roger Sherman, they were at least grouped together—but at the end of
the Constitution, like the afterthought they were, not at its beginning, as
with most state declarations of rights. Moreover, they did not open, like the
Virginia declaration of rights and other state documents modeled on it, with
a declaration that all men had "certain inherent rights" or any of the other
general principles Americans had come to expect in bills or declarations of
rights. The proposed amendments lacked even the abbreviated statement of
basic principles that Madison wanted "prefixed" to the Constitution. And
the amendments included no assertion, like that in the Virginia declaration,
of the people's right to choose their legislative representatives freely and not
to be "taxed or deprived of their property for public use without their consent, or that of their representatives."[94]

Congress's first two proposed amendments did not look like part of a bill
of rights. The first mandated that Congress increase and reapportion seats in
the House of Representatives according to certain set rules. Its proponents
understood it as "a constitution[al] barrier to prevent encroachments on the
liberty of the people" by assuring "that the dearest privilege of the people"—to
a full and free representation—"would not be left to stand upon so flimsy a
foundation as the whim or pleasure of their representatives."[95] The amendment
did not, however, assert a basic right so much as it laid out a way to implement
that right. And what did the second proposed amendment, on Congressional
salaries, have to do with basic rights? Only by default—because the first two
amendments were not ratified—did the third proposed amendment become
the first, so the list began "Congress shall make no law respecting an establishment of religion, or prohibiting the free exercise thereof."

Moreover, a federal bill of rights was supposed to do more than protect
the rights of the people on the model of the state documents. It was also
supposed to define the rights of the several states. Both Samuel Adams in
Massachusetts and Samuel Spencer in North Carolina said an amendment
stating that the states retained all powers not specifically delegated to the
United States might alone serve as a federal bill of rights or, as Spencer put
it, prevent the need for a more detailed bill of rights. Similarly, Rhode Island's statement of rights included an emphatic assertion of the state's right
to appoint its own officers and exercise all powers not explicitly given to the
federal government.

To assure the continued existence of the states in a genuinely federal
system of government was, for the critics of the Constitution, nothing less

than an essential support of the rights of the people. The division of power between the states and the nation, like that among the branches of the federal government, provided a structural check on potentially oppressive power. In fact, the vertical division between levels of government seemed if anything more important than the separation of functions within the federal government. According to Madison, the most extreme opponents of a strong central government considered the state legislatures "sure guardians of the people's liberty" against violations by the federal government.[96] During the ratification debates, several leading Federalists—Fisher Ames, Theophilus Parsons, even Alexander Hamilton—had also argued that the states would protect the people against any federal infringements on their rights.

Madison himself had more confidence in the state legislatures as protectors of rights than he had in the courts: He told the House of Representatives on June 8 that the state legislatures would "jealously and closely watch the operations" of the central government and would "be able to resist with more effect every assumption of power *than any other power on earth can do.*" State legislatures had a far better track record, given their opposition to Parliament's violations of colonial rights, than the courts, whose power to invalidate legislative acts was not yet established.[97] In 1798 and 1799, Madison and Jefferson would turn to the legislatures of Virginia and Kentucky (by then the fifteenth state), not the courts, to oppose the violation of basic rights by the Alien and Sedition Acts. The Supreme Court would not use a "rights" amendment against an act of Congress until more than half a century later—in the Dred Scott decision (1857), which used the "due process" clause to affirm the property rights of slaveholders.[98]

For men like Richard Henry Lee, the amendments Congress proposed failed to give the states sufficient protection to assure their continued existence. Because the Tenth Amendment—which "reserved to the States respectively, or to the people," all powers "not delegated to the United States by the Constitution, nor prohibited by it to the States"—lacked the word "expressly" before "delegated," it left the new government free to claim broad powers under the "necessary and proper" clause. The amendments left Congress's power to tax fully in place, with no source of revenue designated for the states. In the fall of 1789, Lee and his senatorial colleague William Grayson were still hoping for amendments that would prevent "the annihilation of the State Governments."[99] Any constitution that left the future of the states at issue was, in their eyes, a threat to the rights of the people.

That contemporaries did not call the first ten amendments a bill of rights was not peculiar to them. According to the legal historian Akhil Reed Amar, before the enactment of the Fourteenth Amendment to the Constitution in 1868, "the Supreme Court never—not once—referred to the 1792 decalogue as 'the' or 'a' bill of rights." As late as 1880, a Supreme Court justice could say that the federal Constitution, "unlike most modern ones, does not contain any formal declaration or bill of rights." The designation of the first ten amendments as a bill of rights owes less to the First than to the Thirty-ninth Congress, which met during Reconstruction. There Representative John Bingham of Ohio, a principal framer of the Fourteenth Amendment (1868), spoke of the constitutional amendments guaranteeing rights with far more enthusiasm than Madison had done in 1789.[100]

Until then, Americans turned for a statement of their rights not to the first ten amendments to the Constitution but to the Declaration of Independence. It was the only federal founding document that said "all men are created equal" and were "endowed by their Creator with certain inalienable Rights," for the protection of which the people had created governments whose power came exclusively "from the Consent of the Governed." In effect, lacking a "bill of rights" that suited their expectations, Americans recycled a document written for another purpose and made it a sacred statement of their fundamental rights and beliefs.[101] And so it remains.

THE FINAL SCORE

In many ways, the Federalists won. They managed to get the Constitution ratified without prior amendments and successfully avoided the direct tax amendment that, in their view, would have destroyed the creditworthiness of the United States. The amendments that were adopted did not undermine the Constitution. In retrospect, however, the Constitution's critics did not simply "lose." They got almost everything they wanted, though not always in the form they expected or within their lifetimes.

Even without the proposed amendment on representation, Congress responded to the widespread demand for a fuller popular representation in the House of Representatives. After the first census, the 65 members that the Constitution specified for the first House grew to 105, which roughly met the ratio of one representative for 30,000 people. Within a decade the House had 142 members.[102]

Moreover, the Judiciary Act of 1789, which was written at the same time Madison's amendments wound their way through Congress, went far to answer fears of the new federal court system. It set up thirteen federal district courts—for the eleven states then in the union, plus Maine and Kentucky—and three federal circuit courts consisting of a district judge and two itinerant Supreme Court judges for the eastern, middle, and southern states. Litigants would not (as some critics of the Constitution feared) need to travel to the national capital except for appeals to the Supreme Court; justice would come to them. The Judiciary Act also provided for trial by jury in federal courts for both criminal and civil cases, as did the Sixth and Seventh Amendments to the Constitution, but with more detail on the location of trials and the size of juries. Moreover, the act limited federal jurisdiction to cases where the amount in controversy was above a stated minimum and gave state courts substantial concurrent jurisdiction with federal courts, assuring the state courts' continued existence. Senator Richard Henry Lee expressed more satisfaction with the protection of rights in the Judiciary Act than he ever did with the amendments to the Constitution that Congress proposed.[103]

On direct taxes, again, the proponents of amendments lost the battle but won the war for a substantial period of time. Direct taxes did not become a major source of federal revenue in the new republic. Congress levied direct taxes on only three occasions, all of which were, as the Federalists promised, times of war or threat of war—in 1798, during the Quasi-War with France, the War of 1812, and, finally, the Civil War. In the last two instances, it allowed states to raise their quotas and offered a discount on the requisition to cover the cost of collection. That was not exactly what the old direct tax amendment would have mandated, but it came close.[104]

Direct taxes were ultimately abandoned for a reason that nobody in the ratification debates seems to have foreseen. The Constitution said that direct taxes had to be apportioned among the states according to their population, which was calculated by the same formula used in allocating seats in the House of Representatives, i.e., "adding to the whole Number of free Persons, including those bound to Service for a Term of Years, and excluding Indians not taxed, three-fifths of all other Persons," or slaves. The federal Convention adopted the proposal in part to help sell the three-fifths clause in the North: The South might get more seats in the House of Representatives, but it would also have to pay more taxes.[105] However, where per capita wealth is unequal in different states, a tax apportioned among the states according to population alone has the perverse effect of requiring higher tax rates in poorer states than in richer ones to collect the apportioned sum. In 1787, some federal Convention delegates seemed aware of the problem, but they claimed that population was a fair measure of wealth. Others disagreed. Even if wealth was relatively equally distributed in 1787, Rufus King observed, there was no guarantee it would remain so in the future.[106] But the delegates kept the politically useful apportionment provision.

By the 1860s, a federal tax on land—an agreed-upon form of direct taxes—was egregiously unfair: It forced western agricultural states to pay more proportionally than urbanized eastern states with rich commercial and industrial sectors. As a result, Congress preferred to supplement tariff revenue, still the backbone of federal budgets, with new "indirect" taxes on manufactures and incomes.[107] After the Supreme Court decided that an income tax was a direct tax in *Pollock v. Farmers' Loan & Trust Company* (1895), the country enacted the Sixteenth Amendment (1913), which says

Congress can "lay and collect taxes on incomes . . . without apportionment among the Several States." That assured the federal government a major source of revenue without the irrationality of apportioning the tax according to population with no consideration of the people's ability to pay.

Federalists had opposed the original direct tax amendment less because of its impact on federal revenue than because of its anticipated effect on the creditworthiness of the United States in the eyes of foreign lenders. Even there the amendment's probable impact is open to question. As Washington's Secretary of the Treasury, Alexander Hamilton quickly established the country's credit by funding the national debt and paying the annual interest on it from funds raised primarily from customs duties and some excise taxes, including one on distilled liquor. By absorbing the state as well as the national debts and transforming them into long-term federal bonds on which only the interest had to be paid regularly, Hamilton reduced state budgets, which had been heavily dedicated to paying off the states' Revolutionary debts, by as much as 90 percent. That, in turn, ended the states' need to levy the heavy poll and regressively assessed land taxes that lay behind popular sensitivity on direct taxes. The relief was notable in states like Massachusetts, whose extreme fiscal conservatism had provoked rural uprisings that, in turn, prompted fears for the future of the republic among Washington and his correspondents in the late 1780s. With a few exceptions, such as western Pennsylvania's brief Whiskey Rebellion, a new peace settled over the countryside.[108]

The Constitution's critics wanted to avoid the creation of a "consolidated" national government that would destroy the states. Again, their wish was fulfilled beyond their wildest expectations: The states remained the most powerful component of American government for some 150 years after the ratification of the Constitution. Moreover, even without formal term limits, until 1940 presidents followed Washington's precedent and served no more than two terms in office. Then the Twenty-second Amendment (1951) limited the president to two terms, as the ratifying conventions of Virginia, New York, and North Carolina had proposed. Four decades later, the country enacted another amendment that was proposed by the Constitution's critics during the ratification controversy. The Twenty-seventh Amendment prevents senators and representatives from giving themselves a pay increase that takes effect before an election of representatives intervenes. Congress recommended it to the states in 1789; it failed initially, but was finally enacted in 1992.

Eventually, too, the country got a federal Bill of Rights worth having. It emerged from a series of Supreme Court cases, beginning in the 1920s, that used the Fourteenth Amendment to make the first ten amendments powerful protectors of the people's right to "equal protection of the laws" and not to be deprived of "life, liberty, or property without due process of law" by the states as well as the federal government. The document itself—or rather Congress's official copy of the twelve amendments it proposed in September 1789—made its first major public appearance on the 1947 Freedom Train, and a few years later, in 1952, the Bill of Rights went on display in the National Archives along with the Declaration of Independence and the Constitution.[109]

The Bill of Rights we have is, however, different in many ways from the one the Constitution's critics wanted. It says nothing about "no taxation without representation" and "no standing armies in time of peace." And it now takes historical imagination to understand how people could have understood the preservation of the rights of the states as a way of protecting individual rights. The state legislatures have served that role—for example, by passing personal liberty laws before the Civil War to secure the fundamental judicial rights of persons accused of being runaway slaves under the federal fugitive slave laws of 1793 and 1850. Nonetheless, "states rights" today seem more firmly associated with the defense of slavery, disenfranchisement of black voters, and resistance to integration.

Many rights that Americans prize, including freedom of speech, of the press, and of conscience, the right of trial by jury, habeas corpus and other protections of the accused in judicial proceedings, and of course the right to a free and equal representation, had powerful champions in the eighteenth century. The explanation and defense of habeas corpus in the Massachusetts ratifying convention is as relevant now as it was then; and some Americans of the founding period understood freedom of conscience in a way that would still be radical today.[110] In the state ratifying conventions, even some clergymen argued for allowing Jews, Catholics, and Muslims to be eligible for public office against a broad popular conviction that religious freedom and, indeed, freedom in general, was safest in the hands of Protestants. For them, people's religious convictions were for God, not the state, to judge. On the other hand, Congress and the courts have given many rights, including freedom of speech and of the press, a more expanded meaning and have extended civil liberties to far more people—women, racial minorities, persons without property—than most Americans of the Revolutionary era anticipated. American rights and American freedom were not a gift of the country's "founding fathers." They are and have always been a work in progress.

And yet our interest in Americans of the late eighteenth century is not misplaced. The Constitution they gave us proved more successful than its most devoted advocates imagined: It has guided the United States for over two centuries as its boundaries expanded from the Mississippi to the Pacific and its influence spread over the world. The Constitution's success came less from a perfection in its design than from the sacrifices of men like Washington, who took on the presidency with more reluctance than he took to the field with the Continental Army. It also owes much to the dogged commitment of ordinary Americans like the townsmen of Richmond, Massachusetts, and Preston, Connecticut, Madison's testy constituents in the Virginia Piedmont, and the capable delegates they sent to their state ratifying conventions. They refused to be told that the issues of the day were beyond their competence. They put their minds to complicated problems, tried to reconcile the ideals of the Revolution with the needs of the nation, and considered the impact of contemporary decisions not just on their own lives but for the future—for "millions yet unborn," as one person after another put it. They were engaged, often remarkably well informed given the primitive communications of the day, and, with one brief exception, honored majority rule, even when it went against them. They made the republic work.

The Constitution's critics did not get all the amendments to the Constitution they wanted, or even those they thought most important. Without their determined opposition, however, the first ten amendments would not have become a part of the Constitution for later generations to transform into a powerful instrument for the defense of American freedom. "We the People" of 1787 and 1788 inaugurated a dialogue between power and liberty that has continued, reminding us regularly of the principles of 1776 upon which the United States was founded and that have given us direction and national identity. Their example might well be their greatest gift to posterity.

POSTSCRIPT

──── ★ ────

In Memoriam

In the pages of this book, the dead seemed at times to rise from their graves to repeat lines that had earned them a place in American history, a place many of them never received until now. It feels wrong to close without knowing what happened to at least some of them after the ratifying conventions adjourned.

Those who later served in national office are the least obscure. James Iredell was well rewarded for his services at the North Carolina convention in Hillsborough: In February 1790, President Washington nominated him as an associate justice of the Supreme Court. His fellow justices included ratification veterans James Wilson of Pennsylvania, William Cushing of Massachusetts, and Chief Justice John Jay, whose place would later be taken by Connecticut's Oliver Ellsworth. Iredell was delighted with the appointment, which he thought would free him from traveling from court to court in North Carolina to cobble together a decent living. Unfortunately, early Court judges had to "ride circuit," and Iredell was assigned the extraordinarily long and arduous Southern circuit through North Carolina, South Carolina, and Georgia.[1]

His position as an associate Supreme Court justice gave him an opportunity to hear Patrick Henry at court. Iredell seems to have had a bad impression of Henry, and he was agreeably surprised. "Gracious God!" Iredell wrote afterwards, "he is an orator indeed!" Henry spoke "with the most ease, the least embarrassment, the greatest variety, and with an illustration of imagery altogether original but perfectly correct," Iredell reported; and he never said anything "personally offensive." In the end, after spending time with Henry, Iredell concluded that he was "a much more solid character and better reasoner than I expected." Clearly men could not be judged in the light of "Party Prejudices."[2]

Eventually the justices rotated circuits, but Iredell's duties still kept him away from his family for extended periods of time, and the rigors of eighteenth-century travel ate away at his frail health. In the end, they killed him.

He died, back home in Edenton, in October 1799, soon after his forty-eighth birthday.[3]

He had survived Wilson, who, in July of 1798, also died in Edenton, in a small Carolina inn, broken, impoverished, and humiliated after two stints in jail (while still an associate justice of the Supreme Court) for debts from ambitious land speculations that had gone horribly wrong. Barely recovered from malaria and suffering the aftereffects of a stroke, Wilson died a month short of age fifty-six. The contrast between the brilliant man who had held his nose high in Philadelphia, whether or not to keep his spectacles in place, and the pathetic circumstances of his death made the last years of his life an epic tragedy. His colleague Justice Iredell had him buried on the estate of Iredell's brother-in-law, Governor Samuel Johnston.[4] There Wilson rested until 1906, when, finally, Philadelphia reclaimed his remains.

George Washington survived both Iredell and Wilson—and also his neighbor, George Mason, who died peacefully at home in October 1792. He also outlived Patrick Henry, who in June 1799 succumbed to stomach cancer—but not by much. Washington's wish to leave the presidency quickly came to nothing. He served a second term, then issued a final farewell to his country. Iredell recorded the bittersweet mood at Washington's birthday celebration during February 1797, when everyone knew the president would soon leave office. The first lady was moved to tears; the president felt "emotions . . . too powerful to be concealed."[5] Washington lived only a little over two years back at Mount Vernon, until December 1799, when, at age sixty-seven, he died, quite suddenly, of a virulent throat infection. That was not enough time for him to settle his affairs, get his plantation house up to standard, make his farms profitable, or even to complete the agricultural experiments that gave him such pleasure.

Washington's story—like that of Alexander Hamilton, who died after a duel with Aaron Burr in 1804, and Madison, who lived until 1836, when he was the last surviving member of the federal Convention—has often been told. Those of others, who came out of obscurity for a brief, brilliant moment in 1787 or 1788, are less familiar.

Take William Symmes, the young attorney who stood up to his old law teacher, Theophilus Parsons, at the Massachusetts ratifying convention and noted the flaw in Federalist claims that to weaken Congress would be to weaken the people. Symmes never had the brilliant public career for which he seemed destined. His constituents in Andover, Massachusetts, most of whom did not think well of the Constitution, might have resented his "yea" vote on ratification. Or maybe he just found practicing law in rural Andover a hard way to make a living. Whatever the reason, in the fall of 1790 he hung his shingle in the growing commercial town of Portland, Maine, where he became a leading member of the bar. Symmes occasionally wrote essays for local newspapers. He also served three terms in the state legislature and was a member of the Portand School Committee as well as of several other civic organizations, but he never entered national politics. He died in 1807 at age forty-five, still a bachelor, and much respected (despite, it seems, an excessive and unseemly fondness for brandy).[6]

Zachariah Johnston, whose speech endorsing the Constitution seemed to some the best at the Virginia convention, exceeding even those of Patrick Henry, remained a member of the Virginia legislature (and an enthusiast for developing the Potomac River) until a few years before his death in 1800. He was also an elector in the first presidential contest, but chose not to run for Congress.[7] Perhaps he wanted to remain nearer his many children, to whom he had expressed so deep a commitment.

Other backbenchers like Jonathan Smith from Lanesborough, Massachusetts, whose heartfelt endorsement of the Constitution seemed to move the convention in Boston, or Amos Singletary from Sutton, Massachusetts, both of whom served several terms in the state legislature, are all but forgotten. They were part of the rank-and-file that made town democracy and representative state government work. Only rarely do their words survive outside the records of their state ratifying conventions unless—like Singletary, who had complained about monied men, fancy lawyers, and *this here* self-same constitution"—they had a peculiarly memorable way of expressing themselves. The historian of Singletary's home town told a story about him from a period long before 1788, when the town was shaken by a religious revival. A local manufacturer of hoes "being under concern of mind" caught sight of Singletary, who was a justice of the peace and an "earnest Christian," and called out to him: "O Squire! O Squire! What shall I do to be saved?" Singletary had scarcely brought his horse to a stop when he answered: "Put more steel in your hoes." The man never spent a day in school, but he was no fool. He died in 1806, in his mid-eighties.[8]

The political careers of both Gilbert Livingston and Melancton Smith peaked at the New York ratifying convention. Later both served briefly in the state legislature, but neither held further public offices. Smith's "yea" vote had allowed him a safe return home in the summer of 1788, but being in New York City still had its perils. He was the one of the first to die—at age fifty-four—during the city's 1798 yellow fever epidemic.[9]

Smith's convention colleague John Lansing, who in 1788 kept faith with his party and no doubt his conscience by voting "nay," lived longer than Smith and held more public offices. He became a member of the state supreme court in 1790 and later its chief justice. In 1801 he replaced his old convention opponent Robert R. Livingston as the state's chancellor, an extremely distinguished judicial position that he seems to have acquitted honorably. (Reports that Lansing's knowledge of the law was "not extensive,"

which William Pierce repeated in his description of federal Convention delegates, were apparently wrong.) New York City had perils for him, too. On
December 12, 1829, fifteen years after he retired from the chancellorship, the
tall, dignified, seventy-five-year-old Lansing left a Manhattan hotel to mail
some letters. He never returned. A book published a half century later said
he was murdered, apparently by some prominent people, but the evidence,
like Lansing, had long since disappeared.[10]

The last word goes to William Findley, the Irish immigrant who managed at the Pennsylvania ratifying convention to best both James Wilson
and his state's chief justice over the history of jury trials. The Federalists
repeatedly claimed that critics of the Constitution acted out of fear that they
would lose their state jobs. For Findley, however, the Constitution opened
new opportunities. In 1791, when Pennsylvania allowed district elections
of congressmen, he won a seat in the House of Representatives. And there
he remained, except for a four-year hiatus, until 1817, three years before his
death at age eighty, winning the respect of colleagues who fondly referred to
him as "the Venerable Findley."[11] Those long years of service allowed him to
" 'Addrass the chair,' and say 'Myster Spaker,' and avoid being 'parsenal'" at
meetings of Congress in both Philadelphia, to which the new government
quickly moved, and then the new capital, Washington.

In 1796, Findley took the trouble of recording how his thinking on the
Constitution had changed after the Pennsylvania ratifying convention,
where, he recalled with considerable understatement, "some circumstances of
irritation . . . were unfriendly to cool discussion." He watched as other states
took time to deliberate on the Constitution before holding their conventions,
as Pennsylvania had not. When many of those states then decided to recommend amendments for the "consideration and adoption of the first Congress,"
he decided that was the best course to take. The delay involved in calling
a second convention "in the then state of things, would be highly inconvenient." On further reflection, he also decided that not all of his objections to
the Constitution were "well founded." After the first Congress recommended
and the states ratified some of the amendments that he wanted, he became
confident that additional amendments could be enacted "when they became
necessary." He even came to prefer federal direct taxes on land over indirect
excise taxes on American manufactures, such as the 1791 whiskey tax.[12]

In the end, like so many onetime critics of the Constitution, William
Findley "embraced the government as my own and my children's inheritance." He knew the Constitution had defects—and there he had a lot of
company. Perfection was not to be expected in the work of mortal men.
In his mature judgment, the Constitution was, however, not just good or
maybe good enough. Findley came to believe that it was "capable of being
well administered, and on the whole, the best government in the world."[13]

APPENDIX

--- ★ ---

The Constitution of the United States and the First Ten Amendments

We the People of the United States, in Order to form a more perfect Union, establish Justice, insure domestic Tranquility, provide for the common defence, promote the general Welfare, and secure the Blessings of Liberty to ourselves and our Posterity, do ordain and establish this Constitution for the United States of America.

ARTICLE I

Section 1. All legislative Powers herein granted shall be vested in a Congress of the United States, which shall consist of a Senate and House of Representatives.

Section 2. The House of Representatives shall be composed of Members chosen every second Year by the People of the several States, and the Electors in each State shall have the Qualifications requisite for Electors of the most numerous Branch of the State Legislature.

No Person shall be a Representative who shall not have attained to the age of twenty five Years, and been seven Years a Citizen of the United States, and who shall not, when elected, be an Inhabitant of that State in which he shall be chosen.

Representatives and direct Taxes shall be apportioned among the several States which may be included within this Union, according to their respective Numbers, which shall be determined by adding to the whole Number of free Persons, including those bound to Service for a Term of Years, and excluding Indians not taxed, three fifths of all other Persons. The actual Enumeration shall be made within three Years after the first Meeting of the Congress of the United States, and within every subsequent Term of ten Years, in such Manner as they shall by Law direct. The Number of Representatives shall not exceed one for every thirty Thousand, but each State shall have at Least one Representative; and until such enumeration shall be made, the State of New Hampshire shall be entitled to chuse three, Massachusetts eight, Rhode-Island and Providence Plantations one, Connecticut five, New-York six, New Jersey four, Pennsylvania eight, Delaware one, Maryland six, Virginia ten, North Carolina five, South Carolina five, and Georgia three.

When vacancies happen in the Representation from any State, the Executive Authority thereof shall issue Writs of Election to fill such Vacancies.

The House of Representatives shall chuse their Speaker and other Officers; and shall have the sole Power of Impeachment.

Section 3. The Senate of the United States shall be composed of two Senators from each State, chosen by the Legislature thereof, for six Years; and each Senator shall have one Vote.

Immediately after they shall be assembled in Consequence of the first Election, they shall be divided as equally as may be into three Classes. The Seats of the Senators of the first Class shall be vacated at the Expiration of the second Year, of the second Class at the Expiration of the fourth Year, and the third Class at the Expiration of the sixth Year, so that one third may be chosen every second Year; and if Vacancies happen by Resignation, or otherwise, during the Recess of the Legislature of any State, the Executive thereof may make temporary Appointments until the next Meeting of the Legislature, which shall then fill such Vacancies.

No Person shall be a Senator who shall not have attained to the Age of thirty Years, and been nine Years a Citizen of the United States and who shall not, when elected, be an Inhabitant of that State for which he shall be chosen.

The Vice President of the United States shall be President of the Senate, but shall have no Vote, unless they be equally divided.

The Senate shall chuse their other Officers, and also a President pro tempore, in the Absence of the Vice President, or when he shall exercise the Office of President of the United States.

The Senate shall have the sole Power to try all Impeachments. When sitting for that Purpose, they shall be on Oath or Affirmation. When the President of the United States is tried, the Chief Justice shall preside: And no Person shall be convicted without the Concurrence of two thirds of the Members present.

Judgment in Cases of Impeachment shall not extend further than to removal from Office, and disqualification to hold and enjoy any Office of Honor, Trust or Profit under the United States: but the Party convicted shall nevertheless be liable and subject to Indictment, Trial, Judgment and Punishment, according to Law.

Section 4. The Times, Places and Manner of holding Elections for Senators and Representatives, shall be prescribed in each State by the Legislature thereof; but the Congress may at any time by Law make or alter such Regulations, except as to the Places of chusing Senators.

The Congress shall assemble at least once in every Year, and such Meeting shall be on the first Monday in December, unless they shall by Law appoint a different Day.

Section 5. Each House shall be the Judge of the Elections, Returns and Qualifications of its own Members, and a Majority of each shall constitute a Quorum to do Business; but a smaller Number may adjourn from day to day, and may be authorized to compel the Attendance of absent Members, in such Manner, and under such Penalties as each House may provide.

Each House may determine the Rules of its Proceedings, punish its Members for disorderly Behaviour, and, with the Concurrence of two thirds, expel a Member.

Each House shall keep a Journal of its Proceedings, and from time to time publish the same, excepting such Parts as may in their Judgment require Secrecy; and the Yeas and Nays of the Members of either House on any question shall, at the Desire of one fifth of those Present, be entered on the Journal.

Neither House, during the Session of Congress, shall, without the Consent of the other, adjourn for more than three days, nor to any other Place than that in which the two Houses shall be sitting.

Section 6. The Senators and Representatives shall receive a Compensation for their Services, to be ascertained by Law, and paid out of the Treasury of the United States. They shall in all Cases, except Treason, Felony and Breach of the Peace, be privileged from Arrest during their Attendance at the Session of their respective Houses, and in going to and returning from the same; and for any Speech or Debate in either House, they shall not be questioned in any other Place.

No Senator or Representative shall, during the Time for which he was elected, be appointed to any civil Office under the Authority of the United States, which shall have been created, or the Emoluments whereof shall have been encreased during such time: and no Person holding any Office under the United States, shall be a Member of either House during his Continuance in Office.

Section 7. All Bills for raising Revenue shall originate in the House of Representatives; but the Senate may propose or concur with Amendments as on other Bills.

Every Bill which shall have passed the House of Representatives and the Senate, shall, before it become a Law, be presented to the President of the United States; if he approve he shall sign it, but if not he shall return it, with his Objections to that House in which it shall have originated, who shall enter the Objections at large on their Journal, and proceed to reconsider it. If after such Reconsideration two thirds of that House shall agree to pass the Bill, it shall be sent, together with the Objections, to the other House, by which it shall likewise be reconsidered, and if approved by two thirds of that House, it shall become a Law. But in all such Cases the Votes of both Houses shall be determined by Yeas and Nays, and the Names of the Persons voting for and against the Bill shall be entered on the Journal of each House respectively. If any Bill shall not be returned by the President within ten Days (Sundays excepted) after it shall have been presented to him, the Same shall be a Law, in like Manner as if he had signed it, unless the Congress by their Adjournment prevent its Return, in which Case it shall not be a Law.

Every Order, Resolution, or Vote to which the Concurrence of the Senate and House of Representatives may be necessary (except on a question of Adjournment) shall be presented to the President of the United States; and before the Same shall take Effect, shall be approved by him, or being disapproved by him, shall be repassed by two thirds of the Senate and House of Representatives, according to the Rules and Limitations prescribed in the Case of a Bill.

Section 8. The Congress shall have Power To lay and collect Taxes, Duties, Imposts and Excises, to pay the Debts and provide for the common Defence and general Welfare of the United States; but all Duties, Imposts and Excises shall be uniform throughout the United States;

To borrow Money on the credit of the United States;

To regulate Commerce with foreign Nations, and among the several States, and with the Indian Tribes;

To establish an uniform Rule of Naturalization, and uniform Laws on the subject of Bankruptcies throughout the United States;

To coin Money, regulate the Value thereof, and of foreign Coin, and fix the Standard of Weights and Measures;

To provide for the Punishment of counterfeiting the Securities and current Coin of the United States;

To establish Post Offices and post Roads;

To promote the Progress of Science and useful Arts, by securing for limited Times to Authors and Inventors the exclusive Right to their respective Writings and Discoveries;

To constitute Tribunals inferior to the supreme Court;

To define and punish Piracies and Felonies committed on the high Seas, and Offences against the Law of Nations;

To declare War, grant Letters of Marque and Reprisal, and make Rules concerning Captures on Land and Water;

To raise and support Armies, but no Appropriation of Money to that Use shall be for a longer Term than two Years;

To provide and maintain a Navy;

To make Rules for the Government and Regulation of the land and naval Forces;

To provide for calling forth the Militia to execute the Laws of the Union, suppress Insurrections and repel Invasions;

To provide for organizing, arming, and disciplining, the Militia, and for governing such Part of them as may be employed in the Service of the United States, reserving to the States respectively, the Appointment of the Officers, and the Authority of training the Militia according to the discipline prescribed by Congress;

To exercise exclusive Legislation in all Cases whatsoever, over such District (not exceeding ten Miles square) as may, by Cession of particular States, and the Acceptance of Congress, become the Seat of the Government of the United States, and to exercise like Authority over all Places purchased by the Consent of the Legislature of the State in which the Same shall be, for the Erection of Forts, Magazines, Arsenals, dock-Yards, and other needful Buildings;—And

To make all Laws which shall be necessary and proper for carrying into Execution the foregoing Powers, and all other Powers vested by this Constitution in the Government of the United States, or in any Department or Officer thereof.

Section 9. The Migration or Importation of such Persons as any of the States now existing shall think proper to admit, shall not be prohibited by the Congress prior to the Year one thousand eight hundred and eight, but a Tax or duty may be imposed on such Importation, not exceeding ten dollars for each Person.

The Privilege of the Writ of Habeas Corpus shall not be suspended, unless when in Cases of Rebellion or Invasion the public Safety may require it.

No Bill of Attainder or ex post facto Law shall be passed.

No Capitation, or other direct, Tax shall be laid, unless in Proportion to the Census or Enumeration herein before directed to be taken.

No Tax or Duty shall be laid on Articles exported from any State.

No Preference shall be given by any Regulation of Commerce or Revenue to the Ports of one State over those of another: nor shall Vessels bound to, or from, one State, be obliged to enter, clear or pay Duties in another.

No Money shall be drawn from the Treasury, but in Consequence of Appropriations made by Law; and a regular Statement and Account of Receipts and Expenditures of all public Money shall be published from time to time.

No Title of Nobility shall be granted by the United States: And no Person holding any Office of Profit or Trust under them, shall, without the Consent of the Congress, accept of any present, Emolument, Office, or Title, of any kind whatever, from any King, Prince, or foreign State.

Section 10. No State shall enter into any Treaty, Alliance, or Confederation; grant Letters of Marque and Reprisal; coin Money; emit Bills of Credit; make any Thing but gold and silver Coin a Tender in Payment of Debts; pass any Bill of Attainder, ex post facto Law, or Law impairing the Obligation of Contracts, or grant any Title of Nobility.

No State shall, without the Consent of the Congress, lay any Imposts or Duties on Imports or Exports, except what may be absolutely necessary for executing it's inspection Laws: and the net Produce of all Duties and Imposts, laid by any State on Imports or Exports, shall be for the Use of the Treasury of the United States; and all such Laws shall be subject to the Revision and Controul of the Congress.

No State shall, without the Consent of Congress, lay any Duty of Tonnage, keep Troops, or Ships of War in time of Peace, enter into any Agreement or Compact with another State, or with a foreign Power, or engage in War, unless actually invaded, or in such imminent Danger as will not admit of delay.

ARTICLE II

Section 1. The executive Power shall be vested in a President of the United States of America. He shall hold his Office during the Term of four Years, and, together with the Vice President, chosen for the same Term, be elected, as follows:

Each State shall appoint, in such Manner as the Legislature thereof may direct, a Number of Electors, equal to the whole Number of Senators and Representatives to which the State may be entitled in the Congress: but no Senator or Representative, or Person holding an Office of Trust or Profit under the United States, shall be appointed an Elector.

The Electors shall meet in their respective States, and vote by Ballot for two Persons, of whom one at least shall not be an Inhabitant of the same State with themselves. And they shall make a List of all the Persons voted for, and of the Number of Votes for each; which List they shall sign and certify, and transmit sealed to the Seat of the Government of the United States, directed to the President of the Senate. The President of the Senate shall, in the Presence of the Senate and House of Representatives, open all the Certificates, and the Votes shall then be counted. The Person having the greatest Number of Votes shall be the President, if such Number be a Majority of the whole Number of Electors appointed; and if there be more than one who have such Majority, and have an equal Number of Votes, then the House of Representatives shall immediately chuse by Ballot one of them for President; and if no Person have a Majority, then from the five highest on the List the said House shall in like Manner chuse the President. But in chusing the President, the Votes shall be taken by States, the Representation from each State having one Vote; A quorum for this Purpose shall consist of a Member or Members from two thirds of the States, and a Majority of all the States shall be necessary to a Choice. In every Case, after the Choice of the President, the Person having the greatest Number of Votes of the Electors shall be the Vice President. But if there should remain two or more who have equal Votes, the Senate shall chuse from them by Ballot the Vice President.

The Congress may determine the Time of chusing the Electors, and the Day on which they shall give their Votes; which Day shall be the same throughout the United States.

No Person except a natural born Citizen, or a Citizen of the United States, at the time of the Adoption of this Constitution, shall be eligible to the Office of President; neither shall any Person be eligible to that Office who shall not have attained to the Age of thirty five Years, and been fourteen Years a Resident within the United States.

In Case of the Removal of the President from Office, or of his Death, Resignation, or Inability to discharge the Powers and Duties of the said Office, the Same shall devolve on the Vice President, and the Congress may by Law provide for the Case of Removal, Death, Resignation or Inability, both of the President and Vice President, declaring what Officer shall then act as President, and such Officer shall act accordingly, until the Disability be removed, or a President shall be elected.

The President shall, at stated Times, receive for his Services, a Compensation, which shall neither be encreased nor diminished during the Period for which he shall have been elected, and he shall not receive within that Period any other Emolument from the United States, or any of them.

Before he enter on the Execution of his Office, he shall take the following Oath or Affirmation:—"I do solemnly swear (or affirm) that I will faithfully execute the Office of President of the United States, and will to the best of my Ability, preserve, protect and defend the Constitution of the United States."

Section 2. The President shall be Commander in Chief of the Army and Navy of the United States, and of the Militia of the several States, when called into the actual Service of the United States; he may require the Opinion, in writing, of the principal Officer in each of the executive Departments, upon any Subject relating to the Duties of their respective Offices, and he shall have Power to grant Reprieves and Pardons for Offences against the United States, except in Cases of Impeachment.

He shall have Power, by and with the Advice and Consent of the Senate, to make Treaties, provided two thirds of the Senators present concur; and he shall nominate, and by and with the Advice and Consent of the Senate, shall appoint Ambassadors, other public Ministers and Consuls, Judges of the supreme Court, and all other Officers of the United States, whose Appointments are not herein otherwise provided for, and which shall be established by Law: but the Congress may by Law vest the Appointment of such inferior Officers, as they think proper, in the President alone, in the Courts of Law, or in the Heads of Departments.

The President shall have Power to fill up all Vacancies that may happen during the Recess of the Senate, by granting Commissions which shall expire at the End of their next Session.

Section 3. He shall from time to time give to the Congress Information of the State of the Union, and recommend to their Consideration such Measures as he shall judge necessary and expedient; he may, on extraordinary Occasions, convene both Houses, or either of them, and in Case of Disagreement between them, with Respect to the Time of Adjournment, he may adjourn them to such Time as he shall think proper; he shall receive Ambassadors and other public Ministers; he shall take Care that the Laws be faithfully executed, and shall Commission all the Officers of the United States.

Section 4. The President, Vice President and all civil Officers of the United States, shall be removed from Office on Impeachment for, and Conviction of, Treason, Bribery, or other high Crimes and Misdemeanors.

ARTICLE III

Section 1. The judicial Power of the United States, shall be vested in one supreme Court, and in such inferior Courts as the Congress may from time to time ordain and establish. The Judges, both of the supreme and inferior Courts, shall hold their Offices during good Behaviour, and shall, at stated Times, receive for their Services, a Compensation, which shall not be diminished during their Continuance in Office.

Section 2. The judicial Power shall extend to all Cases, in Law and Equity, arising under this Constitution, the Laws of the United States, and Treaties made, or which shall be made, under their Authority;—to all Cases affecting Ambassadors, other public Ministers and Consuls;—to all Cases of admiralty and maritime Jurisdiction;—to Controversies to which the United States shall be a Party;—to Controversies between two or more States;—between a State and Citizens of another State;—between Citizens of different States;—between Citizens of the same State claiming Lands under Grants of different States, and between a State, or the Citizens thereof, and foreign States, Citizens or Subjects.

In all Cases affecting Ambassadors, other public Ministers and Consuls, and those in which a State shall be Party, the supreme Court shall have original Jurisdiction. In all the other Cases before mentioned, the supreme Court shall have appellate Jurisdiction, both as to Law and Fact, with such Exceptions, and under such Regulations as the Congress shall make.

The Trial of all Crimes, except in Cases of Impeachment, shall be by Jury; and such Trial shall be held in the State where the said Crimes shall have been committed; but when not committed within any State, the Trial shall be at such Place or Places as the Congress may by Law have directed.

Section 3. Treason against the United States, shall consist only in levying War against them, or in adhering to their Enemies, giving them Aid and Comfort. No Person shall be convicted of Treason unless on the Testimony of two Witnesses to the same overt Act, or on Confession in open Court.

The Congress shall have Power to declare the Punishment of Treason, but no Attainder of Treason shall work Corruption of Blood, or Forfeiture except during the Life of the Person attainted.

ARTICLE IV
Section 1. Full Faith and Credit shall be given in each State to the public Acts, Records, and judicial Proceedings of every other State. And the Congress may by general Laws prescribe the Manner in which such Acts, Records, and Proceedings shall be proved, and the Effect thereof.

Section 2. The Citizens of each State shall be entitled to all Privileges and Immunities of Citizens in the several States.

A Person charged in any State with Treason, Felony, or other Crime, who shall flee from Justice, and be found in another State, shall on Demand of the executive Authority of the State from which he fled, be delivered up, to be removed to the State having Jurisdiction of the Crime.

No Person held to Service or Labour in one State, under the Laws thereof, escaping into another, shall, in Consequence of any Law or Regulation therein, be discharged from such Service or Labour, but shall be delivered up on Claim of the Party to whom such Service or Labour may be due.

Section 3. New States may be admitted by the Congress into this Union; but no new States shall be formed or erected within the Jurisdiction of any other State; nor any State be formed by the Junction of two or more States, or Parts of States, without the Consent of the Legislatures of the States concerned as well as of the Congress.

The Congress shall have Power to dispose of and make all needful Rules and Regulations respecting the Territory or other Property belonging to the United States; and nothing in this Constitution shall be so construed as to Prejudice any Claims of the United States, or of any particular State.

Section 4. The United States shall guarantee to every State in this Union a Republican Form of Government, and shall protect each of them against Invasion; and on Application of the Legislature, or of the Executive (when the Legislature cannot be convened) against domestic Violence.

ARTICLE V

The Congress, whenever two thirds of both Houses shall deem it necessary, shall propose Amendments to this Constitution, or, on the Application of the Legislatures of two thirds of the several States, shall call a Convention for proposing Amendments, which, in either Case, shall be valid to all Intents and Purposes, as Part of this Constitution, when ratified by the Legislatures of three fourths of the several States, or by Conventions in three fourths thereof, as the one or the other Mode of Ratification may be proposed by the Congress; Provided that no Amendment which may be made prior to the Year One thousand eight hundred and eight shall in any Manner affect the first and fourth Clauses in the Ninth Section of the first Article; and that no State, without its Consent, shall be deprived of its equal Suffrage in the Senate.

ARTICLE VI

All Debts contracted and Engagements entered into, before the Adoption of this Constitution, shall be as valid against the United States under this Constitution, as under the Confederation.

This Constitution, and the Laws of the United States which shall be made in Pursuance thereof; and all Treaties made, or which shall be made, under the Authority of the United States, shall be the supreme Law of the Land; and the Judges in every State shall be bound thereby, any Thing in the Constitution or Laws of any State to the Contrary notwith-standing.

The Senators and Representatives before mentioned, and the Members of the several State Legislatures, and all executive and judicial Officers, both of the United States and of the several States, shall be bound by Oath or Affirmation, to support this Constitution; but no religious Test shall ever be required as a Qualification to any Office or public Trust under the United States.

ARTICLE VII

The Ratification of the Conventions of nine States, shall be sufficient for the Establishment of this Constitution between the States so ratifying the Same.

Done in Convention by the Unanimous Consent of the States present the Seventeenth Day of September in the Year of our Lord one thousand seven hundred and Eighty seven and of the Independence of the United States of America the Twelfth

In witness whereof We have hereunto subscribed our Names,

George Washington—President and deputy from Virginia

New Hampshire: *John Langdon, Nicholas Gilman*

Massachusetts: *Nathaniel Gorham, Rufus King*

Connecticut: *William Samuel Johnson, Roger Sherman*

New York: *Alexander Hamilton*

New Jersey: *William Livingston, David Brearly, William Paterson, Jonathan Dayton*

Pennsylvania: *Benjamin Franklin, Thomas Mifflin, Robert Morris, George Clymer, Thomas FitzSimons, Jared Ingersoll, James Wilson, Gouverneur Morris*

Delaware: *George Read, Gunning Bedford, Jr., John Dickinson, Richard Bassett, Jacob Broom*

Maryland: *James McHenry, Daniel of Saint Thomas Jenifer, Daniel Carroll*

Virginia: *John Blair, James Madison, Jr.*

North Carolina: *William Blount, Richard Dobbs Spaight, Hugh Williamson*

South Carolina: *John Rutledge, Charles Cotesworth Pinckney, Charles Pinckney, Pierce Butler*

Georgia: *William Few, Abraham Baldwin*

AMENDMENT I

Congress shall make no law respecting an establishment of religion, or prohibiting the free exercise thereof; or abridging the freedom of speech, or of the press; or the right of the people peaceably to assemble, and to petition the Government for a redress of grievances.

AMENDMENT II

A well regulated Militia, being necessary to the security of a free State, the right of the people to keep and bear Arms, shall not be infringed.

AMENDMENT III

No Soldier shall, in time of peace be quartered in any house, without the consent of the Owner, nor in time of war, but in a manner to be prescribed by law.

AMENDMENT IV

The right of the people to be secure in their persons, houses, papers, and effects, against unreasonable searches and seizures, shall not be violated, and no Warrants shall issue, but upon probable cause, supported by Oath or affirmation, and particularly describing the place to be searched, and the persons or things to be seized.

AMENDMENT V

No person shall be held to answer for a capital, or otherwise infamous crime, unless on a presentment or indictment of a Grand Jury, except in cases arising in the land or naval forces, or in the Militia, when in actual service in time of War or public danger; nor shall any person be subject for the same offence to be twice put in jeopardy of life or limb; nor shall be compelled in any criminal case to be a witness against himself, nor be deprived of life, liberty, or property, without due process of law; nor shall private property be taken for public use, without just compensation.

AMENDMENT VI

In all criminal prosecutions, the accused shall enjoy the right to a speedy and public trial, by an impartial jury of the State and district wherein the crime shall have been committed, which district shall have been previously ascertained by law, and to be informed of the nature and cause of the accusation; to be confronted with the witnesses against him; to have compulsory process for obtaining witnesses in his favor, and to have the Assistance of Counsel for his defence.

AMENDMENT VII

In Suits at common law, where the value in controversy shall exceed twenty dollars, the right of trial by jury shall be preserved, and no fact tried by a jury, shall be otherwise re-examined in any Court of the United States, than according to the rules of the common law.

AMENDMENT VIII

Excessive bail shall not be required, nor excessive fines imposed, nor cruel and unusual punishments inflicted.

AMENDMENT IX

The enumeration in the Constitution, of certain rights, shall not be constructed to deny or disparage others retained by the people.

AMENDMENT X

The powers not delegated to the United States by the Constitution, nor prohibited by it to the States, are reserved to the States respectively, or to the people.

ACKNOWLEDGMENTS

———— ★ ————

I would still be writing this book if it weren't for the National Endowment of the Humanities, which gave me a research fellowship for 2007–2008 under its "We the People" program, and the support of MIT Provost L. Rafael Reif. He found a way to supplement the NEH grant so I had a full year—really fifteen months with the two summers—to do nothing but scribble away. I should also thank the William Rand Kenan, Jr., Trust, which endowed the chair I hold at MIT; the Provost used the income from that endowment to fund what turned out to be the most productive year of my career. Many of my expenses—books, paper, computers and the like—were paid for out of a research fund associated with the Kenan chair.

Throughout the decade or so that I worked on this book, I benefited from the extraordinary generosity and intellectual support of fellow historians. I never met John Caldwell, the biographer of William Findley, in person, but he patiently answered my e-mail inquiries about politics and travel in western Pennsylvania during the eighteenth century. Then, unsolicited, he sent me copies of studies he'd done of other members of the Pennsylvania ratifying convention.

I did know Jere Daniell, the historian of New Hampshire and professor emeritus at Dartmouth, when we were both in graduate school. I was, however, unprepared for the gift he gave me after I e-mailed him to ask whether the contents of a file at the New Hampshire Archives were worth my driving to Concord. Soon a thick envelope arrived containing copies of articles he'd written on ratification in New Hampshire, many of which I had not yet located on my own, and they were in a category by themselves. Jere knows what happened in New Hampshire's two convention sessions day by day, delegate by delegate, and he knows the ratification politics of the New Hampshire towns with a similar intimacy. He later agreed to read what I'd written on New Hampshire (most of which was informed by his work), and the book is a lot better for his suggestions.

488   *Acknowledgments*

Richard D. Brown, another old graduate school friend, agreed to read my chapters on ratification in Connecticut and Massachusetts and saved me from several mistakes. Richard Beeman did the same service for the chapters on Virginia; Alfred F. Young read those on New York and encouraged me to think more about the social conflicts that fed into that state's political divisions. Todd Estes of Oakland University, who is writing a history of the polemical literature of the ratification controversy, read my chapter on the "War of Printed Words," and later also the Epilogue. Peter H. Wood urged me to do more with the North Carolina convention, its members, and the influence of the Regulator conflict, and even printed out information for my use. At one point when I was drafting the Epilogue, I asked Stanley Kutler, a former colleague at the University of Wisconsin in Madison who knows more legal history than I do, to take a look at it. He read the chapter within a day or two. I did not take his advice to mount a campaign against the advocates of "original intent," but I appreciated his enthusiasm, anyway.

John P. Kaminski, editor of the *Documentary History of the Ratification of the Constitution*, has been a consistent source of help and support. He sent me digital copies of pages from the DHRC that chronicled the last half of the New York ratifying convention before they were in print and even before I knew I needed them. I am also grateful to the members of various seminars—at the National Humanities Center in North Carolina, the Massachusetts Historical Society, the Harvard Law School, and MIT—that read draft chapters and offered suggestions for improvements.

My editor at Simon and Schuster, Bob Bender, noticed sometime in the late 1990s that there was no prominent book on the ratification of the Constitution and went looking for a historian to write one. He contacted my college classmate, friend, and literary agent, Jill Kneerim; she called me. I took about twenty seconds to say I would do it, but the book took far longer to write than I expected (and than my contract allowed). Bob was patient and in the end gave me intelligent feedback on both substance and presentation of a sort writers rarely get from editors anymore. I also want to thank my copy editor, Bob Castillo, who knows a lot of history. He corrected mistakes that got by everyone else, and his enthusiasm ("Excellent point"; "NICE ending!") lifted my spirits. Jessica Maier, an art historian, helped prepare the images in the book with her usual awesome efficiency. Tanya Buckingham of the University of Wisconsin Cartography Laboratory oversaw the preparation of the maps.

My greatest debt, however, is to Richard Leffler, the co-editor emeritus of the DHRC, who volunteered to read the entire manuscript—and on an occasion at the New York Historical Society where he and I met for the first time. He then devoted a good part of his spare time over almost a year to going through the book chapter by chapter, raising questions about the content, suggesting alternative sources, editing the language and even the notes with meticulous care. Now and then he and I would have a terrific fight over something that maybe three people in the world care about, but that forced us both to go back and reexamine the documentary record. Sometimes he won; sometimes I did, but the exchanges were always stimulating. There are parts of the book with which Rich no doubt disagrees. There are probably also mistakes that slipped by the two of us (and all my other readers), or that I clung to stubbornly despite his advice. But the book is much better, and far more accurate, thanks to his gracious and incredibly generous help.

The book is dedicated to the memory of my mother, who never read any of my books but supported my right to do what I wanted with my life, however crazy it seemed to her, and my dear friend and onetime colleague at UMass/Boston, Thomas N. Brown. Tom read every book (except the textbooks) that I've published, including the greater part of this one, and he was one of the best readers in the business. I miss his literary sensitivity, his honesty, and, above all, his good company.

My husband, Charles S. Maier, a historian of modern Europe, let me use his office in Harvard's Widener Library, tolerated the amazing messes I made, read parts of the manuscript on request, and regularly assured me that, in the end, my book would be important. That we have shared both our lives and a profession has been a benefit beyond measure for almost a half century—and still counting.

—Pauline Maier

NOTES

———— ★ ————

ABBREVIATIONS

Conley and Kaminski   Patrick T. Conley and John P. Kaminski, eds., *The Constitution and the States: The Role of the Original Thirteen in the Framing and Adoption of the Federal Constitution.* Madison, Wisconsin, 1988.

DHFFC   Linda Grant DePauw, Charlene Bangs Bickford, Helen E. Veit, and Kenneth R. Bowling, eds., *Documentary History of the First Federal Congress of the United States of America.* Baltimore and London, 1972–.

DHFFE   Merrill Jensen, Robert A. Becker, and Gordon DenBoer, eds., *The Documentary History of the First Federal Elections, 1788–1790.* 4 vols. Madison, Wisconsin, 1976–89.

DHRC   Merrill Jensen, John P. Kaminski, et al., eds., *The Documentary History of the Ratification of the Constitution.* Madison, Wisconsin, 1976–.

DNCB   William S. Powell, ed., *Dictionary of North Carolina Biography.* 6 vols. Chapel Hill, North Carolina, and London, 1979–96.

Farrand   Max Farrand, ed., *The Records of the Federal Convention of 1787*, rev. ed. in 4 vols. New Haven, Connecticut, and London, 1966. Vol. IV, *Supplement to Max Farrand's The Records of the Federal Convention of 1787*, James H. Hutson, ed. New Haven, Connecticut, and London, 1987.

Gillespie and Lienesch   Michael Allen Gillespie and Michael Lienesch, eds., *Ratifying the Constitution.* Lawrence, Kansas, 1989.

JAH   *Journal of American History.*

PAH   Harold C. Syrett, ed., *The Papers of Alexander Hamilton.* Vols. 3–5. New York, 1962.

PGM   Robert A. Rutland, ed., *The Papers of George Mason, 1725–1972.* 3 vols. Chapel Hill, North Carolina, 1970.

PGWCS   W. W. Abbot and Dorothy Twohig, eds., *The Papers of George Washington: Confederation Series.* 6 vols. Charlottesville, Virginia, and London, 1992–97.

PGWPS   W. W. Abbot and Dorothy Twohig, eds., *The Papers of George Washington: Presidential Series.* Vols. 1–4. Charlottesville, Virginia, 1987–93.

PJM   Robert A. Rutland et al., eds., *The Papers of James Madison*, Vols. VIII–
                             XII. Chicago and Charlottesville, Virginia, 1973–79.

PTJ   Julian P. Boyd et al., eds., *The Papers of Thomas Jefferson*. Princeton, New
                             Jersey, 1950–.

Republic of Letters   James Morton Smith, ed., *The Republic of Letters: The Correspondence
                             between Thomas Jefferson and James Madison, 1776–1826.* 3 vols. New York
                             and London, 1995.

Storing   Herbert J. Storing, ed., *The Complete Anti-Federalist.* 7 vols. Chicago,
                             1981.

WMQ   *William and Mary Quarterly*, 3d Series.

Note: Often equally reliable versions of the same document appear in several of these volumes.
DHRC sometimes publishes excerpts relevant to ratification, where the published papers of leading
individuals such as George Washington, Thomas Jefferson, or James Madison include full texts.
Letters can generally be located in alternative publications by their dates, which are supplied here
either in the text or in notes.

INTRODUCTION: PLAYING GAMES
1. Jurgen Heideking, *Die Verfassung vor dem Richterstuhl: Vorgeschichte und Ratifizierung der
   Amerikanischen Verfassung, 1787–1791* (Berlin and New York, 1988); Robert Rutland, *Ordeal
   of the Constitution: The Antifederalists and the Ratification Struggle of 1787–88* (Norman, OK,
   1966); and Craig R. Smith, *To Form a More Perfect Union: The Ratification of the Constitution
   and the Bill of Rights, 1787–1791* (Lanham, MD, New York, and London, 1993), which was
   published by the Center for First Amendment Studies.
2. Forrest McDonald, *We the People: The Economic Origins of the Constitution* (Chicago, 1958);
   Jackson Turner Main, *The Antifederalists: Critics of the Constitution, 1781–1788* (Chapel Hill,
   1961); and *Political Parties Before the Constitution* (Chapel Hill, 1973).
3. Patrick T. Conley and John P. Kaminski, eds., *The Constitution and the States: The Role of the
   Original Thirteen in the Framing and Adoption of the Federal Constitution* (Madison, WI, 1988);
   and Michael Allen Gillespie and Michael Lienesch, eds., *Ratifying the Constitution* (Lawrence, KS, 1989).
4. "A Friend for Liberty," *Massachusetts Centinel*, November 14, 1787, DHRC IV: 231.
5. Ebenezer Bowman to Timothy Pickering, Wilkes-Barre, PA, November 12, 1787, DHRC II:
   257.
6. Findley, *History of the Insurrection in the Four Western Counties of Pennsylvania* (Philadelphia,
   1796; facsimile reprint Spartanburg, SC, 1984), 258. "If we erred," he went on, "it was from
   an excess of zeal for federalism, and a jealousy lest the federal republican principles of the
   government were not sufficiently guarded, and in this we agreed with the majority of citizens
   of the United States." For the use of the term by other critics of the Constitution, see Saul
   Cornell, ed., "Reflections on 'The Late Remarkable Revolution in Government': Aedanus
   Burke and Samuel Bryan's Unpublished History of the Ratification of the Federal Constitution," *Pennsylvania Magazine of History and Biography* CXII (1988), 122, 128, 129.
7. DHRC V: 902.

PROLOGUE: THE VIEW FROM MOUNT VERNON
1. Act of the Virginia general assembly in DHRC I: 198; Randolph to Washington, Richmond,
   December 6, 1786, PGWCS IV: 445 and n1, 445–46.
2. Madison to Washington, Richmond, November 8, 1786, and Washington's reply, November
   18, PGWCS IV: 344–45, 382–83. See also Washington's letter to the Society of the Cincinnati,
   October 31; Madison to Washington, Richmond, December 7; and Washington to Madison,
   December 16, 1786, in ibid., 316–17, 448, 457–59.

3. Washington to Madison, December 16, 1786, PGWCS IV: 457; Minor Myers, Jr., *Liberty without Anarchy: A History of the Society of the Cincinnati* (Charlottesville, 1983), 1–31, 48–69, and "The Institution of the Society of the Cincinnati," 258–62.

4. Washington to Madison, December 16, 1786. PGWCS IV: 457–58. In a letter of November 16, 1786, Jefferson reinforced Washington's misgivings: No good could come from the society, he argued, and it would in time lead to the creation of "an hereditary aristocracy which will change the form of our governments from the best to the worst in the world." He also said that European observers uniformly considered the society "dishonorable & destructive to our governments." Ibid. 364–65. For a brief summary of the controversy over the Cincinnati, see Merrill Jensen, *The New Nation: A History of the United States During the Confederation, 1781–1789* (New York, 1950), 261–65.

5. Washington to Randolph, Mount Vernon, [December 21, 1786], PGWCS IV: 471–72. Washington received Madison's letter, dated December 7, about December 14 but Randolph's, dated December 6, did not arrive until December 20. Ice, it seems, kept Washington from having someone to collect his mail at Alexandria, and perhaps it also slowed the letter's transit over the roughly hundred miles from Richmond to Mount Vernon. That explains why Washington told Madison in a letter of December 16 that he had "received no other than private intimations of my election." Ibid., 458.

6. Randolph to Washington, Richmond, January 4, 178[7], and Madison to Washington, Richmond, December 24, 1786, in PGWCS IV: 500–01, 474–75; and Washington to Henry Knox, Mount Vernon, February 3, 1787, PGWCS V: 8, where he summarized these transactions.

7. Madison to Washington, Richmond, November 8 and December 7, 1786, PGWCS IV: 345, 448. Virginia's original seven-man delegation also included Patrick Henry, who declined, as subsequently did Thomas Nelson and Richard Henry Lee. James McClurg finally accepted the position. DHRC I: n3 at 198.

8. The Articles of Confederation in DHRC I: 93. For a succinct summary of earlier efforts to strengthen the Confederation and, from the mid-1780s on, calls for a convention, see DHRC XIII: 9–34.

9. DHRC I: 192–204; quotations at 197. Under Article V of the Articles of Confederation, individuals could serve as delegates to Congress "for more than three years in any term of six years." Moreover, anyone who held an office under the United States "for which he, or another for his benefit receives any salary or fees of any kind," could not be a member of Congress. That helps explain the Virginia act's reference to persons "disqualified by law." Such people could, however, attend the Philadelphia Convention. See DHRC I: 87.

10. DHRC I: 192–204. New Hampshire's delegates were to attend the convention only if Congress found it advantageous to the union "and not an infringement of the powers granted to Congress by the Confederation" (193–94).

11. Washington to Knox, December 16, 1786, PGWCS IV: 482; and North Callahan, *Henry Knox, George Washington's General* (New York and Toronto, 1958), passim.

12. Frank Landon Humphreys, *Life and Times of David Humphreys* I (New York and London, 1917); and Rosemarie Zagarri, ed., *David Humphreys' "Life of General Washington" with George Washington's "Remarks"* (Athens, GA, and London, 1991), esp.xiv–xix.

13. Washington to Knox Humphreys, December 26, 1786, PGWCS IV: 479.

14. Robert F. Dalzell, Jr., and Lee Baldwin Dalzell, *George Washington's Mount Vernon: At Home in Revolutionary America* (New York and Oxford, 1998), 103–112; quotations at 109 and 111.

15. Ibid., 110; Douglas Southall Freeman, *George Washington: A Biography* V (New York, 1952), 325–28, 401–03.

16. Washington's circular to state executives (which was widely republished in 1787), Newburgh, NY, June 18, 1783, in DHRC XIII: 60–70.

17. Address to Congress on Resigning his Commission [Annapolis, December 23, 1783], in John C. Fitzpatrick, ed., *The Writings of George Washington* XXVII (Washington, 1938), 284–85.

18. Garry Wills, *Cincinnatus: George Washington and the Enlightenment* (Garden City, NY, 1984).

19. Washington to Knox, Mount Vernon, February 20, 1784, and to Lafayette, February 1, 1784, in PGWCS I: 137–38, 87–88.

20. On Mount Vernon, see Zagarri, ed., *Humphreys' "Life of Washington,"* 39–40; Paul Leland Haworth, *George Washington: County Gentleman* (Indianapolis, 1925), esp. 63–64, 66.

21. James Thomas Flexner, *George Washington and the New Nation* (Boston and Toronto, 1970), 39–50; Haworth, *Washington,* 61–63.

22. Flexner, *George Washington and the New Nation,* 45, 49–50, 53–54; Douglas Southall Freeman, *George Washington: A Biography* VI (New York, 1954), 52–62.

23. Quotation in ibid., 43. For Washington's avid agricultural experimentation, see Donald Jackson and Dorothy Twohig, eds., *The Diaries of George Washington* I, 1748–65 (Charlottesville, 1976), xxv–xxxvii.

24. Young to Washington, Bradfield Hall near Burry Suffolk, England, January 7, 1786, and February 1, 1787; Washington to Young, Mount Vernon, August 6, 1786, and November 1, 1787, in PGWCS III: 498–99, n2 at 500; IV: 196–98; V: 3–6 (quotation), 402–05. Washington to James Warren, Mount Vernon, October 7, 1785, ibid. III: 300.

25. Flexner, *George Washington and the New Nation* 44–49 (statement to Lafayette at 49); Jay to Washington, February 3, and Washington to Jay, March 3, 1788, PGWCS VI: 79–80, 138. Zagarri, ed., *Humphreys' "Life of Washington,"* esp. 37–41, 56, and also the fragment of a poem by Humphreys at xxxiii.

26. Jefferson to Washington, Annapolis, March 15, 1784, PGWCS I: 215–18.

27. Washington to Jefferson, Mount Vernon, March 29, 1784, PGWCS I: 237–41. Commerce, he added, had both advantages and disadvantages, but since Americans would not be restrained from trade "it behooves us to place it in the most convenient channels, under proper regulation—freed, as much as possible, from those vices which luxury, the consequence of wealth and power, naturally introduce."

28. Flexner, *Washington and the New Nation,* 70–71; Freeman, *George Washington* VI: 14–27.

29. Flexner, *Washington and the New Nation,* 78–82. For a description of the device and Washington's reaction to it, see Andrea Sutcliffe, *Steam: The Untold Story of America's First Great Invention* (New York, 2004), 2–3.

30. Washington to Henry Knox, Mount Vernon, December 5, 1784, PGWCS II: 170–72.

31. Henry Lee Jr., to Washington, New York, February 16, 1786, PGWCS III: 561.

32. Ibid.; Rufus King to Washington, New York, April 30, 1786, and Charles Petit to Jeremiah Wadsworth, New York, May 27, 1786, in Edmund C. Burnett, ed., *Letters of the Members of the Continental Congress* VIII (Washington, 1963 [orig. 1936]), 346, 369–70. For analyses of public finance in this period, see Max Edling, *A Revolution in Favor of Government: Origins of the U.S. Constitution and the Making of the American State* (Oxford, England, and New York, 2003), esp. 149–62; Roger H. Brown, *Redeeming the Republic: Federalists, Taxation, and the Origins of the Constitution* (Baltimore and London, 1993), esp. 11–21; Edwin J. Perkins, *American Public Finance and Financial Services, 1700–1815* (Columbus, OH, 1994), esp. 85–136, 187–96; and E. James Ferguson, *The Power of the Purse: a History of American Public Finance, 1776–1790* (Chapel Hill, 1961).

33. Washington to James Warren, Mount Vernon, October 7, 1785, PGWCS III: 299–300.

34. Washington to Lafayette, Mount Vernon, August 22, 1785, PGWCS III: 152–53.

35. Brown, *Redeeming the Republic,* 17–21, and DHRC XIII: 24–27, with the final quotation from John Adams, the American minister to Britain, at 24. See also Washington to Henry Lee Jr., April 5, 1786, PGWCS IV: 4, where he said he saw no grounds for negotiations with Morocco and Algiers unless the American negotiators "mean to touch the old string again, and make them dance a while, to the tune of promises."

36. Jacob Read to Washington, Annapolis, August 13, 1784, PGWCS II: 36.

37. Jay to Washington, Philadelphia, June 27, 1786, PGWCS IV: 130–31. The report is in John C. Fitzpatrick, ed., *Journals of the Continental Congress* XXXI (Washington, 1934), 781–874. Jay noted that the British had violated Article VII of the treaty of Paris by carrying away slaves owned by Americans after the war had ended, and also by holding the western posts. However, since American violations of the treaty preceded those by the British, the British could not be blamed for continuing to hold their western posts "until America shall cease to impede her enjoying every essential right secured to her, and her people and adherents, by the treaty"

(867, 868). Although Jay proposed that Congress pass a series of resolutions to end violations of the treaty (869–70), he despaired of getting the states to give Loyalists the "retribution and compensation" they deserved, and he thought Congress should be silent on that issue, "as the United States have neither the power nor the means of doing it without their [the states'] concurrence" (873). For a summary of the proceedings against Loyalists and their outcome, see Jensen, *New Nation*, 265–81.

38. King to Elbridge Gerry, New York, April 30, 1786, in Burnett, ed., *Letters of the Members of Congress* VIII: 345–46.

39. Knox to Washington, Boston, January 31, 1785, PGWCS II: 302. For contemporary statements questioning whether the federal government could continue to exist, see Brown, *Redeeming the Republic*, 27–28.

40. Washington to James Warren, Mount Vernon, October 7, 1785, PGWCS III: 299–300; and to Benjamin Harrison, Mount Vernon, January 18, 1784, PGWCS I: 56–57.

41. Washington, Address to Congress on Resigning his Commission (Annapolis, December 23, 1783), in Fitzpatrick, ed., *Writings of Washington* XXVII; 284–85; to James McHenry, Mount Vernon, August 22, 1785, PGWCS III: 197.

42. Jay to Washington, Philadelphia, June 27, 1786, and Washington to Jay, Mount Vernon, August 15, 1786, PGWCS IV: 131–32, 212–13.

43. Lee to Washington, New York, September 8, 1786, and Humphreys to Washington, Hartford, September 24, 1786, ibid., 240–41, 265, and n4 on 266. On Sullivan's role, see Alan Taylor, "Regulators and White Indians: Forms of Agrarian Resistance in Post-Revolutionary New England," in Robert A. Gross, ed., *In Debt to Shays: The Bicentennial of an Agrarian Rebellion* (Charlottesville and London, 1993), 147–49.

44. October 22, 1786, PGWCS IV: 297.

45. Rufus King to John Adams, New York, October 3, 1786, in Charles R. King, ed., *The Life and Correspondence of Rufus King* I (New York, 1894), 190–91.

46. Knox to Washington, New York, October 23, 1786, PGWCS IV: 300–01. For a detailed study of state fiscal policies, see Max M. Edling and Mark D. Kaplanoff, "Alexander Hamilton's Fiscal Reform: Transforming the Structure of Taxation in the Early Republic," WMQ LXI (2004), 713–44, esp. 719–29. Also Brown, *Redeeming the Republic*, 53–138, and also 156–67, which argues that Federalists everywhere "believed that the presumed weakness and indulgence of the state governments" had accustomed people to breaking the law, so "outbreaks of anarchy would further multiply" (167).

47. Lincoln's report to Washington, which was completed only in March 1787, and Lee to Washington, October 17, 1786, PGWCS IV: 420–1, 295–96. See also Elbridge Gerry to Rufus King, Cambridge, MA, November 29, 1786, reporting on meetings in Vermont "for the purpose of reuniting the American States to the Government of Great Britain," in King, ed., *Life and Correspondence of Rufus King* I: 197.

48. Washington to Knox, Mount Vernon, December 26, 1786; Knox to Washington, New York, October 23, 1786; Humphreys to Washington, New Haven, November 1, 1786; and Lincoln to Washington, February 22, 1787 (but sent in March), PGWCS IV: 482, 300, 325, 422.

49. Richard D. Brown, "Shays's Rebellion and the Ratification of the Federal Constitution in Massachusetts," in Richard Beeman et. al., eds., *Beyond Confederation: Origins of the Constitution and American National Identity* (Chapel Hill and London, 1987), 113–27, esp. 115–21; William Pencak, " 'The Fine Theoretic Government of Massachusetts Is Prostrated to the Earth': The Response to Shays's Rebellion Reconsidered," in Gross, ed., *In Debt to Shays*, 139–41.

50. Washington to Knox, December 26, 1786, to Humphreys on the same date, and to Henry Lee Jr., October 22, 1786, PGWCS IV: 481–83, 478, 318–19.

51. Randolph to Washington, Richmond, January 4, 1787, PGWCS IV: 501.

52. August 15, 1789, PGWCS IV: 213.

53. PGWCS IV: 502–04.

54. Knox to Washington, New York, January 14, 1787, PGSCS IV: 521–22.

55. Ibid., 519–20; commentary and King to Elbridge Gerry, New York, January 7 (on Jay's views), February 11, and February 18, 1787, in King, ed., *Life and Correspondence of Rufus King* I: 200–202; Jay to Washington, New York, January 7, 1787, PGWCS IV: 502–03.

56. Knox to Washington, New York, January 14, 1787, and Jay to Washington, New York, January 7, PGWCS IV: 519–21, 503.

57. Humphreys to Washington, New Haven, January 1, 1787, PGWCS IV: 526–29; Knox to Washington, January 14, ibid., 520: Washington, he said, should come out of retirement only on an "occasion . . . of an unequivocal nature in which the enlightned [sic] and virtuous citizens should generally concur."

58. Washington to Knox, Mount Vernon, February 3, 1787, PGWCS V: 8–9.

59. Knox to Washington, New York, February 12, 1787; Madison to Washington, March 18, 1787; and Humphreys to Washington, March 24, 1787, PGWCS V: 26, 93, 104.

60. DHRC I: 184–85 and 187 for the calls of a convention from Annapolis, September 14, 1787, and Congress, February 21, 1787. The Annapolis resolution called the convention "to take into consideration the situation of the United States, to devise such further provisions as shall appear to them necessary to render the constitution of the Foederal Government adequate to the exigencies of the Union; and to report such an Act for that purpose to the United States in Congress Assembled, as when agreed to, by them, and afterwards confirmed by the Legislatures of every State will effectually provide for the same." Although it did not therefore confine the convention to the "sole and express purpose" of proposing revisions to the Articles of Confederation, the approval process it described suggested that was what it had in mind. On the election of delegates (and also their attendance or nonattendance), see ibid., 192–230. Madison to Washington, New York, March 18, 1787, PGWCS V: 92–93.

61. Washington to Knox, Mount Vernon, April 2, 1787, PGWCS V: 119–20, and n2 on 120–21.

62. Humphreys to Washington, January 20, 1787, PGWCS IV: 527; and Knox to Washington, New York, March 19, 1797, PGWCS V: 97.

63. Charleston, SC, February 23, 1787, PGWCS V: 48.

64. To Humphreys and to Knox, March 8, 1787, PGWCS V: 72, 74–75.

65. Randolph to Washington, March 11, 1787, and Washington's reply, March 28, ibid., 83–84, 112–14.

66. Knox to Washington, New York, March 19, 1787, PGWCS V: 96–97. This letter, which replied to Washington's inquiry of March 8 as whether his nonattendance would be considered a "dereliction to republicanism," arrived by April 2: See Washington to Knox, Mount Vernon, April 2, ibid., 119, which acknowledges receipt. Washington therefore received it before Randolph responded to Washington's equivocal letter of March 28 and before April 9, when Washington accepted his position more clearly. On that correspondence, see below.

67. New Haven, March 24, 1787, PGWCS V: 103.

68. To Knox, April 2, and to Madison, March 31, PGWCS V: 119, 115–16.

69. PGWCS V: 135–36.

70. Franklin to Washington, April 3, Humphreys to Washington, April 9, and Knox to Washington, April 9, 1787, all of which arrived after Washington wrote Randolph accepting his position on the delegation, in PGWCS V: 122, 131–33, 133–34.

71. Madison to Washington, New York, April 16, 1787, PGWCS V: 145–47.

72. Donald Jackson and Dorothy Twohig, eds., *The Diaries of George Washington* V, July 1786–December 1789 (Charlottesville, 1979), 143–50.

73. PGWCS V: 163–66

CHAPTER 1: THE MORNING AFTER

1. DHRC XIII: 200; Leonard Rapport, "Printing the Constitution: The Convention and Newspaper Imprints, August–November 1787," *Prologue: The Journal of the National Archives* II (1970), 69–89, esp. 74 ff. PGWCS V: 333–34, 339–40, and n1 at 340.

2. Donald Jackson and Dorothy Twohig, eds., *The Diaries of George Washington* V (Charlottesville, 1979), 155–56; Washington to Robert Morris, Mount Vernon, May 5, 1787, PGWCS V: 171.

3. Washington to George Augustine Washington, Philadelphia, May 17, 1787, PGWCS V: 189.

4. Farrand I: 17; Washington to Knox, May 31, and to George Augustine Washington, June 3, 1787, PGWCS V: 209–10, 219.

5. Washington to George Augustus Washington, June 3 and July 8, 1787, ibid., 217–19, 250–51.

6. Ibid., 321.

7. Jackson and Twohig, eds., *Diaries of George Washington* V: 185, 178–79. Note too his visit on June 10 to the famous botanical garden of William and John Bartram, which did not particularly impress him, and his visit to another nearby farm where he gathered information on the use of plaster of Paris to increase soil fertility: ibid., 166–69.

8. To Jefferson and to Lafayette, Philadelphia, September 18, 1787, PGWCS V: 333–34.

9. Letter dated September 17, 1787, in DHRC I: 305–06.

10. "Resolutions of the Convention Recommending the Procedures for Ratification and for the Establishment of Government under the Constitution by the Confederation Congress," September 17, DHRC I: 317–18; Jay to Washington, January 7, 1787, PGWCS IV: 504.

11. DHRC I: 305–06.

12. On Madison, see Lance Banning, *The Sacred Fire of Liberty: James Madison and the Founding of the Federal Republic* (Ithaca, NY, and London, 1995). Madison's denial that he was "the writer of the Constitution of the United States," from a letter to William Cogswell, Montpelier, March 10, 1834, in Gaillard Hunt, ed., *The Writings of James Madison* IX (New York and London, 1910), 533–34.

13. Madison to Jefferson, September 6, 1787, and also, explaining himself, October 24, 1787, in PJM X: 163–64, 206–219, esp. 209–14.

14. See Hamilton's description of his ideal plan of government, which he presented to the Convention on June 18, in Farrand I: 291–93; Farrand II: 645–46, for his September 17 remarks.

15. Farrand II: 645, 641–43.

16. To Washington, New York, August 14, 1787, PGWCS V: 293–94.

17. Douglas Southall Freeman, *George Washington: A Biography* VI (New York, 1954), 112.

18. Farrand II: 644.

19. Washington to Hamilton, July 10, 1787, PGWCS V: 257; Farrand I: 551 (Madison on July 7), 568–70 (July 10).

20. Washington to Benjamin Harrison, Mount Vernon, September 24, 1787, PGWCS V: 339. He had assumed that position already in August: See Washington to Knox, August 19, ibid., 297, where he expressed a hope that Congress, the state legislatures, and the community at large would adopt the government proposed by the Convention "because I am fully persuaded it is the best that can be obtained at the present moment, under such diversity of ideas as prevail."

21. Jackson and Twohig, ed., *Diaries of George Washington* V: 186–87.

22. Mason to Jefferson, May 26, 1788, PGM III: 1045; Madison to Jefferson, October 24, 1787, in PJM X: 215. On Mason, see Jeff Broadwater, *George Mason, Forgotten Founder* (Chapel Hill, 2006), and PGM, which includes chronologies and substantial editorial notes.

23. Broadwater, *Mason*, esp. 14–19, 47–53, 64–76 (Fairfax Resolves at 66), 77–87; Mason to the Committee of Merchants in London, June 6, 1766, PGM I: 71.

24. Broadwater, *Mason*, 74–75, 107; Mason to George Washington, April 2, 1776, and to Martin Cockburn, April 18, 1784, in PGM I: 267, II: 799–800. Mason also told Cockburn, however, that "If ever I shou'd see a Time, when I have just Cause to think I can render the Public essential Service, and can arrange my own Domestic Concerns in such a Manner, as to enable me to leave my Family, for any Length of time, I will most cheerfully let the County know it; but this is not the Case, in either Instance, at present."

25. Broadwater, *Mason*, 9, 58, 74–75, 108; Mason to Washington, Gunston Hall, October 14, 1775, PGM I: 255.

26. Broadwater, *Mason*, 8, 80, and passim; Mason to Richard Henry Lee, May 18, 1776, PGM I: 271.

27. Broadwater, *Mason*, 57–58; Peter R. Henriques, "An Uneven Friendship: The Relationship between George Washington and George Mason," *Virginia Magazine of History and Biography* 97 (1989), 185–204.

28. Broadwater, *Mason*, 157–63; Pierce in Farrand III: 94; Mason to George Mason Jr., May 27 and June 1, 1787, PGM III: 884, 892.

29. Broadwater, *Mason*, 136, 151–53, 156 (quotation of James Monroe on Mason's principles); Mason to George Mason Jr., June 1, 1787, PGM III: 892–93.

30. Broadwater, *Mason*, 164–79; Mason in Convention, June 20, Farrand I: 338–40.

31. Broadwater, *Mason*, 164–79; Pierce in Farrand III: 94.

32. Farrand II: 199, 319, 349, 451, 370; Broadwater, *Mason*, 181–97.

33. "Memorandum for the Maryland Delegates" (August 31, 1787), PGM III: 974 and quotation from Madison memo cited at 975; Farrand II: 479.

34. Farrand II: 224, 537–38, 541–42, 527, 550.

35. Ibid., 564–65.

36. Ibid., 636–40; 612 and 623–24 on representation; 587–88; 617, 616–17, 628.

37. Ibid., 587–88.

38. Ibid., 631–32.

39. Ibid., 632–33.

40. Ibid., 637–40; also PGM III: 991–93 and note, 993–94.

41. Ibid., 640, 563–64.

42. Washington to Randolph, November 19, 1786, PGWCS IV: 387.

43. Mason to Washington, October 7, 1787, PGM III: 1001–02.

44. Mason to Elbridge Gerry, October 20, 1787, DHRC XIII: 421.

45. Randolph to the speaker of the Virginia house of representatives, October 10, 1787, DHRC XV: 132–33.

46. Farrand II: 631–32, and William Pierce's description in III: 94.

CHAPTER 2: "TAKE THIS OR NOTHING"

1. Biographical information from George Athan Billias, *Elbridge Gerry: Founding Father and Republican Statesman* (New York, 1976), 2–7, 146–47, and passim.

2. Ibid., 147–52, 123–37; William Pierce's description is in Farrand III: 88.

3. Billias, *Gerry*, esp. chs. 12 and 13, pp. 172–205; Farrand II: 632–33.

4. DHRC XIII: 347.

5. On Lee, see Pauline Maier, *The Old Revolutionaries: Political Lives in the Age of Samuel Adams* (New York, 1980), 164–200, esp. 164–65. Mason's letter to Lee has been lost and is known only because Lee acknowledged receipt. On the circulation of Mason's objections, see DHRC XIII: 346–48, which notes that a copy of them in Whitehill's handwriting is among his papers in the Cumberland County (Pennsylvania) Historical Society. A report that Mason had traveled through the backcountry of Virginia "haranguing the Inhabitants, and pointing out the dangerous effects or consequences which would inevitably [sic] flow from the new Constitution" and also went to North Carolina "on the same Business" is questionable: See Charles Tillinghast to Hugh Hughes, New York, October 12, 1787, ibid., 373. Mason seemed to be home in early October—and, of course, he hated travel.

6. DHRC I: 322. On Congress's deliberations on the Constitution, see also Edmund C. Burnett, *The Continental Congress* (New York, 1941), 693–98. Note that on August 13, Arthur St. Clair, the president of Congress, wrote the governors of five nonattending states—Georgia, Maryland, Connecticut, Rhode Island, and New Hampshire—urging them to send delegates so a "full Congress" would consider the report of the convention. At the time, he noted, Congress was "reduced to six States" legally represented. LDC XXIV: 403–04.

7. DHCR I: 322, and 225–27 for Rhode Island general assembly to the president of Congress, September 15, 1787, and also 227–28 for a protest from the towns of Newport and Providence.

8. Nathan Dane to Caleb Strong, New York, October 10, 1787, DHRC I: 346–47.

9. Carrington to Madison, New York, September 23, 1787, DHRC I: 326.

10. On Mason's letter of September 18, see DHRC XIII: 282, n1, and, with reference also to Randolph's letter of September 17, DHRC XIV: 364 and 366. (Both letters are known mainly by Lee's responses to them.) Also DHRC I: 187, 317–18.

11. The Convention had, in fact, voted against requiring Congress's approbation on two separate occasions: Farrand II: 478–79 (August 31) and 559–63 (September 10). One delegate said "for their approbation" had been struck from the original resolution "to save Congress from the necessity of an Act inconsistent with the Articles of Confederation under which they held their authority" (560), but the delegates also wanted to avoid having the fate of their labors depend on Congress's approval.

12. DHRC I: 327–28 and also DHRC XIII: 231–32. The description of Congress's proceedings here is dependent upon the DHRC editors' careful compilation of accounts by individual members of Congress to supplement the manuscript and final journals of the Congress. Notes on Dane's response to Pierce Butler of Georgia were taken by Melancton Smith of New York, a friend and close colleague who shared Dane's reservations on the Constitution. See the editorial comment and also the transcription of the relevant documents in DHRC XIII: 229–42.

13. DHRC I: 329–30.

14. Ibid., 329–32.

15. Ibid., 332–33.

16. Ibid., 335–37.

17. Ibid.

18. Ibid., 335–36. The surviving records of these debates are fragmentary. On September 30, when the debates were over, Madison sent Washington an account of them that summarized the arguments against congressional amendments with admirable coherence (ibid., 343–45). Melancton Smith's records of the debates, which are far fuller than the official record, suggest that they were not presented with similar coherence in Congress itself.

19. Ibid., 336–37.

20. Ibid.

21. Ibid., 337–38. Lee's amendments are taken from the copy he sent to Elbridge Gerry on September 29. He later sent copies to Mason, William Shippen Jr., and Samuel Adams. Ibid., n24 at 341–42.

22. Ibid., 338–39. Note that the final provision appeared in the copy of his proposed amendments that Lee sent to Elbridge Gerry, but not in those sent to Governor Randolph: DHRC XIV: text to Randolph and n6 at 372.

23. DHRC I: 339–40.

24. Ibid., 340, and Lee to Mason, New York, October 1, 1787, at 345. Washington to Madison, Mount Vernon, October 10, 1787, DHRC XIII: 358.

25. See the transcription of Congress's published journals in DHRC XIII: 231, 232, 233.

26. DHRC I: 323, DHRC XIII: 230, and also DHRC XIV: 365. On the state of the manuscript journals of Congress for the period when it considered the Constitution (essentially, they are full of erasures and blanks), see Burnett, *Continental Congress*, 695.

27. DHRC I: 339, 345.

28. Ibid., 337.

29. DHRC II: 54, 58–61.

30. Ibid., 60–61.

31. Ibid., 54–55, 62–63.

32. Ibid., 65–72.

33. Ibid., 71, 74–75; brief biographies at 728, 733.

34. Ibid., 81–85, 75.

35. Ibid., 90, 92, 78, 72, 84.

36. See denials that the Confederation still existed in ibid., 93 (Hugh H. Brackenridge), and also 89 (Thomas FitzSimons).

37. Ibid., 76–78.

38. Ibid., 76–77, 93.

39. Ibid., 79–80, 85, and also 87–88.

40. Ibid., 86–90, 93.

41. Ibid., 66–67, including n4 at 67; also 55. On the differences between these parties, see Owen S. Ireland, "The Crux of Politics: Religion and Party in Pennsylvania, 1778–1789," WMQ

XLII (1985), 453–75; and Ireland, *Religion, Ethnicity, and Politics: Ratifying the Constitution in Pennsylvania* (University Park, PA, 1995).

42. Ibid., 95–98, including notes on 96 and 98.

43. Ibid., 99–100, 103, 106–07.

44. Ibid., 100, 104, n1 at 110, and 111; and Charles Swift to Robert E. Griffiths, Philadelphia, October 18, 1787, at 199. Swift said that the men who assisted the sergeant at arms were Captain John Barry, Michael Morgan O'Brien, and Jackson. Barry served as captain of the ship *Asia*, which was owned by Robert Morris, a strong supporter of the Constitution; O'Brien was an Irish immigrant and Philadelphia merchant.

45. Ibid., 104–09.

46. Ibid., 100, 109–110.

47. "Address of the Seceding Assemblymen," ibid., 112–114.

48. Ibid., 112–17.

49. DHRC XIV: 365; Lee to Adams, New York, October 5, 1787, DHRC XIII: 323–25.

50. Lee to Gerry, New York, September 29, 1787, DHRC I: 342.

51. Lee to William Shippen Jr., New York, October 2, and to Samuel Adams, October 5, 1787, DHRC XIII: 289, 323–25.

52. Lee to George Mason, October 1, 1787; to Washington, New York, October 11; and to Samuel Adams, October 5, DHRC XIII: 281–83, 367–69, 325.

53. Lee to Washington, New York, October 11, 1787, in which he again insisted that the changes he wanted "do not oppose the exercise of a very competent federal power," in DHRC XIII: 368, n4 at 369; Mason to Washington, October 7; Washington to Madison, October 10; and Madison to Washington, October 18, ibid., 348, 358–59, 408–09.

54. Hamilton, "Conjectures About the Constitution" [September 1787,] DHRC XIII: 277–78.

CHAPTER 3: A WAR OF PRINTED WORDS

1. DHRC XIII: 200n and also xxx–xxxix on the newspapers of the time; Leonard Rapport, "Printing the Constitution: The Convention and Newspaper Imprints, August–November 1787," *Prologue: The Journal of the National Archives* II (1970), 69–89, and "Newspaper Printings of the Constitution: An Unresolved Mystery," *Manuscripts* XXXIX (1987), 327–36.

2. See the list of newspapers of the ratification period in DHRC XIII: xxx–xxxi; also Jeffrey L. Pasley, *"The Tyranny of Printers": Newspaper Politics in the Early American Republic* (Charlottesville and London, 2001), 33, 43, and Appendix I, charts 1 and 2, at 402–03.

3. John K. Alexander, *The Selling of the Constitutional Convention: A History of News Coverage* (Madison, WI, 1990), 150, which describes these essays as resembling "campaign literature," and passim.

4. DHRC II: 146–48.

5. DHRC II: 148–49, and also subsequent commentaries on the exchange, 149–55.

6. DHRC XIII: 312–323, and, for the continuation of the debate in Philadelphia, 573–81; "Fair Play," *Independent Gazetteer*, September 29, 1797, DHRC II: 149.

7. Stephen Botein, "Printers and the American Revolution," in Bernard Bailyn and John B. Hench, eds., *The Press and the American Revolution* (Worcester, MA, 1980), 11–57, esp. 19–23.

8. Leonard W. Levy, *Emergence of a Free Press* (New York and Oxford, 1985); Richard Buel, Jr., "Freedom of the Press in Revolutionary America: The Evolution of Libertarianism, 1760–1820," in Bailyn and Hench, eds., *The Press and the American Revolution*, 59–97. See also James Wilson at DHRC II: 455: "What is meant by the liberty of the press is, that there should be no antecedent restraint upon it; but that every author is responsible when he attacks the security or welfare of the government or the safety, character, and property of the individual."

9. DHRC XIII: xxxiv–xxxv. See also Owen Ireland, *Religion, Ethnicity, and Politics* (University Park, PA, 1995), 161–62.

10. DHRC XIII: xxxv–vi, and 189 for items favoring ratification that Oswald published on August 22, 1787; DHRC II: 148.

11. DHRC XIII: xxxv–vi; Levy, *Emergence of a Free Press*, 206–210, and Jeffery A. Smith, *Printers and Press Freedom: The Ideology of Early American Journalism* (New York and Oxford, 1988), 37–38, 151–53, 155–56, 165.

12. Charles Tillinghast to Hugh Hughes, New York, October 12, 1787, DHRC XIII: 373. See also Samuel Bryan in Saul Cornell, ed., "Reflections on 'The Late Remarkable Revolution in Government,'" *The Pennsylvania Magazine of History and Biography* CXII (1988), 130: "In General it may be said that Col. Oswald was almost the only Printer who published in Opposition in Philadelphia & that he has been injured in Consequence."

13. Pasley, *"The Tyranny of Printers,"* 43, and Jürgen Heideking, "Die Amerikanische Presse und die Verfassungsdebtte," *Amerikastudien/American Studies* XXX (1985), 363–412, which has an abstract in English and lists contemporary newspapers and magazines.

14. DHRC XIII: xxxv–xxxviii, and 315 for a statement in the *New-York Journal*, October 4, 1787. Greenleaf's press was, in fact, attacked by a mob in July 1788.

15. DHRC XIII: 294.

16. See DHRC XIII: 243–45, 255–57, 287–88 (quotation at 288).

17. DHRC XIII: 293–306 (quotation at 294), 592–93; Mason to Elbridge Gerry, Gunston Hall, Fairfax County, Virginia, October 20, 1787, ibid., 421. The full text of the seceding assemblymen's address is in DHRC II: 112–17.

18. Edward Carrington to Thomas Jefferson, New York, October 23, 1787 (opposition in Pennsylvania had become more serious "under circumstances which leave it doubtful whether it is founded in objections to the project or the intemperance of its more zealous friends"); also Madison to Jefferson, New York, October 24 (an "unlucky ferment" in the Pennsylvania assembly has provoked the opposition and "by redoubling the exertions of that party may render the event [outcome] doubtful"); and Nicholas Gilman to President John Sullivan of New Hampshire, New York, October 31, DHRC XIII: 439, 451, 515.

19. DHRC XIII: 326–28. In August, Oswald, in keeping with his current political leanings, had printed an attack on George Bryan: Alexander, *Selling of the Constitutional Convention*, 160. Oswald had also attacked Bryan along with other members of the state supreme court in 1782: Levy, *Emergence of a Free Press*, 207.

20. "Centinel I" and editorial note in DHRC XIII: 326–37 (quotations at 336, 332, 334, and 330).

21. Ibid., 336.

22. Ibid., 336, 329–30.

23. DHRC: XIII, Appendix II, showing circulation figures, esp. 592–94, where the address of the Pennsylvania minority is no. 125A and "Centinel I" is no. 133.

24. DHRC XIII: 337–39.

25. Geoffrey Seed, *James Wilson* (Millwood, NY, 1978), 1–15 and passim.

26. "An Officer of the Late Continental Army," *Independent Gazetteer*, November 6, and "Plain Truth," *Independent Gazetteer*, November 10, 1787, DHRC II: 213, 217.

27. Pierce in Farrand III: 91–92; DHRC XIII: 337. Wilson had also been a member of the Convention's Committee of Detail, which developed a series of resolutions based on the Virginia Plan into a draft constitution, and later (with Morris) of its Committee of Style, which put the document into its final written form except for a few modifications the delegates made in their final days together.

28. The speech is in DHRC XIII: 339–44 (quotation at 339), with editorial comment on 337–39, and also, without such extensive editorial comment, DHRC II: 167–72.

29. DHRC XIII: 339–40.

30. Ibid., 340.

31. Ibid., 340–41.

32. Ibid., 341–43.

33. Ibid., 341.

34. Ibid., 341–42.

35. Ibid., 343.

36. Ibid., 343–44.

37. Ibid., 344.

38. Editorial comment in DHRC XIII: 338–39, n1 at 344, and the tally of printings at 593 (38 in total, of which, it seems, 34 were before December 29, 1787).

39. "A Democratic Federalist," "An Old Whig" II and III, and "Cincinnatus" in DHRC XIII, 386–92, 399–403, 425–29, 529–34 (esp. 531, 387, 400–20). Several replies to Wilson are conveniently grouped together in Bernard Bailyn, ed., *The Debate on the Constitution* I (New York, 1993), 70–126.

40. Richard Henry Lee to Samuel Adams, New York, October 27, 1787, and "Centinel II," DHRC XIII: 484–85, 460, 457.

41. Editorial note in DHRC XIII: 338–39.

42. Ibid., 326, 255, 411.

43. Editorial comment in ibid., 255 and 411, for speculation on who wrote the "Brutus" letters. Another "Antifederalist" series, signed "Federal Farmer" and discussed below, was often and probably incorrectly attributed to Richard Henry Lee: See DHRC XIV: 15–16.

44. These letters, along with those of the "Federal Farmer," are conveniently reprinted in Storing II, part II ("Major Series of Essays at the Outset"), 101–452 (quotation at 363; positive references to "Brutus" at 119 and 161). They are also in DHRC, with letters appearing separately according to their date of publication. For editorial commentary, see DHRC XIII: 255, 326–28, 411–12, and XIV: 14–18.

45. *The Federalist* essays 78–83, on the judiciary, responded to the arguments of "Brutus." Alexander Hamilton, James Madison, and John Jay, *The Federalist*, ed. J. R. Pole (Indianapolis and Cambridge, England, 2005), note at 411; William Jeffrey, Jr., "The Letters of Brutus: A Neglected Element in the Ratification Campaign of 1787–88," *Cincinnati Law Review* XL (1971), 657–61.

46. Cf "Brutus I," DHRC XIII: 420–21, and the "Federal Farmer," Letter V, at DHRC XIV: 49–50, and also 53: "I think the honest and substantial part of the community, will wish to see this system altered," giving "permanency and consistency . . . to the constitution we shall adopt."

47. A separate, "corrected" edition of the first set of "Federal Farmer" letters followed soon after its initial publication, and a third and perhaps a fourth "edition" came out in early 1788. None of these pamphlets identified the publisher, although Thomas Greenleaf, who also published the *New-York Journal*, is a strong candidate, at least for the first two "editions." DHRC XIV: 14–18 (text of the first five letters at 18–54); Storing II, 214–357 for all eighteen letters. For the additional letters, see DHRC XVII: 265–376.

48. DHRC XIII: 255; 327 and n1 at 336; 411, and Appendix II pp. 592–94 (for nos. 103, 133, 134, 178, 190); also DHRC XIV: 16–18 and 531 (for number 242) on the circulation of the "Federal Farmer."

49. DHRC XIII: 486–94, 496; Elizabeth Fleet, ed., "Madison's 'Detached Memoranda,'" WMQ III (1946), 564.

50. Note that the first number of the series promised to demonstrate the Constitution's "analogy to your own state constitution"—i.e., that of New York. DHRC XIII: 496.

51. DHRC XIII: 490–92, 496; DHRC XIV: n5 at 139 and 532 for *Federalist* X and references to modern studies of it. Elaine Crane, "Publius in the Provinces: Where Was The Federalist Reprinted Outside New York City?," WMQ XXI (1964), 589–92. There might have been another anthology of *Federalist* essays printed in Virginia during December 1787, though it does not seem to have been widely circulated: See DHRC XIII: 491. On the "legend" of the essays' importance and impact, see also Jeffrey, "The Letters of Brutus," 661–63.

52. DHRC IV: editorial comment at 30 and 303–04, n1 at 113.

53. Fleet, ed., "Madison's 'Detached Memoranda,'" 565, and Madison to Jefferson, New York, August 10, 1788, PJM XI: 227.

54. "Centinel" XI, January 16, 1788, DHRC XV: 388 and, for other contemporary reactions to *The Federalist*, including both high praise and criticisms from both critics of the Constitution and its supporters, who sometimes found it too "elaborate" and of little use among "the common people," DHRC XIII: 492–94.

55. DHRC XIII: 306–07.

56. Editorial comment in DHRC XIII: 346–48 and XIV: 147–49. The *Massachusetts Centinel*, which supported ratification, published his objections though without Mason's argument for requiring a two-thirds vote in Congress for laws regulating trade to prevent a Northern majority from harming Southern interests. It later claimed that Mason's objection to passing commercial laws by a simple majority had been excised by "a certain antifederal character" who feared it would alienate Northern readers (DHRC XIV: 148). Answers to Mason by Madison, "Civis Rusticus," and "Marcus" (James Iredell) are in Bailyn, ed., *Debate on the Constitution* I: 350–98.

57. Gerry's letter from the *Massachusetts Centinel*, November 3, 1787, in DHRC XIII: 548–50.

58. Ibid.

59. DHRC XIII: 546–48, and Appendix II, esp. 593–95; DHRC IV: 115–16, 121–22, 149. For essays that appeared in the Massachusetts press during the summer and fall of 1787, see DHRC IV, passim. The *Massachusetts Gazette* published one essay criticizing specific provisions of the Constitution on October 9 and was immediately attacked for its "wicked and absurd paragraphs" (pp. 61–62, including quotation by "W.X" in n1 at 62 and 120). Otherwise, essays by "Solon" and "John De Witt I" (October 18 and 22) were devoted mainly to defending the right and obligation of the people to discuss the Constitution freely and propose changes (102–04, 109–113). "John De Witt II," however, published on October 29, criticized the lack of a bill of rights and other problems often cited by critics elsewhere (156–61). For the surge in public debate that began in late October, see DHRC IV: 149–55 and ff.

60. Jackson to Henry Knox, October 28 and November 5, 1787, DHRC IV: 142, 193.

61. "Landholder" IV and V in DHRC XIV: 231–35, 334–39. "Landholder" argued, for example, that the size of the House of Representatives would grow with the American population, and a few good representatives were enough to watch over the limited "general" issues entrusted to the federal government. He said that the provision in Article I, Section 4, allowing Congress to "make or alter" state provisions for congressional elections, assured elections would be held even if a state failed to call them, and so it protected the citizens' right of election. Ellsworth defended congressional power over the military and taxation without mentioning the "necessary and proper clause" in answering Gerry's charge that Congress's powers were ambiguous and dangerous. He also insisted that having the vice president preside over the Senate did not violate separation of powers because the vice president would not be "an executive officer" unless he succeeded the president, at which point he would no longer preside over the Senate.

62. See esp. "Landholder IV," DHRC XIV: 231–32, and "Landholder VIII," DHRC XV, 75–80.

63. Gerry's defense, from the *Massachusetts Centinel* for January 5, 1788, is in DHRC V: 622–23. On his financial holdings, see DHRC IV: 215 n2, and George Athan Billias, *Elbridge Gerry: Founding Father and Republican Statesman* (New York, 1976), 131–37. Gerry could actually have anticipated financial benefits from the ratification of the Constitution, since he was a substantial holder of federal obligations. His politics, therefore, went against his personal financial interests.

64. DHRC XV: 117–21.

65. Ibid., 123–30, esp. 123, 128.

66. Ibid., 131–32.

67. Ibid., 133.

68. Ibid., 133–34.

69. Madison to Washington, January 25, 1788, PGWCS VI: 60; DHRC XV: 120–21 on responses to Randolph's letter.

70. Pierce in Farrand III: 93; DHRC XV: 146–56 for editorial comment and the first segment of the revised speech. For more comment and the entire text, see Storing II: 19–82, and also *Secret Proceedings and Debates of the Convention Assembled at Philadelphia, in the year 1787 . . . Including "The Genuine Information," Laid before the Legislature of Maryland, By Luther Martin, Esquire. . . .* (Richmond, 1839).

71. Martin, "Information to the Legislature of Maryland," in Storing II: 33–34.

72. Ibid., 44–45, and see also 48–49. Although Martin, like other critics of the Constitution, repeated the truism that republics were appropriate only for small units of territory, he char-

acteristically founded his argument on the experience of the American people, who, he said, were always arguing for the division of counties or states so their government would be nearer and more convenient. See p. 48.

73. Ibid., 46, 54–60, 64–65, 67–69, 75–78.

74. Ibid. 34, 43.

75. DHRC XV: 366–70, esp. 369–70.

76. Ibid.; italics mine.

77. Ibid., 366–68.

78. See, for example, Humphreys to Washington, November 16, 1786, PGWCS IV: 373; Linda Grant De Pauw, *The Eleventh Pillar: New York State and the Federal Convention* (Ithaca, NY, 1966), 43, where she says the terms were used as "epithets as men discussed the [proposed federal] impost" but were not used to designate parties until September 1787, when "the Constitution became a subject of political controversy"; and also 170, where De Pauw suggests that the terms went back at least to 1785. Madison to Washington, New York, March 3, 1787, PGWCS V: 93, which refers to an "antifederal party" in New York; and also 103, where Humphreys, in a letter to Washington dated March 24, 1787, refers to "foederal" and "antifoederal" parties in Connecticut politics.

79. For efforts to associate the "Antifederalists" with Loyalists, see "Tar and Feathers," Philadelphia *Independent Gazetteer*, October 2, 1787, DHRC II: 152–53, and also an unsigned piece from the *Pennsylvania Gazette*, October 3, ibid. 157.

80. For an earlier use of the spectrum model, but only with reference to the Virginia ratifying convention, see Jon Kukla, "A Spectrum of Sentiments: Virginia's Federalists, Antifederalists, and 'Federalists Who are For Amendments,' 1787–1788," *Virginia Magazine of History and Biography* XCVI (1988), 277–96. Kukla argues that historians' efforts "to impose a dichotomy of federalists and antifederalists has obscured as much as it explained about Virginia's role in shaping the Constitution and the political heritage of the new nation." In 1788 Virginians held "a full spectrum of sentiments about the Constitution, from ardent support through wary acquiescence to defiant resistance," and an analysis that takes into account those critical but subtle differences requires "something better than the blunt instrument of American dichotomies" (278–79).

81. Madison to Washington, New York, April 16, 1787, PGWCS V, esp. 145–46; Fleet, ed., "Madison's 'Detached Memoranda,'" 565. Differences were also apparent among writers who supported the Constitution and who "did not speak with one voice": Colleen A. Sheehan and Gary L. McDowell, *Friends of the Constitution: Writings of the "Other" Federalists, 1787–1788* (Indianapolis, 1998), xv and passim.

82. Letter VI, "Additional Letters from the Federal Farmer," DHRC XVII: 270–71.

83. Ibid.; Elbridge Gerry, speaking in the first federal Congress, quoted in Francis N. Thorpe, *Constitutional History of the United States* (Chicago, 1901), 238; and *The Federalist* 39 in Pole, ed., *The Federalist*, 206–11.

CHAPTER 4: THE PENNSYLVANIA RATIFYING CONVENTION: ... WITH DELAWARE, NEW JERSEY, AND GEORGIA

1. Morris to Washington, Philadelphia, October 30, 1787, DHRC XIII: 513.

2. For statements that suggest the contrary, see "A Federalist" from the *Independent Gazetteer*. October 10, 1787, DHRC II: 181 ("The distinction of Republican and Constitutionalist in this city has given way to the more important one of Federalist and Antifederalist; such a worthy example will, I trust, be imitated through every part of this state"); and a similar statement in Charles Swift to Robert E. Griffiths, Philadelphia, October 18, ibid., 199. The terms were also used by "One of the Gallery" in the *Pennsylvania Packet*, December 5, ibid., 312–13. However, contenders in the convention did not use those terms, and essayists critical of the Constitution such as "Philadelphiensis I" in Philadelphia's *Freeman's Journal* assiduously avoided either term: See DHRC II: 280–85. Although the terms were used in Pennsylvania mainly by the Constitution's supporters, in January 1788, after the convention had adjourned, writers critical of the Constitution in the *Carlisle Gazette* referred to "Federalists" (see DHRC II: 652,

672); such references to "Federalists" among opposition writers were rare, and to "Antifederalist" almost nonexistent.

3. For brief biographical sketches of these men, see DHRC II: 728, 732, 733. Also William Findley to New Hampshire governor William Plumer, Washington, February 27, 1812, in "William Findley of Westmoreland, PA.," *Pennsylvania Magazine of History and Biography* V (1881), 440–50, esp. 443–44, 449. Only Findley has been the subject of a biography, John Caldwell's *William Findley from West of the Mountains: A Politician in Pennsylvania, 1783–1791* (Gig Harbor, WA, 2000), which offers a graphic description of the route from Westmoreland County to Philadelphia on pp. 13–17, and the account of his accent at 194. Caldwell also wrote *William Findley from West of the Mountains: Congressman, 1791–1821* (Gig Harbor, WA, 2002), but all future references in this chapter are to the first volume. On Whitehill, see also *Dictionary of American Biography* XX (New York, 1936), 131–32.

4. Owen S. Ireland, "The Crux of Politics: Religion and Party in Pennsylvania, 1778–1789," WMQ XLII (1985), 453–75; "The People's Triumph: The Federalist Majority in Pennsylvania, 1787–88," *Pennsylvania History* LVI (1989), 93–113; "The Invention of American Democracy: The Pennsylvania Federalists and the New Republic," *Pennsylvania History* LXVII (2000), 161–71, esp. 164–65; and *Religion, Ethnicity, and Politics: Ratifying the Constitution in Pennsylvania* (University Park, PA, 1995), esp. xvi–xviii, 217–53. Robert L Brunhouse, *The Counter-Revolution in Pennsylvania, 1776–1790* (Philadelphia, 1942), describes the Test Acts at 197–98; he saw the Constitutionalists as radical democrats and the Republicans as antidemocratic conservatives. Terry Bouton, *Taming Democracy: "The People," the Founders, and the Troubled Ending of the American Revolution* (Oxford and New York, 2007), also interprets the conflict as between elite, antidemocratic partisans and "ordinary folk," but describes the complex geographical, ethnic, religious, and historical divisions that shaped Pennsylvania politics at 126–29. Bryan quotation from Saul Cornell, ed., "Reflections on 'The Late Remarkable Revolution in Government': Aedanus Burke and Samuel Bryan's Unublished History of the Ratification of the Federal Constitution," *Pennsylvania Magazine of History and Biography* CXII (1988), 128, where he also says that the self-styled "Republican" party included "most of the Merchants, most of the monied Men, most of the Gentlemen in the late Army & many of the Mob in the Towns," which of course crosses conventional class lines.

5. "William Findley of Westmoreland, PA.," esp. 443–47.

6. Letter in *Freeman's Journal*, October 31, 1787, DHRC II: 207 and n1, stating that "there is no evidence" that copies of the Constitution ordered by the assembly circulated in the backcountry of Pennsylvania. See also Bouton, *Taming Democracy*, 180–81, which adds that "Federalist" postmasters blocked "Antifederalist" mail.

7. DHRC II, esp. editorial comment at 225; William Shippen Jr., to Thomas Lee Shippen, Philadelphia, November 7–18, and Samuel Baird to John Nicholson, Norristown, PA, November 9, 235–237; assembly debates, November 10, 1787, pp. 238–54, esp. 242–43.

8. Ebenezer Bowman to Timothy Pickering, Wilkes-Barre, PA, November 12, 1787, DHRC II: 257. The editors of DHRC incorrectly identify the addresses as Tench Coxe's "An American Citizen IV: On the Federal Government," published at Philadelphia on October 21, 1787 (DHRC II: 257, n.4), which was only one of several Federalist essays the broadside reprinted. The error was corrected in DHRC XIII: 430–31, which identifies the broadside and describes its contents.

9. *Minutes of the Convention of the Commonwealth of Pennsylvania* (Philadelphia, 1787); editorial comment in DHRC II: 39–43.

10. DHRC II: 41; also James H. Hutson, "The Creation of the Constitution: The Integrity of the Documentary Record," in Jack N. Rakove, ed., *Interpreting the Constitution: The Debate over Original Intent* (Boston, 1990), 161 and n.98 on 175. For the Smilie intervention, see DHRC II: 574, 585 n.4. On November 23, John Smilie and Robert Whitehill had opposed Lloyd's petition to be appointed the convention's assistant secretary: See DHRC II: 329. Jonathan Elliot reprinted Lloyd's Debates in *The Debates in the Several State Conventions, on the Adoption of the Federal Constitution . . .* II (2nd ed; Washington, 1836), 415–46, although, as Hutson explains, he understood its inadequacies. The editors of DHRC II, *Ratification by the States: Pennsyl-*

vania, combines Lloyd's version of speeches with those Alexander Dallas published, other newspaper reports, and the private notes of convention delegates to provide a fuller record of the Pennsylvania ratifying convention: See pp. 321–616. The biased and incomplete state of the records helps explain why, so late as 1976, when DHRC II was published, there was "no adequate account of the ratification of the Constitution by Pennsylvania": ibid., 43.

11. Caldwell, *Findley*, 158–59; editorial comment in DHRC II: 40–43.

12. DHRC II: 326–30. Ireland, *Religion, Ethnicity, and Politics*, 71–107, gives an account of the convention that is also based on the DHRC.

13. DHRC II: 330 and n.4 at 331. Information on the meeting hall is from an email message to the author from Karie Diehorn, chief curator, Independence National Park, February 13, 2003. There is no evidence, she said, that the room ever had a balcony; instead spectators sat behind a railing in the back of the room.

14. DHRC II: 328 (*Pennsylvania Herald*).

15. Ibid., 329–32.

16. Ibid., 382. Having accepted the invitation, the convention adjourned on November 28 until Friday.

17. *Minutes of the Convention of the Commonwealth of Pennsylvania*, passim; also DHRC III, 524 (*Pennsylvania Herald*, December 8).

18. Ireland, *Religion, Ethnicity, and Politics*, 74. Bouton, *Taming Democracy*, concedes on p. 182 that the Federalists were able in the fall of 1787 to persuade "large pockets of ordinary people across the state" to support the Constitution. Jackson Turner Main, *The Antifederalists: Critics of the Constitution* (Chapel Hill, 1961), esp. 190–93, emphasizes geographical divisions and the importance of commerce in explaining voters' support for the Constitution.

19. DHRC II: 333–34.

20. Ibid., 335 (*Pennsylvania Herald*) and Francis Hopkinson to Thomas Jefferson, December 14, 1787, quoted in ibid., 339. For newspaper summaries of the speech and also the texts published by Dallas and Lloyd, which provide the basis of the account here and in subsequent paragraphs, see ibid., esp. 342, 347, 352, 349, 362.

21. Ibid., 336–37.

22. Ibid.

23. Ibid., 337, 364–65.

24. Ibid., 370–79, 381.

25. Ibid., 376.

26. *Pennsylvania Packet*, December 5, 1787, ibid., 312–13. "One of the Gallery" is one of a handful of contemporary essays that refers explicitly to "Federalist" and "Antifederalist."

27. DHRC II; 323. Philadelphia candidates did apparently have to declare they would vote for ratification of the Constitution "in toto" prior to the election: William Shippen Jr., to Thomas Lee Shippen, Philadelphia, November 7, 1787, ibid., 235.

28. Ibid., 380–81.

29. Ibid., 382–84.

30. Ibid., 384–86, 393, all from the debates of November 28, 1787.

31. Ibid., 440.

32. Ibid., 411–20.

33. Ibid., 387–91.

34. Ibid., 390–91, and also 440 (November 30, 1787), where Smilie read a copy of the Virginia declaration from *The Remembrancer: or, Impartial Repository of Public Events* (London, 1776), 221–22. (The precise citation is given on 443, n.7.) Smilie said he also had a French translation of the document. Virginia's Revolutionary legislature had enacted the declaration on June 12, 1776, before adopting the state's constitution separately seventeen days later. The declaration was not therefore a part of the state constitution, which probably explains why it wasn't included in *The Constitutions of the Several Independent States of America . . .* (Philadelphia, 1781; reprinted Boston, 1785, and New York, 1786).

35. DHRC II: esp. 391–92 (Smilie), and 398 (Whitehill).

36. On that meeting, held on November 6, 1787, at the Philadelphia home of William Shippen Jr., Lee's brother-in-law, see Shippen to Thomas Lee Shippen, Philadelphia, 7, 13, 15, and November 18, in ibid., 236: Lee stopped in Philadelphia on his way to Virginia and "while here he had a long interesting conference w[ith] Findley, [James] McClean [McLene], [Charles] Pettit, Hutchinson, Bryan, [John] Smiley, and Ab[raham] Smith at my house."

37. DHRC II: 434-35.

38. Ibid., 392-98 (from the *Pennsylvania Herald*, December 12 and 15, 1787).

39. Ibid., 448-49, 471-73, 559.

40. Ibid., 459, 447-49.

41. Ibid., 457, 459.

42. Ibid., 460.

43. Ibid., 465, 459. Whitehill, however, argued for "rejecting the plan" (393).

44. Ibid., 465.

45. Ibid., 465-528 (quotation at 528).

46. Ibid., 527, n.4 and 5 at 531.

47. Ibid., 527-31. There is some uncertainty over the order in which these speeches occurred, including whether McKean spoke before or after the exchange over jury trials in Sweden.

48. Ibid., 529-30. Findley probably received so few votes because he had already announced that he would not attend. He explained later that he refused because the legislature would not pay its delegates, most of whom would have fewer costs than he since they lived in or near Philadelphia. Caldwell, *Findley*, 114.

49. DHRC II: 529-31. The fullest and most coherent contemporary account is from the *Pennsylvania Herald*, December 12, 1787.

50. DHRC II: 532. The citations were from *The Modern Part of an Universal History, From the Earliest Account of Time*, XXXIII, 21-22, and William Blackstone, *Commentaries on the Laws of England. Book the Third* (Oxford, 1768), 349-50, 380-81.

51. Blackstone, *Commentaries* III, 349, 380, 381. John Smilie also made good use of Blackstone's third volume a few days earlier: DHRC II: 525 (Wilson's notes on Smilie's speech of December 8, 1787).

52. DHRC II: 533-47, 548-49.

53. Ibid. 550-51, from the *Pennsylvania Herald*, December 12, 1787.

54. Ibid., esp. 552.

55. Ibid., 553-56, 559-60.

56. Ibid., 560-61, 565, 557.

57. Ibid., 557-58, 563-66, 577-78.

58. Ibid., 566-67.

59. Ibid., esp. 580-84.

60. Ibid., 571 n.4 and 585 n.9.

61. Compare Yeates's notes at ibid., 570-71, on the morning portion of the speech with the text of that part of Wilson's speech as reported by Thomas Lloyd in his *Debates* at 552-70, and Wilson's list of the objections he intended to answer in the morning, 551-52. Lloyd's account of the afternoon speech is at 572-84, Yeates's at 584-85.

62. Ibid., 549 (McKean answered sarcastically that Smilie was "angry—because other folks are pleased") and 587. On Jackson, see William Shippen Jr., to Thomas Lee Shippen, December 18, 1787, quoted in ibid., n.2 at 588, and also n.1 at 110.

63. Items from the *Independent Gazetteer* and the *Freeman's Journal*, both printed on December 5, 1787, in ibid., 264-65. The two items differ in some minor details, and the *Freeman's Journal* does not include the assertion that six other states were certain to reject the Constitution.

64. Ibid., 587 (*Pennsylvania Herald*).

65. DHRC II: 587-88. The speaker was perhaps Thomas Hartley, a delegate from York County in southern Pennsylvania, west of the Susquehanna River and Lancaster County (see n.1 at 381). Bouton, *Taming Democracy*, 183-84, notes that Federalists did not contest the minority's figures and argues that support for the Constitution "may have been even weaker than the vote totals suggest." Owen Ireland, however, insists that "in Pennsylvania supporters far

outnumbered opponents of the Federal Constitution in 1787–1788" and that Pennsylvania voters, unlike those in other critical large states, "knowingly, repeatedly and in overwhelming proportions supported the new frame of government." See "The People's Triumph," 93, 109. Leaving aside the percentage of people who actually participated in elections, which Findley stressed, a modern study concludes that the majority in the Pennsylvania convention represented 65.7 percent of the state's population. Charles W. Roll, Jr., "We, Some of the People: Apportionment in the Thirteen State Conventions Ratifying the Constitution," JAH LVI (1969), 26.

66. DHRC II: 592–96.
67. Ibid., 203–05.
68. Ibid., 205 n.1, and see also George Turner to Winthrop Sargent, Philadelphia, November 6, 1787; at 209, and Francis Murray to John Nicholson, Newtown, PA, November 1, 1787, at 207–08 (I "should like something done like the plan proposed by M.C.").
69. Ibid., 300–03.
70. Excerpt from *A Review of the Constitution Proposed by the Late Convention Held at Philadelphia . . . By a Federal Republican* (Philadelphia, 1787) in DHRC II: 303–06, and also an essay by "An Officer of the Late Continental Army," first published in the *Independent Gazetteer* on November 6, in ibid., esp. 215, 213. Advertisements indicate *A Review of the Constitution* was published on November 28, 1787 (306 n.1).
71. "Many Customers" in ibid., 306–09, and see also "Columbus" from the *Pennsylvania Herald*, December 8, 1787, esp. 314–15.
72. Philadelphia County Petition, December 11, 1787 (which was apparently never presented to the convention), ibid., 316–19 and n.1 at 319, which includes the *Herald* quotation.
73. Ibid., 596.
74. Ibid., 596–99 (mostly from transcripts printed in the *Pennsylvania Herald* on December 15, 1787).
75. Ibid., 597–99.
76. Ibid., 599–600.
77. Ibid., 589–91 and, for purposes of comparison, 364–65. The December 12 vote to ratify the Constitution included all who voted against the motion of November 26, plus Thomas Scott from Westmoreland County, who had voted for a committee of the whole, and Benjamin Elliott from Huntingdon County, also in western Pennsylvania, who was apparently absent for the earlier vote. The negative vote on ratification included all who voted for the committee of a whole except Scott.
78. Ibid., 603.
79. Ibid., 604–610.
80. Ibid., 604–06, 616.
81. Ibid., 617–40. The "Dissent" was also printed as a broadside by Eleazer Oswald.
82. Ibid., 670–84, and 652 for "An Address to the Minority of the Convention" from the *Carlisle Gazette*, January 2, 1788.
83. Ibid., 642–45 (Franklin quotation at 645), 709ff.
84. Gaspare J. Saladino, "Delaware: Independence and the Concept of a Commercial Republic" in Gillespie and Lienesch, 29–51 (quotation at 42).
85. Ibid., 41–43, n.49 at 51. See also DHRC III: 35–115.
86. Sara M. Shumer, "New Jersey: Property and the Price of Republican Politics" in Gillespie and Lienesch, 71–89; and also DHRC III: 117–97, with the quotation from the convention journal for December 14 at 182.
87. For the argument that the Pennsylvania Republicans/Federalists were skilled democratic politicians, see Ireland, "The Invention of American Democracy," esp. 161–62, 164–65.
88. DHRC III, 208–10 (and, for a succinct summary of Georgia's history in the Revolution, 200–11).
89. Documents on Georgia's ratification in DHRC III: 199–311, which includes the convention's journal as well as the assembly's charge of October 26, 1787, at 228, and the local newspaper debate, 233–59.

90. On the significance of the Indian issue, compare Edward J. Cashin, "Georgia: Searching for Security," in Gillespie and Lienesh, 93–116, with the editorial comment in DHRC III: 210–11, and comments by Washington on the situation in Georgia to James Madison, Mount Vernon, December 7 ("the disturbances in Georgia will or at least ought to show the people of it the propriety of a strict union and the necessity there is for a general government") and to Samuel Powel, Mount Vernon, January 18, which is quoted here, ibid., 263–64. Washington was responding to the state assembly's charge to the convention; he had not yet heard the news of Georgia's ratification. See also Albert B. Sayre, "Georgia: Security Toward Union," in Conley and Kaminski, 77–92, esp. 86–90, which argues that "Georgia's exposed and vulnerable location helps to explain its support for a strong national Union" (89).

91. DHRC III: 274–80.

92. See, for example, the debate among Washington and his correspondents in late 1787 in PGWCS V, esp. 465ff.

CHAPTER 5: "WE THE PEOPLE" OF CONNECTICUT AND MASSACHUSETTS

1. "Chronology, 1786–1790" in DHRC III: 26–31, esp. 28–30.

2. Farrand II: 478.

3. To John Langdon, Mount Vernon, December 3, 1787, PGWCS V: 471; Madison to Edmund Randolph, New York, January 10, 1788, DHRC VIII: 290.

4. For example, Madison to Washington, New York, November 18, 1787 ("All my informations from Richmond concur in representing the enthusiasm in favor of the new Constitution as subsiding, and giving place to a spirit of criticism"); Washington to David Stuart, Mount Vernon, November 30, 1787 ("I am sorry to find . . . that the opposition is gaining strength"); and also Washington to Madison, Mount Vernon, December 3, 1787, quoting a letter from a member of the Virginia assembly that said "the Constitution has lost ground so considerably that it is doubtful whether it has any longer a majority in its favor," in PGWCS V: 444, 466, 479.

5. Madison to Washington, New York, October 18, 1787, DHRC XIII: 409; Madison to Randolph, New York, January 10, 1788, DHRC VIII: 289–91; and for the delay in getting firm news on Georgia, Madison to Washington, February 1, 1788, PGWCS VI: 77.

6. Morris to Washington, October 30, 1787, in PGWCS V: 399.

7. Knox to Washington, New York, December 11, 1787; and Madison to Washington, December 7, PGWCS V: 485, 481.

8. Madison to Washington, December 20, 1787, PGWCS V: 500, and also January 20, 1788, PGWCS VI: 51–52.

9. Washington to Madison, January 10, 1788; Lincoln to Washington, January 9–13, 1788, PGWCS VI: 33, 22–23.

10. Lincoln to Washington, January 9[–13], 1788, and Washington to Lincoln, January 31, 1788, PGWCS VI: 22–23, 73–74.

11. The excerpt from Washington's letter to Charles Carter (his Fredericksburg correspondent) as it appeared in the *Maryland Journal* on January 1, and related correspondence, including Washington to Lincoln, January 31, 1788, and to Madison, February 5, with editorial commentary on the episode, is in DHRC VIII: 276–81.

12. To Randolph, Mount Vernon, January 8, 1788, PGWCS VI: 17–18 and also V: 511. Washington's position on amendments was probably influenced by a letter from Madison, New York, December 20, 1787, in which Madison discussed the differences in how George Mason, Richard Henry Lee, and Edmund Randolph proposed to constitute the executive council that they wanted to assume the task of giving advice and counsel to the president. It was "pretty certain," Madison said, that the advocates of amendments differed among themselves on not just that issue but several others. PGWCS V: 499. Later, in the *Pennsylvania Gazette* on January 16, "Philanthropos" (Tench Coxe) summarized several apparent differences among the convention's dissenters and also the minority in the Pennsylvania convention, and he again asked what chance there was for consensus in another convention. See DHRC XV: 391–93.

13. To Edward Newenham, Mount Vernon, December 25, 1787, PGWCS V: 509.

14. DHRC III: 319–20. For accounts of the ratification controversy in Connecticut, see Donald S. Lutz, "Connecticut: Achieving Consent and Assuring Control," in Gillespie and Lienesh, 117–137; Christopher Collier, "Sovereignty Finessed: Roger Sherman, Oliver Ellsworth, and the Ratification of the Constitution in Connecticut," in Conley and Kaminski, 93–112; and Bernard C. Steiner, "Connecticut's Ratification of the Federal Constitution," *Proceedings of the American Antiquarian Society* XXV (1915): 70–127.

15. DHRC III: 320–26 (quotation from the *Connecticut Courant* at 324).

16. Ibid.; David Humphreys to George Washington, New Haven, CT, March 24, 1787, PGWCS V: 103.

17. New Haven, September 28, 1787, PGWCS V: 343; "Observator V," *New Haven Gazette*, September 20 and 27, DHRC III: 348–51.

18. See editorial comment in DHRC III: 329–331, which refers to "the virtual exclusion of anything written against" the Constitution in the Connecticut press and "the virtual blackout of news about opposition to the Constitution within the state," and concludes that, as a consequence, "there was no public debate in Connecticut." Also 372–92 for the apparently bogus "Letter from Massachusetts" and the "Letter from New York" that answered it.

19. DHRC III: 406, and 456–57 for the *Connecticut Courant*. Also "Social Compact," *New Haven Gazette*, October 4, 1787; "A Traveller," *American Mercury* (Hartford), October 8; "excerpt" from a letter by a member of the Connecticut legislature, October 17, ibid., 357, 359, 369.

20. Sherman and Ellsworth to Governor Samuel Huntington, New London, September 26, 1787, DHRC III: 351–2 and n.2 at 353. Connecticut was allowed to send up to seven delegates to the Confederation Congress (although they could collectively cast only one vote). In the new Congress, they would have five representatives and two senators.

21. Ibid., 327–29; Steiner, "Connecticut's Ratification of the Federal Constitution," 81–91.

22. "A Farmer: To the Farmers of Connecticut," *New Haven Gazette*, October 18, 1787; "A Landholder," I and II, *Connecticut Courant*, November 5 and 12, DHRC III: 392–94, 398–403.

23. "Landholder" II, IV and V on Gerry, VI on Mason, and also VIII in DHRC III: 401–03, 476–84, 487–92, and 503–07, quotations at 401–02, 504, 491.

24. Ibid., 456–57 and 476–77, 471, 473, and n.5 at 473.

25. See Hugh Ledlie to John Lamb, Hartford, January 15, 1788, DHRC III: 578–79: "For want of knowing whom to put confidence in, you . . . sent your books into the wrong hands," since none were seen except for a few sent to General James Wadsworth. The others were "all secreted, burnt, and distributed amongst those for the new Constitution in order to torture, ridicule, and make shrewd remarks and may [make] game of, both of the pamphlet and them that wrote and sent them." Also ibid., 458.

26. Ibid., 458 and, for attacks on the New York "Federal Republican" committee, "Landholder" VIII, December 24, 1787, "Connecticutensis," December 31, and, on the background of "Antifederalists," "Landholder" IX, December 31, DHRC III: 503–06, 514, and 516.

27. Ibid., 492–94 and also 457.

28. Resolutions of the legislature, October 17, 1787, DHRC III: 367, 363–64.

29. Text of a speech that Gale might not have actually given, November 12, 1787, DHRC III: 420–29, esp. 420–21, and n.1 at 429. Gale was an opponent of giving Army officers full pay for five years rather than pensions of half pay for life and the Cincinnati, which fed into his opposition to the Constitution. The town of Killingworth apparently agreed with him. Gale wrote to William Samuel Johnson, a delegate to the federal Convention, that 150 voters were at the meeting, but only 14 voted for one delegate and 13 for the other. "All the others would not vote at all and are really against it, but you members of the Convention and Congress have fobbed off our Assembly and the people nicely." Ibid., 429.

30. Ibid., 407, 450–51, 436–37.

31. January 7, 1788, in ibid., 533–34.

32. Ibid., 405–06.

33. Ibid., 442–43, 430–32, 449–50, 416, 411, 441.

34. November 12, 1787, in ibid., 438–41.

35. Ibid., 535 and 540. For an account of the convention, see Steiner, "Connecticut's Ratification of the Federal Constitution," 109–27.

36. Ibid., 336, 535, and, for Perkins's remarks, 554.

37. Hugh Ledlie to John Lamb, Hartford, January 15, 1788, ibid., 576. Ledlie, though a resident of Hartford, was ill with the gout and did not attend the convention, so his information was second-hand.

38. "A Connecticut Farmer," January 28, 1788, ibid., 586.

39. "Letter of a Member of the Connecticut Convention," *Massachusetts Gazette*, February 5, 1788, ibid., 595–96; voting results, 537–39.

40. Knox to Jeremiah Wadsworth, New York, January 13, 1788, ibid., 605. On the distribution of opposition to the Constitution in Connecticut, see Christopher Collier, *All Politics Is Local: Family, Friends, and Provincial Interests in the Creation of the Constitution* (Hanover and London, 2003), esp. 96 for a map of townships indicating how they voted, 110–31, and Appendix C, 149–52, which traces personal linkages among Connecticut "Antifederalists."

41. Cf. Samuel Blachley Webb to Joseph Barrell, New York, January 13, 1788, DHRC III: 605: If Massachusetts rejects the Constitution, "we are ruined. On them depends everything: every Federal Man in this city looks up to your state for our political salvation."

42. Oscar and Mary Handlin, eds., *The Popular Sources of Political Authority: Documents on the Massachusetts Constitution of 1780* (Cambridge, 1966), 190–201 for the proposed constitution of 1778, which was submitted to the towns "for their approbation or disapprobation," esp. 191 and 206. On the tallying of results, see Leonard L. Richards, *Shays's Rebellion: The American Revolution's Final Battle* (Philadelphia, 2002), esp. 70, where he says approval had to be "unqualified"; and Willi Paul Addams, *The First American Constitutions: Republican Ideology and the Making of the State Constitutions in the Revolutionary Era* (Chapel Hill, 1980), esp. 89–92, which notes that "the individual voter, not the corporate entities of the towns," was the basis of decision making, and that the 1778 constitution failed by a vote of 2,083 to 9,972 in some 180 towns (90–91). See also Michael Zuckerman, *Peaceable Kingdoms: New England Towns in the Eighteenth Century* (New York, 1970), 105–06 and 272–73, which stresses the high degree of agreement within towns, not the legislature's method of tabulating results.

43. Resolution of Concord, October 22, 1776, in Handlin, *Popular Sources of Political Authority*, 152–53, and also 315–16. On the emergence and growing popularity of this position, see Robert J. Taylor, *Western Massachusetts in the Revolution* (Providence, RI, 1954), particularly chapter V on the "Berkshire Constitutionalists," radicals in the western part of the state who insisted from 1776 that the people had to ratify a constitution. Taylor notes, however, that the Berkshire Constitutionalists were slower than some other towns to insist that a specially elected convention draft the constitution: See esp. 88 and n. 50 at 191–92. The earliest advocates were apparently the towns of Stoughton, Norton, Middleborough, Attleborough, Lexington, and Concord, all of which were in the eastern part of the state (in Bristol, Middlesex, Plymouth, and Suffolk counties), and also Worcester, in central Massachusetts. By 1777, Taylor indicates that towns in northern Berkshire County, in the far west of Massachusetts, were also adopting that position. In 1778, a convention of towns in Berkshire County called for the election of "a special convention of Delegates" to form a bill of rights and constitution: Handlin, *Popular Sources of Political Authority*, 366–68.

44. L. H. Butterfield, ed., *Diary and Autobiography of John Adams* III (New York, 1954), 351–52.

45. Handlin, *Popular Sources of Political Authority*, 23.

46. S. E. Morison, "The Struggle over the Adoption of the Constitution of Massachusetts, 1780," *Proceedings of the Massachusetts Historical Society*, vol. L, October 1916–June 1917 (Boston, 1917), 353–412, esp. 354–60, including the convention's resolution on ratification, which was sent to town selectmen, at 359–60. Proceedings of the Convention, March 2, 1780, in Handlin, *Popular Sources of Political Authority*, 432–33, and the Convention's Address of March 1780, 434–40 (quotation at 434). Those procedures were not forgotten: "Solon" quoted the Convention's Address on the interest and obligations of the people in the *Independent Chronicle* (Boston) for October 18, 1787. "It is when men consent to forms of Government," he said, "that they should express their sentiments respecting them." DHRC IV: 103.

47. In Handlin, *Popular Sources of Political Authority*, 441–42.

48. Morison, "Struggle over the Adoption of the Constitution of Massachusetts," esp. 357–58, 364–411.

49. Richard D. Brown, *Revolutionary Politics in Massachusetts: The Boston Committee of Correspondence and the Towns, 1772–1774* (Cambridge, 1970); Pauline Maier, *American Scripture: Making the Declaration of Independence* (New York, 1997), 59ff.

50. Samuel Banister Harding, *The Contest over the Ratification of the Federal Constitution in the State of Massachusetts* (New York, 1896), 5: Palmer objected to giving the Confederation power over war and peace, which the town thought should instead be vested in the people; Amesbury shared that objection and also thought the costs of the Confederation should be shared among the states in proportion to "Personal income as well as Real Estate"; Bridgewater thought all congressional enactments should require the assent of eleven states; Westborough wanted more protection for Protestantism and more recognition of God; Lexington wanted the states' freedom and independence better protected and more checks on scheming rulers. It also said the states should be able to propose amendments to the Articles. Massachusetts and other states proposed amendments to the Articles, but Congress rejected them all: See DHRC IV: xxviii. The states' ratifications of the Articles, with proposed amendments, are in DHRC I: 96–137.

51. Harding, *Ratification in Massachusetts*, 1–8 (quotation at 7–8). Harding asserts that the people had never been confined "to a mere acceptance or rejection in its entirety of the instrument proposed to them" but were always free "to reject specific sections and to propose amendments," such that "every citizen of the State was . . . admitted to an active participation in the constitution-making, as well as in the administration of government, of this epoch" (7). The rules for ratifying the constitution of 1778 are to some extent an exception to that generalization, although even then the town reports indicated which parts of the Constitution their voters found objectionable. See Addams, *First American Constitutions*, 91.

52. These town resolves, from the manuscript collections of the Massachusetts Archives, CLVI, 131 and 368, are quoted in Harding, *Ratification in Massachusetts*, 2–3 and n.1 at 3.

53. DHRC IV: li–lvii; quotation from "A Friend for Liberty" in the *Massachusetts Centinel*, November 14, 1787, p. 231. Powers later resumed publication in the inland town of Worcester, which was far more hospitable toward criticisms of the Constitution than Boston, although another local publication, the *Worcester Magazine*, was staunchly Federalist.

54. DHRC IV: 124–48, esp. 144, 130–32, 140.

55. Ibid., 125, 138.

56. Ibid., n.1 at 145–46 and 18–21; also DHRC II: n.1 at 207. The pamphlet was simply titled *The Constitution or Frame of Government for the United States of America . . .* (Boston, 1787). All copies of the Pittsfield, MA, *American Centinel* have disappeared, so it is impossible to know if it too published the Constitution.

57. Chapter I, Section III, Article II of the 1780 Massachusetts constitution in Handlin, *Popular Sources of Political Authority*, 454. For a definition of ratable polls, see Addams, *First American Constitutions*, 241, and Robert E. Brown, *Middle-Class Democracy and the Revolution in Massachusetts, 1691–1780* (Ithaca, NY, 1955), 44, 49. DHRC V: 891, which notes that not all of Boston's 1782 ratable polls were qualified to vote.

58. DHRC V: 888 and Handlin, *Popular Sources of Political Authority*, 455, for Chapter I, Section III, Article IV of the 1780 state constitution.

59. DHRC V: 949–50.

60. DHRC V: 889–91, 1031 for Nathaniel Gorham to Henry Knox, Boston, January 6, 1788, on Nantucket. DHRC VI: 1107 for the total number of delegates elected and, for comparisons with the legislature, Richard D. Brown, "Shays's Rebellion and the Ratification of the Federal Constitution in Massachusetts," in Richard Beeman et al., eds., *Beyond Confederation: Origins of the Constitution and American National Identity* (Chapel Hill and London, 1987), 122–23. Brown argues that the surge in participation was a response to the Bowdoin administration's repressive policies after Shays's Rebellion, and it "threatened to swamp the Constitution in a wave of antigovernment, antilawyer, antiestablishment reaction that was less related

to the particular contents of the document itself than to the power and privilege its leading advocates symbolized" (ibid. at 122). Evidence examined here shows, however, that the towns paid considerable attention to the Constitution, and their responses probably contributed significantly to the increase in convention participation.

61. This and the following discussion are based on the editorial introduction and an extraordinary collection of town records and related documents that report the proceedings of towns that convened to elect delegates to the state ratifying convention in DHRC V: 888–1076, esp. 897 (Adams), 972 (Ipswich), and 954 (Fryeburg).

62. Ibid., 1013–14.

63. "Marcus" in the *Massachusetts Centinel*, January 9, 1788, and "Propriety" in the *Worcester Magazine*, December 13, 1787, DHRC V: 1019, 1074.

64. Thomas Bourne to the townsmen of Sandwich, in the *Massachusetts Centinel* for January 12, in ibid., 1020.

65. Ibid., 906, 944–46, 1013.

66. Ibid., 1062, 897–98, 1014.

67. Ibid., 980, 1024–25, 944.

68. Ibid., 995–98. On Henshaw (Harvard 1773), see DHRC IV: n.1 at 101.

69. DHRC V: 995–98.

70. Ibid., 900, 1029–30 (note that there were two other towns named Sherburne in other counties). In the end, the delegates from Northampton, Easthampton, Becket, and Sherburne all voted to ratify.

71. Ibid., 1000–01.

72. Ibid., 900–03. In the end, the delegates from Belchertown and Oakham voted to reject the Constitution.

73. Ibid., 951, 1044, 1047–48, and the similar instructions for Chesterfield (Hampshire County) at 948 and Westminster (Worcester County) at 1065, including n.1.

74. Ibid., 967 (this vote was apparently meant to serve as an instruction to the town's convention delegate), 940–41, 955, 904.

75. Ibid., 904.

76. Ibid., 977, 1012, 978, 955.

77. Ibid., 1003.

78. Ibid., 968–69. Even Harvard, however, understood that the United States needed a government "adequate for the support of the Union," a standard that it apparently thought the current Confederation did not meet.

79. This and the following paragraph draw particularly upon the instructions of Belchertown (both an early and the final draft), Fryeburg, Harvard, and Townshend, ibid. 901–903, 955, 968–69, 1055–57.

80. Nathaniel Gorham to King, Charlestown, December 12, in ibid., 1074. Christopher Gore to Rufus King, December 23, 1787, (where he reported keeping a list of known opponents of the Constitution who were elected as convention delegates) and January 6, 1787, in Charles R. King, ed., *The Life and Correspondence of Rufus King*, vol. I, *1755–1794* (New York, 1894), 265, 312.

CHAPTER 6: THE MASSACHUSETTS RATIFYING CONVENTION I: THE "CONVERSATION" BEGINS

1. DHRC IV: 126, 124. For general accounts of the ratification in Massachusetts, see Samuel Bannister Harding, *The Contest over the Ratification of the Federal Constitution in the State of Massachusetts* (New York, 1896), and Michael Allen Gillespie, "Massachusetts: Creating Consensus," in Gillespie and Lienesch, 138–167.

2. "Oriental Junius" in the *Cumberland Gazette*, December 13, 1787, DHRC V: 1009. That interest did not, however, always lead to active political participation: The author castigated the town of Portland for low attendance at the meeting to replace its convention delegate, who had "declined the office."

3. Samuel P. Savage to George Thatcher, Weston, January 11, 1788; Mathew Cobb to George Thatcher, January 24; and Silas Lee to George Thatcher, February 7, in DHRC V: 692, 796, 875.

4. Gorham to Henry Knox, Boston, January 6; Christopher Gore to Rufus King, Boston, December 23, and to George Thatcher, December 23, and also January 9 in DHRC V: 629, 506–07, 505, 656; Lincoln to Washington, January 13, 1788, PGWCS VI: 23.

5. *Massachusetts Gazette*, January 18, 1788; "Cassius VI," "A Friend to Honesty," and a January 8 item from the *New Hampshire Spy* that was reprinted in the *Massachusetts Gazette* on January 18, DHRC V: 744, 501, 687, 654–55. On Massachusetts politics, see Van Beck Hall, *Politics without Parties; Massachusetts, 1780–1791* (Pittsburgh, 1972), which analyzes the shifting factions in a system of "preparty politics" but uses the terms "Federalist" and "Antifederalist" in discussing the convention as if there were two settled sides.

6. "Candidus III," January 3, 1788, in DHRC V: 609.

7. For the recommendation of "Agrippa," see ibid., 725–26.

8. Ibid., 944–46.

9. To George Thatcher, Boston, December 23, 1787, DHRC V: 505. On Gore (Harvard 1776), see DHRC IV: 434–35.

10. Dummer Sewall Journal in DHRC VII: 1517–22.

11. Ibid. and also DHRC VI: 1510, 1514.

12. DHRC VII: 1518 and convention records in DHRC VI: 1161–62.

13. DHRC V: 932. Harlow Giles Unger, *John Hancock: Merchant King and American Patriot* (New York, 2000), 309–11; William M. Fowler, Jr., *The Baron of Beacon Hill: A Biography of John Hancock* (Boston, 1980), 265–66. For a careful description of what happened to the Shaysite insurgents under the Bowdoin and Hancock administrations, see Robert A. Feer, *Shays's Rebellion* (New York and London, 1988), a 1958 Harvard Ph.D. dissertation published by Garland Press in dissertation form, esp. 413–25.

14. DHRC IV: 126.

15. King to Horatio Gates, Boston, January 30, 1788, DHRC VII: 1538–39. On Cushing, who graduated from Harvard in 1744, see DHRC IV: 433, and Rufus King to Henry Knox, Boston, October 28, DHRC IV: 155–56.

16. Boston, January 30, 1788, DHRC VII: 1561.

17. DHRC VI: 1161. On individual delegates, see DHRC IV: 437, 439, 433, and V: 897.

18. Edward Bangs to Thatcher, Worcester, January 1, 1788, DHRC V: 571, and excerpts of letters ibid., 1034–36; Samuel Henshaw to Henry Van Schaak, Northampton, October 18, and Henry Van Schaak to David Van Schaack, Pittsfield, October 31, DHRC IV: 100–01, 185, and also n.1 at 64.

19. For Maine town returns, see DHRC V: 905–06, 906–09, 940–41 (for Bristol, Lincoln County, which "voted to Except the Constitution with amendments"), 944 (Brunswick, Cumberland County, which voted 23–7 for the Constitution "as it now Stands"), 952–53, 954–56 (Fryeburg), 966–67, 975, 979–80, 994–95, 999–1000, 1007–12, 1023, 1033, 1054–55 (Topsham), 1059–62, 1063–64, 1070–71, 1072–73. For private statements explaining reservations on the Constitution, which also resemble those of people outside Maine and say nothing about separate statehood, see Nathaniel Barrell to George Thatcher, Boston, January 15, 1788 (Barrell was in Boston representing York, Maine, at the ratifying convention); Silas Lee to Thatcher, Biddeford, ME, January 23 and February 7, DHRC V: 717–19, 780–84, 874–75.

20. New York, January 14, 1788, DHRC V: 706–07.

21. DHRC IV: 155. On King, see Charles R. King, *Life and Correspondence of Rufus King* I (New York, 1894), esp. 1–15, and DHRC IV: 435. George Thatcher of Biddeford was another Federalist who worked to convince his numerous correspondents in Maine that the Constitution should be ratified. Thatcher, however, remained in New York, where he was representing Massachusetts in the Confederation Congress, and so worked mainly through written communications.

22. Gorham to King, Charlestown, December 29, 1787, DHRC V: 549.

23. DHRC V: n. 2 at 549.

24. DHRC VII: 1519 and n. 13 at 1522.

25. Ibid. Henry Jackson to Henry Knox, Boston, November 11, 1787, DHRC IV: 215, and also VI: 1108–09. Despite his reputation as a "high Federal man," Stillman might have had some doubts about the Constitution, which were resolved during the convention. See George Benson to Nicholas Brown, Boston, January 29, DHRC VII: 1557.

26. Portrait of Samuel Adams in Pauline Maier, *The Old Revolutionaries: Political Lives in the Age of Samuel Adams* (New York, 1980), 3–50.

27. To Knox, February 18, 1787, quoted in DHRC IV: n. 13 at 462, and see 453–54 for the instructions adopted on February 22 but subsequently repealed.

28. Adams to Lee, Boston, December 3, 1787, DHRC IV: 349–50. For Lee's letters to Adams, New York, October 5 and also 27, when he resubmitted the earlier letter, suspecting Adams had not received it, see DHRC XIII: 323–25 and 484–86. Adams apparently waited to reply until the legislative session ended, since his duties as president of the state senate claimed much of his time.

29. On the Boston elections, DHRC V: 909–11, 932–33; Gore to King, Boston, December 23, 1787, ibid., 506–07.

30. King to Jeremiah Wadsworth, New York, January 6, 1788, and Gore to King, Boston, January 6, DHRC V: 626, 627.

31. DHRC V: 629–33.

32. DHRC VI: 1162 and n. 2 at 1163, 1175, 1182 and n. 2 at 1183, 1189, 1346. Also Winthrop Sargent to Knox, January 12, 1788, and Jeremy Belknap to Ebenezer Hazard, January 13, both Boston, DHRC VII: 1526–28.

33. Quotation from Jeremy Belknap and Knox to Egbert Benson, New York, January 20, 1788, DHRC V: 630, 753.

34. DHRC VI: 1248 and n.1 at 1249, 1332–33 and n. 2 at 1333; William V. Wells, *The Life and Public Services of Samuel Adams* III, 2nd ed. (Freeport, NY, 1969 [orig. 1888]), 255. Benjamin Lincoln Jr., a Boston lawyer, was a contemporary of King; both graduated from Harvard in 1777 (DHRC V: n. 2 at 636, and IV: 435). For the intensity of debates on the afternoon of January 23, when the convention decided not to adjourn until the next morning so members could attend the Lincoln funeral, see below.

35. DHRC VI: 1111, 1167, 1169–74.

36. Ibid., 1107; Parsons to Michael Hodge, Boston, January 14, 1788, DHRC V: 708.

37. DHRC VI: 1183 and n.1 at 1183–84; commentary at 1128–29.

38. Ibid., 1109–10, 1163–65, 1199; Dwight Foster (a spectator) to Rebecca Foster, Boston, January 16, 1788, and Henry Jackson to Knox, Boston, January 20, DHRC VII: 1529, 1536–37. On Belknap (Harvard 1762), who had already written the first volume of *A History of New Hampshire* (1784), see DHRC IV: n.1 at 24.

39. Jackson to Knox, January 20, 1788, DHRC VII: 1536–37, n. 3 at 1538.

40. William Heath Diary, DHRC VII: 1523; DHRC V: 624–25.

41. DHRC VI: 1182; Sewall journal in DHRC VII: 1519.

42. DHRC VI: 1107; King to James Madison, Boston, January 16, 1788, DHRC VII: 1530–31.

43. King to Knox, January 27, 1788, DHRC VII: 1553; Parsons to Michael Hodge, Boston, January 14, DHRC V: 708.

44. DHRC VI: 1175–77; King to Madison, January 16, and Lincoln to Washington, January 20, 1788, DHRC VII: 1530, 1541. The convention's journal did not record the votes for and against inviting Gerry to attend; Justin Dwight said the division was 175–110, so there was a majority of 65 with 285 delegates voting, but Theodore Sedgwick said it passed by a majority of 20 in a house of about 320. DHRC VI: 1183, 1176, and VII: 1801.

45. King to Madison, January 16, 1788, DHRC VII: 1530; DHRC VI: 1177–79.

46. Ibid., 1179–80.

47. *Massachusetts Centinel*, January 26, and convention debates for January 28, ibid., 1249, 1360–61, and also 1128–1144 for an overview of sources on the Massachusetts ratifying convention. The book edition of the debates also omitted some speeches reported in the press and added others that had not been reported earlier.

48. Note that the Dwight notes published in DHRC VI are from an imperfect transcription made by a high-school student in the late 1980s, before the original manuscript was stolen from the Stone House Museum in Belchertown. Fortunately, the original was recovered after DHRC VI went to press, and a transcription of it appears as an appendix in DHRC VII: 1799–1824, which includes a description by the editors of the journal's history. That transcription should be used rather than the passages from the Dwight journal in DHRC VI. Dwight's notes are fragmentary and succinct to a fault. They say nothing of some important speeches reported at length in the press but are extremely useful for days in late January, when there are few or no other accounts of the debates. Dwight also sometimes mentions opposition speeches that went unreported elsewhere.

49. Benjamin Lincoln to Washington, Boston, January 20, 1788, DHRC VII: 1542; DHRC VI: 1184ff. with quotation (Dr. John Taylor) at 1185.

50. Ibid., 1185–86, 1189. Article V, para. 1 and 2 of the Articles of Confederation, DHRC I: 87.

51. DHRC VI: 1189–93, 1185.

52. Ibid., 1193, 1186.

53. Ibid., 1193–1209 (quotation at 1203).

54. Ibid., 1196, 1200 (from a speech that began in the morning and completed on the afternoon of January 15); DHRC VII: 1802–03.

55. DHRC VI: 1185, 1188–89, 1193, 1198. The newspaper report says Theophilus Parsons called Dench to order (1185), but Parsons's own notes say Dana called him to order and that he, Parsons, intervened against a subsequent speaker (1198).

56. Ibid., 1215, 1224–26 and 1230 (Turner), 1213–14 (Peirce), and also 1210–11 (Dr. John Taylor).

57. Ibid., 1210–11, 1217–19, 1226.

58. Ibid., 1214–15, 1218–19.

59. Ibid., 1232–33.

60. Ibid., 1236, 1240. This is one of several cases where Theophilus Parsons's notes indicate that far more delegates spoke than the newspapers recorded. Parsons said that both Abraham White and Ebenezer Peirce argued for property qualifications and put Thompson on the other side.

61. See Sedgwick to King, Boston, June 18, 1787, in King, ed., *Life and Correspondence of Rufus King* I: 224: "Every man of observation is convinced that the end of government security cannot be attained by the exercise of principles founded on democratic equality."

62. DHRC VI: 1236, 1240–41.

63. Ibid., 1241–47, quotation at 1241.

64. Ibid., esp. 1242–43, and also 1231 and 1246–47 (Holten) in Parsons's notes; the newspapers did not apparently cover Holten's speech (see 1243–46). Dwight's notes summarize the Holten speech and say that Holten also answered delegates who suggested the states might collect federal taxes levied on their people. That practice, Holten argued, would create a "power within a power" and violate federal sovereignty. DHRC VII: 1804–05.

65. DHRC VI: 1239, 1244–45.

66. Ibid., 1247–48, 1237–38.

67. Ibid., 1254–55, 1259, 1262, 1264–65. The published debates, based on the newspapers, are especially inadequate here; the notes of Jeremy Belknap and Theophilus Parsons add essential information. Only Parsons mentions skipping paragraphs. Dwight's journal is silent on the session for January 19 (DHRC VII: 1805). On Singletary, see William A. Benedict and Hiram A. Tracy, *History of the Town of Sutton, Massachusetts* (Worcester, 1873), 727–28, and DHRC IV: 437.

68. DHRC VI: 1263, and 1267–71 for Gerry's "state of facts."

69. Ibid., 1255–56.

70. Ibid., 1257, 1262, 1263.

71. Ibid., 1277–1282. The system of allocating equal representation to towns despite differences in population, which the Federalists condemned, was, of course, similar to the equal representation of states in the Senate, which they defended.

72. Ibid., 1283, 1294–95; DHRC VII: 1806.

73. DHRC VI: 1283–85, 1295.

74. Ibid., 1285–87.

75. Ibid., 1287–92, 1295–97.

76. Ibid., 1296–1305, and also, for Dana's earlier speech on the same subject, 1250–52.

77. Ibid., 1291–92, 1297–03, 1313–15.

78. Ibid., 1307, and, on Symmes, DHRC IV: n.1 at 244–45.

79. DHRC VI: 1308–11.

80. Ibid., 1309, 1311.

81. Ibid., 1324–28.

82. Ibid., 1323–24.

83. Ibid., 1332–33. For a suggestion that the motion was made to prevent Federalists from persuading more delegates to support the Constitution, see George Benson to Nicholas Brown, Boston, January 29, 1788, ibid., 1556–57.

84. Ibid., 1335–36.

85. Ibid., 1336: The motion was "negatived without a return of the house." See, however, George Benson to Nicholas Brown, Boston, January 29, 1788, DHRC VII: 1557: "A Vote was Call'd & not more than 30 appeard for the Motion."

CHAPTER 7: THE MASSACHUSETTS CONVENTION II: ". . . WITH CORDIALITY"

1. Jeremy Belknap to Ebenezer Hazard, Boston, January, 20 and 25–26, and Nathaniel Freeman Jr. to John Quincy Adams, Medford, January 27, 1788, DHRC VII: 1533–34, 1549, 1551. See also John Forbes to John Quincy Adams, Boston, January 19, ibid., 1532; and George Benson to Nicholas Brown, Boston, January 29, ibid., 1557: "I am highly pleas'd in attending the Convention & heard Parsons, Sedgwick, & King this Day with Unspeakable pleasure, tis emphatically 'a feast of reasons.'"

2. Belknap and Freeman letters cited above, and reporters' responses to Dana's eloquence at DHRC VI: 1249. On Dana, see DHRC IV: 434.

3. Forbes to John Quincy Adams, January 19, Belknap to Hazard, January 20, and King to Madison, January 27, 1788, all Boston, DHRC VII: 1532, 1533–34, 1554; and also Henry Jackson to Henry Knox, Boston, January 20, at 1537.

4. DHRC VI: 1244, 1345–46.

5. DHRC IV: 438 (Turner, Class of 1752, M.A. 1755), n.1 at 244–45 (Symmes, Class of 1780); DHRC VI: n.21 at 1294 (Kingsley, Class of 1778), n.12 at 1305 (Willard, Class of 1767).

6. DHRC VI: 1231, 1247 (quotations), n.8 at 1229 (summarizing Holten's career). Holten was probably not a great orator. On one occasion, he spoke so softly that the newspaper reporters were unable to hear him (1228), a problem, it seems, they never had with men like Francis Dana.

7. Nasson to Thatcher, January 22; King to Madison, January 23; Gorham to Madison, Lincoln to Washington, and King to Madison, all January 27, 1788, DHRC VII: 1545, 1546, 1552–55.

8. King to Madison, January 20, and to Knox, January 27, 1788, DHRC VII: 1539, 1553. See also Belknap to Hazard, January 25–26, ibid., 1547: The objections made to the Constitution "appear to arise more from an Enmity to all or any Government than from any defects in the proposed form." Those comments were, of course, out of keeping with the surviving town votes, which are not hostile toward government or amendments, which suggests that the Federalists' comprehension of their opponents was imperfect.

9. King to Horatio Gates, January 20, and to Madison, January 23, 1788; Gorham to Madison, January 27, DHRC VII: 1539, 1546, 1552.

10. DHRC VI: 1338–40, 1345.

11. Ibid., 1346–52.

12. DHRC VII: 1519, and VI: 1346 and, on Smith, n.6 at 1233. The Federalists failed to make maximum use of the speech, which also suggests it was not the result of their contriving. The text was first published in an Exeter, NH, newspaper, which received it from a private correspondent (possibly John Langdon of Portsmouth, NH) and appeared only weeks later in the

Massachusetts press. See editorial comment (and more testimonials to the speech's power) at DHRC VI: 1344–45.

13. DHRC VI: 1352–1360 (Thompson at 1353; 1359–60 on habeas corpus), and also Justin Dwight's notes at DHRC VII: 1812–13.
14. DHRC VI: 1360–63, esp. Jeremy Belknap's notes at 1361–62, and Justin Dwight's notes at DHRC VII: 1813.
15. DHRC VI: 1362.
16. DHRC VI: 1362–64, and DHRC V: n.6 at 657 on White; DHRC VII: 1814–15.
17. DHRC VI: 1363; DHRC VII: 1815–17.
18. DHRC VI: 1366–1373; DHRC VII: 1816–17, which is somewhat at odds with the published debates.
19. DHRC VII: 1817; also DHRC VI: 1373.
20. DHRC VI: 1373–75; DHRC VII: 1818. Note that Dwight includes Heath's speech in his notes for January 31, which makes more sense that the printed debates, which indicate that it was given on the morning of January 30 (DHRC VI: 1370–71). See also DHRC VI: n.11 at 1372.
21. DHRC VI: 1375–1377; DHRC VII: 1816 (Singletary) and 1818, which reports that Theophilus Parsons said "a Relig[i]ous test would answer no purpos[e] but to keep out good men" from office, "not bad men."
22. DHRC VI: 1375–55.
23. Ibid.; King to Madison, January 30, 1788, DHRC VII: 1561.
24. DHRC VI: 1362; George Benson to Nicholas Brown, Boston, January 30, 1788, DHRC VII: 1558.
25. Francis Baylies, *Eulogy on the Hon. Benjamin Russell. . . . March 10, 1845* (Boston, 1845), in DHRC VI: 1781; also Thomas C. Amory, *Life of James Sullivan with Selections from His Writings*, vol. I (Boston, 1859), 225. Hancock also had to be carried out of the hall: See contemporary newspaper account in DHRC VI: 1495–96.
26. Tristram Dalton to Michael Hodge and Gorham to Knox, Boston, January 30, 1788, DHRC VII: 1560–61. See also DHRC VI: 1119, where the editors mention Charles Jarvis and George Cabot as members along with Dalton, Gorham, Dana, King, and Parsons. Another Boston delegate, Christopher Gore, might well also have been a participant.
27. DHRC V: 806–810. On Sullivan, see Amory, *Life of James Sullivan*, esp. vol. I, passim.
28. DHRC V: 806–809.
29. DHRC V: 807 and, for an assertion that Cushing favored amendments, see the statement from a "statesman of the period" in Amory, *Sullivan* I: 223.
30. Sullivan, *Biographical Sketch of the Life and Character of His Excellency Governor Hancock* (Boston [1793]), 13–14; also Michael Gillespie, "Massachusetts: Creating Consensus," in Gillespie and Liensch, 153–54.
31. Francis Baylies to John H. Clifford, Taunton, MA, April 19, 1842; and Baylies, *Eulogy*, in DHRC VII: 1774–1777, 1780–1781.
32. Ibid., 1781.
33. King to Knox, Boston, February 3, 1788, DHRC VII: 1572. See also John Trumbull to John Adams, March 30, 1790, DHRC VI: n.49 at 1126. Trumbull said Hancock "supposed himself almost sure" of the vice-presidential position in return for his "grand manoeuvre of limping forth . . . to propose nonsensical amendments to the convention of Massachusetts," unaware "that the whole affair was planned & conducted as a political measure by men of more discernment than himself."
34. Dalton to Michael Hodge, Boston, January 30, 1788, DHRC VII: 1560–61.
35. King to Madison, Boston, January 30, 1788, DHRC VII: 1561. See also editorial comment at DHRC VI: 1116–1121.
36. Gorham to Knox, January 30, and Dalton to Hodge, January 30, 1788 (with Parsons's postscript), DHRC VII: 1560–61.
37. DHRC VI: 1377.
38. Ibid., 1377–78.
39. Ibid., 1378–79.

40. Ibid., 1379; Henry Jackson to Knox, February 3, 1788, DHRC VII: 1570.
41. DHRC VI: 1386–87, 1380–84.
42. Ibid., 1381–82 (from the convention journal).
43. Belknap to Hazard, February 3, 1788, and Minot's journal in DHRC VII: 1566, 1599. Also Theophilus Parsons (son of the delegate), *Memoir of Theophilus Parsons, Chief Justice of the Massachusetts Supreme Judicial Court* . . . (Boston, 1859), 71–76, which insists that Parsons wrote the amendments; and also the account of Colonel Joseph May, who found a copy of the amendments in Parsons' hand among Hancock's papers, in William V. Wells, *The Life and Public Services of Samuel Adams* III (Freeport, NY, 1969 [orig. 1888]), 258–60.
44. May's account and also the testimony of Joseph Vinal, who said he saw Hancock and Adams in conversation with a Federalist committee, in Wells, *Adams* III: 258–260. Wells said that a copy of the amendments in the handwriting of someone who served as an amanuensis for Adams (whose hands sometimes trembled too much for him to write), with interlineations in Adams's handwriting, was found among Adams's papers (259). James Sullivan's grandson Thomas C. Amory discovered another copy of the amendments in James Sullivan's handwriting among Sullivan's papers. Amory claimed that Benjamin Russell, who attended the convention to take notes for his *Massachusetts Centinel*, said that Hancock read his amendments at the convention from a copy in Sullivan's handwriting. However, Amory also cited "a statesman of the period, who had abundant opportunity of knowing the truth," in arguing that the amendments were the result of negotiations and that it was "very immaterial" in whose handwriting they finally appeared. Amory, *Sullivan* I: 223–24. Another account, from 1789, probably by Stephen Higginson, a political opponent of Hancock, denied that Hancock had any hand in defining the amendments: See "The Writings of Laco" in DHRC VII: 1771–72. For a general discussion of the amendments' preparation and subsequent testimony on that issue, see DHRC VI: 1118–1121.
45. For a good statement of the case that Hancock and others in his circle, along with Adams, had an active and perhaps a primary role in formulating the amendments, see Gillespie, "Massachusetts: Creating Consensus," esp. 153–56.
46. Dalton to Stephen Hooper, January 31, 1788, DHRC VII: 1563; DHRC VI: 1380–85.
47. DHRC VI: 1385 and 1401; George Benson to Nicholas Brown, February 3, 1788, DHRC VII: 1567. Belknap's journal suggests there was a far more complicated argument after Hancock spoke on January 31 than either the newspapers or Benson indicate: See DHRC VI: 1386.
48. DHRC VI: 1390–1407.
49. DHRC VI: 1407 and, on Whitney, who was "an active Shaysite sympathizer," n.2 at 1407, and account by Dalton, February 3, DHRC VII: 1569. See also editorial comment at DHRC VI: 1410–11, and Lincoln to Washington, February 3, 1788, DHRC VII: 1573.
50. Sewall's journal at DHRC VII: 1520; convention journal at DHRC VI: 1406.
51. Sullivan to John Langdon, Belknap to Hazard, Gore to Thatcher, and King to Madison, all February 3, 1788, DHRC VII: 1574, 1566, 1569, 1572; and also Dalton to Stephen Hooper, January 31, at 1563: "I tremble at the approach, and dread the feelings I shall have when the Names and Answers are called and markd! Yea—Yea, Nay—Nay—says the Scripture! Heaven will determine in our favor, unless we deserve Ruin." For Belknap's text, from Deuteronomy 30:19, n.2 at 1567; for Dalton's, Matthew 5:37, n.3 at 1563.
52. Van Schaack to Theodore Sedgwick, Pittsfield, MA, February 4, 1788, DHRC VII: 1577–78 and n.1–3 at 1577–78. The New York legislature actually called a ratifying convention before learning that Massachusetts had voted to ratify.
53. Jackson to Knox, February 3, 1788, DHRC VII: 1571.
54. DHRC VI: 1412–15.
55. Ibid., 1410–1412.
56. Ibid., 1421–23. An earlier, eloquent argument for ratification by the Reverend Thomas Thacher, the pastor of Dedham's Third Congregational Church, came before the committee presented its report: ibid., 1415–21. Dwight's notes, DHRC VII: 1819, do not mention Backus's speech but briefly summarizes Thacher's.
57. DHRC VI: 1423–24, 1444.

58. Ibid., 1424–26, 1446.

59. Ibid., 1428, 1373; George Benson to Nicholas Brown, January 30, and Henry to Peter Van Schaack, February 4, 1788, DHRC VII: 1558, 1575–76. Stoughton vote in DHRC V: 1043–44.

60. DHRC VI: 1444–48.

61. Ibid., 1448–50.

62. Ibid., 1442–43, 1451–52; Jackson to Knox, February 6, Backus's convention journal, Lincoln to Washington, February 6, 1788, and Dwight's journal in DHRC VII: 1581, 1596, 1582, 1819–20.

63. DHRC VI: 1452–53, 1395; Belknap to Hazard, February 10, 1788, DHRC VII: 1584.

64. DHRC VI: 1454–61; Ephraim Ward to Enos Hitchcock, Brookfield, MA, March 2, 1788, DHRC VII: 1591.

65. Jackson to Knox and Sewall journal, both February 6, DHRC VII: 1580, 1520. The word "Sellar" perhaps referred not to the basement (or "cellar," in the modern sense) but to an upper room of the church.

66. Clifford K. Shipton, *Sibley's Harvard Graduates: Biographical Sketches of Those Who Attended Harvard College* XIII (Boston, 1965), 293–99 (quotations at 295).

67. DHRC VI: 1471–75, and n.1 at 1277 on Turner, n.2 at 1208 on Southworth.

68. DHRC VII: 1820–21.

69. DHRC VI: 1475–76.

70. Sewall's journal and Widgery to Thatcher, February 9, 1788, DHRC VII: 1520, 1690. On the vote taking and recording, see DHRC VI: 1461–63. The convention secretary, George Minot, arranged the "yea" and "nay" votes in separate columns—see 1463–67—but the list on 1479–87 represents more faithfully how the vote was taken.

71. *Massachusetts Gazette*, February 8, 1788, DHRC VII: 1611.

72. DHRC VI: 1484–86; and, on Baptists, n.3 at 1460–61, and also Backus diary, DHRC VII: 1594.

73. DHRC VIII: n.2 at 426, reporting on a March 7, 1788, debate by the Virginia Baptist General Committee in Goochland County, Virginia. Baptists also shared other objections: See the Reverend John Leland's objections to the Constitution, ibid., 425–26 and n.4 at 426–27.

74. County breakdowns in DHRC VI: 1479–87. Suffolk County, which included Boston, voted in favor 34–5, Essex 38–6, Plymouth 21–6, Barnstable (Cape Cod) 7–2. Only Dukes County—the island of Martha's Vineyard—had no "nay" votes: It cast both of its two votes for ratification.

75. Caleb Gibbs to Washington, Boston, February 9, and Knox to Washington, New York, February 10, 1788, DHRC VII: 1687, 1587. Gibbs had been one of Washington's bodyguards during the Revolution and fought at Yorktown. Curiously, he himself seems to have been in some financial difficulty: See n.1 at 1687–88. See also the statement of Nathaniel Barrell, the delegate from York, ME, who changed his mind in the course of the convention and voted "yea," on the character of the opposition in a letter to George Thatcher, York, February 20, 1788, DHRC VII, 1589–90: There were "various sorts of opposers . . . all of them dangerous," including Loyalists, debtors, "honest ignorant minds" who fear for their liberties, and "not a few of those Insurgents" who "want no Government but . . . Anarchy." He said the minority, with which he mingled, was "a set of the most unprincipled of men."

76. New York, February 10, 1788, DHRC VII: 1587. See also Dalton to John Langdon, February 6; Lincoln to Washington, February 9, 1788; and also John Quincy Adams's account of Theophilus Parsons's stories from the convention, which notes that Parsons's emphasis on "the formidable opposition . . . naturally enhances the merit of the victory." Ibid., 1579, 1688, 1690–91.

77. Backus diary and Dalton to Stephen Hooper, Boston, January 31, 1788, DHRC VII: 1594, 1563.

78. Adams's diary, Newburyport, February 11, 1788, DHRC VII: 1690–91.

79. DHRC VI: 1487–89.

80. Ibid., 1494.

81. DHRC VII: 1648. The same statement appeared in other Boston newspapers: See DHRC VI: 1494 and n.5 at 1497.

82. DHRC VI: 1492–94; DHRC VII: 1657–58. Also house resolution, March 29, and George Cabot to Nathan Dane, May 9, 1788, DHRC VII: 1662, 1663.

83. DHRC VI: 1495, for the convention resolution, and also DHRC VII: 1628–29, including n.2. On February 8 an unofficial proclamation by "THE PEOPLE" announced the change in name. The convention had, however, already referred to "Federal Street" the day before.

84. DHRC VI: 1495–97.

85. DHRC VII: 1613–14 (descriptions by newspapers and Henry Jackson); Jeremiah Hill to Thatcher, Biddeford, MA, February 14, and Widgery to Thatcher, February 9, 1788, ibid., 1696, 1690.

86. DHRC VII: 1664–66.

87. Jeremiah Hill to Thatcher, February 14, and Belknap to Hazard, February 10, 1788, DHRC VII: 1696, 1584. Hill's statement, like so many others by delegates to the Massachusetts convention, had a scriptural basis: Revelation 12 (n.3 at 1697).

88. Convention payroll report in DHRC VI: 1498–1514, which lists the amount due to Bachus as "9.16.0" (nine pounds, sixteen shillings). The list also included payments to the convention's secretary, George Minot, a messenger, and the sexton of Long Lane Congregational Church, and bonus pay to some officials, particularly Hancock and Cushing, who presided over the convention. Backus's diary, February 8; Backus to Susanna Backus, February 1, 1788, and Dwight's journal, DHRC VII: 1596, 1564, 1821–22.

89. DHRC VII: 1520, and, for other descriptions, 1615–23.

90. Ibid., including Heath at 1623.

91. Ibid., 1520–21.

92. Ibid.

CHAPTER 8: A ROUGH ROAD TO RICHMOND: NEW HAMPSHIRE, RHODE ISLAND, MARYLAND, AND SOUTH CAROLINA

1. Washington to John Jay, January 20, 1788, to Madison, February 5, and to John O'Connor, March 30, all Mount Vernon, PGWCS VI: 49–50, 184.

2. Madison to Washington, New York, January 20, 25, and 28, and February 3, 1788, ibid., 51–52, 60–61, 72–73, 82–83.

3. Washington to Madison, February 5, 1788, ibid., 89.

4. Madison to Washington, February 15; Washington to Henry Knox, March 3, to Benjamin Lincoln, February 29, and to Madison, March 2, and to Jay, March 3, 1788, ibid., 115, 140, 134, 136–37, 139.

5. Washington to Jonathan Trumbull Jr., February 5, and Madison to Washington, February 8, 1788, ibid., 92–93, 101–02.

6. Caleb Gibbs to Washington, Boston, February 9; Knox to Washington, New York, February 15, and Madison to Washington, New York, February 14, 1788, ibid., 103, 114, 115. See also Lawrence Guy Straus, "Reactions of Supporters of the Constitution to the Adjournment of the New Hampshire Ratification Convention—1788," *Historical New Hampshire* XXIII no. 3 (Autumn 1968), 38 and n. 10 at 47.

7. Washington to Knox, March 3, and to Jay, March 3; Caleb Gibbs to Washington, Boston, February 9, 1788, PGWCS VI: 140, 139, 101, 103.

8. Washington to Madison, February 5, 1788, ibid., 89.

9. James to Ambrose Madison, New York, November 8, 1787, DHRC IX: 597; Madison to Washington, February 20, PGWCS VI: 123. For letters urging Madison to stand for election to the convention, see DHRC VIII: 196 and 302 (Archibald Stuart, December 2 and January 14), 224 (Henry Lee, December 7), 284 (Edmund Randolph, January 3); and 424–26 (Joseph Spencer, February 28) on the obstacles Madison faced in gaining a convention seat from Orange; also DHRC IX: 595–601 for letters urging Madison to return to Virginia.

10. Washington to Madison, March 2, 1788, PGWCS VI:137. Madison left for Orange County in early March, stopping at Mount Vernon on the way: See ibid., n.1 at 141.

11. Jere Daniell, "Ideology and Hardball: Ratification of the Federal Constitution in New Hampshire," in Conley and Kaminski, esp. 181–83, and, for a more detailed account (with

references), Daniell, *Experiment in Republicanism: New Hampshire Politics and the American Revolution, 1741–1794* (Cambridge, MA, 1970), 95–179, 210.

12. Daniell, *Experiment in Republicanism*, 145–62, 198.

13. Ibid., 208–212.

14. Ibid., 212–213; Lynn Warren Turner, *The Ninth State: New Hampshire's Formative Years* (Chapel Hill and London, 1983), 70–71, and Albert Stillman Batchellor, ed., *Early State Papers of New Hampshire* XXI (Concord, NH, 1892), 157–61, 165, 151–52 for the legislative records.

15. Langdon to Washington, Portsmouth, NH, February 28, and also Tobias Lear to Washington, June 2, 1788, PGWCS VI: 132, 307. Turner, *Ninth State*, 71–72; Daniell, *Experiment in Republicanism*, 213. As an example of the campaign against instructions, see "A Federalist," *New-Hampshire Recorder*, February 5, 1788, p. 1.

16. The most precise study of town actions (and also convention voting) is Jere Daniell, "Counting Noses: Delegate Sentiment in New Hampshire's Ratifying Convention," *Historical New Hampshire* XLIII, no. 2 (Summer 1988), 136–55, esp. 141–49, which includes a detailed, town-by-town table, based on a careful study of the documentary record. Some delegates were instructed by town vote, others by a committee appointed by the town; in either case, Daniell shows, delegates took their instructions very seriously. See also Daniell, *Experiment in Republicanism*, 213–14, n.13 at 213, and "Ideology and Hardball," 190. John Sullivan put the number of towns that instructed their delegates at thirty, though he suggested incorrectly that all were instructed to vote against ratification: Sullivan to the Reverend Jeremy Belknap, Durham, NH, February 26, 1788, in Otis G. Hammond, ed., *Letters and Papers of Major-General John Sullivan* III, 1779–1795 (Concord, New Hampshire, 1939), 567.

17. Convention records in Nathaniel Bouton, ed., *New Hampshire Provincial and State Papers* X (Concord, NH, 1877), 12–14; and Daniell, "Ideology and Hardball," 191–93.

18. Bouton, *New Hampshire Provincial and State Papers* X, 13–14; Daniell, "Ideology and Hardball," 192–93.

19. The one speech, by John Sullivan, is in Hammond, *Sullivan Papers* III: 569–71, where it's dated March 1788, which is the date of its first publication in the *Freeman's Oracle*. For a few more fragmentary reports on the debates gathered mainly from newspapers, see Daniell, *Experiment in Republicanism*, 214; Bouton, *New Hampshire Provincial and State Papers* X, 14; Daniell, "Ideology and Hardball," 193; also Joseph B. Walker, *Birth of the Federal Constitution: A History of the New Hampshire Convention. . . . 1788* (Boston, 1888), 3–5 on the paucity of sources, and passim on the convention.

20. Bouton, *New Hampshire Provincial and State Papers* X, 14–15, and Daniell, "Ideology and Hardball," 193. The New Hampshire constitution of 1784 in Francis Newton Thorpe, ed., *The Federal and State Constitutions . . .* IV (Washington, 1909), 2460–63, 2465, 2467.

21. *New Hampshire Spy*, February 22, 1788.

22. Langdon to Washington, February 28, PGWCS VI: 132–33, and the similar account in Sullivan to the Reverend Jeremy Belknap, Durham, NH, February 26, 1788, in Hammond, *Sullivan Papers* III: 567 (but note that Sullivan claimed that thirty delegates who were bound by instructions to vote against ratification said their convictions had changed, which was unlikely since it would have included virtually all instructed delegates); Walker, *New Hampshire Convention*, 27–30. The best analysis of the vote for adjournment is Daniell, "Counting Noses," esp. 150–152 (*Spy* citation at 150).

23. Langdon to Washington, February 28, PGWCS VI: 132; Sullivan to Belknap, February 26, 1788, in Hammond, *Sullivan Papers* III, 566.

24. Langdon to Washington, February 28, and Knox to Washington, New York, March 10, 1788, PGWCS VI: 133, 150–51.

25. Gilman to Sullivan, New York, March 22, 1788, in Batchellor, *Early State Papers of New Hampshire* XXI, 845.

26. Ibid.; Madison to Edmund Randolph, New York, March 3, and to Washington, March 3, 1788, PJM X: 554–56.

27. Washington to Knox, March 30, 1788, PGWCS VI: 183.

28. Ibid.

29. "Editors' Note" on "The Raising of the First Three Pillars" (and later ones) in DHRC V: 524–26, and *Massachusetts Centinel*, February 27, 1788.

30. Patrick T. Conley, "First in War, Last in Peace: Rhode Island and the Constitution, 1786–1790," in Conley and Kaminski, 269–94, esp. 272–75, including a copy of the general assembly's vote calling for a referendum on 275. This essay was also published separately, under the same title, as a richly illustrated pamphlet ([Providence] 1987). See also John P. Kaminski, "Rhode Island: Protecting State Interests," in Gillespie and Lienesh, 368–390, and, for a more detailed account, Irwin H. Polishook, *Rhode Island and the Union, 1774–1795* (Evanston, IL, 1969), esp. 198–99, on the assembly's decision for a referendum.

31. "Report of the Committee appointed by the General Assembly relative to accepting the new Constitution of the United States," in John Russell Bartlett, ed., *Records of the State of Rhode Island and Providence Plantations* X, 1784 to 1792 (Providence, 1865), 275. The figures in secondary accounts, except for Polishook, *Rhode Island*, 199, differ slightly (and Polishook says the vote in Little Compton was 63–52 rather than 63–57). Conley, "First in War," 274, says it was 243–2711, and Kaminski, "Rhode Island," 379, gives it as 239–2711. See also William R. Staples, *Rhode Island in the Continental Congress* (Providence, 1870), 589–608, which includes Governor John Collins to the president of Congress, April 5, 1788, announcing the result, the names of voters on both sides in each of the towns, and petitions for a convention. The total referendum vote was unusually low, in part because of the boycotts: 4,287 voters participated in the spring gubernatorial election of 1787 (ibid., 606).

32. Kaminski, "Rhode Island," 368–75, and Polishook, *Rhode Island*, 103–29.

33. Ibid., including Polishook, 127, on the paper money's loss of value, and also 157–61 for evidence that the use of paper money to defraud private creditors was relatively modest and not central to its purpose, and that merchants, who opposed paper money, also used it, even to retire debts, which suggests the system "might not have been so dastardly" as its mercantile critics claimed.

34. Conley, "First in War," 279–85; Polishook, *Rhode Island*, 22–23, on the state's government.

35. Madison to Edmund Randolph, New York, March 3, 1788, DHRC IX: 602, and n.30 at 605.

36. On the weather see, for example, John Page to Jefferson, March 7, and Richard Henry Lee's comment to Samuel Adams, April 23, 1788, DHRC IX: 591, 765. Madison to Eliza House Trist, Orange, March 25, ibid., 603; Joseph Spencer to Madison, Orange County, February 28, DHRC VIII: 424–26, including n.4; Tobias Lear to John Langdon, Mount Vernon, April 3, DHRC IX:, 699. Also Richard R. Beeman, *Patrick Henry: A Biography* (New York, 1974), 132–33.

37. DHRC IX: 581–82, including Carrington to Knox, Fredericksburg, VA, January 12, 1788; also Mason to Washington, Gunston Hall, October 7, DHRC VIII: 43.

38. Nicholas to Madison, Charlottesville, April 5, 1788, DHRC IX: 703.

39. Madison to Washington, New York, October 18, 1787, DHRC VIII: 77; Henry to Washington, Richmond, October 19, PGWCS V: 384.

40. DHRC VIII: 110–20, and 525 on Corbin.

41. Ibid., and, on Marshall, 527; Leonard Baker, *John Marshall: A Life in Law* (New York and London, 1974), 4 and passim.

42. DHRC VIII: 118 and n.11–12 at 119–20. In the colonial period, candidates needed only to own the requisite amount of land in a county to qualify as a freeholder; they did not need to live there. Men could also vote in any county where they qualified as freeholders. See John Gilman Kolp, *Gentlemen and Freeholders: Electoral Politics in Colonial Virginia* (Baltimore and London, 1998), 15, 34, 40. The 1776 state constitution, however, required that members of both houses of the legislature be resident freeholders of their districts: DHRC VIII: 533–34.

43. DHRC VIII: 183–93.

44. Ibid., and Stuart to Madison, Richmond, December 2, 1787, ibid., 195–96.

45. Beeman, *Henry*, 1–3.

46. Ibid., 4–10.

47. Ibid., 11–32, 110, and Stan. V. Henkels, "Jefferson's Recollections of Patrick Henry," *Pennsylvania Magazine of History and Biography* XXXIV (1910), 385–418, esp. Jefferson to William Wirt, Monticello, August 4, 1805, 386–88, 390–91. Jefferson recalled that Henry "said the strongest things in the finest language, but without logic, without arrangement, desultorily" (390), and yet, it seems, very effectively. See also Jefferson's description of Henry's defense of the Virginia Resolves (1765) in the house of burgesses, cited in William Wirt Henry, *Patrick Henry: Life, Correspondence, and Speeches* I (New York, 1891), 83: "He appeared to me to speak as Homer wrote."

48. Beeman, *Henry*, 25, citing St. George Tucker, Spencer Roane, and Peter Lyons; Henkels, "Jefferson's Recollections," 390–93. DHRC VIII: 526.

49. Beeman, *Henry*, 129–34; Jefferson to Madison, Paris, December 8, 1784, *Republic of Letters* I: 353–54. Parts of the passage were written in cipher (i.e. code).

50. Jefferson to Madison, Paris, December 20, 1787, *Republic of Letters* I: 512–14; Dumas Malone, *Jefferson and the Rights of Man*, vol. II (Boston, 1951), 162–72.

51. Beeman, *Henry*, 132–33; Jefferson to William Wirt, Monticello, August 4, 1805, in Henkels, "Jefferson's Reflections," 387.

52. Madison to Randolph, New York, January 10, 1788, and Lear to John Langdon, Mount Vernon, December 3, 1787, in DHRC VIII: 289, 197.

53. DHRC VIII: 309 and IX: 755. Carrington's logic was not altogether persuasive: "I cannot learn that he [Henry] has ever specified the amendments he would have, and therefore, it is fairly to be concluded, his views are a dismemberment of the Union." Carrington to Knox, February 10, 1788, DHRC IX, 606.

54. Madison to Jefferson, New York, December 9, 1787, DHRC VIII: 226–28.

55. For a forceful and persuasive argument in support of this observation, see Jon Kukla, "A Spectrum of Sentiments: Virginia's Federalists, Antifederalists, and 'Federalists Who are For Amendments,' 1787–1788," *Virginia Magazine of History and Biography* XCVI (1988), 277–96.

56. Madison to Jefferson, New York, December 9, 1787, and also to Archibald Stuart, December 14, 1787, and to Edmund Pendleton, February 21, 1788, DHRC VIII: 227, 238, 398.

57. William Short to Thomas Lee Shippen, Paris, May 31, 1788, DHRC IX: 895, and George Lee Tuberville to Madison, Richmond, VA, December 11, 1787, DHRC VIII: 234.

58. Edward Carrington to Henry Knox, Manchester, VA, February 10, DHRC IX: 606. Madison, however, was not so happy about the prospect of instructions from Kentucky, since they were more likely to lock delegates into voting against ratification: Madison to John Brown, Orange, May 27, 1788, DHRC IX: 884.

59. On Virginia elections, see Kolp, *Gentlemen and Freeholders*, and Charles S. Sydnor, *Gentlemen Freeholders: Political Practices in Washington's Virginia* (Chapel Hill, 1952). Although both books concentrate on colonial elections, Sydnor includes several examples from the 1780s and 1790s (though none from the 1788 elections of convention delegates). The practices they describe often persisted into the early nineteenth century. Surviving March 1788 election records, along with letters and other relevant sources, are collected in DHRC IX: 561–631. For an excellent overview of Virginia government and political culture, see Richard R. Beeman, *The Varieties of Political Experience in Eighteenth-Century America* (Philadelphia, 2004), 31–68.

60. Madison to Jefferson, New York, December 9, 1787, DHRC VIII: 227. On the public's interest, see, for example a letter from Alexandria, March 26, 1788, DHRC IX, 585: "Politics engross the attention of all ranks of people here." About the only contrary report came from Boutetourt County in the mountainous west, where an observer said, "We have few Politicians, nor do the People seem to concern themselves much about the New federal Constitution." William Fleming to Thomas Madison, Belmont, Botetourt County, February 19, 1788, DHRC VIII: 383.

61. Carrington to Madison, Manchester, VA, February 10, DHRC VIII: 359, and to Knox, February 10, 1788, DHRC IX: 606.

62. David Stuart to Washington, Abingdon, VA, February 17, 1788, DHRC IX: 583–84.

63. DHRC VIII: 23–24. See also the endorsement of the Constitution by a meeting "of a respectable number of the inhabitants of Berkeley County," who, in one version of their resolutions, seemed to covenant with each other to work for ratification. Ibid., 22 and n.1.

64. DHRC VIII: 39–40 (and n.2 at 40: Williamsburg freeholders also expressed their views on several other issues), 91–93, 85–86. See also an item of January 18, calling a public meeting at the courthouse in Frederick, where people could state objections to the Constitution and give its supporters a chance to answer them, in DHRC IX: 588.

65. DHRC IX: 615–17. The depositions were taken because of a furor that arose after the candidate, Cole Digges, voted for ratification without previous amendments.

66. DHRC IX: 611–13. The objections correspond closely with those Monroe mentioned in a rather wordy pamphlet he wrote after the election. See ibid., 844–77.

67. Randolph's recollection, June 9; letter from Virginia in the *Maryland Journal*, April 11, 1788, DHRC IX: 593, 736, and, for Monroe, 844–77. Monroe said he suppressed his pamphlet because the printed version was delayed and "incorrectly made," and the argument seemed to him too "loosely drawn." He also doubted the propriety of "interfering with the subject in that manner in that late stage of the business." Ibid., 845.

68. Item on Mason's speech in Philadelphia *Independent Gazetteer*, April 4, 1788 (which explained that "it is usual for candidates for a seat in the public bodies in Virginia, which are in the gift of the people, to declare their sentiments by making a short speech on the election ground"); Madison to Eliza House Trist, Orange, March 25; John Page to Jefferson, Rosewell, March 7, in DHRC IX: 614, 603, 590–91.

69. Edward Carrington to Madison, Richmond, April 8; John Blair Smith to Madison, to Hampden Sydney, June 12; and Hugh Williamson to John Gray Blount, New York, June 3, 1788, DHRC IX: 606–09. On Grayson's speech, see also John Vaughan to John Dickinson, Philadelphia, April 19, ibid., 603–04.

70. Account of Littleton Waller Tazewell, who said he was "reciting a Greek lesson" to Wythe when the procession arrived, in DHRC IX: 622–26.

71. Nicholas to Madison, Charlottesville, April 5; Randolph to Madison, Richmond, April 17; Lee to Washington, Richmond, April 11; Washington to Thomas Johnson, Mount Vernon, April 20, DHRC IX: 703, 741, 735, 743; and see also Madison to Jefferson, Orange, April 22, 1788, at 744: The returns so far make it seem "probable, though not absolutely certain that a majority of the members elect[ed] are friends to the Constitution."

72. See the excellent brief summary in Lance Banning, "Virginia: Sectionalism and the General Good" in Gillespie and Lienesch, 263–68, and DHRC XIII: 149–52.

73. DHRC IX: 704. Both James Monroe and William Grayson, who became critics of the Constitution, were Virginia congressmen at the time and registered powerful arguments against changing Jay's instructions. Madison, however, was no less a defender of Virginia's interests: see DHRC VIII: xxx, and Banning, "Virginia," 266–67.

74. William Waller Hening, ed., *The Statutes at Large . . . of Virginia* XII (Richmond, 1833), 242. George Morgan Chinn, *Kentucky: Settlement and Statehood, 1750–1800* (Frankfort, KY, 1975), 442–54; Lowell H. Harrison, *Kentucky's Road to Statehood* (Lexington, KY, 1992), esp. 55–57; Patricia Watlington, *The Partisan Spirit: Kentucky Politics, 1779–1792* (New York, 1972), 80, 106–32, 147–56.

75. Madison to Nicholas, Orange, April 8; Brown to Madison, New York, May 12, 1788, DHRC IX: 709, 794; also, for background material on the Kentucky issue in Congress and on Brown, DHRC VIII: n.2 at 330–31, 525. See also Brown to Madison, June 7, 1788, PJM XI: 88–90, in which he says that Alexander Hamilton led the opposition "from an apprehension that a compliance might embarrass the New Constitution" and was supported by all the "eastern" states—i.e., New England—"least it might add to the Southern Interest." Brown presumed that, if Congress failed to act, which seemed almost certain, Kentucky would declare its independence and remain outside the union. Although he didn't mention it, a separate alliance with Spain was a possibility in that case. He had avoided writing Kentucky's delegates in Richmond, he said, for fear his irritation at Congress's inaction would essentially harden their opposition to ratification.

76. Ann Price, "Notes on the Political Club of Danville and Its Members," *Filson Club History Quarterly* XXXV (1961), 333–52; Thomas Speed, *The Political Club, Danville, Kentucky, 1786–1790* (Louisville, 1894), 19–30 on Danville, and passim on the political club and its members, esp. 143–51 for its debates on the Constitution. Curiously, the club seems to have conceded that navigation of the Mississipi was not an "immediate" imperative for Kentucky's development: See 107–11. DHRC VIII: 408–17, 433–36.

77. Madison to Brown, Orange, April 9; Brown to Madison, New York, May 12 (acknowledging receipt of letters of April 9 and also April 21, which has been lost); Madison to Nicholas, Orange, May 17, 1788, DHRC IX: 711–12, 793, 804–11, and also Nicholas to Madison, Charlottesville, April 4 and May 9, asking for written information for use in Kentucky, at 704 (and n.7 at 705), 793.

78. Brown to Madison, New York, May 12, 1788, DHRC IX: 793–94. On Muter and Innes, see Speed, *Political Club*, 47–50, 42–45. Innes's brother James was attorney general of Virginia and a member of the Virginia ratifying convention. Innes to Brown, February 20, cited in Watlington, *Partisan Spirit*, 149–50.

79. Madison to Brown, Orange, May 27, 1788, DHRC IX: 884. Watlington, *Partisan Spirit*, 150, suggests that the opponents of the Constitution, who were members of a "court party" in Kentucky politics, "abandoned the idea of instructions once a majority of antifederalist delegates was elected" in the district. On the revised delegate count, see Henry Knox to Jeremiah Wadsworth, New York, April 27, DHRC IX: 761–62 and n.2 at 762, which explains that this "statement" of votes probably came from David Henley, a Virginia commissioner to Congress charged with settling expenses due to Virginia for defending and maintaining the Northwest Territory before Virginia ceded the area to the United States. Henley, however, listed 85 Federalists, 66 opponents of ratification, and 3 neutrals.

80. F. Claiborne Johnston, Jr., "Federalist, Doubtful, and Antifederalist; A Note on the Virginia Convention of 1788," *Virginia Magazine of History and Biography* XLVI (1988), 333–44, esp. 337, which speculates that Nicholas sent the account to Edward Carrington, who had gone to New York, and Carrington gave it to Henley. Madison to Washington, Orange County, April 10, 1788, PGM XI: 20.

81. Carrington to Jefferson, New York, April 24, 1788, DHRC IX: 755. Kukla, "A Spectrum of Sentiments," esp. 283–91, which discusses who were in the category of those favoring amendments. He includes Edmund Pendleton, whom Madison had put with those who were for ratification without amendments, as well as Mason, Randolph, Richard Henry Lee, James Monroe, John Dawson, and possibly George Wythe.

82. Kukla, "A Spectrum of Sentiments," 283–4 (Pendleton), 287–88 (Randolph), 289–90 (R.H. Lee), 293 (Benjamin Harrison). Commercial regulation was apparently of more interest to these Virginians than Congress's power with regard to slavery or the slave trade, on which the federal Convention made concessions—to satisfy delegates from Georgia and South Carolina—in return for the simple majority on commercial laws. John Tyler, another delegate who favored amendments, particularly condemned the "wicked clause" allowing the slave trade to continue until 1808: Ibid., 293.

83. Carrington to William Short, April 25, 1788, DHRC IX: 758. See also Madison to Washington, April 10, ibid., 732: He had seen only a partial list of delegates, and, "being unacquainted with the political characters of many of them, I am a very incompetent prophet of the fate of the Constitution."

84. Nicholas to Madison, Charlottesville, April 5, 1788, DHRC IX: 703.

85. Madison to Washington, Orange, April 10, and Griffin to Madison, New York, April 28, 1788, DHRC IX: 732–33, n.6 at 733, 764. Most of these letters have been lost: See PJM XI: 21, which tentatively identifies the "friend" as Charles Pinckney.

86. DHRC IX: 732–33, 743–44. Johnson later denied a report that he had resented Washington's intervention: Edward S. Delaplaine, *The Life of Thomas Johnson* (New York, 1927), 458–60.

87. McHenry to Washington, Baltimore, April 20; Washington to McHenry, Mount Vernon, April 27, 1788, PGWCS VI: 219, 234–35.

88. On the ratification contest in Maryland, see L. Marx Renzulli, Jr., *Maryland: The Federalist Years* (Rutherford, Madison, and Teaneck, NJ, 1972), chapter 2, 50–103, esp. 57–60; Philip A. Crowl, "Anti-Federalism in Maryland, 1787–1788," WMQ IV (1947), 446–69, esp. 450, 458–59; Crowl, *Maryland During and After the Revolution* (Baltimore, 1943); and Gregory Stiverson, "Necessity, the Mother of Union; Maryland and the Constitution, 1785–89," in Conley and Kaminski, 131–52.

89. Renzulli, *Maryland*, 60–79 (citing *Pennsylvania Gazette* at 78); Crowl, "Anti-Federalism in Maryland," 449, 459; Stiverson, "Necessity, the Mother of Union," 146. Jenifer to Washington, Annapolis, April 15, PGWCS VI: 210 and n.1 at 211 with a somewhat garbled version of Washington's reply of April 27; Randolph to Madison, Richmond, April 17, 1788, DHRC IX: 741. Edward C. Papenfuse, Jr., "The 'Amending Fathers' and the Constitution" in Robert J. Haws, ed., *The South's Role in the Creation of the Bill of Rights* (Jackson, MS, and London, 1991), 67–68, notes that even in the most hotly contested elections in Maryland, only about 42 percent of voters participated. Moreover, the high property requirements imposed under Maryland's constitution limited the electorate to about 66 percent of free white males over twenty-one, so that figure represented only a small minority of adult white males. Forrest McDonald in *We the People: The Economic Origins of the Constitution* (Chicago, 1958) claims that the turnout in convention elections was larger than normal, but he bases his analysis on the turnout in six contested constituencies without consideration of the fact that most elections elsewhere—some three-quarters of the total—were uncontested (see 149 and n.79). Popular interest was, of course, greater when elections were contested.

90. From an account of the convention by Alexander Contee Hanson, which Hanson said was reviewed by two other members of the Federalist majority, and which Hanson sent to Madison from Annapolis on June 2, 1788, in *Documentary History of the Constitution of the United States of America, 1786–1870*, IV (Washington, 1905), 645–64, esp. 650. Volume II of that *Documentary History of the Constitution* (Washington, 1894), 97–122, reprints the convention's journal, including a copy of the Constitution and Maryland's form of ratification. Hanson's account was originally designed to answer an earlier narrative of the convention by delegates most of whom voted against ratification: See "A Fragment of Facts, Disclosing the Conduct of the Maryland Convention, on the Adoption of the Federal Constitution" in an "Address to the People of Maryland," [misdated] April 21, 1788, in Jonathan Elliot, ed., *The Debates in the Several State Conventions on the Adoption of the Federal Constitution . . .* II (2nd ed., Philadelphia, 1863), 547–56. These sources generally agree on the course of the convention until its end, and the information they offer on what occurred is more complementary than contradictory. The journal, however, suggests that the convention concluded on Monday, April 28, when the members signed the ratification instrument, but Hanson (660) indicates that it adjourned on Tuesday, April 29. Thomas Lloyd, the shorthand specialist who published the (incomplete) debates of the Pennsylvania convention, attended the Maryland convention and took notes but never published them, at least in part because the speeches were almost all by critics of the Constitution, whom Federalists refused to answer. Members of the Maryland majority compensated him for his expense. See Marion Tinling, "Thomas Lloyd's Reports of the First Federal Congress," WMQ XVIII (1961), 524–26.

91. *Documentary History of the Constitution* II: 97–103.

92. Ibid., II: 103 and IV: 651–52; Elliot, *Debates* II: 548. See also Johnson to Washington, Frederick, October 10, 1788, in Delaplaine, *Thomas Johnson*, 459–60. In a convention committee that considered amendments, Johnson's position was closer to that of Paca and Chase than that of others in the majority: Elliot, *Debates* II: 554. For an analysis of the dissenters' ineffectiveness, see James Haw, "Samuel Chase and Maryland Antifederalism: A Study in Disarray," *Maryland Historical Magazine* 83 (1988), 36–49.

93. *Documentary History of the Constitution* II: 104–05 and IV: 651–53; Elliot, ed., *Debates* II: 547–49. Washington to Chastellux, Mount Vernon, April 25 [–May 1], 1788, PGWCS VI: 230.

94. Elliot, *Debates* II, 549–52.

95. Elliot, *Debates* II: 552–55; also *Documentary History* IV: 654–63. For a more detailed account of the negotiations over amendments that draws on William Tilghman's manuscript notes at the Maryland Hall of Records, see Gregory A. Stiverson, "Maryland's Antifederalists and the Perfection of the U.S. Constitution," *Maryland Historical Magazine* 83 (1988), 18–35, esp. 30–32.

96. Elliot, *Debates* II: 552–55; Delaplaine, *Johnson*, 460.

97. Elliot, *Debates* II, 547–56, esp. 555; *Documentary History* IV: 645. For the influence of the proposed Maryland amendments on other states, see Papenfuse, "The 'Amending Fathers' and the Constitution," 63–67, and Stiverson, "Maryland's Antifederalists and the Perfection of the U.S. Constitution," 32–33.

98. Stiverson, "Necessity, the Mother of Union," passim; Peter S. Onuf, "Maryland, The Small Republic in the New Nation," in Gillespie and Lienesch, esp. 183–94.

99. Crowl, "Anti-Federalism in Maryland," 456, 462–69; Crowl, *Maryland During and After the Revolution*, 133–35; Renzulli, *Maryland*, 70–73. See also McDonald, *We the People*, esp. 153–61.

100. May 2, 1788, PGWCS VI: 258.

101. Michael E. Stevens, ed., *Journals of the [South Carolina] House of Representatives, 1787–1788* (Columbia, SC, 1981), viii–x, which notes that Lowndes had at first tried to prevent the debates and so deny the Federalists a "platform for their cause." Quotation from David Ramsay (a member of the legislature) to John Elliot, January 19, 1788, in Robert L. Brunhouse, "David Ramsay on the Ratification of the Constitution in South Carolina, 1787–1788," *Journal of Southern History* IX (1943), 550. For excellent brief accounts of the ratifying process in South Carolina, see Robert M. Weir, "South Carolina: Slavery and the Structure of Union" in Gillespie and Lienesch, esp. 218–29, and Jerome J. Nadelhaft, *The Disorders of War: The Revolution in South Carolina* (Orono, ME, 1981), 173–90.

102. From Elliot, *Debates* IV (2nd ed; Philadelphia, 1861), 253–317, esp. 265–66, 287–88, 272–73 ("negroes" at 272, "freightage" 288, "bargain" 273). Elliot apparently took his account from the *Charleston City Gazette* or a pamphlet that reprinted newspaper accounts of the debates. See Stevens, *House Journals*, ix. The record of the debates in the legislature is far fuller than that of debates in the South Carolina ratifying convention.

103. Elliot, *Debates* IV: 289.

104. Ibid., 267–71 (treaties), 276–81 (migrations); 272, 283–86, 298, 296 (slave trade), 292 ("shackles").

105. Ibid., 301–02.

106. Ibid., 305–06.

107. Nadelhaft, *Disorders of War*, 155–172, esp. 166–68.

108. Elliot, *Debates* IV: 300, 312–16.

109. Stevens, *House Journals*, 330; qualifications for voting are from Article XIII of the South Carolina constitution of 1778, in Thorpe, *Federal and State Constitution* VI: 3250.

110. Stevens, *House Journals* x, 330–33, 401–04; Nadelhaft, *Disorders of War*, 180; Burke to John Lamb, June 23, 1788, printed in George C. Rogers, Jr., "South Carolina Ratifies the Federal Constitution," *Proceedings of the South Carolina Historical Association* for 1961 (Columbia, SC, 1962), 59–61. On the extreme maldistribution of seats in South Carolina, see also Charles W. Roll, Jr., "We, Some of the People: Apportionment in the Thirteen State Conventions Ratifying the Constitution," JAH LVI (1969), 26, 30–31.

111. *Journal of the Convention of South Carolina which ratified the Constitution of the United States May 23, 1788* (Atlanta, GA, 1928), which is a facsimile of the original, handwritten journal, 1–12.

112. Ramsay to Rush, Charleston, April 21, 1788, in Brunhouse, "David Ramsay on the Ratification of the Constitution in South Carolina," 553–55; speech of Patrick Dollard in Elliot, *Debates* IV:336–38.

113. Burke to Lamb, June 23, 1788, in Rogers, "South Carolina Ratifies the Constitution," 59–61.

114. *Convention Journal*, 13–23; David Ramsay, *History of South Carolina* (Newberry, S.C., 1858), II: 239n.

115. *Convention Journal*, 24, 3.

116. Ibid., 25–39.

117. Ibid., 39–54; Elliot, *Debates*, IV: 340–41.

118. Burke to Lamb, June 23, 1788, in Rogers, "South Carolina Ratifies the Constitution," 59; Roll, "We, Some of the People," 26, 22. Roll lists 15 nonvoting delegates (including some who never attended the convention). Elliot lists 14 in *Debates* IV: 340–41.

119. Roll, "We, Some of the People," 24; Banning, "Virginia," 268.

CHAPTER 9: THE VIRGINIA CONVENTION I: A BATTLE OF GIANTS

1. DHRC IX: 897; Mary Newton Stanard, *Richmond: Its People, and Its Story* (Philadelphia and London, 1923), 59.

2. Ibid., 37 (quotation).

3. James Duncanson to James Maury, Fredericksburg, VA, June 7 and 13, 1788, DHRC X: 1582–84.

4. Stanard, *Richmond*, 37–39, 45–47, 56–57; John P. Little, *History of Richmond* (Richmond, 1933), 64, 72–73.

5. DHRC VIII: 525, 528.

6. DHRC VIII: 528, and David J. Mays, *Edmund Pendleton, 1721–1803: A Biography* (Cambridge, 1952), passim.

7. In Jonathan Elliot, ed., *Debates in the Several State Conventions* IV (2nd ed., Philadelphia, 1861), 318.

8. Cabot to Nathan Dane, Beverly, MA, May 9, 1788, DHRC VII: 1663–64, n.3 at 164, and editorial note on the circulation of the book version of *The Federalist* in DHRC IX: 652–54. Hamilton to Madison, New York, May 19, and Nicholas to Madison, Charlottesville, April 5, 1788, PJM XI: 54, including n.1, and 10. Richard R. Beeman, *The Old Dominion and the New Nation, 1788–1801* (Lexington, KY, 1972), 2.

9. Madison to Rufus King and to Washington, Richmond, June 4, 1788, DHRC X: 1573–74; DHRC IX: 909–912.

10. DHRC IX: 912, and editorial comment at 902–906; Mason to John Mason, July 21 and December 18, 1788, PGM III: 1126, 1137.

11. DHRC IX: 902, 905–06, including quotation from a memorandum by a lawyer, Thomas H. Bayley, describing an 1832 conversation he had with Marshall; Robertson's note for June 20 that "Here Mr. Madison spoke too low to be understood," at DHRC X: 1418.

12. DHRC IX: 913–15; Hugh Blair Grigsby, *The History of the Virginia Federal Convention of 1788* I (Richmond, 1890), 3–4. The *Official Journal of the Convention of Virginia* ([Richmond,] 1788) is nonetheless, with 42 pages, longer than that of Pennsylvania.

13. DHRC IX: 914–15; William Grayson to Nathan Dane, Richmond, June 4, 1788, DHRC X: 1572–73, and Lee to Mason, Chantilly, May 9, 1788, DHRC IX: 784–87.

14. DHRC IX: 917–29.

15. Ibid., 929–31.

16. Farrand I: 18–23.

17. DHRC IX: 931–36. For the length of the speech, see Bushrod to George Washington, Richmond, June 7, 1788, DHRC X: 1581 and also n.2.

18. DHRC IX: 932–33.

19. Madison to Washington and Grayson to Nathan Dane, both Richmond, June 4; Washington to unnamed recipient, Mount Vernon, June 8, 1788, DHRC X: 1572–74, 1585–86. For one notable, angry exchange between Randolph and Henry, see DHRC IX: 1081–87, esp. 1082, and n.1 at 1087.

20. Lee to Mason, Chantilly, May 9, 1788, DHRC IX: 784–88.

21. Ibid., 936–37.

22. Ibid., 937–40.

23. Madison to Washington and also to Rufus King, Richmond, June 4, 1788, DHRC X: 1572–74.

24. Grayson to Nathan Dane, Richmond, June 4, ibid.

25. DHRC IX: 940–41.

26. Ibid., 944–48.

27. Ibid., 948–49.
28. Ibid., 949–51 (Lee) and 951–68 (Henry).
29. Ibid., 951–52.
30. Ibid., 959–60.
31. Ibid., 952, 956–57.
32. Ibid., 951–68. The phrase "from time to time" also appears in Article I, Section 5, paragraph 3, which says each house should keep journals of their proceedings and publish them "from time to time." Henry objected to that, too: See DHRC IX: 1066–67.
33. Ibid., 951–68, esp. 963–64, 962, 957.
34. Ibid., esp. 953–55, 967.
35. Ibid., 951, 955–56, 966–67.
36. Ibid., 968, 973, 1096, and, for other examples of complaints (by Nicholas and Madison), 1127–28, 1142, 1154. Listener's comment quoted in Robert D. Meade, *Patrick Henry: Practical Revolutionary* (Philadelphia, 1969), 360.
37. DHRC IX: 971; John J. Reardon, *Edmund Randolph: A Biography* (New York, 1975), esp. 5, 19–23, 30–34.
38. Lee to John Lamb, Chantilly, June 27, 1788, DHRC IX: 826.
39. Henry Lee in the Virginia convention, June 9, 1788, ibid., 1073. For an earlier version of the argument here on generations, see the chapter "On Faith and Generations in Revolutionary Politics" in Pauline Maier, *The Old Revolutionaries: Political Lives in the Age of Samuel Adams* (New York, 1980), 269–94.
40. DHRC IX: 985, 1034.
41. Ibid., 984–85, 1001, 971–73.
42. Ibid., 978–79, 1033–35; also DHRC XIII: 60–70 for Washington's circular of June 18, 1783, which was frequently reprinted in 1787 and 1788.
43. DHRC IX: 1028–31.
44. Ibid., 995–96, 1010.
45. Ibid., 1010, 987–88, 1124.
46. Ibid., 1010–11.
47. Ibid., 990.
48. Madison to Hamilton, June 9 and 16; to King, June 9 and 13, and to Tench Coxe, June 11, 1788, all from Richmond, DHRC X: 1589–90, 1618, 1630, 1595; also n. 2 at 1589 on the weather and n.3 at 1635 for Cyrus Griffin (the president of Congress) to Madison, June 18.
49. DHRC IX: 1055, 1064.
50. Ibid., 1072–73.
51. See, for example, ibid., 1014–15, 1024, 1026.
52. Ibid., 999–1000, 1011–12, 1021–23, 997. For a discussion of credit as part of Federalist "state building," see Max Edling, *A Revolution in Favor of Government: Origins of the U.S. Constitution and the Making of the American State* (New York, 2003).
53. DHRC IX: 1017–1020 (Randolph), and 1142–47 (Madison).
54. Ibid., 1012, 1024–26, 996, 999–1000.
55. Ibid., 973–81, and also Madison at 1145.
56. Ibid., 977–83.
57. Ibid., 988–89, and also Madison at 1145.
58. News from Virginia in the *Massachusetts Centinel*, June 25, 1788, DHRC X: 1684.
59. DHRC IX: 1051–52, n.6 at 1088, and also X: 1210.
60. DHRC IX: n.7 at 1088; DHRC X: 1223, 1201–02.
61. DHRC IX: 1127–28, 1154, and ff.
62. DHRC X: 1228–29.
63. Ibid., 1619–20 and n.2 at 1630 for Hamilton to Madison, June 8, 1788 (received circa June 16).
64. Ibid., 1229–39, 1247.
65. Ibid., 1239–42. Under the Constitution, voting in the Senate would not be by states. Madison assumed, however, that on issues of obvious local importance, a state's senators would vote the same way.

66. Ibid., 1249–55.

67. Ibid., 1256, William Heth diary, June 13, and Pendleton to R. H. Lee, Richmond, June 14, 1788, at 1622, 1628.

68. Grayson to Dane, June 18, and Madison to Hamilton, June 16, 1788, both Richmond, ibid., 1636, 1630.

69. James to John Breckinridge, Richmond, June 13, 1788, ibid., 1620.

70. Provisionally dated June 14, 1788 (given Morris's chronology and considering that the convention's debates began on its third day and it did not meet on Sundays), in ibid., 1628–29, and n.1 at 1629.

71. Madison to Hamilton, June 9 and 16, and Henry Lee to Hamilton, June 16, 1788, all Richmond, ibid., 1589, 1630, 1631.

72. Letter from Virginia, June 13, from *Pennsylvania Packet*, ibid., 1672, and Henry Lee to convention, June 4, 1788, DHRC IX: 915.

73. Editorial note and Clinton to Randolph, New York, May 8, 1788, DHRC IX: 788–92.

74. Editorial comment and Lamb to Richard Henry Lee, New York, May 18, 1788, ibid., 811–15. The letter to Mason has apparently been lost: See PGM III: 1788. Neither it nor the letters to Henry and Grayson are among the John Lamp papers at the New York Historical Society.

75. Ibid.

76. Editorial comment and Grayson, Henry, and Mason to Lamb, Richmond, June 9; and Lamb to Clinton, New York, June 17, 1788, DHRC IX: 813, 816–23.

77. Lamb to Clinton, New York, June 17, 1788, ibid., 823–24.

78. DHRC X: 1258–99.

79. See, for example, the interventions at ibid., 1290 (Nicholas) and 1294–95 (Madison).

80. Ibid., 1259–69.

81. Ibid., 1269–72, and also Henry at 1274–78.

82. Ibid., 1272–74, and also 1269.

83. Ibid., 1278–83, 1304, 1306–07, 1312.

84. Ibid., 1292, 1320–21, 1317–19.

85. Ibid., 1338–39, 1341.

86. Ibid., 1340–42.

87. Ibid., 1344.

88. Ibid., 1345–46, 1331.

89. Ibid., 1328.

90. Ibid., 1348–50.

91. Ibid., 1332–33.

92. Ibid., 1331, 1347, and also 1354.

93. Ibid., 1354–63.

94. Ibid., 1365–95.

95. Ibid., esp. 1374–77, 1383.

96. Ibid., 1398–1401.

97. Ibid.

98. Ibid., 1401–09.

99. Ibid. Despite Radolph's later assurances, Mason's fears were well founded. Litigation over land titles, including the claims of the Fairfax family, filled the federal courts in their first decades and produced several landmark decisions, including *Martin v. Hunter's Lessee* (1816). Large landowners, moreover, pushed for the expansion of federal over state court jurisdiction. See "Federalist Policy and the Judiciary Act of 1801" in Kathryn Preyer, *Blackstone in America* (New York, 2009), 29–33, esp. 31–32 and n.113 at 32.

100. DHRC X: 1409–10, 1412–18.

101. Ibid., 1415–19.

102. Ibid., 1419, 1422–23.

103. Ibid., 1419–25.

104. Ibid., 1425–26, 1436, and see also Randolph at 1453.

105. Ibid., 1425–29, 1430–39.

106. Ibid., esp. 1431, 1437, 1430, 1429.
107. Ibid., 1454–56.
108. Ibid., 1464–73.
109. Ibid., n.1 at 1472.

CHAPTER 10: THE VIRGINIA CONVENTION II: UNDER THE EYES OF HEAVEN

1. DHRC IX: 897.
2. Madison to Hamilton, Richmond, June 22, 1788, DHRC X: 1665.
3. Madison to James Madison Sr., June 20; to Hamilton, June 22, DHRC X: 1657, 1665; to King, June 22, 1788, PJM XI: 167.
4. Madison to Hamilton, June 22, DHRC X: 1665, and to King, June 22, 1788, PJM XI: 167.
5. To King, June 22, PJM XI: 167, and Madison to Washington, June 23, 1788, DHRC X: 1668–69. Henry restated his position of June 23 the next day in responding to a comment by Randolph: See DHRC X: 1482.
6. DHRC X: 1473–74, and, for Randolph's proposed form of ratification, 1456. "If in the ratification," he said, "we put words to this purpose,—that all authority not given, is retained by the people, and may be resumed when perverted to their oppression; and that no right can be cancelled, abridged, or restrained, by the Congress, or any officer of the United States," that would "manifest the principles on which Virginia adopted it," and Virginia would "be at liberty to consider as a violation of the Constitution, every exercise of a power not expressly delegated therein."
7. The text of Wythe's resolution is not in the convention record, which simply says it was read by the clerk and refers readers to the report of the committee of the whole to the convention on June 25, as if those texts were identical. See DHRC X: 1474, and, for the committee report, 1537–38. Unfortunately, several descriptions of Wythe's motion by members of the convention suggest that it included provisions that do not appear in the committee's report. See ibid., 1474–75. (Henry: Wythe specifically retained "the three great rights—the liberty of religion, liberty of the press," and also "trial by jury," which was not mentioned in the committee report; also, according to the proposed resolution, "the ratification will cease to be obligatory unless they accede to these amendments"); 1501–02 (Madison, who, like Henry, said Wythe enumerated three rights, not the two in the committee report, and that his motion said that the powers granted by the people "may be resumed by them when perverted to their oppression," which is not in the committee report); 1505 (Henry: Wythe had proposed "that a Committee should be appointed to consider what amendments are necessary"); and 1506 (Nicholas: Wythe's resolution said the powers vested by the Constitution came from the people "and might be resumed by them whensoever they should be perverted to their injury and oppression," which, again, is not in the committee report). These descriptions of Wythe's motion have some similarity to the convention's final form of ratification, which includes the provision about the people's right to resume powers perverted to their oppression but says nothing about Virginia's ratification ceasing if no amendments were enacted. Ibid., 1542. The simplest explanation of these discrepancies would be that Robertson's version of the committee report was incomplete, but the text he gives is the same as that in the official *Journal of the Convention of Virginia* (Richmond [1788]), 25. The description of Wythe's motion here takes into account the descriptions of it by convention members.
8. DHRC X: 1475; Lee to Mason, Chantilly, May 7, 1788, DHRC IX: 784–87.
9. DHRC IX: 1070, 1072 (June 9, 1788), and X: 1476–77.
10. DHRC X: 1474–77.
11. Ibid., 1478–80.
12. Ibid., 1478–79.
13. Ibid., 1480–81.
14. Ibid., 1479, 1500, 1485–87.
15. Ibid., 1485–87 for Randolph, whose comments should be compared with the draft amendments Mason sent Lamb on June 9, 1788, at DHRC IX: 819–23, and n.7 at 1508. The amend-

ments that Robertson said were close to Henry's, and which do in fact track closely with Randolph's description of Henry's proposals, are at DHRC X: 1551–56. See also Lance Banning, *The Sacred Fire of Liberty: James Madison and the Founding of the Federal Republic* (Ithaca and London, 1995), 255, which argues that "not slavery, but the Mississippi was the issue that transfixed contemporary minds" and seemed to predict future sectional conflicts.

16. DHRC X: 1478, 1481–84.
17. Ibid., 1484–88.
18. Ibid., 1500–03, 1507.
19. Ibid., 1506, 1502; Madison to King, Richmond, June 22, 1788, PJM XI: 167.
20. DHRC X: 1499–1504.
21. Ibid., 1496–97, 1504–06.
22. Ibid., 1517 (Grayson).
23. Ibid., 1506.
24. Ibid., 1506–07 and also 1511–12.
25. Ibid., 1516–17. For subsequent comments on the amendments Nicholas proposed to recommend, see ibid., 1525–26 (Tyler) and 1535 (Henry).
26. Ibid., 1507, and, on Ronald, a wealthy planter and merchant of Scottish origin who had served in the house of delegates for several years, n.31 at 1510–11.
27. Ibid., 1488–95, and also DHRC VIII: n.1 at 17.
28. DHRC X: 1488–95.
29. Ibid., 1516–18.
30. Ibid., 1519.
31. Ibid., 1524–29; Harrison at 1518.
32. Ibid., 1519–24.
33. Ibid.
34. Ibid., 1530, 1533, and n.13 at 1544. *Dictionary of American Biography* X (New York, 1933), 154–55.
35. DHRC X: 1530–31.
36. Ibid., 1530–33.
37. Ibid., 1532–34.
38. Ibid., 1534–37.
39. Ibid.
40. Ibid., 1537–38, and also editorial commentary, 1512–15. The DHRC editors say that Mathews reported that the committee of the whole "had resolved that the Constitution be ratified" (1513), although, according to Robertson, Mathews said the committee had "come to several resolutions thereupon" (1537). Robertson's *Debates* does not mention a vote on the Wythe motion in the committee of the whole. An account in the Petersburg *Virginia Gazette* for June 26, which seems at first to report a vote in the committee of the whole, was probably describing subsequent votes in the convention; ibid., 1686. The only evidence that the committee of the whole endorsed the Wythe motion (or a version of it) seems to be in the wording of the resolutions as they were presented to the convention, which says they represented "the opinion of this Committee."
41. DHRC X: 1538–40.
42. See for example, the *Virginia Herald*, June 26, 1788, in ibid., 1687.
43. Ibid., 1540–41 and 1513. Madison said the two absentees were divided, and the Kentucky delegate—Notley Conn from Bourbon County—was probably the one opposed to ratification. See Madison to unnamed, June 25, and also to Jefferson on July 24, 1788, from New York: ibid., 1675 and n.2 at 1676, 1707. Also William Heth diary, June 25, ibid., 1677, and letter from Richmond, June 25, in the New York *Daily Advertiser*, July 3, ibid., 1699.
44. DHRC X: 1541.
45. Ibid.
46. Ibid., 1542 (and compare to 1537–38, the Wythe resolutions as reported to the convention), 1545.
47. Ibid., 1551–56.

48. Ibid. For a careful comparison of the amendments endorsed by the Wythe committee with a set of "Draft Structural Amendments" found in the papers of George Mason—probably an updated version of the amendments opposition members of the Virginia convention had sent to New York—see ibid., 1547–50.

49. Ibid., 1551–56.

50. See the amendments favored by the opposition, ibid., 1547–50, and also those Henry advocated in the committee of the whole, described above.

51. Ibid., 1556–57, and 1553–54 for Virginia's version of the direct tax amendment.

52. Pendleton to Richard Henry Lee, Richmond, June 14, 1788, ibid., 1623–28, in which, however, Pendleton said that he saw "no propriety in making requisitions necessary From one body of our Rep[resentativ]es to another, & we have seen the Fatal effects of such a measure" (1626), which makes his support for the tax amendment puzzling. In the convention, Pendleton disparaged comparisons of congressional direct taxes with Parliamentary taxation of the colonists: ibid., 1198–99 (June 12). For Lee's views, see his letters to Mason, May 7; to Samuel Adams, April 28; and to Pendleton, May 26, all from Chantilly, DHRC IX: 784–87, 765–66, 878–82.

53. DHRC X: 1558, 1545, and n.2, 1564–68.

54. Corbin to Benjamin Rush, Richmond, July 2; Madison to Hamilton and also to Washington, June 27, 1788, DHRC X: 1697, 1688.

55. Henry on June 25, 1788, ibid., 1535.

56. Martin Oster to Comte de la Luzerne, Richmond, June 28; William Nelson Jr.—who reported what others said about the speakers—to William Short, York, July 12; Roane to Philip Aylett, Richmond, June 26; and Madison to Washington, Richmond, June 27, 1788, ibid., 1690, 1701–02, 1713, 1689.

57. Ibid., and also, on Pendleton (and some other speakers), James Monroe to Thomas Jefferson, Fredericksburg, July 12, 1788, at 1704.

58. Oster to Luzerne, June 28, *Massachusetts Gazette*, June 25, and Nelson to Short, July 12, 1788, DHRC X: 1690, 1684, 1702, and 1704 for Monroe's statement that Madison "took the principle share in the debate" in defense of the Constitution.

59. Nelson at ibid., 1701, and also 1560–62 for accounts of the meeting and Mason's address, including one that claims Henry spoke against continued resistance to the Constitution. Jeff Broadwater, *George Mason: Forgotten Founder* (Chapel Hill, 2006), 236–37.

60. Editorial comment and Mason's resolutions, circa June 28, at DHRC IX: 789–90, 792–93. Mason to John Mason, Gunston Hall, December 1, 1788, PGM III: 1136.

61. Editorial summary and Lamb to Clinton, New York, June 17; Clinton to Lamb, Poughkeepsie, June 21; and Yates to Mason, Poughkeepsie, June 21, 1788, DHRC IX: 811–13, 823–25.

62. Henry to Lamb, Richmond, June 9, DHRC IX: 817; Madison to Jefferson, New York, July 24, 1788, DHRC X: 1707–08.

63. Roane to Aylett, June 26, 1788, DHRC X: 1713, and Philadelphia newspaper items quoted in n.2.

64. Editorial comment and newspaper accounts of Norfolk celebrations, DHRC X: 1709, 1713–14.

65. Washington to Charles Cotesworth Pinckney, June 28, 1788, and editorial note on the express system in DHRC X: 1714, 1672–74.

66. Washington to Charles Cotesworth Pinckney, June 28; to Tobias Lear, June 29, 1788, both Mount Vernon, in DHRC X: 1714–16 and also DHRC XXI: 1210–21, which has several of the messages forwarded from one state to another and reports on when news arrived where.

67. *Virginia Journal*, July 3, 1788, DHRC X: 1716–17.

68. To Charles Cotesworth Pinckney, June 28, and to Tobias Lear, June 29, DHRC X: 1714–15; and also to Benjamin Lincoln, June 29, 1788, PGWCS VI: 365–66.

69. See Sullivan to Belknap, Durham, NH, February 26, 1788, in Otis G. Hammond, *Letters and Papers of Major-General John Sullivan* III (Concord, NH, 1939), 567.

70. Jere Daniell, "Ideology and Hardball: Ratification of the Federal Constitution in New Hampshire" in Conley and Kaminsky, 194–96. For the complicated story of the Lincoln/

Franconia "delegate," see Daniell, "Frontier and the Constitution: Why Grafton County Delegates Voted 10 to 1 for Ratification," *Historical New Hampshire* XLV (Fall 1990), 223–28.

71. Daniell, "Ideology and Hardball," 196–97; attendance records and convention journal in Nathaniel Bouton, ed., *New Hampshire Provincial and State Papers* X (Concord, NH, 1877), 2–7, 16; Pierce Long to Paine Wingate, July 7, 1788, quoted in Jere Daniell, "Counting Noses: Delegate Sentiment in New Hampshire's Ratifying Convention," *Historical New Hampshire* XLIII (Summer 1988), 139.

72. Daniell, "Ideology and Hardball," 196–97; attendance records and convention journal in *New Hampshire Provincial and State Papers* X, 2–7, 16–18; Daniell, "Counting Noses," 152–53.

73. Daniell, "Counting Noses," esp. 139–40 (includes Pierce quotation), and 152–54. The article as a whole, 136–55, offers a brilliant tabulation of delegates and votes with a careful analysis by which Daniell identifies the swing voters. As he notes on p. 140, the neglected sources he discovered lay to rest an old story that New Hampshire ratified because Timothy Walker kept several opposition delegates from voting by holding them at a sumptuous noontime meal. Daniell also makes clear "just how close the struggle remained until the end." Federalists apparently underestimated by one the number of delegates present, thinking there were 107 instead of 108 in the hall, so the 54 votes they relied upon would not have been a majority without the abstainers and the "surprise" votes. See also Daniell, "Frontier and the Constitution," 207–229, for a graphic study of Federalist local politics and an explanation of why one county in western New Hampshire voted Federalist (its leading men had ties with the eastern part of the state). The Sullivan prediction is in Henry Knox to George Washington, New York, March 10, 1788, PGWCS VI: 151.

74. The states' lists of proposed amendments are conveniently available in Helen E. Veit et al., eds., *Creating the Bill of Rights: The Documentary Record from the First Federal Congress* (Baltimore and London, 1991), 14–21 (14–17 for Massachusetts and New Hampshire).

75. PGWCS VI: 350.

76. To Tobias Lear, Mount Vernon, June 29, 1788, PGWCS VI: 364.

77. Washington to Madison, Mount Vernon, June 23, 1788, ibid., 351 and n.1.

78. DHRC X: 1489, 1498, and 1705 for Monroe to Jefferson, Fredericksburg, July 12, 1788.

79. Washington to Benjamin Lincoln, Mount Vernon, June 29, 1788, PGWCS VI: 365.

CHAPTER 11: ON TO POUGHKEEPSIE

1. DHRC XIX: 11–14.

2. John P. Kaminski, *George Clinton: Yeoman Politician of the New Republic* (Madison, WI, 1993), 124–31. Editorial summary of the episode; "Inspector I"; Hamilton to Washington, New York, October 8–10, and Washington to Hamilton, Mount Vernon, October 18, 1787, DHRC XIX: 9–11, 31–36.

3. Kaminski, *Clinton*, 5.

4. Ibid., 5–7; Linda Grant De Pauw, *The Eleventh Pillar: New York State and the Federal Convention* (Ithaca, NY, 1966), 19–20.

5. Kaminski, *Clinton*, 11–21 (quotation at 21).

6. Ibid., 23–25. Essentially all yeoman farmers could vote, and the property qualifications did not eliminate tenant voters since "tenants with leases of 21 years or more qualified as freeholders, as they did before the Revolution, and landlords had the same stake as before in seeing their property evaluated high enough to qualify their tenants in the £100 category." Other tenants qualified as "40-shilling renters." Alfred F. Young, *The Democratic Republicans of New York: The Origins, 1763–1797* (Chapel Hill, 1967), 84.

7. Staughton Lynd, *Class Conflict, Slavery, and the United States Constitution* (Indianapolis and New York, 1967), esp. 75–77, and, more generally, "The Tenant Uprising at Livingston Manor, May 1777," in Ibid., 63–77. Clinton, who was fighting Loyalists, said the insurgents should be hanged (76).

8. Schuyler to Jay, July 14, 1777, in the Papers of John Jay digital edition (ID 7114) at http://www.columbia.edu/cu/lweb/digital/jay/ (accessed April 2, 2010).

9. On the politics of Revolutionary New York, see Edward Countryman, *A People in Revolution: The American Revolution and Political Society in New York, 1760–1790* (Baltimore and London, 1981), esp. 236–37, and 198–200 on the "new men" of Revolutionary New York; and Young, *Democratic Republicans of New York*, esp. chapters 1–4, and, on patronage, 37–38, 46–51.

10. Kaminski, *Clinton*, 23–37, quotations at 26. Kaminski speculates that Clinton's defense of the forts might have persuaded British general Henry Clinton (a distant cousin of the governor) to return to Manhattan rather than push upriver to meet General John Burgoyne, who was coming down from Canada and would be defeated at Saratoga in October 1777 (34–35). Young, *Democratic Republicans of New York*, 47–48 on Lamb.

11. Washington to Clinton, December 28, 1783, cited in DHRC XXII: n.17 at 2007; Kaminski, *Clinton*, 41–43, 63, and passim. For a succinct summary of New York's wartime efforts to strengthen Congress, see DHRC XIX: xxvi–xxx.

12. Kaminski, *Clinton*, 59–111 (proceeds from confiscated estates at 78); DHRC XIX: xxxi–xxxii.

13. Kaminski, *Clinton*, 89–96; DHRC XIX: xxxvi–xl.

14. Kaminski, *Clinton*, 96–106.

15. Ibid., 90–94. On Yates, opposition to the impost, and New York's "antifederal reputation," see also De Pauw, *Eleventh Pillar*, 28–31.

16. Kaminski, *Clinton*, 27 (speech of September 10, 1777), 90–96. For another instance of Clinton's hesitation "to move one tittle beyond the constitution" and his agonizing over even "the most trivial exercises of discretionary power," see De Pauw, *Eleventh Pillar*, 23–24.

17. Hamilton to Robert R. Livingston [April 25, 1785]. PAH III: 609; Kaminski, *Clinton*, 79; Young, *Democratic Republicans of New York*, 62–69; Countryman, *A People in Revolution*, 169–75, 254–55, 257, and 266–67.

18. Countryman, *A People in Revolution*, 253–65, 286.

19. Kaminski, *Clinton*, 94.

20. Ibid., 122–23.

21. Clinton was suspected of writing the essay signed "A Republican" that defended him against Hamilton's attack in the *New-York Journal* on September 6, and also the series of letters signed "Cato," although his authorship has never been proven. "A Republican" claimed to be a private citizen with "but a slight personal acquaintance with the governor." He said it would be improper for "the first magistrate of a respectable state" to engage in a newspaper fight with "an anonymous scribbler." See DHRC XIX: 10, 17, and, on the controversy over the authorship of "Cato," 58–59. De Pauw, *Eleventh Pillar*, 283–92, argues that "Cato" was more likely the experienced newspaper writer Abraham Yates. See also Kaminski, *Clinton*, 126, 131–35, and n.45 at 309–10 (on De Pauw), and 135: "During the public debate over the Constitution in New York, Clinton refused to take a public stand on the new form of government."

22. To William Short, New York, DHRC XIII: 454; Abigail Adams Smith to Abigail Adams, New York, June 15, 1788, DHRC XX: 1173.

23. See, for example, John Francis to Nicholas Brown, New York, July 23, 1788, DHRC XXI: 1336; *Massachusetts Centinel*, February 20, 1788, DHRC XVI: 521.

24. "One of Yourselves," a broadside of April 30, 1788, perhaps by Hamilton, in DHRC XXI: 1517; De Pauw, *Eleventh Pillar*, 160–63, 174.

25. DHRC XX: 693; 687–91.

26. Madison to Washington, New York, January 20, DHRC XX: 696–97, and also 751; Van Schaack to Theodore Sedgwick, Pittsfield, MA, February 4, 1788, DHRC VII: 1577, n.2 at 1577–78.

27. DHRC XX: 690, 702–14, and Egbert Benson letter, February 1, 1788, 728–29.

28. Ibid., 714–28.

29. Ibid., 705–07, 690–91; Young, *Democratic Republicans of New York*, 19.

30. DHRC XX: 690–91, 729.

31. See, for example, "Democritus," a critic of the Constitution, in the *New-York Journal*, December 14, 1787, which quoted a Federalist reference to "antifederalists" but then, when speaking in his own voice, referred instead to "republicans," in DHRC XIX: 421; also item of April 30, 1788, DHRC XXI: 1519. On the different language of politics in the "southern part of the

state . . . and particularly in the city," see Isaac Q. Leake, *Memoir of the Life and Times of General John Lamb* (Albany, 1857), 306.

32. Walter to John Rutherfurd, late January 1788, and other comments on Clinton at DHRC XX: 688, and in Kaminski, *Clinton*, 135–37; Clinton to John Lamb, Poughkeepsie, June 21, DHRC IX: 824.

33. The Anti-Federal Committee did not at first use that name, but see XXI: 1372, 1407, for circulars of March 15 and April 23, and also 1375 for the Federal Committee (circular of March 26). On terminology, see also De Pauw, *Eleventh Pillar*, 170–72.

34. There is dispute over the extent to which Clintonians and anti-Clintonians constituted parties in New York previous to the Constitution. De Pauw, *Eleventh Pillar*, 24 ff, contends that there were no such parties and factional divisions formed only slowly during the Confederation period; Kaminski, *Clinton*, 3, says this analysis is "simply wrong." Neither, however, disputes that those groups divided over the Constitution. See also Countryman, *A People in Revolution*, which traces the development of New York's precociously partisan politics.

35. Circular of April 23, 1788, DHRC XXI: 1406.

36. Leonard to Peter Gansevoort, Albany, February 13, and William North to Knox, Albany, February 13, 1788, DHRC XXI: 1358, 1359.

37. "Fabius," February 18; "W.M." in *Albany Journal*, March 10; and "J.M." in *Albany Journal*, March 15, 1788, DHRC XXI: 1360, 1366, 1373.

38. DHRC XXI: 1370–73. See also "A Tenant," circa April 10, 1788, ibid., 1386–87. On Jeremiah Van Rensselaer, an heir to Rensselaerswyck and Philip Schuyler's brother-in-law, and his cousin Henry K. Van Rensselaer, see Young, *Democratic Republicans of New York*, 45–46, 337; also 96–98 on the limited impact of the secret ballot. For a contrary view, see Lynd, *Class Conflict, Slavery, and the U.S. Constitution*, 38–39.

39. DHRC XXI: 1371–72.

40. Ibid., 1368–69.

41. Ibid., 1374–75.

42. Oothoudt to John McKesson, April 3, and Schuyler to Robert R. Livingston, Albany, March 29, 1788, DHRC XXI: 1375–77; also 1477–78, and n.1 at 1478, 1573.

43. Ibid., 1439–40 (Dutchess), 1530 (Orange, for which the record on political organization seems somewhat ambiguous), 1542–43 (Ulster), and 1575 (Westchester). George Dangerfield, *Chancellor Robert R. Livingston of New York, 1746–1813* (New York, 1960), 214–20, describes the split in the Livingston family—over a mill and land rights—that complicated the election of convention delegates in Columbia County.

44. DHRC XXI: 1542 and ff.

45. Ibid.; also Melancton Smith to Cornelius C. Schoonmaker, New York, April 6, 1788, ibid., 1556–57. Kaminski, *Clinton*, 139–45. On the caucus and committee of correspondence, one member of which sparked controversy, see DHRC XXI: 1543, and also Schoonmaker to Peter Van Gaasbeek, Shawangunk, NY, April 4, ibid., 1553–56.

46. Abraham to Evert Bancker, Staten Island, May 4, 1788, ibid., 1534.

47. DHRC XXI: 1536–41.

48. Ibid., 1468–76, 1481–1529, esp. 1504–06, 1511, 1496–98, 1502.

49. DHRC XXI: 1355.

50. See, for example, a letter from Westchester County in New York *Daily Advertiser*, June 2, in DHRC XXI: 1577–78.

51. Severyn T. Bruyn to Peter Van Gaasbeek, Bruynswyke, NY, March 23, 1788, DHRC XXI: 1547.

52. Peter Ten Broeck to Peter Van Gaasbeek, Manor Livingston, NY, April 7, 1788, DHRC XX: 901; issue of July 8, 1788, DHRC XXI: 1300.

53. DHRC XIX: lvi–lxv on New York newspapers of the period; Abraham G. Lansing to Abraham Yates Jr., Albany, January 31, 1788, DHRC XX: 678–79 and 834–36.

54. DHRC XXI: 1379–85.

55. Ibid., 1388–1401.

56. Ibid., 1405–07, 1408–12, 1402.

57. North to Knox, Albany, February 13, 1788, DHRC XX: 766; DHRC XVI: 273–74. The New York Federal Republican Committee had also sent pamphlets to Connecticut and, later, to Virginia and North Carolina.

58. DHRC XVI: 272–91.

59. DHRC XX: 894–98, which includes the New York Federal Republican Committee's circular letter, New York, April 6; its list of persons to whom pamphlets were sent in early April, and the Albany Anti-Federal Committee to the New York Federal Republican Committee, Albany, April 12, 1788.

60. Ibid.

61. Albany Anti-Federal Committee circulars of April 10 and 23, 1788, DHRC XXI: 1384, 1406.

62. DHRC XX: 878–80, citing Kent at 879–80; Archibald M'Lean to Stephen Van Rensselaer, New York, April 10, and Leonard Gansevoort to Stephen Van Rensselaer, New York, April 11, 1788, ibid., 906–07, 913.

63. DHRC XX: 766.

64. For the reasons "A Citizen of New York" was rejected as the pseudonym of *The Federalist*, see Madison to James K. Paulding, July 23, 1818, cited in DHRC XX: 879. (Madison was not a New York citizen, and "the publication had diffused itself among most of the other States.")

65. DHRC XX: 927–32, and also 922–27.

66. Ibid., 933–34.

67. Ibid., 934.

68. Ibid., 934–38 and, for the attack on "Publius," "Centinel XI" in DHRC XV: 388.

69. DHRC XX: 938–40.

70. Ibid., 940–41.

71. Ibid., 923–24, including Livingston citation; Samuel Blachley Webb to Joseph Barrell, New York, April 27, 1788, DHRC XXI: 1509.

72. DHRC XX: 924–27.

73. Ibid., 942–43, 959. See also Robert H. Webking, "Melancton Smith and the Letters from the Federal Farmer," WMQ, XLIV (1987), 510–28; William Jeffrey, Jr., "Letters of Brutus: A Neglected Element in the Ratification Campaign of 1787–88," *Cincinnati Law Review* XL (1971), 643–63; and John P. Kaminski, who argues that Elbridge Gerry wrote the "Federal Farmer" in "The Role of Newspapers in New York's Debate over the Federal Constitution" in Stephen L. Schechter and Richard B. Bernstein, eds., *New York and the Union* (Albany, 1990), 285–87.

74. DHRC XX: 943–50.

75. Ibid., 949–53.

76. Ibid., 954–59, and n.12–14 at 963, on the financial records, which generally support Smith's numbers.

77. Ibid., 959–62.

78. Ibid., 1104.

79. DHRC XXI: 1355.

80. Young, *Democratic Republicans of New York*, chapter 4, "The Electorate," 83–105, esp. 85, 89–94, n.22 at 90, 100–02, and also 74 (quotation). DHRC XXI: 1358, which notes that the close range of votes for candidates in Albany County (4,657 to 4,681 for Antifederalists, 2,610 to 2,627 for Federalists) suggests voters were supporting the slates proposed by county committees; 1481–82, where the figures for New York City and County—2,836 votes cast for convention delegates, 1,650 for assemblymen—are slightly different from Young's, and 1575 for Westchester.

81. DHRC XXI: 1356; Havens to Smith, Sag Harbor, NY, April 7, 1788, at 1538 and 1536.

82. DHRC XX: 1124–28; Hamilton to Madison, New York, May 19, 1788, and the Comte de Moustier to Comte de Montmorin, New York, May 29, 1788, ibid., 1103, 1120.

83. Hamilton to Madison and also to Gouverneur Morris, New York, May 19, 1788, ibid., 1103–04. See also Abraham Yates Jr. to Abraham G. Lansing, New York, June 1: "It is expected that South Carolina Will adopt the New Constitution[.] I wish they may not but Wether they Do or not Will make no alteration With me nor do I think [it] ought to make an alteration in the State" (ibid., 1123).

84. William Bingham to Tench Coxe, New York, June 12 ("The most Sanguine Advocates for the federal System only flatter themselves with the hopes that the Convention will adjourn, & not reject") and Abraham Yates to Abraham G. Lansing, New York, June 15, 1788, ibid., 1150, 1174.
85. Jay to Washington, May 29, and to Jefferson, June 9, 1788, New York, ibid., 1119, 1137.
86. Yates to Lansing, New York, May 28; Lansing to Yates, Albany, June 1; and New York Federal Republican Committee circular letter, June 6, 1788, ibid., 1115, 1121, 1133–34.
87. Yates to Abraham Lansing, New York, June 15, and Lansing to Yates, Albany, June 15, 1788, ibid., 1172–74.

CHAPTER 12: THE NEW YORK CONVENTION I: A FAILURE OF ORATORY

1. DHRC XXII: 1669 and, on the Poughkeepsie *Country Journal*, XIX: xiv.
2. Linda Grand De Pauw, *The Eleventh Pillar: New York State and the Federal Constitution* (Ithaca, 1966), 195, citing the *Country Journal*.
3. De Pauw, *Eleventh Pillar*, 195–200; Smith in DHRC XXII: 2019 (convention June 30, 1788).
4. Clinton's statement in Rufus King memorandum, New York, June 12, 1789, in Charles R. King, *Life and Correspondence of Rufus King*, I (New York, 1894), 357, where Clinton also claimed the country members were "ridiculed and their speeches improperly taken and published by Childs." Smith commented that most delegates were from "the middling class of people" at DHRC XXII: 1820 (June 23).
5. De Pauw, *Eleventh Pillar*, 199, citing statements by William Duer and Kent.
6. Pierce in Farrand III: 90; DHRC XIX: 497–98; *Country Journal* cited in De Pauw, *Eleventh Pillar*, 196.
7. Convention journal and John Lansing, Jr., to Abraham Yates, Poughkeepsie, June 19, 1788, DHRC XXII: 1678–79, 1702. The "Antis" on the rules committee were Samuel Jones, John Lansing, Jr., and John Haring; the Federalists were James Duane and Judge Richard Morris. Also, on the "Promptitude" with which the Antifederalists arrived, James M. Hughes to John Lamb, Poughkeepsie, June 18, 1788, DHRC XXI: 1202.
8. Convention journal in DHRC XXII: 1679–81.
9. Ibid., including n.5 at 1681, and John Lansing, Jr., to Abraham Yates, Poughkeepsie, June 19, 1788, at 1702.
10. Robert Yates to George Mason, Poughkeepsie, June 21, 1788, DHRC XXII: 1799.
11. DHRC XXII: 1681–1701 (quotation at 1688).
12. Yates to George Mason, June 21, 1788, DHRC XXII: 1799.
13. Abraham G. Lansing to Abraham Yates Jr., Albany, June 22, 1788, DHRC XXI: 1207–08; John Lansing, Jr., to Abraham Yates, Poughkeepsie, June 19, DHRC XXII: 1702.
14. Robert Yates to George Mason, Poughkeepsie, June 21, 1788, DHRC XXII: 1799–1801. See also Hamilton to Madison, Poughkeepsie, June 21, PJM XI: 165: "The object of the party at present is undoubtedly conditional amendments." Note too that Gilbert Livingston, an Antifederalist delegate, told the convention on July 26 that the members of the majority had met sometime after the convention first convened and determined that most Antifederalist delegates did not want to reject the Constitution but to amend it. DHRC XXIII: 2322.
15. See DHRC XXII: 1681, for the June 19 convention journal, which specified that the committee would meet from ten o'clock until two, and subsequent entries in *Journal of the Convention of the State of New York: held at Poughkeepsie . . . the 17th of June 1788* (Poughkeepsie, 1788 [Evans 21313]), passim.
16. *The Debates and Proceedings of the Convention of the State of New York, Assembled at Poughkeepsie, on the 17th of June, 1788* (New York, 1788 [Evans 21310]). See also DHRC XIX: lvii, lxix–lxx.
17. DHRC XIX: lxviii–lxx. The extraordinary number of documents needed to understand the New York ratifying convention were never pulled together in print until the publication of DHRC XXII and XXIII in 2008 and 2009. Although New York in the late 1780s has been the subject of an immense body of respectable scholarship (see DHRC XIX: lxx–lxxix), the importance of those volumes for understanding the politics of ratification may well exceed that for any other state that the series covered to the point they appeared.

18. DHRC XXII: 1704–08.

19. Ibid., 1708.

20. Ibid., 1712–22, esp. 1715–17.

21. Ibid., 1717–18.

22. Ibid., 1722–26 and newspaper comments at 1742–43.

23. Clinton to Lamb, June 21, and Kent to Robert Troup, June 20, both Poughkeepsie, in DHRC XXII: 1798, 1703; also Charles Tillinghast to John Lamb, Poughkeepsie, June 21, 1788, which referred to Hamilton's "*retailing, in Convention, Publius*" (ibid. 1796). For purposes of comparison, see the discussion of previous confederacies in *The Federalist* essays 18, 19, and 20, identified as written by Madison "with the Assistance of Alexander Hamilton" in Jacob E. Cooke, ed., *The Federalist* (Middletown, CT, 1961), 110–29, and Hamilton's discussion of the defects of the Confederation in numbers 21 and 22, ibid., 129–46.

24. Smith to Nathan Dane, June 28, 1788, DHRC XXII: 2015–16.

25. Ibid., 1727–30 and other accounts of the speech to 1737.

26. Poughkeepsie, June 21, 1788, ibid., 1795.

27. Clinton to Lamb, June 21, and Yates to George Mason, June 21, 1788, both Poughkeepsie, ibid., 1798–1800.

28. Ibid., 1748–67, esp. 1748, 1754.

29. Ibid., 1750–51.

30. Ibid., 1750–53, 1820.

31. Cooke, ed., *The Federalist*, 56–65, esp. 62. See also Gordon S. Wood, "Interests and Disinterestedness in the Making of the Constitution," in Richard Beeman et. al., *Beyond Confederation: Origins of the Constitution and American National Identity* (Chapel Hill, 1987), 69–109.

32. DHRC XXII: 1767–80, esp. 1768, 1772–73.

33. Poughkeepsie, June 21, 1788, DHRC XXII: 1796.

34. Ibid., esp. 1767–71.

35. Ibid., esp. 1771–72.

36. Ibid., 1773.

37. Ibid., 1784–86. Clinton said very little, even during meetings of the committee of the whole, when he was not presiding. The texts of three long speeches that Clinton apparently prepared have survived, but it is uncertain that he actually presented them to the convention. No report of debates on the days he was most likely to give them mentions a substantial speech by Clinton. Moreover, only copies of the speeches survive, since the original versions were destroyed in a 1911 fire, so no handwriting analysis can help establish their provenance. See headnote at DHRC XXII: 1971.

38. Ibid., 1787–93, esp. 1789–91.

39. From New York, in DHRC XX: 1104. See also Hamilton to Madison, May 19, 1788, ibid., 1102–03, in which Hamilton says he learned that Clinton "has in several conversations declared his opinion of the inutility of the UNION" from "the most direct intelligence," although he could not make it public. John P. Kaminski, *George Clinton: Yeoman Politician of the New Republic* (Madison, WI, 1993), 149, says Hamilton "appears to have had a spy in Clinton's inner circle." It's also possible that Hamilton's source—here and for the comments that supposedly prompted his attack on Clinton in the summer of 1787—was either nonexistent or unreliable.

40. DHRC XXII: 1793.

41. Ibid., 1811–12, 1819, and newspaper accounts of Livingston's speech at 1829–32 (quotation at 1832).

42. Ibid., 1822–27, esp. 1822–25; *Daily Advertiser*, June 28, 1788, at 1830. For an appreciative analysis of Jay's role in the convention, see Richard B. Morris, "John Jay and the Adoption of the Federal Constitution in New York: A New Reading of Persons and Events," *New York History* LXIII (1982), 133–64.

43. George Dangerfield, *Chancellor Robert R. Livingston of New York, 1746–1813* (New York, 1960), 229; Alfred F. Young, *The Democratic Republicans of New York: The Origins, 1763–1797* (Chapel Hill, 1967), 46–47. Gilbert Livingston owned some tenanted land and did work as a lawyer

for his uncle, the lord of Livingston manor, who was, as Dangerfield notes, involved in a nasty fight with Robert R. Livingston. Gilbert was, as Young put it, "no more than a poor relation" to Robert R. Livingston.

44. DHRC XXII: 1836–41, esp. 1836–38.
45. Ibid., 1845.
46. Ibid., 1853.
47. Ibid., 1854.
48. Ibid., 1790 (June 21), and see Melancton Smith's observation of the contradiction at 1880 (June 25).
49. Ibid., 1861–62.
50. Ibid., 1871, 1858–59.
51. Ibid., 1877–80.
52. Ibid., 1864, 1871, 1880, 1881.
53. Hamilton to Madison, July 2, PJM XI: 185; Jay to Washington [June 1788], PGWCS VI: 367 ("there is no reason to think that either Party has made much Impression on the other").
54. July 17, 1788, DHRC XXIII: 2219.
55. Clinton to Lamb and to Abraham Yates Jr., and Smith to Nathan Dane, all Poughkeepsie, June 28, 1788, cited, with other statements to the same effect, in DHRC XXII: 1875–77, esp. 1876.
56. DHRC XXII: 1877–99, esp. Hamilton at 1891.
57. Ibid., 1899, 1902, 1903.
58. Ibid., 1904–05, 1910–16.
59. Ibid., 1916–17.
60. Ibid., 1917–19.
61. Ibid., 1944.
62. Ibid., 1921–35, esp. 1921–26.
63. Ibid., esp. 1931–32 for Smith's notes on the speech, which cite the familiar arguments against large republics, note the argument that they do not apply to representative governments, and says instead that "we must . . . reason . . . from our own experience, and that of others so far as they apply." On the percentage of requisitions the states actually paid by March 31, 1788, in response to congressional levies imposed October 1781 and October 1786, see DHRC XIX: n.4 at 14. New York, at 67 percent, was at the top of the list; then Pennsylvania, 57 percent; South Carolina, 55 percent; Virginia, 44 percent; Massachusetts and Delaware, both 39 percent; Maryland, 29 percent; Rhode Island, 24 percent; Connecticut, 20 percent; New Jersey, 19 percent; New Hampshire, 12 percent; North Carolina, 3 percent; and Georgia, which paid nothing.
64. Ibid., 1939–42. On Federalist nation-building, see Max M. Edling, *A Revolution in Favor of Government: Origins of the U.S. Constitution and the Making of the American State* (Oxford and New York, 2003).
65. DHRC XXII: 1942–44, 1956, 1959.
66. Ibid., 1936.
67. Ibid., 1969, 1973.
68. Ibid., 1953.
69. Ibid., 1957–60, 1966.
70. Ibid., 1976–1980.
71. Ibid., 1980–82, 1986–87.
72. Ibid., 1988–89, 1939–40.
73. Ibid., 1989–90.
74. Ibid., 1998–2000.
75. Ibid., 2001–02.
76. Ibid., 2004–05 and also 2009–14 on the Lansing-Hamilton altercation, esp. Lansing to Abraham Yates Jr., June 28, 1788, 2010–11. On the plan Hamilton presented at the federal Convention, see ibid., n.34 at 2009, and Farrand I: 291–93, esp. Article X, which said that, to prevent laws contrary to the Constitution from being adopted by the states, "the Governour

or president of each state shall be appointed by the General Government and shall have a negative upon the laws about to be passed."

77. DHRC XXII: 2016–17, and 2013 for the account in the *Daily Advertiser*, July 4.

78. Ibid., 2020–21.

79. Ibid., 2024–27.

80. Ibid., 2027.

81. Ibid., 1940. Article I, Section 9, paragraph 4 of the Constitution identified poll taxes as direct taxes by referring to "No capitation [poll], or other direct, Tax." Excise taxes on, for example, liquor were also excluded since Article I, Section 8, paragraph 1 said "all Duties, Imposts and Excises" had to be uniform throughout the United States, and the requirement that direct taxes had to be allocated among the states in proportion to their population, using the same formula as for representation, meant that they would not be uniform throughout the country. The amendment proposed by John Williams also suggested that excise taxes were not direct taxes since it would preclude Congress from levying direct taxes unless the revenue "from the impost and excise" was "insufficient for the public exigencies."

82. DHRC XXII: 2045.

83. Smith seems to have argued on July 1, 1788, that excise taxes should be left to the states because they would "operate unequally" if levied by the general government. That comment appeared in McKesson's notes on his speech but not other accounts: ibid., 2047–49. Jay's carriage tax was obviously not for him an excise tax: It was on property already owned, like homes and land. The issue of what "direct taxes" included beyond land and poll taxes later carried over into the courts and is still debated by legal scholars. See, for example, Bruce Ackerman, "Taxation and the Constitution," *Columbia Law Review* XCIX (1999), 1–58; Calvin H. Johnson, "Apportionment of Direct Taxes: The Foul-Up in the Center of the Constitution," *William and Mary Bill of Rights Journal* VII (1999), 1–160; and Johnson, "The Four Good Dissenters in Pollock," *Supreme Court Law Review* XXXII (2007), 162–77, which uses the carriage-tax example (addressed by the court in *Hylton v. United States* [1796]) at 163.

84. DHRC XXII: 2049–56, esp. 2049–51.

85. Ibid., 2056, and Schoonmaker to Peter Van Gaasbeek, Poughkeepsie, July 2, 1788, at 2083.

86. Ibid., 2058–69, and newspaper responses at 2079–82, where the response of the *Daily Advertiser* differs from that of the Antifederalist/Republican *New-York Journal*.

87. Ibid., 2069–75.

88. *Daily Advertiser* account, July 8, 1788, ibid., 2080, and also 2084–87; Hamilton letters, PJM. XI: 183, 185.

89. Abraham G. Lansing to Abraham Yates Jr., Albany, June 29, 1788, DHRC XXI: 1235.

90. Comment from the *Massachusetts Gazette*, July 16, 1788, cited with other testimony to the same effect in DHRC XXII: 2085.

91. See Comment of a Federalist delegate, July 3, from the *Daily Advertiser*, July 7, 1788, in ibid., 2093: "We find that the powers of eloquence and argument are unavailing; we shall therefore refrain from any further exertions in defence of the Constitution."

92. Ibid., 2077 and 2090 for the *Daily Advertiser*, July 8, 1788.

93. Ibid., 2069.

94. Ibid., 2087–93.

95. Ibid., 2094–97. See also the amendments Melancton Smith wrote, which were more elaborate than those actually introduced, at 2097–98.

96. Ibid., 2099–2117.

97. Ibid., 2107–2109.

98. Ibid., 2109–13, and 2115 for Jay to Washington, Poughkeepsie, July 4 and 8, 1788.

99. Ibid., 2030, 2108.

100. Ibid., 2112; also 2113–14.

101. Ibid., 2117–18.

102. Newspaper accounts in DHRC XXI: 1290–91, and n.3 at 1291; Jay to Sarah Jay, Poughkeepsie, July 5, 1788, DHRC XXII: 2098–99, and n.1 at 2099.

103. DHRC XXI: 1291, including n.4–6 at 1291–92.

104. Ibid., 1275–77.

105. Ibid., 1284–90.

106. Ibid., 1281, and 1283–84 for a similar toast by "a number of . . . respectable gentlemen" in the town of Lansingburgh, Albany County, who added "May their wise and patriotic examples be speedily followed by the remaining three."

107. Ibid., 1277–78, 1282–83.

108. See the several accounts, not all entirely consistent, in DHRC XXI: 1264–75.

109. Ibid.

110. To William Smith, Poughkeepsie, July 7, 1788, DHRC XXII: 2115–16. Smith's earlier letter to Schoonmaker has been lost, but see his letter to Abraham Yates Jr., Manor St. George (his home), June 12, DHRC XX: 1150–51, which expressed "Amaisement that Good Whiggs Who Suffered and underwent what they Did Should turn tail too and Act a Simmulal part With the Brittish Nation."

111. Compare Smith's admission "that the powers of the general government ought to operate upon individuals to a certain degree" at DHRC XXII: 1748 (in convention, June 21) with Clinton's comments on Hamilton at 1798 and n.9 at 1801 and Clinton's prepared convention speech, circa July 11, at 2142–47, in which he argued that the proposed Constitution was not a "federal republic" because it did not receive its power from the states and act upon them but took its power from the people and operated immediately upon the people (esp. 2144). However, unlike other defenders of the Confederation such as Luther Martin, Clinton thought "suitable amendments" confining the general government to "general objects" would make the Constitution acceptable (2147).

112. Smith to Dane, Poughkeepsie, June 28, 1788, DHRC XXII: 2015.

113. Ibid.

114. New York *Daily Advertiser*, July 16, and Jay to Washington, Poughkeepsie, July 4 and 8, 1788, DHRC XXII: 2113–15. Already on July 2, Hamilton wrote Madison that some leaders of the opposition to ratification "appear to me to be convinced by circumstances [rather than by the Federalists' arguments] and to be desirous of a retreat. This does not apply to the Chief, who wishes to establish Clintonism on the basis of Antifoederalism." PAH V: 140–41.

115. Lansing to Abraham Yates Jr., Albany, July 9, 1788, DHRC XXI: 1306–07.

116. Letter from Poughkeepsie, July 3, in *Daily Advertiser*, July 7, 1788, DHRC XXII: 2093–94.

117. DHRC XXI: 1250–53.

118. Madison to Washington, New York, July 21, 1788, PGWCS VI: 392–93.

119. DHRC XXII: 2099, 2094.

120. Swann to James Iredell, New York, July 7, 1788, DHRC XXI: 1294–95.

CHAPTER 13: THE NEW YORK CONVENTION II: IN OR OUT?

1. PGWCS VI: 361–62. James Madison and what he called the "intelligent Citizens" of New York City saw the flaw in that strategy: It would as effectually keep New York out of the new union, at least for the present, as an unqualified rejection. To Washington, New York, July 21, 1788, ibid., 392.

2. DHRC XXII: 2118–27.

3. Ibid., 2111, 2119, and original act of January 26, 1787, at DHRC XIX: 504–06; Pauline Maier, "Rights, Revolution, and New York's Ratification of the Constitution," *New York Legal History* I (2005), 157–69.

4. Lansing's draft list lacks a provision that no standing army could be raised without a two-thirds vote of Congress, which, however, a letter from Poughkeepsie in the *Daily Advertiser* included among the "conditional" amendments: See DHRC XXII: 2126–28.

5. Abraham to Evert Bancker, Poughkeepsie, July 12, ibid., 2149.

6. Ibid., 2128–29.

7. Ibid., 2130–35.

8. Ibid., 2135.

9. Ibid., 2136–38.

10. Ibid., 2138–41.

11. DeWitt Clinton to Charles Tillinghast, Poughkeepsie, July 12, ibid., 2150–51.

12. Ibid. On July 10, according to the *New-York Journal*, Lansing expressed hope that the bipartisan committee that would consider the proposed form of ratification and amendments might "bring the business to a quick and friendly decision." Ibid., 2129. Later Melancton Smith said, "We have manifested a disposition to recede—[that] the Gent opposed in Sentiment have not mani[fested]." Ibid., 2154.

13. Abraham to Evert Bancker, July 12, 1788, ibid., 2149.

14. Ibid., 2164.

15. DHRC IV: 434. Also Thomas Shevory, "Melancton Smith and the Articulation of New York Antifederalism" in Stephen L. Schechter and Richard B. Bernstein, eds., *New York and the Union* (Albany, 1990), 536.

16. On Dane, see Andrew Jay Johnson, *The Life and Constitutional Thought of Nathan Dane*, a Ph.D. Dissertation, Indiana University, June 1964, which was published in dissertation form in a series of "Outstanding Dissertations" on American Legal and Constitutional History edited by Harold Hyman and Stuart Bruchey (New York and London, 1987). Johnson argues that Dane was throughout his life "a consistent supporter of the Union and a devoted friend of the Federal Constitution" (iv). That inaccurate assertion probably comes from Johnson's inattention to the September 1787 proceedings of Congress, and also to the fact that Dane, like Melancton Smith, was near the center of opinion on the Constitution, where critics and supporters of the Constitution were relatively close in their views.

17. Dane to Smith, New York, July 3, 1788, DHRC XXI: 1254–59.

18. July 15, 1788, DHRC XXII: 2164.

19. Smith to Dane, Poughkeepsie, circa June 15, DHRC XXIII: 2369, and June 28, 1788, DHRC XXII: 2015.

20. Osgood to Smith and Jones, New York, July 11, 1788, DHRC XXI: 1308–10.

21. Smith to Dane, June 28, and Osgood to Smith and Jones, July 11, 1788, DHRC XXII: 2015, XXI: 1309. For an argument supporting Smith's critical role—and dismissing earlier, unpersuasive arguments crediting Hamilton's oratory with persuading the convention to ratify—see Robin Brooks, "Alexander Hamilton, Melancton Smith, and the Ratification of the Constitution in New York," WMQ XXIV (1967), 339–58.

22. DHRC XXIII: 2171–75.

23. Ibid., 2177–78, 2181.

24. Ibid., 2178–79; New York *Daily Advertiser*, July 17, at 2175, and Schuyler to Stephen Van Rensselaer, Poughkeepsie, July 15, 1788, at 2176. DeWitt Clinton wrote in his journal that Hamilton's amendments included one that precluded poll taxes "as a bait to take in [John] Williams," who had spoken against them. Ibid., 2183.

25. Ibid., 2179–83.

26. Ibid., 2184–91.

27. Ibid., 2191–94, 2198.

28. Ibid., 2193–98.

29. Ibid., 2199 (compare with DHRC XXII: 1676–77) and 2219.

30. Ibid., 2198. Smith and Hobart also expressed a wish for some way to conciliate the two sides: 2199.

31. Ibid., 2199–2203.

32. Ibid., 2205–08 and n.19 at 2218.

33. Ibid., 2210.

34. Ibid., 2211–13.

35. Ibid., 2213–15.

36. Ibid., 2191.

37. Ibid., 2212.

38. Ibid., 2213, 2216, 2225, and DeWitt Clinton to Charles Tillinghast, Poughkeepsie, July 19, 1788, at 2230.

39. Abraham to Evert Bancker, Poughkeepsie, July 18; Jay to Washington, July 18, convention debates, and New York *Daily Advertiser*, July 21, 1788, ibid., 2226–28, 2231–33.

40. DeWitt Clinton journal, July 18; Schoonmaker to Peter Van Gaasbeek, Poughkeepsie, July 18, 1788, in ibid., 2232–33, 2229; and also 2219 for DeWitt Clinton's journal for July 17, where he said Smith's proposal "was brought on too rapidly" and "the minds of the Members ought to have been prepared gradually for it."

41. Ibid., 2234–42; also Smith's proposal at 2200–2203, and Lansing's of July 10 at DHRC XXII: 2118–27. These texts and the relationships among them are complicated and occasionally ambiguous. See DHRC XXIII: n.17 at 2217–18, and notes 2 and 7 at 2250–51. Gilbert Livingston's notes for July 19 indicate that the motion (by Lansing) was "to take up the first proposition of Smith as the basis" of discussion (ibid., 2242). The phrasing subsequently discussed by the committee of the whole makes most sense with reference to Smith's text.

42. Ibid., 2243; Clinton's speech at 2220–2225, and John P. Kaminski, *George Clinton: Yeoman Politician of the New Republic* (Madison, WI, 1993), 158–60. It is not certain whether Clinton actually gave this or two other substantial speeches for which texts survive. See DHRC XXII: 1971.

43. DHRC XXIII: 2243–54.

44. Ibid., 2255–2276, esp. 2257, 2267–69.

45. Ibid., 2254.

46. Ibid., 2277–79. The word "confidence" had first been used in place of "condition" in Hamilton's earlier motion (see 2205).

47. Ibid., 2279. Unlike the earlier passage, the ratification statement differs slightly in wording from Smith's first proposal, as read in the convention on July 17, 1788, and printed in the *Daily Advertiser*: See ibid., 2202–03. It is closer to Smith's proposal of July 15 as it appears in the official convention journal: ibid., 2177.

48. Ibid., 2279–80 and 2282–83, esp. 2283, 2280.

49. Ibid., 2281–82, 2284–87, including Jay to Washington, Poughkeepsie, July 23, 1788, at 2286.

50. For a description and contemporary documents on the event, see DHRC XXI, appendix I, 1584–1666. Several articles, cited at 1588, also describe the event, and, for an analysis of it, see Jürgen Heideking, "The Federal Processions of 1788 and the Origins of American Civil Religion," in *Soundings: An Interdisciplinary Journal* LXXVII (1994), 367–87.

51. DHRC XXI, esp. 1592–93, 1598–1600, 1605–09, 1612–14, 1654–55, and Don Diego de Gardoqui to Conde de Floridablanca, New York, July 24, 1788, at 1610; Heideking, "Federal Processions," 373.

52. Ibid., 1586–87, 1655–59.

53. Ibid., esp. 1655.

54. Ibid., 1657.

55. DHRC XXIII: 2288–90.

56. Ibid., 2290–2291; Madison to Hamilton, New York, Sunday Evening [July 20, 1788], PAH V: 184–85. Hamilton had asked only about the possibility of New York's being received into the union, supposedly by the current Congress, if it adopted a form of ratification qualified by a reservation of the right to secede if amendments weren't considered within a certain number of years, "perhaps five or seven." Hamilton to Madison, Poughkeepsie, July 19, PAH V: 177–78.

57. DHRC XXIII: 2292–97, 2300–01. I have assumed that, in the report of Lansing's speech of July 24 taken from Gilbert Livingston's notes (ibid., 2293), which says that "the Latter states the matter as an impression of the Moment—or as an opinion," the word "Latter" meant "letter." Madison had begun his answer to Hamilton "My opinion is . . ." On the letter's possible influence on Smith, see Brooks, "Ratification in New York," 355, which suggests that Smith might have been shown the letter by Federalists previous to July 24. It took only a day for Madison to receive Hamilton's letter of inquiry, dated July 19, and to write his reply, which probably arrived in Poughkeepsie on July 21 or 22 (Monday or Tuesday). Assuming that Smith had already seen Madison's letter, it could explain Smith's reference during the debates on July 23 to "the sentiments of persons abroad" as a factor in his conclusion that such a form of ratification would not be accepted by Congress. Ibid., 2283.

58. Ibid., 2301–2311.

59. Ibid., 2311–21. Jay's proposal also said the president, vice president, and all members of Congress had to be natural-born citizens, have become citizens before July 4, 1776, or to have held a military commission under the United States during the war. Lansing tried to get the phrase "and who shall be freeholders" removed, but his motion failed, 18–34, with Schoonmaker, Jones, Melancton Smith, and several other "Antis" voting "nay." Ibid., 2312–13.

60. Ibid., 2321–24 and n.8 at 2326.

61. Ibid., 2324–25 and n.1 at 2336–37.

62. Ibid., 2326–30. The two secretaries were John McKesson, who took his own private notes on the debates, and Abraham B. Bancker, from Kingston in Ulster County, who was also clerk of the state senate and must be distinguished from Abraham Bancker, the delegate from Richmond County. See DHRC XX: n.1 at 782.

63. DHRC XXIII: 2330–34.

64. Ibid., 2335–36, and also drafts by Melancton Smith (Smith's was apparently written earlier, probably when he introduced his second proposal, which included a provision for a circular letter) and Jay, 2337–40, and n.1 at 2340.

65. Ibid., 2402.

66. DHRC XXI: 1614–19, including the "offensive" passage on 1616; DHRC XIX: lxi, and Thomas Greenleaf, "To the Public," *New-York Journal*, August 7, 1788, DHRC XXIII: 2407–10, and 2438–41 for accounts from New York in the *Massachusetts Gazette*, August 1, and the *Massachusetts Centinel*, August 2, 1788.

67. Alfred F. Young, *The Democratic Republicans of New York* (Chapel Hill, 1967), 120–21; DHRC XXI: 1615; John P. Kaminski, "The Role of Newspapers in New York's Debate over the Federal Constitution," in Stephen L. Schechter and Richard B. Bernstein, eds., *New York and the Union* (Albany, 1990), 289–91, with Oswald citation at 290.

68. Schoonmaker to Peter Van Gaasbeek, Poughkeepsie, July 25, 1788, DHRC XXIII: 2298–99.

69. Platt to William Smith, Poughkeepsie, July 28, 1788, ibid., 2432–33.

70. Ibid., 2321–23.

71. Ibid., 2323.

72. Rufus King memorandum, June 12, 1789, in Charles R. King, ed., *Life and Correspondence of Rufus King* I (New York, 1894), 355.

73. DHRC XXIII: 2283.

74. The broadside was issued on Monday, July 28, 1778 (Evans 21172). It is much longer than the introductory paragraph in DHRC XXIII: 2402, and includes the copy of a letter from Poughkeepsie, of Friday, July 25, at ibid., 2282–85, which describes in detail Smith's speech in the committee of the whole the previous Wednesday, supporting Samuel Jones's critical motion to ratify "in full confidence" rather than "upon condition" that a convention would be called for proposing amendments. "I was so well pleased with Smith's speech," it said, "that I have given you the substance of it with fidelity, and nearly as I could in his own language." The broadside also showed the division on Jones's motion, with Smith voting for it.

CHAPTER 14: SOME FINAL TWISTS: THE NORTH CAROLINA CONVENTION, A MEETING IN PENNSYLVANIA, AND THE RATIFICATION STORY DRAWS TO AN END

1. New York, July 28, 1788, PGWCS VI: 405.

2. From New York, August 11 and 24, 1788, PGWCS VI: 438–39, 468–69.

3. Jay to Washington, New York, September 21, 1788, PGWCS VI, 528; circular letter at DHRC XXIII, 2336. For evidence in support of Jay's assessment, see Alfred F. Young, *The Democratic Republicans of New York* (Chapel Hill, 1967), 119–23.

4. Louise Irby Trenholme, *The Ratification of the Federal Constitution in North Carolina* (New York, 1932), 100–105, 107. The legislative resolutions are in Walter Clark, ed., *State Records of North Carolina* XX (Goldsboro, NC, 1907), 196–97. Stephen E. Massengill, *North Carolina Votes on the Constitution: A Roster of Delegates to the State Ratification Conventions of 1788 and 1789* ([Raleigh, NC], 1988), 67–70, lists all the delegates to the 1788 convention, including those from seven boroughs (Edenton, Fayetteville, Halifax, Hillsborough, New Bern,

Salisbury, and Wilmington). In the end, however, the convention's committee on elections decided Fayetteville did not have a right to a seat: Clark, *State Records* XXII, 12–13.

5. Trenholme, *Ratification in North Carolina*, 135–36.

6. Ibid., 11–13, 16–20, 104–05; Alan D. Watson, *Society in Colonial North Carolina* (rev. ed., Raleigh, NC, 1996), 100–11, esp. 107; and Watson, *An Index to North Carolina Newspapers* (Raleigh, NC, 1992), xix.

7. DHRC XIII: xxxi. Both Edenton and New Bern had papers called the *North Carolina Gazette*. New Bern also had the *State Gazette of North Carolina*. The state's fourth newspaper was the Wilmington *Centinel*. Trenholme, *Ratification in North Carolina*, 26–28, says that between 1783 and 1789 the state had eight newspapers, including a couple published in interior towns. Some had ceased publishing by 1788, and no issues survive of another, which was supposedly published at the town of Halifax. For a more detailed account, which largely confirms Trenholme's summary, see Watson, *Index to North Carolina Newspapers*, esp. x–xii, xiv, and, for a list of the few surviving issues of these newspapers, xxvi–xxviii.

8. Trenholme, *Ratification in North Carolina*, 12, 16–19, 108; Watson, *Society in Colonial North Carolina*, esp. 11–14..

9. Marvin L. Michael Kay, "The North Carolina Regulation, 1766–1776: A Class Conflict," in Alfred F. Young, ed., *The American Revolution: Explorations in the History of American Radicalism* (DeKalb, IL, 1976), 70–123 (quotation at 75). Tryon's successor, Josiah Martin, later affirmed that dishonest officials and lawyers had subjected the people to "every sort of rapine and extortion." Ibid., 104. See also Marjoleine Kars, *Breaking Loose Together: The Regulator Rebellion in Pre-Revolutionary North Carolina* (Chapel Hill and London, 2002), 207–08, and, on the Regulators' grievances and futile efforts to get redress, 111–205.

10. Kars, *Breaking Loose Together*, 208–10; Pauline Maier, *From Resistance to Revolution: Colonial Radicals and the Development of American Opposition to Britain, 1765–1776* (New York, 1972), 195–97.

11. North Carolina constitution of 1776 in Francis Newton Thorpe, ed., *Federal and State Constitutions . . .* (Washington, 1909), 2787–2794, esp. 2788. The 1776 constitution allowed each county to choose annually two delegates to the lower and one to the upper house of the legislature; the seven borough towns could each send an additional member to the lower house (or "House of Commons"). Together, those two houses elected the governor (chosen annually), other executive offices, judges, and state militia officers.

12. Kay, "The North Carolina Regulation," and Kars, *Breaking Loose Together*. I am also indebted to Professor Michael Gillespie of Duke University for access to an unpublished article he wrote titled "The Question of Representation and the Rejection of the Constitution in North Carolina."

13. Kars, *Breaking Loose Together*, 187–88, 1–3.

14. Donna Kelly and Lang Baradell, eds., *The Papers of James Iredell* III, 1784–1789 (Raleigh, NC, 2003), 325–28.

15. Jonathan Elliot, ed., *Debates in the Several State Conventions . . .* IV (2nd ed., Philadelphia, 1861), 202, 215. For an earlier reference to instructions in Northampton County, see James to Hannah Iredell, Elk Marsh, NC, March 28, 1774, *Iredell Papers* III: 42.

16. Newspaper account dated April 16, 1788, originally from the *North Carolina Gazette* (New Bern), in William K. Boyd, "News, Letters, and Documents Concerning North Carolina and the Federal Constitution," in the *Trinity College Historical Society's Historical Papers*, series XIV (Durham, NC, 1922), 75–76. For a more detailed account, drawing on convention papers, see Trenholme, *Ratification in North Carolina*, 111–15.

17. Boyd, "News Letters, and Documents," 75–76; Trenholme, *Ratification in North Carolina*, 112, gives slightly different numbers on the vote.

18. Account of the second encounter from the *State Gazette of South Carolina*, July 28, 1788, in ibid., 76–77; *Journal of the Convention of North Carolina* (Hillsborough, 1788), as republished in Clark, *State Records* XXII: 10–11.

19. Bloodworth to Lamb, North Carolina, July 1, and Person to Lamb, Goshen, August 6, 1788, in Boyd, ed., "News, Letters, and Documents," 77–81; Trenholme, *Ratification in North Carolina*, 111.

20. Trenholme, *Ratification in North Carolina*, remains the fullest account of its subject, but see also Albert Ray Newsome, "North Carolina's Ratification of the Federal Constitution," *North Carolina Historical Review* XVII (1940), 287–301; Michael Lienesch, "North Carolina: Preserving Rights," in Gillespie and Lienesch, 343–67; and Alan D. Watson, "North Carolina: States' Rights and Agrarianism Ascendant," in Conley and Kaminski, 251–68.

21. Clark, *State Records* XXII, 11. Galloway also asked that the list include the North Carolina Assembly Act of January 6, 1787, appointing delegates to a convention in Philadelphia "for the purpose of revising the Federal Constitution" and Congress's resolution of February 21, 1787, calling a Convention in Philadelphia "for the purpose of revising the said articles of confederation." He probably wanted to show that the Federal Convention had exceeded its powers. The journal does not include them among the documents that were read.

22. William Davie to James Iredell, [no place, November 1788] and Halifax, December 19, 1788, in Kelly and Baradell, *Iredell Papers* III, 457–59, including n.2, and 461–62. James H. Hutson, in a generally useful discussion of the surviving records of state ratifying conventions, identifies the stenographer as David Robertson, who recorded the Virginia convention's debates, and cites the second of these letters as his source. However, Davie clearly refers to "Mr. Robinson," as do the editors of the Iredell papers (see n.2 at 458). If, however, the stenographer was Robertson—and Davie's second letter suggests that "Robinson" was in Virginia—his loss of interest would be understandable. He must have been overwhelmed transcribing the massive Virginia debates for publication. See Hutson, "The Creation of the Constitution: The Integrity of the Documentary Record," in Jack N. Rakove, ed., *Interpreting the Constitution: The Debate over Original Intent* (Boston, 1990), 161–62.

23. *The Proceedings and Debates of the Convention of North Carolina, Convened at Hillsborough on Monday, the 21st day of July, 1788 . . .* (Edenton, 1789), 280.

24. Griffith J. McRee, *Life and Correspondence of James Iredell* II (New York, 1858), 235, said that "neat copies" of the manuscript were made in Edenton by an Englishman named Lorimer "from the notes of a stenographer, a Mr. Robinson," and "as far as practicable, the speeches were submitted to their authors for correction." McRee gave no source for his assertions.

25. *The Proceedings and Debates* as republished in Elliot, *Debates* IV, 3–4. Elliot eliminated the documents that opened the 1789 edition and also the note about the transcription at p. 280. Massengill, *North Carolina Votes*, 21, lists two Galloways from Rockingham County, Charles and James, who were uncle and nephew of each other. The records are imprecise on which Galloway spoke, but James seems to have been the more active speaker. The published debates are here at odds with the official journal in Clark, *State Records* XXII, 11, which says nothing about these motions by Galloway and Jones but simply reports that the convention put off until the next day the issue of how it would discuss the Constitution.

26. Trenholme, *Ratification in North Carolina*, 18, 129–30, including n.133; DNCB III: 330–31; Massengill, *North Carolina Votes*, 34. Iredell described Jones as leader of the convention's majority in a letter to Hannah Iredell, Hillsborough, August 3, 1788, Kelly and Baradell, *Iredell Papers* III, 413.

27. Elliot, *Debates* IV: 4; Massengill, *North Carolina Votes*, 47; DNCB V: 74–75.

28. Elliot, *Debates* IV: 4–6. See also Iredell's address to his constituents after being elected to the convention in DHRC XVI: 498–99.

29. See the excellent brief biography in Kelly and Baradell, *Iredell Papers* III, xxv–xlvi, esp. xxv–xxviii.

30. Ibid.

31. Ibid., 341–70. Installments of Iredell's *Answers to Mr. Mason's Objections to the New Constitution . . .* , signed "Marcus," were printed as newspaper essays in February and March, then it appeared as a 12-page pamphlet in March 1788. See DHRC XVI: 161–69. The reference to Iredell's speech impediment, by the minister who spoke at his funeral, is from Natalie

Wexler, *A More Obedient Wife: A Novel of the Early Supreme Court* (no place, 2006), 438, citing McRee, *Life and Correspondence of Iredell* I:76.

32. Elliot, *Debates* IV, 7–8; Clarke, *State Records* XXII: 11–12.

33. DNCB II: 28–29 and V: 403–04.

34. Contrast Iredell's and Maclaine's statements in Elliot, *Debates* IV:41–42, and see also Maclaine at 43, 47. For "Publicola," see DHRC XVI: 435–41, 493–98. There too he dismissed many arguments against the Constitution as made by ignorant, dishonest people who had not even read the Constitution, and confessed "some degree of contempt for their selfish meanness" (436). In the end, he acknowledged that his remarks might reveal a certain "asperity" (497). DNCB IV: 166.

35. Elliot, *Debates* IV, 28–30.

36. Ibid., 52.

37. Ibid., 50–52; DNCB V: 412–13. Spencer to William Tryon, Anson County, April 28, 1768, in William S. Powell et al., eds., *The Regulators in North Carolina: A Documentary History, 1759–1776* (Raleigh, 1971), 92–96.

38. Elliot, *Debates* IV, 50–56 and ff.; DNCB I: 177.

39. Ibid., 75–77.

40. Ibid.

41. Ibid., 77–80.

42. Ibid., 80–82.

43. Ibid., 87–88; Massengill, *North Carolina Votes*, 38–39.

44. Elliot, *Debates* IV, 93, and also 30, where Goudy opposed calculating a state's portion of federal direct taxes on the basis of three-fifths of its slaves as well as its white population, which he said would increase the Southern states' tax burden.

45. Ibid., 33–37.

46. Ibid., 100–01. Galloway also feared that the tax allowed on imported slaves was so written that it would affect "all persons whatsoever," and so discourage white immigration, which North Carolina needed more than the Northern states.

47. For the discussion of paper money and state bills of credit, see below and ibid., 180–91.

48. Ibid., 102–06.

49. Ibid., 107–114 and, for the corresponding comments on an executive council and the presidential power to pardon in Iredell's answer to Mason, Kelly and Baradell, *Iredell Papers* III, 348–55.

50. Elliot, *Debates* IV, 114–35, esp. 116–18, and Iredell's comments on Spencer's proposal at 128, 134.

51. Ibid., 136–39, 164.

52. Ibid., 137–38, 152–54, 163.

53. Ibid., 141–42, 146–47, and also Maclaine at 163.

54. Ibid., 140–42, 148–49, 164.

55. Ibid., 142–43.

56. Ibid., 153–55, 149–51, 167.

57. Ibid., 176–78.

58. Ibid., 178–80.

59. Ibid., 180–91.

60. Ibid., 185–87.

61. Ibid., 180.

62. Ibid., 191–96.

63. Ibid., 199–200. Article XXXII of the North Carolina constitution of 1776 in Thorpe, *The Federal and State Constitutions . . .* V 2793. Not all delegates shared the position of Iredell and Spencer. Another delegate expressed a wish, even after Iredell and Spencer had spoken, "that the Constitution had excluded Popish priests from office." Elliot, *Debates*, IV: 212.

64. Ibid., 200–01.

65. Ibid., 201–23.

66. The motion is not included in the printed debates for July 30, but its text is in the record for the next day: See ibid., 242–47, and also Clark, *State Records* XXII, 16–23. On the ambiguity over what happened in the committee of the whole, see also Trenholme, *Ratification in North Carolina*, 181.

67. Elliot, *Debates* IV: 223–26.

68. Ibid., 240–51, and Clark *State Records* XXII: 16–26 (vote at 24–26).

69. Clark, *State Records* XXII: 29–31; Trenholme, *Ratification of the Constitution in North Carolina*, 163–65, including the map between 164 and 165. Trenholme gives the vote as 184–93 rather than 184–83, as in the *State Records*.

70. Elliot, *Debates* IV: 242–47.

71. Ibid., 251–52.

72. James to Hannah Iredell, August 3, 1788, Kelly and Baradell, *Iredell Papers* III, 413. Clark, *State Records* XX: 197, 199, for the legislature's charge to the convention on the capital, and XXII: 33–35, for the convention's choice of what would become Raleigh, North Carolina.

73. DHFFE I: 239–240. The letter went out as the result of resolutions passed at a Cumberland County meeting, also July 3, 1788, at 239.

74. Blyth to John Nicholson (who coordinated the petition campaign), near Shippenburg, February 11, 1788, and documents on the petition campaign in DHRC II: 715, 709–25.

75. DHFFE I: 260–64.

76. Ibid., 262.

77. Ibid., 263–64. The amendments would restrict Congress to exercising powers "explicitly given to that body by the Constitution" and reserve to the states all powers not explicitly granted to Congress; assure representation at one for every twenty thousand people until the House of Representatives had two hundred members; allow a senator to be recalled by his state legislature before his six-year term of office had expired; restrict Congress's power to regulate congressional elections; require a two-thirds vote of Congress to raise and maintain a regular army in peacetime; limit Congress's control over state militias; confine federal courts' appellate jurisdiction to cases involving less than three thousand dollars; and require Congress to requisition the states for all direct taxes and allow the federal government to collect those taxes only if a state failed to act. The petition also said no treaty should be the supreme law of the land until the House of Representatives assented to it.

78. Madison to Jefferson, New York, August 23 and September 21, 1788; Madison to James Madison Sr., September 6, PJM XI: 238, 257, 248; also John Dawson to Madison, Fredericksburg, August 20, at 237: "The plan proposd in Govr. Clintons circular Letter is much approv'd of, and not [sic] doubt, will be forwarded by the legislature of this State."

79. Randolph to Madison, Richmond, August 13 and September 3, 1788, PJM XI: 231, 247.

80. Madison to Randolph, New York, August 22, and to Jefferson, August 23 and September 23, 1788, PJM XI: 237, 238–39, 257–58.

81. Madison to Jefferson, New York, September 21, 1788, PJM XI: 257.

82. Randolph to Madison, Richmond, August 13; Madison to Jefferson, New York, August 23, PJM XI: 231, 238; and also James Gordon Jr., to Madison, Germanna, VA, August 31, at 245–46. Washington to Jefferson, Mount Vernon, August 1788, PGWCS VI: 493.

83. Tench Coxe to Madison, Philadelphia, July 23, 1788, PJM XI: 194.

84. Madison to Washington, August 11, 1788, PJM XI: 230.

85. Madison to Randolph, New York, August 11; to Jefferson, August 23, and to Washington, August 24, 1788, PJM XI: 227–28, 239, 240–42.

86. Madison to Randolph, New York, August 11, and to Washington, August 24, 1788, PJM XI: 228, 241–42.

87. Madison to Jefferson, August 23, where his comments on Kentucky are in code, and to Washington, August 24, 1788, where he speaks of "reasons . . . of too confidential a nature for any other than verbal communication," 239–41, including n.1 at 240, which explains that the Spanish minister, Diego de Gardoqui, had told John Brown, a congressman from Kentucky, that he was authorized to negotiate a commercial treaty with Kentucky once it cut its ties with the United States.

88. Madison to Randolph, New York, September 14, PJM XI: 253, and also to Washington, September 14, 1788, PGWCS VI: 513–14.

89. DHFFE I: 261.

90. See Jon Kukla, "A Spectrum of Sentiments: Virginia's Federalists, Antifederalists, and 'Federalists Who Are For Amendments,' 1787–1788," *Virginia Magazine of History and Biography* 96 (1988), 277–96, esp. 283–91, for a discussion of the "pivotal figures" in the middle of the political spectrum at Virginia's ratifying convention. The Maryland convention also had a contingent of Federalists who favored amendments, as the shifting votes after that on ratification revealed.

91. Washington to Madison, Mount Vernon, September 23, PJM XI: 262; and to Henry Lee, Jr., September 22, 1788, PGWCS VI: 529.

92. Citations in George Athan Billias, *Elbridge Gerry: Founding Father and Republican Statesman* (New York, 1976), 215–16, 224. On the subject in general, see Steven R. Boyd, *The Politics of Opposition: Antifederalists and the Acceptance of the Constitution* (Millwood, NY, 1979), and David J. Siemers, *Ratifying the Republic: Antifederalists and Federalists in Constitutional Time* (Stanford, CA, 2002), 25–46, which discusses other scholarly analyses of the postratification acceptance of the Constitution by former "Antifederalists."

93. Yates cited in Alfred F. Young, *The Democratic Republicans of New York* (Chapel Hill, 1967), 121, with a similar statement made by Jonathan Havens of New York's Suffolk County in April 1788, before the New York convention. Abraham G. Lansing to Abraham Yates Jr., Albany, August 3, 1788, DHRC XXIII: 2443.

94. Burr cited in Young, *Democratic Republicans of New York*, 122; DHFFE III: 197.

95. Joshua Atherton to John Lamb, Amherst, February 23, 1789, DHFFE I: 839. Boyd, *Politics of Opposition*, esp. 161. There were fifty-nine seats filled rather than the sixty-five specified in the Constitution because Rhode Island and North Carolina did not take their seats. For more detailed records on the elections, see DHFFE, vol. I–III.

96. Boyd, *Politics of Opposition*, 139–64, and 146 on George Thacher, a Federalist who won in Maine with the support of oldtime critics of the Constitution William Widgery and Samuel Nasson. In western Massachusetts, Theodore Sedgwick was forced, like Madison in Virginia, to state that he had been and was still "a zealous advocate of amendments" before winning his hotly contested seat in the House for Hampshire and Berkshire Counties. DHFFE I, 232, 148, 438 (Massachusetts had district elections, but the districts favored the Federalist coast over western parts of the state) and 728–31, including Sedgwick to Samuel Henshaw, Stockbridge, Mass., April 6, 1789, 729–30; Sedgwick to Benjamin Lincoln, July 19, 1789, in Helen E. Veit et al., eds., *Creating the Bill of Rights* (Baltimore and London, 1991), 263–64. On voters' interest in amendments, see also Kenneth Bowling, " 'A Tub to the Whale': The Founding Fathers and Adoption of the Federal Bill of Rights," *Journal of the Early Republic*, VIII (1988), 230–34.

EPILOGUE: "PLAYING THE AFTER GAME": AMENDMENTS, RIGHTS, AND THE FUTURE OF THE REPUBLIC

1. Thomson probably also read, or at least presented to Washington, a brief, formal notification of his election from John Langdon, the former governor of New Hampshire and one of Washington's correspondents, who, as temporary president of the Senate, had read and counted the electoral votes in the presence of both houses of Congress, as the Constitution directs. PGWPS II: 54–57.

2. Ibid., 56.

3. Knox to Washington, New York, April 2, 1789, ibid., 8; Morris to Washington, Philadelphia, October 30, 1787, PGWCS V: 399–400.

4. Lafayette to Washington, Paris, January 1, 1788, PGWCS VI: 5. Douglas Southall Freeman, *George Washington: A Biography* VI (New York, 1954), 145–55, esp. 146–47.

5. Lee to Washington, New York, September 13, 1788, PGWCS, VI: 512; Hamilton to Washington, New York, September 1788, and Lincoln to Washington, Hingham, Massachusetts, September 24, PGWPS I: 23–24, 5–8.

6. Washington to Lincoln, Mount Vernon, October 26, 1788, PGWPS I: 71–73.

7. Washington to Lee, Mount Vernon, September 22, 1788, PGWCS VI: 529–31, esp. 531.

8. Washington to Hamilton, October 3, 1788, PGWPS I: 31–33.

9. PGWPS II: esp. 153, 158–73.

10. Ibid., 160–62, 169.

11. Knox to Washington, New York, February 16, March 23, and 30, 1789, PGWPS I: 316, 434, and n.6 at 434–35, 463; Washington to Knox, Mount Vernon, April 1, PGWPS II: 2. Freeman, *Washington* VI, 157–58, 162–64.

12. Washington to George Augustine Washington, PGWPS I: 472–75; Charles Lee to Washington, Richmond, April 17, 1788, PGWCS VI: 214–15, and Freeman, *Washington* VI, 144–45, 159–62.

13. Washington to Clinton, Mount Vernon, March 25, 1789; to Madison, March 30, and to Clement Biddle, March 30, PGWPS I: 443–44, 464–65, n.2 at 465, 463; Freeman, *Washington* VI, 163, 182.

14. Washington to Knox, Mount Vernon, April 1, 1789, PGWPS II: 2.

15. PGWPS II: 155, which includes the Ames quotation and William Maclay's more often-quoted description, which stressed Washington's awkwardness.

16. PGWPS II: 173–75; PJM XII: 120–21 on Madison's speechwriting for Washington.

17. PGWPS II: 176.

18. Washington to Madison, Mount Vernon, November 17, 1788; Richard Bland Lee to Madison, Richmond, October 29, PJM XI: 351, 323.

19. George Lee Turberville to Madison, November 16, 1788; Randolph to Madison, Richmond, November 10 (which reports that Lee received 98 votes, Grayson 86, and Madison 77, and some other candidates not formally nominated received scattered votes, and also that some of Madison's supporters were unaccountably absent); Henry Lee to Madison, Alexandria, VA, November 19, PJM XI: 347, 338–39, 356. Richard Labunski, *James Madison and the Struggle for the Bill of Rights* (Oxford and New York, 2006), 133–37.

20. Madison to Randolph, October 17 and November 23, 1788, PJM XI: 305, 362.

21. See the succinct summary at PJM XI: 301–04, and a more detailed one in Labunski, *Madison and the Bill of Rights*, 133–77, which observes, at 141, that the residency requirement probably violated the Constitution, which requires only that members of the House be inhabitants of their states.

22. Labunski, *Madison and the Bill of Rights*, 137, 144–62. See also Nicholas to Madison, January 2, 1789, and Madison to Randolph, Alexandria, March 1, 1789, PJM XI: 406–09, 453.

23. Madison to George Eve, January 2, 1789, and also to Thomas Mann Randolph, Louisa, January 13, and to a resident of Spotsylvania County [no place, January 27, 1789], PJM XI: 404–05 (quotations), 415–17, 428–29.

24. Ibid., esp. 405.

25. To George Thompson, ibid., 433–36.

26. Ibid., 436–37.

27. Madison to Randolph, Alexandria, March 1, 1789, and Edward Carrington to Madison, Richmond, February 16, PGM XI: 453, 445, and also 304 and n.1–2 at 438–39; Labunski, *Madison*, 173–77.

28. DHRC X: 1507 (Virginia convention, June 24, 1788).

29. Jefferson to Madison, Paris, December 20, 1787, in *Republic of Letters* I: 512–13.

30. Madison to Jefferson, New York, August 10, August 31, and also September 21, 1788, ibid., 547–53, esp. 550, 552. Madison acknowledged receipt of the December 20 letter from Jefferson on July 24: ibid., 541.

31. Madison to Jefferson, New York, October 17, 1788, ibid., 563–64. The enclosure was *The Ratifications of the New Federal Constitution, Together with the Amendments Proposed by the Several States* (Richmond, 1787). Evans 21529.

32. Jefferson to Madison, Paris, December 20, 1787, *Republic of Letters* I: 512–13. Jefferson, like Madison, Washington, and others, was acutely aware of the importance of credit to national security. Consequently, he wanted the new government to fund its foreign loan quickly,

which would require an adequate and secure stream of income. See also Jefferson to Madison, Paris, May 3 and November 18, 1788, ibid., 536–38, 568–78.

33. DHRC X: 1531, where Zachariah Johnston refers back to the debates of June 23, when David Robertson, the stenographer, was absent.

34. Madison to Jefferson, October 17, 1788, *Republic of Letters* I: 564.

35. Ibid., 564–66.

36. Jefferson to Madison, Paris, March 15, 1789, ibid., 587–88, and also Madison to Jefferson, New York, May 27, at 613, acknowledging receipt of the letter.

37. Jefferson to Madison, March 15, 1789, *Republic of Letters* I: 588. His belief that the executive would become a threat to liberty perhaps explains Jefferson's discontent with the constitutional provision allowing the suspension of habeas corpus during insurrections and rebellions, when persons arrested could still be charged with well-defined crimes. "If the public safety requires that the government should have a man imprisoned on less probable testimony in those than in other emergencies," he wrote Madison on July 31, 1788, "let him be taken and tried, retaken and retried, while the necessity continues, only giving him redress against the government for damages." Ibid., 545.

38. Jefferson to Madison, March 15, 1789, and November 18, 1788, ibid., 587–88, 567.

39. Madison to Jefferson, March 29, 1789, and December 8, 1788, ibid., 606, 580.

40. Madison to Jefferson, New York, June 30, 1789, PJM XII: 268.

41. Helen E. Veit et al., eds., *Creating the Bill of Rights: The Documentary Record from the First Federal Congress* (Baltimore and London, 1991), 64.

42. Speech of June 8, 1789, in PJM XII: 196–99, and Veit, *Creating the Bill of Rights*, 72–73, 77–78.

43. In Veit, *Creating the Bill of Rights*, 75.

44. Ibid., 78–80.

45. Madison's proposed amendments are in PJM XII: 200–03. Veit, *Creating the Bill of Rights* lists the amendments apart from Madison's June 8, 1789, speech at 11–14.

46. Compare with the Virginia constitution at DHRC VIII: 530, and see Charles Cotesworth Pinckney's statement in Jonathan Elliot, ed., *The Debates in the Several State Conventions . . .* IV (2nd ed, Philadelphia, 1861), 316. John D. Cushing, "The Cushing Court and the Abolition of Slavery in Massachusetts: More Notes on the 'Quock Walker Case,'" *American Journal of Legal History* V (1961), 118–44, notes that Massachusetts courts actually freed some captured South Carolina slaves (though not, in that case, using the "born equal" statement). Madison's speech of June 8, 1789, in PJM XII: 203.

47. PJM XII: 200, 207. When, in his campaign letter to Thomas Mann Randolph, January 13, 1789, Madison said that he had unsuccessfully advocated in the federal Convention "several of the very amendments" that Virginia and other states recommended, he was almost certainly thinking of the provisions on representation. He believed the Senate should be based on proportional representation and tried unsuccessfully to double the size of the first House of Representatives. He also told Randolph that increasing the size of the House of Representatives should not be left to Congress's discretion, which recalled the arguments of Melancton Smith and other critics of the Constitution. PJM XI: 416; Farrand I: 568–70.

48. Proposed amendment from Massachusetts and New Hampshire in Veit, *Creating the Bill of Rights*, 14, 16 (also 14, 21, 25). When a member of the House of Representatives proposed an amendment to confine Congress's power under Article I, Section 4, to situations where the states failed to act (not where they acted unfairly), Madison observed that it was unlikely to get the consent of two-thirds of the House or three-fourths of the state legislatures. "I have considered the subject with some degree of attention," he said, "and upon the whole, am inclined to think the constitution stands very well as it is." Ibid., 200. Also Madison in the Virginia ratifying Convention, DHRC X: 1260.

49. PJM XII: 200–01, 207–08.

50. PJM XII: 201–02; Veit, *Creating the Bill of Rights*, 18–19, 22. The final provision echoed the Seventeenth Amendment proposed by Virginia: See ibid., 21.

51. PJM XII: 202, 208.

52. PJM XII: 202. He added "nor shall any fact triable by jury, according to the course of common law, be otherwise re-examinable than may consist with the principles of common law." One of Madison's correspondents supposed that meant federal appeals courts could not reexamine facts except with a jury, though he remained uncertain what was its "true meaning." Joseph Jones to Madison [probably Fredericksburg, VA], June 28, 1789, in Veit, *Creating the Bill of Rights*, 253–54.

53. PJM XII: 202.

54. Ibid.; Veit, *Creating the Bill of Rights*, 14, 15, 19, 21; Elliot, *Debates* IV: 244.

55. PJM XII: 203; to Jefferson, May 27, 1789, *Republic of Letters* I: 614. In going through his proposed amendments, Madison skipped from his third, on congressmen's compensation, to his fifth, the provision prohibiting states from violating basic rights, apparently because he had discussed the fourth, the several provisions on rights to be inserted in Article I, Section 9, along with the first. PJM XII: 207–08.

56. Ibid., 205–06.

57. Ibid., 206–07.

58. Ibid., 204–05.

59. Ibid., 209; Madison to Jefferson, New York, June 30, 1789, *Republic of Letters* I 622.

60. The committee report and Vining's statement are in Veit, *Creating the Bill of Rights*, 29–33, 170; Madison to Wilson Cary Nicholas, New York, August 2, 1789, PJM XII: 321. For the legislative history of the amendments, see Robert Allen Rutland, *The Birth of the Bill of Rights, 1776–1791* (Boston, 1991 [orig. Chapel Hill, 1955]), 206–15, and Kenneth R. Bowling, " 'A Tub to the Whale': The Founding Fathers and the Adoption of the Federal Bill of Rights," *Journal of the Early Republic* VIII (1988), 223–51, esp. 239–46.

61. In Veit, *Creating the Bill of Rights*, 175 (August 15) and also n.26, which explains that the last metaphor was beholden to Jonathan Swift's "Tale of a Tub" (1704).

62. Ibid., 104–213, esp. 199–201 (August 21); 206 (August 22); 184–85 (August 17); also 193, 197, 199, and, for a compendium of proposed amendments, 34–36.

63. Ibid., 105–07, 117–28, 197–98, and the final House report of August 24 at 37–41; Madison to Alexander White, New York, August 24, 1789, PJM XII: 352–53.

64. House and Senate amendments, in Veit, *Creating the Bill of Rights*, 37–41, 47–49; Bowling " 'A Tub to the Whale,' " 245–46.

65. Conference Committee Report, September 24, in Veit, *Creating the Bill of Rights*, 49–50; Rutland, *Birth of the Bill of Rights*, 214–15.

66. House Resolution, September 24, in Veit, *Creating the Bill of Rights*, 50; Washington's circular to the states, PGWPS IV: 125–27, which includes the final version of the amendments.

67. Lee to Patrick Henry, September 14, 1789, and Grayson to Henry, September 29, in Veit, *Creating the Bill of Rights*, 295–96, 300, and also what seems to be a somewhat different version of Lee's letter to Henry in James Curtis Ballagh, ed., *The Letters of Richard Henry Lee* II (New York, 1970 [orig. 1914]), 502.

68. To Pendleton, New York, September 14, and also to Edmund Randolph, September 23, 1789, PJM XII: 402, 418–19.

69. To Richard Peters, New York, August 19, 1789, ibid., 346–48. See also Madison to Samuel Johnston, New York, June 21, 1789: The amendments aimed "at the twofold object of removing the fears of the discontented and of avoiding all such alterations as would either displease the adverse side, or endanger the success of the measure." Ibid., 250.

70. Sedgwick to Benjamin Lincoln, July 19; Morris to Francis Hopkinson, August 15, 1789; George Clymer to Tench Coxe, June 28, in Veit, *Creating the Bill of Rights*, 263, 278, 255.

71. DHFFC III: 47–50 (House Journals, May 5 and 6); Veit, *Creating the Bill of Rights*, 57–62; Alfred F. Young, *The Democratic Republicans of New York: The Origins, 1763–1797* (Chapel Hill, 1967), 122–24. See also Edward P. Smith, "The Movement Toward a Second Constitutional Convention in 1788," in J. Franklin Jameson, ed., *Essays in the Constitutional History of the United States in the Formative Period, 1775–1789* (Boston and New York, 1889), 46–115, esp. 95–111 on state responses to the New York circular letter; and Linda Grant De Pauw, "The Anticlimax of Antifederalism: The Abortive Second Convention Movement, 1788–89," in

Prologue: The Journal of the National Archives II (1970), 98–114. The circular was popular in North Carolina, which had not ratified and so had no say on the issue, but not in Rhode Island. The Massachusetts legislature, following Governor Hancock's advice, decided a new convention might endanger the union, and Pennsylvania said there was no need for amendments.

72. To Patrick Henry, September 14, 1789, in Ballagh, ed., *Letters of Richard Henry Lee* II: 502–03. See also Lee to Henry, New York, June 10, 1790, which said there was no prospect of further amendments in the current congressional session and recommended that Virginia adopt the proposed amendments because they at least inculcated in the minds of the people "just ideas of their rights." Lee also hoped "that by getting as much as we can at different times, we may at last come to obtain the greatest of our wishes." Ibid. 524–25.

73. Young, *Democratic Republicans of New York*, 122–23; Smith to Gilbert Livingston, New York, January 1, 1789, DHRC XXIII: 2496–97.

74. Carrington to Madison, Richmond, September 9, 1789, and Madison to Washington, November 20, PJM XII: 392–93, 453; Mercy Otis Warren, *History of the Rise, Progress and Termination of the American Revolution* (Indianapolis, 1994 [orig. 1805]), II: 661.

75. Louise Irby Trenholme, *The Ratification of the Federal Constitution in North Carolina* (New York, 1992), 192–232, gives an excellent account of the movement toward ratification in North Carolina after the Hillsborough convention.

76. Ibid., 196–239, and John C. Cavanagh, *Decision at Fayetteville: The North Carolina Ratification Convention and General Assembly of 1789* ([North Carolina Division of Archives and History], 1989). The convention's official journal, which records members present as well as motions and votes when the delegates sat as a convention, is reprinted in Walter Clark, ed., *The State Records of North Carolina* XXII (Goldsboro, NC, 1907), 36–53; the final vote, on November 21, is at 48–49. The vote is listed there as 195–77 because one delegate who voted in favor was counted twice: Trenholme, *Ratification in North Carolina*, n.25 at 238–39.

77. Madison to Johnston, June 21 and July 31, 1789, PJM XII: 250, 317.

78. Davie to Madison, Halifax, NC, June 10, 1789, PJM XII: 210–11; convention journal for November 18 in Clark, *State Records* XXII, 43.

79. Clark, *State Records* XXII, 45–47, 49–52. The convention did, however, ask that the additional amendments it proposed be considered "agreeable to the second mode proposed by the fifth article" of the Constitution—i.e., a convention (ibid., 51). North Carolina remained more receptive to the New York circular letter than most states in the union: See Trenholme, *Ratification in North Carolina*, 205, and also n.28 at 239.

80. Dawson to Iredell, Fayetteville, November 22, 1789, in Donna Kelly and Lang Baradell, *The Papers of James Iredell* III (Raleigh, 2003), 539. The recommended amendments are in Clark, *State Records* XXII: 51–52. They called for limiting Congress's power to set aside state provisions for congressional elections under Article I, Section 4; preventing Congress or the federal judiciary from interfering with the redemption of paper money "already emitted and now in circulation, or in liquidating and discharging the public securities of any one of the States"; excluding senators and representatives from holding other federal offices during their terms in Congress; requiring that Senate and House journals be published at least once a year (except for parts relating to issues that require secrecy); requiring the annual publication of the federal government's receipts and expenditures, and requiring a two-thirds vote of Congress for navigation laws or laws regulating commerce. They also said soldiers could not enlist for terms longer than four years or, during wars, the continuation of the war, and that tribunals other than the Senate should be provided to try impeachments of senators.

81. John P. Kaminski, "Rhode Island: Protecting State Interests," in Lienesch and Gillespie, esp. 378–82; letter from the Rhode Island legislature to the president and Congress "of the eleven United States of America," September 1789, and vote of October in William R. Staples, *Rhode Island in the Continental Congress* (Providence, 1870), 622–25. Staples calls this the seventh time the assembly voted down a convention, Kaminski the ninth time. Also Douglas Southall Freeman, *George Washington: A Biography* VI (New York, 1954), 274.

82. Kaminski, "Rhode Island," 382–84; Irwin H. Polishook, *Rhode Island and the Union, 1774–1795* (Evanston, IL, 1969), 211–23, n.23 at 212–13.

83. Kaminski, "Rhode Island," 385–86.

84. On the states' complex responses to the proposed amendments—a strangely neglected subject, perhaps because the records are meager—see Clair W. Keller, "The Failure to Provide a Constitutional Guarantee on Representation," *Journal of the Early Republic* XIII (1993), 23–54, esp. 37–39, including a helpful chart on 39, and 38–54 on the states' response to the first proposed amendment, which Pennsylvania debated with particular thoroughness (45–52). One Pennsylvania legislator argued that the proposed amendment would actually reduce the size of the House when the population went from eight to nine million. That amendment said: "After the first enumeration, required by the first Article of the Constitution, there shall be one representative for every thirty thousand, until the number shall amount to one hundred, after which the proportion shall be so regulated by Congress, that there shall be not less than one hundred representatives, nor less than one representative for every forty thousand persons, until the number of representatives shall amount to two hundred, after which the proportion shall be so regulated by Congress, that there shall not be less than two hundred Representatives, nor more than one Representative for every fifty thousand persons." PGWPS IV: 126. If the response of some of Rhode Island's towns to the second amendment was characteristic, it failed because opponents thought the state legislatures should control their representatives' compensation (and also have the power of recall). See Staples, *Rhode Island and the Continental Congress*, 664–66, and also the Newport convention's recommendation on Congress's proposed amendments at 674.

85. Bernard Schwartz, ed., *The Bill of Rights: A Documentary History* II (New York, 1971), 1172, 1203.

86. Mason to Jefferson, Gunston Hall, March 16, 1790, and Jefferson to Mason, New York, June 13, 1790, PGM III: 1189, 1202, and also 1172 for Mason to Samuel Griffin, September 8, 1789, which says he had "received much Satisfaction from the Amendments to the federal Constitution" lately approved by the House of Representatives, and "cou'd chearfully" put his "Hand & Heart" to the Constitution if a list of other amendments were added to them. He says nothing about a bill of rights. Madison to Edmund Pendleton, New York, September 23, 1789; to Washington, Orange County, November 20 and December 5, 1789, PJM XII: 418, 453, 458; and see also Edward Carrington to Madison, Richmond, December 20, ibid., 463–65, which adds that the people expected those amendments proposed to be adopted "and that others will be supplied as further deliberation and experience shall discover the want of them."

87. Keller, "The Failure to Provide a Constitutional Guarantee on Representation," 37; Hancock to Massachusetts legislature, January 19, 1790, and House Journal for February 2, 1790, in Schwartz, *Bill of Rights* II: 1173–75. The state senate agreed to all but the first two and eventually went along with the house on the twelfth proposed amendment. However, it seems that Massachusetts did not officially ratify amendments three through twelve in 1790 or 1791 because a joint committee appointed to prepare a declaration of their assent failed to report and nobody noticed that failure until Jefferson asked what was going on. See Christopher Gore to Jefferson, Boston, August 18, 1791, in ibid., 1175–76.

88. Virginia Senate Journal cited in John P. Kaminski, "The Making of the Bill of Rights: 1787–1792," in Stephen L. Schechter and Richard B. Bernstein, eds., *Contexts of the Bill of Rights* (Albany, 1990), 58–59, and, for a summary of state proceedings, including the complicated fight in Virginia, 51–61. Also Patrick T. Conley and John P. Kaminski, *The Bill of Rights and the States* (Madison, Wisconsin, 1992).

89. Hardin Burnley to Madison, Richmond, November 28, 1789, PJM XII: 456. Richard R. Beeman, *Patrick Henry: A Biography* (New York, 1974), 171.

90. See for example the *Hampshire Chronicle*, December 2, 1789; a letter from Wilmington, NC, the *Boston Gazette*, October 19, 1789; a letter from the First Presbytery of the Eastward to Washington, Newburyport, MA, October 28, 1789, in the *Pennsylvania Packet*, December 2, 1789. The same is true of the excerpts from newspapers in Schwartz, *Bill of Rights* II: 1176–84,

and, in fact, the documents reproduced under "Ratification by the States," 1171–1203. The term "bill of rights" is used there by the editor but not in the eighteenth-century documents he reprints. This evidence disputes the assertion in Bowling, "'A Tub to the Whale,'" 250, with no evidence, that by the time the first ten amendments to the Constitution were ratified they were "widely referred to as the Bill of Rights."

91. Rhode Island instrument of ratification, May 29, 1790, in Staples, *Rhode Island and the Continental Congress*, 674–80, esp. 674–75.

92. Ibid., esp. 675–80. Rhode Island also ratified "in confidence" that until its proposed amendments were ratified, Congress would forbear exercising certain of its powers in the state, including that of levying direct taxes, until the state had been given an opportunity to raise the sum; to interfere with state elections under Article I, Section 4, or to take the militia out of the state for more than six weeks without the legislature's permission. The proposed amendment (no. 17) on the slave trade was more an instruction to Congress than an amendment to the Constitution. The issue was very important in Rhode Island, which had a large population of Quakers.

93. Presentment of the Circuit Court for the District of Georgia, October 18, 1791, in Maeva Marcus, et al., eds., *The Documentary History of the Supreme Court of the United States, 1789–1800* II, *The Justices on Circuit, 1790–1794* (New York, 1988), 224, 333.

94. Virginia Declaration of Rights, 1776, in DHRC VIII: 530–31.

95. Quotations from William Findley and William Bingham in the Pennsylvania debates on the first proposed amendment in Keller, "Failure to Provide a Constitutional Guarantee on Representation," 51; also Madison to Thomas Mann Randolph, Louisa, January 13, 1789, PJM XI: 416: a periodical increase in the size of the House should be provided for in the Constitution "instead of being left to the discretion of government."

96. Quotation from Madison's speech to Congress, June 8, 1789, PJM XII: 207.

97. Ibid. (italics mine), and Gordon S. Wood, "The Origins of Judicial Review Revisited, or How the Marshall Court Made More out of Less," *Washington and Lee Law Review* LVI (1999), 787–809.

98. Akhil Reed Amar, *The Bill of Rights: Creation and Reconstruction* (New Haven and London, 1998), 205.

99. Virginia Senators to the Speaker of the Virginia House of Representatives, New York, September 28, 1789, in Ballagh, ed., *Letters of Richard Henry Lee* II: 508.

100. Amar, *The Bill of Rights*, 284–87 and, on Bingham and the Thirty-ninth Congress, 181ff. Amar found only one reference in all of the antebellum United States Reports to the amendments as a bill of rights: in an argument of 1840, C. P. Van Ness spoke of "the amendments to the Constitution of the United States, commonly called the bill of rights" (at 286).

101. Pauline Maier, *American Scripture: Making the Declaration of Independence* (New York, 1997), esp. 175–208.

102. Akhil Reed Amar, *America's Constitution: A Biography* (New York, 2005), 81–82. Amar also notes that, unlike the old Confederation Congress and the federal Convention, the House of Representatives had open sessions that were covered in newspapers, and within a few years the Senate also threw its doors open to visitors. That, too, undercut any popular suspicions of Congress.

103. Judiciary Act of 1789 at www.constitution.org/uslaw/judiciary_1789.htm, accessed March 24, 2009; Maeva Marcus and Natalie Wexler, "The Judiciary Act of 1789: Political Compromise or Constitutional Interpretation?" in Maeva Marcus, ed., *Origins of the Federal Judiciary: Essays on the Judiciary Act of 1789* (New York, 1992), 13–39, esp. n.21 at 32 for a summary of the complicated minimum jurisdictional amounts specified in the act, 29 on jury trials, and 28 for a statement by Lee that the act remedied so far as possible in a law certain "defects in the Constitution" with regard to the rights of the people.

104. Paul Douglas Newman, *Fries's Rebellion: The Enduring Struggle for the American Revolution* (Philadelphia, 2004), 72–78 and passim; Lee Soltow, "America's First Progressive Tax," *National Tax Journal* XXX (March 1977), 53–58; Charles F. Dunbar, "The Direct Tax of 1861," *Quarterly Journal of Economics* III (1889), 436–61, esp. 441–46; and Roger Foster, *Commentaries*

on the Constitution of the United States, Historical and Juridical I (Boston, 1896), 413–15. See also Max Edling, *A Revolution in Favor of Government: Origins of the U.S. Constitution and the Making of the American State* (Oxford and New York, 2003), esp. 212–16. Under the tax of 1813, seven of the eighteen states in the union paid their quotas, and four of the eighteen in 1815 and 1816. All the Northern states except Delaware and Colorado paid their quota under the direct tax levied in 1861, often with credits for military equipment and service. The obligations of Confederate states, which Congress considered still under its jurisdiction, were sometimes collected with the sale of lands in seized territory, but, as Dunbar explains at length, they remained an issue into the late nineteenth century.

105. Article I, Section 2, paragraph 3. Federal Convention debates of July 12, 1787, in Farrand I: 591–97. Bruce Ackerman, "Taxation and the Constitution," *Columbia Law Review* 99 (1999), 1–58, emphasizes the "tainted" character of the direct tax provision because of its association with slavery, which William Paterson later asserted in *Hylton v. U.S.* (1896) (cited at 22).

106. Farrand I: 582–88, 593, and 595 (King), from the debates of July 11 and 12, 1787. See also Robin L. Einhorn, *American Taxation, American Slavery* (Chicago and London, 2006), 157–99. The Constitution does not define direct taxes except for poll taxes, and there is some evidence that the federal Convention members had no clear understanding of what the term meant. On August 20, 1787, when Rufus King "asked what was the precise meaning of direct taxation? No one answ[ere]d." Farrand II: 350. Modern scholars still argue over the eighteenth-century meaning of "direct taxes." See Ackerman, "Taxation and the Constitution," esp. n.50 at 15–16; Calvin H. Johnson, "The Apportionment of Direct Taxes: The Foul-Up in the Core of the Constitution," *William and Mary Bill of Rights Journal* VII (1998), 1–160, and also Johnson, "The Four Good Dissenters in *Pollock*," *Journal of Supreme Court History* XXXII (2007), 162–77.

107. Heather Cox Richardson, *The Greatest Nation of the Earth: Republican Economic Policies During the Civil War* (Cambridge and London, 1997), 103–38 on "tariff and tax legislation," esp. 112–13, 116–17, 119–22, 130–32.

108. Edling, *A Revolution in Favor of Government*, 157–59, 191, 207–09, 211–12; Edling and Mark D. Kaplanoff, "Alexander Hamilton's Fiscal Reform: Transforming the Structures of Taxation in the Early Republic," WMQ LXI (2004): 713–44.

109. For a careful account of how, after many setbacks, the Court used the Fourteenth Amendment to make the first eight powerful protectors of Americans' rights, see Richard C. Cortner, *The Supreme Court and the Second Bill of Rights: The Fourteenth Amendment and the Nationalization of Civil Liberties* (Madison, WI, 1981). Maier, *American Scripture*, xiii, xv.

110. See, for example, Irving Brant, "Madison: On the Separation of Church and State," *William and Mary Quarterly*, 3d ser., III (1951), 3–24. Madison thought even chaplains for Congress and the army were proscribed by the First Amendment.

POSTCRIPT: IN MEMORIAM

1. Willis P. Whichard, *Justice James Iredell* (Durham, North Carolina, 2000).

2. Iredell cited in Ibid., 222.

3. Ibid., For an engaging, semifictional but well-researched story of Iredell's relationship with Wilson, and even more with Hannah Gray Wilson, the very young Boston woman whom Wilson married late in life, told in good part from the perspective of Iredell's long-suffering wife, Hannah Johnston Iredell, see Natalie Wexler, *A More Obedient Wife: A Novel of the Early Supreme Court* (Washington, 2006).

4. Charles Page Smith, *James Wilson, Founding Father, 1742–1798* (Chapel Hill, 1956), esp. 382–88, and Geoffrey Seed, *James Wilson* (Millwood, NY, 1978). The circumstances of Wilson's death are graphically described in Wexler, *A More Obedient Wife*. Wilson's remains were transferred in 1906 to Christ Churchyard in Philadelphia.

5. Whichard, *Iredell*, 99.

6. I am indebted to Conrad Wright of the Massachusetts Historical Society for access to a draft sketch of Symmes prepared for a future volume of *Sibley's Harvard Graduates: Biographical Sketches of Graduates of Harvard University...* (Cambridge, 1873–). See also Claude M. Fuess,

Andover: Symbol of New England ([Andover, MA.,] 1959), 197–200, and L. H. Hazen, "A Memorial Discourse on William Symmes, Esq.," *Essex Institute Historical Collections* IV (1862), 193–240.

7. *Dictionary of American Biography* X (New York, 1943), 154–55.

8. DHRC VI: n.6 at 1233, IV: 437; William A. Benedict and Hiram A. Tracy, *History of the Town of Sutton, Massachusetts* (Worcester, 1878), 727–28.

9. *Dictionary of American Biography*, XVII (New York, 1943).

10. Ibid., X, 608–09; DHRC XIX: 497–98; Farrand III: 90. *Memoir of Thurlow Weed* (Boston, 1884), 33–35, which was published by Weed's grandson, Thurlow Weed Barnes, claimed that an informant had told Weed about the murder, gave him papers with the details, and told him to reveal them when the principal participants in the crime had died. After their deaths, in 1870, Weed realized that others closely associated with them were still "occupying high positions and enjoying public confidence" and decided not to reveal the crime. By 1884, Weed, a prominent journalist and political boss, was dead and papers entrusted to him had apparently been lost or destroyed.

11. John Caldwell, *William Findley from West of the Mountains: Congressman, 1791–1821* (Gig Harbor, WA, 2002), 374 and passim.

12. Findley, *History of the Insurrections in Four Western Counties of Pennsylvania* (Philadelphia, 1796; facsimile reprint Spartanburg, SC, 1984), 257, 327.

13. Ibid., 257.

INDEX

★

farmers: in Connecticut, 129; and
Massachusetts debates, 160; in New
York State, 322, 323, 324, 345, 360; in
North Carolina, 405, 406; and taxes,
15, 31, 324
federal Convention. See Philadelphia
Convention
"Federal Farmer," 83, 85–86, 93, 94, 95,
164, 280, 334, 339, 345, 356
Federal Republican Committee (New
York), 280, 326, 328, 334, 335, 340, 344,
353, 430, 456
federal-state relations: and Articles of
Confederation, 81, 417; and bill of
rights, 462–63; and congressional
debate on amendments, 450, 453,
454; and future of republic, 466;
and Hamilton's analysis of odds
of ratification, 69; and Harrisburg
convention, 425; and Madison-
Jefferson correspondence, 444; and
Massachusetts debates, 152, 177, 187, 190,
450; and New Hampshire debates, 450;
and New York debates, 351, 359–60, 362,
363, 364, 367, 371; and North Carolina
debates, 413–14, 417, 419, 450; and
Pennsylvania debates, 65, 66, 109, 110,
113, 119; and Philadelphia Convention
debates, 32; and print debate, 71, 76, 80,
81, 90; and proposals for Philadelphia
Convention, 24–25; and South Carolina
debates, 450; and Virginia debates,
263–64, 450. See also specific person
The Federalist by "Publius" (Madison,
Hamilton, and Jay): 83, 84–85, 257, 270,
271, 335–36, 352, 355, 401, 430, 446
Federalists: and amendments to
Constitution, 128, 431–32, 454, 464; and
bill of rights, 450–51; characteristics of,
93–94; and coordination among states,
281; and delays in calling ratification
conventions, 125; and divisions within
states, 430; domination of Congress by,
440, 456; election to first U.S. congress
of, 433–34; Hancock deal with,
194–95, 211–12; impact of Massachusetts
convention on, 210; and importance
of Virginia to ratification, 293; and
instructions versus convictions of
delegates, 148; and name calling, 92–95;
as orators, 360–61; and Oswald trip to
Virginia, 279; and print debate, 78, 80,

81, 87; and ratification of Constitution,
464; and second convention, 427,
428–29; and taxes, 428–29, 465, 466; as
a term, xv, 92–95; and Wilson's State
House speech, 78, 80, 81. See also specific
person, state, or state convention
Findley, William: attacks on, 100; as
Constitutionalist party member,
98; death of, 472; and Harrisburg
Convention, 424; Henry compared
with, 229; and juries, 289; as moderate,
99; as orator, 186; and Pennsylvania
Assembly "big rush," 60, 61, 63, 66;
and Pennsylvania debate, 98, 99, 100,
101, 106, 110, 111, 112, 113, 115, 116, 472;
personal and professional background of,
98; as Philadelphia Convention delegate,
112; post-convention career of, 472
First Amendment, 453, 462
Fourteenth Amendment, 463, 464, 466–67
Franklin, Benjamin, 23, 37, 43–44, 45, 59,
66, 75, 76, 122, 131, 268, 387
Freeman's Journal, 71, 73, 74, 81, 82, 99, 115, 120

Galloway, James, 408, 409, 410, 415, 419
Georgia: and amendments to Constitution,
123, 447, 459, 461–62; Confederation
Congress delegation from, 123;
and Creek Wars, 124; and electoral
system, 286; Philadelphia Convention
delegation from, 4, 123; and print
debate, 92; ratification of amendments
to Constitution by, 459, 461–62;
ratification of Constitution by, 123–24,
125, 126, 215; requisitions from, 11;
security of, 282; and slavery, 43, 123, 248,
284; and Spain-U.S. negotiations, 238
Gerry, Elbridge: "all or nothing" views
of, 87, 89; and amendments to
Constitution, 52, 87, 88, 90; and bill of
rights, 44, 87; and Congressional power,
45, 87, 452–53; and Connecticut debates,
132, 133; Constitution, concerns over,
44, 45, 51; and diversity among critics of
the Constitution, 93; elections, views of,
87; fears about nation of, 87; Federalists'
views of, 87; and House debate about
amendments, 446, 452–53; House of
Representatives views of, 87; Judiciary,
views of, 87; and Lee (Richard Henry)
proposed amendments, 66; letter to
Massachusetts legislature of, 87–89;

and professional background of, 39–41; personality and character of, 39, 41–42, 43; and Philadelphia Convention, 3, 39, 41–44, 45, 46–49; Pierce comments about, 43; and Potomac River project, 41; and presidency, 44, 47, 286; and print debate, 75, 76, 86–87; and ratification of amendments to Constitution, 460; and record of Virginia convention, 258; refusal to sign Constitution, 29, 45, 49, 53, 226; and representation, 42; and republicanism, 270; reputation after Virginia convention, 311; and second convention, 45, 48, 49, 68, 76, 231; and Senate, 43, 46, 47; and separation of powers, 47, 48; and slavery, 43, 283–84; and standing army, 46, 282; as "star" at Virginia convention, 256, 300; and state conventions, 52; and state legislatures, 42, 46; and statehood, 291; and states, 42; support for Constitution, 312; and taxes, 42, 46–47, 262, 273, 308; and trade/commerce, 43, 46, 132, 241; and treason, 43; and treaties, 43; and vetos, 42; and vice presidency, 44; and Virginia convention, 305; and Virginia debates, 126, 226, 227, 232, 241, 259, 262–63, 266, 271–73, 276, 282–84, 286–88, 290, 291, 293, 296, 308; and Virginia Declaration of Rights, 108; and Virginia state constitution, 39; and war powers, 43; and Washington, 41, 48, 67, 321

Massachusetts: and Articles of Confederation, 141; and bill of rights, 459; Connecticut compared with, 142; Constitution, criticisms in, 142–47; Declaration of Rights in, 448; elections of 1787 in, 16–17; elections to first U.S. Congress in, 433; growing support for Constitution in, 433; land claims in New York of, 323; and political parties, 156–57; popular sovereignty in, 138–41, 146, 153; and print debate, 71–72, 75, 76, 83, 85, 87, 88, 89; ratification of amendments to Constitution by, 459; representation in first Congress from, 30; salaries of legislators in, 179; state constitution for, 16, 138–42, 144, 150, 160, 174, 189;

support for Philadelphia Convention by, 21; taxes in, 15, 466; town meetings in, 140, 141–52, 153; "We the People" of, 138–41, 146, 153. *See also* Massachusetts convention; Shays's Rebellion; *specific person or topic*

Massachusetts Centinel, 71–72, 86, 87, 89, 146, 166, 170, 184, 187, 193, 221, 223

Massachusetts convention: address to the people from, 210–11; adjournment/dissolution of, 209, 211, 220; and amendments to Constitution, 128, 149–51, 157, 160, 163, 164, 167, 174, 187, 191–208, 210, 215, 251, 262, 272, 275, 280–81, 293, 295, 301, 308, 316, 317, 330, 362, 421, 424, 450; call for, 88; Committee of the Pay Roll of, 196, 210, 212; Committee of Twenty-five of, 199–207; and Connecticut ratification, 214; contested elections to, 160, 165; "with cordiality" at, 207–13; critics of the Constitution in, 157, 160, 185–87, 209; deal made with Hancock, 192–98; decision time at, 198–207; difficulty of predicting political division in, 127, 147, 153, 156; discussion as a whole at, 191–92, 195–207; diversity of delegates at, 152–53, 165, 168; election of delegates to, 88, 143–45; Federalists at, 126–27, 138, 142, 146, 148–50, 152, 153, 156–58, 160–62, 164, 167–73, 176–80, 182–86, 189, 190, 193–95, 197–204, 208, 210–12, 220, 223, 233, 251, 257, 259, 360, 369; Gerry-Dana conflict at, 169; "Grand Procession" following, 212; Hancock addresses to, 196–97, 206–7, 211; Hancock as president of, 159, 160; Hancock proposal at, 196–97, 198, 199, 200, 201, 204, 206–7; importance of ratification by, 214–15; influence of other states/conventions on, 138, 143, 150, 155, 195, 204, 214; influence on other states/conventions of, 126–27, 155, 198, 200, 214, 215, 218, 222, 251, 275, 316, 317, 350, 408, 421; instructions to delegates at, 134–36, 138, 145–49, 150, 151, 203–4, 233; meeting places for, 166; "monitors" at, 160; Nasson motion at, 182–83, 186; and Northampton-Easthampton address, 147–48, 149; opening of, 125, 167–69; optimisim about, 126; "other side" in, 185–87, 214;

ILLUSTRATION CREDITS

———— ★ ————

1   Portrait by Charles Willson Peale, Pennsylvania Academy of Fine Arts.

2   Painting by Edward Savage.

3   Painting by Charles Willson Peale, National Portrait Gallery, Washington, D.C.

10   *Columbian Magazine*, June 1787.

13   Painting by Rembrandt Peale, Independence National Historical Park.

16   Painting by Edward Augustus Brackett.

17   Portrait by John Singleton Copley, Museum of Fine Arts, Boston.

23   *Patrick Henry: Life, Correspondence and Speeches, Volume I*, by William Wirt Henry, New York: 1891.

7, 9, 11, 12, 19   John Sanderson and Robert Waln, Jr., *Biography of the Signers to the Declaration of Independence*, vols. 2–9. Philadelphia, 1822–27.

4–6, 8, 14, 15, 21, 22, 24-30   John Fiske, *The Critical Period of American History 1783–1789*. Cambridge, Massachusetts, 1898.

31   Martha J. Lamb, *History of the City of New York*, vol. II. New York, 1896.

18, 20, 32   Library of Congress.